Lab Sheet Annotations

Lore Rasmussen
Robert Hightower
Peter Rasmussen

The Miquon School
Miquon, Pennsylvania

Third Edition
© 1985, 1977, 1964 by Lore Rasmussen. All rights reserved.
Printed in the United States of America. ISBN 0-913684-64-3

Key Curriculum Press
1150 65th Street
Emeryville, California 94608
E-mail: editorial@keypress.com
http://www.keypress.com

12 11 10 9 8 7   04

Contents

A Letter from the Author   1

The Miquon Math Lab Materials   5

Lab Sheet Annotations   7

Lab Sheet Level Chart   9

A   Counting   10

B   Odd-even   27

C   Addition   37

D   Subtraction   59

E   Addition and subtraction   82

F   Multiplication   106

G   Addition, subtraction, and multiplication   133

H   Fractions   140

I   Addition, subtraction, multiplication, and fractions   166

J   Division   173

K   Addition, subtraction, multiplication, fractions, and division   186

L   Equalities and inequalities   198

M   Place value   210

N   Number lines and functions   224

O   Factoring   239

P   Squaring   246

Q   Simultaneous equations   256

R   Graphing equations   261

S   Geometric recognition   282

T   Length, area, and volume   290

U   Series and progressions   306

V   Grid and arrow games   316

W   Mapping   323

X   Clock arithmetic   331

Y   Sets   341

Z   Word problems   352

Scope and Sequence Chart   363

A Letter From the Author

Dear Reader-Colleagues:

The Miquon Math Lab Materials were developed by the children of the Miquon School and myself during the early days of the post-Sputnik mathematics education reform. I was fortunate at the time to be teaching in a school atmosphere where creativity and inquiry were encouraged; where children and subject matter were genuinely respected.

At that time laboratory "hands-on" techniques for teaching mathematics were rare in America. Few good structural teaching aids existed. No one had heard of the British Primary School reforms.

Those of us who were dissatisfied with the prevailing mathematics teaching methods had to steer our own course and travel far to find allies. What we wanted to change, we had to invent and test. (We couldn't buy it.) What we wanted to incorporate of the traditional curriculum, we had to vitalize. For me, as I developed materials at the time, *the children were my teachers.* They let me know clearly when they were bored, confused or didn't understand and were frustrated. The curriculum that emerged was developed according to the signals they gave me.

I was also fortunate at the time to receive generous encouragement, knowledge and support from some leading mathematicians and mathematics educators who were becoming aware of the ease with which young children could grasp basic mathematical notions that had previously been presented only to older children. A new era of optimistic reform seemed to be opening up as sophisticated topics from college and high school curricula found their way into the elementary school.

Coached by the experts, I, too, tried many of these ideas. Some worked. Others confused and depressed me as well as the children. The "new ideas" to which the children responded positively became the collection of materials known as the Miquon Math Lab Materials. They also contained enough practice papers in basic skills to assure cautious parents that arithmetic computation was still held important. In this way my teaching and writing became a fabric jointly woven by children and parents on the one hand and inspiring professional mathematicians on the other.

Fifteen years have passed since then. Those years produced many diverse and sometimes pedagogically unsound innovations in mathematics teaching. The swing of the pendulum has now moved back to the new-old overconcern with "basic" skills. I feel good after restudying my materials in 1977. Their development in a classroom setting made for a common sense synthesis of both points of view.

What *are* then some of the significant aspects of the program that made it stand the test of time?

- Few word reading skills are required in the materials, but the program builds up a large vocabulary of mathematical reading skills: notation, chart reading, map reading, diagram reading. The materials allow the non-word-reader a fair chance at success.

- Most concrete learning aids suggested in these materials are teacher or student made or are easily collected from the everyday environment. Only a few, carefully selected, commercially available aids are suggested. (I still consider the Cuisenaire® rods the best all-purpose aid.)

- Both metric and common English units of measurement are used. No other American series did that a generation ago. Cuisenaire® rods, based on the centimeter scale, are used from the start to measure in metric units.

- Number lines are used in a variety of ways that range from ordering numbers (whole numbers, fractions, integers) to beginning functions. 10 by 10 arrays are used with similar variety, from counting to making tables for basic operations.

- Practice in computing is given through the creation and analysis of varied number patterns and series. Also included are instructions for card games, lotto, number line races, spinner and dice games.

- All four arithmetic operations and work with fractions are introduced in the first year. Experience in building models for concepts precedes all written work. The development of mathematical notation arises out of the children's own needs to record the results of experiments.

- Lab sheets do not have a commercial appearance and are not overcrowded. The pages are often handwritten or typed and deliberately varied. There is space for children to add their own problems. This serves as an encouragement for teachers and children to create their own additional materials. If pages are too slick, home-made materials can't compete with them.

- Ideas about sets are introduced with fun activities. Sorting games, for example, are used to introduce Venn diagrams. Many textbooks introduce an artificial and stilted formal language of sets in the early grades—only to give up any reference to sets by grades 4 and 5. This is ridiculous!

- Our base ten system of numeration is shown in many ways without overburdening the children by formal references to expanded notation.

- A variety of types of open sentences are introduced early in the series and continued throughout.
  $5 + 3 = \square$ (Five plus three equals what?)
  $\square = 5 + 3$ (What equals five plus three?)
  $8 = 5 + \square$ (Eight equals five plus what?)
  $5 + \square = 8$ (Five plus what equals eight?)

- Perforations in the workbook pages allow greater flexibility in their use. Children can remove lab sheets for correction or to take home. Lab sheets can also be arranged in different sequences and stapled together as units. Extra sheets can go into a classroom collection for use by other children. The progress charts on the inside back covers of the workbooks can be used to keep track of the completed work of the children.

Over the years I have had the opportunity to keep in close touch with many of the children I taught and whose mathematical education started with these materials. It gives me pleasure and satisfaction to know that a high proportion of students kept their love for the subject and experienced success in mathematics throughout their schooling. Many chose careers requiring advanced mathematics. They still recall with pleasure episodes from our math lab. My personal experience has been reinforced by my discovery this year that many of the schools that participated in the first large tryouts years ago are still using the books—and still consider them the best materials available.

Although I have learned much about teaching mathematics since 1960, I do not hesitate to sign my name again to them in 1977.

Lore Rasmussen

Philadelphia, Pennsylvania
June 1977

3

The Miquon Math Lab Materials

The Miquon Math Lab Materials were developed by Lore Rasmussen at the Miquon School, Miquon, Pa., in the early 1960's. The children's materials, 650 pages of lab sheets collected into six workbooks, reflect the author's profound belief that young children can understand and enjoy mathematical concepts not usually taught in

the primary grades in this country. The teacher's materials, published in four parts, reflect the same attitude about teachers, that they too can understand and enjoy the mathematics they teach. Originally tested in 150 classrooms, the Miquon Math Lab Materials have since been used by many thousands of children and their teachers. The materials are as unique today as when they were written.

Teacher's materials

The teacher's component of the Miquon Math Lab materials consists of three dialogues between author and teacher, each serving a distinct purpose. The three books are: *Notes to Teachers, Lab Sheet Annotations,* and *First-Grade Diary.*

Notes to Teachers is a philosophical and pedagogical statement about children, learning, and teaching. It is the THIS I BELIEVE statement embedded in the Miquon Math Lab Materials.

Lab Sheet Annotations contains the specific instructions for use of the children's lab sheets. It is the daily teaching companion of teachers using the Miquon Math Lab Materials. Each topic is introduced by a discussion of the mathematics underlying the children's work along with teaching suggestions and anecdotes.

First-Grade Diary is a day-by-day account of the activities in the author's mathematics classroom. It gives an intimate view of the author as teacher dealing with real children's problems and progress. *One* model of *one* class for *one* year, it illustrates personal uniqueness, spontaneity, and flexibility inherent in a teaching-learning situation where "workbooks" (even the ones in this collection) do not dominate. It is a ready source of stimulating ideas.

Lab Sheet Annotations

This book, *Lab Sheet Annotations,* contains a complete set of the 650 pupil lab sheets (reduced in size) that appear in the workbooks of the Miquon Math Lab Materials. The intervening text indicates the objectives of the sheets and ways in which the pupils may use them. Included are preliminary activities, teaching suggestions, and follow-up activities for many of the lab sheets. The annotations provide questions that the teacher can ask to reinforce the concepts underlying the problems on the sheets. The text also suggests activities for practice in applying those concepts. Where the procedures and objectives are apparent at a glance, lab sheets are not annotated.

Using the annotations

Following are some recommendations for the use of *Lab Sheet Annotations:*

1   Before beginning work on a topic with the children, the teacher should read the mathematics background material on that topic included in *Lab Sheet Annotations.* The teacher should also continually refer to *First-Grade Diary* for teaching suggestions and games.

2   Answers to only the most difficult or the trickiest problems are provided in the annotations. The teacher should use an extra set of the workbooks and work through *all* of the problems in order to be

familiar with the concepts involved and the relative difficulty of the sheets. Thus teachers become their own first pupils as they transform their personal copies of the workbooks into answer books.

3 The divisions between Levels 1 to 6 are somewhat arbitrary. The teacher should feel free to dip into any level at any time that this is warranted for a particular pupil or group of pupils. No child should necessarily have to finish every sheet in a given level before advancing to the next level. Since the divisions between levels are artificial, all levels have been combined in *Lab Sheet Annotations*. This allows the teacher to develop a topic beyond the pages available in a particular workbook. It also allows each teacher to get a complete overview of the entire sequence of learning tasks for children. First grade teachers can look ahead, third grade teachers can look back.

4 The teacher should understand the organization of the material in *Lab Sheet Annotations*. Each student lab sheet is labeled with a dot-letter-number sequence. The dots indicate the lab sheet's level of difficulty and locate it in a particular workbook. The letter identifies the topic of the lab sheet. The number indicates the position of the lab sheet within its topic. Hence "••• F23" means that this lab sheet is in Level 3 (The Blue Book) and is the twenty-third lab sheet on Topic F, Multiplication. Similarly, " ••••• S9" means that this lab

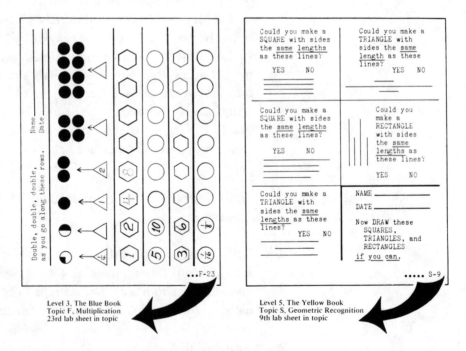

Level 3, The Blue Book
Topic F, Multiplication
23rd lab sheet in topic

Level 5, The Yellow Book
Topic S, Geometric Recognition
9th lab sheet in topic

sheet is in Level 5 (The Yellow Book) and is the ninth lab sheet on Topic S, Geometric Recognition. *Lab Sheet Annotations* is organized according to topic, not according to level. The Lab Sheet Level Chart that follows provides a quick reference guide for the levels and topics of lab sheets.

Lab Sheet Level Chart

Section	Topic	Level 1 • Orange Book	Level 2 •• Red Book	Level 3 ••• Blue Book	Level 4 •••• Green Book	Level 5 ••••• Yellow Book	Level 6 •••••• Purple Book
A	Counting	A1-A24					
B	Odd–Even		B1-B12	B13-B20			
C	Addition	C1-C11	C12-C25	C26-C34	C35-C36	C37-C46	
D	Subtraction	D1-D4	D5-D12	D13-D16	D17-D18	D19-D22	D23-D44
E	Addition and Subtraction	E1-E25	E26-E41	E42-E49		E50-E53	E54-E57
F	Multiplication	F1-F12	F13-F22	F23-F42	F43-F46	F47-F50	F51-F56
G	Addition, Subtraction, and Multiplication	G1-G8	G9-G12	G13-G20			
H	Fractions	H1-H6	H7-H24	H25-H42		H43-H56	H57-H64
I	Addition, Subtraction, Multiplication, and Fractions		I1-I8	I9-I16			
J	Division		J1-J12		J13-J18	J19-J26	J27-J32
K	Addition, Subtraction, Multiplication, Fractions, and Division		K1-K8	K9-K16		K17-K22	
L	Equalities and Inequalities	L1-L4	L5-L10		L11-L16	L17-L20	L21-L24
M	Place Value				M1-M16	M17-M20	M21-M24
N	Number Lines and Functions	N1-N4			N5-N10	N11-N18	
O	Factoring		O1-O4		O5-O6	O7-O12	
P	Squaring				P1-P16		P17-P18
Q	Simultaneous Equations					Q1-Q8	
R	Graphing Equations						R1-R30
S	Geometric Recognition	S1-S4		S5-S8		S9-S11	
T	Length, Area, and Volume	T1-T8			T9-T20	T21-T28	
U	Series and Progressions				U1-U6	U7-U12	
V	Grid and Arrow Games			V1-V6		V7-V8	V9-V10
W	Mapping				W1-W12		
X	Clock Arithmetic	X1-X10			X11-X14	X15-X16	X17-X18
Y	Sets						Y1-Y10
Z	Word Problems						Z1-Z13

A Counting

A robin will come back to its nest when one of four of its eggs has been removed. A robin will desert its nest when one of three eggs has been removed. Can a robin count to three?

A pre-schooler rattles off number words from one to twenty with lightning speed. Does this pre-schooler necessarily know how to count?

What is involved in counting? Is counting the first rung in man's—or the child's—climb up the mathematical ladder?

Counting is not the very beginning of man's mathematical development. Counting implies that we can extract a common feature, "threeness," from three elephants and three years. It also implies that we consider this "threeness" as *less* than the "fourness" embodied in four mice and four minutes.

The robin recognized a group of "more than two." The pre-schooler memorized a "word sequence." Neither activity is enough to be called counting. The ideas of one-to-one correspondence and number sequence, and a special generalized vocabulary to express the two ideas, are prerequisites for counting. Let us illustrate them.

Matching, or one-to-one correspondence

We see many examples of one-to-one correspondence in our everyday experience. We enter a lecture hall with friends and all get seats. Others come into the hall and take seats. When all seats are taken, the number of seats matches the number of people. For every person in the audience, there is a corresponding chair. For every chair, there is a corresponding person. If one person is without a chair, the "set of chairs" is one less than the "set of persons"—whether there are 50 chairs, 10 chairs, or 300 chairs. We know this without having to count the chairs or the people. If one chair is without a person, the set of persons is one less than the set of chairs. Again, we do not have to count to know that .his is true.

Children do this kind of matching when they pass out candy, pencils, paper, and other objects. Will there be enough? Let's give each child a piece of candy. If the supply of candy is exhausted at the same time that all of the children have gotten their candy, then the groups (candy, children) are matched and are equal. We do not need number names, nor do we need to count. We either "have enough," "have more than enough," or "do not have enough."

Early man used matching or tallying in this way to keep track of his herds and other possessions. The word *tally* comes from the Latin word *talea*, which means "stick" or "cutting," and probably refers to the cutting of notches into sticks to make a record of some possession. For example, seven notches refer to seven sheep let out to pasture.

The word *calculate* is from the Latin word *calculus*, meaning "pebble," and is a reminder of our ancestors' use of piles of pebbles to keep track of their possessions. Therefore a tally

or a pile of pebbles

served as a check of the herd. If the herd, upon its return, did not match with the tally or the pile of pebbles, then the missing animal(s) had to be sought. The herd was intact only when the set of tally marks or pebbles was in one-to-one correspondence with the set of animals.

Fingers—and toes—have been man's most convenient matching device. The fact that our own system of numeration (that is, system of counting) is a base-ten system is an outgrowth of the early use of fingers and toes for matching. Other systems of numeration have been used, such as base five (number of fingers on one hand), base twenty (number of fingers and toes), base twelve (still used in our dozens and in inches in a foot), etc. The modern computer uses base two, the same system we use in measuring dairy products (cup, pint, quart, half gallon, gallon).

From the crude beginnings of tallying, pebbling, or fingering, a shorter method of grouping tallies, pebbles, or fingers arose.

 was probably easier to read than $||||$

was probably easier to read than $||||$

Later, picture numerals and picture words were used instead of repeated tallies. Picture symbols, such as those below, were used to refer to different numbers of things. From these beginnings simpler numerals developed. Our own number words and numerals probably had such a beginning.

sun	wings	leaf	deer	hand
1	2	3	4	5

From directly matching two groups of things (for example, matching pebbles with sheep), matching could be extended. Groups could be matched indirectly.

As an example, each child is given a pencil. The set of children in the group is thereby matched with the set of pencils. The children go out for recess but leave their pencils on their desks. Can the set of children be matched, during their absence, with a set of paper? Yes. We can match a set of paper with the set of pencils on the desks and thereby indirectly match the paper with the set of children.

A set of children	is matched with	B set of pencils
B set of pencils	is matched with	C set of paper

therefore,

A. set of children	is matched with	C set of paper

There are certain sets whose elements are easily counted. Examples are a formation of dots on a domino or the set of lines in a tally.

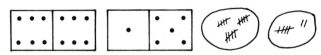

By establishing a one-to-one correspondence between such a "model" set and an arbitrary given set, we can determine the number of elements in the given set.

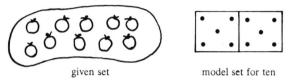

given set   model set for ten

In the picture above, by matching each apple with each dot on the domino, we can prove that altogether there are ten apples.

Suggested activities

The following nine activities are ones that can be used to suggest to children the concept of one-to-one correspondence. Use any collection, or set, of things: children, leaves, geometric solids, blocks, books, letters of the alphabet, etc.

1   Boys are matched with girls.

Larry   Peter   Danny   Carl
  ↕   ↕   ↕   ↕
Mary   Ann   Toni   Betty

2   Capital letters are matched with small letters.

3   Names are matched with girls.

4   Dots are matched with capital letters.

The number of the sets of dots matches the number of the set of capital letters.

5   Geometric shapes are matched.

The number of the set of circles matches the number of the set of triangles.

6   Individual shapes are matched with a row of identical shapes.

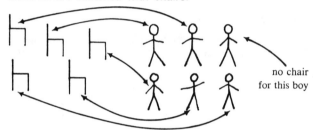

The number of the set of single squares matches the number of the row of squares.

7   Children are matched with chairs.

no chair for this boy

The set of chairs does *not* match the set of boys.

8   Rods of different lengths are matched.

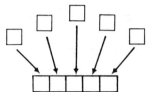

The number of the set of white rods matches the number of the set of red rods.

Number sequence

We may have many of the kinds of "model" sets which we found on dominoes and still not have a number system. To establish a number system, we must have a systematic way of arranging the model sets in the order of their magnitude. When we develop a way to obtain a successor to each number, we have established a counting system. The usual way in which to obtain the successor to a number is by adding one to it.

In the Mathematics Laboratory program, the Cuisenaire® rods are recommended as a basic model-making device for giving children experiences in matching and counting. Once a child has selected a model for the set of one, he can pass on to models for the sets of two, three, four . . . and on and on. The "rod stairs" illustrate this.

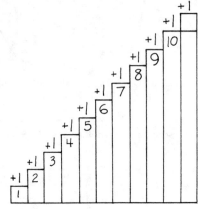

Thus,

$$1 = 1$$
$$(1) + 1 = 2$$
$$(1 + 1) + 1 = 3$$
$$(1 + 1 + 1) + 1 = 4 \text{ (etc.)}$$

From this experience, the child perceives that every number has a successor. The successor to a number is found by adding one to the number.

Suggested activities

Below are sketchy outlines for activities that introduce children to the notion of number sequence.

1   With children

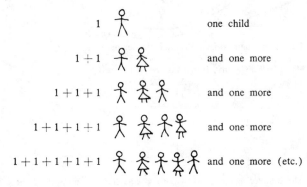

Whenever we stop, we can always go backward, getting one less until "all are gone." When "all are gone," then the number of children or objects is zero, written '0.'

2   On the number line

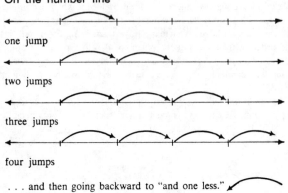

one jump

two jumps

three jumps

four jumps

. . . and then going backward to "and one less."

3   With rods

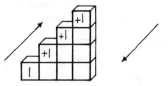

. . . and one more and one more, or backward to "and one less."

4   With fingers

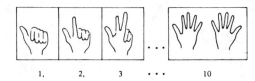

1,   2,   3   . . .   10

and backwards

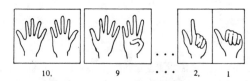

10,   9   . . .   2,   1

Number vocabulary and numerals

After the preceding activities, it will not be difficult to associate number words (one, two, three, etc.) and numerals (1, 2, 3, etc.) with groups of discrete objects and length.

Suggested activities

Repeat many of the previous activities, using children, jumps on the number line, blocks, or fingers. However, this time make a verbal and visual association between number words, numerals, and objects.

1   Use of rods

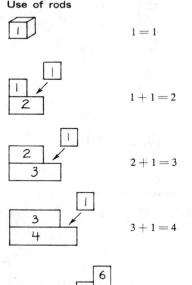

$$1 = 1$$

$$1 + 1 = 2$$

$$2 + 1 = 3$$

$$3 + 1 = 4$$

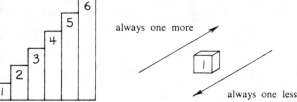

always one more

always one less

2   Use of numeral cards

Each child should have a deck of numeral cards for the numbers 0 through 10. They may eliminate the need for early writing, or they can assist the child who is learning to write numerals.

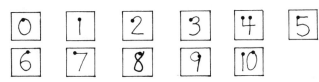

They can be made from 3 x 5″ file cards. Dots should be put at the spot where each stroke is started as the numeral is written. The child then can put these cards at the top of his desk to serve as models when he writes. He can place his finger on the dot and trace the numeral first when he is confused about how to write it.

These numeral cards may be used in such activities as the following:

a. Children match number of things with cards.

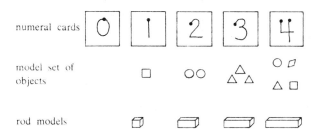

b. Children arrange numeral cards in counting sequence: 1, 2, 3, 4, 5, . . . [etc.] or 10, 9, 8, 7, . . . [etc.].

c. Children use numeral cards as answer cards for large-scale single problems the teacher has made on strips of oaktag.

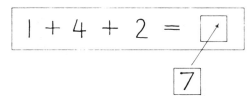

Transition from activity to writing

The lab sheets in Section A will require the children to write for the first time.

Not all children will make the transition from model building to written work at the same time. Some reasons for this are the children's varying degree of fine-muscle control for writing, reversal tendencies, varying rates of committing new symbols to memory, differing backgrounds, and varying intelligence.

It is therefore very important that teachers do not press children too hard and too early on matters of neatness, correct numeral form, and quick memorization of symbols.

Following are some examples of children's work which show that they *understand* the task at hand but have trouble because of unfamiliarity with numerals.

1   John built this model of the counting sequence 1 through 7. He placed the rods on a sheet of paper on which he had written:

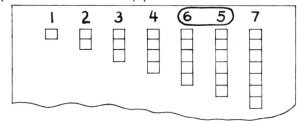

John had the right mathematical idea but mixed up the numerals 5 and 6. He will learn their proper placement soon!

2   Ann made a fine model for $3 + 4 = \square$

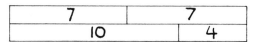

and then called out, "It's the black rod! It's the black rod! What is its name?" The teacher asked her to line up the white rods under it and find out. "Oh, it's seven, but how do you make a seven?"

3   Gary made up problems of his own and was very proud of them. Here is one:

$$7 + 7 = 41$$

What was his mistake? The teacher asked Gary to read his problem out loud to her. Gary read, "Seven plus seven equals fourteen. And I'll show you with my rods!"

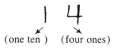

Gary is a good thinker. He wrote:

(four   teen)

It was not his fault that our language and our numerals do not match! The teacher showed him from his model that we write:

1   4

(one ten)   (four ones)

Note: It might be fun to make a game of inventing new names for ten, twenty, thirty, as follows. Such words would be consistent with their numerals.

. . . eight, nine, onety, onety-one, onety-two, etc.
    8   9   10   11   12

twoty	twoty-one	twoty-two, etc.
20	21	22

threety	threety-one
30	31

fourty	fourty-one
40	41

4   Louis is excellent in computation, but his writing is full of reversals.

$$4 + 2 = 9 \qquad 5 + 3 = 2$$

The teacher has to be a detective to tell he knows the answers. But she gives him the benefit of the doubt.

Work with children during their *handwriting lesson* on writing numerals. On arithmetic papers do not make the children take time out to correct their reversals or sloppy rendering of numerals.

•A1–A3

These lab sheets are arranged in order of complexity. Each sheet contains nine collections (sets) of objects which vary in number from one item to nine items (elements).

A-1   All sets contain circles of uniform size and in an orderly arrangement.

A-2   Sets contain elements in a variety of shapes and sizes.

A-3   Elements are less neatly arranged and vary in shape and size.

Suggested uses of lab sheets

1   Pupils match each element in each set (picture group) with an object such as a rod or a bead.

2   Pupils check off each element in a set with a tally mark.

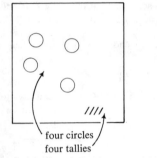

four circles
four tallies

three things
three tallies

3   Pupils match each element in a set with a white rod to get a model set. Then they arrange the rods in a row and exchange the row of white rods for a single rod of that length.

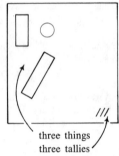

| Set of 4 elements | is matched with 4 white rods. | White rods are placed in a row, and | white rods are exchanged for 1 purple rod. |

The purple rod now represents the original set of 4 curved lines.

4   Pupils count the elements in each set and match each set with a numeral card.

5   Sample questions appropriate for all three pages:

Which collection (group, set)
. . . is the smallest (the least)?
. . . is the largest (most)?
. . . has one more than three things?
. . . has twice as many as two things?

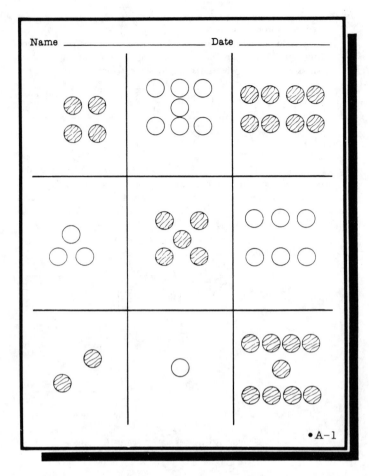

Name _____   Date _____

•A–1

6   Coloring activity for lab sheet A1.

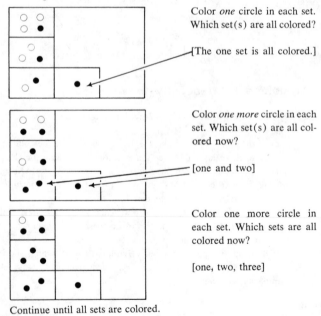

Color *one* circle in each set. Which set(s) are all colored?

[The one set is all colored.]

Color *one more* circle in each set. Which set(s) are all colored now?

[one and two]

Color one more circle in each set. Which sets are all colored now?

[one, two, three]

Continue until all sets are colored.

7   Lotto

Each child is given one sheet (either A1, A2, or A3). A "caller" holds up a Cuisenaire® rod—for example, a yellow rod. The children find on their sheets the set containing five elements and lay a yellow rod on that picture. The game is over when all the sets are matched with rods. The same game should also be played with numeral cards instead of rods.

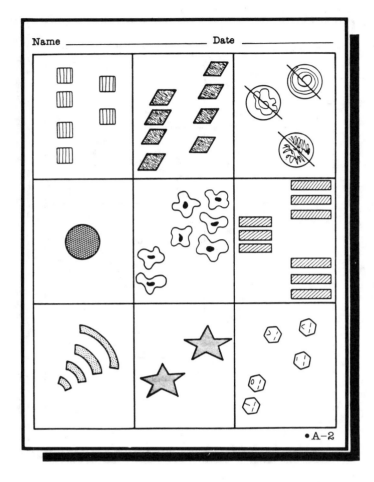

• A-2

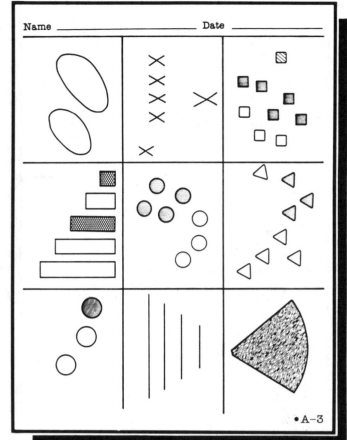

• A-3

8   Special use of A3

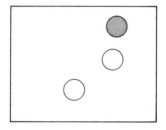

How many circles in the set? [3]
How many are white? [2]
How many are colored? [1]

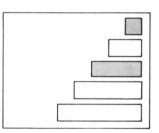

How many things? [5]
How many white? [3]
What color is the smallest? [blue]
What color is the largest? [white]
What color is the middle one?
[blue]

Special use of A1 and A2. After children have learned some addition
sentences, they can reuse these sheets, writing a problem of their
own to go with each picture.

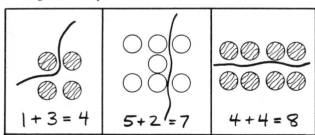

$1 + 3 = 4$ $5 + 2 = 7$ $4 + 4 = 8$

A a A	B b B b	b B b B	F f
D D D	d d d d	M	r R R r
E e E	e e e	G g G G	N n N N n N N N

• A-3a

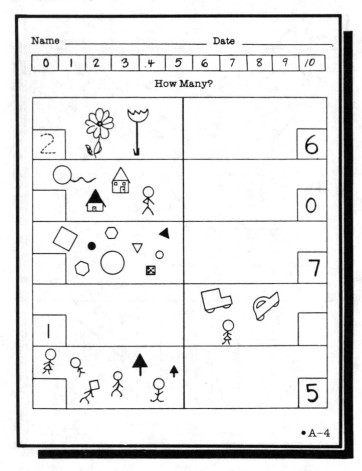

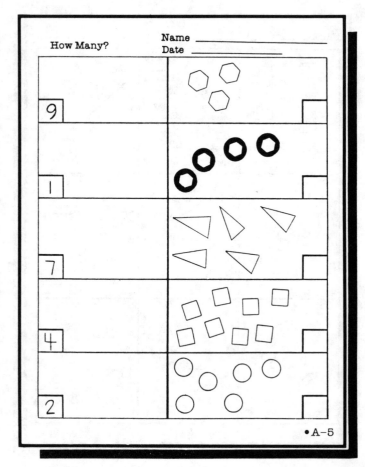

•A4, A5

Matching numerals with size of set

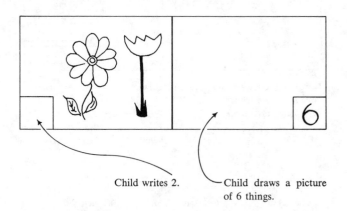

Child writes 2.

Child draws a picture of 6 things.

A5 is essentially the same as A4. Geometric shapes—hexagons, circles, triangles, squares—are used instead of representative pictures. Children may be introduced to the correct names for those shapes.

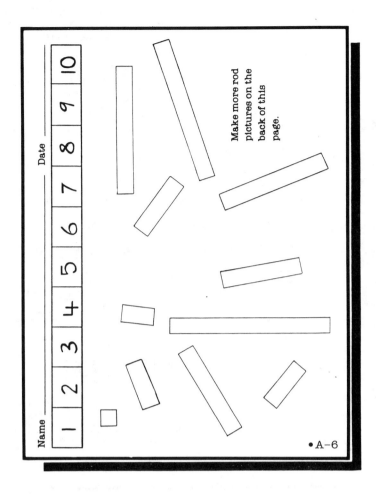

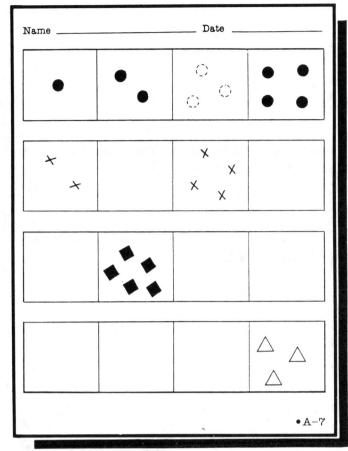

·A6

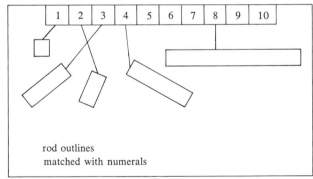

rod outlines
matched with numerals

or

numerals written
into outlines

Children match the rod outlines with Cuisenaire® rods and identify
the outlines with the proper numerals in either of the ways shown.
Children may want to color the rod outlines the same colors as the
matching rods.

·A7

This is a rather difficult lab sheet. The teacher should precede its use
with similar exercises on the chalkboard.

Child completes lab sheet A7 in either of two ways:

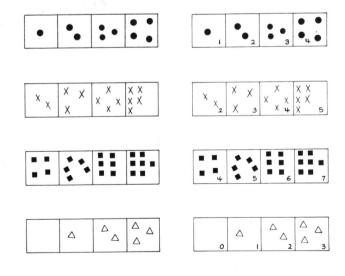

Child completes each row of
pictures so that the number of
things increases by one from
left to right.

Child completes each row of
pictures and also writes the corresponding numerals.

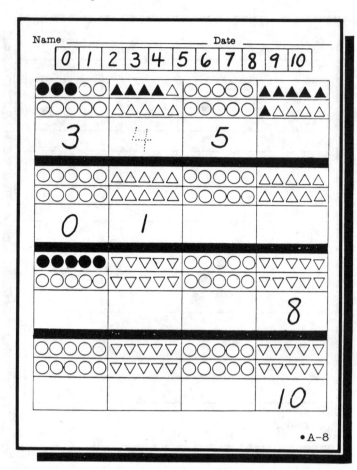

A8

On this sheet the first two rows completed will look like the picture below. To get the activity started, the teacher may ask the children to give suggestions as to how they think the sheet should be done.

●●●○○ / ○○○○○	▲▲▲▲△ / △△△△△	●●●●● / ○○○○○	▲▲▲▲▲ / ▲△△△△
3	**4**	**5**	**6**

Three things are shaded, and the corresponding numeral is written.

four things five things six things

○○○○○ / ○○○○○	▲△△△△ / △△△△△	●●○○○ / ○○○○○	▲▲▲△△ / △△△△△
0	**1**	**2**	**3**

zero things one thing two things three things

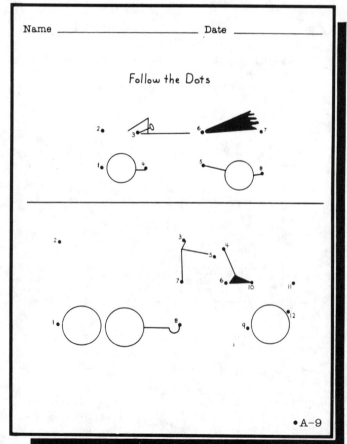

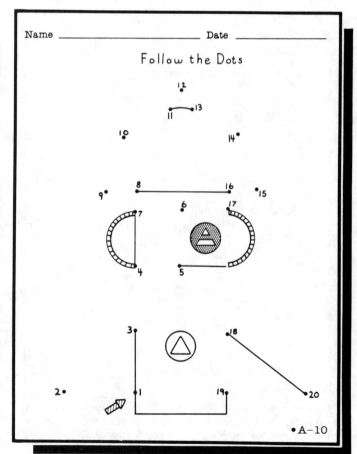

·A11, A12

Some number lines are labeled. Each mark (point) has a name. Children are to complete the labeling of some of the lines and then draw in "jumps" or "hops" of various sizes.

"one" hops

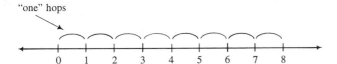

"two" hops

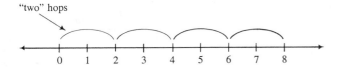

a jump from 5 to 8 . . . or a jump from 8 to 5

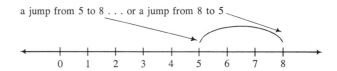

Zero is the starting place. It is "home," or where we begin our trip. We move along the line from 0 to 1 to 2 to 3, etc. We cannot get to 3 without passing 1 and 2.

Each mark on the line has a name. Name '1' comes before name '2,' etc.

It does not matter which way the line slants. We can always use it for our trips.

The distance between the numbers can be different for different lines. The distance between numbers must remain the same on any one line.

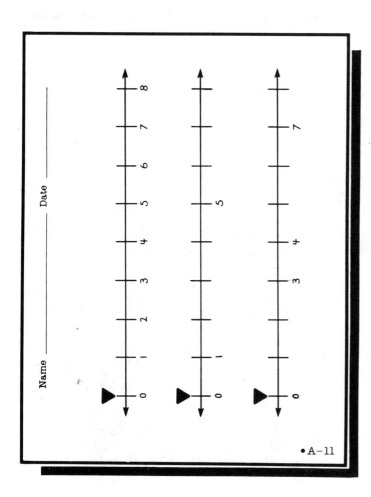

•A-11

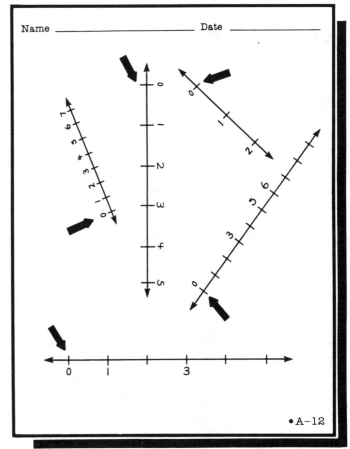

•A-12

·A13

The number line introduced

Here the number line is introduced as "a road to be traveled." There are signs on the way—equal spaces apart.

Zero is the starting place for the trips on this number line. We travel to the right. The first and second trips are already drawn in. Children may trace them with their fingers, stopping at each sign.

When the lab sheet is completed, *all* road signs are labeled and the following "trips" have been taken:

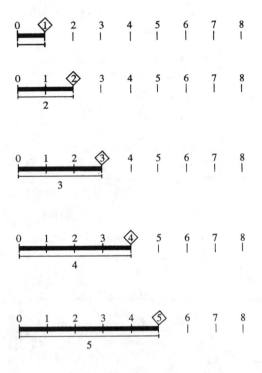

Sample questions

Which trip is the longest?
Which trip is the shortest?
What is the longest trip we *could* take on this road?
How long is the second trip? The third?

Note: The association of "to the right" with "greater value" is arbitrary but follows mathematical convention.

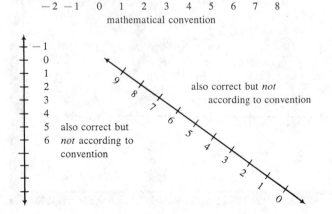

mathematical convention

also correct but *not*
according to convention

also correct but *not* according to convention

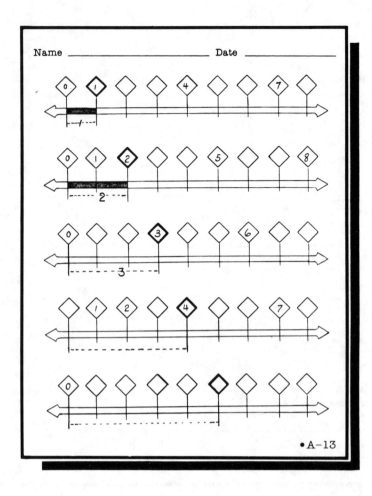

Name _____   Date _____

•A–13

·A14

Writing the missing numerals

1, 2, 3, □, 5 . . . What counting number comes after 3 and before 5?
2, 3, 4, □, □ . . . What are the next two counting numbers?
6, □, 8 . . . What counting number is between 6 and 8?

Class aids

1 A number chart for the wall

1	2	3	4	5	6	7	8	9	10
11	12	13	14	15	16	17	18	19	20
21	22	23	24	25	26	27	28	29	30
31	32	33	34	35	36	37	38	39	40
41	42	43	44	45	46	47	48	49	50
51	52	53	54	55	56	57	58	59	60
61	62	63	64	65	66	67	68	69	70
71	72	73	74	75	76	77	78	79	80
81	82	83	84	85	86	87	88	89	90
91	92	93	94	95	96	97	98	99	100

Name _____   Date _____

1, 2, 3, □, 5

2, 3, 4, □, □

6, □, 8

9, □, 11

14, 15, □

18, 19, □, 21

10, □, □, 13

• A–14

Name _____   Date _____

Finish the chart.

0	1		3	4			7		
10		12			15				19
		23			26		28		
30		32		34		36		38	
	41		43		45		47		49
50			53			56			59
	61				65				
	71	72	73	74		76	77	78	
80			83		85		87		89
90				94	95	96			99

• A–15

---

2   A chalkboard number line stretching across the top of the chalkboard

0 1 2 3 4 5 6 7 8 9 10 11

on as far as
there is space ....

•A15

Filling in the grid

A sample procedure follows:

Make a color stairs with the rods. Look at the chart. What goes into the empty spaces in the first row? [2, 5, 6, 8, 9]

Find the place for '2' and write it in.

Find the place for '5' and write it in.

Write in all the missing numerals in the first row.

Can you tell the name for the smallest number in the second row?

Can you tell the name for the largest number in the second row?

Count from 10 to 19. Point to the space where '11' should go, '13' should go, etc.

Make a rod stairs beginning with 10.

Your stairs will help you write the missing number names for the second row.

Find '10' on your chart. Point to your model of 10 in your stairs. What comes after 10 in your stairs? What would you write after '10' in your chart? Write '11' in that space. 11 means 1 ten and 1 one.

After the second row is filled in, children may then be asked to build models of the numbers, in stair fashion, from 20 through 29. They might try to write the missing numerals unaided.

For many children this is enough for one lesson. The chart need not be finished in one day. Others may want to finish on their own.

10 11 12 13
rod stairs

(10 + 1) = 11
(10 + 2) = 12
(10 + 3) = 13

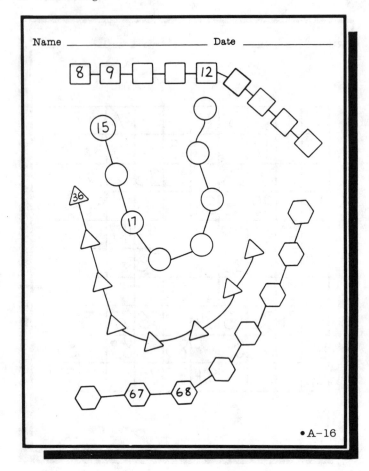

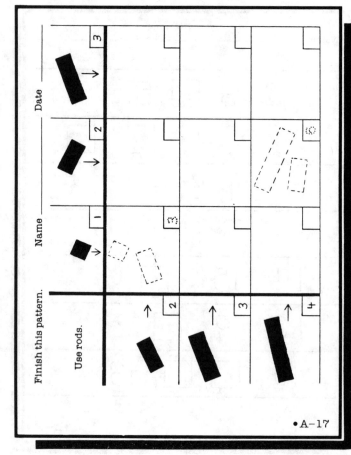

·A16

Fill in the missing numerals so that each chain has numerals for consecutive whole numbers.

Suggested procedures

1 Look at the chain of squares. There are some empty spaces. What do you think goes into the square after '9'? [10] Write it in.

2 And what comes after '10'? [11] Write it in, etc.

3 Look at the chain of circles. There are some empty spaces . . . etc.

Or, children could begin at 1 and count aloud up to 7; then beginning with 8, tap each square with their fingers as they count along the chain. (Do the same for the chain of circles.)

Or, look at lab sheet A15. The chart will help children complete A16. The number chart on the wall (like A15) will also help them complete A16.

Note: For many children, it will be enough to do only the square chain and the circle chain. The other chains can be finished from a chalkboard model or at a later date.

·A17
Suggested procedures

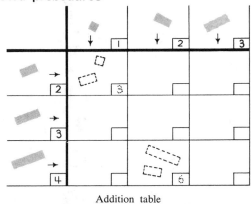

Addition table

At first, this sheet should be used only as an activity sheet. No writing! (Use Cuisenaire® rods.)

1 Find a rod to fit each rod shadow. Cover each shadow with the correct rod.

2 Now we can play a "sliding" game. The rods on the *side* can move only *to the right*. The rods on the *top* can only move *straight down*.

3 Move the red *side* rod one space over to the right. Only one other rod is allowed to go into the space. Which one is it? [the *top* white rod] Put it there.

4 Now put the red rod and the white rod back onto their "shadow places."

5 Move the red *side* rod *two spaces* over to the right. There is only *one* other rod that can meet it there. It is . . . [the *top* red rod] Put it there. Now what is in the box? [two red rods]

6 Move the rods back onto their shadows.

7 Where can the *side* red rod and the *top* green rod meet? Put them there.

8 Where can the *side* green rod and the *top* white rod meet?

9 Where can the *side* purple rod meet the *top* green rod?

10 Where can the *side* green rod meet the *top* green rod? Etc. (Play until interest wanes.)

Other suggestions

1 The children may try to trace around the two rods that meet in a box. (Two samples are done.) Do not insist on neatness. The rods slip!

2 As an extra activity, let those children who are able to do so write in the numerals.

(How many white rods would we need to cover the pair of rods in each box?)

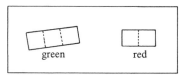

Five white rods cover the pair of rods in this box.

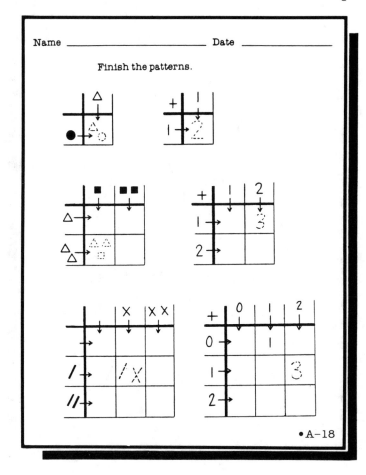

Name _____ Date _____

Finish the patterns.

·A-18

·A18

Lab sheet A18 is an extension of A17. Let the children study each example and tell you what has been done.

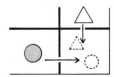

Put a finger next to the red circle on the side. Put a finger next to the triangle at the top.

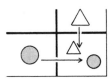

Pretend that the circle moved into the box; pretend that the triangle moved into the box. Draw them. How many things are in the box? [two things]

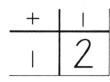

This is how we write what happened.

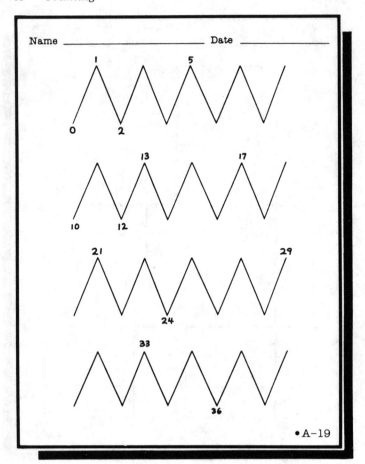

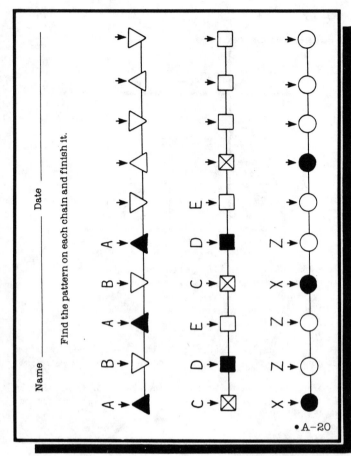

•A19

Up and Down the Mountain

This is a mountain road. We start from "home" at zero. The even
numbers are "down," and the odd numbers are "up."

•A20,   A21

Lots of patterns should be clapped, shouted, tapped, drawn, built,
etc. Children can "talk the pattern" as they finish each chain.

Name _____ Date _____

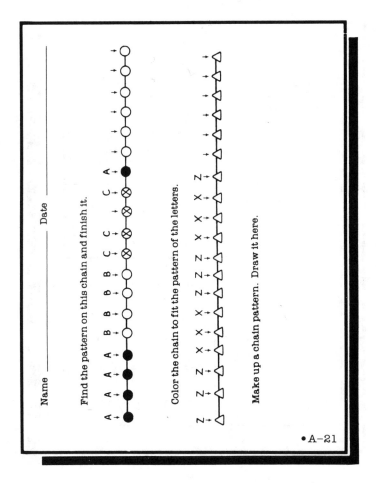

Name _____ Date _____

Fit the right rod on each part of the rod picture.

How many white rods long
is your train? ☐

How many red rods long
is your train? △

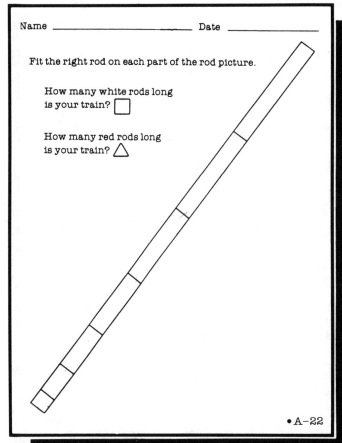

• A-21

• A-22

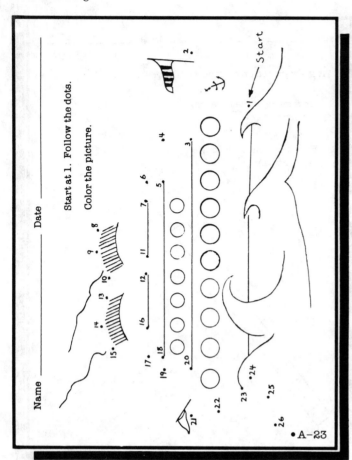

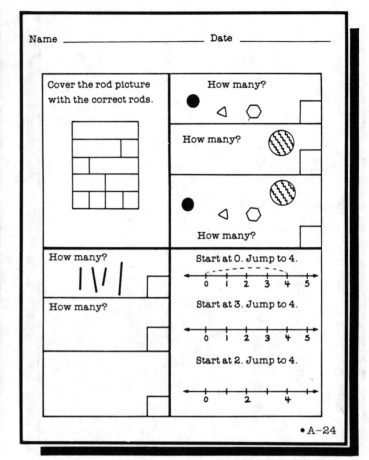

B Odd-even

The fact that the set of whole numbers can be divided into two subsets—the subset of odd whole numbers and the subset of even whole numbers—can be a useful tool in learning arithmetic. There are several ways in which the sets of even and odd whole numbers can be described.

1 **The set of even whole numbers** consists of those numbers left over after we cross out every second whole number starting with 1.

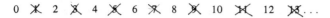

0 ✗ 2 ✗ 4 ✗ 6 ✗ 8 ✗ 10 ✗ 12 ✗ . . .

The set of odd whole numbers consists of those numbers left after we cross out every second whole number starting with 0.

✗ 1 ✗ 3 ✗ 5 ✗ 7 ✗ 9 ✗ 11 ✗ 13 . . .

2 **We get the set of even whole numbers** from

$$2 \times \square$$

if $\square$ is the placeholder for *every* whole number. We get the set of odd numbers from

$$(2 \times \square) + 1$$

if $\square$ is the placeholder for *every* whole number.

Whole Numbers $\square$	Even Whole Numbers $2 \times \square$	Odd Whole Numbers $(2 \times \square) + 1$
0	0	1
1	2	3
2	4	5
3	6	7
4	8	9
5	10	11
6	12	13
7	14	15
8	16	17
9	18	19
10	20	21
.	.	.
.	.	.
.	.	.

3 **The even whole numbers are members of the set of whole numbers** which, when divided by 2, produce another whole number. (The number 6 is an even whole number, because 6 divided by 2 equals 3, another whole number.)

The odd whole numbers are the members of the set of whole numbers which, when divided by 2, do *not* produce another whole number. (The number 7 is an odd whole number, because 7 divided by 2 is not equal to any whole number.)

4 **If the small white rod is our unit**, then any length which can be built out of red rods *alone* represents an even number. Any length which can be built out of red rods and *one* white rod stands for an odd number.

0		1	I
2	2	3	2 | 1
4	2 | 2	5	2 | 2 | 1
6	2 | 2 | 2	7	2 | 2 | 2 | 1
8	2 | 2 | 2 | 2	9	2 | 2 | 2 | 2 | 1

5 **A collection contains an even number of objects** if each object in the collection can be paired with some other object in the collection and no unpaired object remains. A collection contains an odd number of objects if one object in the collection remains unpaired.

·· B1–B3

The purpose of these sheets is to enable children to find out something about collections without necessarily counting their elements. Children can determine whether a collection contains an even or an odd number of elements by *pairing* them. If the pairing comes out even, then the number of elements in the collection is *even*. If one element is left over after pairing (that is, if there is an "odd" element in the collection), then the collection contains an *odd* number of elements. Some children will be able to pair mentally. Others will circle their pairs. Children should not be discouraged from using either of these methods. After determining whether a collection is even or odd the children should count its elements.

Preliminary activities

Before attempting any of the first three odd–even lab sheets, it is well worth the time to play some classroom games, do some pattern building with Cuisenaire® rods, and to improvise some story problems, using the chalkboard.

Musical chairs

Musical chairs can be adapted to introduce the odd-even principle, as follows:

No one loses—even
Choose 6 children and put up 6 chairs. When the music (or the singing) stops, all children find chairs and there are 6 child–chair pairs. There are no losers: no chair, no child is left over. This can be repeated with other numbers of children and chairs.

One person loses—odd
Six children and 5 chairs make only 5 child–chair pairs with one child left standing. He is the "odd" one. He does not have a chair as a "partner."

A game with Cuisenaire® rods

Let the children choose any rod or train of rods and then measure them with *red* rods only. All of the lengths of the rod trains will then fall into two groups:

□ × red	or	(□ × red) + white
purple = 2 reds orange + red = 6 reds [etc.]		blue = 4 reds + white black = 3 reds + white [etc.]

If we now call the white rod "one" and the red rod "two," we can make a table of numbers.

Even		Odd	
build in twos only		build in twos plus a one	
2	2	3	(2 + 1)
(2 + 2)	4	5	(2 + 2 + 1)
(2 + 2 + 2)	6	7	(2 + 2 + 2 + 1)
(2 + 2 + 2 + 2)	8	9	(2 + 2 + 2 + 2 + 1)
(etc.)	10	11	(etc.)
	12	13	

"Chalk" story

The teacher uses illustrations to help tell a story:

"Father is sorting socks that he just washed. He arranges all the socks by color. Here is what he finds. [Draw the following on the chalkboard.]

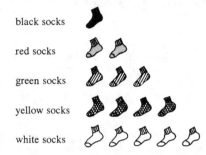

black socks

red socks

green socks

yellow socks

white socks

"He calls his daughter Janie and says, 'Janie, look in your closet and under your bed. Some of your socks are missing.' "

Questions to children:
a. How does father know that some socks are missing?
b. What colors are the missing socks?
c. How many socks does Janie wear at one time?
d. What is the color of the socks that can be arranged into one pair with one sock left over?
e. What is the color of the two pairs of socks with no sock left over?
f. If Janie does not find her missing socks will she be able to wear a pair of black socks?
g. Father asks Janie to arrange all her socks into pairs and bring him the leftover socks. Janie brings him a _____ sock, a _____ sock, and a _____ sock. These are her odd socks.

When we have a number of things that can be arranged by twos without a leftover thing, the number is even.

Lab sheets B1, B2, and B3 should be used for concrete activity before children write on them. Provide the children with a number of small objects, such as pennies, paper clips, or rods, which they can place on the sheets and arrange into groups.

·· B1

Lab sheet B1 may serve as the cover of a booklet on the topic odd-even. It is also a sample page to "talk about."

The groups of squares on the page are sorted according to the odd-even criterion.

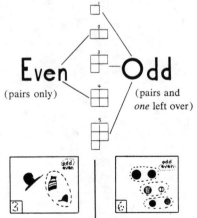

Pictured are 3 hats: one *pair* of hats and 1 hat *left over;* 3 is an *odd* group.

Pictured are 6 balls: 3 *pairs* of balls; 6 is an *even* group.

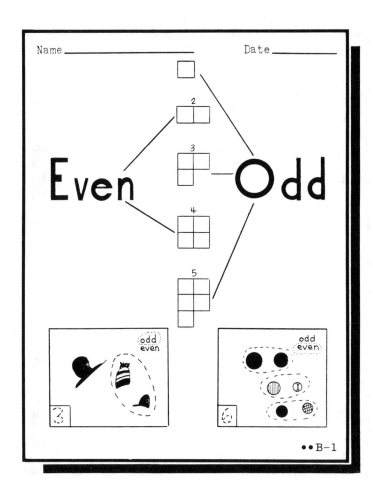

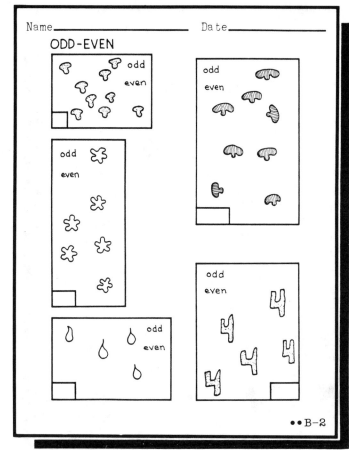

•• B3

Below are two completed examples from the second row of B3:

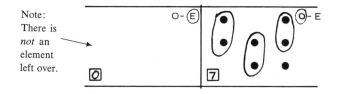

Note:
There is *not* an element left over.

Questions relevant to these problems are: Is *every* collection of 7 elements odd? Is *every* collection of 0 elements even? By answering questions such as these, the children will form generalizations about numbers. Seven will become an *odd* number to them. Zero will become an *even* number to them.

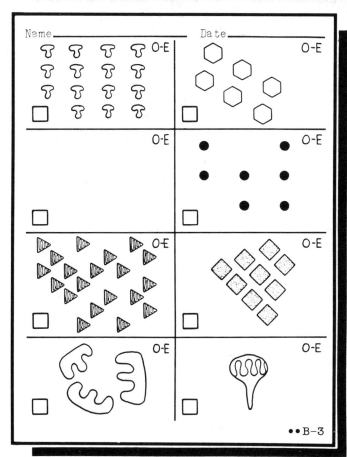

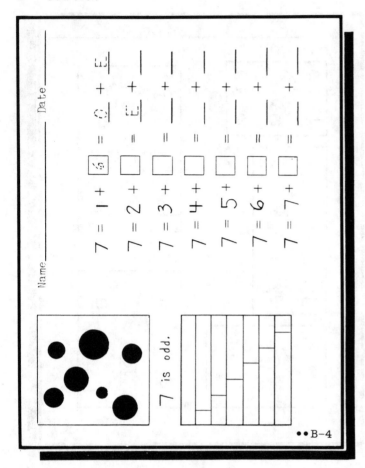

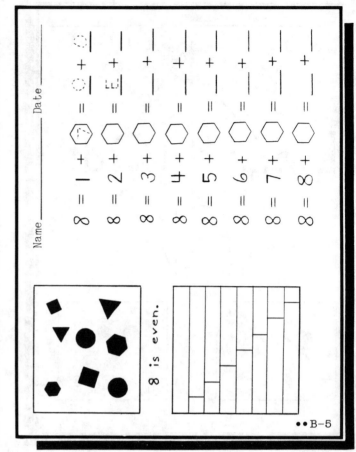

•• B4, B5

Let the children study these lab sheets silently. Then ask *them* for suggestions as to how to proceed. They will notice that on B4 there is a rod pattern for the black rod and on B5 there is a rod pattern for the brown rod. They can fit their rods over the pattern as they work. The geometric designs (7 things on B4, 8 things on B5) can also be used.

7 circles equal 1 circle and 6 circles.

     (1)   and   (3 pairs)
    odd   +   even

7 circles equal 2 circles and 5 circles.

   (a pair)   and   (2 pairs + 1)
    even   +   odd

When the children have completed B4 and B5, they may have noticed that in every case the number 7 was made up of an *odd* addend and an *even* addend

$$O + E = O$$
$$E + O = O$$

and that the number 8 has either 2 *odd* addends or 2 *even* addends.

$$O + O = E$$
$$E + E = E$$

The question should be raised whether these patterns hold only for 7 and 8 or for other odd and even numbers. The children themselves can verify this experimentally by making two-addend patterns for other numbers and testing their hunches.

B-6 Worksheet

Name _____   Date _____

Draw an <u>odd</u> number of things.	Draw an <u>even</u> number of things.
Draw <u>five</u> <u>pairs</u> of things. O-E	Draw <u>five</u> things. O-E
Draw one pair of things and one extra thing. O-E	Draw two pairs of things and one extra thing. O-E

•• B-6

B-7 Worksheet

Name _____   Date _____

Collection	Number of things	Number of Odd or Even?	Number of pairs	Number Left Over
(example, X's)	□ THINGS	even	⬡ PAIRS	◯ LEFT OVER
(crowns)	□ THINGS		⬡ PAIRS	◯ LEFT OVER
(shapes)	□ THINGS		⬡ PAIRS	◯ LEFT OVER
(striped shape)	□ THINGS		⬡ PAIRS	◯ LEFT OVER

•• B-7

•• B6–B8

For B6 the teacher may need to read the directions aloud. The children should do B6 in preparation for B7 and B8. Additional chalkboard work or individual work, similar to B6, may be helpful to some children.

On B7 the children should study the dotted example, trace over the dots, and then complete the lab sheet along the following lines:

a. Arrange the collection into pairs.
b. How many *things* in the collection?
c. Is the collection even or odd?
d. How many *pairs* in the collection?
e. After pairing, how many things are left over?

The activity on B8 is similar to that on lab sheet B7, except that the order of the questions is changed.

Collection	Pairs	Left over	Odd/Even	Things
(ovals)	④ pairs	◯ left over	even	⑧ things
	◯ pairs	◯ left over	even	◯ things

B-8 Worksheet

Name _____   Date _____

Collection	Number of Pairs	Number Left Over	Odd or Even?	Number of Things
(shapes)	◯ Pairs	⬡ Left Over		□ Things
(Pr sp v)	◯ Pairs	⬡ Left Over		□ Things
(shapes)	◯ Pairs	⬡ Left Over		□ Things
(shapes)	◯ Pairs	⬡ Left Over		□ Things

•• B-8

31

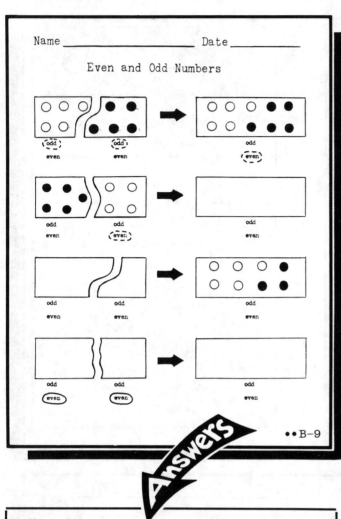

Name _____ Date _____

Even and Odd Numbers

•• B-9

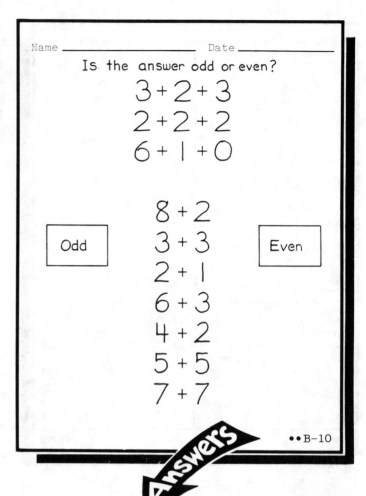

Name _____ Date _____

Is the answer odd or even?

$$3 + 2 + 3$$
$$2 + 2 + 2$$
$$6 + 1 + 0$$

Odd   Even

$$8 + 2$$
$$3 + 3$$
$$2 + 1$$
$$6 + 3$$
$$4 + 2$$
$$5 + 5$$
$$7 + 7$$

•• B-10

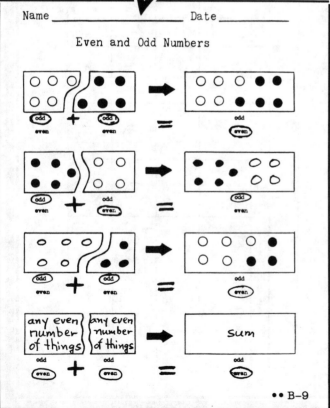

Name _____ Date _____

Even and Odd Numbers

•• B-9

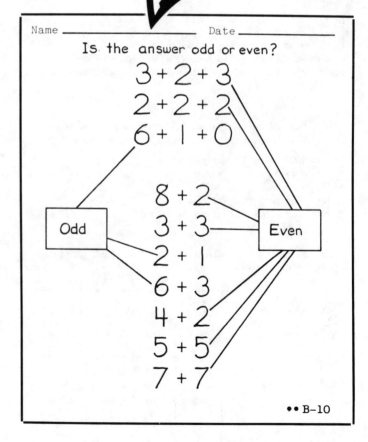

Name _____ Date _____

Is the answer odd or even?

$$3 + 2 + 3$$
$$2 + 2 + 2$$
$$6 + 1 + 0$$

Odd   Even

$$8 + 2$$
$$3 + 3$$
$$2 + 1$$
$$6 + 3$$
$$4 + 2$$
$$5 + 5$$
$$7 + 7$$

•• B-10

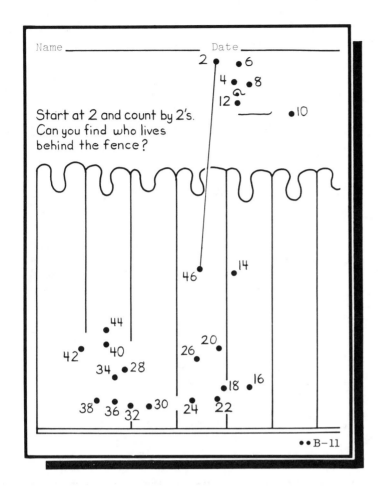

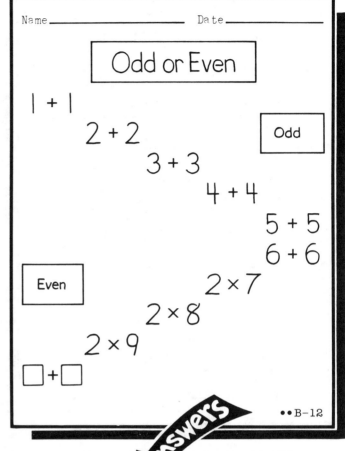

·· B9

Again, it is good pedagogy to let the children puzzle out what this lab sheet is about.

The following comments are typical of those children make: "This could be about torn strips of paper that have to be pasted together." "The first pieces are fixed already, and the second pieces have to be fixed by us and drawn in."

A completed sheet will resemble the following:

·· B10, B12

Before these sheets are used, children should be able to distinguish between the even numbers and the odd numbers. Not only should they know that the numerals 0, 2, 4, 6, and 8 stand for even numbers, but they should also have made the generalization that any numeral whose last digit is 0, 2, 4, 6, or 8 also stands for an even number. Likewise they should know that any numeral whose last digit is 1, 3, 5, 7, or 9 stands for an odd number.

Thus, they should have no trouble recognizing that 37 is odd or that 3078 is even. The problems on these sheets call on this ability. Additional problems of this type may be done on the chalkboard.

The purpose of these sheets is to provide opportunities for the children to make generalizations such as, "The sum of any two even numbers is always even." (B10) Similarly,

$$odd + odd = even$$
$$odd + even = odd$$
$$even + odd = odd$$

Another generalization is: "Two times any whole number is even." (B12)

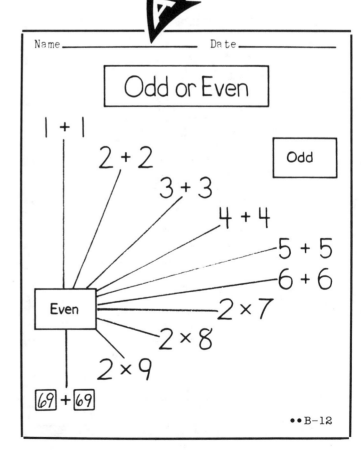

Name _____ **Date** _____

3 + 1 = ☐	Odd	Even
5 + 5 = ☐	Even	Odd
7 + 3 = ☐	Even	Odd
11 + 5 = ☐	Odd	Even
9 + 13 = ☐	Odd	Even
7 + 1 = ☐	Even	Odd
23 + 15 = ☐	Odd	Even
41 + 33 = ☐	Even	Odd
165 + 235	Even	Odd
4003 + 3001	Odd	Even
	Odd	Even
	Odd	Even

•••B-13

•••B13–B15

Fill in the frame and then put a loop around the correct word.

At the bottom of each lab sheet are some three-digit and four-digit addends, but no frames are provided for their respective sums. It is hoped that some children will attempt to generalize from their previous work whether the sums will be odd or even. *They are not expected to know the exact answers.*

$$165 + 235$$
$$\downarrow \qquad \downarrow$$
$$\text{odd} + \text{odd} = \text{even}$$

Of course, no child should be prevented from writing the sums.

There is space on all three sheets for the children to make up their own problems.

Name _____ **Date** _____

4 + 4 = ☐	Even	Odd
8 + 0 = ☐	Even	Odd
2 + 6 = ☐	Odd	Even
12 + 6 = ☐	Even	Odd
26 + 2 = ☐	Odd	Even
18 + 14 = ☐	Odd	Even
24 + 16 = ☐	Even	Odd
302 + 124	Odd	Even
6328 + 3572	Odd	Even
	Even	Odd
	Odd	Even
	Even	Odd

•••B-14

Name _____ **Date** _____

Odd	Even	☐ = 3 + 4
Even	Odd	☐ = 5 + 6
Even	Odd	☐ = 1 + 8
Odd	Even	☐ = 7 + 0
Even	Odd	☐ = 13 + 4
Odd	Even	☐ = 21 + 10
Odd	Even	319 + 124
Even	Odd	45 + 202
Odd	Even	3981 + 4328
Even	Odd	
Even	Odd	
Odd	Even	

•••B-15

Worksheet B-16

Name_____ Date_____

Cross out all the odd numbers.

6	9	11	0	4	12	35
28	36	63	101	427	666	555
1234	7	72	110	1	724	2345

Make these even:

3 + △	8 + ○	☐ + 1
17 + ☐	⬡ + 100	9 − △
6 − ○	43 + ☐	639 + ☐
803 − ⬡	△ x 3	☐ x 4
☐ x △	½ x ☐	⅓ x ⬡

•••B-16

Worksheet B-17

Name_____ Date_____

Start at zero and count by twos.

0				

How many even numbers are listed? ☐
How many odd numbers are listed? ☐

Start at one and count by twos.

1				

How many even numbers are listed? ☐
How many odd numbers are listed? ☐

Start at three hundred and count by twos.

300				

How many even numbers are listed? ☐
How many odd numbers are listed? ☐

•••B-17

B16

To do the first exercise on this lab sheet, the child must realize that the digit farthest to the right in a numeral (in the decimal system of numeration) tells us whether the number is odd or even.

427 is an odd number because 7 is odd.
724 is an even number because 4 is even.

Note: There are many correct answers to the problems in the second exercise. Any correct answer is acceptable. Here is a sample:

3 + [1]	8 + [0]	[1] + 1
17 + [1]	[0] + 100	9 − [1]
6 − [0]	43 + [1]	639 + [1]
803 − [1]	[2] × 3	[2] × 4
[2] × [△1]	½ × [0]	⅓ × [6]

Worksheet B-18

Name_____ Date_____

Start at three hundred and one; count by twos.

301				

How many even numbers are listed? ☐

How many odd numbers are listed? ☐

Start at sixty-three and count backward by twos.

63				

How many even numbers are listed? ☐

How many odd numbers are listed? ☐

•••B-18

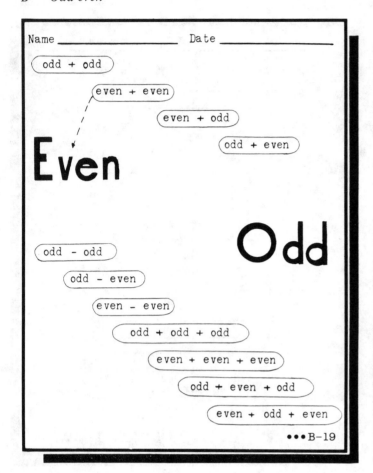

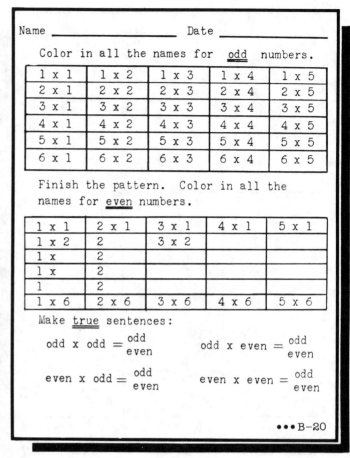

··· B19, B20

Until now all of the lab sheets have dealt with the recognition and addition of *specific* odd and even numbers. Here now is a first attempt to get children to generalize about *all* odd and *all* even numbers.

Primary-grade children are too young to be really sure of their first efforts at generalization. They cannot "prove" what they have reason to expect. They try to say to themselves that they know no exceptions—but they *know* that they do not know all numbers. Still, they have good reason to trust the regular pattern of odd and even.

Following are two arguments given by young children about zero being an even number:

1 Between any two odd numbers there is *always* an even number; between any two even numbers is *always* an odd number. Zero *must* be even or the pattern breaks its own rule.

2

A	B	C	D
odd	odd	even	even
+ odd	+ even	+ odd	+ even
even	odd	odd	even

Let's *pretend* zero is odd. Then, according to the above,

    A. 5 + 0 = an even number
    B. 0 + 6 = an odd number
    C. 6 + 0 = an odd number

None of the preceding is true. Therefore, zero cannot be odd. Now let's *pretend* zero is even. Then, according to the above,

    B. 5 + 0 = odd
    C. 0 + 5 = odd
    D. 0 + 6 = even

All of the preceding are true. Therefore, zero must be an even number or our rules for all other numbers won't hold.

··· B20

Children should color all names for *odd* numbers.

1 × 1	1 × 2	1 × 3	1 × 4	1 × 5
2 × 1	2 × 2	2 × 3	2 × 4	2 × 5
3 × 1	3 × 2	3 × 3	3 × 4	3 × 5
4 × 1	4 × 2	4 × 3	4 × 4	4 × 5
5 × 1	5 × 2	5 × 3	5 × 4	5 × 5
6 × 1	6 × 2	6 × 3	6 × 4	6 × 5

Color names for *even* numbers.

1 × 1	2 × 1	3 × 1	4 × 1	5 × 1
1 × 2	2 × 2	3 × 2	4 × 2	5 × 2
1 × 3	2 × 3	3 × 3	4 × 3	5 × 3
1 × 4	2 × 4	3 × 4	4 × 4	5 × 4
1 × 5	2 × 5	3 × 5	4 × 5	5 × 5
1 × 6	2 × 6	3 × 6	4 × 6	5 × 6

C Addition

After children have learned to count and to recognize and write numerals, they are ready to begin working with them.

The first fundamental operation to be introduced is *addition*. This is an extension of the successor concept. The successor concept defines any integer (whole number) as the preceding integer plus one. (See Section A, Counting, "Number Sequence," page 11) As we now take up addition, we no longer limit ourselves to the sum of "any number plus one" but include other sums.

Before any written work is done involving addition, the children should have done a considerable amount of "pattern building" with the Cuisenaire® rods. They should know, for instance, that there are many different rod "trains" equal in length to a given "train."

8							
4				4			
5			3				
1	7						
1	1	1	1	1	1	1	1

(In this illustration, the white rod, 1, is considered the unit.)

Once this concept is fully understood, the children need only to learn a way of transcribing what they see and understand. The relationships shown in the preceding diagram may be expressed by the following notations:

$$8 = 4 + 4$$
$$8 = 5 + 3$$
$$8 = 1 + 7$$
$$8 = 1 + 1 + 1 + 1 + 1 + 1 + 1 + 1$$
$$5 + 3 = 1 + 7$$
$$4 + 4 = 5 + 3$$
$$1 + 1 + 1 + 1 + 1 + 1 + 1 + 1 = 4 + 4$$
etc.

Properties of addition

Although one purpose of the problems on the Section C lab sheets is to give children practice in arithmetical computation, the problems also serve as an opportunity for children to discover some of the basic properties of the addition of whole numbers. The whole numbers are the numbers in the set {0, 1, 2, 3, 4, . . .}.

An important property of addition of whole numbers, which is frequently taken for granted, is that any two whole numbers can be added to produce another whole number. In mathematical terms,

if $\square$ and $\bigcirc$ are whole numbers,
then $\square + \bigcirc$ is also a whole number.

Commutative property

Another of the basic properties of addition is illustrated by the following pair of problems from lab sheet C1:

$$4 = 1 + \square$$
$$4 = \square + 1$$

When, with the aid of his Cuisenaire® rods, a child discovers that '3' goes into both $\square$'s, he will see that $1 + 3$ and $3 + 1$ are both equal to 4. Other problems on these lab sheets will show that

$$0 + 4 = 4 + 0$$
$$3 + 2 = 2 + 3$$
$$4 + 1 = 1 + 4$$

After a child has done enough problems of this type, he should be able to form the generalization that

$$\square + \bigcirc = \bigcirc + \square$$

is *always* true, provided we obey the rule which tells us to place the same number in every $\square$ and place the same number in every $\bigcirc$ in any one problem. This property—that the sum of two numbers equals the sum of the same two numbers in the reverse order—is called the *commutative property* of addition.

Associative property

The next property of addition is illustrated by the problems on lab sheets C19, C20, and C23. This property, which applies to the addition of three or more numbers, indicates that the order in which we add does not affect the sum. For example:

$$(3 + 4) + 2 = 7 + 2 = 9$$
$$3 + (4 + 2) = 3 + 6 = 9$$

Regardless of the pair of numbers added first, the sum is 9. Therefore we can say that

$$3 + 4 + 2 = 9$$

or, in general terms, the *associative property of addition* tells us that

$$\left(\square + \triangle\right) + \bigcirc = \square + \left(\triangle + \bigcirc\right)$$

We recommend using loops, rather than parentheses, with young children.

Identity element

Another important property of addition is illustrated by the following examples:

$$4 + 0 = 4$$
$$1167 + 0 = 1167$$
$$11 + 0 = 11$$

Adding zero to a number gives us as the sum the identical number with which we started. In mathematical language, we can say that

$$\square + 0 = \square$$

Inverse operation

It is an important fact that addition has an inverse operation. Subtraction, the inverse of addition, is dealt with extensively in Section D, Subtraction.

Frames

Frames, such as

are placeholders in equations and inequalities. There are two ways in which they are used:

1   **Frames are used to express unknown quantities** in precisely the same manner that we used *x*'s, and *z*'s in our high school algebra courses. The advantage of using frames instead of letters is that frames can be filled in. In comparing the following two solutions of the same problem, we see that there is less writing involved:

$$x + 7 = 10 \qquad \square + 7 = 10$$
$$x = 3 \qquad\qquad \text{fill in '3'}$$

2   **Frames are also used in writing open sentences** which are *always* true. For example:

$$\square + 0 = \square.$$

This open sentence is always true *regardless* of what number is placed in the two $\square$s.

Some others are as follows:

$$1 \times \square = \square$$
$$\triangle + \bigcirc = \bigcirc + \triangle$$
$$(\square + \triangle) + \bigcirc = \square + (\triangle + \bigcirc)$$
$$\square + (4 \times \square) = 5 \times \square$$

So that no mistake is made in using frames, study carefully the two examples given below.

Some of the solutions to the open sentence

$$\square \; + \; \triangle \; + \; \bigcirc \; = \; 6$$

are

$$\boxed{2} + \triangle\!\!\!\!0 + \textcircled{4} = 6$$
$$\boxed{0} + \triangle\!\!\!\!3 + \textcircled{3} = 6$$
$$\boxed{2\tfrac{1}{2}} + \triangle\!\!\!\!1 + \textcircled{2\tfrac{1}{2}} = 6$$
$$\boxed{2} + \triangle\!\!\!\!2 + \textcircled{2} = 6$$

This open sentence also has many other solutions.

The open sentence

$$\square \; + \; \square \; + \; \square \; = \; 6$$

has only one solution:

$$\boxed{2} + \boxed{2} + \boxed{2} = 6$$

Why does this open sentence have only *one* solution? Why doesn't it have *many* solutions, as the open sentence in the first example does? For the reason, study the following frame rule.

Frame Rule: In an open sentence, all frames which have the same shape stand for the same number. Frames with different shapes *can* stand for the same number, but *may* stand for different numbers.

Suggested activities: partner games

The three games that follow are examples of simple addition and/or multiplication drill which are easily done in the classroom. Children like playing them and will invent new games to be played with their cards.

Numeral Card Game 1:   Make Ten

Equipment
Two decks of numeral cards in contrasting colors, each deck containing numerals 0 through 10.

Rules
1   Each child has a colored deck. He shuffles his deck and places it face down in front of him.

2   First player places his top card face up in the center.

3   Second player now places his top card face up in the center. If he can make a two-color combination which equals 10, he wins the pair of cards. If not, his card remains in the center.

4   Game continues until all cards are paired and "owned" by one or the other of the players. The player with the most pairs is the winner.

5   If a player fails to see a possible pair when it is his turn, the other player may claim it without losing his own turn.

6   Follow the same procedure for "Make 9," "Make 11," and other such games.

Numeral Card Game 2:   Odd or Even

This game has two versions; it can be both an addition game and a multiplication game.

Equipment
Two decks of numeral cards in contrasting colors, each deck containing numerals 0 through 10, each numeral duplicated.

Rules
1   The two players decide who will claim odd numbers and who will claim even numbers.

2   One deck is placed face down in front of each child.

3   Each child puts one card face up in the middle of the table. If the sum (or product) is odd, Child A claims the pair. If the sum (or product) is even, Child B claims the pair. The winner is the child with the most pairs.

Numeral Card Game 3:   Make Ten

This game has the same equipment and rules as the other game "Make Ten," except that each pair of numbers is multiplied and a score is kept of each product. The winner is the child who has the highest score. For example:

$$
\begin{array}{lrl}
\text{Child A claimed:} & 1, 9 = & 9 \\
& 2, 8 = & 16 \\
& 0, 10 = & 0 \\
\hline
& & 25 \\
\end{array}
$$

$$
\begin{array}{lrl}
\text{Child B claimed:} & 3, 7 = & 21 \\
& 4, 6 = & 24 \\
& 8, 2 = & 16 \\
\hline
& & 61 \\
\end{array}
$$

Child B won.

· C1–C10

Cuisenaire® rods should be available to the children for use with these lab sheets. The following diagrams illustrate ways in which the rods may be used to solve problems involving addition.

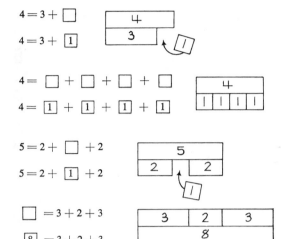

$4 = 3 + \square$

$4 = 3 + \boxed{1}$

$4 = \square + \square + \square + \square$

$4 = \boxed{1} + \boxed{1} + \boxed{1} + \boxed{1}$

$5 = 2 + \square + 2$

$5 = 2 + \boxed{1} + 2$

$\square = 3 + 2 + 3$

$\boxed{8} = 3 + 2 + 3$

There is more than one way of representing a problem in addition. The preceding problems can also be pictured very easily on number lines.

$4 = 3 + \square$

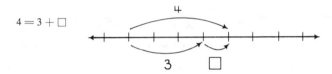

$4 = \square + \square + \square + \square$

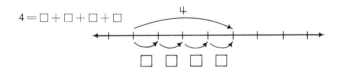

$5 = 2 + \square + 2$

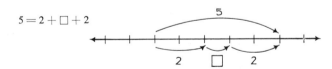

$\square = 3 + 2 + 3$

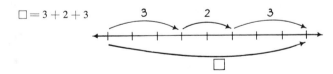

Many of these early lab sheets contain enough extra space to allow children to make up their own problems or the teacher to dictate problems for the children to solve.

Name _____ Date _____

⬡ 4

Use rods.

$3 + \square$

$2 + \square$

$1 + \square$

$0 + \square$

$\square + 2$

$\square + 1$

$\square + \square + \square + \square$

$\square + 4$

· C–1

Name _____ Date _____

⬡ 5

$3 + \square$

$4 + \square$

$2 + \square$

$\square + 1$

$\square + 3$

$2 + \square + 2$

$\square + \square + \square + \square + \square$

Make up your own.

_____   _____

_____   _____

· C–2

C-3

Name _____ Date _____

⑦

Seven

6 + □
5 + □
4 + □
□ + 3
□ + 2
□ + 1
3 + 3 + □
□ + □ + □ + □ + □ + □ + □

•C-3

C-4

Name _____ Date _____

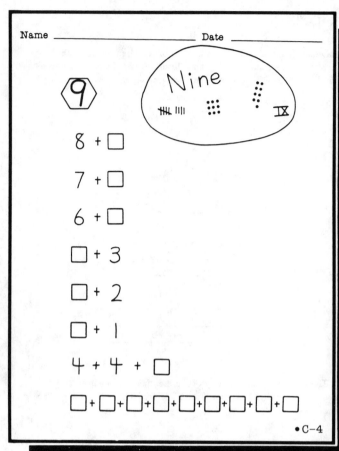

⑨

Nine

8 + □
7 + □
6 + □
□ + 3
□ + 2
□ + 1
4 + 4 + □
□ + □ + □ + □ + □ + □ + □ + □ + □

•C-4

C-5

Name _____ Date _____

2 + 1 = □

5 + 2 = □

6 + 3 = □

4 + 4 = □

3 + 3 = □

1 + 1 + 1 + 1 = □

•C-5

C-6

Name _____ Date _____

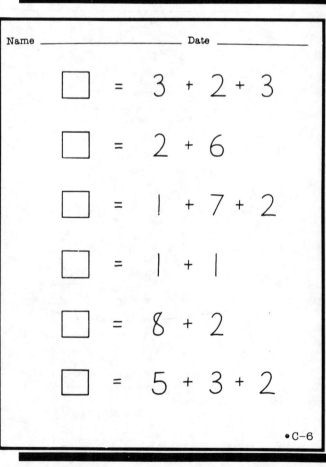

□ = 3 + 2 + 3

□ = 2 + 6

□ = 1 + 7 + 2

□ = 1 + 1

□ = 8 + 2

□ = 5 + 3 + 2

•C-6

Name _____ Date _____

$1 + 2 = \square$

$4 + 3 = \square$

$\square = 2 + 4$

$5 + 3 = \square$

$\square = 2 + 2$

• C-7

Name _____ Date _____

$1 + 3 = \square$

$2 + 4 = \square$

$\square = 5 + 2$

$\square = 4 + 3$

$6 + 1 = \square$

$7 + 3 = \square$

• C-8

• C5–C10

You may have noticed that the problems on these sheets are written in two different ways. The position of the frame varies from the right to the left of the equation. This is done to keep children from relying solely on one manner of presentation of the problem. Children should understand that the problems in the following pairs are equivalent:

$6 + 3 = \square$ $5 + 5 = \square$
$\square = 6 + 3$ $\square = 5 + 5$

Six plus three equals what?   Five plus five equals what?
What equals six plus three?   What equals five plus five?

• C9, • • C14
Repeated addition

These two lab sheets provide problems in *repeated addition* and may serve as an introduction to the material on the lab sheets of Section F, Multiplication.

$1 + 1 = 2 \times 1 = 2$
$2 + 2 = 2 \times 2 = 4$
$3 + 3 = 2 \times 3 = 6$
$4 + 4 = 2 \times 4 = 8$

$3 + 3 + 3 + 3 = 4 \times 3 = 12$
$4 + 4 + 4 + 4 = 4 \times 4 = 16$
$5 + 5 + 5 + 5 = 4 \times 5 = 20$

(See also lab sheets E24, E25, F1–F5, F7–F10.)

Name _____ Date _____

$1 + 1 = \square$

$2 + 2 = \square$

$\square = 3 + 3$

$4 + 4 = \square$

$\square = 5 + 5$

$6 + 6 = \square$

• C-9

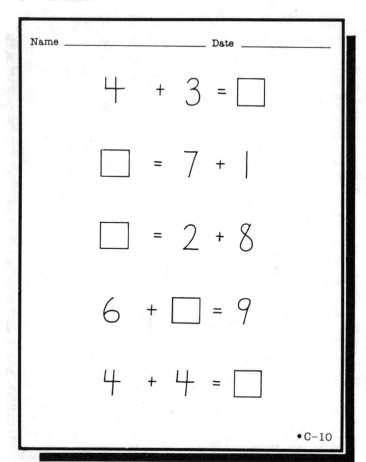

Name _____ Date _____

$$4 + 3 = \square$$

$$\square = 7 + 1$$

$$\square = 2 + 8$$

$$6 + \square = 9$$

$$4 + 4 = \square$$

• C–10

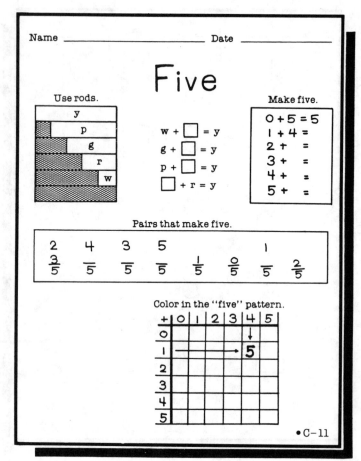

Name _____ Date _____

Five

Use rods.

w + $\square$ = y

g + $\square$ = y

p + $\square$ = y

$\square$ + r = y

Make five.

0 + 5 = 5
1 + 4 =
2 + =
3 + =
4 + =
5 + =

Pairs that make five.

$\frac{2}{3}$ ...	$\frac{4}{5}$	$\frac{3}{5}$	$\frac{5}{5}$	$\frac{1}{5}$	$\frac{0}{5}$	$\frac{}{5}$	$\frac{2}{5}$

Color in the "five" pattern.

+	0	1	2	3	4	5
0					↓	
1	→	→	→	→	**5**	
2						
3						
4						
5						

• C–11

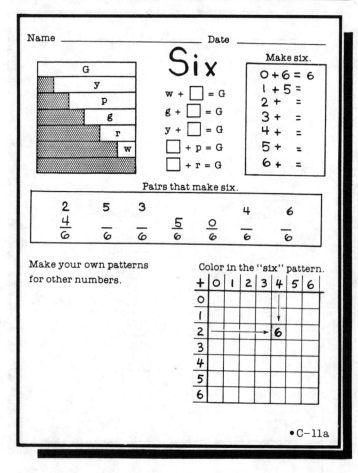

Name _____ Date _____

Six

Make six.

0 + 6 = 6
1 + 5 =
2 + =
3 + =
4 + =
5 + =
6 + =

w + $\square$ = G

g + $\square$ = G

y + $\square$ = G

$\square$ + p = G

$\square$ + r = G

Pairs that make six.

$\frac{2}{4}$	$\frac{5}{6}$	$\frac{3}{6}$	$\frac{}{6}$	$\frac{0}{6}$	$\frac{4}{6}$	$\frac{6}{6}$

Make your own patterns for other numbers.

Color in the "six" pattern.

+	0	1	2	3	4	5	6
0							
1							
2	→	→	→	→	**6**		
3							
4							
5							
6							

• C–11a

• C11

This page could be approached as a puzzle page. The teacher may suggest: "Let's have a 'thinking silence' and each get an idea of what we could do with this page."

1 Yes, rods fit on the staircase picture. The letters stand for the color names of our rods: *y*ellow, *p*urple, *g*reen, etc.

2 w + $\boxed{p}$ = y is a sentence about the rod picture. (white + $\boxed{purple}$ = yellow)

3 "Make five" is a game for writing true sentences about the picture, using numerals instead of color names.

4 "Pairs that make five" is another puzzle about the same thing. We fill in the missing numerals.

5 "Color in the five patterns" will look like this when finished:

+	0	1	2	3	4	5
0					↓	▓
1	→	→	→	→	**5**	
2				▓		
3			▓			
4		▓				
5	▓					

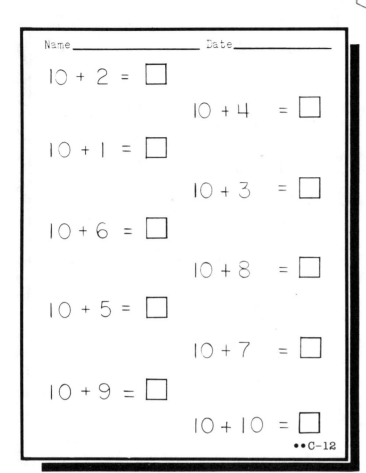

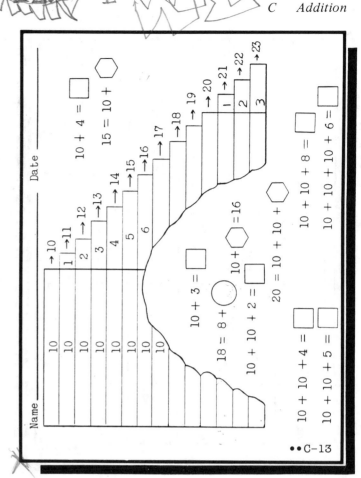

··C12, C13, C15, C19, C23

With these lab sheets we are beginning to deal with numbers greater than 10 for the first time. When introducing two-digit numbers, it is very important that the children realize that the place which a digit occupies in a numeral determines its value. In the numeral 27 the '2' stands for two tens. The '7' stands for seven ones.

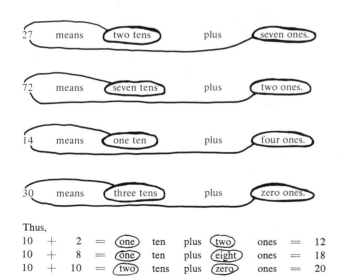

The problems on sheets C13, C15, and C23 can be solved more easily by arranging the addends into groups equal to ten before adding. Below is a problem solved in this manner:

$$6 + 5 + 3 + 4 + 5 = \boxed{23} \quad \text{(two tens plus three ones)}$$

We are justified in adding in this manner because a sum is independent of the order in which the addends are combined.

··C13

On C13 the "rod stairs" are continued from 10 through 23:

$$10 + 1 = 11$$
$$10 + 2 = 12$$
$$10 + 3 = 13, \text{ etc.}$$

Intentionally the paper is "torn" in the middle so that the child has to imagine what the whole length is. The last visible pair of rods is $10 + 6 = 16$; the next pair is one unit longer, or $10 + 7 = 17$. The last row must be $10 + 10 + 3 = 23$. The child can verify his guess by matching that length with two orange rods and a light green rod.

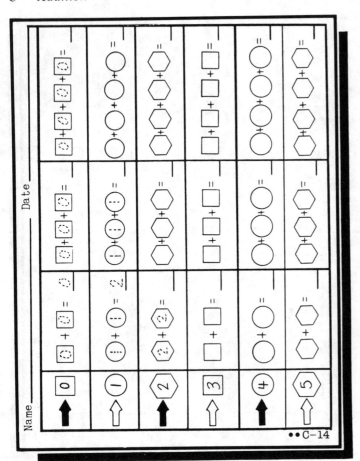

$$1 + 9 + 5 + 5 = \square$$

$$2 + 8 + 4 + 6 = \bigcirc$$

$$\hexagon = 3 + 7 + 8 + 2$$

$$5 + 5 + 6 + 4 = \triangledown$$

$$\bigcirc = 7 + 3 + 9 + 1$$

$$2 + 2 + 6 + 2 + 8 = \hexagon$$

$$8 + 1 + 1 + 4 + 6 = \bigcirc$$

$$5 + 5 + 7 + 1 + 2 = \hexagon$$

••C-15

••C14

This repeated addition is a preliminary to multiplication. The sheet also introduces the *frame rule*.

Within the same problem, frames of the same shape hold the place for the same number. Thus:

$$\boxed{3} + \boxed{3} + \boxed{3} = 9 \quad \text{is correct.}$$

$$\boxed{3} + \boxed{2} + \boxed{4} = 9 \quad \text{is not correct.}$$

C14 also introduces several series. Series are treated extensively in Section U, Series and Progressions.

••C15
Decompositions of 20

Lab sheet C15 is about various decompositions of 20. It also reinforces addition facts about 10.

$$\overset{10}{\overbrace{(1+9)}} + \overset{10}{\overbrace{(5+5)}} = 20$$

$$\overset{10}{\overbrace{(2+8)}} + \overset{10}{\overbrace{(4+6)}} = 20$$

Encourage children to put loops around groups of 10; also encourage them to verify their answers with rods.

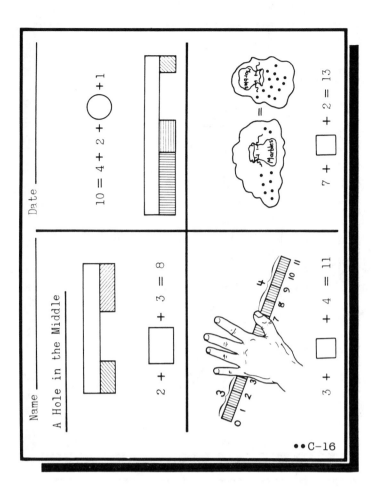

C-16

A Hole in the Middle

Name _____ Date _____

$10 = 4 + 2 + \bigcirc + 1$

$7 + \square = 13$

$2 + \square + 3 = 8$

$3 + \square + 4 = 11$

Name _____ Date _____

From	Lab sheet made by some six-year-olds.
Cindy	$2 + \square + 2 = 10$
Ilsa	$3 + \square + 2 = 7$
Jason	$5 + \square + 1 = 10$
Jen	$3 + \square + 5 = 10$
RM	$4 + \square + 1 = 10$
Benjie	$8 + \square + 1 = 10$

C-17

•• C16–C18, C20, C21

Lab sheet C16 is a teaching page that introduces problems with a "hole in the middle" (a name given to this kind of problem by several groups of six-year-olds).

Do this page with the whole group together. Put rods over the rod pictures. Read the problem. What is the missing rod? Place that rod in the hole. Write in the frame the numeral which makes the sentence true.

Look at the picture of the hand on the ruler. (If the children have rulers, they could get them out and cover the same part as shown on the picture.) How long is the segment that is covered by the hand? Fill in the frame to make the sentence true.

Look at the picture of the partially filled marble bag and then the picture of the completely emptied marble bag.

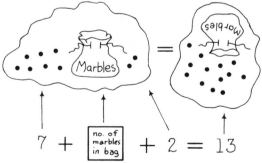

When the bag is emptied, there are 13 marbles. How many marbles were in the bag originally?

$$7 + \boxed{4} + 2 = 13$$

The problems on C17, C18, C20, and C21 are similar to the "hole in the middle" type. Let the children use rods to set up models.

Name _____ Date _____

From	Lab sheet made by some six-year-olds.
Hal	$4 + \square + 4 = 10$
Toni	$4 + \square + 1 = 9$
David	$6 + \square + 3 = 10$
Jeff	$3 + \square + 4 = 8$
Valery	$2 + \square + 5 = 8$

C-18

Card C-19

Name_____ Date_____

Put loops ◯ around tens and then add.

$7 + (\widehat{2 + 8}) = \square$

$3 + 7 + 4 + 6 = \square$

$9 + 1 + 9 = \square$

$5 + 3 + 2 + 6 = \square$

$24 + 3 + 7 = \square$

$5 + 5 + 40 = \square$

$3 + 4 + 5 + 6 + 7 = \square$

$8 + 1 + 2 + 9 + 3 = \square$

$12 + 8 + 3 + 7 = \square$

$6 + 5 + 2 + 4 + 5 = \square$

$4 + 3 + 2 + 1 + 9 + 8 + 7 + 6 = \square$

•• C-19

Card C-20

Name _____ Date_____

From	Lab sheet made by some six-year-olds.
Cindy	$2 + 2 + \square + 3 = 10$
Billy	$10 + \square + 4 = 20$
Ruth	$1 + 1 + 1 + 1 + 1 + \square + 1 + 1 + 1 + 1 = 10$
Carol	$2 + 2 + 2 + \square + 2 = 10$
David	$2 + 2 + 3 + \square + 2 = 10$

Why don't you make up some lab sheets now?

•• C-20

Card C-21

Name_____ Date_____

From	Lab sheet made by some six-year-olds.
Joan	$10 = \square + 3 + 3$
Bobby	$2 + 2 + \square + 3 = 10$
Peter	$10 = 1 + 2 + 3 + \square$
Verna	$10 = 1 + \square + 3 + 4$
David	$\square + 3 + 4 = 10$
Jon	$\square + 1 + 1 + 1 + 1 + 1 + 1 + 1 + 1 + 1 = 10$

•• C-21

Card C-22

Name _____ Date _____

$(\widehat{3 + 4}) + 2 = \square + 2$

$3 + (\widehat{4 + 2}) = 3 + \square$

$(\widehat{3 + 4 + 2}) = \square$

$5 + 2 + 1 = \square + 1$

$5 + 2 + 1 = 5 + \square$

$5 + 2 + 1 = \square$

Make up some problems of your own.

•• C-22

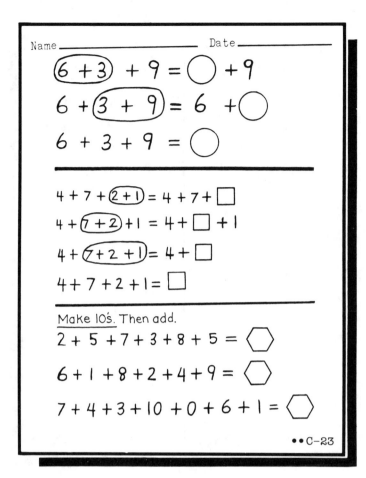

Name＿＿＿＿＿＿＿ Date＿＿＿＿

$(6 + 3) + 9 = \bigcirc + 9$

$6 + (3 + 9) = 6 + \bigcirc$

$6 + 3 + 9 = \bigcirc$

$4 + 7 + (2 + 1) = 4 + 7 + \square$

$4 + (7 + 2) + 1 = 4 + \square + 1$

$4 + (7 + 2 + 1) = 4 + \square$

$4 + 7 + 2 + 1 = \square$

Make 10's. Then add.

$2 + 5 + 7 + 3 + 8 + 5 = \hexagon$

$6 + 1 + 8 + 2 + 4 + 9 = \hexagon$

$7 + 4 + 3 + 10 + 0 + 6 + 1 = \hexagon$

•• C-23

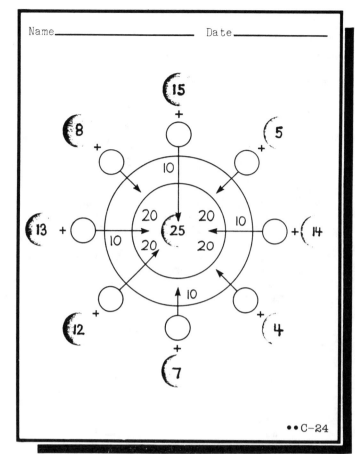

Name＿＿＿＿＿＿＿ Date＿＿＿＿

•• C-24

•• C22, C23

When adding a long string of numbers, it makes no difference in which order the adding is performed. The sum will be the same each way. This is so because addition is an *associative* operation. Below are rod diagrams and solutions to four of the problems on lab sheet C23:

4	7	2	1
4	7	3	

$4 + 7 + (2 + 1) = 4 + 7 + \boxed{3}$

4	7	2	1
4	9		1

$4 + (7 + 2) + 1 = 4 + \boxed{9} + 1$

4	7	2	1
4	10		

$4 + (7 + 2 + 1) = 4 + \boxed{10}$

$4 + 7 + 2 + 1 = \boxed{14}$

Children should be encouraged to look for easy combinations to make when doing long addition problems. For example, the following problem from lab sheet C23 can be done by "finding 10's":

$7 + 4 + 3 + 10 + 0 + 6 + 1 = \langle 31 \rangle$

There are three 10's and a 1, for a total of 31.

·· C25

Cat and Mouse

This is a simple addition game for partners.

Materials needed: buttons or coins,

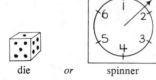

die   *or*   spinner

Directions: Let us say that Rodney is the mouse and Felice is the cat. Rodney begins play by throwing the die (or by spinning the spinner). He throws a 4, so he advances 4 steps toward the mouse hole $(0 + 4 = 4)$. Now it is Felice's turn. She throws a 3, so she advances 3 steps $(0 + 3 = 3)$. Rodney throws a 1, so he advances 1 step $(4 + 1 = 5)$. After each player has landed on a number, he draws a circle around that number with a crayon. Play alternates either until the mouse escapes by arriving first at the mouse hole or until the cat arrives first at the mouse hole and waits to catch the mouse.

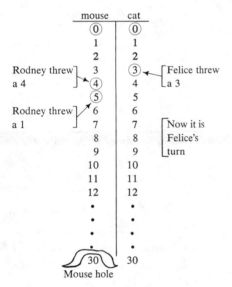

If the teacher wants to use this game sheet more than once, then have the children use buttons to keep track of their numbers instead of writing on the lab sheet. This game can also be played using dice and centimeter rulers. Cuisenaire® rods can be used to build models of the moves.

··· C26

This lab sheet is similar to C22 and C23 except that the format is different.

$$2 + 4 + 1 + 3 = \boxed{6} + 1 + 3$$
$$\boxed{6} + 1 + 3 = \boxed{6} + \boxed{4}$$
$$\boxed{6} + \boxed{4} = \triangle{10}$$

You might want to make up more problems like this on the chalkboard or make a stencil lab sheet. The children can make their own problems with rods:

2	2	1	3
4		1	3
4			4
8			

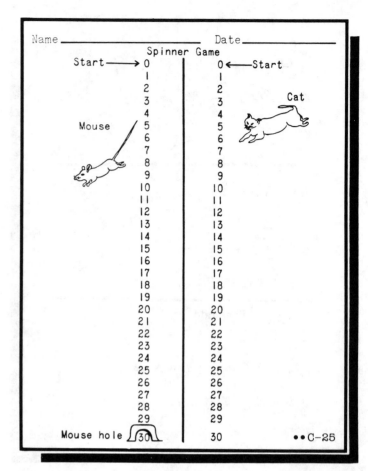

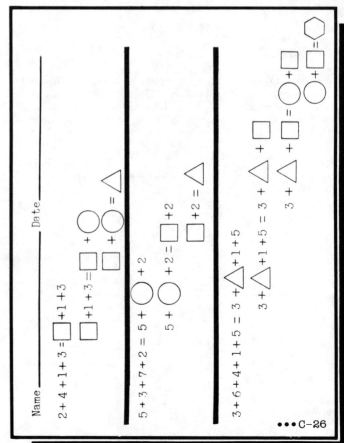

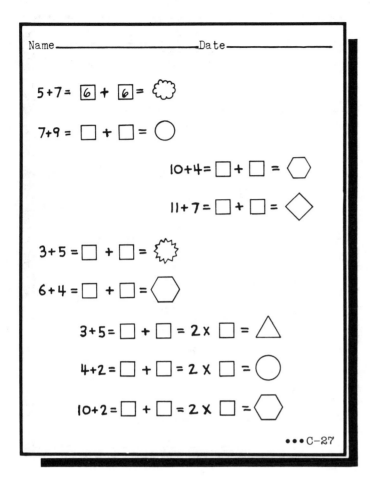

Worksheet C-27:

Name_____Date_____

$5+7 = \boxed{6} + \boxed{6} = $ ⬡

$7+9 = \square + \square = \bigcirc$

$10+4 = \square + \square = $ ⬡

$11+7 = \square + \square = \diamondsuit$

$3+5 = \square + \square = $ ✦

$6+4 = \square + \square = $ ⬡

$3+5 = \square + \square = 2 \times \square = \triangle$

$4+2 = \square + \square = 2 \times \square = \bigcirc$

$10+2 = \square + \square = 2 \times \square = $ ⬡

•••C-27

Worksheet C-28:

Name_____Date_____

$7 + \square = 10$ $7 + 4 = 10 + \triangle$ $7 + 4 = \bigcirc$	$9 + \square = 10$ $9 + 6 = 10 + \triangle$ $9 + 6 = \bigcirc$
$8 + \square = 10$ $8 + 5 = 10 + \triangle$ $8 + 5 = \bigcirc$	$7 + \square = 10$ $7 + 6 = 10 + \triangle$ $7 + 6 = \bigcirc$
$9 + \square = 10$ $9 + 8 = \bigcirc$	$8 + \square = 10$ $8 + 7 = \bigcirc$
$8 + \square = 10$ $8 + 6 = \bigcirc$	$7 + 3 = \square$ $7 + 9 = \bigcirc$
$15 + \square = 20$ $15 + 8 = \bigcirc$	$46 + \square = 50$ $46 + 9 = \bigcirc$

•••C-28

• • • C27

Following are solutions to some of the problems on C27:

$5 + 7 = \boxed{6} + \boxed{6} = ⬡ 12$

$7 + 9 = \boxed{8} + \boxed{8} = ⬡ 16$

$10 + 4 = \boxed{7} + \boxed{7} = ⬡ 14$

$11 + 7 = \boxed{9} + \boxed{9} = ⬡ 18$

$3 + 5 = \boxed{4} + \boxed{4} = 2 \times \boxed{4} = \triangle 8$

$10 + 2 = \boxed{6} + \boxed{6} = 2 \times \boxed{6} = ⬡ 12$

• • • C28

It is important that the children practice making addition combinations for 10.

The activity on this sheet involves finding a missing addend to make 10 as a first step for finding other sums.

In the problem $8 + 5 = \square$ what name for 5 is most helpful? [$\boxed{2 + 3}$ because $8 + 2 = 10$, $10 + 3 = 13$.]

8		
8	2	3
10		3

$$8 + 5 = 8 + \boxed{2 + 3} = \boxed{8 + 2} + 3 = 13$$

In the problem $15 + 8 = \square$ what do I need to add to 15 to make the next 10?

$$15 + 5 = 20$$
$$15 + 8 = 20 + 3$$
$$15 + 8 = 23$$

Give the children some oral practice:

If I want to add $7 + 5$, what name for 5 would help me most? [$\boxed{3 + 2}$ because $7 + 3 = 10$, and 2 more is 12.]

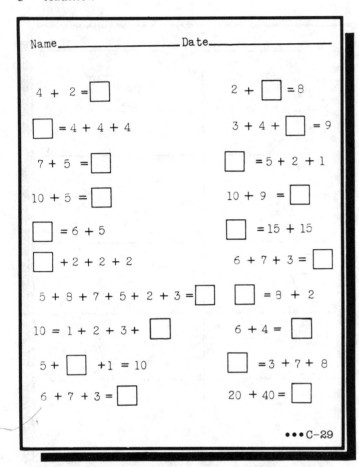

4 + 2 = ☐   2 + ☐ = 8

☐ = 4 + 4 + 4   3 + 4 + ☐ = 9

7 + 5 = ☐   ☐ = 5 + 2 + 1

10 + 5 = ☐   10 + 9 = ☐

☐ = 6 + 5   ☐ = 15 + 15

☐ + 2 + 2 + 2   6 + 7 + 3 = ☐

5 + 8 + 7 + 5 + 2 + 3 = ☐   ☐ = 8 + 2

10 = 1 + 2 + 3 + ☐   6 + 4 = ☐

5 + ☐ + 1 = 10   ☐ = 3 + 7 + 8

6 + 7 + 3 = ☐   20 + 40 = ☐

•••C-29

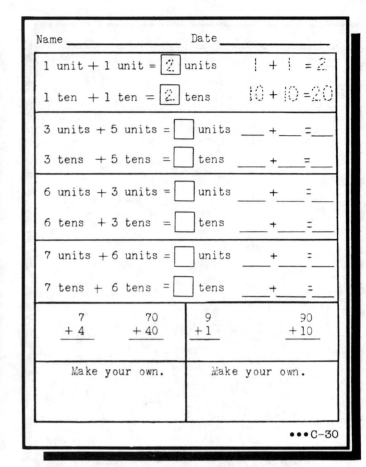

| 1 unit + 1 unit = 2 units | | 1 + 1 = 2 |
| 1 ten + 1 ten = 2 tens | | 10 + 10 = 20 |

3 units + 5 units = ☐ units   ___ + ___ = ___
3 tens + 5 tens = ☐ tens   ___ + ___ = ___

6 units + 3 units = ☐ units   ___ + ___ = ___
6 tens + 3 tens = ☐ tens   ___ + ___ = ___

7 units + 6 units = ☐ units   ___ + ___ = ___
7 tens + 6 tens = ☐ tens   ___ + ___ = ___

| 7
+ 4 | 70
+ 40 | 9
+ 1 | 90
+ 10 |
| Make your own. | | Make your own. | |

•••C-30

••• C30

C30 is designed to show that adding tens is similar in pattern to adding units. We can demonstrate this easily with orange rods, using the rods as tallies. The children can work the problem, first using white rods for units; then they can work the corresponding problem, using orange rods for tens.

It is important to review the numerals for tens.

one ten   no units   two tens   four units

7 tens + 6 tens = 13 tens
70   + 60   = 130 [13 tens = 1 hundred + 3 tens]

••• C31–C33
Grid addition

Grid addition is another way of increasing the child's mental flexibility. Besides introducing a new way to read instructions, grid addition presents a large number of practice problems without boring the child.

One problem on C32 is given here to explain the technique of grid addition.

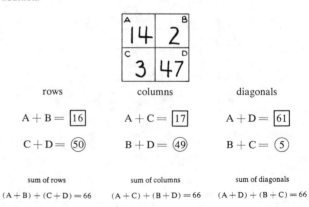

	rows	columns	diagonals
	A + B = 16	A + C = 17	A + D = 61
	C + D = 50	B + D = 49	B + C = 5
	sum of rows	sum of columns	sum of diagonals
	(A + B) + (C + D) = 66	(A + C) + (B + D) = 66	(A + D) + (B + C) = 66

Questions to ask:
Why does the sum of two columns equal the sum of the two rows? Of the two diagonals?   [Addition may be done in any order.]

Name_____ Date_____

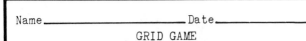
GRID GAME

DIRECTIONS: Starting from the "zero" box, make only ⊞ jumps and ⊟ jumps. Write in each box the number of jumps needed to arrive at it from the "zero" box. A few boxes have already been filled in for you.

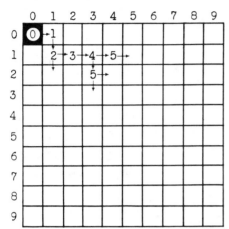

Now, can you figure out a way to find the numbers that go in the different boxes, using only the numbers at the tops of their columns and to the left of their rows?

•••C-31

On C33 the children choose their own numbers for A, B, C, D and fill in the grid. The numbers they choose may be as difficult as they can handle. If the sums of the rows, columns, and diagonals match, they are likely to be correct.

Let the children make many problems of their own. After they understand the procedure, the letters may be omitted from the grid.

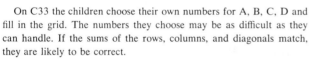

rows	columns	diagonals
9 + 8 = 17	9 + 14 = 23	9 + 25 = 34
14 + 25 = 39	8 + 25 = 33	8 + 14 = 22
sum of rows	sum of columns	sum of diagonals
17 + 39 = 56	23 + 33 = 56	34 + 22 = 56

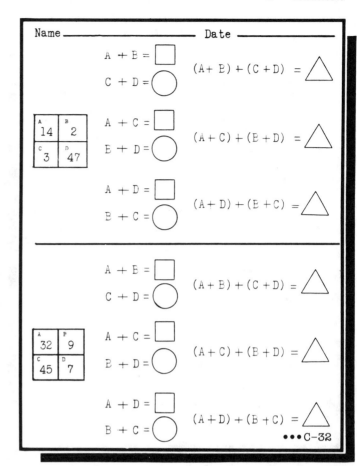

Name_____ Date_____

A + B = □   (A + B) + (C + D) = △
C + D = ○

A + C = □   (A + C) + (B + D) = △
B + D = ○

A + D = □   (A + D) + (B + C) = △
B + C = ○

| A 14 | B 2 |
| C 3 | D 47 |

A + B = □   (A + B) + (C + D) = △
C + D = ○

A + C = □   (A + C) + (B + D) = △
B + D = ○

A + D = □   (A + D) + (B + C) = △
B + C = ○

| A 32 | B 9 |
| C 45 | D 7 |

•••C-32

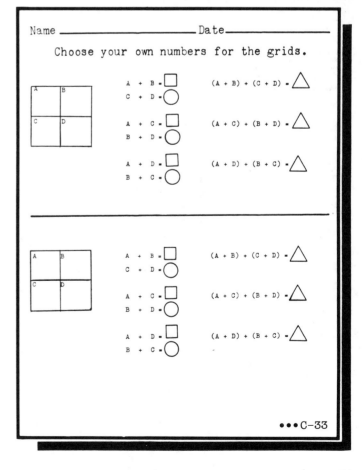

Name_____ Date_____

Choose your own numbers for the grids.

A + B = □   (A + B) + (C + D) = △
C + D = ○

A + C = □   (A + C) + (B + D) = △
B + D = ○

A + D = □   (A + D) + (B + C) = △
B + C = ○

A + B = □   (A + B) + (C + D) = △
C + D = ○

A + C = □   (A + C) + (B + D) = △
B + D = ○

A + D = □   (A + D) + (B + C) = △
B + C = ○

•••C-33

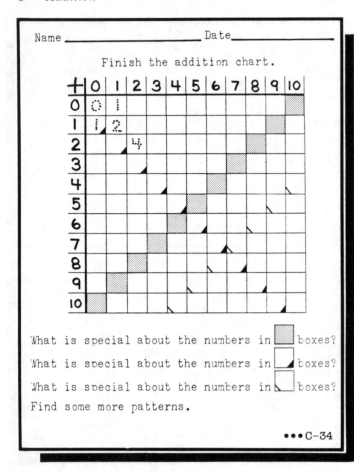

Name _____ Date _____

Finish the addition chart.

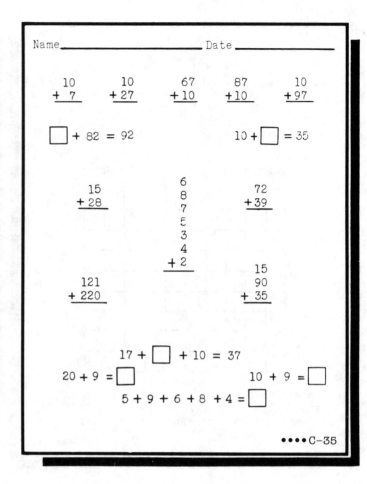

Name _____ Date _____

What is special about the numbers in ▨ boxes?

What is special about the numbers in ◹ boxes?

What is special about the numbers in ◸ boxes?

Find some more patterns.

•••C–34

••••C–35

••• C34

An addition table

If children have difficulty filling out this table, they should be allowed to use their rods for practice.

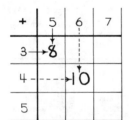

Example: Each numeral across the top can be represented by a rod of a certain size. These rods can only move straight down. Each numeral on the left can be represented by a rod of a certain size. These rods can only move to the right. In which square would the seven rod (black) meet the five rod (yellow)? $[7 + 5 = 12]$ Write '12' into that square and continue in the same manner.

•••• C35, C36

At this point in the sequence, the lab sheets are difficult for most children. C35 and C36 should be used mainly as diagnostic sheets to discover which problems children can puzzle out. *The children should not be rushed.* They should be allowed to use any learning aids they want—rods, wall number chart, number line, meterstick and rods, etc.

In every class there will be some children who will have "taught" themselves to do many of these problems correctly. Do not force the children to do those problems that are too difficult for them.

Note: Pupils should now work in Section M, Place Value (M1–M16), where the foundation for computation with large numbers is laid, before they work on Level 5 Addition sheets.

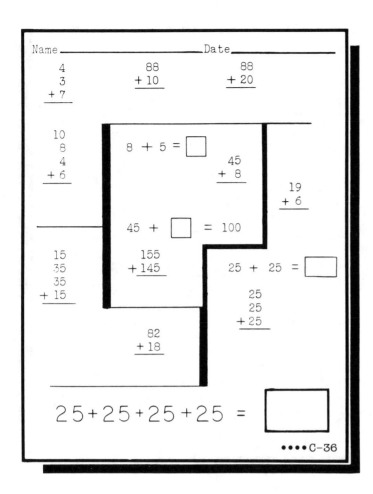

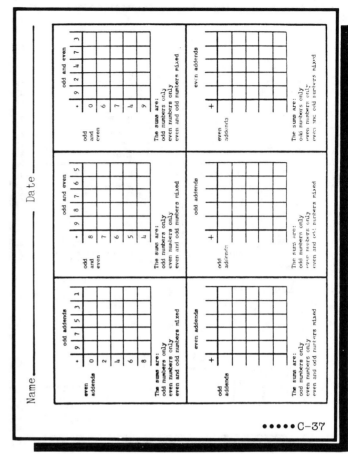

•••••C37–C39

Addition tables

The addition tables on these lab sheets have several purposes: (a) they provide computation practice; (b) they show regularities or patterns that lead to generalization; and (c) they introduce math vocabulary.

0	+	9	=	9
addend 1	plus	addend 2	equals	sum

9	−	0	=	9
sum	minus	addend 1	equals	addend 2

9	−	9	=	0
sum	minus	addend 2	equals	addend 1

C37

Three grids without numerals are provided to let children choose their own addends. However, their addends must fit the odd-even specifications given beneath each grid. Thus children are reminded that:

even addend + odd addend = odd sum
odd addend + odd addend = even sum
even addend + even addend = even sum

Note: It is important, before children do the addition tables on C37–C39, to make sure that they have done the work on place value (lab sheets M1–M16 in Level 4). Annotations for these sheets discuss addition techniques to use with large numbers. Following are some examples from Section M, Place Value.

$500 + 30 + 3 = \square$ hundreds $+ \bigcirc$ tens $+ \triangle$ units

$533 = 500 + \square + 3$

$$533 = \begin{array}{|c|c|c|} \hline H & T & U \\ \hline 5 & 3 & 3 \\ \hline \end{array}$$

$$14 \text{ tens} = \begin{array}{|c|c|c|} \hline H & T & U \\ \hline & 14 & \\ \hline \end{array} = \begin{array}{|c|c|c|} \hline H & T & U \\ \hline 1 & 4 & \\ \hline \end{array} = 140$$

$$26 \text{ units} = \begin{array}{|c|c|c|} \hline H & T & U \\ \hline & & 26 \\ \hline \end{array} = \begin{array}{|c|c|c|} \hline H & T & U \\ \hline & 2 & 6 \\ \hline \end{array} = 26$$

$$\begin{array}{|c|c|} \hline T & U \\ \hline 1 & 7 \\ +6 & 3 \\ \hline 7 & 10 \\ \hline \end{array} \text{ or } \begin{array}{c} \text{1 ten, 7 units} \\ \underline{+6 \text{ tens, 3 units}} \\ \text{7 tens, 10 units} \\ \\ \text{8 tens, 0 units} \end{array}$$

$$\begin{array}{|c|} \hline 80 \\ \hline \end{array}$$

53

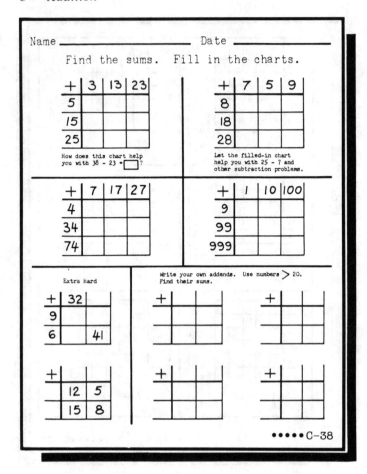

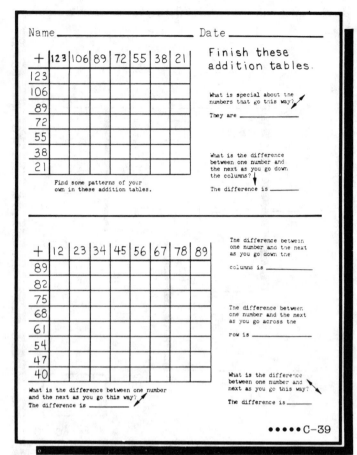

····· **C38**

Use C38 for addition *and* subtraction practice.

+	1	10	100
9	10	19	109
99	100	109	199
999	1000	1009	1099

The preceding chart is especially helpful in writing large numbers. It could be extended to include 9,999 and 10,000.

+		12	5
		15	8

The chart above has no unique solution.

+	8	1
4	will work.	
7		

+	7	0
5	will work.	
8		

+	9	2
3	will work, etc.	
6		

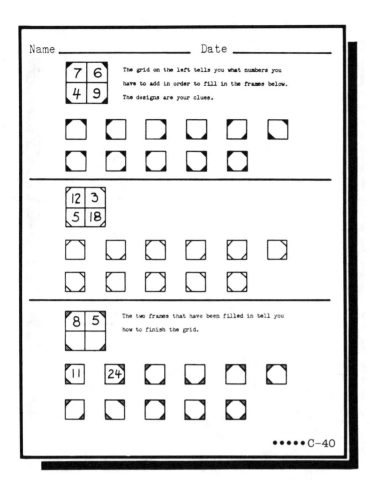

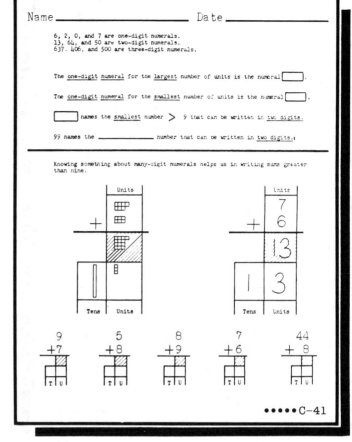

•••••C40

The top and middle panels are worked in the same way, according to the directions given on the sheet.

In the bottom panel children are to fill in the two blank frames in the grid, using the sums 11 and 24 to find the missing addends. Then they continue as before.

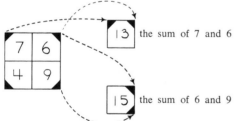

$\boxed{11}$ is a sum.
One of the addends is $\boxed{8}$.
The other addend must be $\boxed{3}$.

$\boxed{24}$ is a sum.
One of the addends is $\boxed{5}$.
The other addend must be $\boxed{19}$.

Make up more practice sheets like C40. Let the children suggest addends.

•••••C41

Preparing for the addition algorithm

$$
\begin{array}{r}
{\scriptstyle 1\ \ 1} \\
2\ 4\ 3 \\
+\quad 6\ 9 \\
\hline
3\ 1\ 2
\end{array}
$$

C41

Following are the answers for the top half of the sheet:

The one-digit numeral for the largest number of units is the numeral $\boxed{9}$.

The one-digit numeral for the smallest number of units is the numeral $\boxed{0}$.

$\boxed{10}$ names the smallest number > 9 that can be written in two digits.

99 names the largest number that can be written in two digits.

On the lower half of C41, simple addition problems illustrate the multidigit nature of a place-value notational system. Every digit to the left of the first stands for an additional power of ten.

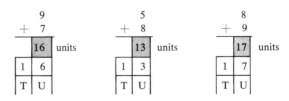

The shaded box, in which the total units are recorded, will eventually be eliminated from the lab sheets.

55

C   Addition

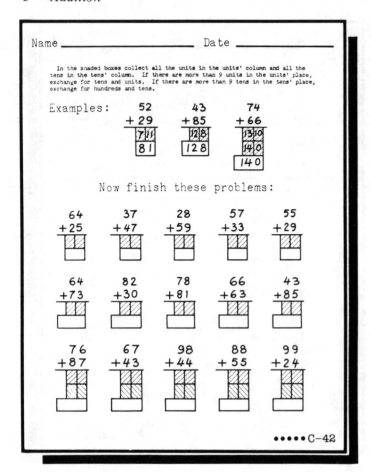

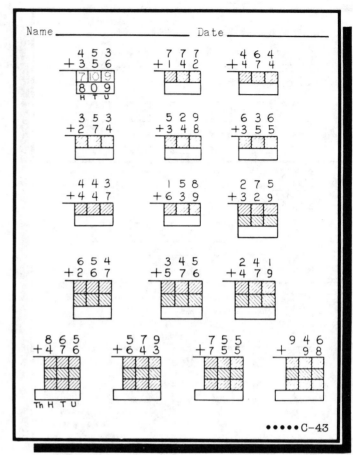

•••• C42, C43

After children have completed C41, C42, and C43 you may ask them for suggestions about how this process could be shortened. Accept all reasonable suggestions and try them. *Only then* inform the children what many adults do:

$$\begin{array}{r} 11 \\ 667 \\ +\ 295 \\ \hline 962 \end{array}$$

Now, they may appreciate the "elegance" of the addition algorithm introduced on C44.

Oral and chalkboard work

Give more oral and chalkboard practice similar to the following:

1   Find the smallest number, greater than 90, which is written in three digits.   [100]

2   Find the largest number, greater than 90, which is written in three digits.   [999]

3   Find the smallest number, greater than 900, which is written in four digits.   [1000]

4   Find the largest number, greater than 900, which is written in four digits.   [9999]

5   84 + 16   The sum is written as a

two-digit numeral

(three-digit numeral)

6   981 + 17   The sum is written as

(a three-digit numeral)

a four-digit numeral

7   ■ ■ 3   This was a three-digit numeral and someone scribbled over it. What is the largest number it could have named?   [993]   What is the smallest number it could have named?   [103, or perhaps you may have to accept 003!]

Name _____ Date _____

A Shorter Way of Adding
A teaching page

$$35 + 47 = \boxed{}$$

[✓] 35 +47 — 2	5 and 7 have already been added. 12, their sum, equals 1 ten plus 2 units Find where the 1 ten is written. Find where the 2 units are written.
[✓] 35 +47 — 2	Now add up all the tens.

```
 □
 46        6 + 8 = 14   Where do you write the units?
+23                     where do you write the tens?
                        Add up all the tens.
```

```
  □        □        □        □        □
  29      143      637      533      182
 +55      +28     +134     +257     +508


  □        □        □        □        □
 348      379      666      734      203
+524     +420     +226     +229     +407
```

•••••C-44

Name _____ Date _____

```
  □        □        □
 382      541      444
+427     +376     +375


  □        □□       □
 724      245      372
+146     +255     + 85


  □        □□       □□
 439      439      599
+ 58     + 78     + 99
```

```
  34       48       76       57
+ 27      +45      +38      +35


 124      365      277
+128     +325     +322


 463      624      325
+253     +280     +495
```

•••••C-45

·····C44, C45

The addition algorithm

Small boxes above the tens and hundreds columns remind children to record extra tens. On the lower half of C45 the boxes are omitted.

```
 □
 45
+38
```

It seems certain that children will need more addition practice than the lab sheets provide. Encourage children to make up their own problems. Duplicate sheets of practice problems for the class.

Additional suggestions

Lab sheets E54 and E55 are useful for making up addition problems. Children may also (a) collect cash-register slips from their families' grocery bags, cut them up, paste them on paper, and find the totals; (b) open a book at random several times, record the page numbers, and compute the results. Such activities will lend variety to making up computation problems.

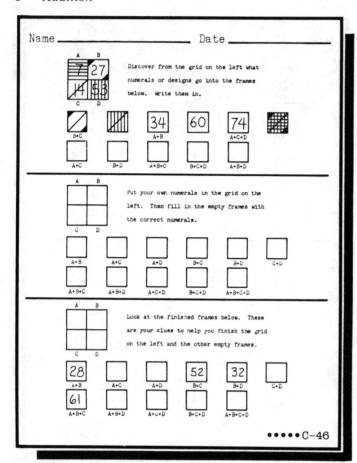

●●●●●C-46

·····**C46**

Addition puzzles

This is a puzzle page. It is important to give children time to puzzle it out for themselves.

1

given   solution

B + C   B + C

The designs of frames B and C are given. Children are to write the sum of 27 and 14 inside. They follow the same procedure for other composite designs.

2

given   solution

A + B   A + B

The sum (34) of frames A and B (7 + 27) is given. Children are to draw in the composite design of A and B.

3

given   solution

60

A+D

Children are to figure out which frames 60 is the sum of.   [A + D] Then they draw in the composite design of those frames.

4

given   solution

A + C   A + C

Children write the sum of A and C, and draw in the composite design of A and C.

A reasoning problem

The puzzle at the bottom of C46 is a good exercise in reasoning. How can I find the values of A, B, C, and D when I know that:

$$A + B = 28$$
$$A + B + C = 61$$
$$B + C = 52$$
$$B + D = 32$$

Solution

$$(A + B + C) - (A + B) = C$$
$$61 \quad - \quad 28 \quad = 33 \qquad \mathbf{C = 33}$$

I write 33 in the C section of the grid. Now I can substitute 33 for C in the equations.

$$B + C = 52$$
$$B + 33 = 52$$
$$52 - 33 = 19 \qquad \mathbf{B = 19}$$

B = 19 because 19 + 33 = 52. Now I can substitute 19 for B.

$$A + B = 28$$
$$A + 19 = 28$$
$$A = 28 - 19$$
$$A = 9 \qquad \mathbf{A = 9}$$

Now I can substitute 9 for A.

$$B + D = 32$$
$$19 + D = 32$$
$$32 - 19 = 13 \qquad \mathbf{D = 13}$$

I can substitute 13 for D. Now I can work the other problems, and fill in the remaining frames.

D Subtraction

The second arithmetic operation to be introduced is subtraction. Subtraction is very closely related to addition; *whatever has been grouped together by addition can be taken apart again by subtraction.* In this sense, subtraction *undoes* addition. Notice that in the equation below we start with 4 and end with 4.

Adding	is undone	subtracting
five	by	five.
$4 + 5 = 9$		$9 - 5 = 4$

This relationship can be expressed more briefly by the following equation.

$$(4 + 5) - 5 = 4$$

We can also see that addition undoes subtraction. Notice that we also start and stop with the same number.

Subtracting	is undone	adding
three	by	three.
$4 - 3 = 1$		$1 + 3 = 4$

The following equation expresses this relationship:

$$(4 - 3) + 3 = 4$$

Operations which undo each other are called *inverse* operations. Thus subtraction is the inverse of addition, and addition is the inverse of subtraction. In mathematical terms, these generalizations may be expressed as follows:

$$(\boxed{} + \bigcirc) - \bigcirc = \boxed{}$$

$$(\boxed{} - \bigcirc) + \bigcirc = \boxed{}$$

The fact that addition and subtraction are inverse operations accounts for the small number of lab sheets containing only simple subtraction problems in this section. Section E, Addition and Subtraction, contains most of the early subtraction work.

Discovering the relation between addition and subtraction

Children should be allowed ample time with Cuisenaire® rods, number lines, and other materials to discover the basic relationship between addition and subtraction. Do *not* stop the use of models by insisting on the quick memorization of "facts." The extra time spent here will be saved later when these ideas are put to use.

Note: In this program we work with children under the age of ten. We want to teach them good mathematics, but we do not at any time want to push more symbolism and mathematical conventions (agreements among mathematicians) on them than is necessary to think clearly and to communicate clearly with others in the writing of mathematical sentences. We also want to encourage them to make up temporarily their own symbols when the need arises and when those symbols can be clearly understood.

Some examples of symbolism which we *must* teach to children quickly and must insist on their correct use are the Hindu-Arabic numerals, the operational symbols, and the relations symbols. (We cannot allow a child to write '7' when he means the number eight. We cannot allow a child to persist in writing ✳ for ✕, when he means "times," etc.)

We feel differently about the use of parentheses for this age group. Our experience has been that children must invent something like parentheses (usually loops) which communicate clearly what they mean when they run into ambiguous situations. These situations usually arise when the children have built concrete rod models and want to represent them by an equation or when an equation has been written and a rod model is to be built to represent it. Ambiguous situations will also arise with the use of the number line. As an example:

$$8 - 4 + 1 = \square$$

This expression can mean either $8 - (4 + 1)$ or $(8 - 4) + 1$, which are different in value.

We have not felt that it is wise to insist on parentheses here. We accept as the answer either $8 - 4 + 1 = 5$ or $8 - 4 + 1 = 3$ until children become aware of the ambiguity. Then parentheses (or loops) make sense to them, and they will begin to use them correctly and with understanding in order to signal their meaning.

$$8 - \!\!\overline{(4 + 1)} = 3$$
$$\overline{(8 - 4)} + 1 = 5$$

Adding and subtracting with rods

1 Take a yellow rod.

yellow

2 Take a red rod.

red

3 Place these rods end-to-end.

yellow	red

4 Find one rod that is the same length as the yellow and red rods placed end-to-end.

5 If we consider the white rod to be one unit in length, then
the yellow rod = 5 units
the red rod = 2 units
the black rod = 7 units.

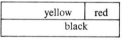

The relationship between the lengths of the rods can now be expressed in mathematical terms as:

$$5 + 2 = 7$$

6 From the arrangement of the rods, remove the red rod. Only the black and yellow rods remain.

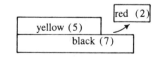

This new relationship, which involves "taking away," is expressed mathematically as:

$$7 - 2 = 5$$

We have now performed an operation and its inverse. The operation—adding two—took us from 5 to 7.

$$5 + 2 = 7$$

The inverse operation—subtracting two—took us from 7 back to 5.

$$7 - 2 = 5$$

Adding and subtracting with the number line

In work involving a horizontal number line, to add means "to jump to the right." To subtract means "to jump to the left." Therefore, starting at point 2 on the number line and jumping 3 units to the right is written:

$$2 + 3$$

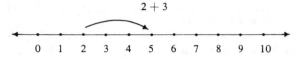

├──┤ This length has been chosen as the unit.

After making this jump, we find that we have landed at point 5. We then write

$$2 + 3 = 5$$

We are now at point 5, and we wish to return to point 2. What jump must we make? We must jump three units to the left,

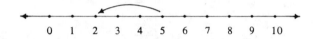

which is written:

$$5 - 3 = 2$$

Now we are back at the point where we began. We have performed an operation—jumping three units to the right, or adding 3—and we have performed its inverse—jumping three units to the left, or subtracting 3.

$$(2 + 3) - 3 = 2$$

There is another equally useful interpretation of subtraction, namely that of finding the missing addend, as in the example

$$3 + \square = 5$$

This is perhaps most clearly illustrated to children by vertical number-line models such as the thermometer, a pupil's growth record, the elevator in an apartment building.

1   Temperatures in degrees C

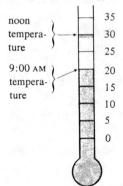

noon temperature	35
	30
	25
9:00 AM temperature	20
	15
	10
	5
	0

How much warmer is it at noon than at 9 AM?

$$20 + \square = 30$$
$$30 - 20 = \square$$
$$30 - \square = 20$$

2   Height records in centimeters

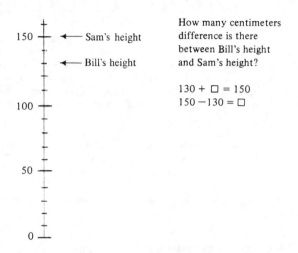

150 ◄── Sam's height

◄── Bill's height

100

50

0

How many centimeters difference is there between Bill's height and Sam's height?

$$130 + \square = 150$$
$$150 - 130 = \square$$

Such a scale can be made of masking tape on a door jamb or wall.

Properties of subtraction

Section C described several properties of addition. We shall now discuss subtraction with respect to these properties.

Not all subtraction problems have an answer within the whole numbers. It is *not* true that any two whole numbers can be subtracted to produce *another* whole number.

Addition	Subtraction
$7 + 6 = 13$	$7 - 6 = 1$
$4 + 2 = 6$	$4 - 2 = 2$
$9 + 6 = 15$	$9 - 6 = 3$
$5 + 5 = 10$	$5 - 5 = 0$
$4 + 6 = 10$	$4 - 6 =$
$2 + 7 = 9$	$2 - 7 =$

As can be seen from the preceding examples, there is no whole number equal to $4 - 6$ or $2 - 7$. (Remember that the set of whole numbers is $\{0, 1, 2, 3, \ldots\}$.) Later in their mathematical growth, children will discover that there *are* solutions to these problems. The solutions are *negative numbers,* which belong to the *set of integers.*

If a subtraction problem *does* have an answer which belongs to the set of whole numbers, then that answer is a *unique* answer.

Commutative property

Addition is commutative. *Subtraction, however, is not commutative.*

$9 + 2 = 2 + 9$	$9 - 2 \neq^* 2 - 9$
$5 + 7 = 7 + 5$	$5 - 7 \neq 7 - 5$
$6 + 3 = 3 + 6$	$6 - 3 \neq 3 - 6$

In general terms, these relationships may be expressed as follows:

$\square + \bigcirc = \bigcirc + \square$	$\square - \bigcirc = \bigcirc - \square$
is an identity.	is *not* an identity.

An interesting consequence of the *commutativity of addition* is illustrated by the following pairs of subtraction equations:

$4 - 3 = 1$	$10 - 4 = 6$
$4 - 1 = 3$	$10 - 6 = 4$
$7 - 0 = 7$	$9 - 2 = 7$
$7 - 7 = 0$	$9 - 7 = 2$

* $\neq$ means "is not equal to."

In general, this property may be formulated as follows:

If $\bigcirc - \triangle = \square$ is true,
then $\bigcirc - \square = \triangle$ is also true.

Associative property

Addition is associative. *Subtraction, however, is not associative.*

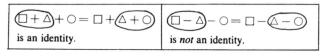

$$(9+5)+2=9+(5+2) \qquad (9-5)-2 \neq 9-(5-2)$$
$$14 \ + 2 = 9 + \ 7 \qquad \quad 4 \ -2 \neq 9 - \ 3$$
$$16 = 16 \qquad\qquad\qquad 2 \neq 6$$

In general,

$(\square + \triangle) + \bigcirc = \square + (\triangle + \bigcirc)$	$(\square - \triangle) - \bigcirc = \square - (\triangle - \bigcirc)$
is an identity.	**is *not* an identity.**

Since $(\square - \triangle) - \bigcirc$ and $\square - (\triangle - \bigcirc)$ are not necessarily the same thing, we shall always mean $(\square - \triangle) - \bigcirc$ when we write $\square - \triangle - \bigcirc$. This means that problems of the type

$$\square - \triangle - \bigcirc$$

must be performed *from left to right.*

Identity element

Zero is the identity element for addition. *Zero is also the identity element for subtraction.*

$$5 + 0 = 5 \qquad\qquad 5 - 0 = 5$$
$$17 + 0 = 17 \qquad\quad 17 - 0 = 17$$

In general,

$$\square + 0 = \square \qquad\qquad \square - 0 = \square$$

is an identity.   is *also* an identity.

Another important property of subtraction is that a number subtracted from itself is always equal to zero, the identity element.

$$8 - \ 8 = 0$$
$$17 - 17 = 0$$

In general,

$$\square - \square = 0$$

is an identity.

The properties of addition and subtraction which we have discussed are repeatedly stressed in the lab sheets of sections D and E. These items should *not* be presented to the children as "rules" to memorize. The lab sheets provide exercises through which the children themselves may discover these properties.

Why problems are presented in line form

The teacher may wonder why problems involving addition and subtraction (and, later, the other operations) are introduced in these materials in line form rather than in column form. This is done because equations and inequalities are expressed in line form. *Equations and inequalities are mathematical sentences.* It is by means of these sentences that relationships of equality and inequality are expressed in mathematics. Although numerals in a column are very convenient to work with, one should realize that a column of numerals does not constitute a mathematical sentence. The column form is merely a useful working arrangement which facilitates computation.

Examples of rote arithmetic

Following are solutions to three problems involving addition and subtraction. (These three solutions are included for *illustrative purposes only.* We do not recommend this approach.)

1   **Problem:** $23 + 40 = \square$

$$\begin{array}{r} 23 \\ + 40 \\ \hline \end{array} \qquad\qquad \begin{array}{r} 23 \\ + 40 \\ \hline 63 \end{array}$$

"3 plus nothing is 3. Write down '3.'
2 plus 4 is 6. Write down '6.' Therefore, 23 plus 40 is 63."

2   **Problem:** $27 + 64 + 45 = \square$

$$\begin{array}{r} 27 \\ 64 \\ + 45 \\ \hline \end{array} \qquad\qquad \begin{array}{r} 1 \\ 27 \\ 64 \\ + 45 \\ \hline 136 \end{array}$$

"7 plus 4 is 11, plus 5 more is 16.
Write down '6'; carry '1.'
1 plus 2 is 3, plus 6 is 9, plus 4 is 13.
Write down '13.'
Therefore, 27 plus 64 plus 45 is 136."

3   **Problem:** $94 - 68 = \square$

$$\begin{array}{r} 94 \\ - 68 \\ \hline \end{array} \qquad\qquad \begin{array}{r} 8\,1 \\ \cancel{9}\cancel{4} \\ - 68 \\ \hline 26 \end{array}$$

"You can't subtract 8 from 4, so you have to borrow 1 from 9.
8 from 14 is 6. Write down '6.'
6 from 8 is 2. Write down '2.'
Therefore, 94 minus 68 is 26."

The answers to these problems have been obtained through the use of the traditional addition and subtraction algorithms. These results are certainly correct, but the steps preceding them do not lead one to feel that the problem-solver had a true understanding of the mathematics involved in the problems. His solutions appear to be more the result of mechanical manipulations than of reasoned calculations. In the first problem, for example, how can one conclude from "3 plus nothing is 3" and "2 plus 4 is 6" that "23 plus 40 is 63"? In the second problem, what does it mean "to write down '6' and carry '1'"? Or, in the third problem, what allows us to "borrow 1 from 9" when we find that we "can't subtract 8 from 4"?

Although most children learn to solve arithmetic problems without ever knowing the answers to questions such as those above, it is certainly to their advantage to have an understanding of the structure of multidigit numerals so that they will be able to see why the operational techniques taught them lead to correct results. One way to help bring about this understanding is to encourage children to develop their own ways of solving problems. Do not introduce short cuts such as the borrowing and carrying algorithms—which make use of the column form—until the children themselves have discovered and used their own methods of solving problems.

Children's solutions to problems

Following are several mathematically explicit solutions to each of the three preceding problems. We have observed these solutions being "invented" by individual children of this age group. All primary children should be encouraged to use their inventiveness in tackling such problems.

1   Problem: $23 + 40 = \square$

Solution A

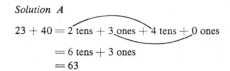

$$23 + 40 = 2 \text{ tens} + 3 \text{ ones} + 4 \text{ tens} + 0 \text{ ones}$$
$$= 6 \text{ tens} + 3 \text{ ones}$$
$$= 63$$

Solution B

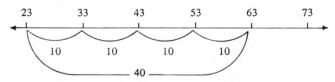

Solution C (using rods)

If we let the white rod equal one, then the orange rod equals ten. Using *only* white and orange rods, we can see that

$$23 = 2 \text{ orange rods} + 3 \text{ white rods}$$
and $$40 = 4 \text{ orange rods} + 0 \text{ white rods}$$
therefore, $$23 + 40 = 6 \text{ orange rods} + 3 \text{ white rods}$$

2   Problem: $27 + 64 + 45 = \square$

Solution A

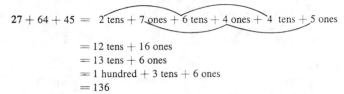

$$27 + 64 + 45 = 2 \text{ tens} + 7 \text{ ones} + 6 \text{ tens} + 4 \text{ ones} + 4 \text{ tens} + 5 \text{ ones}$$
$$= 12 \text{ tens} + 16 \text{ ones}$$
$$= 13 \text{ tens} + 6 \text{ ones}$$
$$= 1 \text{ hundred} + 3 \text{ tens} + 6 \text{ ones}$$
$$= 136$$

Solution B

$$60 + 40 = 100; \qquad 4 + 5 = 9$$
therefore, $$64 + 45 = 109$$
$$109 + 20 = 129; \qquad 129 + 7 = 136$$
therefore, $$64 + 45 + 27 = 136$$

Solution C

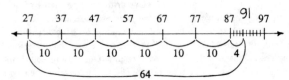

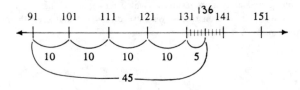

Solution D (using rods)

If we let the white rod equal one, then the orange rod equals ten. Using *only* the white and orange rods, we can see that:

$$27 = 2 \text{ orange rods} + 7 \text{ white rods}$$
$$64 = 6 \text{ orange rods} + 4 \text{ white rods}$$
$$45 = 4 \text{ orange rods} + 5 \text{ white rods}$$

Therefore,
$$27 + 64 + 45 = 12 \text{ orange rods} + 16 \text{ white rods}$$
$$= 13 \text{ orange rods} + 6 \text{ white rods}$$
$$= \qquad 130 \qquad + \qquad 6$$
$$= \qquad \qquad 136$$

3   Problem: $94 - 68 = \square$

Solution A

$$94 - 68 = (9 \text{ tens} + 4 \text{ ones}) - (6 \text{ tens} + 8 \text{ ones})$$
$$= (8 \text{ tens} + 14 \text{ ones}) - (6 \text{ tens} + 8 \text{ ones})$$
$$= (8 \text{ tens} - 6 \text{ tens}) + (14 \text{ ones} - 8 \text{ ones})$$
$$= \qquad 2 \text{ tens} \qquad + \qquad 6 \text{ ones}$$
$$= \qquad \qquad 26$$

Solution B

$$94 - 68 = 96 - 70 = 26$$

Solution C

$$94 - 68 = (94 - 60) - 8 = \quad 34 - 8$$
$$= (34 - 4) - 4$$
$$= \quad 30 - 4$$
$$= \quad 26$$

Solution D

Since $68 + \square = 94$ is just another way of saying $94 - 68 = \square$ and it is easier to solve on the number line than $94 - 68 = \square$, we shall use $68 + \square = 94$ in demonstrating this solution.

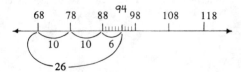

Solution E (using rods)

If we let the white rod equal one, then the orange rod equals ten. Using only the white and orange rods, we can see that

$$94 = 9 \text{ orange rods} + 4 \text{ white rods}$$
$$68 = 6 \text{ orange rods} + 8 \text{ white rods}$$

Therefore,
$$94 - 68 = (9 \text{ orange} + 4 \text{ white}) - (6 \text{ orange} + 8 \text{ white})$$
$$= (8 \text{ orange} + 14 \text{ white}) - (6 \text{ orange} + 8 \text{ white})$$
$$= (8 \text{ orange} - 6 \text{ orange}) + (14 \text{ white} - 8 \text{ white})$$
$$= 2 \text{ orange rods} + 6 \text{ white rods}$$
$$= 26$$

The solutions presented rely heavily on an understanding of *place value*—the role played by *position* in denoting the *values* signified by multidigit numerals. Before attempting to solve problems resembling those above, children should be well aware, for instance, that the '2' in

'2634' stands not for two ones, but for two thousands; the '6' stands for six hundreds; the '3,' for three tens; and the '4,' for four ones.

2 thousands + 6 hundreds + 3 tens + 4 ones

For further discussion of Place Value, see Section M, page 210 ff.

Exploring several subtraction techniques

We believe strongly that the subtraction algorithm

$$\begin{array}{r} {}^{5}\not6\,{}^{12}\not3\,{}^{14}\not4 \\ -\ 2\,7\,5 \\ \hline 3\,5\,9 \end{array}$$

should *not* be taught prematurely to children for the following reasons. (This section is a summary of the work presented on lab sheets D17, 19, 20, 21, 22.)

1   The subtraction algorithm is not appropriate for mental subtraction, even though it is a convenient paper–pencil method. We want to encourage skill in mental arithmetic first.

2   It is only one of many useful ways of subtracting.

3   The algorithm can easily become a rote process. Children may use it even when an answer can be read off at a glance.

$$\begin{array}{r} 3\,0\,0 \\ -\,2\,9\,9 \\ \hline 1 \end{array} \left\{ \begin{array}{l} \text{noticeable} \\ \text{at a glance} \end{array} \right. \qquad \begin{array}{r} {}^{2}\not3\,{}^{9}\not0\,{}^{10}\not0 \\ -\ 2\,9\,9 \\ \hline 1 \end{array} \left\{ \begin{array}{l} \text{inefficient use} \\ \text{of algorithm} \end{array} \right.$$

Let us try some "pre-algorithm" methods of finding the difference between 634 and 275. *Children and teachers should be encouraged to devise more such methods of their own.*

1   Billy's method (see D17)

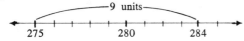

$$275 \xrightarrow{\qquad \Box \qquad} 634$$

I first add 25 to get to an even hundred. Then I add the other 334.

So: $275 + \textcircled{25} = 300$

$300 + \textcircled{334} = 634$

So: $275 + \textcircled{25 + 334} = 634$

$$275 \xrightarrow{\qquad \boxed{359} \qquad} 634$$

2   Pam's method (see D19, 20)

$$275 \xrightarrow{\qquad \Box \qquad} 634$$

I am at 275 on the number line. I want to go to 634. That's far off. I first go

9 units

| | | | | | | | |
275   280   284

from 275 to 284. Now I travel by tens to the right number of tens.

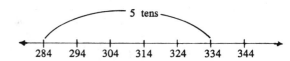

5 tens

284   294   304   314   324   334   344

Now I travel by hundreds to the right number of hundreds.

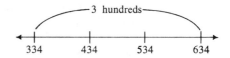

3 hundreds

334   434   534   634

So the trip is 9 units plus 5 tens plus 3 hundreds long. That's 359 units long.

$$275 \xrightarrow{\qquad \boxed{359} \qquad} 634$$

3   Ted's method (see D21, 22)

$$634 - 275 = \Box$$

Ted says to himself: "It is easier to take 300 away than 275. I can do that if I first add 25 to both 634 and 275. So my easier problem is $659 - 300$. The answer to that is 359."

$$(634 + 25) - (275 + 25) = \\ 659 \quad - \quad 300 \quad = 359$$

4   Lynn's method

$$634 - 275 = \Box$$

Lynn begins by taking away hundreds and takes 200 away from 634 and has 434 left. Then she takes 70 away from 434 and has 364 left. Then she takes 5 away from 364 and has 359 left.

$$634 - 275 = [(634 - 200) - 70] - 5 \\ [434 \quad - 70] - 5 \\ 364 \qquad - 5 \\ 359$$

5   George's method

This youngster's method deserves special attention. Several third-graders have invented this technique and are *very* fast with it. Obviously they understand negative numbers!

$$\begin{array}{r} 634 \\ -\ 275 \\ \hline 400 - 40 - 1 = 359 \end{array}$$

George starts his subtraction at the left with $600 - 200 = 400$. Then he does the subtraction $30 - 70 = -40$. Then he does $4 - 5 = -1$. His answer is then $400 - 40 - 1 = 359$. Try this method. It works every time!

Working toward the subtraction algorithm

Our goal is to take the children *slowly* through a rationale which makes the subtraction algorithm below meaningful. (This represents a summary of lab sheets D23 through D42.

$$\begin{array}{r} {}^{6}\not7\,{}^{11}\not2\,{}^{14}\not4 \\ -\ 3\,8\,6 \\ \hline 3\,3\,8 \end{array}$$

D Subtraction

1 **We first concentrate** on those decompositions of numbers into addends of hundreds, tens, and units that are useful for subtraction. (Note: h = hundreds, t = tens, u = units.)

$$434 = 400 + \boxed{30} + 4$$
$$= 400 + 20 + \boxed{13}$$
$$= \boxed{300} + 130 + 4$$
$$= 300 + 120 + \boxed{13}$$

$$434 = 4h + \boxed{?}t + 4u$$
$$= 4h + 2t + \boxed{?}u$$
$$= \boxed{?}h + 13t + 4u$$
$$= 3h + 12t + \boxed{?}u$$

This form is introduced: three hundred fifty-four, or 354, as:

h	t	u	
3		4	$300 + \square + 4 = 354$
3	4		$300 + 40 + \square = 354$
2		4	$200 + \square + 4 = 354$
2	14		$200 + 140 + \square = 354$

2 **Next we show some scaled pictures** representing hundreds, tens, and units in the regroupings needed for subtraction.

	hundreds	tens	units	
A				$3h + 2t + 1u = 321$
B				$2h + 12t + 1u = 321$
C				$3h + 1t + 11u = 321$
D				$2h + 11t + 11u = 321$

The table below summarizes the preceding regroupings.

A	3	2	1
B	2	12	1
C	3	1	11
D	2	11	11

Then we follow this with some subtraction problems in which the child must choose the best regrouping for the number. (See lab sheets D29, 30, 31, 32.)

the best regrouping
is item B in the table above

the problem:
321
− 141

B→
h	t	u
2	12	1

3 2 1
−1 4 1
1 8 0

3 **On lab sheets D33 and D34,** the child shades in the picture, represented by the chart.

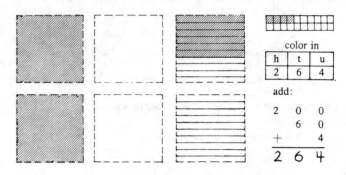

color in
h	t	u
2	6	4

add:

```
  2 0 0
    6 0
+     4
  2 6 4
```

4 **Next, on lab sheets D35 and D36,** the child's attention is directed to a subtraction problem, and he is to decide whether he has enough hundreds, tens, and units in each column.

527
− 451

	h	t	u
enough		✓		✓
not enough			✓	

The child has enough units (7) to subtract 1. He checks "enough" for units. He has not enough tens (2 tens) to subtract 5 tens. He checks "not enough" for tens and puts a loop around the 2 in the tens column. He has enough hundreds. He checks "enough" for hundreds. Finally he must think of a regrouping of 527 that will give him enough tens. After he has worked as shown below he checks for enough units, tens, and hundreds again and finds that he has *enough*.

5②7
−4 5 1

h	t	u
4	12	7

−4 5 1
76

	h	t	u
enough	✓	✓	✓
not enough			

5 **On lab sheets D37, 38, and 39** the process is shortened. The child thinks: I examined each column and found there were not enough tens. I circled the two tens. In the boxes I regrouped 426 into 3h, 12t, and 6u. This makes the subtraction easy.

h	t	u
3	12	6

4 ② 6
−2 3 5
1 9 1

6 **Lab sheets D41 and D42** present regular column subtraction where all steps are done by pupils.

7	9	10

8 0 0
−3 1 1
4 8 9

Note: Move slowly through these pages. Do not rush. Make up more lab sheets if they are needed.

· D1–D4, ·· D5–D8

The children should be free to make use of concrete materials, especially number lines and Cuisenaire rods, when doing work on the subtraction sheets through D8.

$4 - 3 = \square$

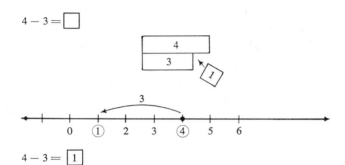

$4 - 3 = \boxed{1}$

$13 - 7 = \square$

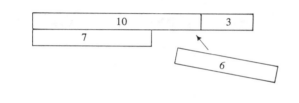

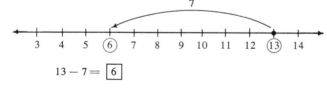

$13 - 7 = \boxed{6}$

Name _____ Date _____

$4 - 3 = \square$

$5 - 2 = \square$

$7 - 5 = \square$

$3 - 1 = \square$

$8 - 4 = \square$

$10 - 3 = \square$

● D–1

Name _____ Date _____

$\square = 9 - 2$

$\square = 6 - 4$

$\square = 2 - 1$

$\square = 5 - 4$

$\square = 10 - 5$

$\square = 7 - 3$

● D–2

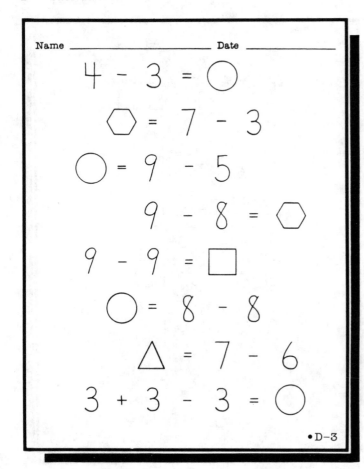

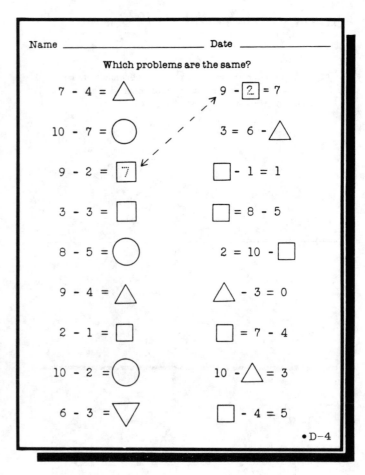

· **D4**

Children may use rods to complete all problems on this page.

After completing the problems (writing the equations) the children should match each sentence in the left column with a sentence in the right column.

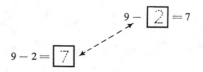

All equations can be matched except

$$10 - 2 = \bigcirc$$
$$2 = 10 - \square$$

Note: Most of the early subtraction problems are in Section E, Addition and Subtraction.

Name _____   Date _____

8 - 1 = ☐	4 - 2 = ☐
6 - 1 = ☐	8 - 2 = ☐
4 - 1 = ☐	6 - 2 = ☐
9 - 1 = ☐	3 - 2 = ☐
10 - 1 = ☐	9 - 1 = ☐
3 - 1 = ☐	10 - 2 = ☐
12 - 1 = ☐	11 - 2 = ☐
15 - 1 = ☐	13 - 2 = ☐
5 - 1 = ☐	2 - 2 = ☐
2 - 1 = ☐	5 - 2 = ☐
7 - 1 = ☐	12 - 2 = ☐
11 - 1 = ☐	7 - 2 = ☐

20, 19, 18, ☐, ☐, ☐, ☐, ☐, ☐

20, 18, 16, ☐, ☐, ☐, ☐, ☐, ☐, ☐

••D-5

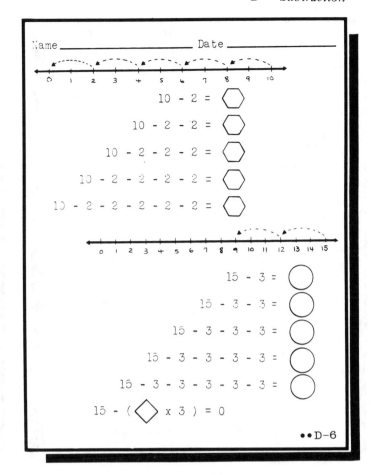

Name _____   Date _____

10 - 2 = ⬡

10 - 2 - 2 = ⬡

10 - 2 - 2 - 2 = ⬡

10 - 2 - 2 - 2 - 2 = ⬡

10 - 2 - 2 - 2 - 2 - 2 = ⬡

15 - 3 = ◯

15 - 3 - 3 = ◯

15 - 3 - 3 - 3 = ◯

15 - 3 - 3 - 3 - 3 = ◯

15 - 3 - 3 - 3 - 3 - 3 = ◯

15 - (◇ x 3) = 0

••D-6

·· D6

Repeated subtraction

To introduce repeated subtraction—actually a prelude to division—have the child trace with his finger the "10 − 2 jump" on the number line at the top of D6. He will land at point 8. Then he can trace the "10 − 2 − 2 jump" on the number line and land at 6, etc.

The following questions can be asked:

a. How many "−2 jumps" did we make from 10 to 6?
b. How many from 10 to 4? From 10 to 2?
c. If we start at 10 how many "−2 jumps" must we take to reach 0?
d. When we jump toward 0 on this number line, do we jump to the left or to the right?

Other activities

1   Trace with your finger the "8 − 2 jump." Write down the sentence for it.

$8 - 2 = 6$ *or* $6 \overset{2}{\frown} 8$ *or* $6 \xleftarrow{2} 8$

2   Trace with your finger the "8 − 2 − 2 jumps." Where do you land? [at 4]   Could you make that trip in *one* jump? How would you write the problem for that jump?

$8 - 4 = 4$ *or* $4 \overset{4}{\frown} 8$ *or* $4 \xleftarrow{4} 8$

Repeat this for "8 − 4 − 2."

3   Trace the "−2 jumps": 10 − 2 − 2. You land at 6. Now go back by "+2 jumps" to 10. How would you write that?

$10 - 2 - 2 = 6$ $6 \overset{2}{\frown} \overset{2}{\frown} 10$ $6 \xleftarrow{2} \xleftarrow{2} 10$

    or   *or*

$6 + 2 + 2 = 10$ $6 \overset{2}{\frown} \overset{2}{\frown} 10$ $6 \xrightarrow{2} \xrightarrow{2} 10$

Here we see clearly that addition is the inverse of subtraction. Whatever subtraction does, addition can *undo*.

Pose a tricky question: Trace two "−2 jumps" from 4 to 0. Could you make *three* "−2 jumps" from 4 in the 0 direction?

Yes, you could, but you would land at the edge of the paper where there is no more line. Suggest that children make the line a little longer and mark the spot where they think they would land. What would they call that spot?

Many suggestions such as the following will be made. Accept them all if they are logical.

"2 on the other side of 0"
"2 below zero" (from thermometer)
"2 minus"
"wrong 2"
(etc.)

(These are all answers from first- and second-graders.)

67

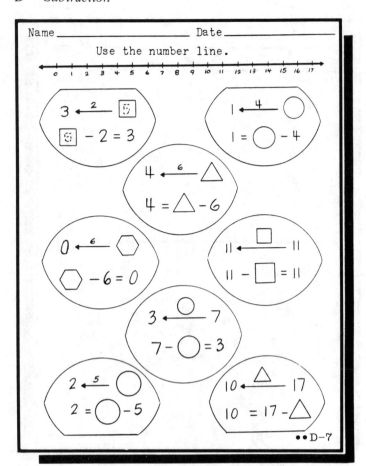

•• D-7

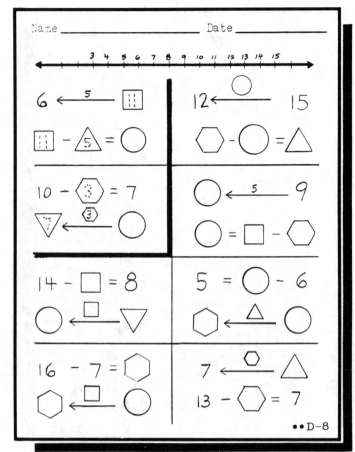

•• D-8

•• D7, D8

The number line as a tool

On D7 and D8 let the children trace the jumps with their fingers.

Problem 1

What does $3 \xleftarrow{2} \square$ mean?

What does $\longleftarrow$ mean?   [a trip to the left]

What does $\xleftarrow{2}$ mean?   [a "2 jump" to the left]

Where did the $\xleftarrow{2}$ take us?   [to point 3]

Where did it start?   [at 5]

$$3 \xleftarrow{2} \boxed{5}$$

Trace that trip with your finger.

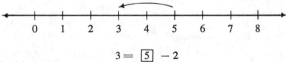

$$3 = \boxed{5} - 2$$

Problem 6

What does $3 \xleftarrow{\bigcirc} 7$ mean?   [Start at 7; jump $\bigcirc$; land at 3.]

With your finger, trace it on the number line. How big was your jump? [It was a "4 jump."] Write '4' in the frame.

$$3 \xleftarrow{\textcircled{4}} 7$$

$$7 - \textcircled{4} = 3$$

You might now want to use the number-line sheets N1 and N2 or make up some like them.

On these sheets the children draw in the "hops" or "jumps," and then play games:

$$0 \xrightarrow{2} \boxed{2} \qquad \boxed{0} \xleftarrow{2} 2 \quad \text{etc.}$$

$$\square \xrightarrow{4} 8 \qquad 4 \xrightarrow{4} \square \quad \text{etc.}$$

Look at sheet N2. On the top number line, put your finger on *any one* of the cross lines; write zero under it:

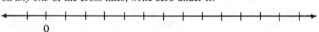
0

Under the next cross line in this direction ($\longrightarrow$) write 1. Now label the number line all the way:

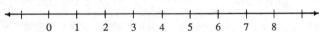
0 1 2 3 4 5 6 7 8

Different children will have different last numbers, depending on where they started.

Ask: What is your largest number, John? What is your largest number, Mary? Why is Mary's largest number smaller than John's? etc.

Now look at the cross lines on the other side of 0. How should we mark them? (Marking them with a red crayon is an easy way to differentiate positive and negative numbers.)

Put your finger on the red 1 and make a "$\xrightarrow{2}$" jump." Where did you land? Children will answer such things as: "on the dark 1," "on the pencil 1," etc.

Make many moves like that.

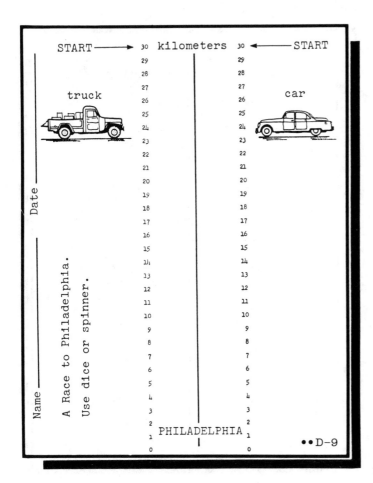

START ⟶ 30 kilometers 30 ⟵ START

truck   car

truck	car
29	29
28	28
27	27
26	26
25	25
24	24
23	23
22	22
21	21
20	20
19	19
18	18
17	17
16	16
15	15
14	14
13	13
12	12
11	11
10	10
9	9
8	8
7	7
6	6
5	5
4	4
3	3
2	2
1	1
0	0

PHILADELPHIA

Name

Date

A Race to Philadelphia.
Use dice or spinner.

••D-9

Have a Race Game

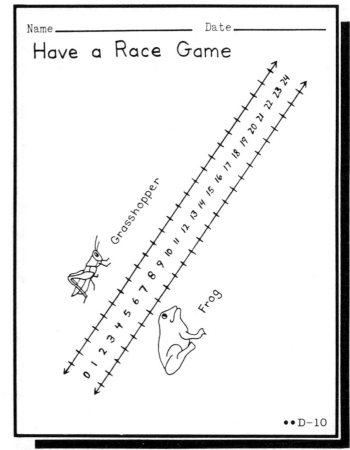

Grasshopper

Frog

0 1 2 3 4 5 6 7 8 9 10 11 12 13 14 15 16 17 18 19 20 21 22 23 24

••D-10

••D9, D10
Driving to Philadelphia

This is a simple subtraction game for partners.

Materials needed: coins or buttons,

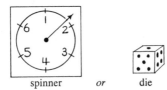

spinner   *or*   die

Directions: Let us say that Jill is the truck driver and Joe is driving the car. Jill begins the game by throwing the die. She throws a 2, so she advances 2 km toward Philadelphia ($30 - 2 = 28$).

Next Joe takes a turn. He throws a 5, so he advances 5 km ($30 - 5 = 25$). After each throw, the player circles the number landed on with a crayon. Play continues to alternate in this manner until a player reaches Philadelphia. That player wins.

If the lab sheet is to be used more than once, then students should use buttons or some other markers instead of writing on the lab sheet. The game can also be played on centimeter rulers beginning at 30 cm, using rods to lay out the distances covered. Whoever gets to 0 first wins.

The game on D10 is played similarly. Children can also make up their own games.

$\square = 9 - 8$ $\square = 5 - 3$

$6 - 6 = \square$ $8 - 2 - 2 - 2 = \square$

$\square - 7 = 2$ $16 - 12 = \square$

$14 - 4 = \square$ $5 = 10 - \square$

$\square = 7 - 2 - 2 - 2$ $7 - 7 = \square$

$7 - 2 = \square$ $8 - 5 = 2 + \square$

$\square - 2 = 3$ $14 - 7 = \square$

$12 = 17 - \square$ $\square - 3 = 1$

$11 - \square = 11$ $15 - 5 = \square$

$5 - 0 = \square$ $15 - 6 = \square$

$\square = 8 - 4$ $12 = 14 - \square$

$9 - 7 = \square$ $11 - 3 = \square$

Use rods to check your answers.

••D-11

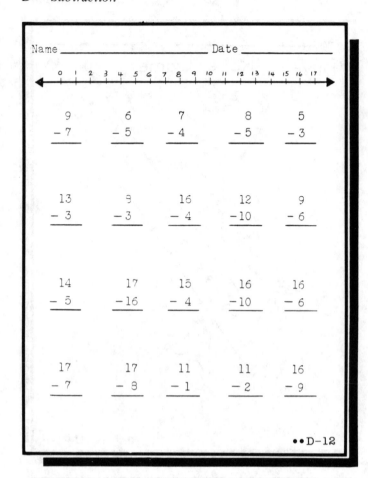

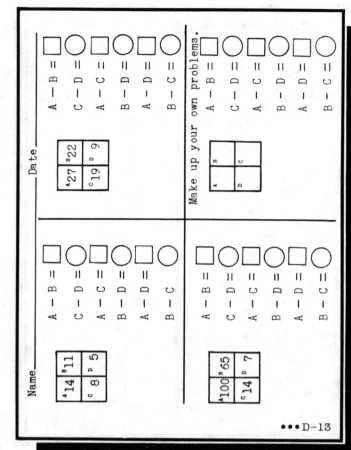

••D12
Subtraction in column form

The authors feel that children should not be given problems whose solutions involve "borrowing" and "carrying" techniques until after they themselves have discovered and used their own methods of solving similar problems. After the children have mastered the concept of place value (see Section M), they should have no difficulty solving the problems on this lab sheet by "regrouping" numbers whenever necessary. The words "carry" and "borrow" need never be introduced.

Problems of this type may be solved in a variety of ways.

Number lines and rods should be available to those children who cannot yet do these computations mentally.

•••D13

The grid on D13 is used for subtraction.

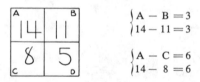

$$\begin{cases} A - B = 3 \\ 14 - 11 = 3 \end{cases}$$

$$\begin{cases} A - C = 6 \\ 14 - 8 = 6 \end{cases}$$

There is also enough room on the lab sheet for the children to write the sums.

Note

$$A - C \neq C - A \quad but \quad A + C = C + A$$
Not commutative   Commutative
$$14 - 8 \neq 8 - 14 \quad\quad 14 + 8 = 8 + 14$$

Warning: When children write their own numerals in the empty grid, they may get negative numbers as answers! If you want to avoid this "nice" problem, suggest that $A > B > C > D$. That is, make

    A the biggest number.
    B a little smaller than A.
    C a little smaller than B.
    D the smallest number.

···D15

Let the children trace the jumps on the number line:

$16 - 6 = \boxed{10}$

land   6   start
10 11 12 13 14 15 16

$26 - 6 = \boxed{20}$

20 21 22 23 24 25 26

$36 - 6 = \boxed{30}$

30 31 32 33 34 36 36

The children can use imaginary number-line segments to trace the jumps for the next two problems.

$46 - 6 = \boxed{40}$ 40   46

$56 - 6 = \boxed{50}$ 50   56

If you start at 86 and jump to the left 6, where will you land?

$86 - 6 = \boxed{80}$ 80   86

If you start at 106 and jump to the left 6, where will you land?

$106 - 6 = \boxed{100}$ 100   106

The children should be able to generalize that:

$[(\square \times 10) + 6] - 6 = \square \times 10$

$(\square \times 10)$ $[(\square \times 10) + \triangle{6}]$

land $\triangle{6}$ start

$16 - 7 = \boxed{9}$	$46 - 7 = \boxed{39}$
$26 - 7 = \boxed{19}$	$56 - 7 = \boxed{49}$
$36 - 7 = \boxed{29}$	$66 - 7 = \boxed{59}$

These are problems of the type:

$[(\square \times 10) + 6] - 7 = (\square \times 10) - 1$

$9 - 7 = \boxed{2}$	$29 - 7 = \boxed{22}$
$19 - 7 = \boxed{12}$	$39 - 7 = \boxed{32}$

These are problems of the type:

$[(\square \times 10) + 9] - 7 = (\square \times 10) + 2$

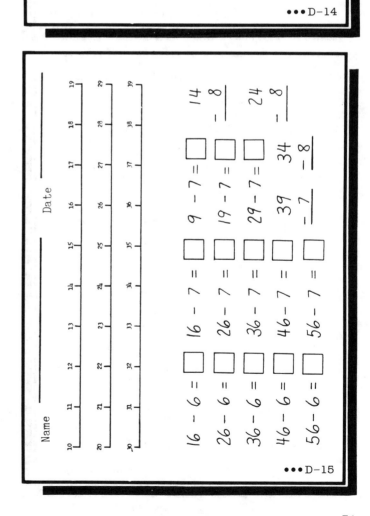

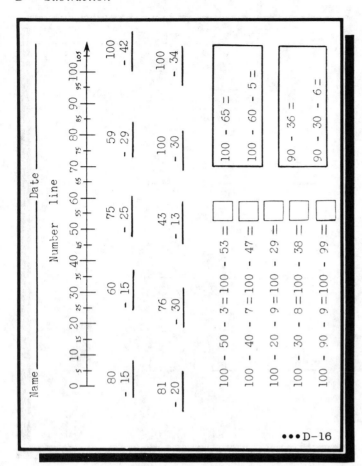

••• D-16

···D16

$$100 - 65 = 100 - 60 - 5 = 35$$

The child may think: "When jumping tens *and* units, I may first jump the tens and *then* jump the units." This is a convenient method for mental subtraction.

Name_____ Date_____

1. How big are the jumps?

24 →▢→ 59   84 →▢→ 102

32 →▢→ 60   56 →▢→ 63

62 →▢→ 64   56 →▢→ 93

2. Where did we start?

▢ →9→ 29   ▢ →18→ 104

▢ →18→ 42   ▢ →8→ 112

▢ →28→ 42   ▢ →5→ 86

▢ →7→ 63   ▢ →14→ 75

▢ →17→ 73   ▢ →3→ 186

▢ →38→ 129   ▢ →25→ 36

••••D-17

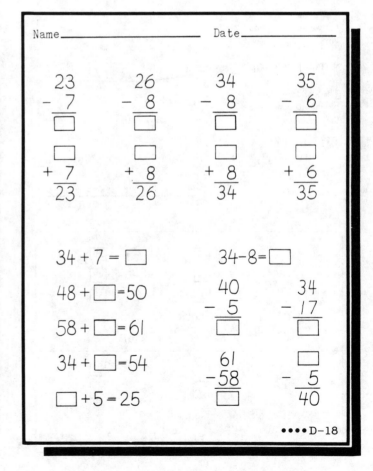

••••D-18

·····D19, D20

Additive subtraction

1   Problem:

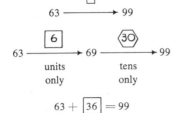

$$63 \longrightarrow 99$$

Solution

$$63 \xrightarrow{\boxed{6}} 69 \xrightarrow{\langle 30 \rangle} 99$$

units only   tens only

$$63 + \boxed{36} = 99$$

2   Problem:

$$123 \longrightarrow 380$$

Solution

$$123 \xrightarrow{\boxed{7}} 130 \xrightarrow{\langle 50 \rangle} 180 \xrightarrow{\langle 200 \rangle} 380$$

units   tens   hundreds

a. Beginning on the left, first jump to the correct units place.
b. Jump to the correct tens place.
c. Jump to the correct hundreds place.
d. Add all previous jumps.

$$123 + \left(7 + 50 + 200\right) = 380$$
$$123 + \boxed{257} = 380$$

3   Problem:

$$89 \longrightarrow 632$$

Solution

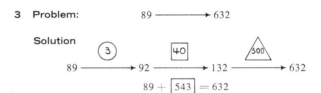

$$89 \xrightarrow{3} 92 \xrightarrow{\boxed{40}} 132 \xrightarrow{\triangle 500} 632$$

$$89 + \boxed{543} = 632$$

Remember to work these lab sheets yourself before the children begin them.

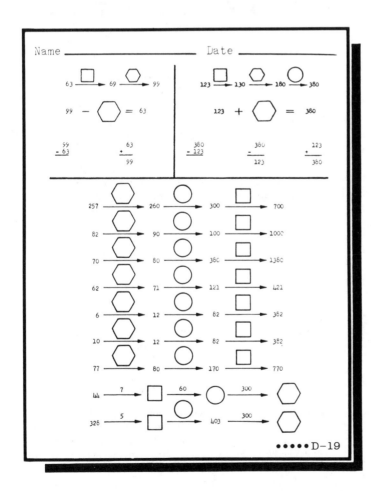

·····D–19

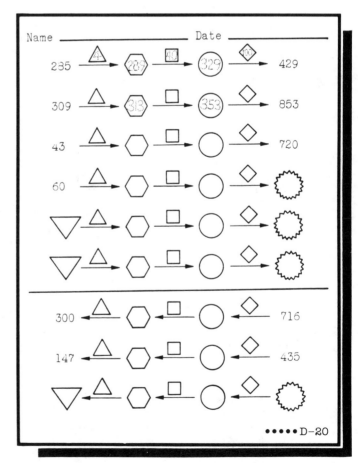

·····D–20

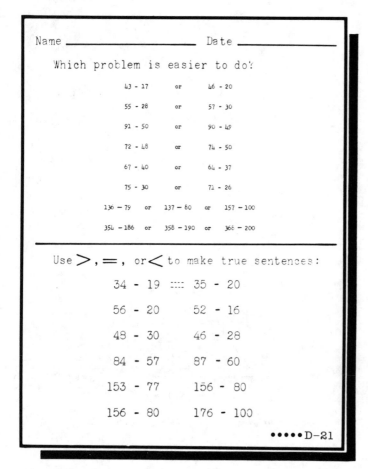

Name _____ Date _____

Which problem is easier to do?

43 - 17	or	46 - 20
55 - 28	or	57 - 30
91 - 50	or	90 - 49
72 - 48	or	74 - 50
67 - 40	or	64 - 37
75 - 30	or	71 - 26
136 - 79	or 137 - 80 or	157 - 100
354 - 186	or 358 - 190 or	368 - 200

Use $>$, $=$, or $<$ to make true sentences:

34 - 19 ⸭⸭⸭ 35 - 20	
56 - 20	52 - 16
48 - 30	46 - 28
84 - 57	87 - 60
153 - 77	156 - 80
156 - 80	176 - 100

•••••D-21

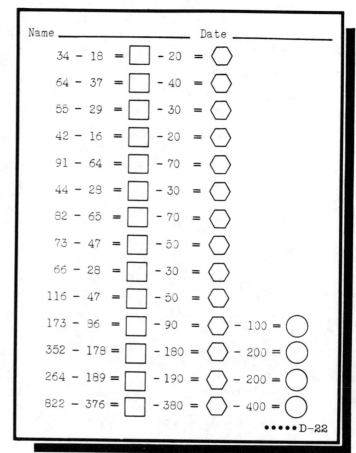

34 - 18 = ☐ - 20 = ⬡
64 - 37 = ☐ - 40 = ⬡
55 - 29 = ☐ - 30 = ⬡
42 - 16 = ☐ - 20 = ⬡
91 - 64 = ☐ - 70 = ⬡
44 - 28 = ☐ - 30 = ⬡
82 - 65 = ☐ - 70 = ⬡
73 - 47 = ☐ - 50 = ⬡
66 - 28 = ☐ - 30 = ⬡
116 - 47 = ☐ - 50 = ⬡
173 - 36 = ☐ - 90 = ⬡ - 100 = ◯
352 - 178 = ☐ - 180 = ⬡ - 200 = ◯
264 - 189 = ☐ - 190 = ⬡ - 200 = ◯
822 - 376 = ☐ - 380 = ⬡ - 400 = ◯

•••••D-22

·····D21

Preliminary activity

Look at the two pictures below.

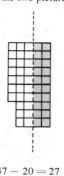

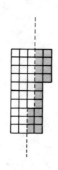

$$47 - 20 = 27 \qquad\qquad 44 - 17 = 27$$

It is easier to take 20 away from 47 than to take 17 away from 44.

One can think: "I don't like taking 17 away from 44. I'd rather take (17 + 3), or 20, away from (44 + 3), or 47. Both have the same answer."

35 − 18	is harder than	37 − 20	(35 + 2) − (18 + 2)
362 − 189	is harder than	373 − 200	(362 + 11) − (189 + 11)

In fact, in mental arithmetic it is generally easier to subtract tens only or hundreds only, rather than units and tens, or units, tens, and hundreds.

Since $\Box - \triangle = (\Box + \bigcirc) - (\triangle + \bigcirc)$, we may change a subtraction problem to one which is easier to work.

$$16 - 9 = 17 - 10 = 7$$
$$23 - 8 = 25 - 10 = 15$$

Try this technique with the rods and see how convenient it is.

On lab sheet D21, children are asked which of each pair of problems is easier to do. Because they might never realize that each pair has the same difference, problems that make this clear were included at the bottom of the page.

·····D22

$$34 - 18 = \boxed{36} - 20 = \langle 16 \rangle$$
$$264 - 189 = \boxed{265} - 190 = \langle 275 \rangle - 200 = \textcircled{75}$$

Before a definite method of subtraction is taught, children should be encouraged to invent their own methods. This is why we have taken them through 21 subtraction lab sheets without forcing them to use one uniform procedure. We are showing them several sensible ways to do mental subtraction.

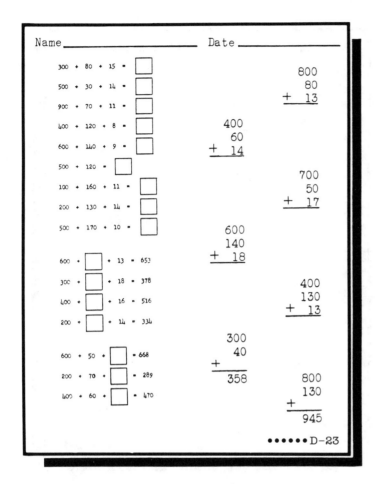

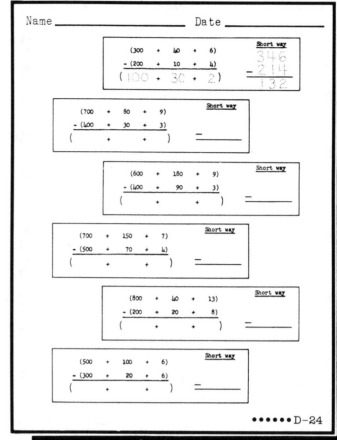

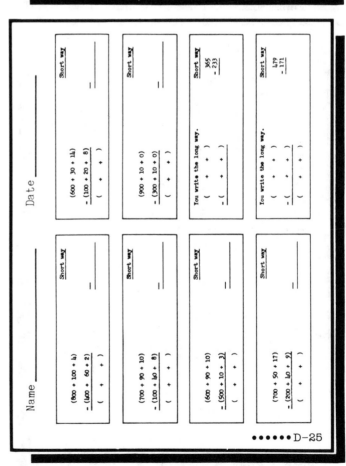

······ D23 ,   D26–D28

Regrouping of hundreds, tens, and units

These sheets are provided to establish firmly in children's minds that regrouping does not change the simple three-digit name of a number.

$$2h + 13t + 13u = 3h + 4t + 3u = 343$$

Note: Cut out of oaktag or cardboard a stack of squares, 10 cm. × 10 cm., and use them with orange rods and white rods as models for hundreds, tens, and units. (Perhaps a handy parent or custodian could cut 10-cm. squares from plywood and paint them orange.) You can then demonstrate regrouping as follows:

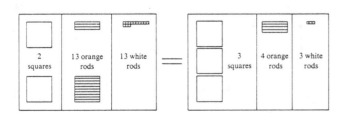

Name _____   Date _____

435 = 400 + 30 + [ ]
435 = 400 + 20 + [ ]
435 = 300 + [ ] + 5
435 = 300 + [ ] + 15

362 = 300 + [ ] + 2
    = 300 + [ ] + 12
    = 200 + 160 + [ ]
    = 200 + 150 + [ ]

711 = [ ] + 10 + 1
    = [ ] + 0 + 11
    = [ ] + 110 + 1
    = [ ] + 100 + 11

888 = 8h + [ ]t + 8u
    = 8h + [ ]t + 18u
    = [ ]h + 18t + 8u
    = 7h + 17t + [ ]u

•••••• D-26

Name _____   Date _____

h = hundreds
t = tens
u = units

7h + 5t + 11u = [761]   3h + 17t + 5u = [ ]
9h + 6t + 11u = [ ]   2h + 19t + 6u = [ ]
3h + 4t + 17u = [ ]   14t + 3u = [ ]
      7t + 19u = [ ]   6h + 9t + 10u = [ ]
3h + 0t + 12u = [ ]   7h + 9t + 10u = [ ]
7h + 14t + 0u = [ ]   3h + 9t + 10u = [ ]
8h + 16t + 0u = [ ]   3h + 10t + 10u = [ ]
4h + 10t = [ ]   5h + 10t + 10u = [ ]
5h + 15t = [ ]   7h + 11t + 10u = [ ]
6h + 10t = [ ]   6h + 14t + 12u = [ ]
4h + 10t = [ ]   3h + 17t + 15u = [ ]
9h + 10t = [ ]   8h + 15t + 14u = [ ]
4h + 10t + 3u = [ ]   3h + 13t + 14u = [ ]
5h + 10t + 7u = [ ]   6h + 16t + 17u = [ ]
3h + 10t + 1u = [ ]   8h + 18t + 19u = [ ]
8h + 15t + 1u = [ ]   8h + 17u = [ ]
6h + 13t + 8u = [ ]   4h + 12u = [ ]

•••••• D-27

Name _____   Date _____

five hundred thirty-two 532

h	t	u
5	(3)	2
4	2	2
5	12	12
4	12	12

500 + [ ] + 2 = 532
400 + [ ] + 2 = 532
500 + [ ] + 12 = 532
400 + [ ] + 12 = 532

six hundred fifty 650

h	t	u
6	5	(0)
5	15	
6	4	
5	14	

600 + 50 + [ ] = 650
500 + 150 + [ ] = 650
600 + 40 + [ ] = 650
500 + 140 + [ ] = 650

seven hundred thirty-six 736

h	t	u
	3	6
6	2	6
7		6
6		16

six hundred 600

h	t	u
6	0	0
	10	0
5		0
5	9	

four hundred five 405

h	t	u
	0	5
	10	5
3		5
3		15

•••••• D-28

Name _____   Date _____

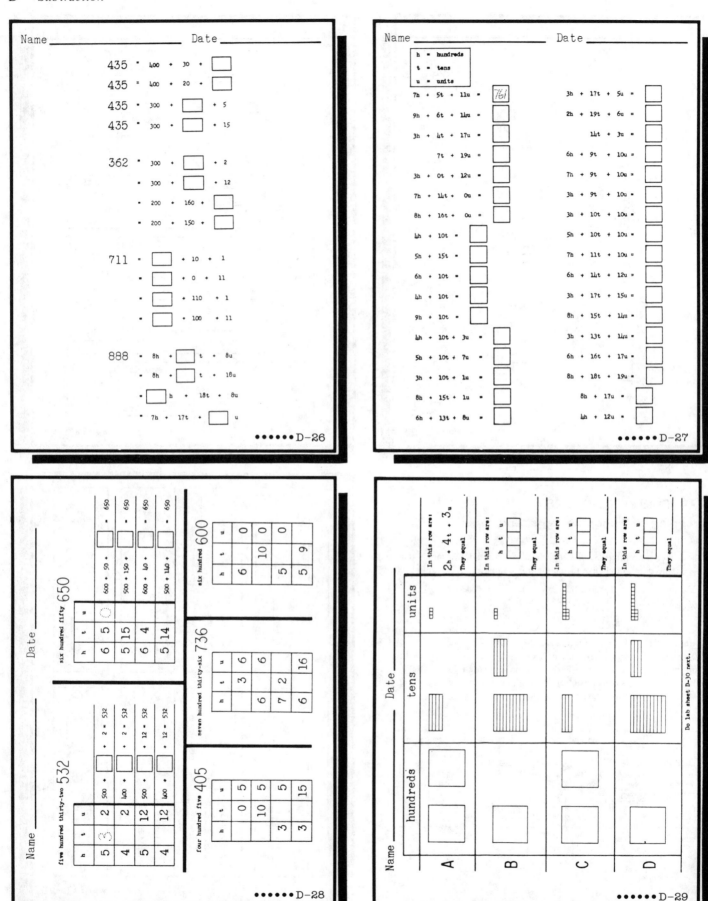

	hundreds	tens	units
A			
B			
C			
D			

A In this row are: 2h + 4t + 3u   They equal [ ]
B In this row are: __ h __ t __ u   They equal [ ]
C In this row are: __ h __ t __ u   They equal [ ]
D In this row are: __ h __ t __ u   They equal [ ]

Do lab sheet D-30 next.

•••••• D-29

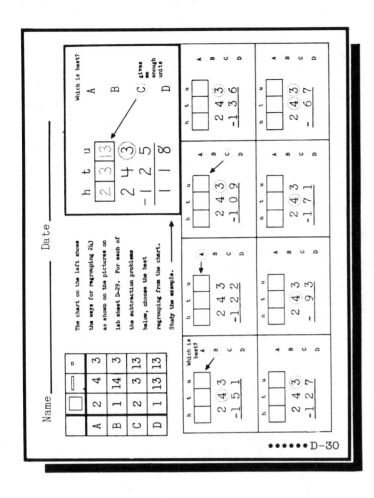

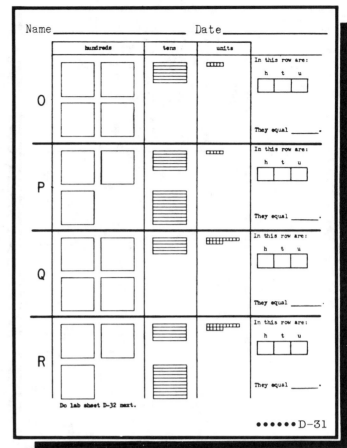

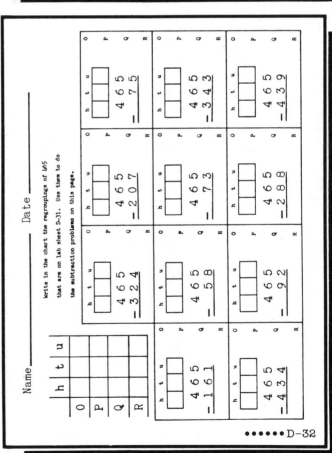

······ D29– D32

D29 and D31 demonstrate the preceding suggestion for using rods and cardboard squares to show regrouping.

D30 and D32 are each about the numbers represented in pictures on lab sheets D29 and D31. D30 is about the number 243. D32 is about the number 465.

h	t	u
2	(4)	3
−1	5	1

Questions a child must ask himself:

Do I have enought units in the units column to take away one unit? [Yes.]

Do I have enough tens in the tens column to take away 5 tens?   [No. I have only 4 tens.]

I circle the 4 tens to remember that I do not have enough.

h	t	u	
1	14	3	A
2	(4)	3	(B)
−1	5	1	C
	9	2	D

Which regrouping of 243 will give me enough tens.   [The regrouping labeled "B" on the chart on D30.]

I regroup 243 according to B, that is, 1, 14, 3. Now I can subtract units from units, tens from tens, and hundreds from hundreds.

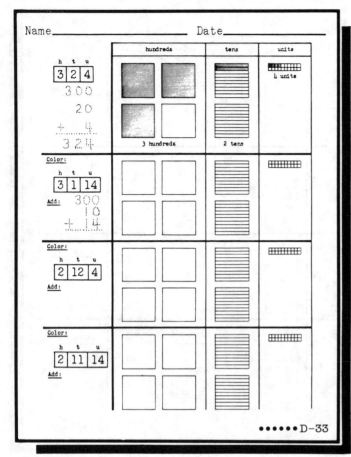

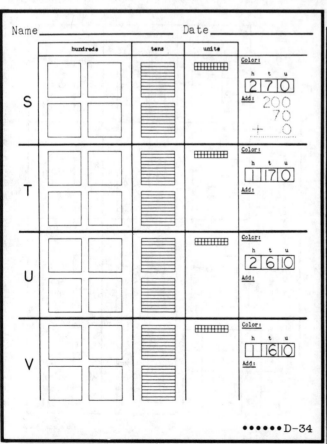

······ D35
Closer to the algorithm

Problem 1

$$
\begin{array}{ccc}
5 & ② & 7 \\
-4 & 5 & 1 \\
\end{array}
$$

Not enough tens (checked on the chart); I must regroup.

Now I have enough in each column to subtract.

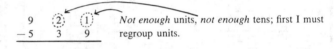

$$
\begin{array}{|c|c|c|}
\hline
4 & 12 & 7 \\
\hline
\end{array}
$$
$$
-4 \quad 5 \quad 1
$$

Problem 3

$$
\begin{array}{ccc}
6 & 7 & 8 \\
-3 & 2 & 7 \\
\hline
3 & 5 & 1 \\
\end{array}
$$

Enough units, enough tens, enough hundreds; I can subtract.

Problem 4

$$
\begin{array}{ccc}
9 & ② & ① \\
-5 & 3 & 9 \\
\end{array}
$$

Not enough units, *not enough* tens; first I must regroup units.

$$
\begin{array}{|c|c|c|}
\hline
9 & ① & 11 \\
\hline
\end{array}
$$
$$
-5 \quad 3 \quad 9
$$

Enough units, *not enough* tens; now I must regroup tens.

$$
\begin{array}{|c|c|c|}
\hline
8 & 11 & 11 \\
\hline
\end{array}
$$
$$
\begin{array}{ccc}
-5 & 3 & 9 \\
\hline
3 & 8 & 2 \\
\end{array}
$$

Enough units, tens, hundreds; I can subtract.

······ D37

$$
\begin{array}{ccc}
h & t & u \\
\end{array}
$$
$$
\begin{array}{|c|c|c|}
\hline
6 & 11 & 2 \\
\hline
\end{array}
$$
$$
\begin{array}{ccc}
7 & ① & 2 \\
-1 & 7 & 0 \\
\hline
5 & 4 & 2 \\
\end{array}
$$

Not enough tens; put a loop around the 1 ten. Regroup in the boxes; subtract.

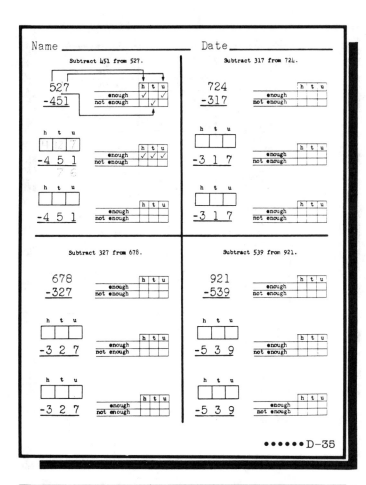

Name _____ Date _____

Subtract 451 from 527.

527
−451

enough / not enough

Subtract 317 from 724.

724
−317

Subtract 327 from 678.

678
−327

Subtract 539 from 921.

921
−539

•••••• D-35

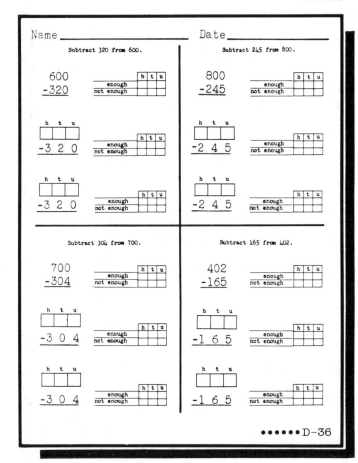

Name _____ Date _____

Subtract 320 from 600.

600
−320

Subtract 245 from 800.

800
−245

Subtract 304 from 700.

700
−304

Subtract 165 from 402.

402
−165

•••••• D-36

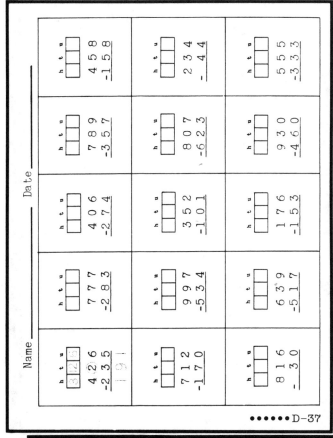

Name   Date

	458 −158	234 −44	555 −333
	789 −357	807 −623	930 −460
	406 −274	352 −101	176 −153
	777 −283	997 −534	639 −517
	426 −235	712 −170	816 −30

•••••• D-37

Name   Date

	830 −417	786 −629	684 −408
	969 −78	803 −350	309 −264
	583 −236	934 −92	448 −236
	784 −350	606 −275	890 −96
	337 −164	293 −160	532 −307

•••••• D-38

79

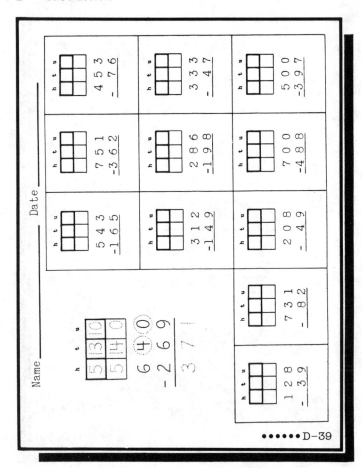

Date _____ Name _____

h t u 453 − 76	h t u 333 − 47	h t u 500 −397
h t u 751 −362	h t u 286 −198	h t u 700 −488
h t u 543 −165	h t u 312 −149	h t u 208 − 49

h t u 731 − 82

5 3 10 6 4̸0 − 269 371

h t u 128 − 39

•••••• D-39

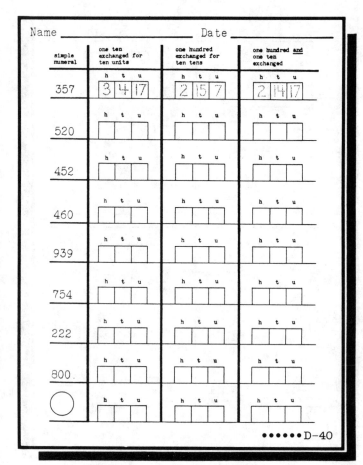

Name _____ Date _____

simple numeral	one ten exchanged for ten units			one hundred exchanged for ten tens			one hundred and one ten exchanged		
	h	t	u	h	t	u	h	t	u
357	3	4	17	2	15	7	2	14	17
520									
452									
460									
939									
754									
222									
800									
◯									

•••••• D-40

Name _____ Date _____

800	245	235	915	709
−311	− 67	−128	−726	−524

518	598	754	91	28
−329	−296	−555	− 57	− 25

605	780	59	777	70
−513	−684	− 22	−688	−59

380	707	700	150	215
− 98	−686	− 49	− 20	− 19

•••••• D-41

Name _____ Date _____

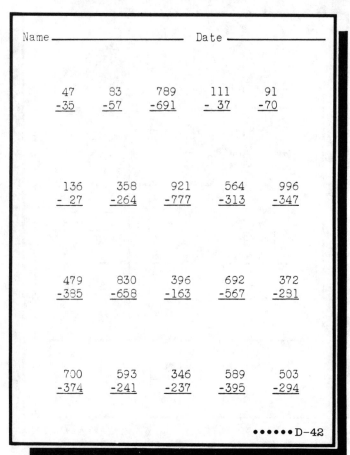

47	83	789	111	91
−35	−57	−691	− 37	−70

136	358	921	564	996
− 27	−264	−777	−313	−347

479	830	396	692	372
−385	−658	−163	−567	−231

700	593	346	589	503
−374	−241	−237	−395	−294

•••••• D-42

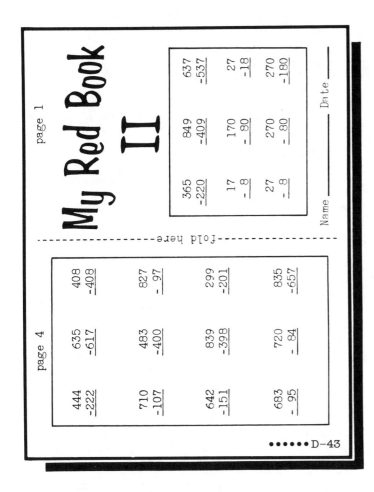

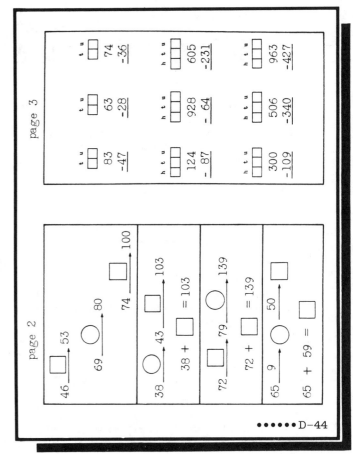

······ **D43, D44**

Diagnostic achievement book on subtraction

Teachers may want to keep this booklet for their records. This is not a standardized test in the usual sense. It should serve to spot the range of achievement in the class and particular difficulties each child may be having. The need for small-group review or individual practice can be determined by these diagnostic sheets.

E   Addition and subtraction

The lab sheets of this section contain most of the beginning work in subtraction. Addition and subtraction operations should be taught together, because subtraction is introduced as the operation that *undoes* addition. It is the inverse operation of addition. In the problem below, one starts with 8 and ends with 8.

Adding	is undone	subtracting
seven	by	seven.
$8 + 7 = 15$		$15 - 7 = \mathbf{8}$

This relationship can be expressed more briefly by the following equation:

$$(8 + 7) - 7 = 8$$

The children are also taught that addition is the operation that undoes subtraction. Thus, *addition and subtraction are the inverse operations of each other.* In the problem below notice that again one starts with one number and ends with the same number.

Subtracting	is undone	adding
seven	by	seven.
$8 - 7 = 1$		$1 + 7 = \mathbf{8}$

$$(8 - 7) + 7 = 8$$

The problems on lab sheets E7–E14 are very useful in bringing out this fundamental relationship between addition and subtraction.

Comparison of the properties of addition and subtraction

If $\square$, $\bigcirc$, and $\triangle$ are understood to be placeholders for whole numbers, then the following general laws apply to addition and subtraction.

1   Closure and uniqueness properties

$\square + \bigcirc$ is always a unique whole number.

$\square - \bigcirc$ is not always a whole number. If it is a whole number, then it is unique.

2   Commutative property

$\square + \bigcirc = \bigcirc + \square$ is an identity.

$\square - \bigcirc = \bigcirc - \square$ is *not* an identity.

3   Associative property

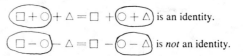

$(\square + \bigcirc) + \triangle = \square + (\bigcirc + \triangle)$ is an identity.

$(\square - \bigcirc) - \triangle = \square - (\bigcirc - \triangle)$ is *not* an identity.

4   Identity element

$\square + 0 = \square$ is an identity.

$\square - 0 = \square$ is an identity.

$\square - \square = 0$ is an identity.

5   Inverse property

$(\square + \bigcirc) - \bigcirc = \square$ is an identity.

$(\square - \bigcirc) + \bigcirc = \square$ is an identity.

6   Equality

If $\square + \bigcirc = \triangle$

then $\triangle - \bigcirc = \square$

and $\triangle - \square = \bigcirc.$

Vocabulary for addition and subtraction

Following are some suggestions for vocabulary-building activities in addition and subtraction. We have deliberately kept technical vocabulary at a minimum, but some teachers may feel we went too far in that direction. If you are one of those teachers, the following sample chalkboard activities may be to your liking.

Put this list on the chalkboard.

A.	addition	H.	equals
B.	subtraction	I.	greater than
D.	sum	J.	less than
E.	difference	K.	odd
C.	addends	L.	even
F.	minus	M.	equation
G.	plus	N.	open sentence

Then write, one at a time, the following sentences. Write nothing on or under the blank line. The children are to fill in a letter from the list above. The correct answers are shown below the lines.

1. $4 + 6 = \square$ is an ___(N)___
   (open sentence)

2. The ___(D)___ is missing in $4 + 6 = \square$.
   (sum)

3. 4 and 6 are the ___(C)___ .
   (addends)

4. The sum of 4 and 6 will be ___(I)___ 4 or 6.
   (greater than)

5. 4 and 6 are ___(L)___ numbers.
   (even)

6. The sum will be an ___(L)___ number.
   (even)

7. $4 + 6 = 10$ is an ___(M)___ .
   (equation)

8. 4, 6 are a pair of numbers. The difference between 4 and 6 is an ___(L)___ number.
   (even)

9. Write the equation for number 8 above: _____
   $(6 - 4 = 2)$

10. To get the difference we _____ .
    (subtract)

11. The sum of 4 and 6 is an ___(L)___ number.
    (even)

12. To get the sum we _____ .
    (add)

13. 32, 41 are a pair of numbers. Set up an open sentence to find their sum. _____
    $(32 + 41 = \square)$ or $(41 + 32 = \square)$

14. Their sum is an ___(K)___ number.
    (odd)

15. Set up an open sentence to find their difference.
    $(41 - 32 = \square)$ or $(32 + \square = 41)$

16. Their difference is an ___(K)___ number.
    (odd)

17. 2, 5, 7 are a triplet of numbers. One of these is the sum of the other two numbers. Write the equation to show this.
    $(2 + 5 = 7)$ or $(5 + 2 = 7)$

18. If 7 is the sum of 2 and 5, then 2 and 5 are the ___(C)___ .
    (addends)

19. When we subtract the *addend* 2 from the *sum* 7, we get the addend _____ .
    (5)

The following seatwork activities may be given.

1. Write four open sentences.
2. Write five equations.
3. Make up addition problems.
4. Make up seven subtraction problems.
5. Make up two addition problems with only odd addends.
6. Make up two subtraction problems in which the missing addend is an even number.

Suggested activities: Lotto

Equipment
Cuisenaire® rods or sets of numeral cards (0-10) and lotto cards made from light-colored construction paper. The lotto cards should represent several difficulty levels which children may choose from. Below are some sample lotto cards. *Notice that all sums, differences, and products are numbers 10 or under.*

Easy			Average		
4+5	3+4	2+6	12-9	14-8	18-9
3+2	2+4	6-4	13-5	19-18	12-10
0+1	7+3	8-5	17-17	11-7	15-10

Average			Difficult		
$\begin{matrix}14\\-6\end{matrix}$	$\begin{matrix}16\\-9\end{matrix}$	$\begin{matrix}23\\-20\end{matrix}$	43-42	17-9	3×2
			101-98	64-55	2×2×2
			$\frac{1}{2} × 14$	$\frac{1}{3} × 6$	8÷2

Rules

1 The class is divided into groups of 6 children. In each group there is a "caller–checker" and 5 players.

2 The caller holds up a rod or a numeral card. The 5 players look over their lotto cards to see if they have a problem (or problems) whose answer corresponds to the rod or card that was held up.

3 If a player has such a problem, he places a rod or numeral card on the problem.

4 The winner is the first player to have "three in a row" covered or the first player to have his whole card covered.

5 The caller–checker must check the winning card before he can declare the winner and call the game finished.

E1 – E6

On these sheets the plus and minus signs are printed in contrasting ways to help children who have difficulty differentiating between the two symbols. It will also help if the children put a frame around every subtraction problem *before* attempting to solve the problems.

$3 + 7 = \square$

$5 + 2 = \square$

$\boxed{9 - 5 = \square}$

$\boxed{6 - 3 = \square}$

$4 + 2 = \square$

$\boxed{7 - 6 = \square}$

Name _____ Date _____

$3 + 7 = \square$

$5 + 2 = \square$

$9 - 5 = \square$

$6 - 3 = \square$

$4 + 2 = \square$

$7 - 6 = \square$

• E-1

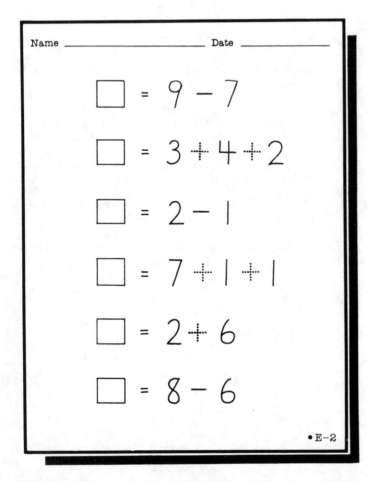

Name _____ Date _____

$\square = 9 - 7$

$\square = 3 + 4 + 2$

$\square = 2 - 1$

$\square = 7 + 1 + 1$

$\square = 2 + 6$

$\square = 8 - 6$

• E-2

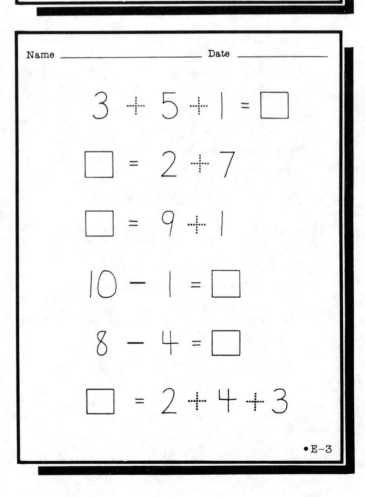

Name _____ Date _____

$3 + 5 + 1 = \square$

$\square = 2 + 7$

$\square = 9 + 1$

$10 - 1 = \square$

$8 - 4 = \square$

$\square = 2 + 4 + 3$

• E-3

Name _____ Date _____

$$3 + 1 + 2 = \square$$

$$\square = 5 + 5$$

$$6 - 4 = \square$$

$$3 + 3 = \square$$

$$7 + \square = 10$$

• E-4

Name _____ Date _____

$$3 + 3 = \square$$

$$3 + \square = 6$$

$$\square = 9 - 4$$

$$5 + \square = 9$$

$$2 + 2 = \square$$

$$\square = 5 + 5$$

• E-5

Name _____ Date _____

$$2 + 2 = \square$$

$$3 + 0 = \square$$

$$1 + 1 = \square$$

$$3 - 1 = \square$$

$$4 - 2 = \square$$

$$2 + 1 = \square$$

$$3 + 2 = \square$$

$$2 + \square = 4$$

$$5 - 3 = \square$$

$$4 + 3 = \square$$

$$7 - 3 = \square$$

Make up some problems of your own.

• E-6

Use rods.

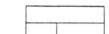

$$4 + 2 = \square$$

$$\square = 2 + 4$$

$$6 - 2 = \square$$

$$\square = 6 - 4$$

$$6 - \square = 2$$

$$\square - 2 = 4$$

$$\square - 4 = 2$$

$$6 - \square = 4$$

Name _____

Date _____

Make up your own problems for this rod picture.

• E-7

85

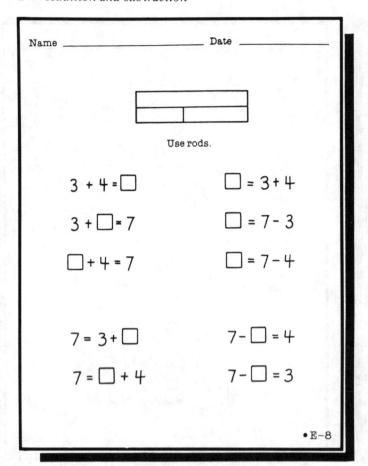

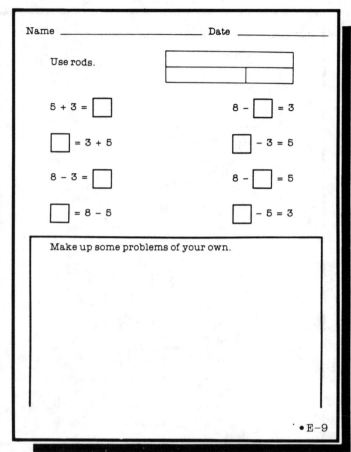

· **E7–E13**

At the top of E7, E8, E9, E10, and E11 are rod outlines upon which children may place their rods if necessary. They will find that the simple relationships among the rods illustrate every problem on the respective sheets. Only three or four numbers are involved in any one set of problems. In this way children become aware of the variety of relationships that can exist among three or four numbers.

To get children accustomed to writing equations and inequalities, the teacher might present them with a concrete relationship and ask them to write as many true mathematical sentences as they can to describe what they see. For instance, three rods may be held up by the teacher (as in one of the arrangements pictured on E7) and the following can be established:

dark green	
purple	red

If the white rod $= 1$,
then the purple rod $= 4$,
the red rod $= 2$,
and the dark green rod $= 6$.

Then <u>some</u> of the following true mathematical sentences about the rods can be written:

$$4 + 2 = 6 \qquad 6 - 4 - 2 = 0$$
$$2 + 4 = 6 \qquad 6 - 2 - 4 = 0$$
$$6 = 4 + 2 \qquad 0 = 6 - 4 - 2$$
$$6 = 2 + 4 \qquad 0 = 6 - 2 - 4$$

$$6 - 4 = 2 \qquad 6 > 4$$
$$6 - 2 = 4 \qquad 6 > 2$$
$$2 = 6 - 4 \qquad 4 < 6$$
$$4 = 6 - 2 \qquad 2 < 6$$

$$6 \neq 4 \qquad 6 \not> 4 + 2$$
$$6 \neq 2 \qquad 6 \not> 2 + 4$$
$$4 \neq 6 \qquad 4 + 2 \not< 6$$
$$2 \neq 6 \qquad 2 + 4 \not< 6$$

$$4 + 2 \not> 6 \qquad 6 - 4 \not< 2$$
$$4 + 4 \not> 6 \qquad 6 \not< 2$$
$$6 \not< 4 + 2 \qquad 2 \not> 6 \qquad 6 > 4 > 2$$
$$6 \not< 2 + 4 \qquad 4 \not> 6 - 2 \qquad 2 < 4 < 6$$

Lab sheets E12 and E13 are similar to the preceding sheets but do not have rod patterns at the top.

86

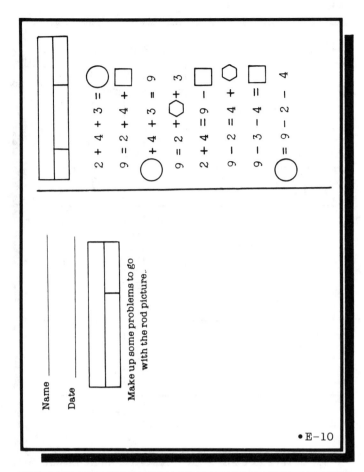

Name ____
Date ____

Make up some problems to go
with the rod picture.

$2 + 4 + 3 = \bigcirc$

$9 = 2 + 4 + \square$

$\bigcirc + 4 + 3 = 9$

$9 = 2 + \square$

$2 + 4 = 9 - \hexagon$

$9 - 2 = 4 + \square$

$9 - 3 - 4 = \square$

$\bigcirc = 9 - 2 - 4$

• E-10

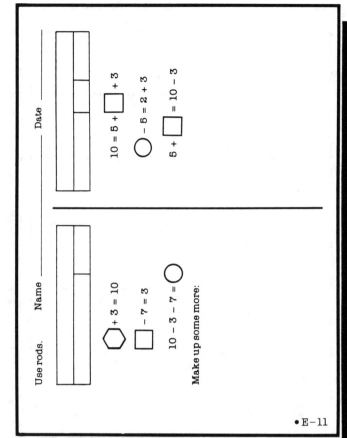

Use rods.   Name ____   Date ____

$10 = 6 + \square + 3$

$\bigcirc - 6 = 2 + 3$

$5 + \square = 10 - 3$

$\hexagon + 3 = 10$

$\square - 7 = 3$

$10 - 3 - 7 = \bigcirc$

Make up some more:

• E-11

Name ____   Date ____

$8 = 7 + \square$

$1 + 7 = \square$

$8 - 1 = \square$

$8 - \square = 1$

$8 - \square = 7$

$7 + \square = 8$

$6 - 6 = \square$

$6 - \square = 0$

$0 + 6 = \square$

$0 = 6 - \square$

• E-12

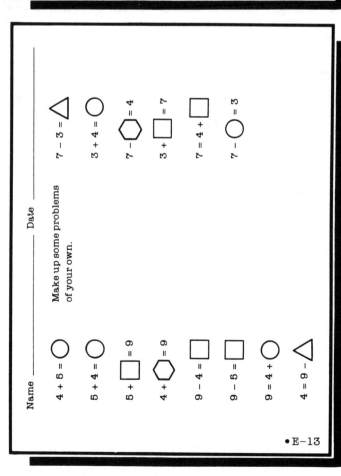

Name ____   Date ____

$4 + 5 = \bigcirc$

$5 + 4 = \bigcirc$

$5 + \square = 9$

$4 + \hexagon = 9$

$9 - 4 = \square$

$9 - 5 = \square$

$9 = 4 + \bigcirc$

$4 = 9 - \triangle$

Make up some problems
of your own.

$7 - 3 = \triangle$

$3 + 4 = \bigcirc$

$7 - \hexagon = 4$

$3 + \square = 7$

$7 = 4 + \square$

$7 - \bigcirc = 3$

• E-13

87

Name   Date

This picture shows:

$$10 - 3 = \square \qquad 7 + 3 = \square$$
$$10 - 7 = \square \qquad 3 + 7 = \square$$

What does this picture show?

$$10 - 4 = \square \qquad 6 + \bigcirc = \square$$
$$10 - 6 = \square \qquad 4 + \triangle = \square$$

What does this picture show?

Put a loop around <u>nine things</u>.
The picture shows:

$$10 - 9 = \square \qquad \square + 9 = 10$$
$$10 - \square = 9 \qquad 9 + \square = 10$$

Put a loop around <u>two things</u>.
What does the picture show?

What does the picture show?

• E–14

Name   Date

$\square = 5 + 3$	$\square = 5 - 3$
$\square = 7 + 4$	$\square = 7 - 4$
$\square = 10 + 7$	$\square = 10 - 7$
$\square = 9 + 2$	$\square = 9 - 2$
$\square = 3 + 3$	$\square = 3 - 3$
$\square = 2 + 1$	$\square = 2 - 1$
$\square = 6 + 3$	$\square = 6 - 3$
$\square = 4 + 3$	$\square = 4 - 3$
$\square = 8 + 5$	$\square = 8 - 5$
$\square = 9 + 4$	$\square = 9 - 4$

• E–15

• E14

On this sheet children analyze a collection of things from the standpoint of subtraction and addition facts, always getting the inverse of each statement.

Encourage pupils to make their own papers, using other sets of things—9 things, 11 things, etc.—and writing their own true sentences about them.

Other questions to ask: How many dark things? How many light things? How many circles? How many squares? How many boats (trapezoids)?

Examples of problems which originate in the classroom:

a. There are 10 boys and 12 girls in the room. That's _____ children.

b. If there are 22 children in the room and if 12 of them are girls, then _____ of them are boys.

• E15–E17

These sheets are intended especially for children who have difficulty in distinguishing between the symbols for addition and subtraction. (See also E1–E6.)

Children should notice that whenever we add a number greater than 0 to another number, we make the number larger, and that whenever we subtract a number greater than 0 from another number, we make the number smaller.

On E16 children must write in the operational symbols (+ or −) in order to make the sentences true.

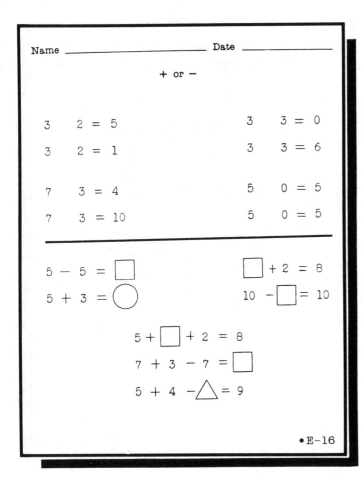

Name _____ Date _____

+ or −

3 2 = 5		3 3 = 0
3 2 = 1		3 3 = 6
7 3 = 4		5 0 = 5
7 3 = 10		5 0 = 5

$5 - 5 = \square$ $\square + 2 = 8$

$5 + 3 = \bigcirc$ $10 - \square = 10$

$5 + \square + 2 = 8$

$7 + 3 - 7 = \square$

$5 + 4 - \triangle = 9$

● E–16

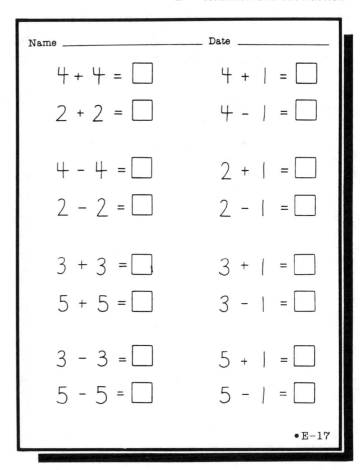

Name _____ Date _____

$4 + 4 = \square$ $4 + 1 = \square$

$2 + 2 = \square$ $4 - 1 = \square$

$4 - 4 = \square$ $2 + 1 = \square$

$2 - 2 = \square$ $2 - 1 = \square$

$3 + 3 = \square$ $3 + 1 = \square$

$5 + 5 = \square$ $3 - 1 = \square$

$3 - 3 = \square$ $5 + 1 = \square$

$5 - 5 = \square$ $5 - 1 = \square$

● E–17

· E18–E20

Before these lab sheets are given to the children, the teacher should do related number-line work on the chalkboard with them.

These sheets are very useful in helping children who have difficulty visualizing problems written in standard mathematical notation. To a child who has trouble understanding what $5 + 4 = \square$ means,

$$5 \xrightarrow{\quad 4 \quad} \square$$

may prove to be very meaningful. Here he can "act out" the problem. It requires him to start at the point labeled '5' on the number line and to jump four units to the right. It asks him where he landed.

In this type of number-line problem, three numbers are involved: the number of the point at which we start, the number and arrow which tell us how far and in which direction we jump, and the number which tells us where we land. In each problem we are given two of these numbers. From this information we can always determine the third.

After children have worked out several problems on the number line, most of them will begin to perform the indicated operations in their heads.

Frequently, in doing work with the number line, children will make up problems similar to the following.

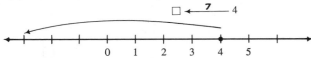

What number goes in the box? Some children will say, "Three below zero." Others will say, "Three to the left," "three minus," "negative three," or "three less than zero." Any answer to this effect should be accepted.

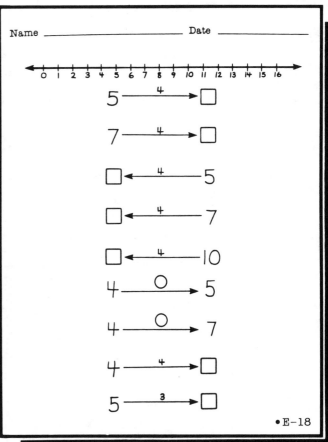

Name _____ Date _____

● E–18

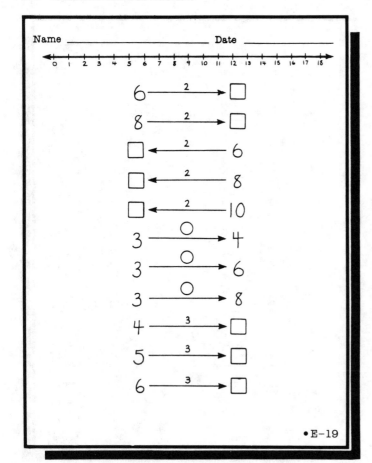

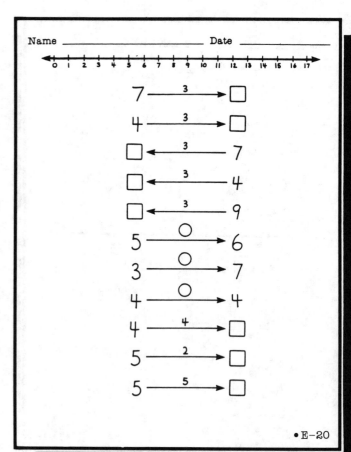

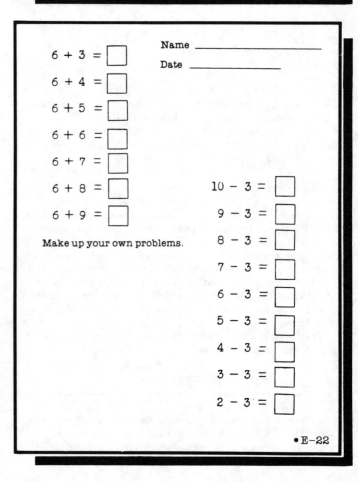

5 + 1 = ☐   Name _____

5 + 2 = ☐   Date _____

5 + 3 = ☐

5 + 4 = ☐

5 + 5 = ☐

5 + 6 = ☐

5 + 7 = ☐

You make up some
more problems.

6 − 1 = ☐

7 − 2 = ☐

8 − 3 = ☐

9 − 4 = ☐

10 − 5 = ☐

11 − 6 = ☐

12 − 7 = ☐

• E-23

Name _____   Date _____

5 + ☐ = 6   Your own problems.

5 + ☐ = 7

5 + ☐ = 8

5 + ☐ = 9

5 + ☐ = 10

5 + ☐ = 11

5 + ☐ = 12

Your own problems.

6 − ☐ = 5

7 − ☐ = 5

8 − ☐ = 5

9 − ☐ = 5

10 − ☐ = 5

11 − ☐ = 5

12 − ☐ = 5

• E-23a

· E22, E23

Experimenting with sequences of related problems such as those appearing on these two sheets is certain to lead to interesting results. The teacher will probably find that before most children have completed a given sequence of problems, they will have discovered the "rule" which tells the answers to the remainder of the problems. After making this discovery they will probably hurriedly complete the sequence without even having to work out the problems.

The "rule" which tells the answers to the problems in the lower sequence on E22 is: *The answer is one less than the preceding answer.*

$$10 - 3 = \boxed{7}$$
$$9 - 3 = \boxed{6}$$
$$8 - 3 = \boxed{5}$$
$$7 - 3 = \boxed{4}$$
$$6 - 3 = \boxed{3}$$
$$5 - 3 = \boxed{2}$$
$$4 - 3 = \square$$
$$3 - 3 = \square$$
$$2 - 3 = \square$$

What is the answer to the next problem in the sequence? [The answer is 1, since 1 is the number that is 1 less than 2. $4 - 3 = \boxed{1}$.]

What is the answer to the next problem? [It is 0, since 0 is the number which is 1 less than 1. $3 - 3 = \boxed{0}$.]

What is the answer to the next problem in the sequence? [The answer is that number which is 1 less than 0. We can call this number "negative one" and write it "−1." $2 - 3 = \boxed{-1}$.]

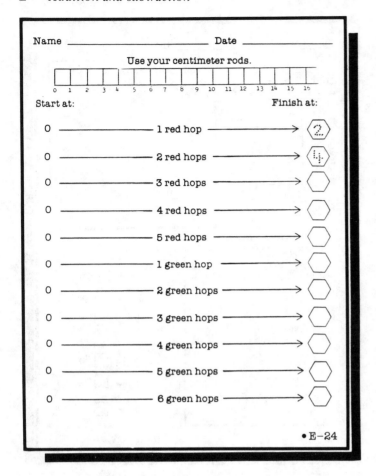

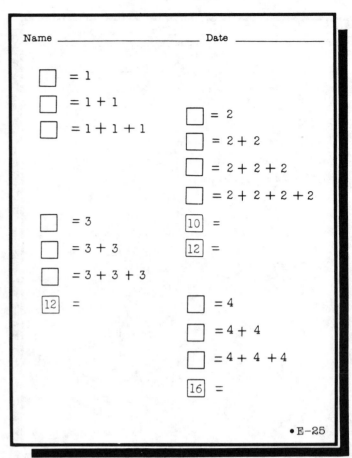

· E24, E25

Introduction to multiplication

On E24 the number line is like a track on which the rods fit. A "red hop" means a hop as long as one red rod.

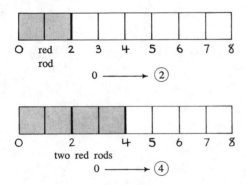

Later this can be written as $2 \times 2 = 4$, meaning *two two's equal four*.

On E25 we find repeated addition, which serves as an introduction to multiplication.

1, 2, 3, 4, ... (counting by one's series)
2, 4, 6, 8, ... (counting by two's series)
3, 6, 9, 12, . . . (counting by three's series)
4, 8, 12, 16, . . (counting by four's series)

With rods:

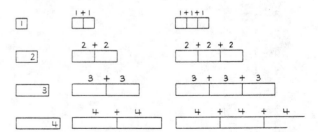

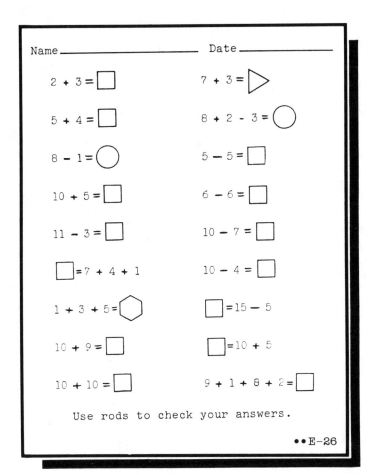

Name _____   Date _____

2 + 3 = ☐   7 + 3 = ▷

5 + 4 = ☐   8 + 2 - 3 = ◯

8 - 1 = ◯   5 - 5 = ☐

10 + 5 = ☐   6 - 6 = ☐

11 - 3 = ☐   10 - 7 = ☐

☐ = 7 + 4 + 1   10 - 4 = ☐

1 + 3 + 5 = ⬡   ☐ = 15 - 5

10 + 9 = ☐   ☐ = 10 + 5

10 + 10 = ☐   9 + 1 + 8 + 2 = ☐

Use rods to check your answers.

•• E-26

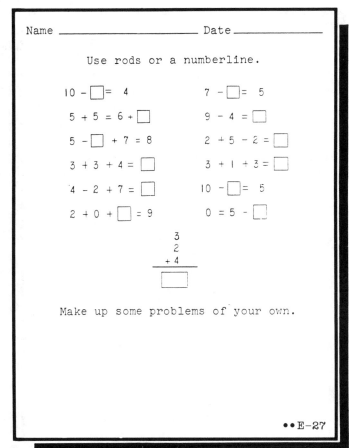

Name _____   Date _____

Use rods or a numberline.

10 - ☐ = 4   7 - ☐ = 5

5 + 5 = 6 + ☐   9 - 4 = ☐

5 - ☐ + 7 = 8   2 + 5 - 2 = ☐

3 + 3 + 4 = ☐   3 + 1 + 3 = ☐

4 - 2 + 7 = ☐   10 - ☐ = 5

2 + 0 + ☐ = 9   0 = 5 - ☐

$$\begin{array}{r} 3 \\ 2 \\ +\,4 \\ \hline \boxed{} \end{array}$$

Make up some problems of your own.

•• E-27

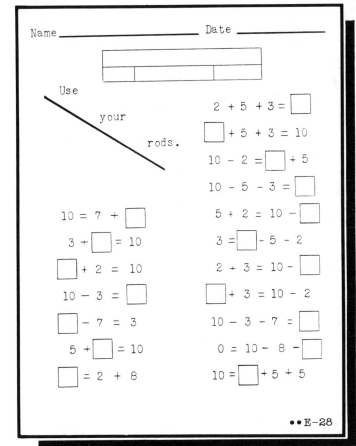

Name _____   Date _____

Use your rods.

2 + 5 + 3 = ☐

☐ + 5 + 3 = 10

10 - 2 = ☐ + 5

10 - 5 - 3 = ☐

10 = 7 + ☐   5 + 2 = 10 - ☐

3 + ☐ = 10   3 = ☐ - 5 - 2

☐ + 2 = 10   2 + 3 = 10 - ☐

10 - 3 = ☐   ☐ + 3 = 10 - 2

☐ - 7 = 3   10 - 3 - 7 = ☐

5 + ☐ = 10   0 = 10 - 8 - ☐

☐ = 2 + 8   10 = ☐ + 5 + 5

•• E-28

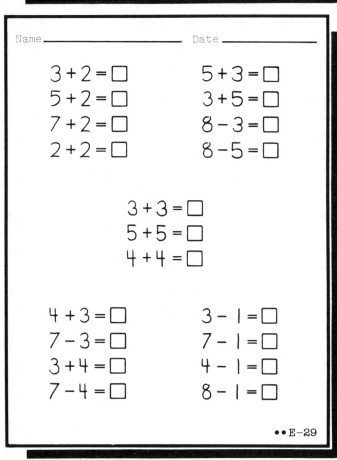

Name _____   Date _____

3 + 2 = ☐   5 + 3 = ☐
5 + 2 = ☐   3 + 5 = ☐
7 + 2 = ☐   8 - 3 = ☐
2 + 2 = ☐   8 - 5 = ☐

3 + 3 = ☐
5 + 5 = ☐
4 + 4 = ☐

4 + 3 = ☐   3 - 1 = ☐
7 - 3 = ☐   7 - 1 = ☐
3 + 4 = ☐   4 - 1 = ☐
7 - 4 = ☐   8 - 1 = ☐

•• E-29

Name _____ Date _____

$10 - 2 = \square$ $5 - 5 = \square$

$7 - 4 = \square$ $4 + 3 = \square$

$2 + 2 + 1 + 3 = \square$ $5 + 2 = \square$

$5 + 3 = \square$ $3 + 3 + 1 = \square$

$3 + 3 + 2 = \square$ $7 + 2 + 1 = \square$

$4 + 2 + 2 = \square$ $5 + \square = 9$

$4 + 4 = \square$ $3 + \square + 4 = 10$

$7 + 1 = \square$ $5 - \square = 2$

$9 - 1 = \square$ $10 - 5 = \square$

•• E–30

Name _____ Date _____

Make up your
own problems.

$5 + 2 + 1 = \square$
$3 + \square = 7$
$2 + 2 + 2 + 2 = \square$
$\square = 5 - 4 + 7$
$3 + 3 - 2 + 2 = \square$
$\square = 10 - 4$
$6 + 4 = \square$ Make up your
$2 + \square = 8$ own problems.
$10 - 10 = \square$
$7 - \square = 7$

•• E–31

•• E32, E33

Column addition and subtraction, which have been infrequently used up to this point, are presented to the children in doubling and halving, for which they seem to have an early affinity.

On E32, these simple problems appear in order; on E33 they are mixed up. On the latter the children are also given the choice of adding *or* subtracting. They should put in the operational symbols themselves.

•• E34
Using "doubles" to help with "near doubles"

Children love the rhythm of doubles. They first memorize $1 + 1$, $2 + 2$, $3 + 3$, etc.

At first these doubles are dotted in as clues to help the child solve a problem involving a "near double."

Clue	helps you solve
$\begin{array}{r} 6 \\ + 6 \\ \hline 12 \end{array}$	$\begin{array}{r} 7 \\ + 6 \\ \hline 13 \end{array}$

Then the child is presented with a problem: $\begin{array}{r} 5 \\ + 4 \\ \hline \end{array}$

He must provide his own clue, the double $\begin{array}{r} 4 \\ + 4 \\ \hline 8 \end{array}$

$4 + 4 = 8$, therefore $5 + 4 = (4 + 1) + 4 = 9$, or "one more than $4 + 4$." He might provide as his own clue the double $\begin{array}{r} 5 \\ + 5 \\ \hline 10 \end{array}$

$5 + 5 = 10$, therefore $5 + 4 = 5 + (5 - 1) = 9$, or "one less than $5 + 5$."

E-32

Name_____ Date_____

$\begin{array}{r}2\\+2\\\hline\end{array}$ $\begin{array}{r}3\\+3\\\hline\end{array}$ $\begin{array}{r}4\\+4\\\hline\end{array}$ $\begin{array}{r}5\\+5\\\hline\end{array}$ $\begin{array}{r}6\\+6\\\hline\end{array}$

$\begin{array}{r}7\\+7\\\hline\end{array}$ $\begin{array}{r}8\\+8\\\hline\end{array}$ $\begin{array}{r}9\\+9\\\hline\end{array}$ $\begin{array}{r}10\\+10\\\hline\end{array}$ $\begin{array}{r}11\\+11\\\hline\end{array}$

$\begin{array}{r}12\\+12\\\hline\end{array}$ $\begin{array}{r}13\\+13\\\hline\end{array}$ $\begin{array}{r}14\\+14\\\hline\end{array}$ $\begin{array}{r}15\\+15\\\hline\end{array}$

$\begin{array}{r}4\\-2\\\hline\end{array}$ $\begin{array}{r}6\\-3\\\hline\end{array}$ $\begin{array}{r}8\\-4\\\hline\end{array}$ $\begin{array}{r}10\\-5\\\hline\end{array}$ $\begin{array}{r}12\\-6\\\hline\end{array}$ $\begin{array}{r}14\\-7\\\hline\end{array}$

$\begin{array}{r}16\\-8\\\hline\end{array}$ $\begin{array}{r}18\\-9\\\hline\end{array}$ $\begin{array}{r}20\\-10\\\hline\end{array}$

•• E-32

E-33

Name_____ Date_____

$\dfrac{\quad\textbf{+}\quad or\quad \textbf{–}\quad}{}$

12 12	3 3	14 14	10 10
8 8	20 20	16 16	17 17
2 2	11 11	30 30	9 9
16 8	18 9	10 5	20 10
30 15	22 11	24 12	6 3

•• E-33

E-34

Name_____ Date_____

(grid of problems labelled "clue")

4 +3	15 −7	19 −9
clue	clue	clue
6 +7	13 −7 (6)	13 −6
clue	clue	clue
5 +4	9 +10	7 −4
clue	clue	clue
8 +7 (7 +7)	8 +9	11 −6
clue	clue	clue
7 +6 (13)	5 +6	17 −9
clue	clue	clue

•• E-34

E-35

Name_____ Date_____

10 10 +10	5 10 +5	11 +11	9 11 +11 +9
10 11 +9	11 9 11 +9	3 +3 3 +4	4 +4 4 +5
4 3 3 +10	4 5 +10	1 +9 1 9 10	1 2 3 +4
1 2 3 +10	1 2 3 4 +5	2 3 4 9 +1	1 2 3 4 9 +10
20 −10	20 −1	20 −19	20 −20 20 −0

•• E-35

95

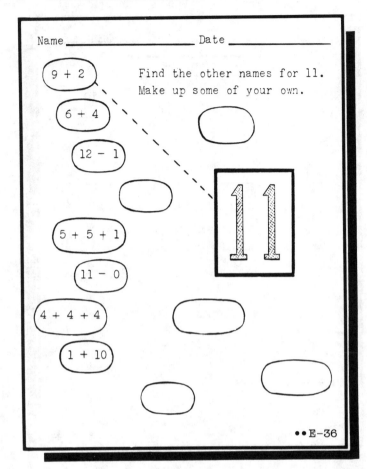

Find the other names for 11.
Make up some of your own.

9 + 2
6 + 4
12 − 1
5 + 5 + 1
11 − 0
4 + 4 + 4
1 + 10

11

•• E-36

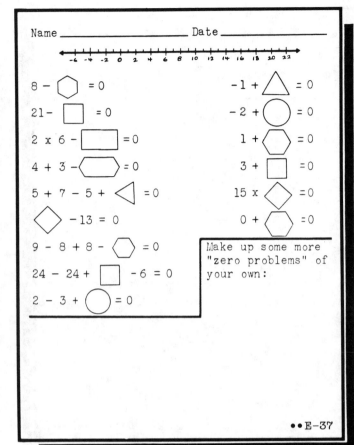

8 − ⬡ = 0
21 − ☐ = 0
2 x 6 − ▭ = 0
4 + 3 − ⬡ = 0
5 + 7 − 5 + △ = 0
◇ − 13 = 0
9 − 8 + 8 − ⬡ = 0
24 − 24 + ☐ − 6 = 0
2 − 3 + ◯ = 0

−1 + △ = 0
− 2 + ◯ = 0
1 + ⬡ = 0
3 + ☐ = 0
15 x ◇ = 0
0 + ⬡ = 0

Make up some more
"zero problems" of
your own:

•• E-37

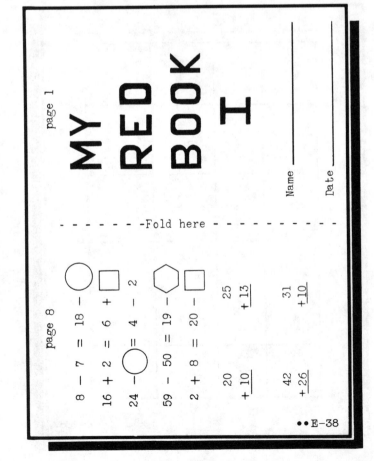

page 1

MY
RED
BOOK
I

Name
Date

- - - - - Fold here - - - - -

page 8

8 − 7 = 18 − ◯
16 + 2 = 6 + ☐
24 − ◯ = 4 − 2
59 − 50 = 19 − ⬡
2 + 8 = 20 − ☐

25
+13

31
+10

20
+10

42
+26

•• E-38

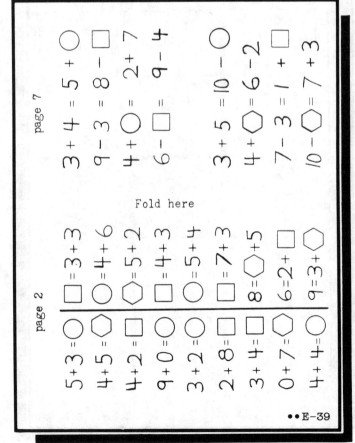

page 7

3 + 4 = 5 + ◯
9 − 3 = 8 − ☐
4 + ◯ = 2 + 7
6 − ☐ = 9 − 4

3 + 5 = 10 − ◯
4 + ⬡ = 6 − 2
7 − 3 = 1 + ☐
10 − ◇ = 7 + 3

Fold here

☐ = 3 + 3
◯ = 4 + 6
◇ = 5 + 2
☐ = 4 + 3
◯ = 5 + 4
☐ = 7 + 3
8 = ⬡ + 5
6 = 2 + ☐
9 = 3 + ⬡

page 2

5 + 3 = ◯
4 + 5 = ⬡
4 + 2 = ☐
9 + 0 = ◯
3 + 2 = ◯
2 + 8 = ☐
3 + 4 = ☐
0 + 7 = ⬡
4 + 4 = ◯

•• E-39

·· E37
Zero

There are many names for zero.

$$8 - \textcircled{8} = 0$$
$$21 - \textcircled{21} = 0$$
$$-1 + \triangle\!\!\!1 = 0$$
$$1 + \text{\textcircled{-1}} = 0$$
$$3 + \boxed{-3} = 0$$

Again, the number line can be used as a learning aid. Children can trace each trip to 0 with their fingers and record it in the frame.

$$\xrightarrow{\hspace{2cm}} \quad \text{is a "+ trip."}$$

$$\xleftarrow{\hspace{2cm}} \quad \text{is a "- trip."}$$

·· E38–E41
My Red Book I

These four pages are used together and folded to make a booklet. They can be used as an informal diagnostic or achievement test. The difficulty increases from page to page. Only page 8 deals with numbers greater than 10.

Depending upon the maturity of the children, this work can be attempted with or without rods. Most children should be allowed to use rods when they need them. They are quite willing to write "R" next to the problems for which they used rods.

For many children this booklet is too long for one sitting. Therefore, extend its use over two days. *Don't make a serious affair out of this.* The children should not even know that you plan to look this over very carefully. Keep the booklet and use it to give the children some tailor-made work of your own devising if you find that they need more practice on a particular facet of the work.

Don't expect many perfect papers. Don't expect many finished papers.

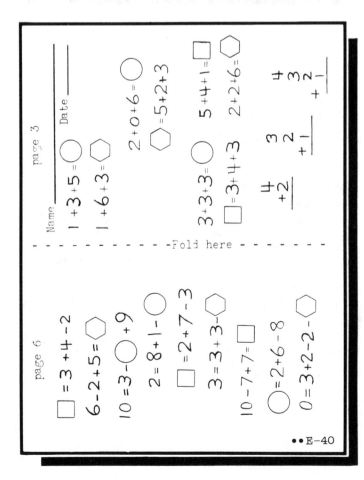

·· E-40

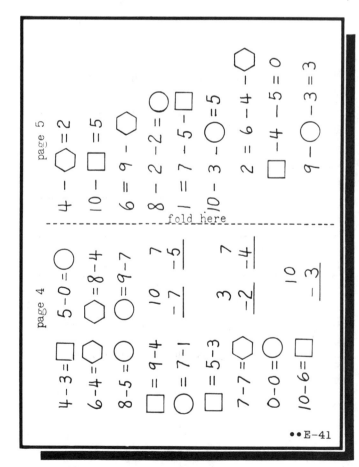

·· E-41

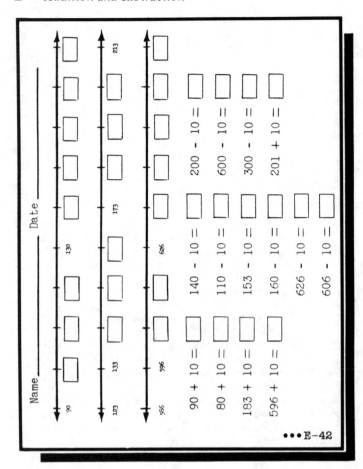

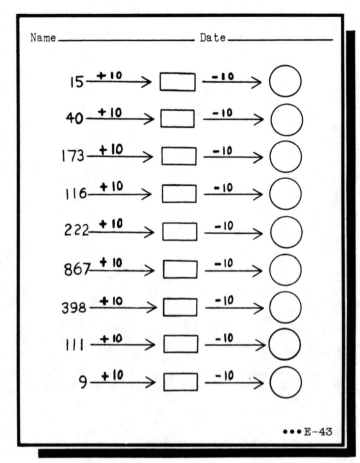

··· E42
Adding tens, hundreds, and their inverses

Children are to label the missing points (by tens) on the number line.

Special difficulty:

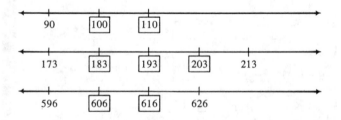

Introduce this activity at the chalkboard. Then have the children fill in the number lines on the lab sheet. The number lines can then be used to find (or check) the answers to the problems at the bottom of the lab sheet.

··· E43

Lab sheet E43 is the same as E42 except that no number line is given. The difficult problem is

$$398 \xrightarrow{+10} \boxed{408} \xrightarrow{-10} \bigcirc$$

Lotto games for drill

Equipment
Cuisenaire® rods or sets of numeral cards (0–10) and Lotto cards made from light-colored construction paper. These cards should represent several levels of difficulty for the children to choose from. *Notice that all sums, differences, and products are numbers ten or under.*

Easiest			Average		
$4+5$	$3+4$	$2+6$	$12-9$	$14-8$	$18-9$
$3+2$	$2+4$	$6-4$	$13-5$	$19-18$	$12-10$
$0+1$	$7+3$	$8-5$	$17-17$	$11-7$	$15-10$

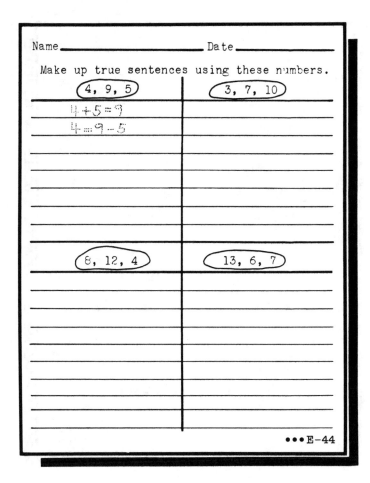

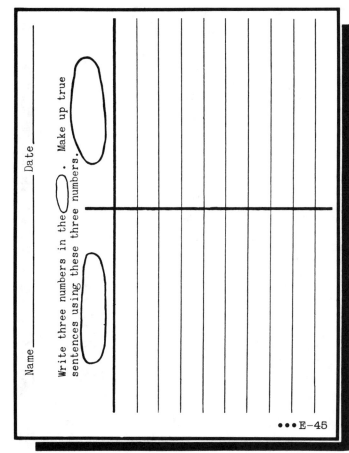

··· **E44, E45**

These lab sheets are similar to E7 through E14.

Using the numbers 4, 9, and 5, the most obvious true sentences are the following equations:

$$4+5=9 \qquad 9=4+5$$
$$5+4=9 \qquad 9=5+4$$
$$9-4=5 \qquad 5=9-4$$
$$9-5=4 \qquad 4=9-5$$

Below are more true sentences that can be made from these three numbers:

$4 \neq 9+5$	$4 \neq 5+9$	$9 \not> 4+5$
$5 \neq 9+4$	$5 \neq 4+9$	$9 \not> 5+4$
$9+5 \neq 4$	$5+9 \neq 4$	$9 \not< 4+5$
$9+4 \neq 5$	$4+9 \neq 5$	$9 \not< 5+4$
$4-5 \neq 9$	$4+5 \not> 9$	$5 \not> 9-4$
$5-4 \neq 9$	$5+4 \not> 9$	$4 \not> 9-5$
$9 \neq 4-5$	$4+5 \not< 9$	$5 \not< 9-4$
$9 \neq 5-4$	$5+4 \not< 9$	$4 \not< 9-5$
$5 \neq 4-9$	$9-4 \not> 5$	$9 > 5 > 4$
$4 \neq 5-9$	$9-5 \not> 4$	$4 < 5 < 9$
$4-9 \neq 5$	$9-4 \not< 5$	$9 \not< 5 \not< 4$
$5-9 \neq 4$	$9-5 \not< 4$	$4 \not> 5 \not> 9$

(left page, E-44)

Name _____ Date _____

Make up true sentences using these numbers.

(4, 9, 5)   (3, 7, 10)

4 + 5 = 9
4 = 9 − 5

(8, 12, 4)   (13, 6, 7)

··· E-44

(right page, E-45)

Name _____   Date _____

Write three numbers in the ◯. Make up true sentences using these three numbers.

··· E-45

(bottom left)

Average

14 − 6	16 − 9	23 −20

Most Difficult

43 − 42	17 − 9	3×2
101 − 98	64 − 55	$2 \times 2 \times 2$
$\frac{1}{2} \times 14$	$\frac{1}{3} \times 6$	$8 \div 2$

Procedure

1   Divide the class into groups of six children. In each group there is one "caller-checker" and five players.

2   The caller holds up a rod or a numeral card. The five players look over their Lotto cards to see if the answer to any of their problems corresponds with the rod or numeral card held up.

3   If a player has such an answer, he places a rod or numeral card on the problem.

4   The winner is the first player to have "three in a row" or the first player to have his whole card covered. The caller-checker must check the problem before he declares a winner.

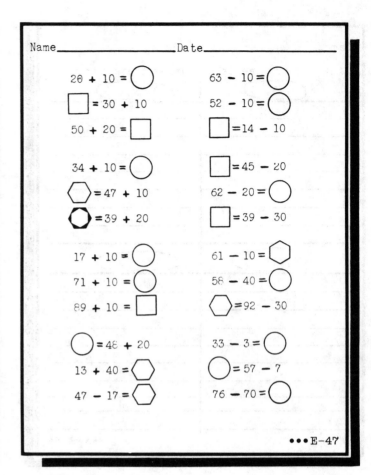

Name_____ Date_____

```
  829          10                20
 -211          10                20
               10                20
               10               +20
              +10

  532          10                30
 -500          20                30
               30                30
               10               +30
               20
              +30

 3642
 -642
                6                60
                4                40
                7                70
                3                30
                8                80
$430.50         2                20
-200.20         9                90
$              +1               +10
```

●●●E-46

Name_____ Date_____

```
20 + 10 = ◯          63 - 10 = ◯
☐ = 30 + 10          52 - 10 = ◯
50 + 20 = ☐          ☐ = 14 - 10

34 + 10 = ◯          ☐ = 45 - 20
⬡ = 47 + 10          62 - 20 = ◯
⬣ = 39 + 20          ☐ = 39 - 30

17 + 10 = ◯          61 - 10 = ⬡
71 + 10 = ◯          58 - 40 = ◯
89 + 10 = ☐          ⬡ = 92 - 30

◯ = 48 + 20          33 - 3 = ◯
13 + 40 = ⬡          ◯ = 57 - 7
47 - 17 = ⬡          76 - 70 = ◯
```

●●●E-47

●●● E46

This is a diagnostic page to find out which children can do the problems easily without having been specifically "taught."

There *will* be children who will say to themselves:

"Oh, 5 tens! That's 50!

Oh, 20, 40, 60, 80!

Oh, 60 and 60, . . . 120!

Oh, ⟨6⟩   10
     ⟨4⟩

    ⟨7⟩   10
    ⟨3⟩

    ⟨8⟩   10
    ⟨2⟩

    ⟨9⟩   10
    ⟨1⟩
    ___
     40

```
  3,642
-   642
 _____
  3,000
```

I can't read it, but that's the answer."

100

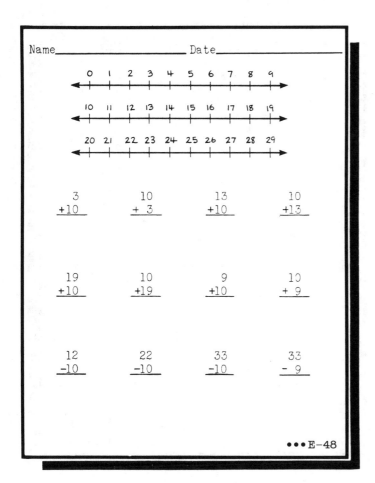

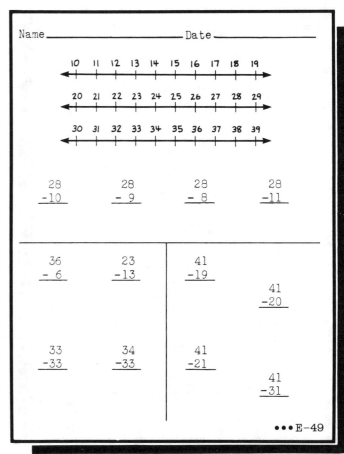

· · · E48, E49

On these sheets number lines are provided to help children solve the problems. When ten is added to a number, one merely jumps to the corresponding point on the number line below. If ten is subtracted from a number, the jump is to the corresponding point on the number line above.

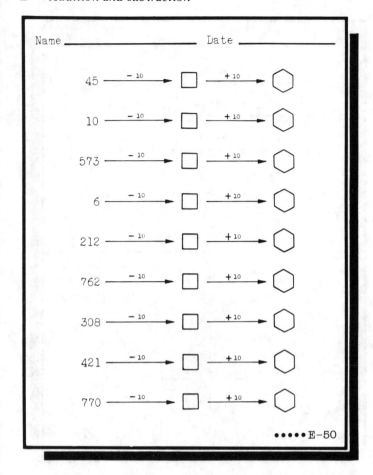

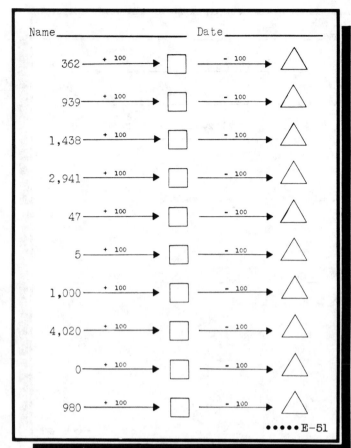

· · · · · **E50**

Bridging hundreds (or thousands) by adding or subtracting tens is difficult for some children. Another trouble area is subtraction problems that lead to negative numbers. In both instances give the children supplementary practice, using the number line as a visual model.

The most difficult problems are the following:

$$308 \xrightarrow{-10} \boxed{298} \xrightarrow{+10} \hexagon$$

$$6 \xrightarrow{-10} \boxed{-4} \xrightarrow{+10} \hexagon$$

· · · · · **E51**

The most difficult problems are:

$$939 \xrightarrow{+100} \boxed{1039}$$

$$2941 \xrightarrow{+100} \boxed{3041}$$

$$980 \xrightarrow{+100} \boxed{1080}$$

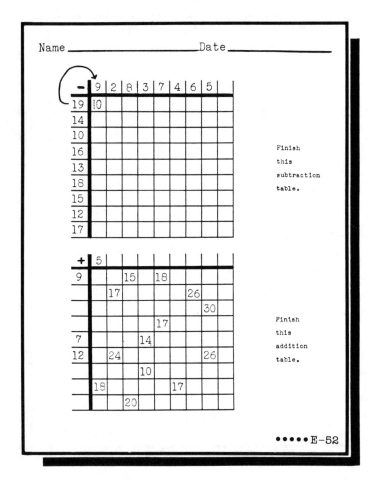

Finish this subtraction table.

Finish this addition table.

•••••E-52

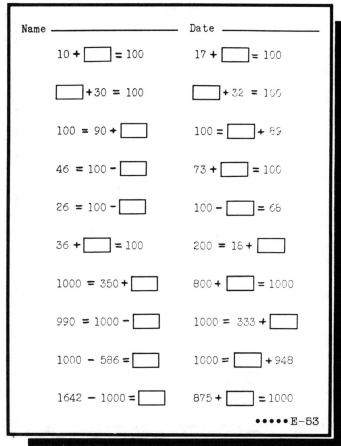

•••••E-53

····· **E52**
Subtraction and addition tables

The top chart is a subtraction table.

$$\text{sum} \quad - \quad \text{addend} \quad = \quad \text{addend}$$
$$\downarrow \qquad\qquad \downarrow \qquad\qquad \downarrow$$
$$9 \quad - \quad 4 \quad = \quad 5$$

The main purpose of the chart is to provide a quick review of basic subtraction facts. It also can be used to introduce vocabulary—*addends* and *sum*.

For a basic subtraction vocabulary, it is preferable to use the same terms used for addition—but in inverse order. Thus we say:

$$\text{addend} \quad + \quad \text{addend} \quad = \quad \text{sum} \quad \text{(addition)}$$
$$\text{sum} \quad - \quad \text{addend} \quad = \quad \text{addend} \quad \text{(subtraction)}$$

When the top chart is contrasted with the bottom chart we see the different placement of one of the addends and the sums.

The bottom chart has enough information to fill out the table. We must puzzle out where to start, and we will get some information by both addition and subtraction. *Do this page yourself first.*

50	41	62	33	74	25	86
17	98	9	49	40	61	32
73	24	85	16	97	8	48
39	60	31	72	23	84	15
96	7	47	38	59	30	71
22	83	14	95	6	46	37

How <u>to</u> <u>make</u> <u>your</u> <u>own</u> <u>practice</u> <u>problems:</u>

1. Cut out the numeral squares.
2. Put them all in an envelope.
3. Take two squares out of the envelope and write the two numbers on a piece of paper.
4. Find the sum of these two numbers.
5. Find their difference.
6. Pick two other numbers from the envelope and do the same thing.

LOOK AT THE PICTURES ON THE NEXT LAB SHEET IF YOU DON'T UNDERSTAND.

••••••E-54

538	259	766	100	238	345	888
472	643	804	510	789	901	777
325	591	317	300	456	890	555
154	620	692	800	123	567	678
345	642	765	987	321	135	911
543	754	876	109	159	333	214

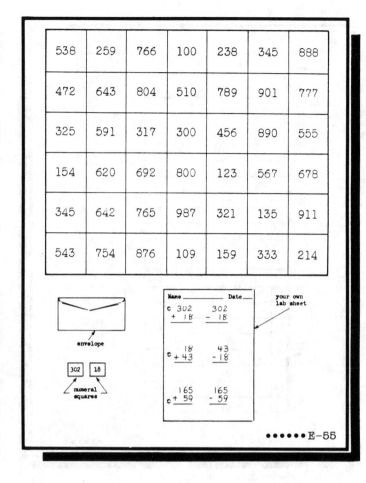

••••••E-55

•••••• **E54 , E55**

Very often some children find it difficult to make up their own problems. They tend to repeat themselves. For this reason we included two sheets of cut-out numerals which the child places in an envelope. (He can initial them on the backs.) He can make it a game—to take two numerals out of the envelope at random and add and subtract the numbers.

Believe it or not, for the 42 numerals on E54 alone, there are 861 two-numeral combinations that can be made! The formula is:

$$\frac{n \times (n-1)}{2} \qquad \frac{42 \times 41}{2}$$

For both lab sheets there are 3,486 different combinations of two numerals!

The teacher will find the job of correcting the children's papers made from these sheets virtually impossible. Let the children exchange papers and "proofread" for one another. They—*not you*—need the computation practice! Here is a good opportunity to introduce the children to hand minicalculators. They will enjoy using the calculators to check their work.

A good feature for the slow child is the fact that he can always "hunt" for a combination of numbers he *can* add and subtract, since he can throw back what is too difficult for him at the present.

What will happen when a child subtracts a larger number from a smaller number? He will get a negative number.

$$\begin{array}{r} 59 \\ -95 \\ \hline -40+4= -36 \end{array} \qquad \text{instead of} \qquad \begin{array}{r} 95 \\ -59 \\ \hline 36 \end{array}$$

Note: These numerals can also be used for other purposes: (1) Pick a number, write it down, divide it by 5. (2) Pick a number, write it as a product. Etc.

It is impossible to determine the exact amount of computation practice each child profits by. Regular chalkboard drill is also tedious for the teacher—and boring to the child.

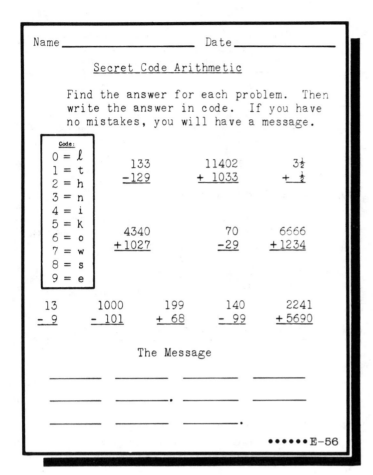

Name_____ Date_____

Secret Code Arithmetic

Find the answer for each problem. Then write the answer in code. If you have no mistakes, you will have a message.

Code:
0 = l	
1 = t	
2 = h	
3 = n	
4 = i	
5 = k	
6 = o	
7 = w	
8 = s	
9 = e	

```
  133      11402       3½
 -129      + 1033      + ½

  4340       70        6666
 +1027      -29       +1234

 13     1000    199    140    2241
- 9    - 101   + 68   - 99   +5690
```

The Message

_____ _____ _____ _____

_____ _____. _____ _____

_____ _____ _____.

•••••• E-56

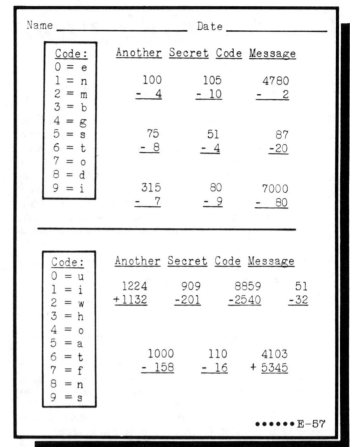

Name_____ Date_____

Code:
0 = e	
1 = n	
2 = m	
3 = b	
4 = g	
5 = s	
6 = t	
7 = o	
8 = d	
9 = i	

Another Secret Code Message

```
  100      105     4780
 -  4     - 10     -  2

   75       51       87
 -  8     -  4     -20

  315       80     7000
 -  7     -  9     -  80
```

Code:
0 = u	
1 = i	
2 = w	
3 = h	
4 = o	
5 = a	
6 = t	
7 = f	
8 = n	
9 = s	

Another Secret Code Message

```
  1224     909    8859     51
 +1132    -201   -2540    -32

  1000     110    4103
 - 158    - 16   + 5345
```

•••••• E-57

•••••• **E56, E57**

Secret codes

On E56 the message is: "I think I know it well. I see how it went." Here is another message you may write on the chalkboard.

```
6,000      100      600      100     1,000     7,000
−  779    −  18    −130     −  88    −  707    −  797
```

Code:
0 = r	5 = g
1 = d	6 = m
2 = o	7 = a
3 = e	8 = s
4 = f	9 = n

Message: Good so far. Do one more.

F *Multiplication*

Multiplication as repeated addition

Just as subtraction arises out of the need for an operation to *undo* addition, the third arithmetical operation, mutiplication, arises from the need of a short way in which to add a number repeatedly. When we wish to know what $3 + 3$ or $3 + 3 + 3 + 3 + 3$ equals, it is a simple task to perform the indicated operations. But if we want to determine what 3 repeatedly added to itself 37 times (or 1037 times) equals, we must take into consideration the limitations of human endurance. To avoid this difficulty, we devise a new operation, multiplication, which can be used to simplify expressions involving repeated addition.

We define

2×3 to mean $3 + 3$ (2 addends)

5×3 to mean $3 + 3 + 3 + 3 + 3$ (5 addends)

and

1037×3 to mean $3 + 3 + 3 + \ldots + 3$ (1037 addends)

When we begin work in multiplication we define $\square \times \bigcirc$ to mean $\bigcirc + \bigcirc + \bigcirc + \ldots + \bigcirc$ ($\square$ addends), where $\square$ and $\bigcirc$ are place-holders for two *whole* numbers. Later we must extend our definition of multiplication to take care of such situations as $\frac{1}{4} \times \frac{3}{7}$, where neither factor is a whole number and the repeated-addend model no longer holds. This kind of situation will be dealt with later on.

Repeated addition can be represented easily with the Cuisenaire® rods. If we use the small white rod as our unit, then 2×3 can be represented as

2 addends

| 3 | + | 3 |

| green | green |

5×3 can be represented as

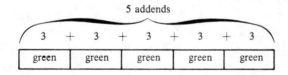

5 addends

1037×3 can be represented as

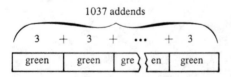

1037 addends

When representing a multiplication problem with the rods, it is usually more convenient to place the rods side-by-side rather than end-to-end. For this reason the muliplication problem $5 \times 3 = \square$ would be represented as follows:

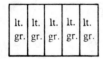

$5 \times 3 = \square$

The same problem represented as repeated addition would be:

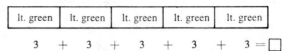

| lt. green | lt. green | lt. green | lt. green | lt. green |

$3 + 3 + 3 + 3 + 3 = \square$

With the help of the white rods, which have been chosen as our units, we can demonstrate the equivalence of these two configurations. Each is completely covered by 15 white rods. Therefore we have shown that

$$5 \times 3 = 3 + 3 + 3 + 3 + 3 = 15$$

Multiplying with the number line

Using the number line, the product of two numbers can be interpreted as the distance covered by a number of jumps of a certain size. Following are several examples of how this may be done.

1 Problem: $6 \times 2 = \square$

Related Question: What distance is covered by 6 two-unit jumps?

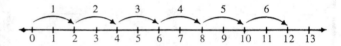

Each jump is 2 units long.

Solved Problem: $6 \times 2 = \boxed{12}$

2 Problem: $4 \times \square = 12$

Related Question: Four jumps of what length cover a distance of twelve units? The distance is divided into 4 equal parts.

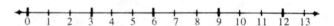

Each part is 3 units long.

Solved Problem: $4 \times \boxed{3} = 12$

3 Problem: $\square \times 3 = 15$

Related Question: How many three-unit jumps must one make in order to cover a distance of fifteen units?

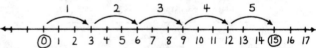

Each jump is 3 units long. Thus, it takes 5 jumps to reach 15.

Solved Problem: $\boxed{5} \times 3 = 15$.

Multiplication with arrays

Let us represent the numbers 3, 5, 2, and 1 by four rows of dots:

| 3 | 5 | 2 | 1 |
| • • • | • • • • • | • • | • |

We can now represent two 3's, two 5's, two 2's, and two 1's, by the following arrays of dots:

2×3	2×5	2×2	2×1
• • •	• • • • •	• •	•
• • •	• • • • •	• •	•

The arrays of dots for 3×3, 3×5, 3×2, and 3×1 are

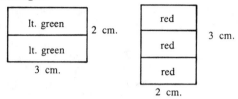

In like manner we can write an array of dots for the product of any two whole numbers. If $\square$ and $\bigcirc$ are placeholders for any two whole numbers, $\square \times \bigcirc$ is represented by an array of $\square$ rows of dots with $\bigcirc$ dots in each row. If $\triangle$ is the total number of dots in the array, we can say that

$$\square \times \bigcirc = \triangle.$$

We can demonstrate by means of arrays that multiplication of whole numbers has the *commutative property*. For example, let us repeat the arrays for 2×3 and 3×2.

We see that 2×3 and 3×2 really have the same arrays. The only difference lies in their positions. Since there are six dots in each of these arrays, we can say that

$$2 \times 3 = 6$$

and

$$3 \times 2 = 6.$$

In general, we make the rule that

$$\square \times \bigcirc = \bigcirc \times \square$$

is an identity.

Note: The commutative principle of multiplication does not imply that *all* aspects of two array situations are alike. Study the three examples which all deal with $2 \times 3 = 3 \times 2$.

1   Lumber

two 3' boards   three 2' boards

Questions
• Can both be used to make three steps? (no)
• Do they both have a 6' length? (yes)

2   Groups of people

Group A: three people in each of two cars on the same road from New York to Chicago.

Group B: two people in each of three cars on the same road from New York to Chicago.

Questions
• Do both groups use the same amount of gas? (no)
• Do both groups bring the same number of people to Chicago? (yes)

3   Rectangles

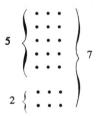

Questions
• Do they both make rectangles of identical color? (no)
• Do they both make rectangles using the same number of pieces of wood? (no)
• Do they both make rectangles of equal area and equal shape? (yes)

To what aspect of all three situations does $\bigcirc \times \square = \square \times \bigcirc$ (the commutative law) apply? The commutative law applies to all questions answered by *yes*.

Another property which can be demonstrated very effectively with arrays is the *distributive property of multiplication* with respect to addition. By placing a 5 X 3 array and a 2 X 3 array together, we can form a 7 X 3 array. This is an important preliminary activity to understanding the multiplication algorithm for multidigit numbers.

In this way we can show that

$$(5 \times 3) + (2 \times 3) = (5 + 2) \times 3 = 7 \times 3.$$

Below is an array which shows us that

$$(2 \times 7) + (4 \times 7) = (2 + 4) \times 7 = 6 \times 7.$$

In each of the foregoing examples, the two arrays that were added together had the same number of dots in their rows. We can also add arrays that have different numbers of dots in their rows but the

107

same number of rows. For example, let us add a

4 × 3 array   to a   4 × 5 array

```
• • •            • • • • •
• • •            • • • • •
• • •            • • • • •
• • •            • • • • •
```

We get a 4 × 8 array. Thus we can see that

$$(4 \times 3) + (4 \times 5) = 4 \times (3 + 5) = 4 \times 8.$$

Each of the examples above has been an illustration of the *distributive law*. In general terms, the distributive law tells us that

and

$$\square \times (\triangle + \bigcirc) = (\square \times \triangle) + (\square \times \bigcirc)$$
$$(\triangle + \bigcirc) \times \square = (\triangle \times \square) + (\bigcirc \times \square)$$

are identities when $\square$, $\triangle$, and $\bigcirc$, are placeholders for whole numbers.

Properties of multiplication

We shall now examine some important properties of multiplication. With respect to some of these properties, multiplication is very similar to addition.

If $\square$ and $\triangle$ are whole numbers,

then $\square \times \triangle$ is also a whole number.

When we multiply whole numbers the product is always a whole number. Since any two whole numbers have only one correct product, we say that *multiplication of whole numbers has the uniqueness property.*

Commutative property

The commutative property of multiplication of whole numbers is emphasized by the use of many problems that illustrate this property on the introductory lab sheets of this section. By completing sets of problems such as

$4 \times 2 = \square$	$3 \times 5 = \square$
$2 \times 4 = \square$	$5 \times 3 = \square$

which appear on lab sheets F1, F7, F9, F13, F14, F19, F20, F22, F43, and F44, the children should discover that one doesn't even have to compute in order to know that $67 \times 21 = 21 \times 67$. In general, the commutative property of multiplication tells us that

$$\square \times \triangle = \triangle \times \square$$

is always true, provided we obey the rule which tells us to place the same number in every $\square$ and place the same number in every $\triangle$ in the same problem.

Associative property

The associative property of multiplication of whole numbers, which applies to the multiplication of three or more numbers, tells us that it makes no difference into what pairs we group numbers to multiply. In general terms, the associative property may be expressed as follows:

$$(\square \times \triangle) \times \bigcirc = \square \times (\triangle \times \bigcirc)$$

Identity element

Like addition, multiplication has an identity element. The identity element for multiplication is the number one. The following problems are from lab sheets in this section.

$$7 \times 1 = \boxed{7}$$
$$1 \times 1 = \boxed{1}$$
$$3 \times 1 = \boxed{3}$$
$$6 \times 1 = \boxed{6}$$

The number one is called the identity element because any number times one gives us, as the product, the number with which we began. In mathematical language,

$$\square \times 1 = \square$$

Inverse operation

Division, the inverse of multiplication, will be dealt with in Section J.

Zero property for multiplication

This property is illustrated by the following equations:

$$7 \times 0 = 0$$
$$13 \times 0 = 0$$
$$921 \times 0 = 0$$

In general,

$$\square \times 0 = 0$$

Distributive property of multiplication with respect to addition

The distributive property is illustrated by the solutions to the following problems from lab sheets G9 and G13.

$$(4 + 2) \times 3 \quad = \quad 6 \times 3 = 18$$
$$(4 \times 3) + (2 \times 3) = 12 + 6 = 18$$

$$(2 \times 6) + (2 \times 4) = 12 + 8 = 20$$
$$2 \times (6 + 4) \quad = \quad 2 \times 10 = 20$$

$$(2 \times 4) + (2 \times 3) = \quad 2 \times 7 = 14$$
$$(4 \times 4) + (4 \times 3) = \quad 4 \times 7 = 28$$
$$(3 \times 4) - (3 \times 3) = \quad 3 \times 1 = 3$$

In general terms, the distributive law may be stated as follows:

$$\square \times (\bigcirc + \triangle) = (\square \times \bigcirc) + (\square \times \triangle)$$
$$(\bigcirc + \triangle) \times \square = (\bigcirc \times \square) + (\triangle \times \square)$$
$$\square \times (\bigcirc - \triangle) = (\square \times \bigcirc) - (\square \times \triangle)$$

• F1–F10

Multiplication as repeated addition

The problems on these lab sheets demonstrate the equivalence of multiplication and repeated addition when dealing with whole numbers.

Children may be asked to calculate the answer to each of the problems on sheets F4 and F5.

On F4, the problems 7×2 and $2 + 2 + 2 + 2 + 2 + 2$ are not equal. It is fascinating to see the varied reactions of the children. Some ignore this inequality; some silently add another $+2$; some complain, and others report with joy that they found a "mistake."

On F8 the equivalent problems are not next to each other. After children have done the problems, ask them to connect with lines those that are equivalent.

$$3 \times 5 = \boxed{15} \qquad 6 + 6 = \boxed{12}$$
$$4 \times 4 = \boxed{16} \qquad 3 + 3 + 3 + 3 = \boxed{12}$$
$$2 \times 6 = \boxed{12} \qquad 5 + 5 + 5 = \boxed{15}$$
$$4 \times 3 = \boxed{12} \qquad 4 + 4 + 4 + 4 = \boxed{16}$$

Name _____ Date _____

$$3 \times 2 = \square$$
$$4 \times 2 = \square$$

$$2 \times 4 = \square$$
$$2 \times 3 = \square$$

$$2 + 2 + 2 = \square$$
$$2 + 2 + 2 + 2 = \square$$
$$4 + 4 = \square$$
$$3 + 3 = \square$$

• F–1

Name _____ Date _____

$2 \times 6 = \square$ $6 + 6 = \square$	$4 \times 4 = \square$ $4 + 4 + 4 + 4 = \square$
$3 \times 3 = \square$ $3 + 3 + 3 = \square$	$2 \times 10 = \square$ $10 + 10 = \square$
$3 \times 5 = \square$ $5 + 5 + 5 = \square$	$5 \times 3 = \square$ $3 + 3 + 3 + 3 + 3 = \square$
$2 \times 4 = \square$ $4 + 4 = \square$	$1 \times 1 = \square$ $1 + 0 = \square$
$7 \times 1 = \square$ $1 + 1 + 1 + 1 + 1 + 1 + 1 = \square$	

• F–2

Name _____ Date _____

$3 \times 1 = \square$ $1 + 1 + 1 = \square$	$2 + 2 + 2 = \square$ $3 \times 2 = \square$
$4 \times 2 = \square$ $2 + 2 + 2 + 2 = \square$	$3 + 3 = \square$ $2 \times 3 = \square$
$3 \times 4 = \square$ $4 + 4 + 4 = \square$	$5 + 5 + 5 + 5 = \square$ $4 \times 5 = \square$
$2 \times 6 = \square$ $6 + 6 = \square$	$10 + 10 + 10 + 10 = \square$ $4 \times 10 = \square$
$4 \times 3 = \square$ $3 + 3 + 3 + 3 = \square$	$7 + 7 + 7 = \square$ $3 \times 7 = \square$
$5 \times 2 = \square$ $2 + 2 + 2 + 2 + 2 = \square$	$1 + 1 + 1 + 1 + 1 + 1 = \square$ $6 \times 1 = \square$

• F–3

Name _____ Date _____

Which problems are the same?

8 + 8	3 × 5
3 + 3 + 3 + 3 + 3	4 × 2
4 + 4 + 4	2 × 8
5 + 5 + 5	3 × 4
6	5 × 3
2 + 2 + 2 + 2	1 × 6
2 + 2 + 2 + 2 + 2 + 2 + 2	5 × 4
5 + 5 + 5 + 5	7 × 2
4 + 4 + 4 + 4 + 4	4 × 5

• F-4

• F6, F11, F12

These sheets can be very effective in helping children who have difficulty distinguishing between the signs for addition and multiplication. The children should be aware that addition and multiplication, although related, are distinct operations.

When □ and △ are placeholders for whole numbers,

$$\square + \triangle = \square \times \triangle$$

is true *only* when '0' or '2' is written in both □ and △.

• F7, F9
Commutativity of multiplication

The problems on these sheets bring out the commutative property of multiplication. This property means that the product of two numbers equals the product of the same two numbers in the reverse order.

Name _____ Date _____

Which problems are the same?

4 × 5	3 + 3 + 3 + 3 + 3 + 3 + 3
3 × 2	1 + 1 + 1 + 1 + 1
7 × 3	2 + 2 + 2
2 × 4	5 + 5 + 5 + 5
5 × 1	2 + 2 + 2 + 2 + 2 + 2 + 2 + 2
2 × 6	4 + 4
8 × 2	6 + 6
1 × 9	6 + 6 + 6 + 6 + 6 + 6
6 × 6	9

• F-5

3 + 5 = □	2 × 4 = □
3 × 5 = □	2 + 4 = □
3 × 3 = □	4 + 3 = □
3 + 3 = □	4 × 3 = □
2 × 5 = □	5 × 2 = □
2 + 5 = □	5 + 2 = □
2 + 2 = □	3 × 2 = □
2 × 2 = □	3 + 2 = □
1 + 1 = □	5 + 1 = □
1 × 1 = □	5 × 1 = □

• F-6

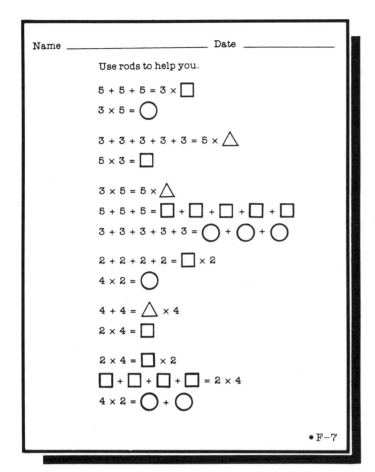

Use rods to help you.

5 + 5 + 5 = 3 × ☐

3 × 5 = ◯

3 + 3 + 3 + 3 + 3 = 5 × △

5 × 3 = ☐

3 × 5 = 5 × △

5 + 5 + 5 = ☐ + ☐ + ☐ + ☐ + ☐

3 + 3 + 3 + 3 + 3 = ◯ + ◯ + ◯

2 + 2 + 2 + 2 = ☐ × 2

4 × 2 = ◯

4 + 4 = △ × 4

2 × 4 = ☐

2 × 4 = ☐ × 2

☐ + ☐ + ☐ + ☐ = 2 × 4

4 × 2 = ◯ + ◯

• F–7

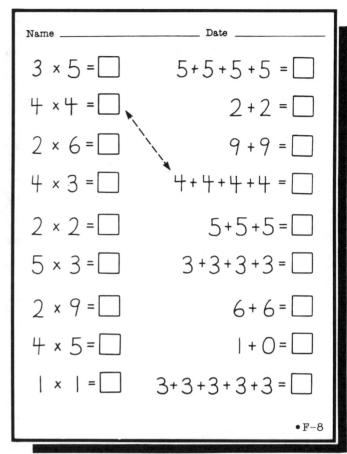

3 × 5 = ☐   5 + 5 + 5 + 5 = ☐

4 × 4 = ☐   2 + 2 = ☐

2 × 6 = ☐   9 + 9 = ☐

4 × 3 = ☐   4 + 4 + 4 + 4 = ☐

2 × 2 = ☐   5 + 5 + 5 = ☐

5 × 3 = ☐   3 + 3 + 3 + 3 = ☐

2 × 9 = ☐   6 + 6 = ☐

4 × 5 = ☐   1 + 0 = ☐

1 × 1 = ☐   3 + 3 + 3 + 3 + 3 = ☐

• F–8

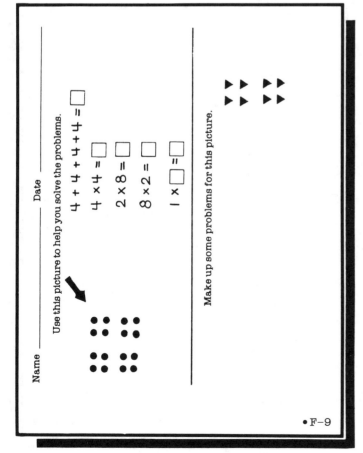

Use this picture to help you solve the problems.

4 + 4 + 4 + 4 = ☐

4 × 4 = ☐

2 × 8 = ☐

8 × 2 = ☐

1 × = ☐

Make up some problems for this picture.

• F–9

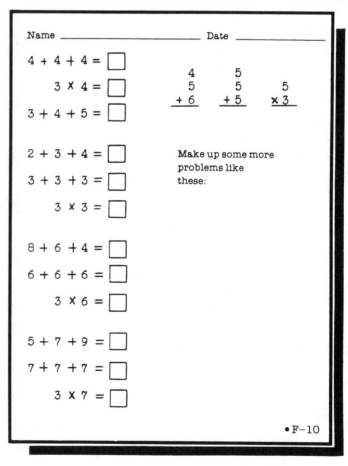

4 + 4 + 4 = ☐

3 × 4 = ☐

3 + 4 + 5 = ☐

2 + 3 + 4 = ☐

3 + 3 + 3 = ☐

3 × 3 = ☐

8 + 6 + 4 = ☐

6 + 6 + 6 = ☐

3 × 6 = ☐

5 + 7 + 9 = ☐

7 + 7 + 7 = ☐

3 × 7 = ☐

```
  4        5
  5        5          5
+ 6      + 5        × 3
```

Make up some more problems like these:

• F–10

Name _____   Date _____

3 x 3 = ☐	3 + 3 = ☐
2 x 4 = ☐	2 + 4 = ☐
5 x 3 = ☐	5 + 3 = ☐
4 x 5 = ☐	4 + 5 = ☐
2 x 6 = ☐	2 + 6 = ☐
1 x 1 = ☐	1 + 1 = ☐
3 x 2 = ☐	3 + 2 = ☐
4 x 2 = ☐	4 + 2 = ☐
2 x 7 = ☐	2 + 7 = ☐
2 x 8 = ☐	2 + 8 = ☐

• F–11

•• F13

Following is one of the problems on F13 and several ways in which the commutative property may be illustrated.

$$3 \times 5 = \square$$
$$5 \times 3 = \square$$

Solution 1

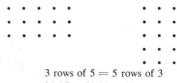

3 rows of 5 = 5 rows of 3
$$3 \times 5 = 5 \times 3 = 15$$

Solution 2

$$3 \times 5 = 5 \times 3 = 15$$

Solution 3

$$3 \times 5 \quad = \quad 5 \times 3 \quad = \quad 15$$

Name _____   Date _____

5 x 3 = ☐

4 x 2 = ☐

6 x 2 = ☐

    5 + 3 = ☐

    4 + 2 = ☐

    6 + 2 = ☐

3 x 3 = ☐

4 x 4 = ☐

5 x 2 = ☐

    3 + 3 = ☐

    4 + 4 = ☐

    5 + 2 = ☐

• F–12

Name _____   Date _____

3 x 5 = ☐ 5 x 3 = ☐	☐ = 6 x 10 ☐ = 10 x 6
7 x 3 = ☐ ☐ = 3 x 7	2 x 3 = ☐ 3 x 2 = ☐
4 x 3 = ☐ 3 x 4 = ☐	5 x 6 = ☐ ☐ = 6 x 5
☐ = 2 x 7 ☐ = 7 x 2	5 x 7 = ☐ 7 x 5 = ☐
☐ = 3 x 6 ☐ = 6 x 3	4 x 6 = ○ 6 x 4 = ○

•• F–13

·· F14

Here are related multiplication problems which we easily solve by
doubling.

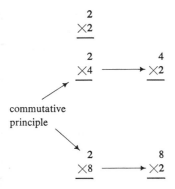

$$\begin{array}{r} 2 \\ \times 2 \\ \hline \end{array}$$

$$\begin{array}{r} 2 \\ \times 4 \\ \hline \end{array} \longrightarrow \begin{array}{r} 4 \\ \times 2 \\ \hline \end{array}$$

commutative
principle

$$\begin{array}{r} 2 \\ \times 8 \\ \hline \end{array} \longrightarrow \begin{array}{r} 8 \\ \times 2 \\ \hline \end{array}$$

Since doubling is an easily learned skill, 2 times, 4 times, and 8
times a number are easily obtained products.

Name			Date	
2 X 2			3 X 2	2 X 3
2 X 4	4 X 2		3 X 4	4 X 3
2 X 8	8 X 2		3 X 8	8 X 3
4 X 2	2 X 4		5 X 2	2 X 5
	4 X 4		5 X 4	4 X 5
4 X 8	8 X 4		5 X 8	8 X 5

·· F-14

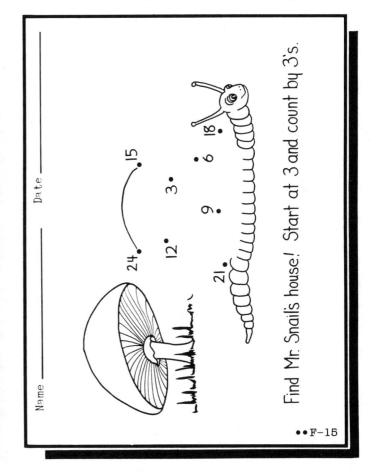

Name ___

Date ___

Find Mr. Snail's house! Start at 3 and count by 3's.

·· F-15

Name _____ Date _____

$3 \times \square = 6$ $3 \times \square = 9$

$2 \times \square = 18$ $2 \times \square = 4$

$1 \times \square = 10$ $1 \times \square = 1$

$\square \times 4 = 12$ $3 \times 6 = \square$

$\square \times 5 = 15$ $5 \times 4 = \square$

$4 \times \square = 16$ $9 \times 2 = \square$

$4 \times 6 = \square$

•• F-16

Name _____ Date _____

Important: The same number must be
named in each $\triangle$ in $(\triangle \times \triangle)$ or $(\triangle + \triangle + \triangle)$.

$2 \times 15 = \square$

$3 \times 10 = \square$

$5 \times 5 = \square$

$6 \times 6 = \square$

$5 \times 4 = \square$

$3 \times 8 = \square$

$30 = 2 \times \square$ $36 = \triangle \times \triangle$

$\square \times 3 = 30$ $5 \times \square = 12 + 8$

$\triangle \times \triangle = 25$ $\triangle + \triangle + \triangle = 24$

•• F-17

•• F16

This is the first sheet containing multiplication problems which does not merely ask the child to determine the product of two numbers. These problems may be solved as in the illustrations below:

Problem 1: $3 \times \square = 6$

Related question: Three of what number equals 6? [Three 2's equal 6.]

Solved problem: $3 \times \boxed{2} = 6$

Problem 2: $\square \times 4 = 12$

Related question: How many 4's equal 12? [Three 4's equal 12.]

Solved problem: $\boxed{3} \times 4 = 12$

Some children may also want to use their rods in solving these problems.

Problem 1: $3 \times \square = 6$

Related question: Three of what rod equals the dark green rod? [Three red rods equal the dark green rod.]

dark green		
red	red	red

Solved problem: $3 \times \boxed{2} = 6$

Problem 2: $\square \times 4 = 12$

Related question: How many of the four-rods are the same length as a ten-rod plus a two-rod? [Three four-rods equal 1 ten-rod plus 1 two-rod.]

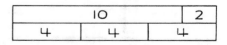

10		2
4	4	4

Solved problem: $\boxed{3} \times 4 = 12$

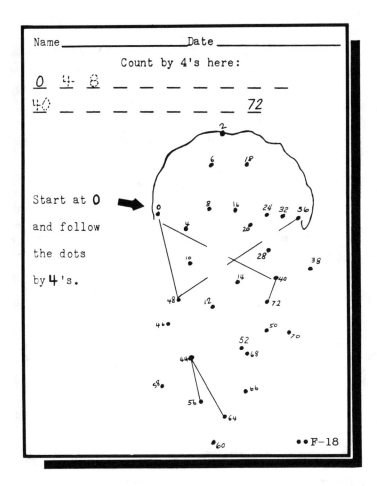

Name _____ Date _____

Count by 4's here:

0   4   8   __ __ __ __ __ __ __

40 __ __ __ __ __ __   72

Start at **0**
and follow
the dots
by **4**'s.

•• F-18

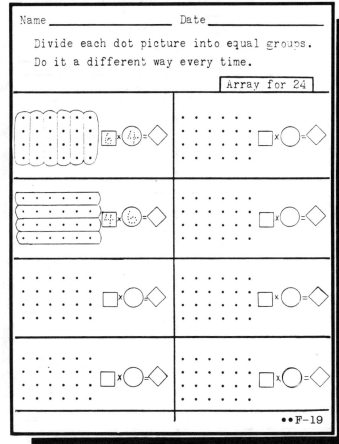

Name _____ Date _____

Divide each dot picture into equal groups.
Do it a different way every time.

| Array for 24 |

$\square \times \bigcirc = \diamondsuit$

•• F-19

·· F18, F21
Following-the-dots multiplication

Children count by fours and write out the multiples across the top of F18. They then use these numbers to draw the ice cream cone.

If the teacher feels that some children need to make lists of the multiples of 5 and 6 before attempting F21, they should write them on a separate piece of paper. (The picture is a Christmas tree with a red chain on it.)

·· F19, F20, F22
Factoring a number

Children are to subdivide the arrays, as illustrated in the following sample for the number 12. They write into the $\square$ the number of equal groups. They write into the $\bigcirc$ the size of each equal group.

The sample is filled in to illustrate the commutative law of multiplication.

Children will not usually do this in such a systematic fashion, but after they have filled in the arrays the teacher should give chalkboard examples which point out the commutative law.

Problem

$$\square \times \bigcirc = \diamondsuit$$

Solutions

$12 \times \textcircled{1} = \langle 12 \rangle$

$1 \times \textcircled{12} = \langle 12 \rangle$

$2 \times \textcircled{6} = \langle 12 \rangle$

$6 \times \textcircled{2} = \langle 12 \rangle$

$4 \times \textcircled{3} = \langle 12 \rangle$

$3 \times \textcircled{4} = \langle 12 \rangle$

The factor pairs of 12 are: 1,   2,   3,   4,   6,   12.

Name _____ Date _____

Divide each dot picture into equal groups.
Do it a different way every time.

| Array for 32 |

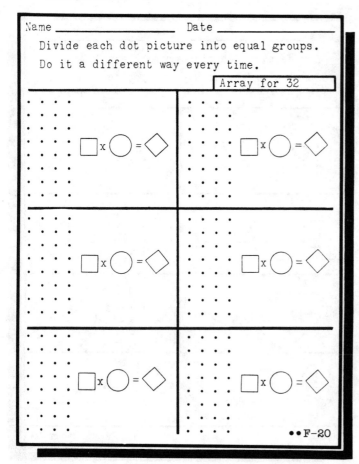

□ x ○ = ◇   □ x ○ = ◇

□ x ○ = ◇   □ x ○ = ◇

□ x ○ = ◇   □ x ○ = ◇

•• F-20

Name _____ Date _____

Start at 0 and go by 5's in <u>green</u>.
Start at 0 and go by 6's to 30 in <u>red</u>.

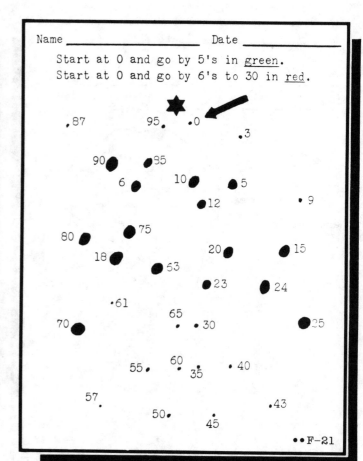

•• F-21

Name _____ Date _____

Divide each dot picture into equal groups.
Do it a different way every time.

| Array for 36 |

□ x ○ = ◇   □ x ○ = ◇

□ x ○ = ◇   □ x ○ = ◇

□ x ○ = ◇   □ x ○ = ◇

•• F-22

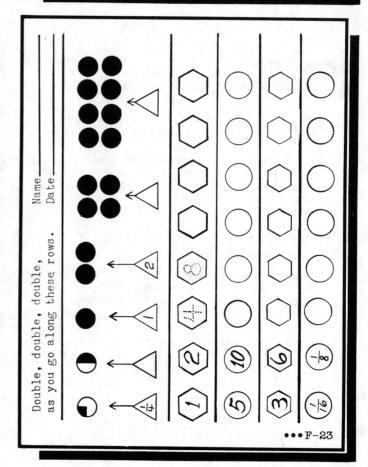

••• F-23

···F23, F25–F27
Doubling and halving

Doubling and halving are other ways to build up children's independence in learning specific multiplication and division facts.

Preliminary activities

1   With Cuisenaire® rods:

Take a red rod. Double it. Now you have how many red rods?   [2]

Double the two red rods. Now you have how many red rods?   [4]

Double the four red rods. Now you have how many red rods?   [8]

Put the red rods back in your pile of rods.

Now *double, double* the red rod. How many red rods do you now have?   [4]

Put the red rods back in your pile of rods.

Double, double, double the red rod. How many red rods do you now have?   [8]

2   Repeat the same procedure for the light green rod.

3   Without rods:

Put the rods away. How many times the red rod is *double* the red rod? [2 $\times$ the red rod or 2 $\times$ 2.]

How many times the red rod is *double, double* the red rod?   [4 $\times$ the red rod or 4 $\times$ 2.]

How many times the red rod is *double, double, double* the red rod? [8 $\times$ the red rod or 8 $\times$ 2.]

4   Repeat this procedure for the light green rod.

5   Repeat the same procedure with a group of children.

Two children
Two children [doubled]
Two children [doubled and doubled again]

6   Let's choose a number

number	5
doubled	10
doubled, doubled	20
doubled, doubled, doubled	40

5 is how many times the starting number?   [1 $\times$ 5]

10 is how many times the starting number?   [2 $\times$ 5]

20 is how many times the starting number?   [4 $\times$ 5]

40 is how many times the starting number?   [8 $\times$ 5]

7   Each child chooses a secret number and writes it on a piece of paper. "Double your number. Double again. Double again."

Each child writes down his last number.

Teacher calls on a child: "Johnny, tell us your starting number." He tells it. "Class, tell us Johnny's last number." Class responds. "Are they right, Johnny?" Repeat for several other children's numbers.

Then have some children give their second number and ask the class if they can figure out what the starting number was.

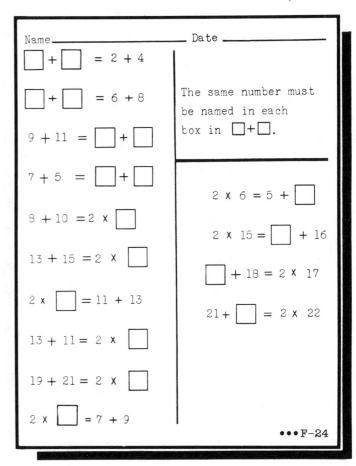

8   To practice halving a number, do the inverse of the previous suggestions. You must now start with the large number. Take the number 12. Halve it. [6] Halve it again. [3] 3 is half of half of 12.

Take 2. Double, double it. [8] Take 8. Halve, halve it. [2]

$$2 \times 2 \times 2 = 8$$
$$8 \div 2 \div 2 = 2$$
$$4 \times 2 = 8$$
$$8 \div 4 = 2$$

Generalizations

Multiplying by 2, 4, 8

$$2 \times \square = \square + \square$$
$$4 \times \square = (\square + \square) + (\square + \square)$$
$$8 \times \square = (\square + \square + \square + \square) + (\square + \square + \square + \square)$$

Dividing by 2, 4, 8

$$(2 \times \square) \div 2 = \square$$
$$(4 \times \square) \div 4 = \square$$
$$(8 \times \square) \div 8 = \square$$

Thus, by doubling repeatedly we can figure out what 2 or 4 or 8 or 16 times a number is. By halving repeatedly we can figure out what a number divided by 2 or 4 or 8 or 16 is.

Name _____ Date _____

Double down these columns:

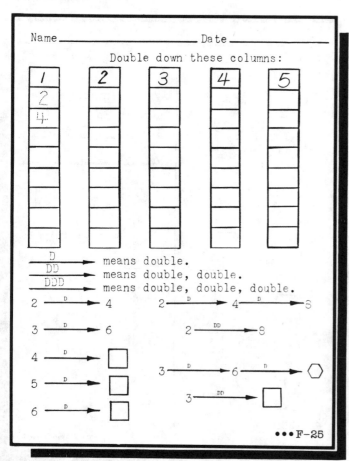

D ——▶ means double.
DD ——▶ means double, double.
DDD ——▶ means double, double, double.

2 —D→ 4   2 —D→ 4 —D→ 8

3 —D→ 6   2 —DD→ 8

4 —D→ ☐   3 —D→ 6 —D→ ⬡

5 —D→ ☐   3 —DD→ ☐

6 —D→ ☐

•••F-25

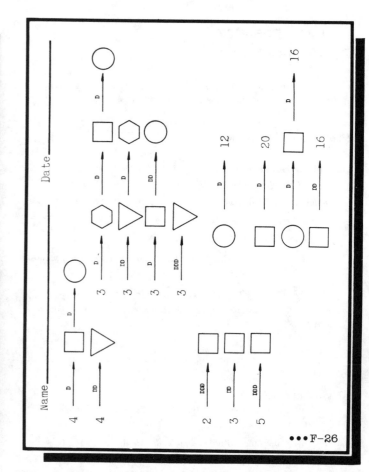

•••F-26

Name _____ Date _____

Finish the chart.

X	1	2	3	4	5	6	7	8	9	10
1	1	2								
2	2	4								
4		8								
8										

Use the chart to do these problems:

1 X 4 = ☐   1 X 10 = ⬡   1 X 7 = ◯
2 X 4 = ☐   2 X 10 = ⬡   2 X 7 = ◯
4 X 4 = ☐   4 X 10 = ⬡   4 X 7 = ◯
8 X 4 = ☐   8 X 10 = ⬡   8 X 7 = ◯

Find 36 on the chart.

36 = 4 X ☐

Find 64 on the chart.

64 = ◯ X ◯

•••F-27

Name _____ Date _____

Find the other names for 16, 32, and 40.
Write them inside the boxes.

2 x 2 x 10

2 X 16

10 x 2 x 2

(8 x 2)

8 x 5

2 x 5

10 x 4

5 x 5 x 2

Names for 16

8 x 2

2 x 2 x 2 x 5   4 x 4

2 x 2 x 2 x 2 x 2

(2 x 20)

5 x 4 x 2

4 x 8

Names for 40

2 x 20

Names for 32

2 x 2 x 2 x 2

5 x 4 + x 2

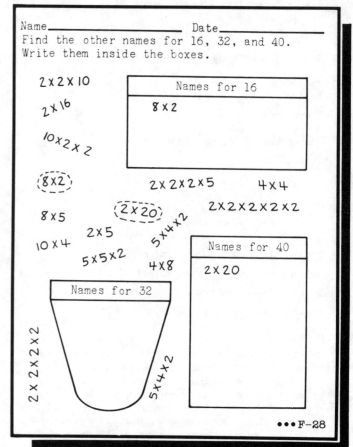

•••F-28

··· F25, F26
Double down these columns

Very few children will be able to go *all the way* down the column alone. Let them stop when they are stuck.

Children may discover the relationship between the 1, 2, and 4 columns.

An occasional child gets so "turned on" by this doubling that she or he does not want to stop and for days keeps on doubling at home and at school. One very bright first grader once kept going into the trillions! Dont stop such a child.

$$\text{DD} \xrightarrow{\quad} \text{(double, double)} = 4 \times \text{a number}$$

$$\text{DDD} \xrightarrow{\quad} = 8 \times \text{a number}$$

··· F28
Many names for a number

This lab sheet might best be used as a "teaching page" supervised by the teacher. There will be more such pages later. The children will then be able to do the others independently.

As the children "find" one of the names for 16, they can put a loop around it before they write it in the block labeled "Names for 16."

··· F29

The lab sheet is divided into columns, each giving practice on a particular technique useful in mental arithmetic.

Left Column

$$\square \times \triangle = \tfrac{1}{2}\,\square \;\times\; 2\,\triangle$$
$$4 \times 8 = (\tfrac{1}{2} \times 4) \times (2 \times 8)$$
$$4 \times 8 = \quad 2 \quad \times \quad 16$$

Right Column

By doubling four times a number, we will know eight times the number.

$$4 \times 3 = 12$$
$$8 \times 3 = 24$$

Name _____   Date _____

4 x 8 = ☐ x 16

8 x 3 = 4 x ☐

☐ x 10 = 4 x 5

8 x 6 = ☐ x 12

4 x ☐ = 2 x 6

☐ x 14 = 4 x 7

6 x 5 = ☐ x 10

8 x ☐ = 4 x 4

4 x 10 = 2 x ☐

4 x 3 = ☐

8 x 3 = ☐

4 x 5 = ☐

8 x 5 = ☐

☐ = 4 x 4

☐ = 8 x 4

☐ = 4 x 6

☐ = 8 x 6

20 = 4 x ☐

40 = 8 x ☐

18 = ☐ x 9

36 = ☐ x 9

●●● F–29

Name _____   Date _____

1 X 1 = ☐

4 X 2 = ☐

☐ = 3 X 3

0 X 6 = ☐

10 = 5 X ☐

2 X 5 = ☐

☐ = 3 X 4

5 X ☐ = 20

5 X 5 = ☐

1 X 2 X 3 = ☐

☐ = 3 X 2

(4 X 2) X 1 = ☐

4 X 4 = ☐

☐ = 4 X 5

☐ = 5 X 3

8 X ☐ = 16

7 X 2 = ☐

1 X 2 X 3 X 4 X 5 = ☐

☐ = 6 X 6

☐ = 6 X 3

3 X 3 X 3 = ☐

☐ = 2 X 4

4 X ☐ = 8

7 X 7 = ☐

●●● F–30

···F31–F40
The Pattern Book

The Pattern Book represents another approach to multiplication skills. It places previously acquired "scattered" knowledge into a carefully arranged sequence.

Lab sheets F31 through F40 are divided into two completely separate pattern types. Children should complete the top half of each lab sheet F31 through F40 before attempting the lower half.

Staple lab sheets F31 through F40 together. You can make two separate booklets out of them by cutting the pages in half horizontally. This way they make two very nice "flip books."

Preliminary chalkboard work

The teacher draws a large 10 × 10 grid on the chalkboard and fills in certain key numerals.

1	2	3	4	5	6	7	8	9	10
11	12	13							20
							28		
31			35						40
							48		50
		53							
									70
		74							
							88		
									100

Children are asked to fill in missing numerals.
Complete the second row.
Complete the first column.
Write in the next three numerals after 91, etc.

When the chart is filled in, questions such as the following may be asked:

What is the same about all the numerals in the first column? [All end with '1'] In the last column? [All end with '0'] The numbers in the second row are the numbers from 11 to ____?

Children now fill in the grid on F31.

Teacher erases columns 1, 3, 5, 7, and 9 from the chalkboard chart.

Question: What numbers are left?

Children's answers: Every other number. Counting by 2's. Even numbers.

Children fill in their own grid on F32.

The teacher draws three rows of another grid and places *X*'s in every third square.

	X		X		X
X		X		X	
X		X		X		X
		?			

She then adds another row and asks the children if they can figure out which squares should be marked with an *X*.

Question: Who can tell something about the way these squares are marked?

Answer: Counting by 3's.

What numeral could we write in the first ☒ square? (3)

in the second ☒ square? (6)

in the third ☒ square? (9)

This pattern is called the "pattern of 3." In your pattern books, find the page for the "pattern of 3." Fill in this pattern.

The first three patterns might be done as a group activity. Then many children will be able to go on independently. They can check back to the pattern of 1 if they need help.

Discussion after the ten patterns are completed

1 Studying a pattern

What numbers showed up in the pattern of 1?
What numbers are missing in the pattern of 2?
How many numbers 1–100 are missing in the pattern of 2?
How many numbers 1–100 are left in the pattern of 2?
How many 2's are in 100?
Is 41 a numeral in the pattern of 2? Is 54? 86? 99?
If we made the chart bigger, would 112, 165, 180, 210 be in the pattern of 2?
What is special about the pattern of 3?
Do *only* even numbers show up?
Do *all* the even numbers show up? etc.

2 Comparing patterns

Look at the pattern of 4; then look at the pattern of 2.
How are they alike? How are they different?
Could you make a 4 pattern out of the 2 pattern?
How does the 9 pattern compare with the 3 pattern?
    (Repeat the questions for previous patterns of 2 and 4.)
How do the 5 pattern and the 10 pattern compare?
    Repeat the questions for previous patterns.)

3   Some informal division

Which pattern helps you tell how many 2's there are in 100?

How many

3's in 100?	3's in 10?
4's in 100?	4's in 10?
5's in 100?	5's in 10?

4   Detective work

How many patterns do 4, 10, 42, 49, etc., appear in?

[4] is in the ①, ②, 3, ④, 5, 6, 7, 8, 9, 10 patterns.

[10] is in the ①, ②, 3, 4, ⑤, 6, 7, 8, 9, ⑩ patterns.

[42] is in the ①, ②, ③, 4, 5, ⑥, ⑦, 8, 9, 10 patterns.

[49] is in the ①, 2, 3, 4, 5, 6, ⑦, 8, 9, 10 patterns.

Which numbers can you *not* find on any pattern except the 1 pattern? [11, 13, 17, 19 and all the other *prime* numbers between 10 and 100.] (See the annotation for F42.)

Supplementary suggestion for patterns

Special "look-through" pattern charts made by the teacher will be helpful in pattern exercises. To make these charts, you will need 11 posterboards 24″ × 24″, in assorted colors, a razor-blade knife, and a felt-point marker. Allow for a 2″ frame around each posterboard. Draw on each posterboard a 20″ × 20″ square. Subdivide each large square into one hundred 2″ squares, and write the numerals from 1 through 100 on one grid. The chart will be the same as the completed top half of lab sheet F31. This becomes the basic number chart.

The other 10 sheets are used to make large duplicates of the patterns on the top half of lab sheets F31 through F40. To make the pattern of 2, for example, cut out the pattern of the white squares that appears on lab sheet F32. These are the spaces for even numbers. For patterns 3 through 10 cut out white sections of these charts in the same way.

When one of these look-through patterns is placed on top of the basic number chart, the numbers in that pattern are revealed.

Sample of 3 pattern	Sample of 3 pattern laid over basic number chart
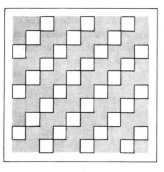	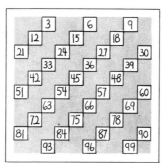
Blank squares are cut out.	Numerals are seen through holes in pattern.

With such a collection of large class charts many interesting observations can be made.

1   Example

When both the 3 pattern and the 2 pattern are laid over the basic number chart, the 6 pattern is revealed. (2 and 3 are the factors of 6.)

2   When both the 3 pattern and the 5 pattern are laid over the basic number chart, the 15 pattern is produced. (3 and 5 are the factors of 15.)

The following questions were asked by six children of the rest of their group. The questions are the result of their independent work with the charts.

Mike: Which numbers will show when we put the 8 pattern on top of the 10 pattern?

Donna: Which numbers will show when we put the 10 pattern on top of the 9 pattern?

Mary: Which numbers will show when we put the 4 pattern on top of the 7 pattern?

Tracy: Which numbers will show when we put all the patterns on the chart?

Peter: Which numbers will show when we put the 3, 5, 7, 9 patterns on top of one another?

Mark: Which numbers will show when we put all the *even* patterns on top of one another?

The children guessed that 11, 49, 29, 41, and 51 would *not* show up on the patterns 2 through 10. They were wrong about 49 and 51.

11	(did)	(did not)	show up
49	(did)	(did not)	show up
29	(did)	(did not)	show up
41	(did)	(did not)	show up
51	(did)	(did not)	show up

The children guessed that 48, 18, 100, 8, and 38 would show up in more patterns than other numbers. Were they right?

48 showed up in patterns

②, ③, ④, 5, ⑥, 7, ⑧, 9, 10

18 showed up in patterns

②, ③, 4, 5, ⑥, 7, 8, ⑨, 10

100 showed up in patterns

②, 3, ④, ⑤, 6, 7, 8, 9, ⑩

8 showed up in patterns

②, 3, ④, 5, 6, 7, ⑧, 9, 10

38 showed up in patterns

②, 3, 4, 5, 6, 7, 8, 9, 10

One child asked what numbers *never* show up. These numbers are covered by each of the patterns 2 through 10:

11, 13, 17, 19, 23, 29
31, 37, 41, 43, 47, 53
59, 61, 67, 71, 73, 79
83, 89, 97.

They are called prime numbers. (See annotation for lab sheet F42.) 2, 3, 5, and 7 are also prime numbers, but they do show up in their own pattern.

Introduction of the multiplication table

On the lower half of each lab sheet F31 through F40 is a multiplication table. The grids are drawn slightly smaller than a centimeter scale, but children will be able to use Cuisenaire® rods as a learning aid in the completion of the tables.

The teacher should show the group how to make a table. It is advisable to start with the table of 3 or 4.

Sample procedure
Find the pattern of 3 (F33). Look at the large square at the bottom of the page.

1   About rows
Move your finger across row 1.
Move your finger across row 2.
Move your finger across row 7.

How do you know it is row 1?
How do you know it is row 2?
How do you know it is row 7?   [I counted]

How could you know without counting which row I am talking about? [There is a numeral on the left side of each row that tells.]

2   About columns
Move your finger down column 1.
Move your finger down column 2.
Move your finger down column 8.

How did you know which is column 8?   [By counting.]
How could you know which column it is without counting?   [The numeral at the top of the column tells which column it is.]

3   Locating squares in the white column
Place your finger on the square that is both in row 1 *and* in column 3.
Place your finger on the square that is both in row 2 *and* in column 3.
Place your finger on the square that is both in row 6 *and* in column 3.
What color are all these squares?

4   Locating squares in the white row
Place your finger on the square that is both in row 3 *and* in column 1.
Place your finger on the square that is both in row 3 *and* in column 2.
Place your finger on the square that is both in row 3 *and* in column 6.
What color are all these squares?

5   Making rows of three with grid and rods
Get a pile of light green rods.

Place a light green rod on row 1. How many squares does it cover? Write a '3' in the square which is both in row 1 and column 3.

Leave the rod on the row. Place another light green rod on row 2. How many squares do the two rods cover? Write a '6' in the square which is in both row 2 and column 3.

Leave the two rods and get another green rod. Place the new rod on row 3. How many squares do three rods cover? Write a '9' in the square which is in both row 3 and column 3. Continue this procedure through row 10.

6   Making columns of three with grid and rods
The method is the same as the one for rows except that now rods are placed vertically and instructions for rows and columns are reversed.

Place a light green rod on column 1. How many squares does it cover? Write a '3' in the square which is both in column 1 and row 3.

Leave the rod on column 1. Place another light green rod on column 2. How many squares do the two rods cover? Write a '6' in the square which is in both column 2 and row 3.
Continue through column 10.

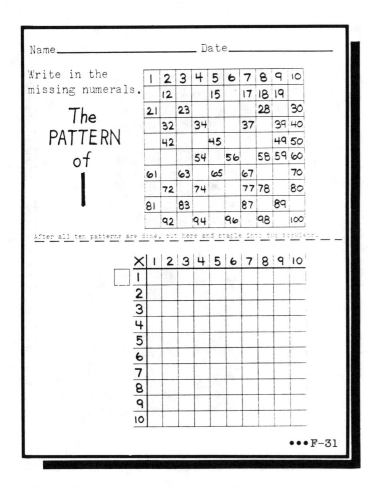

Name_____ Date_____

Write in the missing numerals.

The PATTERN of 1

1	2	3	4	5	6	7	8	9	10
	12			15		17	18	19	
21		23					28		30
	32		34			37		39	40
	42			45				49	50
			54		56		58	59	60
61		63		65		67			70
	72		74			77	78		80
81		83				87		89	
	92		94		96		98		100

After all ten patterns are done, cut here and staple into two booklets.

X	1	2	3	4	5	6	7	8	9	10
1										
2										
3										
4										
5										
6										
7										
8										
9										
10										

•••F-31

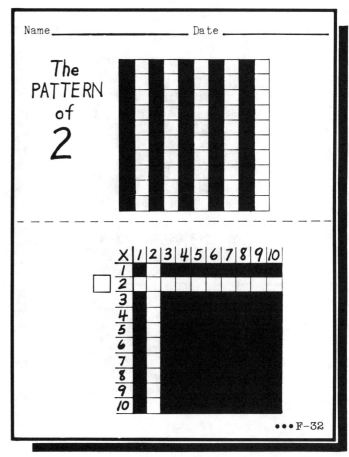

Name_____ Date_____

The PATTERN of 2

•••F-32

7 Discussion about the filled-in chart

Read the numbers in the white row.

Read the numbers in the white column.

What is special about these numbers?

Which number tells about 2 rows of 3?

Which number tells about 2 columns of 3?

Which of those two numbers covers more squares?

Find the number that tells about five 3's. [There are 5 rows of three and there are 5 columns of three.]

How many 9's are written in your chart? [One]

Why is there only one 9? [It is the square of three.]

How can the chart help us find the answer to 7 × 3? [It is in the square which is *row 7, column 3* or in *row 3, column 7.*]

Other charts

1 Filling in the other multiplication tables

By using rods, some children will be able to go on without help to fill in the other tables. Others will have to be started by the teacher.

No one should be encouraged to proceed without rods. Some children will quickly see that they are recording in these charts the first 10 numbers of the patterns developed on the upper half of each page.

2 Locating the charts

The teacher should ask the children to locate the charts on which the following patterns can be found:

Find the chart for 8 × 7, 6 × 4, 2 × 1, etc.

Name_____ Date_____

The
PATTERN
of
3

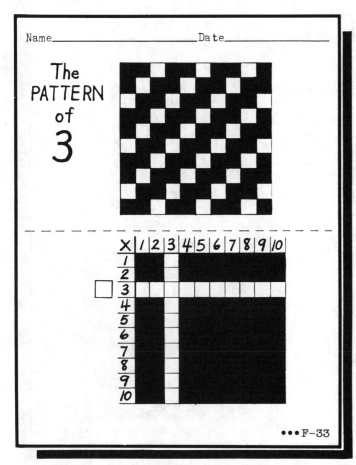

Name_____ Date_____

The
PATTERN
of
4

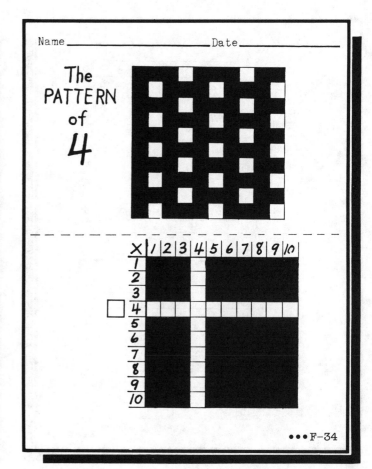

Name_____ Date_____

The
PATTERN
of
5

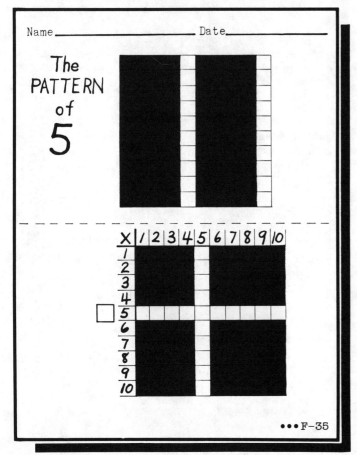

Name_____ Date_____

The
PATTERN
of
6

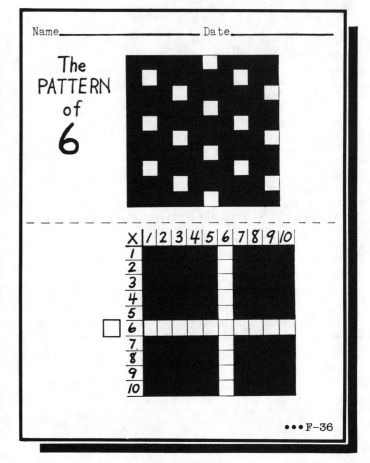

F   Multiplication

Name_____ Date_____

The
PATTERN
of
7

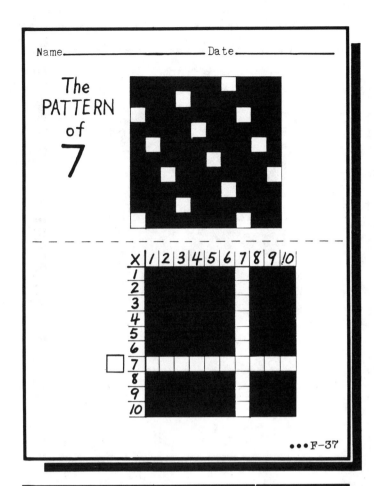

X	1	2	3	4	5	6	7	8	9	10
1										
2										
3										
4										
5										
6										
7										
8										
9										
10										

•••F–37

Name_____ Date_____

The
PATTERN
of
8

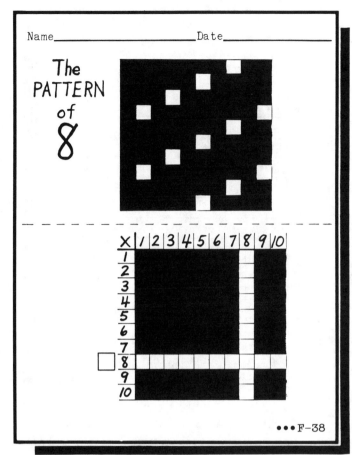

X	1	2	3	4	5	6	7	8	9	10
1										
2										
3										
4										
5										
6										
7										
8										
9										
10										

•••F–38

Name_____ Date_____

The
PATTERN
of
9

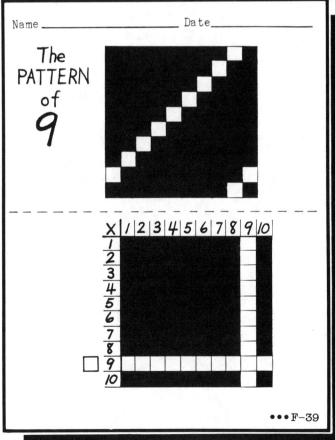

X	1	2	3	4	5	6	7	8	9	10
1										
2										
3										
4										
5										
6										
7										
8										
9										
10										

•••F–39

Name_____ Date_____

The
PATTERN
of
10

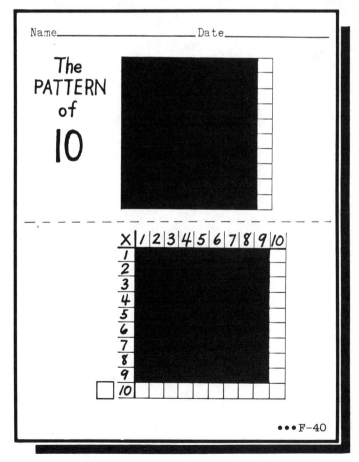

X	1	2	3	4	5	6	7	8	9	10
1										
2										
3										
4										
5										
6										
7										
8										
9										
10										

•••F–40

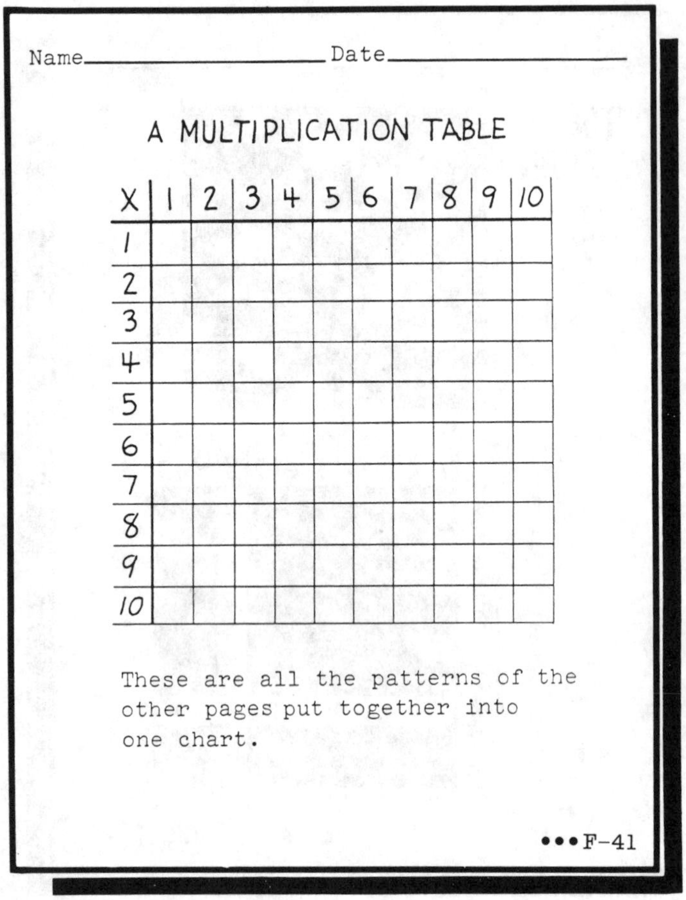

Name_____ Date_____

A MULTIPLICATION TABLE

X	1	2	3	4	5	6	7	8	9	10
1										
2										
3										
4										
5										
6										
7										
8										
9										
10										

These are all the patterns of the other pages put together into one chart.

•••F-41

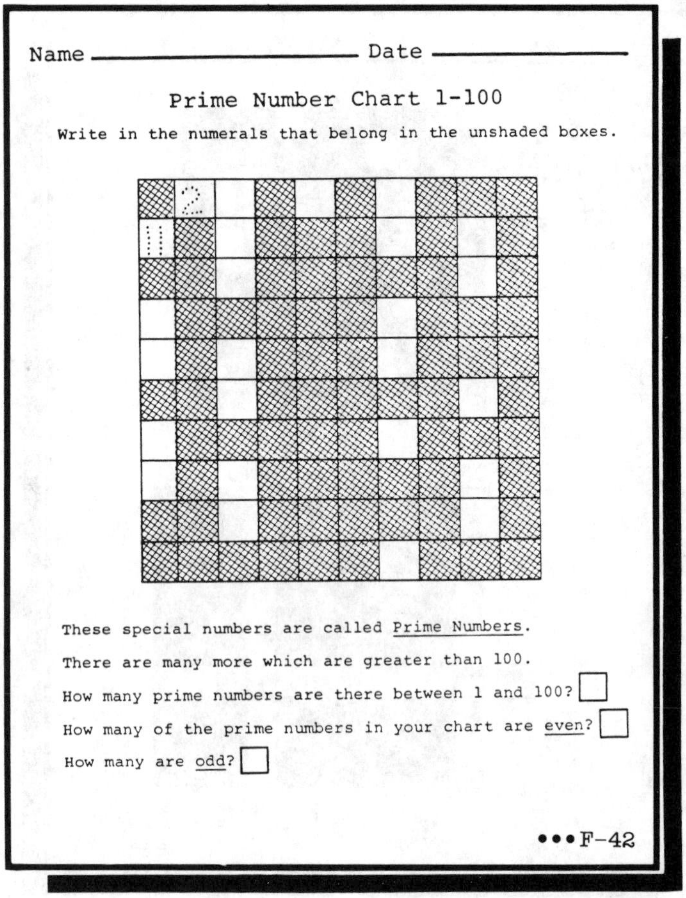

Name _____ Date _____

Prime Number Chart 1-100
Write in the numerals that belong in the unshaded boxes.

These special numbers are called <u>Prime Numbers</u>.

There are many more which are greater than 100.

How many prime numbers are there between 1 and 100? ☐

How many of the prime numbers in your chart are <u>even</u>? ☐

How many are <u>odd</u>? ☐

•••F-42

•••F41
The multiplication table

Lab sheet F41 is the chart on which *all* of the previous ten patterns from the bottoms of lab sheets F31-F40 are recorded. Suggest that pupils leaf slowly through the ten patterns before beginning work on this sheet.

•••F42
Prime number chart

The prime number chart shows whole numbers which have as factors only 1 and themselves.

One can easily see from this chart that the prime numbers do not present a predictable pattern. No mathematician has yet worked out a way to predict where very large prime numbers will occur. They are infinite in number, but they thin out as the numbers increase. No other span of 100 numbers has as many as 25 prime numbers in it.

See Section O, Factoring, for more work on prime numbers.

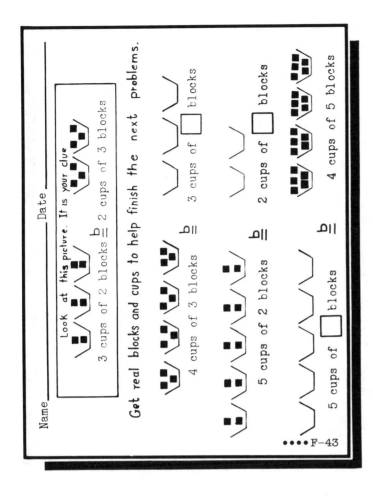

F-43 (worksheet)

Name _____ Date _____

Look at this picture. It is your clue.

3 cups of 2 blocks $\overset{b}{=}$ 2 cups of 3 blocks

Get real blocks and cups to help finish the next problems.

3 cups of ☐ blocks

2 cups of ☐ blocks

4 cups of 5 blocks

4 cups of 3 blocks $\overset{b}{=}$ 3 cups of ☐ blocks

5 cups of 2 blocks $\overset{b}{=}$ 2 cups of ☐ blocks

5 cups of ☐ blocks

••••F-43

Name _____ Date _____

Check your answers with real cups and blocks

3 cups of 7 blocks $\overset{b}{=}$ 7 cups of ☐ blocks

6 cups of 5 blocks $\overset{b}{=}$ 5 cups of ☐ blocks

5 cups of ☐ blocks $\overset{b}{=}$ 1 cup of 5 blocks

4 cups of 6 blocks $\overset{b}{=}$ 6 cups of ☐ blocks

9 cups of 3 blocks $\overset{b}{=}$ 3 cups of ☐ blocks

2 cups of ☐ blocks $\overset{b}{=}$ 8 cups of 2 blocks

••••F-44

••••F43

Commutativity of multiplication

The children should be given cups and blocks to use in working the problems.

If it is difficult to get paper cups to fill with blocks, the children might each use a three-row egg carton instead. The twelve compartments of the egg carton can be substituted for cups.

Change

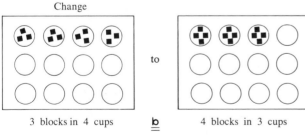

3 blocks in 4 cups $\quad\overset{b}{=}\quad$ 4 blocks in 3 cups

$\overset{b}{=}$ means "The number of blocks is equal."

In another variation of this activity, children can build towers out of blocks. Then problems can be made up similar to the following one:

3 towers of 4 blocks $\overset{b}{=}$ 4 towers of 3 blocks

This way no containers are needed.

F-45 Worksheet

Name_____ Date_____

3 × 4 units = ☐   units   3 × 4   = ☐
3 × 4 tens = ☐   tens   3 × 40 = ☐
3 × 4 hundreds = ☐ hundreds 3 × 400 = ☐

5 × 3 units = ☐   units   5 × 3   = ☐
5 × 3 tens = ☐   tens   5 × 30 = ☐
5 × 3 hundreds = ☐ hundreds 5 × 300 = ☐

6 × 3 units = ☐   units   6 × 3   = ☐
6 × 3 tens = ☐   tens   6 × 30 = ☐
6 × 3 hundreds = ☐ hundreds 6 × 300 = ☐

5	50	500	Make up your own problems.
×2	× 2	× 2	
4	40	400	
×6	× 6	× 6	
3	30	300	
×7	× 7	× 7	

•••• F-45

F-46 Worksheet

Name_____ Date_____

3 × 2 =   3 × 5 =   7 × 5 =
3 × 20 =   30 × 5 =   7 × 50 =

7 × 4 =   9 × 1 =   6 × 10 =
7 × 40 =   90 × 1 =   6 × 100 =

3 × 6   =   8 × 4   =
3 × 60 =   8 × 40 =
3 × 600 =   8 × 400 =

5   × 6 =   7 × 6   =
50 × 6 =   7 × 60 =
500 × 6 =   7 × 600 =

13 × 2   =   5   × 15 =
13 × 20 =   50 × 15 =
13 × 200 =   500 × 15 =

9 × 60 =   30 × 12 =

50 × 9 =   6 × 400 =

8 × 900 =   600 × 9 =

•••• F-46

•••• F45, F46
Multiplication with units, tens and hundreds

The children should be divided into small groups of three or four. Each group should have enough Cuisenaire® rods for this activity.
Give each group several 10 cm. × 10 cm. oaktag squares. These squares are to be used to represent 100 in the model-building activity.

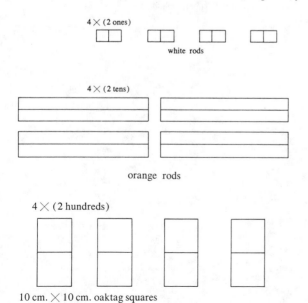

4 × (2 ones)

white rods

4 × (2 tens)

orange rods

4 × (2 hundreds)

10 cm. × 10 cm. oaktag squares

Questions	On chalkboard

How many ones in
  4 × (2 ones)?
  8 ones
	4 × 2 = 8

How many tens in
  4 × (2 tens)?
  8 tens
	4 × 20 = 80

How many hundreds in
  4 × (2 hundreds)?
  8 hundreds
	4 × 200 = 800

then	

How many thousands in
  4 × (2 thousands)?
  8 thousands
	4 × 2000 = 8000

(See annotations for Section M, Place Value, for other activities.)

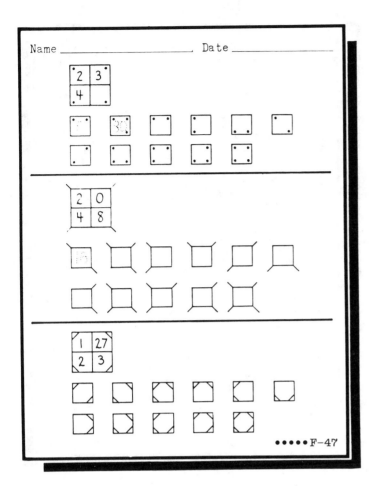

•••••F-47

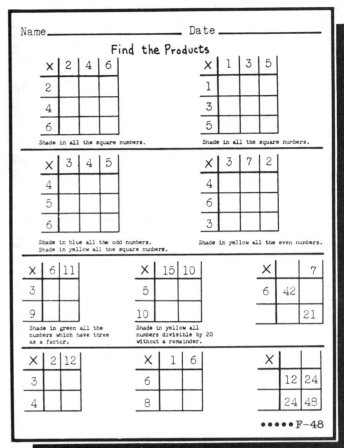

Find the Products

•••••F-48

•••••F47
Multiplication puzzles

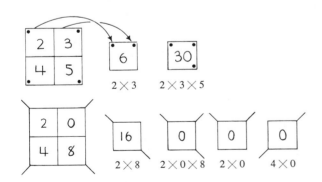

Most answers are zero because $\square \times 0 = 0$.

Let children make up some multiplication puzzles of their own.

•••••F48
Multiplication charts

$\times$	6	11
3	18	33
9	54	99

All numbers except 11 have 3 as a factor.

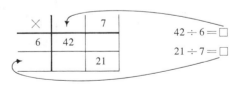

$42 \div 6 = \square$

$21 \div 7 = \square$

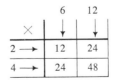

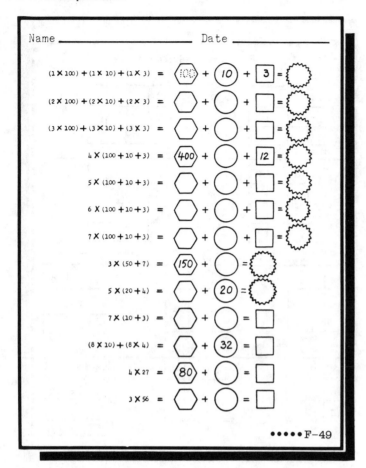

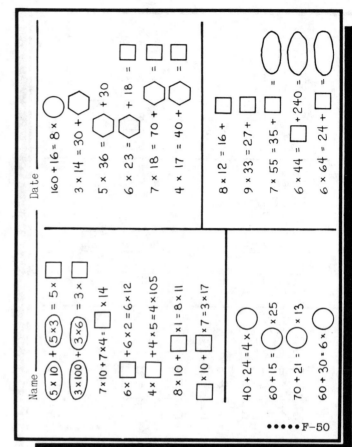

• • • • • F49, F50

These sheets are designed to help the child get ready for the multiplication algorithm by using the distributive law of multiplication with respect to addition.

With paper squares and rods:

3 times 115

$$3 \times 100 + 3 \times 10 + 3 \times 5$$
$$300 \quad + \quad 30 \quad + \quad 15$$
$$345$$

$$3 \times 1 \text{ ft. } 5 \text{ in.} = 3 \times 1 \text{ ft.} + 3 \times 5 \text{ in.}$$
$$= \quad 3 \text{ ft.} \quad + \quad 15 \text{ in.}$$
$$4 \text{ ft. } 3 \text{ in.}$$

$$5 \times 1\frac{1}{2} \text{ hrs.} = 5 \times 1 \text{ hr.} + 5 \times \frac{1}{2} \text{ hrs.}$$
$$= \quad 5 \text{ hrs.} \quad + \quad \frac{5}{2} \text{ hrs.}$$
$$= \quad 5 \text{ hrs.} \quad + \quad 2\frac{1}{2} \text{ hrs.}$$
$$= \quad \quad 7\frac{1}{2} \text{ hrs.}$$

$$9 \times 1 \text{ wk. } 2 \text{ days} = 9 \text{ wks.} + 18 \text{ days}$$
$$= 9 \text{ wks.} + 2 \text{ wks.} + 4 \text{ days}$$
$$= \quad 11 \text{ wks.} \quad + 4 \text{ days}$$

The technique used here starts with multiplying hundreds first, then tens only, then units only, and then getting the sum of these partial products.

F-51

Name _____ Date _____

$6 \times 21 = (6 \times \square) + (6 \times \hexagon) = \bigcirc$

$4 \times 18 = (4 \times \square) + (4 \times \hexagon) = \bigcirc$

$7 \times 15 = (7 \times \square) + (7 \times \hexagon) = \bigcirc$

$4 \times 34 = (4 \times \square) + (4 \times \hexagon) = \bigcirc$

$5 \times 23 = (5 \times \square) + (5 \times \hexagon) = \bigcirc$

$9 \times 105 = (9 \times \square) + (9 \times \hexagon) = \bigcirc$

$4 \times 42 = (\square \times 2) + (\hexagon \times 40) = \bigcirc$

$6 \times 27 = (\square \times 7) + (\hexagon \times 20) = \bigcirc$

$3 \times 82 = (\square \times 80) + (\hexagon \times 2) = \bigcirc$

```
   2 3              3 6              2 7
 x   4            x   3            x   4
  1 2 (4 x 3)      1 8 (3 x 6)      +
+ 8 0 (4 x 20)    +    (3 x 30)
  9 2
```

•••••• F-51

F-52

Name _____ Date _____

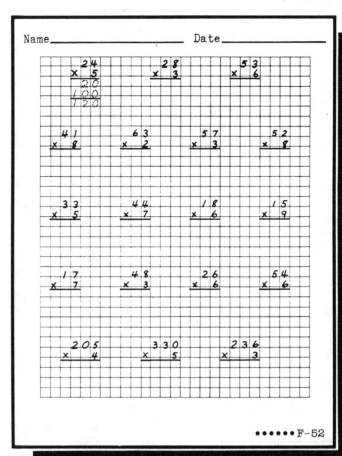

```
    2 4           2 8           5 3
  x   5         x   3         x   6
    2 0
  1 0 0
  1 2 0
```

```
    4 1           6 3           5 7           5 2
  x   8         x   2         x   3         x   8
```

```
    3 3           4 4           1 8           1 5
  x   5         x   7         x   6         x   9
```

```
    1 7           4 8           2 6           5 4
  x   7         x   3         x   6         x   6
```

```
  2 0 5         3 3 0         2 3 6
 x    4        x    5        x    3
```

•••••• F-52

F-53

Name _____ Date _____

```
  1 0 0       1 0 1       1 1 0       1 1 1
 x     3     x     3     x     3     x     3

  2 0 0       2 0 2       2 2 0       2 2 2
 x     4     x     4     x     4     x     4

  2 0 0       2 0 3       2 1 0       2 1 3
 x     6     x     6     x     6     x     6

  3 0 0       3 0 1       3 3 0       3 3 1
 x     3     x     3     x     3     x     3

  1 0 0       1 0 1       1 2 0       1 2 1
 x     7     x     7     x     7     x     7

  2 0 0       2 0 9       2 5 0       2 5 9
 x     5     x     5     x     5     x     5

  4 0 0       4 0 3       4 4 0       4 4 3
 x     2     x     2     x     2     x     2
```

•••••• F-53

F-54

Name _____ Date _____

| 24 | 28 |

Add the same number for each dot.

Add the same number for each line.

Fill the correct numerals in the frames below.

(frames with dots)

| 200 | 200 | 200 | 200 | | |

| 9 | 9 | 9 | 9 | | |

(frames)

| | | 18 | 209 | | |

These double boxes go with the pattern above.
Try to figure them out.

(double box patterns)

•••••• F-54

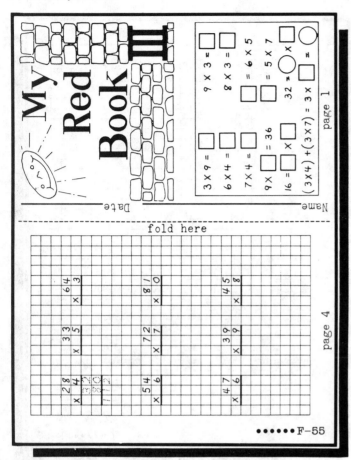

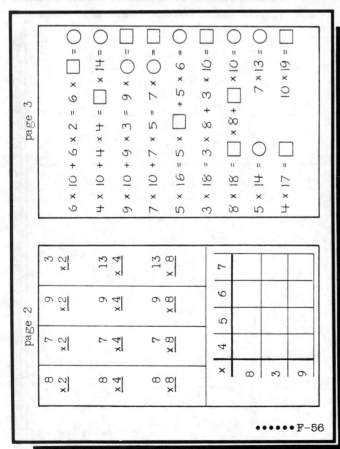

G Addition, subtraction, and multiplication

$3 \times 4 = \square$

$5 + 2 = \square$

$3 + 4 = \square$

$5 \times 2 = \square$

$4 - 3 = \square$

$2 \times 5 = \square$

$4 \times 3 = \square$

$5 - 2 = \square$

$2 \times 4 = \square$

$4 \times 2 = \square$

• G-1

$5 - \square = 3$ $4 - \square = 1$

$\square - 2 = 3$ $\square - 3 = 1$

$\square \times 4 = 12$ $2 \times \square = 8$

$4 \times \square = 12$ $\square \times 2 = 8$

$\begin{array}{r} 5 \\ +6 \\ \hline \end{array}$ $\begin{array}{r} 10 \\ +11 \\ \hline \end{array}$ $\begin{array}{r} 4 \\ +5 \\ \hline \end{array}$ $\begin{array}{r} 6 \\ +7 \\ \hline \end{array}$ $\begin{array}{r} 3 \\ +4 \\ \hline \end{array}$

$\begin{array}{r} 15 \\ +6 \\ \hline \end{array}$ $\begin{array}{r} 20 \\ +11 \\ \hline \end{array}$ $\begin{array}{r} 14 \\ +5 \\ \hline \end{array}$ $\begin{array}{r} 16 \\ +7 \\ \hline \end{array}$ $\begin{array}{r} 13 \\ +4 \\ \hline \end{array}$

• G-2

$3 + 4 = \square$ $2 \times 3 = \square$

$7 + 7 = \square$ $\square = 2 \times 4$

$\square = 9 - 7$ $\square = 4 \times 2$

$8 + 0 = \square$ $3 \times 2 = \square$

$\square = 3 \times 5$ $9 - 4 = \square$

$12 - 10 = \square$ $4 + 5 = \square$

$12 - 2 = \square$ $5 + \square = 9$

$10 + \square = 12$ $7 + 2 + 3 = \square$

Make up your own problems.

$\square = 8 - 0$

$8 - 8 = \square$

• G-3

133

Name _____ Date _____

Find the TENS and ADD.

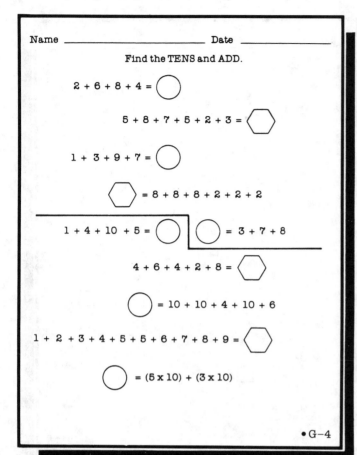

$2 + 6 + 8 + 4 = \bigcirc$

$5 + 8 + 7 + 5 + 2 + 3 = \hexagon$

$1 + 3 + 9 + 7 = \bigcirc$

$\hexagon = 8 + 8 + 8 + 2 + 2 + 2$

$1 + 4 + 10 + 5 = \bigcirc$ $\bigcirc = 3 + 7 + 8$

$4 + 6 + 4 + 2 + 8 = \hexagon$

$\bigcirc = 10 + 10 + 4 + 10 + 6$

$1 + 2 + 3 + 4 + 5 + 5 + 6 + 7 + 8 + 9 = \hexagon$

$\bigcirc = (5 \times 10) + (3 \times 10)$

• G–4

Name _____ Date _____

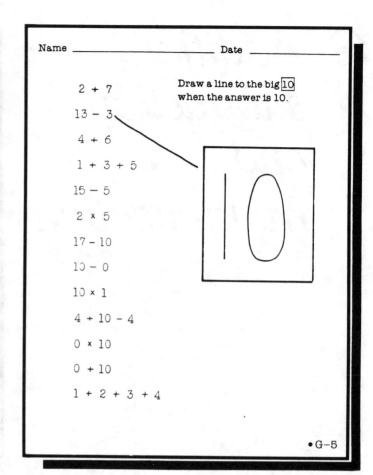

Draw a line to the big ☐10 when the answer is 10.

$2 + 7$

$13 - 3$

$4 + 6$

$1 + 3 + 5$

$15 - 5$

2×5

$17 - 10$

$10 - 0$

10×1

$4 + 10 - 4$

0×10

$0 + 10$

$1 + 2 + 3 + 4$

• G–5

Name _____ Date _____

Draw a line to the big ▽9 when the answer is 9.

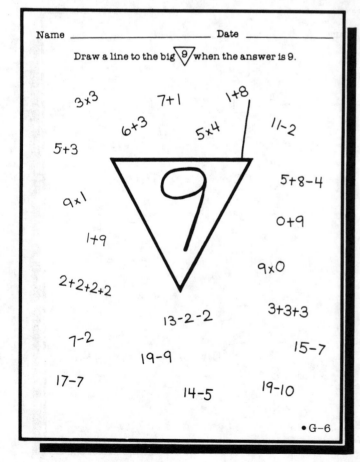

3×3 $7 + 1$ $1 + 8$

$6 + 3$ 5×4 $11 - 2$

$5 + 3$

$5 + 8 - 4$

9×1

$0 + 9$

$1 + 9$

9×0

$2 + 2 + 2 + 2$

$13 - 2 - 2$ $3 + 3 + 3$

$7 - 2$

$19 - 9$ $15 - 7$

$17 - 7$

$14 - 5$ $19 - 10$

• G–6

Name _____ Date _____

Draw a line to the big ☐12 when the answer is 12.

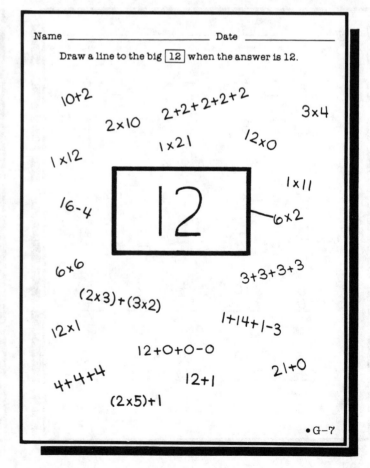

$10 + 2$

2×10 $2 + 2 + 2 + 2 + 2$ 3×4

1×12 1×21 12×0

$16 - 4$ 1×11

6×2

6×6

$3 + 3 + 3 + 3$

$(2 \times 3) + (3 \times 2)$

12×1 $1 + 14 + 1 - 3$

$12 + 0 + 0 - 0$

$4 + 4 + 4$ $12 + 1$ $21 + 0$

$(2 \times 5) + 1$

• G–7

• G5–G8
"Loop" problems

To complete lab sheets containing "loop" problems, draw a loop around all combinations and connect those that equal the "big" number to the "big" number box, or simply cross out the combinations that do not equal the "big" number. On sheets with blank loops, the child should write combinations that do not appear on the page.

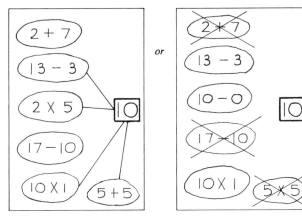

Name _____ Date _____

Fill in the frames with names for 100.

•• G9

The problems in the first group have the two operations addition and multiplication. Those in the second group have multiplication and subtraction. In these problems both the multiplications should be performed before the addition or subtraction is done. To help the children perform the operations in the correct order, have them put a loop around each multiplication part. Below is an example.

$$2 \times 4 + 2 \times 3 = \boxed{}$$
$$\overset{8}{\underbrace{(2 \times 4)}} + \overset{6}{\underbrace{(2 \times 3)}} = \boxed{14}$$

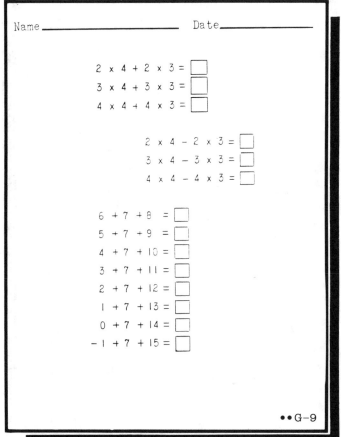

Name _____ Date _____

Find all the names for 16
Make up some of your own.

8 + 7

10 + 5 + 1

8 x 2

11 + 4

9 + 3 + 3

2 + 2 + 2 + 2 + 8

16

••G–10

·· G10–G12

See annotations for lab sheets G5-G8.

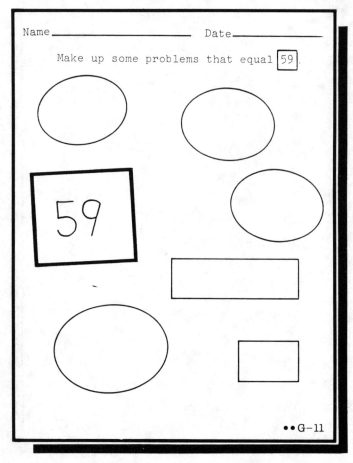

Name _____ Date _____

Make up some problems that equal 59.

59

••G-11

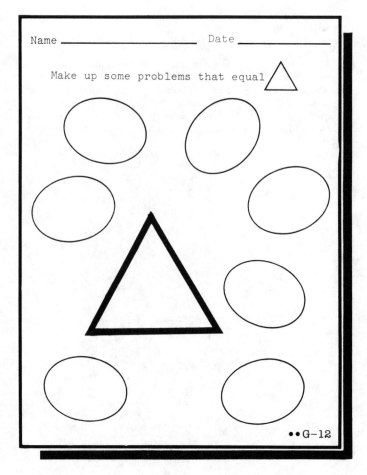

Name _____ Date _____

Make up some problems that equal △

••G-12

Before giving children this lab sheet, children should be given opportunities to go through rod experiences with problems of this sort. (If no rods are available, dot arrays or diagrams on squared paper will do.)

···G13

Distributive law

This lab sheet deals with the distributive law. One can see that the members of each pair of problems on this sheet are equivalent.

Example

$$(4 + 2) \times 3 = 6 \times 3 = 18$$
$$(4 \times 3) + (2 \times 3) = 12 + 6 = 18$$

In general terms, the distributive law tells us that

$$(\square + \triangle) \times \bigcirc = (\square \times \bigcirc) + (\triangle \times \bigcirc)$$

and

$$\bigcirc \times (\square + \triangle) = (\bigcirc \times \square) + (\bigcirc \times \triangle)$$

are always true, provided $\square$, $\triangle$, and $\bigcirc$ are placeholders for whole numbers.

Example A

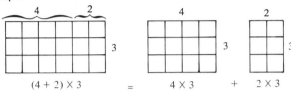

$(4 + 2) \times 3$ = 4×3 + 2×3

Example B

| purple + red | | same length as | dark green |

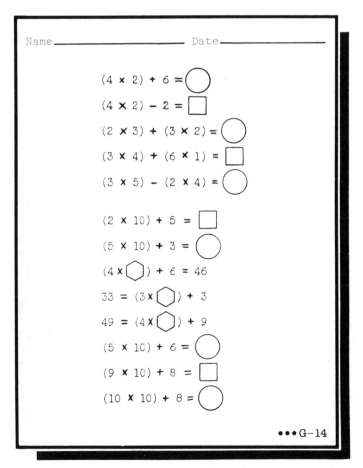

Name _____ Date _____

$(4 + 2) \times 3 = \hexagon$

$(4 \times 3) + (2 \times 3) = \bigcirc$

$3 \times (4 + 2) = \square$

$(3 \times 4) + (3 \times 2) = \hexagon$

$(2 \times 6) + (2 \times 4) = \bigcirc$

$2 \times (6 + 4) = \square$

$(4 \times 3) + (4 \times 1) = \hexagon$

$4 \times (3 + \hexagon) = 16$

$\hexagon \times (3 + 1) = 16$

$(\hexagon \times 3) + (\hexagon \times 1) = 16$

Make up some more problems of your own!

···G-13

Name _____ Date _____

$(4 \times 2) + 6 = \bigcirc$

$(4 \times 2) - 2 = \square$

$(2 \times 3) + (3 \times 2) = \bigcirc$

$(3 \times 4) + (6 \times 1) = \square$

$(3 \times 5) - (2 \times 4) = \bigcirc$

$(2 \times 10) + 5 = \square$

$(5 \times 10) + 3 = \bigcirc$

$(4 \times \hexagon) + 6 = 46$

$33 = (3 \times \hexagon) + 3$

$49 = (4 \times \hexagon) + 9$

$(5 \times 10) + 6 = \bigcirc$

$(9 \times 10) + 8 = \square$

$(10 \times 10) + 8 = \bigcirc$

···G-14

Name_____ Date_____

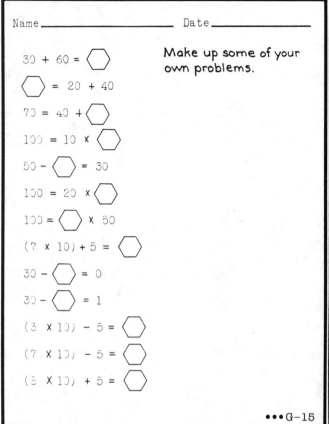

Make up some of your own problems.

$30 + 60 = \bighexagon$

$\bighexagon = 20 + 40$

$70 = 40 + \bighexagon$

$100 = 10 \times \bighexagon$

$50 - \bighexagon = 30$

$100 = 20 \times \bighexagon$

$100 = \bighexagon \times 50$

$(7 \times 10) + 5 = \bighexagon$

$30 - \bighexagon = 0$

$30 - \bighexagon = 1$

$(3 \times 10) - 5 = \bighexagon$

$(7 \times 10) - 5 = \bighexagon$

$(5 \times 10) + 5 = \bighexagon$

•••G–15

Name_____ Date_____

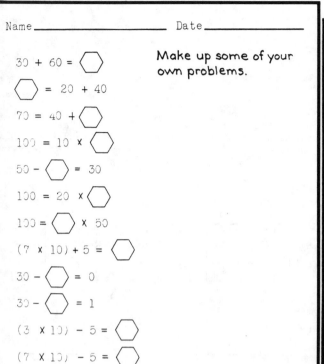

$$\begin{array}{cccc} 30 & 25 & 10 & 15 \\ +30 & +25 & +10 & +15 \end{array}$$

$3 \times 20 = \bigcirc \qquad 8 \times 10 = \bigcirc$

$$\begin{array}{cccc} 10 & 100 & 50 & 15 \\ 10 & 25 & 25 & 15 \\ +10 & +25 & +25 & +15 \end{array}$$

$4 \times 15 = \bigcirc \qquad 3 \times 25 = \bigcirc$

•••G–16

••• **G17–G20**

A reminder

In an open sentence, every frame with the same shape is a placeholder for the same number. Therefore the only correct solution to the open sentence

$$\square + \square + \square + \square + \square + \square = 12$$

is

$$\boxed{2} + \boxed{2} + \boxed{2} + \boxed{2} + \boxed{2} + \boxed{2} = 12$$

Solutions for the open sentence

$$16 = \square \times \square \times \bigcirc \times \bigcirc$$

are

$$16 = \boxed{2} \times \boxed{2} \times ②\times ②$$

or

$$16 = \boxed{1} \times \boxed{1} \times ④\times ④$$

or

$$16 = \boxed{4} \times \boxed{4} \times ①\times ①$$

The only correct solution to the open sentence

$$\bigcirc + \bigcirc + \bigcirc = 24$$

is

$$⑧ + ⑧ + ⑧ = 24$$

••• **G20**

Solutions to tricky problems

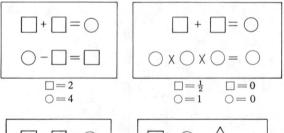

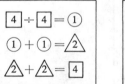

The clue is: $\square \div \square = ①$.
Any number divided by itself is one.
The rest is easy.

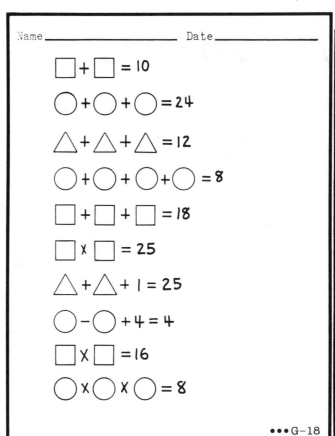

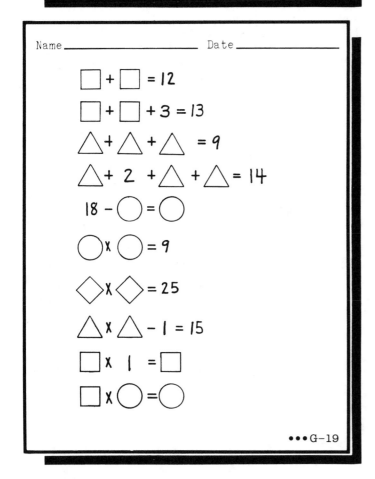

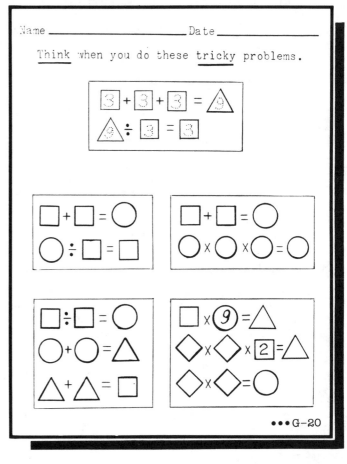

G-17

$\square = 12$

$\square + \square = 12$

$\square + \square + \square = 12$

$\square + \square + \square + \square = 12$

$\square + \square + \square + \square + \square + \square = 12$

$16 = \square \times \square$

$16 = \bigcirc + \bigcirc$

$16 = \square \times \square \times \diamondsuit \times \diamondsuit$

$\square \times 1 = 12$ $12 = 4 \times \square$

$\square \times 2 = 12$ $12 = 6 \times \square$

$\square \times 3 = 12$ $12 = 12 \times \square$

•••G–17

G-18

$\square + \square = 10$

$\bigcirc + \bigcirc + \bigcirc = 24$

$\triangle + \triangle + \triangle = 12$

$\bigcirc + \bigcirc + \bigcirc + \bigcirc = 8$

$\square + \square + \square = 18$

$\square \times \square = 25$

$\triangle + \triangle + 1 = 25$

$\bigcirc - \bigcirc + 4 = 4$

$\square \times \square = 16$

$\bigcirc \times \bigcirc \times \bigcirc = 8$

•••G–18

G-19

$\square + \square = 12$

$\square + \square + 3 = 13$

$\triangle + \triangle + \triangle = 9$

$\triangle + 2 + \triangle + \triangle = 14$

$18 - \bigcirc = \bigcirc$

$\bigcirc \times \bigcirc = 9$

$\diamondsuit \times \diamondsuit = 25$

$\triangle \times \triangle - 1 = 15$

$\square \times 1 = \square$

$\square \times \bigcirc = \bigcirc$

•••G–19

G-20

Think when you do these tricky problems.

$3 + 3 + 3 = \triangle$

$\triangle \div 3 = 3$

$\square + \square = \bigcirc$

$\bigcirc \div \square = \square$

$\square + \square = \bigcirc$

$\bigcirc \times \bigcirc \times \bigcirc = \bigcirc$

$\square \div \square = \bigcirc$

$\bigcirc + \bigcirc = \triangle$

$\triangle + \triangle = \square$

$\square \times 9 = \triangle$

$\diamondsuit \times \diamondsuit \times 2 = \triangle$

$\diamondsuit \times \diamondsuit = \bigcirc$

•••G–20

H Fractions

How is it possible that many first-graders can solve a difficult problem such as

$$(\tfrac{1}{3} \times 9) + (\tfrac{2}{5} \times 10) - (\tfrac{1}{2} \times 8) = \square \quad ?$$

This can be done because these first-graders are learning fractions by making models and because vocabulary is kept to a minimum.

The words *fractions, numerator, denominator, mixed number*, etc., are not necessary to solve the preceding problem. The child already understands "one half of" as a result of sharing candy bars and marbles. We show him other fractional parts through many experiences with Cuisenaire® rods, number lines, paper cutting, and other activities.

The child gathers from these experiences that numbers have many names—some easy, some tricky. The names we use depend on what we need them for. The simple name '3' is handy for telling your age or describing the size of a collection. The tricky name for the number 3, '$\tfrac{1}{3}$ of 9,' is handy to use for measuring a length or sharing 9 things equally among 3 people. '7 − 4' is a good name for 3 when we try to think how much we have left of 7 things after we give away 4. '3 × 1' is a good name for 3 when we watch, with an eagle eye, that we get our share of candy as it is passed around among 3 people.

With this kind of flexibility as a stimulus to his thinking, the child enjoys exchanging tricky names for simple names and is off to a good start in finding answers.

$$(\tfrac{1}{3} \times 9) + (\tfrac{2}{5} \times 10) - (\tfrac{1}{2} \times 8) = \square$$
$$\quad\; 3 \quad + \quad 4 \quad - \quad 4 \quad = \boxed{3}$$

Before making suggestions for classroom activities to begin teaching fractions, we may observe:

1 "$\tfrac{2}{3}$ *of* 9" makes more sense than "$\tfrac{2}{3}$ *times* 9." We say "$\tfrac{2}{3}$ of 9" but write it as "$\tfrac{2}{3} \times 9$."

2 $\qquad\qquad \tfrac{9}{3}, \quad 9 \div 3, \quad 3\overline{)9}$

are all division statements. They *may* all be read as "nine divided by three."

3 Any whole number may be written in a fractional notation. The number 3 may be written as $\tfrac{3}{1}$, or $\tfrac{6}{2}$, or $\tfrac{9}{3}$. When we use fractional notation for a whole number we are not using the simplest name.

Fractions are treated as a form of division. In this program, children are introduced to fractional notation and vocabulary *before* they are introduced to the notation for ordinary division. The reason for this is that the children's own speech and concept development suggests an early introduction to fractions. They use the concepts *half, quarter*, etc., in sharing things and measuring things.

Suggested activities

Instead of providing a theoretical framework about the place of fractions in the number system, these general notes give practical suggestions for introductory work. These suggestions include the use of the chalkboard, sets of objects, rods, and the number line.

Fractions illustrated on the board

1 This circle

is now divided into

. . . [2] equal parts.
Each part is . . . [$\tfrac{1}{2}$] of the circle.

2 This square

is now divided into

. . . [4] equal parts

Now 1 of the 4 parts is colored.

. . . [$\tfrac{1}{4}$]
How many parts are left uncolored? [$\tfrac{3}{4}$]

3 This shape

has 1 part colored. It is 1 out of . . . [3] equal parts of the shape.

The part is called . . . [$\tfrac{1}{3}$] of the shape.

4 A frame

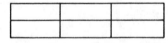

How many equal parts is the frame divided into? [6 parts]
Each part is called . . . [$\tfrac{1}{6}$].
Color 4 of the 6 parts, or . . . [four-sixths] of all the parts.

5 Many figures

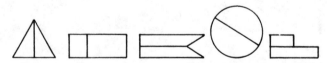

Which shapes are divided into 2 halves? Write '$\tfrac{1}{2}$' in each half. Cross out the shapes that are not divided into 2 halves.

6   Children

There are ☐ children.

☐ children are boys.

☐ children are girls.

How many of the 5 are boys?   [two out of five—$\frac{2}{5}$]
How many of the 5 are girls?   [three out of five—$\frac{3}{5}$]

7   Marbles

Jack gets $\frac{2}{3}$ of 6 marbles.   Peggy gets $\frac{1}{3}$ of 6 marbles.
Jack gets ____ marbles.   Peggy gets ____ marbles.

All of these activities can be done with blocks, paper cutouts, etc. (See *First-Grade Diary* index under "Fractions.")

Fractions illustrated with rods

1   Rod "families": halves, thirds, fourths

Halves
In each rod pair, the *smaller* rod is as long as *one half* of the *larger* rod.

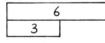
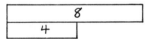
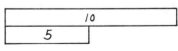
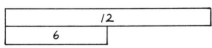

$1 = \frac{1}{2}$ of 2.
$2 = \frac{1}{2}$ of 4.
$3 = \frac{1}{2}$ of 6.

In every pair, the *larger* rod is as long as 2 of the *smaller* rod.

$2 = 2 \times 1$
$4 = 2 \times 2$
$6 = 2 \times 3$

Thirds
In this pair, the small rod is *not* one half of the large rod. What is it? How many small rods will you need to make the large rod? The *small* rod is 1 of the 3 that make the *large* rod.

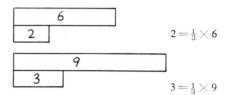   We say, "one-third."

Find other pairs of rods in which the small rod is $\frac{1}{3}$ as long as the large rod.

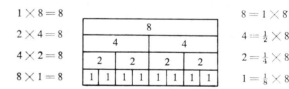

$2 = \frac{1}{3} \times 6$

$3 = \frac{1}{3} \times 9$

In every pair, the large rod is as long as . . . [3]   of the small rods. Prove it with the rods.

$3 \times 2 = 6$ $2 = \frac{1}{3}$ of 6
$3 \times 3 = 9$ $3 = \frac{1}{3} \times 9$
$3 \times 4 = 12$ $4 = \frac{1}{3}$ of 12

Ask children to make "rod families" showing small rods which are $\frac{1}{4}$ of the large rods.

2   One-color patterns of a rod
From the one-color patterns of a rod, we can learn many relationships found in multiplication and fractions.

For example, the pattern of the brown rod (8 white units long) is given.

$1 \times 8 = 8$ $8 = 1 \times 8$
$2 \times 4 = 8$ $4 = \frac{1}{2} \times 8$
$4 \times 2 = 8$ $2 = \frac{1}{4} \times 8$
$8 \times 1 = 8$ $1 = \frac{1}{8} \times 8$

Teacher: Find a rod which is as long as $\frac{3}{8}$ of 8.

$\boxed{3} = \frac{3}{8} \times 8$

Build a rod train of $(\frac{1}{8} \times 8)$ plus $(\frac{1}{2} \times 8)$.

$(\frac{1}{8} \times 8) + (\frac{1}{2} \times 8)$

Build a rod train of $(\frac{2}{4} \times 8)$ plus $(\frac{1}{2} \times 8)$. How long is that train?

$(\frac{2}{4} \times 8) + (\frac{1}{2} \times 8) = \boxed{8}$

3 Comparison of all ten rods with one another

Compare all rods with the light green (3) rod. What part of the light green rod is each rod?

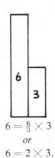

$1 = \frac{1}{3} \times 3$ $2 = \frac{2}{3} \times 3$ $3 = \frac{3}{3} \times 3$
or 1×3

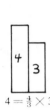 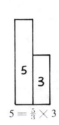

$4 = \frac{4}{3} \times 3$ $5 = \frac{5}{3} \times 3$ $6 = \frac{6}{3} \times 3$
or
$6 = 2 \times 3.$

Fractions illustrated on the number line

1

What should we name the point where the cross is? *It is halfway between 0 and 1. It is "one half of 1." We write* $\frac{1}{2}$. (Children often write $0\frac{1}{2}$. This should be accepted.)

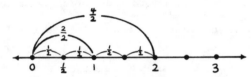

How many $\frac{1}{2}$'s are in 1 unit? *There are two of the* $\frac{1}{2}$'s *in 1 unit.*

$$2 \times \frac{1}{2} = 1$$
$$\frac{2}{2} = 1$$

How many $\frac{1}{2}$'s are in 2 units? *There are four of the* $\frac{1}{2}$'s *in 2 units.*

$$4 \times \frac{1}{2} = 2$$
$$\frac{4}{2} = 2$$

We now have two names for one: 1 and $\frac{2}{2}$.
We have two names for two: 2 and $\frac{4}{2}$.

2

Where is the arrow on our number line? *It is halfway between 0 and* $\frac{1}{2}$. *It is half of one half.* ($\frac{1}{2}$ *of* $\frac{1}{2}$)

How much is this of 1 unit? *It is* $\frac{1}{4}$ *of 1.*

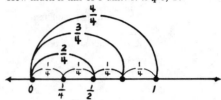

· H1–H3
Identifying fractional parts of one unit

Before the children are given these lab sheets to do, there should be a great deal of non-writing activity.

Suggestions for preliminary work
The teacher can make large oaktag cutouts to illustrate the relative sizes of fractional parts.

a whole   3 thirds   2 halves

She can use homemade plywood puzzles, whose various sets of fractional parts fit into the frame.

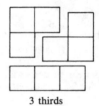

frame   red halves   blue thirds

fourths   sixths   eighths

The teacher can use the chalkboard occasionally to introduce the following notations in a meaningful context:

$\frac{1}{2}$ of $\square$, $\frac{1}{3}$ of $\square$, $\frac{1}{4}$ of $\square$

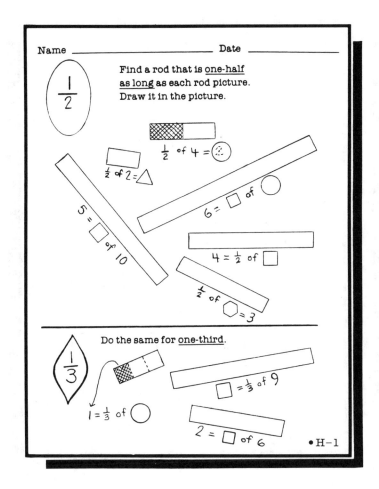

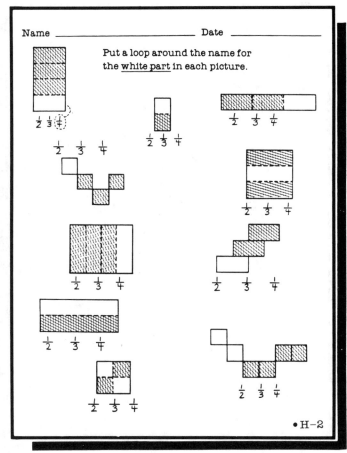

· H2

Sample non-writing activities. The teacher says to the children:

1 Find the rod that is one half of the purple rod. Yes, it is the red rod because two red rods make the purple rod.

2 Let's put away our rods by playing a game. Put away the rod that is one third as long as the light green rod. It is the _____ rod. [On chalkboard: $\frac{1}{3}$ of 3 = □.] Put away the rod that is one third as long as the blue rod. [On chalkboard: $\frac{1}{3}$ of 9 = □.]

3 Now I'll write some more directions on the chalkboard:

$\frac{1}{2}$ of 8   Put that rod away.
$\frac{1}{4}$ of 8   Put that rod away.
$\frac{1}{2}$ of 10   Put that rod away.

On H2, rods fit on the drawings. The children should cover the drawings, one at a time, with rods. Then they should uncover the white part of the drawing.

For the first drawing, 4 red rods are used. *One* of the 4 red rods is removed to uncover the white space. "One out of four" is called "one-fourth" and written:

$$\frac{1}{4} \quad \begin{array}{l} \text{one} \\ \text{out of} \\ \text{four} \end{array}$$

Now ask how many of the 4 rods are left on the picture. *Three* of the 4 are left.

$$\frac{3}{4} \quad \begin{array}{l} \text{three} \\ \text{out of} \\ \text{four} \end{array}$$

In the last two drawings children can discover that several names for the parts are acceptable.

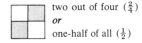

two out of four ($\frac{2}{4}$)
or
one-half of all ($\frac{1}{2}$)

Name _____ Date _____

WHAT PART IS SHADED IN?

$\frac{1}{2}$ $\frac{1}{3}$ $\frac{1}{4}$ $\frac{1}{5}$ $\frac{1}{6}$ $\frac{1}{7}$ $\frac{1}{8}$ $\frac{1}{9}$ $\frac{1}{10}$ $\frac{1}{11}$ $\frac{1}{12}$ $\frac{1}{13}$ $\frac{1}{14}$ $\frac{1}{15}$ $\frac{1}{16}$

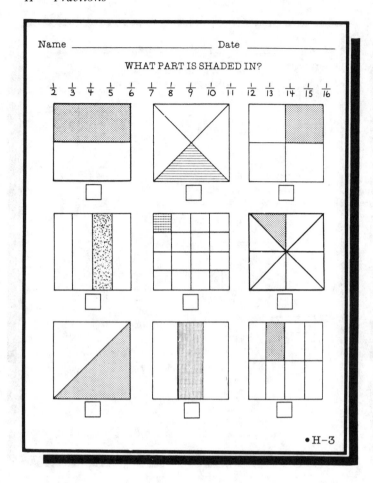

• H–3

Name _____ Date _____

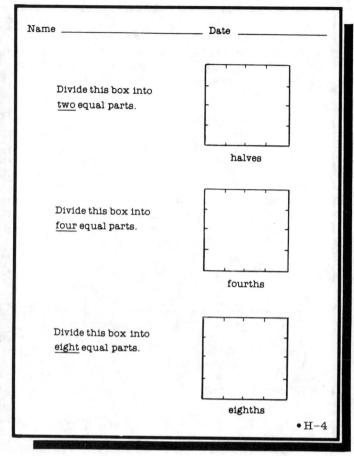

Divide this box into <u>two</u> equal parts.

halves

Divide this box into <u>four</u> equal parts.

fourths

Divide this box into <u>eight</u> equal parts.

eighths

• H–4

· **H3**

On H3 children write the name of the shaded part in the little box under each large square. The fraction numerals at the top of the page assist the children in doing this.

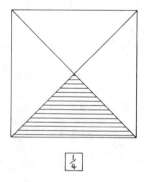

$\frac{1}{4}$

· **H4**
Suggestions for preliminary work

1 Plan activities that involve folding, tearing, or cutting paper into halves, fourths, eighths. (See *Diary* index under "Fractions.")

2 Use the chalkboard for work in distinguishing 2 equal parts of a unit (halves) and 2 unequal parts of a unit, 3 equal parts of a unit (thirds) and 3 unequal parts of a unit, etc.

3 Let the children engage in activities such as slicing pies made out of modeling clay into halves, thirds, fourths, fifths, etc.

There are no unique correct answers to the problems on H4. For example, the first problem may be done correctly in many different ways:

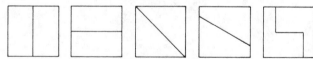

Name _____ Date _____

Use your rods for this:

$$\frac{1}{2} \ of \ 2 = \square$$

$$\frac{1}{2} \ of \ 4 = \square$$

$$\frac{1}{2} \ of \ 6 = \square$$

$$\frac{1}{2} \ of \ 8 = \square$$

$$\frac{1}{2} \ of \ \bigcirc = \square$$

$$\frac{1}{2} \ of \ \bigcirc = \square$$

$$\frac{1}{2} \ of \ 20 = \square$$

• H-5

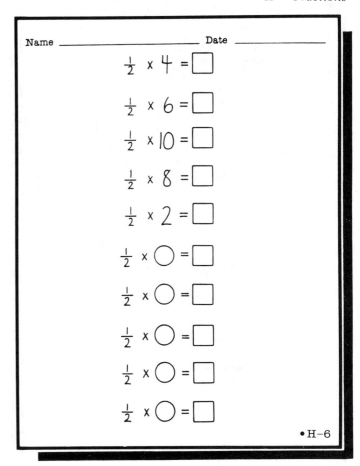

Name _____ Date _____

$$\frac{1}{2} \times 4 = \square$$

$$\frac{1}{2} \times 6 = \square$$

$$\frac{1}{2} \times 10 = \square$$

$$\frac{1}{2} \times 8 = \square$$

$$\frac{1}{2} \times 2 = \square$$

$$\frac{1}{2} \times \bigcirc = \square$$

$$\frac{1}{2} \times \bigcirc = \square$$

$$\frac{1}{2} \times \bigcirc = \square$$

$$\frac{1}{2} \times \bigcirc = \square$$

$$\frac{1}{2} \times \bigcirc = \square$$

• H-6

· H5, H6

These two sheets are the first to contain problems that involve actual computation with fractions. There are many ways in which problems of this type can be represented with concrete materials.

Problem 1: $\frac{1}{2} \times 4 = \square$

Restatement of problem:

$\frac{1}{2}$ of 4 objects are $\square$ objects.

Representation of problem:

Solution: $\frac{1}{2} \times 4 = \boxed{2}$

Problem 2: $\frac{1}{2} \times 8 = \square$

Restatement of problem:

Two jumps of $\square$ units equal 8 units.

Representation of problem:

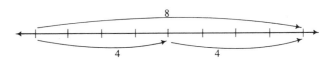

Solution: $\frac{1}{2} \times 8 = \boxed{4}$

All these problems can, of course, be illustrated very easily with the rods, as we have previously suggested.

$\frac{1}{2}$ of 4 $\frac{1}{2}$ of 4

$\frac{1}{2} \times 4 = 2$

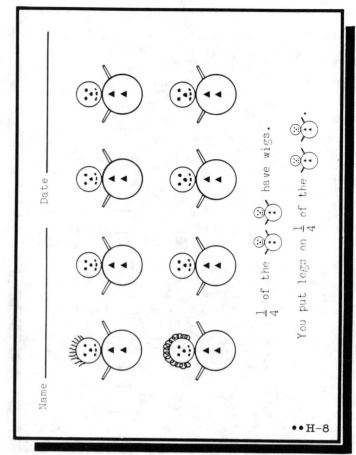

·· H7–H12

Identifying fractional parts of a group

In each problem on these sheets, the children are asked to mark off some fractional part of a group of objects. The problems in which the children are required to mark off $\frac{1}{n}$ of the members of a group are much easier than those on later sheets on which children are asked to mark off $\frac{2}{n}$, $\frac{3}{n}$ or $\frac{4}{n}$ of the members of a group.

Eight Snowmen Booklet

These three sheets, which can be put together in booklet form, are simple enough to be read by first-graders. They contain only fractions whose numerators are 1.

Children can add their own directions on the bottom of the page. As an example, to H10, one child added:

$\frac{1}{2}$ of ⬡⬡ have hair.

$\frac{1}{8}$ of ⬡⬡ have balloons.

Note: "$\frac{1}{2}$ of 6 cookies" means $\frac{1}{2} \times 6$ cookies, but "$2\frac{1}{2}$ of 6 cookies" means just $2\frac{1}{2}$ cookies!

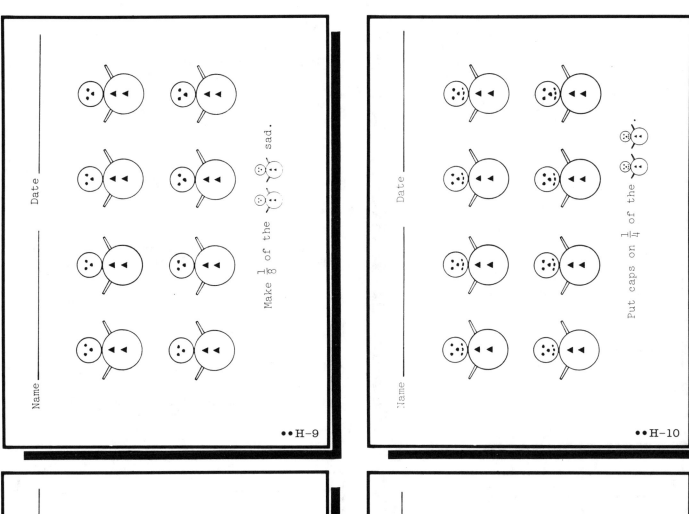

Name _____

Date _____

Make $\frac{1}{8}$ of the 🐞 sad.

•• H–9

Name _____

Date _____

Put caps on $\frac{1}{4}$ of the 🐞.

•• H–10

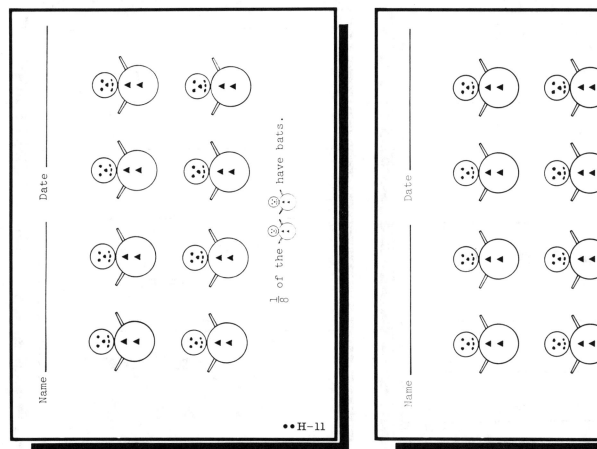

Name _____

Date _____

$\frac{1}{8}$ of the 🐞 have bats.

•• H–11

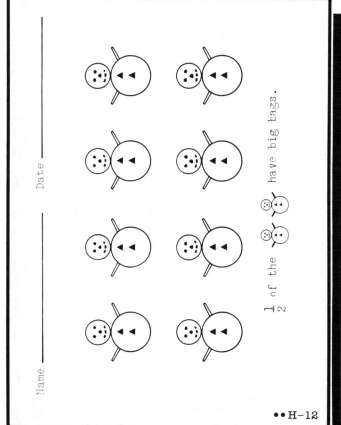

Name _____

Date _____

$\frac{1}{2}$ of the 🐞 have big tags.

•• H–12

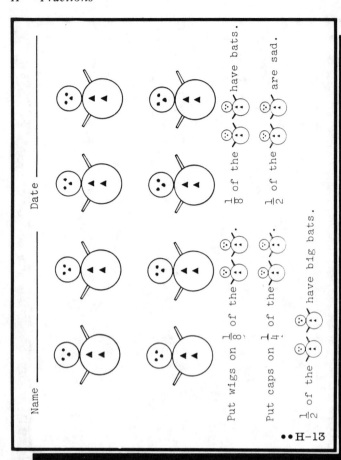

•• H-13

•• H13

This page is similar to the preceding, except for the fact that it contains many more instructions. Children still handle only $\frac{1}{8}$, $\frac{1}{4}$, and $\frac{1}{2}$.

•• H14, H15

These lab sheets are teaching (self-teaching if children can handle them alone) pages about $\frac{2}{3}$, $\frac{3}{5}$, $\frac{2}{4}$, $\frac{6}{9}$, etc.

•• H17–H23

These sheets make another booklet in which pupils are asked to do something to $\frac{3}{3}$ of 6 children, $\frac{2}{3}$ of 6 children, etc.

Name _____ Date _____

Color 1 of the 5 boxes:

☐ ☐ ☐ ☐ ☐

$\frac{1}{5}$ of the boxes.

Color 2 of the 5 boxes:

☐ ☐ ☐ ☐ ☐

$\frac{2}{5}$ of the boxes.

Color $\frac{3}{5}$ of the boxes:

☐ ☐ ☐ ☐ ☐

⬡→ of the boxes are colored:

■ ■ ■ ☐ ■

Color $\frac{2}{3}$ of the boxes:

☐ ☐ ☐

Color $\frac{5}{6}$ of the boxes:

☐ ☐ ☐ ☐ ☐ ☐ ☐

⬡— of the boxes are colored:

■ ■ ☐ ■ ☐ ■

•• H-14

Name _____ Date _____

Color 3 of the 4 boxes:

☐ ☐ ☐ ☐

$\frac{3}{4}$ of the boxes.

Color $\frac{2}{6}$ of the boxes:

☐ ☐ ☐ ☐ ☐ ☐

Color 1 of every 3 boxes:

☐ ☐ ☐   ☐ ☐ ☐

$\frac{1}{3}$ of the boxes.

Color 2 of every 4 boxes:

☐ ☐ ☐
☐ ☐ ☐

$\frac{2}{4}$ of the boxes.

Color $\frac{3}{5}$ of the boxes:

☐ ☐ ☐ ☐ ☐   ☐ ☐ ☐ ☐ ☐

⬡— of these boxes are colored:

■ ■ ☐ ■ ■ ☐ ■ ■ ☐

⬡— of these boxes are colored:

■ ■ ■ ■ ■ ■ ☐ ☐ ☐

•• H-15

Name_____ Date_____

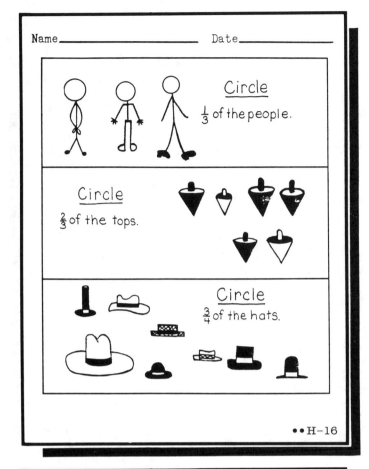

Circle $\frac{1}{3}$ of the people.

Circle $\frac{2}{3}$ of the tops.

Circle $\frac{3}{4}$ of the hats.

••H–16

Name_____ Date_____

My Fractions Book II

Color!

••H–17

Date_____ Name_____

$\frac{3}{3}$ of the 👦 have wigs.

••H–18

Date_____ Name_____

$\frac{1}{3}$ of the 👦 have caps.

••H–19

Name _____   Date _____

Make $\frac{1}{2}$ of the  glad.

•• H-20

Name _____   Date _____

$\frac{1}{6}$ of the  have shoes.

•• H-21

Name _____   Date _____

$\frac{1}{3}$ of the  have bats.

•• H-22

Name _____   Date _____

$\frac{6}{6}$ of the  have wigs. $\frac{2}{6}$ of the  have shoes.

$\frac{3}{6}$ of the  have caps. $\frac{1}{3}$ of the  have bats.

$\frac{2}{3}$ of the  are glad.

•• H-23

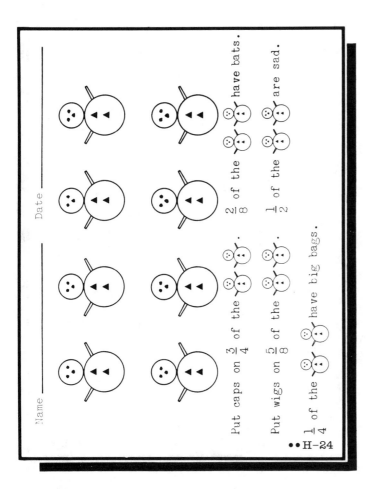

Date _____

Name _____

... have bats.

... are sad.

$\frac{2}{8}$ of the ...

$\frac{1}{2}$ of the ...

Put caps on $\frac{3}{4}$ of the ...

Put wigs on $\frac{5}{8}$ of the ...

$\frac{1}{4}$ of the ... have big bags.

•• H-24

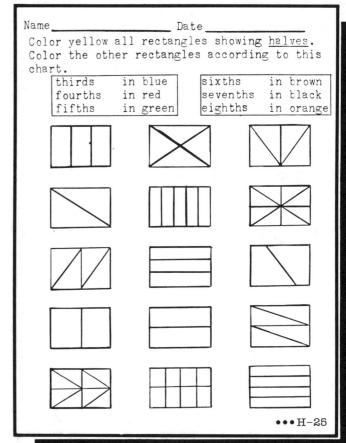

Name _____   Date _____

Color yellow all rectangles showing <u>halves</u>.
Color the other rectangles according to this chart.

thirds	in blue		sixths	in brown
fourths	in red		sevenths	in black
fifths	in green		eighths	in orange

••• H-25

••• H26

Learning names for mixed numbers

One child gave a puzzling, but mathematically correct, answer to the following problem.

Problem

Put a sad mouth on $\frac{1}{4}$ of the faces.
Put hair on $\frac{1}{2}$ of the faces.

Expected answer

Child's answer

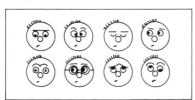

Each face has $\frac{1}{4}$ of a sad mouth.
Each face has $\frac{1}{2}$ head of hair.

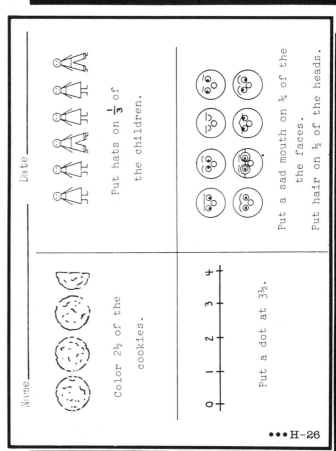

Date _____

Name _____

Put hats on $\frac{1}{3}$ of the children.

Put a sad mouth on $\frac{1}{4}$ of the faces.

Put hair on $\frac{1}{2}$ of the heads.

Color $2\frac{1}{2}$ of the cookies.

Put a dot at $3\frac{1}{2}$.

0   1   2   3   4

••• H-26

151

Name_____ Date_____

Look at each picture. If <u>one</u> <u>fourth</u> $\left(\frac{1}{4}\right)$ is shaded in, shade in <u>another</u> <u>one</u> <u>fourth</u>.

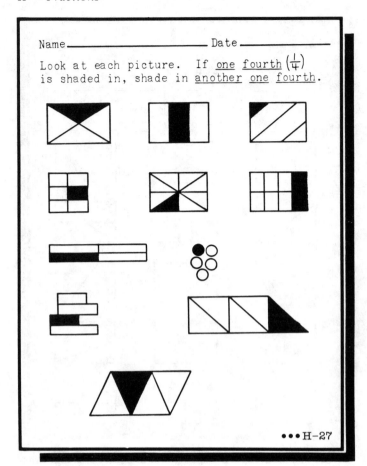

●●● H-27

Name _____ Date_____

Divide these rectangles into sixths.

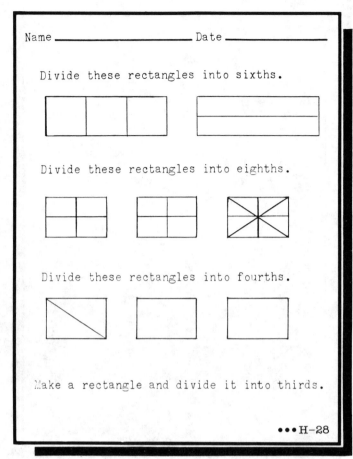

Divide these rectangles into eighths.

Divide these rectangles into fourths.

Make a rectangle and divide it into thirds.

●●● H-28

• • • **H27**

These are not fourths:

not $\frac{1}{4}$

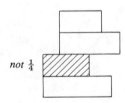

not $\frac{1}{4}$

Only these are fourths:

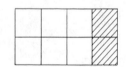

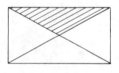

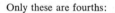

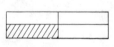

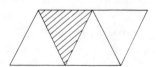

Name _____ Date _____

(1)   (5)   (10)   (25)   (50)

Color in: The coin that is worth $\frac{1}{4}$ of a dollar.

(1)   (5)   (10)   (25)   (50)

Color in: The coin that is worth $\frac{1}{10}$ of a dollar.

(1)   (5)   (10)   (25)   (50)

Color in: The coin that is worth $\frac{1}{2}$ of a dollar.

(1)   (5)   (10)   (25)   (50)

Color in: The coin that is worth $\frac{1}{100}$ of a dollar.

(1)   (5)   (10)   (25)   (50)

Color in: The coin that is worth $\frac{1}{20}$ of a dollar.

••• H-30

••• H30
Parts of a dollar

A great deal of oral work should precede work on this lab sheet. The children may want to make their own play money so that they can "act out" problems.

Suggestion for preliminary work

Oral word problems

I have $\frac{1}{2}$ of a dime and $\frac{1}{10}$ of a dime under a cup. How much money is under the cup. [6 cents.]

Jack has $\frac{1}{5}$ of a dollar. Bill has $\frac{1}{4}$ of a dollar.
Who has more money? [Bill.]
How much money does Jack have? [20 cents.]
How much money does Bill have? [25 cents.]
How much money do they have together? [45 cents.]

The children can also make charts showing the relationship between coins of different denominations.

	Pennies	Nickels	Dimes	Quarters	Half dollars	Dollar bills	Five-dollar bills	Ten-dollar bills
One penny	1	$\frac{1}{5}$	$\frac{1}{10}$					$\frac{1}{1000}$
One nickel	5	1	$\frac{1}{2}$					
One dime	10	2	1					
One quarter	25	5	$2\frac{1}{2}$					
One dollar	100	20	10	4	2	1	$\frac{1}{5}$	$\frac{1}{10}$

Some children might be able to complete the whole chart.

Name_____ Date_____

Fill this cup $\frac{1}{2}$ full.

Fill this cup $\frac{1}{4}$ full.

Fill this cup $\frac{3}{4}$ full.

Fill this cup $\frac{1}{3}$ full.

Fill this cup $\frac{2}{3}$ full.

••• H-31

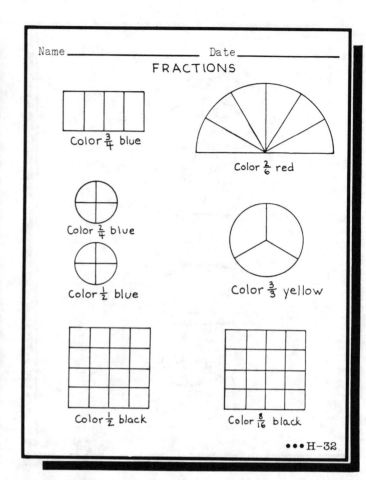

Name_____ Date_____

FRACTIONS

Color $\frac{3}{4}$ blue

Color $\frac{2}{6}$ red

Color $\frac{2}{4}$ blue

Color $\frac{1}{2}$ blue

Color $\frac{3}{3}$ yellow

Color $\frac{1}{2}$ black

Color $\frac{8}{16}$ black

••• H-32

Name_____ Date_____

$\frac{1}{3}$ of the houses have smoke.

$\frac{4}{6}$ of the houses have doors.

$\frac{1}{2}$ of the balloons have strings.

••• H-33

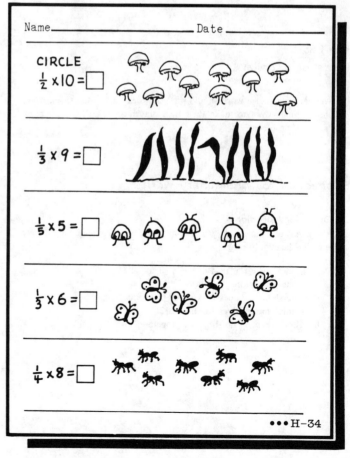

Name_____ Date_____

CIRCLE
$\frac{1}{2} \times 10 = \square$

$\frac{1}{3} \times 9 = \square$

$\frac{1}{5} \times 5 = \square$

$\frac{1}{3} \times 6 = \square$

$\frac{1}{4} \times 8 = \square$

••• H-34

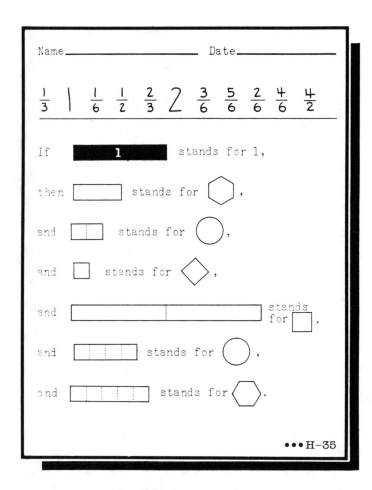

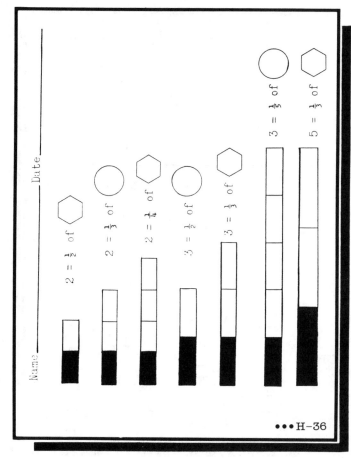

···H35

Fractions with Cuisenaire® rods

Numerals are given at the top of the lab sheet for reference in writing.
The designs match rods.

When completed, the sentence reads as follows:

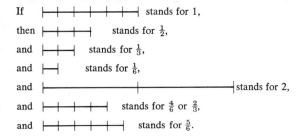

Name _____ Date _____

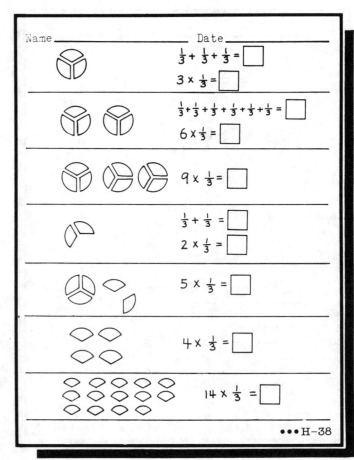

$\frac{1}{2} + \frac{1}{2} = \square$

$2 \times \frac{1}{2} = \square$

$\frac{1}{2} + \frac{1}{2} + \frac{1}{2} + \frac{1}{2} = \square$

$4 \times \frac{1}{2} = \square$

$\frac{1}{2} + \frac{1}{2} + \frac{1}{2} + \frac{1}{2} + \frac{1}{2} + \frac{1}{2} = \square$

$6 \times \frac{1}{2} = \square$

$8 \times \frac{1}{2} = \square$

$\frac{1}{2} + \frac{1}{2} + \frac{1}{2} = \square$

$3 \times \frac{1}{2} = \square$

$5 \times \frac{1}{2} = \square$

• • • H-37

Name _____ Date _____

$\frac{1}{3} + \frac{1}{3} + \frac{1}{3} = \square$

$3 \times \frac{1}{3} = \square$

$\frac{1}{3} + \frac{1}{3} + \frac{1}{3} + \frac{1}{3} + \frac{1}{3} + \frac{1}{3} = \square$

$6 \times \frac{1}{3} = \square$

$9 \times \frac{1}{3} = \square$

$\frac{1}{3} + \frac{1}{3} = \square$

$2 \times \frac{1}{3} = \square$

$5 \times \frac{1}{3} = \square$

$4 \times \frac{1}{3} = \square$

$14 \times \frac{1}{3} = \square$

• • • H-38

Name _____ Date _____

8

$\frac{1}{2} \times 8 = \square$ $\frac{5}{8} \times 8 = \square$

$\frac{2}{8} \times 8 = \square$ $\frac{8}{8} \times 8 = \square$

$\frac{3}{8} \times 8 = \square$ $\frac{9}{8} \times 8 = \square$

$\frac{4}{8} \times 8 = \square$ $\frac{16}{8} \times 8 = \square$

$\frac{1}{4} \times 8 = \square$ $\frac{1}{2} \times 8 = \square$

$\frac{2}{4} \times 8 = \square$ $\frac{2}{2} \times 8 = \square$

$\frac{3}{4} \times 8 = \square$ $\frac{3}{2} \times 8 = \square$

$\frac{4}{4} \times 8 = \square$ $\frac{4}{2} \times 8 = \square$

$1 \times 8 = \square$ $2 \times 8 = \square$

• • • H-39

Name _____ Date _____

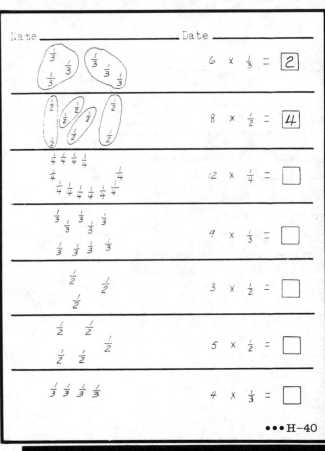

$6 \times \frac{1}{3} = \boxed{2}$

$8 \times \frac{1}{2} = \boxed{4}$

$12 \times \frac{1}{4} = \square$

$9 \times \frac{1}{3} = \square$

$3 \times \frac{1}{2} = \square$

$5 \times \frac{1}{2} = \square$

$4 \times \frac{1}{3} = \square$

• • • H-40

···H37, H38, H40
Repeated addition of fractions

Just as we defined multiplication of two whole numbers in terms of repeated addition, multiplication of a whole number and a fraction can be explained in the same way.

Examples

$$7 \times \tfrac{1}{2} = (\tfrac{1}{2} + \tfrac{1}{2}) + (\tfrac{1}{2} + \tfrac{1}{2}) + (\tfrac{1}{2} + \tfrac{1}{2}) + \tfrac{1}{2} = \tfrac{7}{2} = 3\tfrac{1}{2}$$

$$6 \times \tfrac{1}{3} = (\tfrac{1}{3} + \tfrac{1}{3} + \tfrac{1}{3}) + (\tfrac{1}{3} + \tfrac{1}{3} + \tfrac{1}{3}) = \tfrac{6}{3} = 2$$

$$5 \times \tfrac{1}{5} = (\tfrac{1}{5} + \tfrac{1}{5} + \tfrac{1}{5} + \tfrac{1}{5} + \tfrac{1}{5}) = \tfrac{5}{5} = 1$$

$$\tfrac{1}{3} \times 4 = 4 \times \tfrac{1}{3} = (\tfrac{1}{3} + \tfrac{1}{3} + \tfrac{1}{3}) + \tfrac{1}{3} = \tfrac{4}{3} = 1\tfrac{1}{3}$$

$$\tfrac{1}{2} \times 4 = 4 \times \tfrac{1}{2} = (\tfrac{1}{2} + \tfrac{1}{2}) + (\tfrac{1}{2} + \tfrac{1}{2}) = \tfrac{4}{2} = 2$$

The problems on lab sheets H37, H38, and H40 are designed to bring out this basic relationship between addition and multiplication.

···H39, H41, H42
Using Cuisenaire® rods to do problems

Cuisenaire® rods may be placed over the rod outlines at the top of these lab sheets. Other rods may also be used in determining the answers to the problems on these pages. Since every problem on H39 is about the number eight, the pattern of the brown rod is on the top of the page.

Some of the problems on these lab sheets are arranged in sequence. The problems in the sequence on the lower left part of H39 might be solved as follows:

If ☐ (white rod) is the unit rod

then [   ] is the eight rod.

To find what ¼ × 8 is, we ask, "What rod do we need four of to equal the eight rod?"

red	red	red	red
		8		

Four of the red rods equal the eight rod.

red	

Since the red rod equals two, the answer to the first problem is:

$$\tfrac{1}{4} \times 8 = \boxed{2}$$

We now want to know the answer to

$$\tfrac{2}{4} \times 8 = \boxed{}$$

If $\tfrac{1}{4} \times 8$ equals 2, then $\tfrac{2}{4} \times 8$ must be two 2's (or 4). Therefore,

$$\tfrac{2}{4} \times 8 = \boxed{4}$$

Similarly, $\tfrac{3}{4} \times 8$ must be three 2's (or 6)

$$\tfrac{3}{4} \times 8 = \boxed{6}$$

and $\tfrac{4}{4} \times 8$ must be four 2's (or 8)

$$\tfrac{4}{4} \times 8 = \boxed{8}$$

This last answer makes sense, since $\tfrac{4}{4}$ is the same as 1, and we already know that

$$1 \times 8 = 8$$

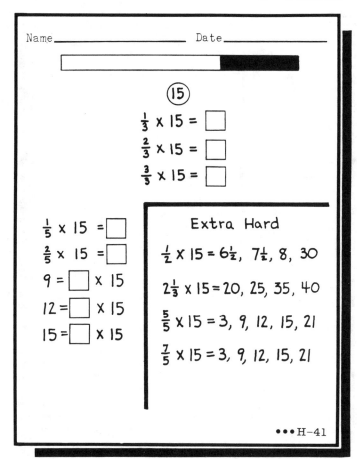

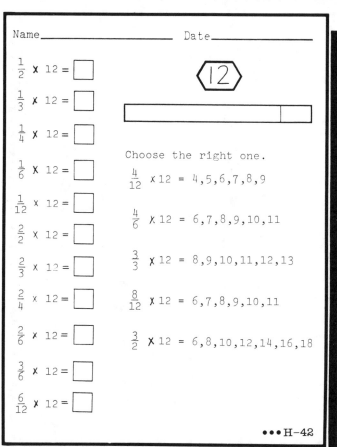

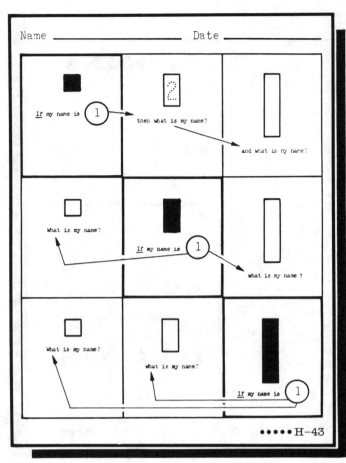

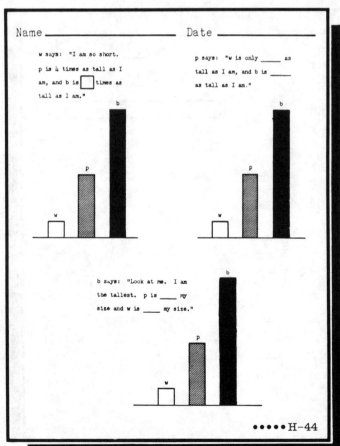

·····H43, H44
Comparing three lengths with one another

Answers for H43

1	2	4
$\frac{1}{2}$	1	2
$\frac{1}{4}$	$\frac{1}{2}$	1

H44

The dialogue among the personified rods is as follows:

White says: "I am so short. Purple is 4 times as tall as I am, and Brown is $\boxed{8}$ times as tall as I am."

Purple says: "White is only $\underline{\frac{1}{4}}$ as tall as I am, and Brown is <u>twice</u> as tall as I am."

Brown says: "Look at me. I am the tallest. Purple is $\underline{\frac{1}{2}}$ [or half] my size and white is $\underline{\frac{1}{8}}$ my size."

You can make up many such rod-comparison stories in the oral work of the class.

·····H47, H49
Computation with fractions

These two lab sheets contain a variety of problems, most of which can be worked out in the same manner as in the illustrations below.

1   **Problem:** $\frac{8}{3} - \Box = 1$

Representation:

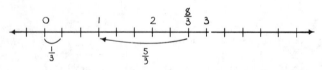

Solution: $\frac{8}{3} - \boxed{\frac{5}{3}} = 1$

2   **Problem:** $\frac{6}{3} \div \frac{2}{3} = \Box$

How many $\frac{2}{3}$ are there in $\frac{6}{3}$? [3]

Representation:

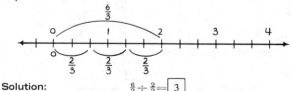

Solution: $\frac{6}{3} \div \frac{2}{3} = \boxed{3}$

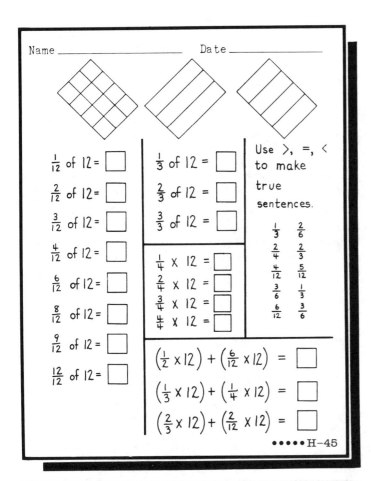

Name _____ Date _____

$\frac{1}{12}$ of 12 = ☐ $\frac{1}{3}$ of 12 = ☐   Use >, =, < to make true sentences.

$\frac{2}{12}$ of 12 = ☐ $\frac{2}{3}$ of 12 = ☐

$\frac{3}{12}$ of 12 = ☐ $\frac{3}{3}$ of 12 = ☐

$\frac{4}{12}$ of 12 = ☐

$\frac{6}{12}$ of 12 = ☐ $\frac{1}{4}$ X 12 = ☐

$\frac{8}{12}$ of 12 = ☐ $\frac{2}{4}$ X 12 = ☐

$\frac{9}{12}$ of 12 = ☐ $\frac{3}{4}$ X 12 = ☐

$\frac{12}{12}$ of 12 = ☐ $\frac{4}{4}$ X 12 = ☐

$\frac{1}{3}$ $\frac{2}{6}$

$\frac{2}{4}$ $\frac{2}{3}$

$\frac{4}{12}$ $\frac{5}{12}$

$\frac{3}{6}$ $\frac{1}{3}$

$\frac{6}{12}$ $\frac{3}{6}$

$\left(\frac{1}{2} \times 12\right) + \left(\frac{6}{12} \times 12\right)$ = ☐

$\left(\frac{1}{3} \times 12\right) + \left(\frac{1}{4} \times 12\right)$ = ☐

$\left(\frac{2}{3} \times 12\right) + \left(\frac{2}{12} \times 12\right)$ = ☐

•••••H-45

Name _____ Date _____

Which is more?   Circle the larger one.

$\frac{1}{3}$ X 12   or $\frac{1}{6}$ X 12

$\frac{1}{2}$ X 6   or $\frac{1}{3}$ X 6

$\frac{1}{9}$ X 9   or $\frac{1}{3}$ X 9

$\frac{1}{5}$ X 10   or $\frac{1}{2}$ X 10

$\frac{2}{5}$ X 15   or $\frac{1}{3}$ X 15

$\frac{10}{100}$ X 100   or $\frac{1}{2}$ X 10

$\frac{1}{3}$ X 6   or $\frac{1}{4}$ X 8

$\frac{7}{10}$ X 10   or $\frac{1}{2}$ X 16

•••••H-46

Name _____ Date _____

Label each point on the number line.

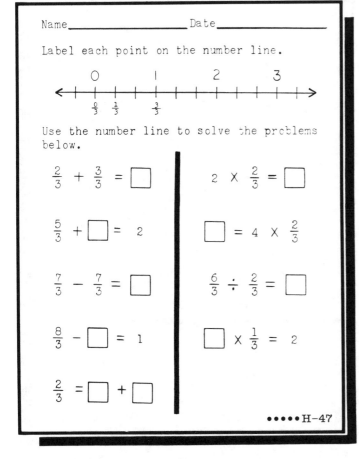

Use the number line to solve the problems below.

$\frac{2}{3} + \frac{3}{3}$ = ☐   2 X $\frac{2}{3}$ = ☐

$\frac{5}{3}$ + ☐ = 2   ☐ = 4 X $\frac{2}{3}$

$\frac{7}{3} - \frac{7}{3}$ = ☐ $\frac{6}{3} \div \frac{2}{3}$ = ☐

$\frac{8}{3}$ - ☐ = 1   ☐ X $\frac{1}{3}$ = 2

$\frac{2}{3}$ = ☐ + ☐

•••••H-47

Name _____ Date _____

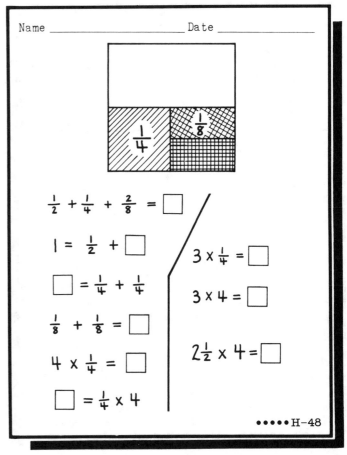

$\frac{1}{2} + \frac{1}{4} + \frac{2}{8}$ = ☐

1 = $\frac{1}{2}$ + ☐

☐ = $\frac{1}{4} + \frac{1}{4}$ 3 X $\frac{1}{4}$ = ☐

$\frac{1}{8} + \frac{1}{8}$ = ☐   3 X 4 = ☐

4 X $\frac{1}{4}$ = ☐ $2\frac{1}{2}$ X 4 = ☐

☐ = $\frac{1}{4}$ X 4

•••••H-48

159

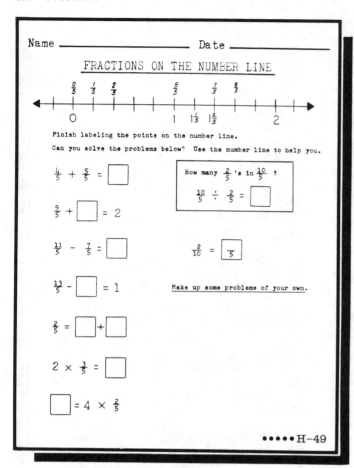

Name _____ Date _____

FRACTIONS ON THE NUMBER LINE

Finish labeling the points on the number line.

Can you solve the problems below? Use the number line to help you.

$\frac{4}{5} + \frac{5}{5} = \boxed{}$

$\frac{9}{5} + \boxed{} = 2$

$\frac{11}{5} - \frac{7}{5} = \boxed{}$

$\frac{13}{5} - \boxed{} = 1$

$\frac{2}{5} = \boxed{} + \boxed{}$

$2 \times \frac{3}{5} = \boxed{}$

$\boxed{} = 4 \times \frac{2}{5}$

How many $\frac{2}{5}$'s in $\frac{10}{5}$?

$\frac{10}{5} \div \frac{2}{5} = \boxed{}$

$\frac{2}{10} = \boxed{\frac{}{5}}$

Make up some problems of your own.

•••••H-49

·····H50–H56

These lab sheets are sequential. They build up systematically the beginning of the concepts of equivalent fractions, mixed numbers, addition of fractions, and division by a fraction.

H50, H51 are about "other names" for 1 and $\frac{1}{2}$. Make up chalkboard exercises like these two sheets and let children take turns choosing the "other names." Extend it to $\frac{1}{3}, \frac{1}{4}, \frac{2}{3}, \frac{3}{4},$ etc.

Children enjoy playing this as a game also. Each child writes five fractional numerals for 1 on a piece of paper. Children take turns reading aloud what they wrote. They get no points for a mistake. They get *one* point for a name someone else has written. They get *three* points for a unique name.

Fraction vocabulary

Not much vocabulary is necessary for this age group. *Fraction, fractional numeral, mixed number* (*top part, bottom part*) are satisfactory.

Don't use the term *improper fraction*. There is nothing "improper" about it. It is a fraction > 1. Remember that *all whole numbers (integers) can be written as fractions.*

We can talk about fractions < 1, fractions $= 1$, fractions > 1.

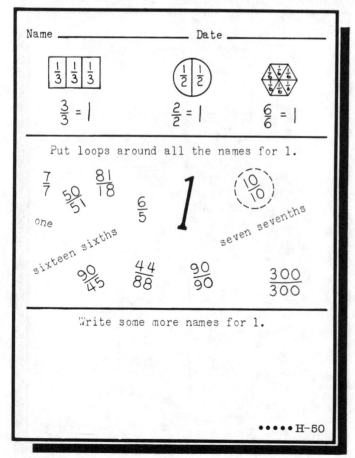

Name _____ Date _____

$\frac{3}{3} = 1$ $\frac{2}{2} = 1$ $\frac{6}{6} = 1$

Put loops around all the names for 1.

$\frac{7}{7}$ $\frac{81}{18}$ $\frac{50}{51}$ $\frac{6}{5}$ **1** $\frac{10}{10}$

one   sixteen sixths   seven sevenths

$\frac{90}{45}$ $\frac{44}{88}$ $\frac{90}{90}$ $\frac{300}{300}$

Write some more names for 1.

•••••H-50

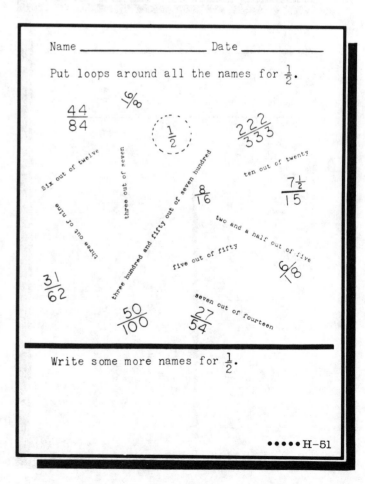

Name _____ Date _____

Put loops around all the names for $\frac{1}{2}$.

$\frac{44}{84}$ $\frac{16}{8}$ $\frac{1}{2}$ $\frac{222}{333}$

Six out of twelve   three out of seven   ten out of twenty

$\frac{7\frac{1}{2}}{15}$

three out of nine $\frac{8}{16}$ three hundred and fifty out of seven hundred

two and a half out of five

five out of fifty $\frac{6}{8}$

$\frac{31}{62}$ $\frac{50}{100}$ $\frac{27}{54}$ seven out of fourteen

Write some more names for $\frac{1}{2}$.

•••••H-51

Concrete problems with fractions

1 Question: Are there enough, not enough, too many window panes to put glass on the window?

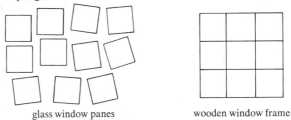

glass window panes   wooden window frame

Answer: We have 11 pieces of glass. Only 9 are needed to fill the frame.

$$\tfrac{11}{9} > \tfrac{9}{9}; \quad \tfrac{9}{9}=1; \quad \tfrac{11}{9}=1+\tfrac{2}{9}; \quad 1+\tfrac{2}{9}=1\tfrac{2}{9}$$

2 Question: Are there enough, not enough, too many $\tfrac{1}{4}$'s to fill the two circles?

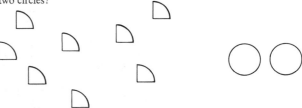

Answer: There are enough $\tfrac{1}{4}$'s. $\tfrac{8}{4}=2$

· · · · · **H52– H55**

Some children may want to verbalize how they can tell from the fractional numeral whether a number is less then one-half, equal to one-half, or greater than one-half. This is one child's way of saying it:

"I look at the top part and the bottom part. If the top part is more than the bottom part, then I know it is a name for more than one. If the top part is less than half of the bottom part, then I know it is a name for something less than one-half.

"If the top part is exactly one-half of the bottom part, then it is another name for one-half. If the top part is exactly three times the bottom part, then it names 3."

Learning names for mixed numbers

Rulers, yardsticks, metersticks, and rods are helpful aids in introducing problems of this type. Related lab sheets in Section N (Number Lines) and Section T (Length, Area, and Volume) may also be used.

Name _____ Date _____

Make true sentences using $>$, $=$, or $<$

$\tfrac{3}{2}$ > $\tfrac{1}{2}$ $\tfrac{6}{11}$ $\tfrac{1}{2}$

$\tfrac{40}{80}$ $\tfrac{1}{2}$ ⬡ $=$ $\tfrac{1}{2}$

$\tfrac{7}{9}$ $\tfrac{1}{2}$ $\tfrac{1}{2}$ $>$ ◯

$\tfrac{6}{13}$ $\tfrac{1}{2}$ $\tfrac{1}{2}$ $<$ ⬡

$\tfrac{6}{12}$ $\tfrac{1}{2}$ $\tfrac{1}{2}$ $>$ ◯

$\tfrac{20}{40}$ $\tfrac{1}{2}$ ⬡ $>$ $\tfrac{1}{2}$

$\tfrac{12}{9}$ $\tfrac{1}{2}$ $\tfrac{1}{2}$ $=$ ◯

⬡ $<$ $\tfrac{1}{2}$

Make up more problems about $\tfrac{1}{2}$.
Use $=,>,<$.

· · · · · H-52

Name _____ Date _____

Find the tricky names for ③, ④, ⑤, and ⑥.

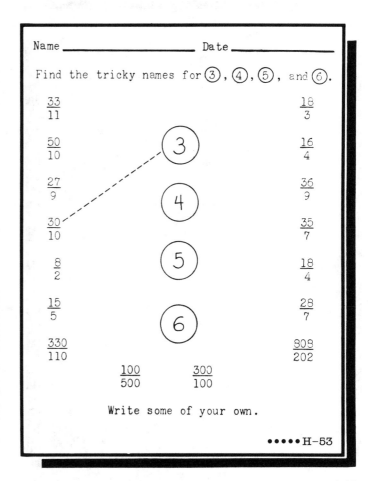

$\tfrac{33}{11}$ $\tfrac{18}{3}$

$\tfrac{50}{10}$ $\tfrac{16}{4}$

$\tfrac{27}{9}$ $\tfrac{36}{9}$

$\tfrac{30}{10}$ $\tfrac{35}{7}$

$\tfrac{8}{2}$ $\tfrac{18}{4}$

$\tfrac{15}{5}$ $\tfrac{28}{7}$

$\tfrac{330}{110}$ $\tfrac{808}{202}$

$\tfrac{100}{500}$ $\tfrac{300}{100}$

Write some of your own.

· · · · · H-53

Name _____ Date _____

Use = , > , and < to make true sentences.

$\frac{1}{3}$	$\frac{1}{2}$
$\frac{1}{4}$	$\frac{1}{2}$
$\frac{1}{3}$	$\frac{1}{4}$
$\frac{1}{5}$	$\frac{1}{3}$
$\frac{1}{4}$	$\frac{1}{5}$
$\frac{1}{6}$	$\frac{1}{5}$
$\frac{1}{3}$	$\frac{1}{6}$
$\frac{1}{3}$	$\frac{2}{6}$
$\frac{1}{2}$	$\frac{3}{4}$
$\frac{2}{4}$	$\frac{1}{2}$

How many $\frac{1}{2}$'s in 1?

$1 \div \frac{1}{2} = \boxed{}$

How many $\frac{1}{2}$'s in 2?

$2 \div \frac{1}{2} = \boxed{}$

How many $\frac{1}{3}$'s in 1?

$1 \div \frac{1}{3} = \boxed{}$

How many $\frac{1}{3}$'s in 3?

$3 \div \frac{1}{3} = \boxed{}$

How many $\frac{2}{3}$'s in 2?

$2 \div \frac{2}{3} = \boxed{}$

How many $\frac{1}{4}$'s in $\frac{1}{2}$?

$\frac{1}{2} \div \frac{1}{4} = \boxed{}$

How many $\frac{2}{5}$'s in $\frac{10}{5}$?

$\frac{10}{5} \div \frac{2}{5} = \boxed{}$

•••••H-54

····· **H54**

Division by a fraction

Notice that we use the same types of questions we used to introduce division by a whole number: How many 4's in 8? How many ½'s in 2?

Procedure for solving the problem with rods:

I am looking for a special kind of rod for which I can also find a rod ½ as long. I'll use the red rod. I'll call it "1." Now the white rod is my "½" rod.

The question now simply is: How many white rods (½-rods) are there in *two* red rods (in two 1-rods)? The answer is 4 (white rods).

$$2 \div \frac{1}{2} = 4$$

······ **H59, H60**

Diagnostic book on fractions

These sheets make another diagnostic booklet. Don't make too much of an occasion out of working these problems.

Answers for Page 3

$A = \langle\!\langle \tfrac{1}{2} \rangle\!\rangle \times C$

$A = \langle\!\langle \tfrac{1}{3} \rangle\!\rangle \times E$

$A = \tfrac{2}{3} \times \triangle{B}$

$2\tfrac{1}{2} \times A = \boxed{D}$

$(\tfrac{1}{5} \times D) + (\tfrac{1}{2} \times A) = \bigcirc{A}$

$\tfrac{3}{2}$ of $C = \triangle{E}$

Answer for Page 4

your apples

<!-- Bottom left panel -->

Name _____ Date _____

Connect the names for the same number.

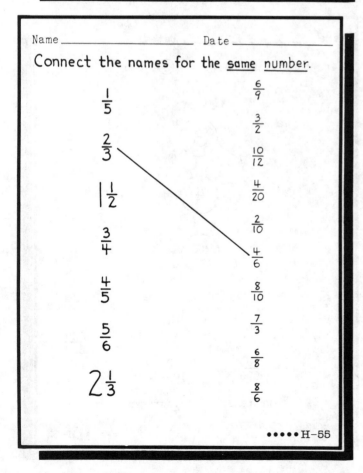

$\frac{1}{5}$	$\frac{6}{9}$
$\frac{2}{3}$	$\frac{3}{2}$
$1\frac{1}{2}$	$\frac{10}{12}$
$\frac{3}{4}$	$\frac{4}{20}$
$\frac{4}{5}$	$\frac{2}{10}$
$\frac{5}{6}$	$\frac{4}{6}$
$2\frac{1}{3}$	$\frac{8}{10}$
	$\frac{7}{3}$
	$\frac{6}{8}$
	$\frac{8}{6}$

•••••H-55

<!-- Bottom right panel -->

Name _____ Date _____

$\frac{33}{11} + \frac{4}{11} = 3\frac{?}{?}$ $\frac{3}{5} + \frac{2}{5} =$

$\frac{8}{8} + \frac{3}{8} = 1\frac{?}{?}$ $\frac{4}{2} + \frac{6}{3} =$

$\frac{10}{5} + \frac{2}{5} =$ Make up more problems like these.

$\frac{14}{7} + \frac{1}{7} =$

$\frac{14}{2} + \frac{1}{2} =$

$\frac{30}{5} + \frac{4}{5} =$

$\frac{5}{5} + \frac{6}{6} =$

$\frac{2}{2} + \frac{3}{3} + \frac{4}{4} =$

$\frac{8}{2} + \frac{3}{3} =$

•••••H-56

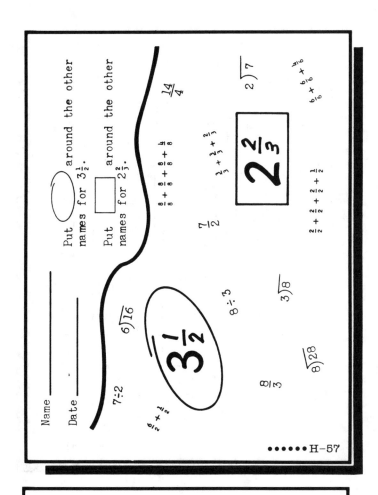

Name _____
Date _____

Put ⬭ around the other
names for $3\frac{1}{2}$.

Put ▭ around the other
names for $2\frac{2}{3}$.

$\frac{14}{4}$

$2\overline{)7}$

$\frac{6}{6}+\frac{6}{6}+\frac{6}{6}$

$\frac{8}{8}+\frac{8}{8}+\frac{8}{8}+\frac{8}{8}+\frac{4}{8}$

$\frac{2}{3}+\frac{2}{3}+\frac{2}{3}$

$\frac{7}{2}$

$2+2\frac{1}{2}+2\frac{1}{2}$

$6\overline{)16}$

$8\div 3$

$3\overline{)8}$

$3\frac{1}{2}$

$2\frac{2}{3}$

$\frac{8}{3}$

$8\overline{)28}$

$\frac{1}{2}+\frac{1}{2}$

•••••• H-57

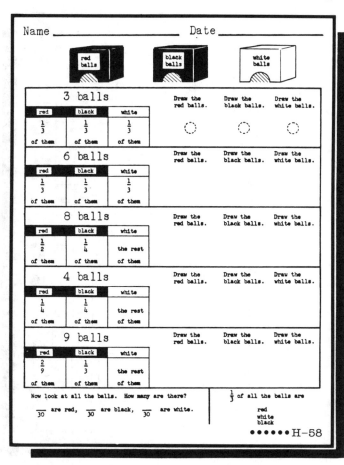

Name _____   Date _____

red balls   black balls   white balls

3 balls			Draw the red balls.	Draw the black balls.	Draw the white balls.
red	black	white	◯	◯	◯
$\frac{1}{3}$	$\frac{1}{3}$	$\frac{1}{3}$			
of them	of them	of them			

6 balls			Draw the red balls.	Draw the black balls.	Draw the white balls.
red	black	white			
$\frac{1}{3}$	$\frac{1}{3}$	$\frac{1}{3}$			
of them	of them	of them			

8 balls			Draw the red balls.	Draw the black balls.	Draw the white balls.
red	black	white			
$\frac{1}{2}$	$\frac{1}{4}$	the rest			
of them	of them	of them			

4 balls			Draw the red balls.	Draw the black balls.	Draw the white balls.
red	black	white			
$\frac{1}{4}$	$\frac{1}{4}$	the rest			
of them	of them	of them			

9 balls			Draw the red balls.	Draw the black balls.	Draw the white balls.
red	black	white			
$\frac{2}{9}$	$\frac{1}{3}$	the rest			
of them	of them	of them			

Now look at all the balls. How many are there?

___/30 are red, ___/30 are black, ___/30 are white.

$\frac{1}{3}$ of all the balls are

red
white
black

•••••• H-58

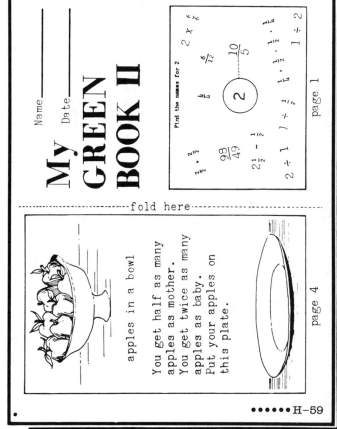

My
GREEN
BOOK II

Name _____
Date _____

Find the names for 2

$2^{3} \times \frac{3}{2}$

$\frac{6}{12}$

$\frac{4}{2}$

$\frac{10}{5}$

2

$2\frac{1}{2} \cdot 1 \cdot \frac{1}{2} \cdot \frac{1}{2} \cdot \frac{1}{2}$

$\frac{1}{2} + \frac{1}{2} \cdot \frac{1}{2}$

$1\div 2$

$2\times \frac{2}{2}$

$\frac{98}{49}$

$2\frac{1}{2}-\frac{1}{2}$

$2\div 1$ $1\div \frac{1}{2}$

$2 \div 1 \cdot 1 \div \frac{1}{2}$

page 1

- - - - fold here - - - -

apples in a bowl

You get half as many
apples as mother.
You get twice as many
apples as baby.
Put your apples on
this plate.

page 4

•••••• H-59

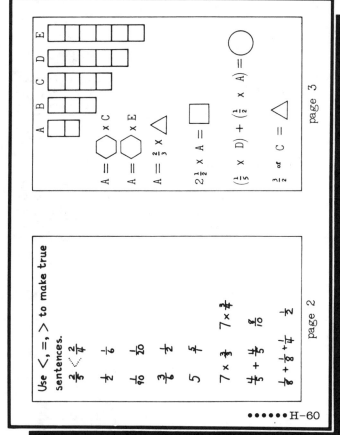

A ▭▭
B ▭▭▭
C ▭▭▭▭
D ▭▭▭▭▭
E ▭▭▭▭▭▭

◯

A = ⬡ × C
A = ⬡ × E
A = $\frac{2}{3}$ × △

$2\frac{1}{2}$ × A = ▢

$(\frac{1}{5} × D) + (\frac{1}{2} × A) =$ △

$\frac{3}{2}$ of C = △

page 3

Use $<$, $=$, $>$ to make true
sentences.

$\frac{2}{5} \;\vee\; \frac{2}{4}$

$\frac{1}{2}$ ___ $\frac{1}{6}$

$\frac{1}{10}$ ___ $\frac{1}{20}$

$\frac{3}{8}$ ___ $\frac{1}{2}$

5 ___ $\frac{5}{4}$

$7 \times \frac{1}{3}$ ___ $7 \times \frac{1}{4}$

$\frac{4}{5} + \frac{1}{5}$ ___ $\frac{6}{10}$

$\frac{4}{8} + \frac{1}{8} + \frac{1}{4}$ ___ $\frac{1}{2}$

page 2

•••••• H-60

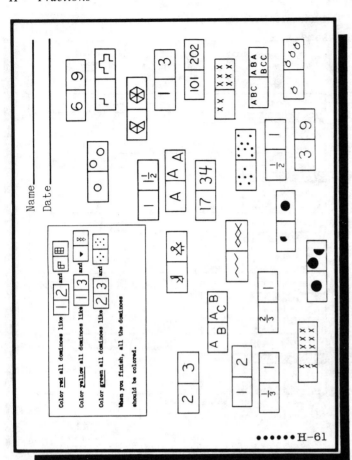

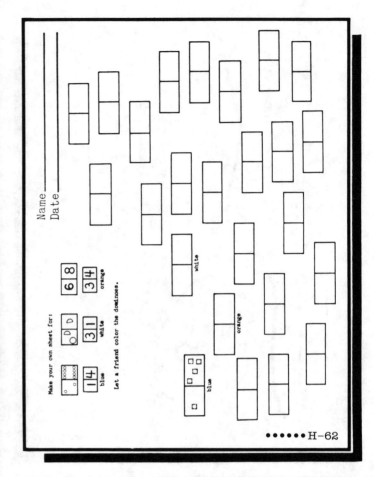

•••••• H-61

•••••• H-62

•••••• H61, H62

Fractions are ordered pairs. $\frac{4}{5}$ means (4, 5). $\frac{5}{4}$ means (5, 4). Fractions are ratios. Ordered pairs are ratios. The *simplest* ratio for (9, 15) is (3, 5). The "reduced" fraction for $\frac{9}{15}$ is $\frac{3}{5}$. (There is no need, however, to bother the children with these terms.)

A fraction card game

Before the children do lab sheet H62 independently, you might let them first make a card game for the class. Each child is given one or two file cards which he divides into two sections. On the chalkboard are written several fractional numerals expressed in their simplest form.

$$\frac{3}{4} \quad \text{or} \quad (3, 4)$$
$$\frac{2}{5} \quad \text{or} \quad (2, 5)$$
$$\frac{1}{3} \quad \text{or} \quad (1, 3)$$

Children choose one of these and draw a "response" picture to it. The cards are later collected and become a "sorting game" for the class.

As an illustration, if (3, 4) is put on the board, response cards might include:

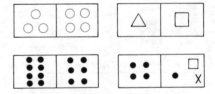

If (5, 2) is put on the board, some correct response cards are:

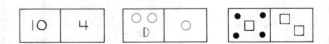

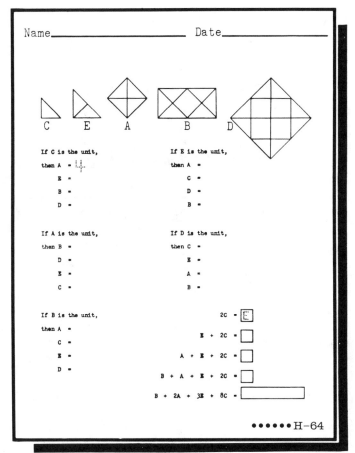

•••••• H63

Word problems

Problem 1

Bill has $\frac{3}{5}$ or ⟨9⟩ marbles.   Nina has ⟨6⟩ marbles.

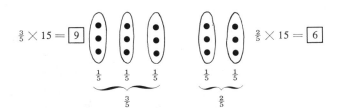

$\frac{3}{5} \times 15 = \boxed{9}$ $\frac{2}{5} \times 15 = \boxed{6}$

Problem 2

One child weighs $\frac{3}{5}$ of 50 kilograms (or 30 kilograms). The other child weighs $\frac{2}{5}$ of 50 kilograms (or 20 kilograms).

$$\frac{3}{5} \times 50 = \boxed{30}$$
$$1 - \frac{3}{5} = \frac{2}{5}$$
$$\frac{2}{5} \times 50 = \boxed{20}$$

•••••• H64

Answers

If C is the unit,   If E is the unit,
then A $= 4$ then A $= 2$
      E $= 2$ C $= \frac{1}{2}$
      B $= 8$ D $= 8$
      D $= 16$ B $= 4$

If A is the unit,   If D is the unit,
then B $= 2$ then C $= \frac{1}{16}$
      D $= 4$ E $= \frac{1}{8}$
      E $= \frac{1}{2}$ A $= \frac{1}{4}$
      C $= \frac{1}{4}$ B $= \frac{1}{2}$

If B is the unit,
then A $= \frac{1}{2}$ $2C = \boxed{E}$
      C $= \frac{1}{8}$ $E + 2C = \boxed{A}$
      E $= \frac{1}{4}$ $A + E + 2C = \boxed{B}$
      D $= 2$ $B + A + E + 2C = \boxed{D}$
                          $B + 2A + 3E + 8C = \boxed{A + B + D + E}$

I Addition, subtraction, multiplication, and fractions

Problems on I1 are similar to the following:

$$\square + \square = 2 \times \square$$
$$8 + 8 = 2 \times 8$$

$$\square - (\tfrac{1}{2} \times \square\,) = \tfrac{1}{2} \times \square$$
$$16 - (\tfrac{1}{2} \times 16\,) = \tfrac{1}{2} \times 16$$

Problems on I2 must be worked carefully since children might easily misread:

$3 \times 3 + 4$	*as*	$3 + 3 + 4$
5×5	*as*	$5 + 5$
10×0	*as*	$10 + 0$
$0 - 10$	*as*	$10 - 0$

The correct answers to the problems on I2 are shown below.

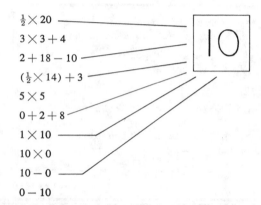

$\tfrac{1}{2} \times 20$

$3 \times 3 + 4$

$2 + 18 - 10$

$(\tfrac{1}{2} \times 14) + 3$

5×5

$0 + 2 + 8$

1×10

10×0

$10 - 0$

$0 - 10$

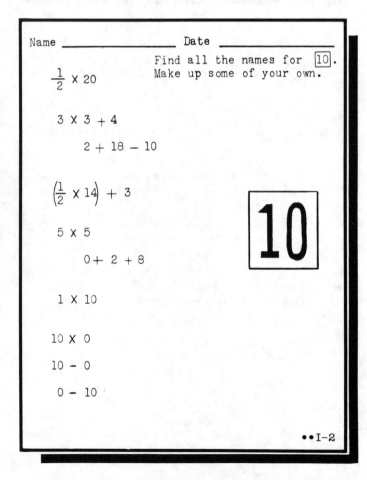

Name _____ Date _____

$$3 + 3 = 2 \times \square$$
$$5 + 5 = 2 \times \square$$
$$2 \times \square = 8 + 8$$
$$2 \times \square = 10 + 10$$
$$4 - 2 = \tfrac{1}{2} \times \square$$
$$6 - 3 = \tfrac{1}{2} \times \square$$
$$\tfrac{1}{2} \times \square = 8 - 4$$
$$\tfrac{1}{2} \times 10 = 10 - \square$$
$$\tfrac{1}{2} \times 6 = 6 - \square$$
$$\tfrac{1}{2} \times \square = 12 - 6$$

·· I-1

Name _____ Date _____

Find all the names for ☐10. Make up some of your own.

$\tfrac{1}{2} \times 20$

$3 \times 3 + 4$

$2 + 18 - 10$

$\left(\tfrac{1}{2} \times 14\right) + 3$

5×5

$0 + 2 + 8$

1×10

10×0

$10 - 0$

$0 - 10$

10

·· I-2

·· **I4**

This lab sheet requires a good deal of thought by the children. Some frames can be filled with many answers, while others take only one answer.

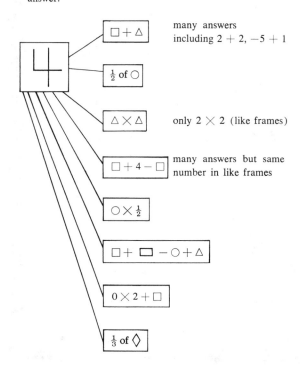

·· **I3**

I3 is similar to I2 except that children put their own problems into the empty spaces.

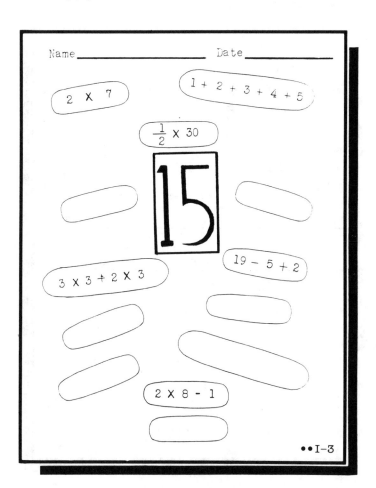

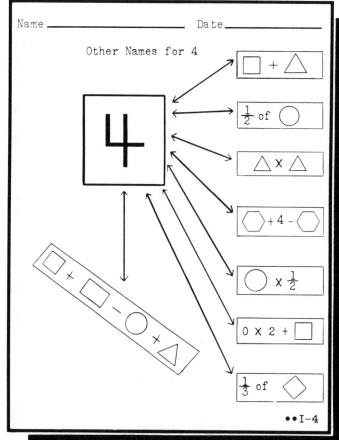

Name _____ Date _____

$\frac{1}{2}$ × 2 = □
2 × 1 = □

$\frac{1}{2}$ × 4 = □
2 × 2 = □

$\frac{1}{2}$ × 6 = □
2 × 3 = □

$\frac{1}{2}$ × 8 = □
2 × 4 = □

$\frac{1}{2}$ × 10 = □
2 × 5 = □

$\frac{1}{2}$ × 12 = □
2 × 6 = □

$\frac{1}{2}$ × 14 = □
2 × 7 = □

$\frac{1}{2}$ × 16 = □
2 × 8 = □

$\frac{1}{2}$ × 18 = □
2 × 9 = □

$\frac{1}{2}$ × 20 = □
2 × 10 = □

2 × □ = 6
$\frac{1}{2}$ × 6 = □

$\frac{1}{2}$ × □ = 10
□ × 5 = 10

2 × □ = 8
$\frac{1}{2}$ × 8 = □

□ × 8 = 16
$\frac{1}{2}$ × 16 = □

••I–5

••I5

On this sheet are related pairs of problems of the type:

$\frac{1}{2} \times 18 = \boxed{9}$
$2 \times 9 = \boxed{18}$

There is one subtle exception:

$\frac{1}{2} \times \boxed{20} = 10$
$\boxed{2} \times 5 = 10$

Children should be encouraged to say these pairs of problems to themselves (using "of" for ×) so that they will get the "rhythm" of the pairs.

••I6

On I6 are more complicated computations with fractions. Some children will *write* a simplified version; others will simplify *mentally*.

Problem: $(\frac{1}{2}\times 4) - (\frac{1}{2}\times 4) = □$
Simplified: $2 \quad - \quad 2 \quad = 0$

Problem: $(\frac{1}{2}\times 6) + (\frac{1}{2}\times 8) = □$
Simplified: $3 \quad + \quad 4 \quad = 7$

Name _____ Date _____

One half of a number.

$(\frac{1}{2} \times 4) - (\frac{1}{2} \times 4) = □$

$□ = (\frac{1}{2} \times 6) + (\frac{1}{2} \times 6)$

$(\frac{1}{2} \times 10) + (\frac{1}{2} \times 2) = □$

$(\frac{1}{2} \times 8) - (\frac{1}{2} \times 2) = □$

$□ = (\frac{1}{2} \times 6) + (\frac{1}{2} \times 8)$

$(\frac{1}{2} \times 12) - (\frac{1}{2} \times 10) = □$

$(\frac{1}{4} \times 4) + (\frac{1}{4} \times 8) = □$

$□ = (\frac{1}{2} \times 14) - (\frac{1}{4} \times 16)$

$(\frac{1}{4} \times 12) + (\frac{1}{2} \times □) = 12$

••I–6

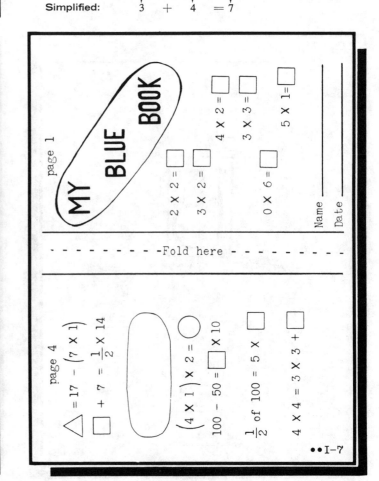

••I–7

··I7, I8
Diagnostic booklets

The teacher may want to keep these as part of a cumulative record for each child. The booklet provides a means to check on trouble spots and to give individual help.

Not all children in a class are ready to work on this booklet at the same time.

···I9
Operations with multiples of ten

One child stated well the purpose of this lab sheet when he said, with a big smile, "That was easy! Every time I thought about ones, I thought the same thing about tens!"

He used his knowledge of the problem $8 + 3$ for getting the answer to $80 + 30$.

He used his knowledge of the problem $\frac{1}{10} \times 10$ for getting the answer to $\frac{1}{10} \times 100$.

Some children "get a feel" for this kind of relationship through their experiences with the Cuisenaire® rods:

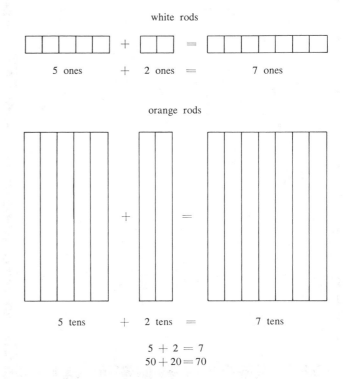

white rods

$$5 \text{ ones} \quad + \quad 2 \text{ ones} \quad = \quad 7 \text{ ones}$$

orange rods

$$5 \text{ tens} \quad + \quad 2 \text{ tens} \quad = \quad 7 \text{ tens}$$

$$5 + 2 = 7$$
$$50 + 20 = 70$$

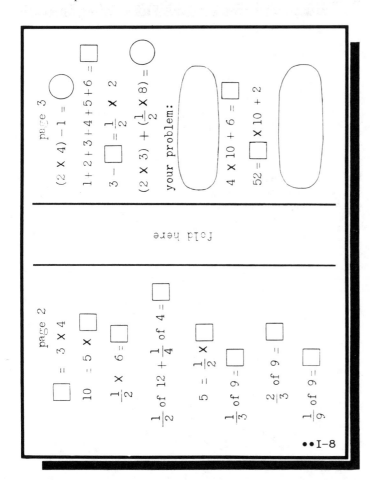

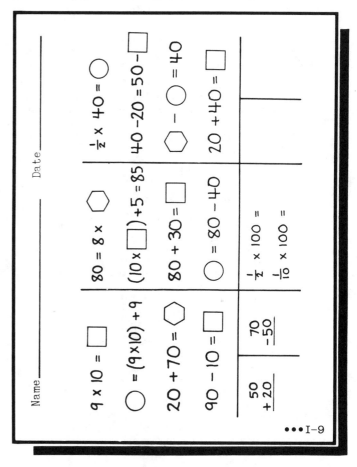

Name _____ Date _____

$$4 \times 3 = \square$$

$$6 \times 4 = \square$$

$$2 \times 3 + 2 \times 4 = \square$$

$$3 + 5 + 7 = \square$$

$$6 + 4 - 7 - 3 = \square$$

$$\tfrac{1}{2} \times 28 = \square$$

$$\square \times 3 = 9$$

$$1 + 2 + 3 + 4 + 9 + 1 = \square$$

$$16 + (\tfrac{1}{2} \text{ of } 16) = \square$$

$$0 = 12 - \square$$

•••I–10

Name _____ Date _____

If it's wrong, cross it out.

$$7 \times 2 = 14 \times 1$$

$$6 \times \tfrac{1}{2} = \tfrac{1}{2} \times 6$$

$$(\tfrac{1}{2} \times 8) + (\tfrac{1}{2} \times 8) = 4$$

$$(\tfrac{1}{2} \times 8) - (\tfrac{1}{2} \times 8) = 0$$

$$6 - 8 = -2$$

$$4 + 3 = (-4) + (-3)$$

$$12 + 12 + 12 + 12 = 3 \times 12$$

$$21 + 21 + 21 + 21 = 4 \times 21$$

•••I–11

•••I10

A few children will try to solve the problem $\frac{1}{2} \times 28$ without using Cuisenaire® rods. Those who solve the problem without rods often use this method:

$$\tfrac{1}{2} \times 28 = \square$$
$$28 = 20 + 8$$
$$\tfrac{1}{2} \times 20 = 10$$
$$\tfrac{1}{2} \times 8 = 4$$

therefore $\qquad \tfrac{1}{2} \times 28 = 10 + 4 = 14$

If children have trouble with such problems, ask them how many of the two's equal twenty-eight?

•••I11

"If it's wrong, cross it out," may be interpreted in two ways. Most children will draw a line through a statement that is wrong, for example,

$$4 + 3 = (-4) + (-3)$$

will be completely crossed out. Occasionally, a child will use the more sophisticated way of crossing out a wrong statement by crossing out the equality symbol, for example:

$$4 + 3 \neq (-4) + (-3)$$

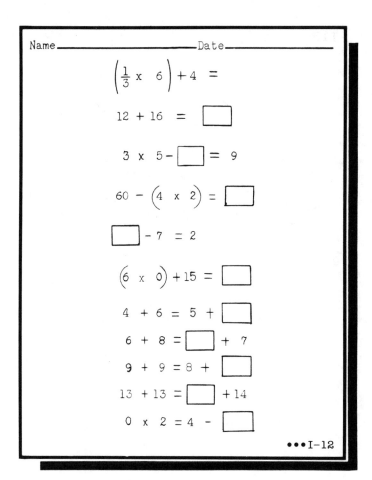

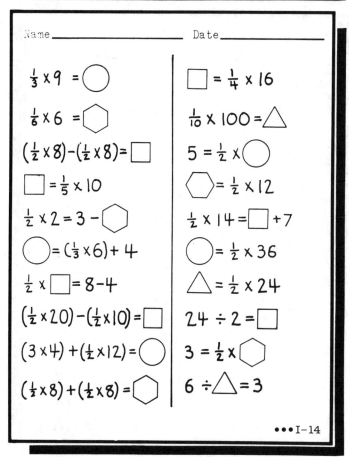

···I12
An important reminder

Solutions to the problems on these lab sheets are given below, but you should work the problems yourself before checking the solutions. Only through your own experience will you arrive at the mathematical concepts the children are intended to discover. Solutions alone are meaningless.

Solutions

$(\frac{1}{3} \times 6) + 4 = \boxed{6}$

$12 + 16 = \boxed{28}$

$3 \times 5 - \boxed{6} = 9$

$60 - (4 \times 2) = \boxed{52}$

$\boxed{9} - 7 = 2$

$(6 \times 0) + 15 = \boxed{15}$

$4 + 6 = 5 + \boxed{5}$

$6 + 8 = \boxed{7} + 7$

$9 + 9 = 8 + \boxed{10}$

$13 + 13 = \boxed{12} + 14$

$0 \times 2 = 4 - \boxed{4}$

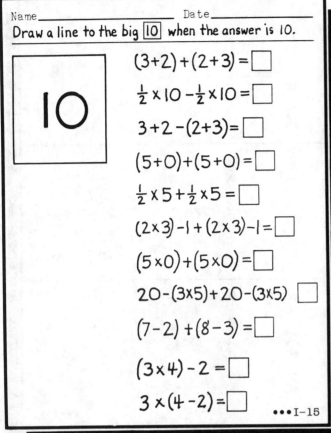

Name_____   Date_____

Draw a line to the big ☐10☐ when the answer is 10.

10

$(3+2)+(2+3)=☐$

$\frac{1}{2}\times10-\frac{1}{2}\times10=☐$

$3+2-(2+3)=☐$

$(5+0)+(5+0)=☐$

$\frac{1}{2}\times5+\frac{1}{2}\times5=☐$

$(2\times3)-1+(2\times3)-1=☐$

$(5\times0)+(5\times0)=☐$

$20-(3\times5)+20-(3\times5)\ ☐$

$(7-2)+(8-3)=☐$

$(3\times4)-2=☐$

$3\times(4-2)=☐$

•••I-15

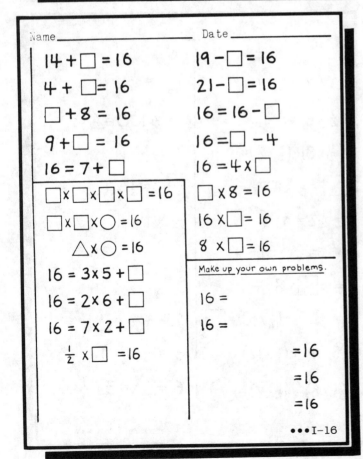

Name_____   Date_____

$14+☐=16$ $19-☐=16$

$4+☐=16$ $21-☐=16$

$☐+8=16$ $16=16-☐$

$9+☐=16$ $16=☐-4$

$16=7+☐$ $16=4\times☐$

$☐\times☐\times☐\times☐=16$ $☐\times8=16$

$☐\times☐\times\bigcirc=16$ $16\times☐=16$

$\triangle\times\bigcirc=16$ $8\times☐=16$

$16=3\times5+☐$ Make up your own problems.

$16=2\times6+☐$ $16=$

$16=7\times2+☐$ $16=$

$\frac{1}{2}\times☐=16$ $=16$

                        $=16$

                        $=16$

•••I-16

•••I15

Solutions

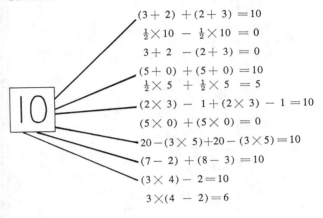

$(3+2)+(2+3)=10$

$\frac{1}{2}\times10-\frac{1}{2}\times10=0$

$3+2-(2+3)=0$

$(5+0)+(5+0)=10$

$\frac{1}{2}\times5+\frac{1}{2}\times5=5$

$(2\times3)-1+(2\times3)-1=10$

$(5\times0)+(5\times0)=0$

$20-(3\times5)+20-(3\times5)=10$

$(7-2)+(8-3)=10$

$(3\times4)-2=10$

$3\times(4-2)=6$

•••I16

This lab sheet is about one number—16.

Problem

$$☐\times☐\times☐\times☐=16$$

Only 2 will make it true.

Problem

$$☐\times☐\times\bigcirc=16$$

$$\boxed{1}\times\boxed{1}\times\circled{16}=16$$

$$\boxed{4}\times\boxed{4}\times\circled{1}=16$$

$$\boxed{2}\times\boxed{2}\times\circled{4}=16$$

$$\boxed{8}\times\boxed{8}\times\circled{\tfrac{1}{4}}=16$$

Many answers are correct as long as the same number is in both ☐'s.

Problem

$$\triangle\times\bigcirc=16$$

$$\triangle_{4}\times\circled{4}=16$$

$$\triangle_{2}\times\circled{8}=16$$

$$\triangle_{\tfrac{2}{3}}\times\circled{24}=16$$

Again, many answers are correct.

J   Division

The fourth arithmetic operation to be introduced is division. Division is related to multiplication in the same way that subtraction is related to addition. Just as subtraction is the operation that *undoes* addition, division is the operation that *undoes* multiplication.

Multiplying	is undone	dividing
by three	by	by three.
$6 \times 3 = 18$		$18 \div 3 = 6$

Notice that one starts with 6 and ends with 6. Combining these two equations, we can say that

$$(6 \times 3) \div 3 = 6$$

We can also see that multiplication is the operation that undoes division. Again we start with the same number that we end with.

Dividing	is undone	multiplying
by three	by	by three.
$6 \div 3 = 2$		$2 \times 3 = 6$

$$(6 \div 3) \times 3 = 6$$

Since multiplication and division are operations which undo each other, we call them *inverse* operations. In mathematical terms, the inverse relationship between multiplication and division may be expressed as follows:

$$\boxed{\square \times \triangle \div \triangle = \square}$$

and

$$\boxed{\square \div \triangle \times \triangle = \square}$$

provided $\triangle \neq 0$.

Why is division by zero ruled out?

We can say that	$12 \div 3 = 4$
because	$4 \times 3 = 12$
or that	$0 \div 7 = 0$
since	$0 \times 7 = 0.$

But in the open sentence

$$5 \div 0 = \square$$

what number can be written in the $\square$ to make the sentence true? If the number is zero, then we should expect the following sentence to be true.

$$0 \times 0 = 5$$

But

$$0 \times 0 \neq 5$$

therefore

$$5 \div 0 \neq 0.$$

We can see that in the open sentence

$$5 \div 0 = \square$$

no number can be written in the $\square$ to make the sentence true, since if we could find such a number, that number would also make the open sentence

$$\square \times 0 = 5$$

true. But this is impossible, since the left side of the sentence will equal zero *regardless* of what number we write in the $\square$.

Multiplication and division vocabulary

If a teacher feels that the children are ready for a more extensive technical vocabulary for multiplication and division than has been presented, she may want to study the material below, which concludes Section J, and work out her own method of presentation. (This was done for addition and subtraction at the end of Section E. It is entirely optional.)

The teacher may explain the following terms to pupils in her own words:

1. Multiplication

2. Multiply

3. Division

4. Divide

5. Factor—factor times factor equals product:
$$5 \times \tfrac{1}{2} = \boxed{\tfrac{5}{2}} \qquad 4 \times 3 = \boxed{12}$$

6. Product—product divided by a factor equals the other factor:
$$12 \div 3 = \boxed{4} \qquad \tfrac{5}{2} \div \tfrac{1}{2} = \boxed{5}$$

7. Numerals (All numerals are names for numbers. The same number has many names.)
   • Roman numeral (IV)
   • (Hindu-Arabic) one-digit numeral (4)
   • fractional numeral ($\tfrac{4}{2}$)
   • two-digit numeral (63)
   • four-digit numeral (2395)

The following kinds of work may be done on the chalkboard. Make names for the number seven from the following:

1. $3 + \square$

2. $\bigcirc \times \square$

3. $28 \div \bigcirc$

4. $\bigcirc - 33$

5. $\tfrac{1}{2}$ of $\triangle$

6. Add some of your own.

Fill in the missing information in each row. Use a letter to tell what operation is involved. (A = addition, S = subtraction, M = multiplication, D = division.)

1st number	2nd number	end number	operation
15	8	7	
6	4		M
	5	5	D
19	7	26	
			S

Make up your own:

··J1–J6
How many □'s in △ ?

We have found that the simplest way to pose the division question
is to ask: How many _____'s in _____?

Question: How many 4's in 8?

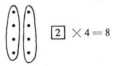

Answer: There are two 4's in 8.

$\boxed{2} \times 4 = 8$

Question: How many purple rods in a brown rod?

brown	
purple	purple

Answer: Two purple rods = one brown rod (that is, two purple rods
end to end are as long as one brown rod). $\boxed{2} \times 4 = 8$

Question: How many 4's in 8?

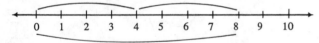

Answer: There are two "4 jumps" in 8. $\boxed{2} \times 4 = 8$

$$8 \div 4 = \boxed{2}$$

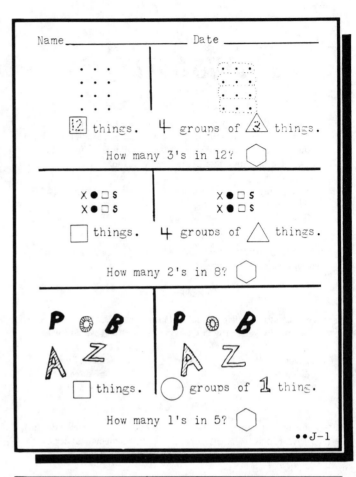

174

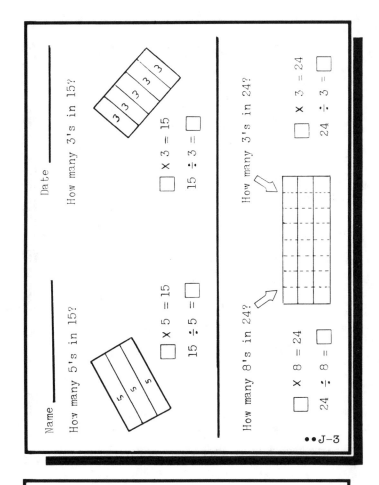

J-3

Name _____ Date _____

How many 5's in 15?

□ × 5 = 15
15 ÷ 5 = □

How many 3's in 15?

□ × 3 = 15
15 ÷ 3 = □

How many 8's in 24?

□ × 8 = 24
24 ÷ 8 = □

How many 3's in 24?

□ × 3 = 24
24 ÷ 3 = □

••J-3

Name _____ Date _____

Rods will fit this picture.

□ × 18 = 18   How many 18's in 18? □   18 ÷ 18 = □
□ × 1 = 18   How many 1's in 18? □   18 ÷ 1 = □
□ × 2 = 18   How many 2's in 18? □   18 ÷ 2 = □
□ × 3 = 18   How many 3's in 18? □   18 ÷ 3 = □
□ × 6 = 18   How many 6's in 18? □   18 ÷ 6 = □
□ × 9 = 18   How many 9's in 18? □   18 ÷ 9 = □

••J-4

Name _____ Date _____

How many 3's in 6? □   6 ÷ 3 = □
How many 1's in 5? □   5 ÷ 1 = □
How many 2's in 4? □   4 ÷ 2 = □

How many 4's in 4? □   4 ÷ 4 = □
How many 2's in 8? □   8 ÷ 2 = □
How many 4's in 8? □   8 ÷ 4 = □

How many 5's in 10? □   10 ÷ 5 = □
How many 2's in 10? □   10 ÷ 2 = □
How many 6's in 12? □   12 ÷ 6 = □

How many 4's in 12? □   12 ÷ 4 = □
How many 3's in 12? □   12 ÷ 3 = □
How many 2's in 12? □   12 ÷ 2 = □

••J-5

Name _____ Date _____

How many 2's in 6? □   6 ÷ 2 = □
How many 10's in 20? □   20 ÷ 10 = □
How many 3's in 12? □   12 ÷ 3 = □
How many 4's in 8? □   8 ÷ 4 = □
How many 4's in 16? □   16 ÷ 4 = □
How many 3's in 9? □   9 ÷ 3 = □
How many 5's in 10? □   10 ÷ 5 = □
How many 4's in 20? □   20 ÷ 4 = □
How many 5's in 15? □   15 ÷ 5 = □
How many 2's in 10? □   10 ÷ 2 = □

••J-6

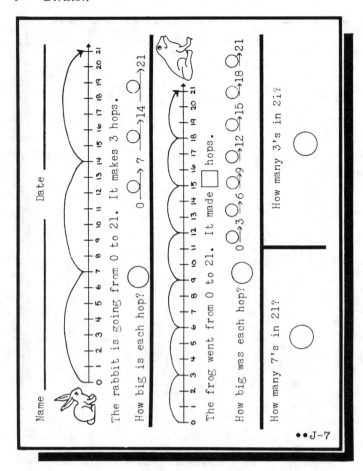

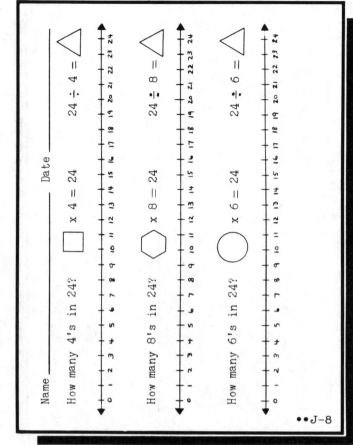

·· J7

Number-line hops illustrate division and multiplication as inverse operations.

The rabbit is going from 0 to 21. When the rabbit has arrived at 21, we can see that it took him 3 hops to get there. In the rabbit story we ask for the *size* of the hops. How big is each hop?

$$3 \times \Box = 27$$

In the frog story we ask for the number of hops *and* the size of the hops.

·· J8

On this lab sheet we ask for the *number* of hops in each case. Children are to draw in the hops and then answer the questions.

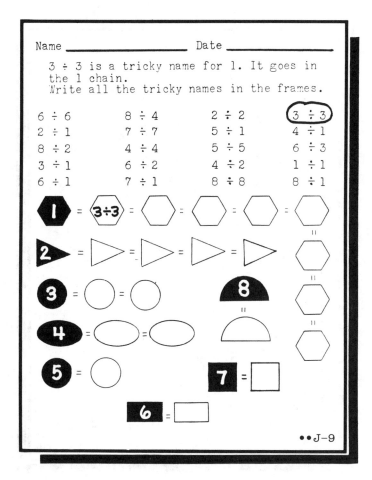

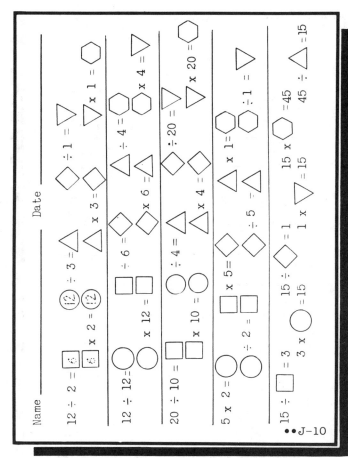

··J9

"Tricky names" for 1, 2, 3, 4, 5, and 6 are given at the bottom of the page. Children are to write each one in the chain that begins with the simple name.

$$\boxed{6} = \boxed{6 \div 1}$$

As a child matches one of the "tricky" names with the simple name, he may want to put a loop around the used-up names.

··J10

We want the frame rule to apply to each of the many problems between the horizontal lines. This seems logical to children and is suggested by the dotted examples.

These chains dramatically illustrate division and its multiplicative inverse.

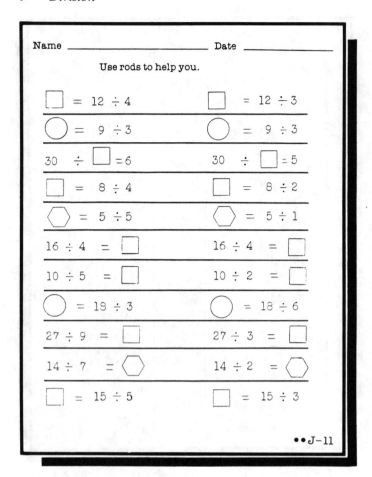

Name _____ Date _____

Use rods to help you.

□ = 12 ÷ 4	□ = 12 ÷ 3
○ = 9 ÷ 3	○ = 9 ÷ 3
30 ÷ □ = 6	30 ÷ □ = 5
□ = 8 ÷ 4	□ = 8 ÷ 2
⬡ = 5 ÷ 5	⬡ = 5 ÷ 1
16 ÷ 4 = □	16 ÷ 4 = □
10 ÷ 5 = □	10 ÷ 2 = □
○ = 18 ÷ 3	○ = 18 ÷ 6
27 ÷ 9 = □	27 ÷ 3 = □
14 ÷ 7 = ⬡	14 ÷ 2 = ⬡
□ = 15 ÷ 5	□ = 15 ÷ 3

••J-11

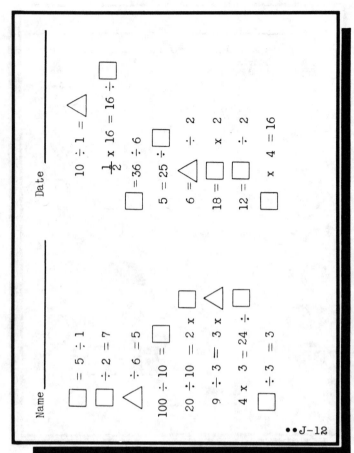

Name _____ Date _____

10 ÷ 1 = △

$\frac{1}{2}$ x 16 = 16 ÷ □

□ = 36 ÷ 6

5 = 25 ÷ □

6 = △ ÷ 2

18 = □ x 2

12 = □ ÷ 2

□ x 4 = 16

□ = 5 ÷ 1

□ ÷ 2 = 7

△ ÷ 6 = 5

100 ÷ 10 = □

20 ÷ 10 = 2 x □

9 ÷ 3 = 3 x △

4 x 3 = 24 ÷ □

□ ÷ 3 = 3

••J-12

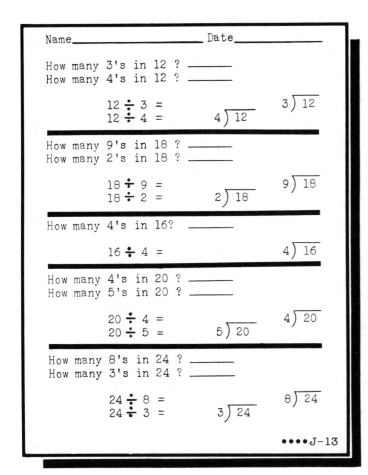

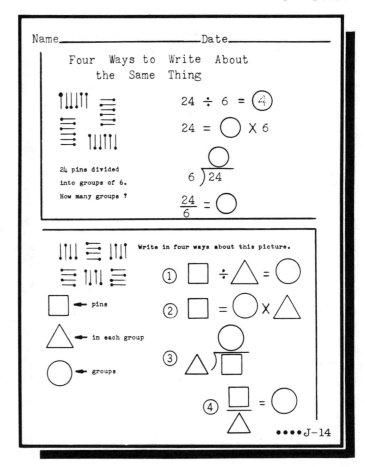

· · · · J13, J14

The division notation $3\overline{)12}$ is introduced as a synonym for $12 \div 3$ and $\square \times 3 = 12$. Children should be reminded that $\frac{12}{3}$ means the same thing.

On lab sheet J14 the fractional notation is given as a fourth way of writing division.

Give the children practice in these four ways of writing division. On chalkboard, write $\frac{15}{5}$. The children should write $5\overline{)15}$, $15 \div 5$, $\square \times 5 = 15$.

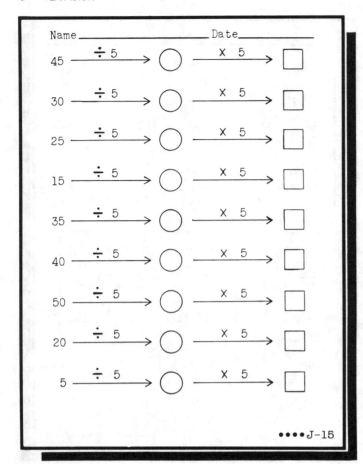

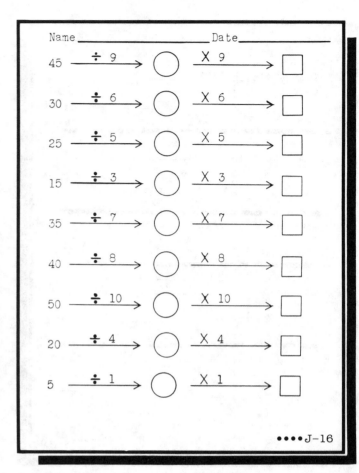

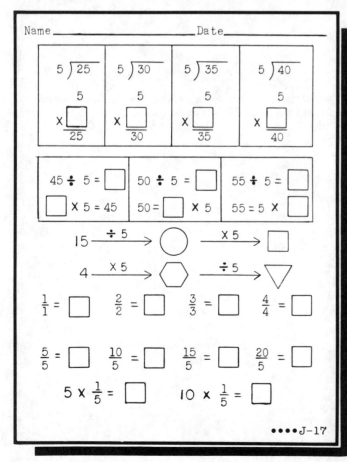

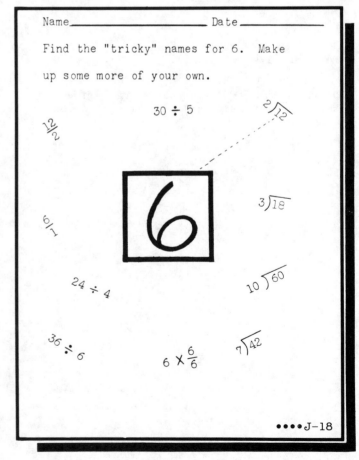

Find the "tricky" names for 6. Make up some more of your own.

Name_____ Date_____

How many 8's are there in 32?

Make a quick guess and write it→ ☐ Guess ☐ Answer

Look at this rod picture
to help you find the correct
answer. ↓

8 ⟌ 32

There are ☐ eights

in 32.

Write in your guesses for _all_
the problems. Check them with your rods.

☐ Guess ☐ Answer ☐ Guess ☐ Answer

9 ⟌ 45   7 ⟌ 35

☐ Guess ☐ Answer ☐ Guess ☐ Answer

8 ⟌ 40   3 ⟌ 27

☐ Guess ☐ Answer ☐ Guess ☐ Answer

8 ⟌ 80   6 ⟌ 48

•••••J-19

Name_____ Date_____

Guess ☐ Answer ☐	Guess ☐ Answer ☐	Guess ☐ Answer ☐
5 ⟌ 25	4 ⟌ 36	3 ⟌ 33
Guess ☐ Answer ☐	Guess ☐ Answer ☐	Guess ☐ Answer ☐
8 ⟌ 56	7 ⟌ 63	6 ⟌ 54
Guess ☐ Answer ☐	Guess ☐ Answer ☐	Guess ☐ Answer ☐
5 ⟌ 60	16 ⟌ 64	7 ⟌ 28
Guess ☐ Answer ☐	Guess ☐ Answer ☐	Guess ☐ Answer ☐
9 ⟌ 96	3 ⟌ 39	9 ⟌ 108
Guess ☐ Answer ☐	Guess ☐ Answer ☐	Guess ☐ Answer ☐
8 ⟌ 48	9 ⟌ 81	9 ⟌ 75

•••••J-20

····J15–J17

Division and its inverse, multiplication

On J15 and J16 the same numbers are divided first by one factor, then
by the other.

Example

(J15) $45 \xrightarrow{\div 5} (9) \xrightarrow{\times 5} \boxed{45}$

(J16) $45 \xrightarrow{\div 9} (5) \xrightarrow{\times 9} \boxed{45}$

Use the same vocabulary built up in multiplication when doing
division.

$$\text{Factor} \times \text{Factor} = \text{Product} \qquad 8 \times 3 = 24$$
$$\text{Product} \div \text{Factor} = \text{Factor} \qquad 24 \div 3 = 8$$

The term *quotient* is used infrequently in the newer programs and
can be introduced later. The quotient *is* one of the factors. The terms
dividend and *divisor* are not needed.

·····J19, J20

These lab sheets are to encourage children to use "hunches," or estimate quickly and then check their estimates. There are legitimate
reasons for being wrong the first time. Practice makes for greater
accuracy than is achieved on the first try.

J20 has a problem in which the quotient is a mixed number.

$$\begin{array}{r} 8\frac{3}{9} \text{ or } 8\frac{1}{3} \text{ or } 8 \text{ r}3 \\ 9 \overline{\smash{)}75} \end{array}$$

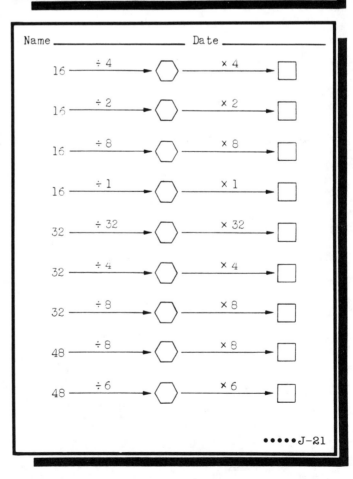

•••••J-21

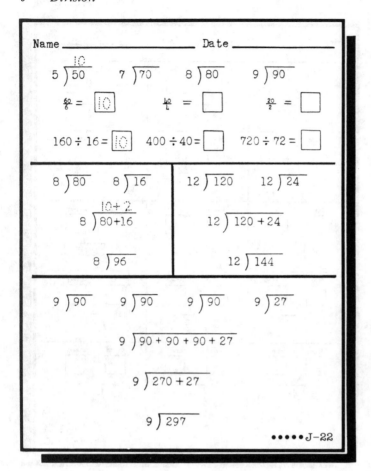

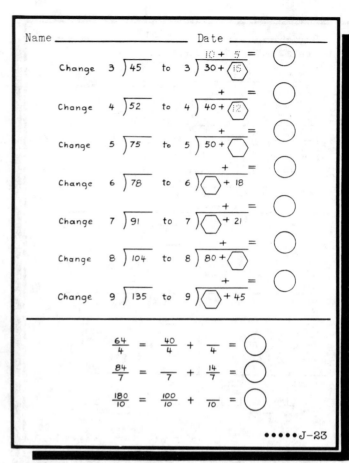

· · · · · J22–J24

These sheets give division practice on problems whose missing factor is 10 or > 10. This prepares children for so-called "short division."

Suggested preliminary practice

$10 \times 5 = \square$
$\square \div 5 = 10$

$$
\begin{array}{c}
6 \\
\times 10 \qquad 10\overline{)\,60}
\end{array}
$$

$180 \div 18 = \square$
$\square \times 18 = 180$ etc.

How many fours in 64? Answer:

        There are   10   fours in 40.
        There are   6   fours in 24.
∴ There are $(10 + 6)$ fours in $(40 + 24)$.
∴ There are   16   fours in 64.

How many eights in 112?

        There are   10   eights in 80.
        There are   4   eights in 32.
∴ There are $(10 + 4)$ eights in $(80 + 32)$.
∴ There are   14   eights in 112.

We write the preceding problem this way:

$$
\frac{14}{8\overline{)112}} = \frac{10 + 4}{8\overline{)80 + 32}}
$$

$$
112 \div 8 = (80 \div 8) + (32 \div 8) = 10 + 4 = 14
$$

$$
\frac{112}{8} = \frac{80}{8} + \frac{32}{8} = 10 + 4 = 14
$$

J-24

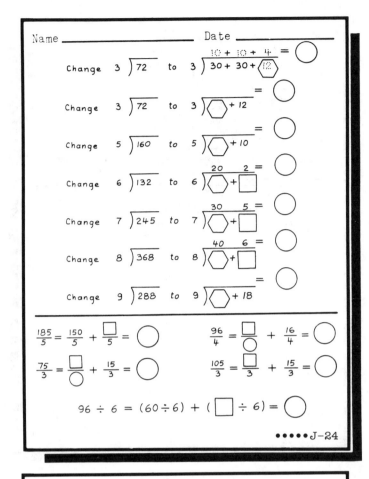

Change $3\overline{)72}$ to $3\overline{)30+30+12}$ ($10+10+4$) = ◯

Change $3\overline{)72}$ to $3\overline{)⬡+12}$ = ◯

Change $5\overline{)160}$ to $5\overline{)⬡+10}$ = ◯

Change $6\overline{)132}$ to $6\overline{)⬡+□}$ ($20 \quad 2$) = ◯

Change $7\overline{)245}$ to $7\overline{)⬡+□}$ ($30 \quad 5$) = ◯

Change $8\overline{)368}$ to $8\overline{)⬡+□}$ ($40 \quad 6$) = ◯

Change $9\overline{)288}$ to $9\overline{)⬡+18}$ = ◯

$\frac{185}{5} = \frac{150}{5} + \frac{□}{5} = ◯$ $\qquad$ $\frac{96}{4} = \frac{□}{◯} + \frac{16}{4} = ◯$

$\frac{75}{3} = \frac{□}{◯} + \frac{15}{3} = ◯$ $\qquad$ $\frac{105}{3} = \frac{□}{3} + \frac{15}{3} = ◯$

$96 \div 6 = (60 \div 6) + (□ \div 6) = ◯$

•••••• J-24

J-25

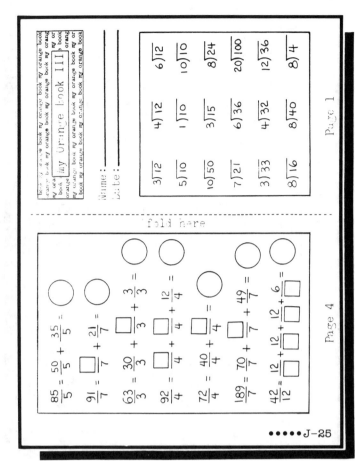

•••••• J-25

J-26

(Page 3)

	true	false
$8 \div 2 > 8 - 2$	T	F
$18 \div 3 = \frac{18}{3}$	T	F
$(5 \times 5) - 5 = 5$	T	F
$3\overline{)6}\,^{\frac{2}{}}\quad 6\overline{)3}\,^{\frac{1}{2}}$	T	F
$5\overline{)20},\ \frac{16}{4},\ 36 \div 9$ are all names for the number four.	T	F
$(75-3)+50 \neq 75$	T	F
$\frac{48}{6} = 18 \qquad \frac{60}{6}$	T	F
$\frac{8}{8} + \frac{7}{7} + \frac{6}{6} + \frac{5}{5} = \frac{26}{26}$	T	F

fold here

(Page 2)

$\frac{66}{11} = □$ $\qquad$ $7\overline{)\,}\,^{6}$

$66 - 11 = □$ $\qquad$ $3\overline{)42}\,^{6}$ $\qquad$ $\frac{9}{3} = ◯$

$3\overline{)27}$ $\qquad$ $\frac{1}{4}$ of $28 = □$ $\qquad$ $100 - 20 = □$

$\frac{1}{3}$ of $9 = ◯$ $\qquad$ $28 \div = 4$ $\qquad$ $100 \div 5 = □$

$\qquad$ $60 \div 30 = \div 3 = □$

$\qquad$ $81 \div 9 = 10 - □$

•••••• J-26

J-27

Name _____ Date _____

Try to do these division problems by thinking
of the steps you followed on lab sheets J-24, J-25, and J-26.

$12\overline{)168}$ $\quad$ think: $12\overline{)120+48}$ ($10+4$) $\quad$ write: $12\overline{)168}$ (14)

$9\overline{)99}$ $\qquad$ $9\overline{)135}$ $\qquad$ $6\overline{)90}$ $\qquad$ $8\overline{)128}$

$4\overline{)96}$ $\qquad$ $2\overline{)86}$ $\qquad$ $3\overline{)81}$ $\qquad$ $5\overline{)105}$

$11\overline{)121}$ $\qquad$ $14\overline{)154}$ $\qquad$ $4\overline{)128}$ $\qquad$ $6\overline{)78}$

$3\overline{)156}$ $\qquad$ $20\overline{)240}$ $\qquad$ $40\overline{)240}$ $\qquad$ $80\overline{)240}$

$\frac{150}{5} = □$ $\qquad$ $\frac{84}{4} = □$ $\qquad$ $\frac{64}{4} = □$

$\frac{52}{2} = □$ $\qquad$ $\frac{96}{8} = □$ $\qquad$ $\frac{330}{10} = □$

•••••• J-27

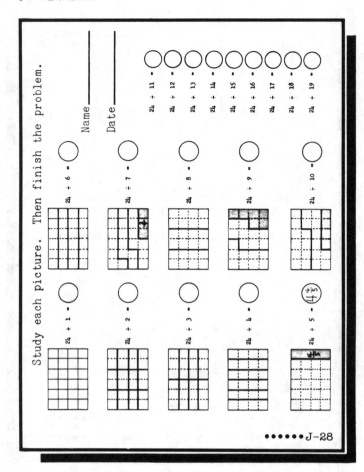

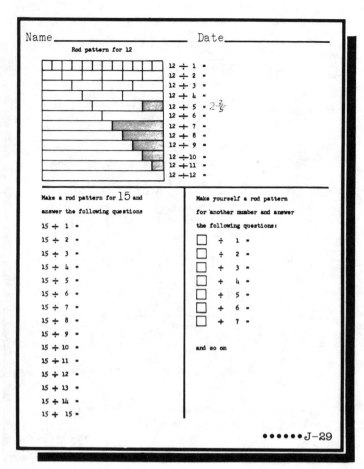

······ J28– J32

Division with a remainder

In this program we prefer to teach children immediately to write a remainder as a fractional part of the divisor.

$$15 \div 8 = 1\tfrac{7}{8}$$
not $15 \div 8 = 1 \text{ r}7$

$$8 \overline{)15} \,\, 1\tfrac{7}{8}$$
not $8 \overline{)15} \,\, 1 \text{ r}7$

To make this clear we think children should go back to the Cuisenaire® rod models.

Example from J29: How many fives in 12? Answer:

There are 2 fives and $\tfrac{2}{5}$ of a five.

10		2
5	5	$\tfrac{2}{5} \times 5$

$$12 \div 5 = 2\tfrac{2}{5}$$

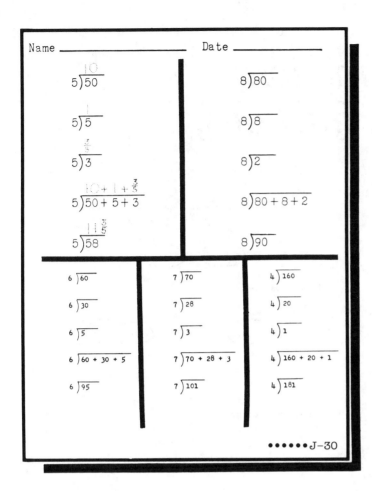

Name _____   Date _____

10
$5\overline{)50}$

1
$5\overline{)5}$

$\frac{3}{5}$
$5\overline{)3}$

$10 + 1 + \frac{3}{5}$
$5\overline{)50 + 5 + 3}$

$11\frac{3}{5}$
$5\overline{)58}$

$6\overline{)60}$ $7\overline{)70}$ $4\overline{)160}$

$6\overline{)30}$ $7\overline{)28}$ $4\overline{)20}$

$6\overline{)5}$ $7\overline{)3}$ $4\overline{)1}$

$6\overline{)60 + 30 + 5}$ $7\overline{)70 + 28 + 3}$ $4\overline{)160 + 20 + 1}$

$6\overline{)95}$ $7\overline{)101}$ $4\overline{)181}$

$8\overline{)80}$

$8\overline{)8}$

$8\overline{)2}$

$8\overline{)80 + 8 + 2}$

$8\overline{)90}$

••••••J-30

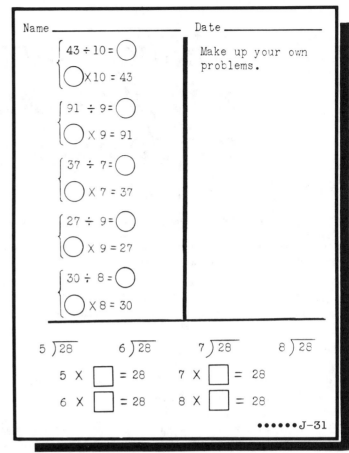

Name _____   Date _____

$\begin{cases} 43 \div 10 = \bigcirc \\ \bigcirc \times 10 = 43 \end{cases}$

$\begin{cases} 91 \div 9 = \bigcirc \\ \bigcirc \times 9 = 91 \end{cases}$

$\begin{cases} 37 \div 7 = \bigcirc \\ \bigcirc \times 7 = 37 \end{cases}$

$\begin{cases} 27 \div 9 = \bigcirc \\ \bigcirc \times 9 = 27 \end{cases}$

$\begin{cases} 30 \div 8 = \bigcirc \\ \bigcirc \times 8 = 30 \end{cases}$

Make up your own problems.

$5\overline{)28}$ $6\overline{)28}$ $7\overline{)28}$ $8\overline{)28}$

$5 \times \boxed{} = 28$ $7 \times \boxed{} = 28$

$6 \times \boxed{} = 28$ $8 \times \boxed{} = 28$

••••••J-31

•••••• **J32**

It takes children a long time to do this lab sheet. Children who have the patience enjoy doing it and checking their answers with Cuisenaire® rods. Children may also be encouraged to use rods to work the problems in the following manner.

	13	or	10	$+$	3
	orange				lt. gr.
	3	3	3	3	1

↖ remainder

13 cannot be divided by 3 without a remainder.

Name _____   Date _____

Which numbers can be divided by $\boxed{5}$ without a remainder? (circle them)

35   39   60   72   45   43   82   66

Which numbers can be divided by $\boxed{3}$ without a remainder?

14   22   27   18   13   33   42   60

Which numbers can be divided by $\boxed{8}$ without a remainder?

24   58   48   70   19   32   36   56

Which numbers can be divided by $\boxed{6}$ without a remainder?

26   42   38   48   20   30   54   72

Which numbers can be divided by $\boxed{9}$ without a remainder?

17   29   61   80   35   84   27   73

••••••J-32

185

K Addition, subtraction, multiplication, fractions, and division

Suggested activity: an algebraic game

No new operations are introduced in this section. These notes are confined to suggestions for preliminary activities.

This game will be useful as preparation for lab sheet K20 and many lab sheets in Section L, Equalities and Inequalities.

Equipment

The group playing the game will need a set of oaktag strips approximately $2'' \times 10''$ and a set of True–False cards.

Preparation

The teacher writes an open sentence on each oaktag strip. These open sentences fall into the following categories:

1 Identities (unconditional equations): equations which are true for any numerical replacements of $\square$ and $\triangle$.

2 Conditional equations: only certain replacements for $\square$ and $\triangle$ will make them true.

3 Unconditional inequalities: all replacements for $\square$ and $\triangle$ will make them true.

4 Conditional inequalities: only certain replacements for $\square$ and $\triangle$ will make them true.

Content

The strips that follow contain open sentences which the teacher may put on the oaktag strips.

1 Identities

$$\square \times \triangle = \triangle \times \square$$

Commutative law of multiplication: always true if we put the same number in both $\square$'s and the same number in both $\triangle$'s.

$$\square + \triangle = \triangle + \square$$

Commutative law of addition

$$\square \times (\triangle + \bigcirc) = (\square \times \triangle) + (\square \times \bigcirc)$$

$$(\square \times 3) + (\square \times 2) = \square \times 5$$

Distributive law

$$(\tfrac{1}{2} \times \square) \times (2 \times \triangle) = (2 \times \square) \times (\tfrac{1}{2} \times \triangle)$$

$$\square \times 1 = \square$$

2 Conditional equations

$$\square \times \triangle = \triangle$$

True when $\square = 1$ and $\triangle =$ any number *or* $\triangle = 0$ and $\square =$ any number.

$$\square + \triangle = \square$$

True when $\triangle = 0$.

$$\square + \square = \square \times \square$$

True when $\square = 0$ *or* $\square = 2$.

$$\square \div \triangle = \triangle \div \square$$

True only when $\square = \triangle$ and neither $= 0$.

3 Non-identities

$$\square + 6 = \square$$

$$\square - 10 = \square$$

Neither of the above types of equations is ever true.

4 Unconditional inequalities

$$\square + 5 > \square$$

This type of equation is always true. ($>$ means "is greater than.")

186

5   Conditional inequalities

$$\square \times 2 > 4$$

True only when $\square$ = any number > 2.

$$\square \times 7 > 35$$

True only when $\square$ = any number > 5.

$$\square \times 5 > 15$$

True only when $\square$ = any number > 3.

$$5 < \square < 6$$

True only when $\square$ > 5 but < 6. (< means "is less than.")

$$432 \neq \boxed{}$$

True for any number except 432.

$$2 \times 3 \times 4 < 2 \times 3 \times \boxed{}$$

Many more open sentences such as these examples may be given.

Playing the game

The following is an actual class record.

Each child has a file card on his desk; the "T" side is turned up. The group has decided to try to make true the open sentence which the teacher will show them. The teacher holds up the oaktag strip with:

$$\boxed{\square + \triangle = \triangle + \square}$$

Teacher: Who can make this true?

Mary: I can! I can!

$$\boxed{3} + \triangle_4 = \triangle_4 + \boxed{3}$$

Johnny: I have another way!

$$\boxed{9} + \triangle_{16} = \triangle_{16} + \boxed{9}$$

Tom: I have one!

$$1000 + 1{,}000{,}000 = 1{,}000{,}000 + 1{,}000$$

Billy: Oh, there are so many ways; we couldn't find them all. It's always true! (The children, excepting Cathy, seem to agree with Billy. Cathy isn't sure.)

Teacher: Turn your cards over to the "F" side. Who wants to try to make this sentence false? She holds up:

$$\boxed{\square + \triangle = \triangle + \square}$$

Cathy: Maybe things like $\frac{1}{2}$ or $\frac{3}{4}$ will make it false; or maybe negative numbers—we haven't tried those. (There is pensive silence, and then a gradually increasing volume of "No, no, it won't work!" is heard in the room.)

Teacher: Let's check for some fractions and negative numbers. (As the children suggest fractions and negative numbers, the teacher writes them in a table on the chalkboard.)

$\square$	$\triangle$	
$\frac{1}{2}$	$\frac{3}{4}$	works
-2	-5	works
0	-3	works
-1	10	works
etc.		

Billy: I won't play any more. This is silly. It can't be made false. (The class echoes, "We won't play.")

Teacher: "Fine, why don't we make the rule that whenever you are asked to make an open sentence true or false, and you think it is impossible, you say, "I won't play." (The new rule is accepted.) "You may now decide for yourselves which side of your card to turn up. If your "T" shows, try to make the next open sentence true; if your "F" shows, try to make it false. You can't change once you have seen the card. Ready?" (She gives:)

$$\boxed{\square + \triangle = 2\square + \tfrac{1}{2}\triangle}$$

There is a long silence. Then the teacher asks to hear from the T's first. Johnny reports he tried 2 for $\square$ and 1 for $\triangle$ and it didn't work. Mary reports she tried 6 for $\square$ and 4 for $\triangle$ and it didn't work. Several other children made similar reports.

Then the teacher asks to hear from the F's. All F's report success.

$$\boxed{0} + \triangle_9 \neq 2 \times \boxed{0} + \tfrac{1}{2} \times \triangle_9$$

$$\boxed{15} + \triangle_8 \neq 2 \times \boxed{15} + \tfrac{1}{2} \times \triangle_8$$

Hands are up from most of the T's. One after the other says, "I won't play" (meaning it can't be made true). The T's sit back complacently. All but one child—Cathy. Cathy's hand is up.

Cathy: I can make it true. I have two numbers for $\square$ and two numbers for $\triangle$ and I think there are more. (The class is surprised. Cathy gives her replacement:)

$$\boxed{1} + \triangle_2 = 2 \times \boxed{1} + \tfrac{1}{2} \times \triangle_2$$

$$\boxed{3} + \triangle_6 = 2 \times \boxed{3} + \tfrac{1}{2} \times \triangle_6$$

The children are awe-struck. Then David gets up and says: "Cathy just conquered the unknown." And Andy adds: "She is an explorer, a mathematical explorer." Cathy blushes and grins. (This happened in a second-grade class on the very day that John Glenn orbited the earth.)

Written signals: parentheses

The point to be made is that just as pauses and inflections in oral speech clear up the meaning, and punctuation clears up ambiguities in written English, so do parentheses clear up ambiguities in mathematical statements. For example, the expression

> That tiger ate Nancy

could mean one of several things. Notice the different stress and punctuation.

> That tiger ate, Nancy.
> *That* tiger ate, Nancy?
> That tiger ate *Nancy!*

Without the proper inflection (or punctuation in a written sentence), we do not know who ate whom.

$$3 + 4 \times 2 + 5 = \square$$

is also an ambiguous statement when one does not know how to use parentheses.

The following happened in a classroom. On the chalkboard the teacher wrote:

$$3 + 4 \times 2 + 5 = \square$$

Teacher: Build a rod model for the open sentence I wrote on the chalkboard. Raise your hand when you know what goes in the box.

Many hands go up. The teacher goes around and has children whisper answers to her. She writes the following answers on the board as she hears them: 16, 16, 19, 19, 16, 49, 16, 49, etc.

There is general alarm. "16 isn't right. It's 49." "No, it's 16." "No, it's 19."

All children insist they can prove their answers with the rods. What has happened? Why the disagreement? The teacher asks for silence.

Teacher: Ruth, you gave 16 as your answer. Tell me the rod train *you* built.

Ruth: Light green, red, red, red, red, yellow. ("That's right, I have that, too," is heard from a small chorus.)

Teacher: Frank, you said the answer is 19. Read off the colors of your train.

Frank: Green, purple, green, purple, yellow. (Several children agree with Frank.)

Teacher: Toni, your answer was 49. What is your train?

Toni: Red, yellow; red, yellow; red, yellow; red, yellow; red, yellow; red, yellow; red, yellow. (Two children agree with Toni.)

Teacher: Isn't that strange? Who can tell what happened?

Jeff: I agree with Ruth: 3—plus four 2's—plus 5 equals 16.

Teacher writes: $\left(3 + \boxed{4 \times 2}\right) + 5 = 16$

Toby: It doesn't say that. It says: 3 plus 4—taken 2 times—plus 5, and that is 19.

Teacher writes: $\left(\boxed{3 + 4} \times 2\right) + 5 = 19$

Teacher: Toni, read it your way.

Toni: 3 plus 4—times—2 plus 5.

Teacher writes: $\boxed{3 + 4} \times \boxed{2 + 5} = 49$

Teacher: Well, who is right?

The children decide they all are right—depending on how they read the problem. They could tell from the voices—where the pauses were—which way was meant.*

The class decides that parentheses and loops are "neat" ways to keep from arguing. Loops or parentheses around the problem tell the same things that voice pauses tell. The children want more problems like the preceding.

The problem is posed: do we need parentheses for each of the following:

1 $5 + 3 + 2 + 9 = \square$ Parentheses: yes (no)

2 $7 - 2 + 3 + 5 = \square$ Parentheses: (yes) no
$7 - 2 + 3 + 5 = 13$
but
$7 - \boxed{2 + 3} + 5 = 7$
and
$7 - \boxed{2 + 3 + 5} = -3$

3 $2 \times 3 + 5 - 2 = \square$ Parentheses: (yes) no
$\boxed{2 \times 3} + 5 - 2 = 9$
$2 \times \boxed{3 + 5} - 2 = 14$
$2 \times \boxed{3 + 5 - 2} = 12$

4 $24 \div 4 \times 2 = \square$ Parentheses: (yes) no
$\boxed{24 \div 4} \times 2 = 12$
$24 \div \boxed{4 \times 2} = 3$

---

*16, however, is the only conventionally "correct" answer to the problem as presented, since mathematical convention dictates that when there are no parentheses, the multiplication must be performed first.

·· K1

Answers

~~0×7=1~~
$0 + 7 = 7$
$1 \times 7 = 7$

~~1÷7=1~~
$7 \div 1 = 7$
~~7÷7=1~~

~~1×0=1~~
$7 - 0 = 7$
$0 \times 7 = 0$

$10 = 2 \times 5$
$10 \div 5 = 2$
$2 \times 5 = 10$

$2 = 10 \div 5$
$5 \times 2 = 10$
$5 = 10 \div 2$

$5 \div 5 = 1$
$5 - 5 = 0$
$5 + 5 = 10$
$5 \times 5 = 25$

$1 \div 1 = 1$
$1 \times 1 = 1$
$1 - 1 = 0$
$1 + 1 = 2$

$6 = 3 + 3$
or
$6 - 3 = 3$

$3 = 6 - 3$

$3 + 3 = 6$

Here is a code puzzle, using the same kind of thinking. Instead of the computational symbols ($+$ $-$ $\div$ $\times$) we use a code.

All of the following code sentences are true.

$$15 \; ✡ \; 5 \; < \; 15 \; ☾ \; 5$$
$$15 \; \infty \; 5 \; > \; 15 \; \odot \; 5$$
$$15 \; \odot \; 5 \; > \; 15 \; ☾ \; 5$$

What operators do ✡ , ∞ , $\odot$, ☾ stand for?

code	key
✡	$\div$
∞	$\times$
$\odot$	$+$
☾	$-$

Thus:

$15 \div 5 < 15 - 5$
$15 \times 5 > 15 + 5$
$15 + 5 > 15 - 5$

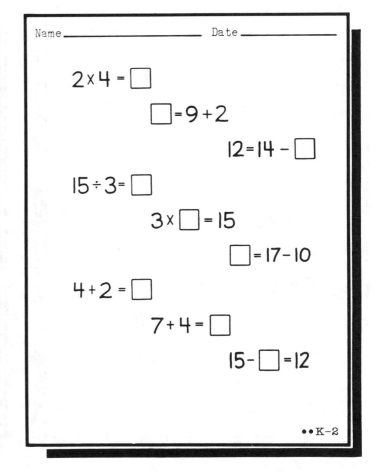

Name_____ Date_____

$9 \div 3 = \square$ $3 \times 5 = \square$

$12 \div 4 = \square$ $\square = 5 \times 3$

$15 \div 5 = \square$ $\square = 4 \times 5$

$8 \div 2 = \square$ $5 \times \square = 20$

$10 \div 5 = \square$ $2 \times 5 = \square$

$20 \div 4 = \square$ $\square = 6 \times 3$

$18 \div 3 = \square$ $12 = 3 \times \square$

$\square = 20 \div 5$ $3 \times \square = 9$

$\square = 16 \div 8$ $4 \times \square = 8$

$5 = \square \div 3$ $8 \times 2 = \square$

•• K-3

Name_____ Date_____

$6 + 5 = \square$ $4 \times 4 = \square$

$2 \times 6 = \square$ $15 - 5 = \square$

$9 - 4 = \square$ $4 + 5 + 2 = \square$

$12 \div 3 = \square$ $10 \div 5 = \square$

$7 + 5 = \square$ $20 - 10 = \square$

$14 - 4 = \square$ $11 + 9 = \square$

$3 \times 5 = \square$ $4 \times 5 = \square$

$9 \div 3 = \square$ $7 - 3 + 6 = \square$

$3 + 4 + 6 = \square$ $8 \div 4 = \square$

$7 - 7 = \square$ $3 \times 10 = \square$

•• K-4

Name_____ Date_____

$3 \times 3 = \square$ $9 \div 3 = \square$

$\square = 4 \times 3$ $\square = 12 \div 4$

$\square = 2 \times 8$ $10 \div 2 = \square$

$\square = 4 \times 5$ $\square = 18 \div 3$

$3 \times 5 = \square$ $18 \div 2 = \square$

$2 \times 4 = \square$ $8 \div 4 = \square$

$5 \times 5 = \square$ $20 = 4 \times \square$

$\square = 7 \times 2$ $20 \div 4 = \square$

$5 \times 2 = \square$ $\square = 12 \div 2$

$2 \times 10 = \square$ $20 \div 2 = \square$

•• K-5

Name_____ Date_____

$2 \times 6 = \bigcirc$ $3 \times 6 = \square$

$12 \div 6 = \bigcirc$ $4 \times 5 = \square$

$14 \div 7 = \bigcirc$ $8 \times 2 = \square$

$16 \div 4 = \bigcirc$ $4 \times 3 = \square$

$20 \div 5 = \bigcirc$ $5 \times 3 = \square$

$20 \div 4 = \bigcirc$ $7 \times 2 = \square$

$20 \div 10 = \bigcirc$ $4 \times 6 = \square$

$20 \div 2 = \bigcirc$ $30 \div 5 = \square$

$100 \div 10 = \bigcirc$ $9 \div 3 = \square$

$40 \div 10 = \bigcirc$ $10 \times 2 = \square$

•• K-6

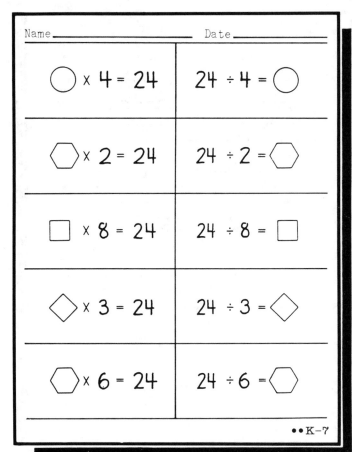

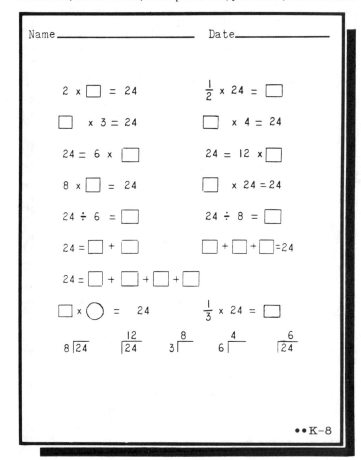

·· K7

Multiplication and division

Both K7 and K8 are about the number 24.

Related problems

$\square \times 3 = 12$
How many 3's equal 12?

$12 \div 3 = \square$
12 divided by 3 equals what?

Additional suggestions

1   Children may be asked to make a list of all the whole numbers that divide 24 without a remainder. These numbers are the *factors* of 24. They are: 1, 2, 3, 4, 6, 8, 12, 24. They come in pairs.

    (1, 24) 1×24 and 24×1.
    (2, 12) 2×12 and 12×2.
    (3, 8) 3×8 and 8×3.
    (4, 6) 4×6 and 6×4.

2   When a rod model of 24 is built, the one-color patterns will tell the factor story.

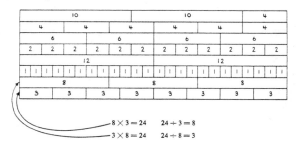

·· K8

Children may be asked, individually or as a group, to make up a paper like K8 for another number—perhaps 16, 18, or 28.

Name _____ Date _____

Make up true sentences using these numbers.

(4, 3, 12)   (8, 3, 24)

(12, 9, 21)   (34, 0, 34)

•••K-9

Name _____ Date _____

Make up true sentences using these numbers.

(7, 21, 3)   (0, 8, 0)

(5, 8, 40)   (22, 7, 15)

•••K-10

•••K9, K10
Number triplets

These lab sheets deal with triplets of numbers related through multiplication and its inverse or through addition and its inverse.

Solutions to K9

(4,   3,   12)   (34,   0,   34)

$4 \times 3 = 12$	$34 + 0 = 34$
$3 \times 4 = 12$	$0 + 34 = 34$
$12 = 4 \times 3$	$34 = 34 + 0$
$12 = 3 \times 4$	$34 = 0 + 34$
$12 \div 4 = 3$	$34 = 34 - 0$
$4 = 12 \div 3$	$34 - 34 = 0$
$3 = 12 \div 4$	$0 = 34 - 34$

Solutions to K10

(0,   8,   0)

$0 \times 8 = 0$	$0 = 0 \times 8$
$8 \times 0 = 0$	$0 \div 8 = 0$
$0 = 8 \times 0$	$0 = 0 \div 8$

Not (8 ÷ 0 = 0.) *We cannot divide by zero!*

Note: Children should be encouraged to make lab sheets like **K9** and **K10** for themselves.

K-11

Name_____ Date_____

How many 100's in 100?	[ ]	100 ÷ 100 =	[ ]
How many 50's in 100?	[ ]	100 ÷ 50 =	[ ]
How many 25's in 100?	[ ]	100 ÷ 25 =	[ ]
How many 20's in 100?	[ ]	100 ÷ 20 =	[ ]
How many 10's in 100?	[ ]	100 ÷ 10 =	[ ]
How many 5's in 100?	[ ]	100 ÷ 5 =	[ ]
How many 2's in 100?	[ ]	100 ÷ 2 =	[ ]
How many 1's in 100?	[ ]	100 ÷ 1 =	[ ]

Make up problems of your own.

$\frac{1}{100}$ of 100 = [ ]

$\frac{1}{50}$ of 100 = [ ]

$\frac{1}{10}$ of 100 = [ ]

$\frac{1}{2}$ of 100 = [ ]

•••K-11

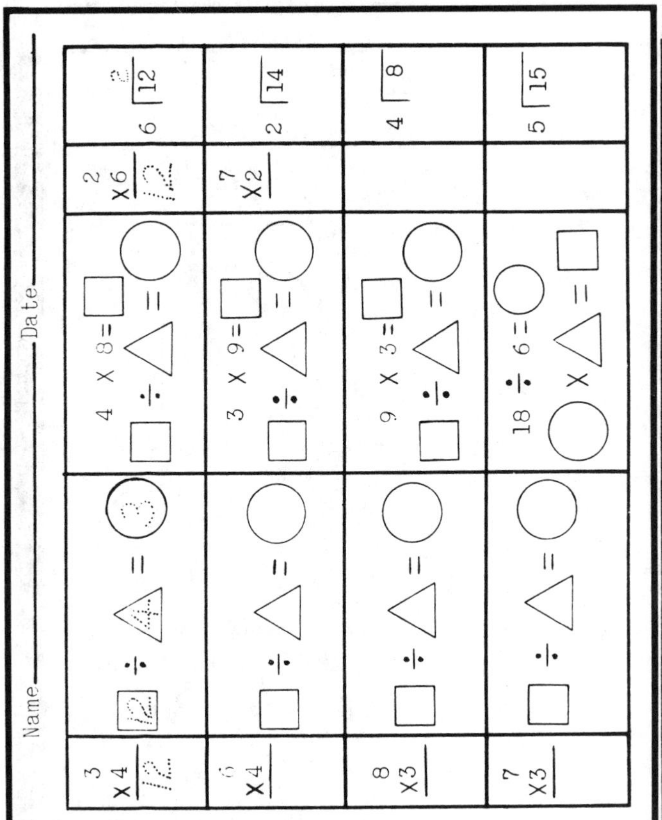

K-12

Name_____ Date_____

Row 1:
- $6\overline{)12}$ = 2
- $2\overline{)14}$
- $4\overline{)8}$
- $5\overline{)15}$

Row 2:
- $\begin{array}{r}2\\ \times 6\\ \hline 12\end{array}$
- $\begin{array}{r}7\\ \times 2\\ \hline \end{array}$

Row 3:
- $4 \times 8 = \square$; $\triangle \div \square =$ $\bigcirc$
- $3 \times 9 = \square$; $\triangle \div \square =$ $\bigcirc$
- $9 \times 3 = \square$; $\triangle \div \square =$ $\bigcirc$
- $18 \div 6 = \square$; $\triangle \times \bigcirc =$ $\square$

Row 4:
- $\triangle \div \square =$ $\bigcirc$ (4 ÷ 12 = 3)
- $\triangle \div \square =$ $\bigcirc$
- $\triangle \div \square =$ $\bigcirc$
- $\triangle \div \square =$ $\bigcirc$

Row 5:
- $\begin{array}{r}3\\ \times 4\\ \hline 12\end{array}$
- $\begin{array}{r}6\\ \times 4\\ \hline \end{array}$
- $\begin{array}{r}8\\ \times 3\\ \hline \end{array}$
- $\begin{array}{r}7\\ \times 3\\ \hline \end{array}$

•••K-12

193

···K13, K14

Children make up their own problems.

Example

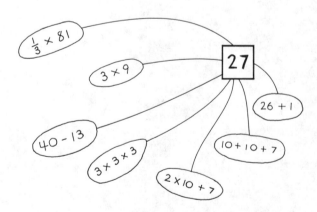

Lab sheet K14 is like K13, except that answers to the problems should equal 105. Since some children confuse 105 with 500, they should be encouraged to make a paper for 500.

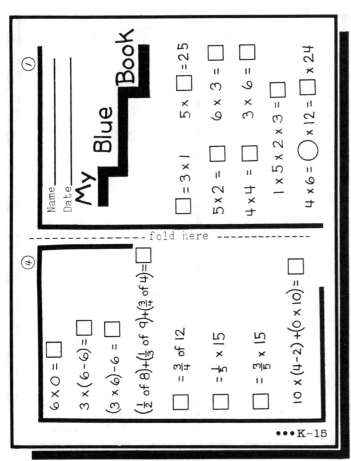

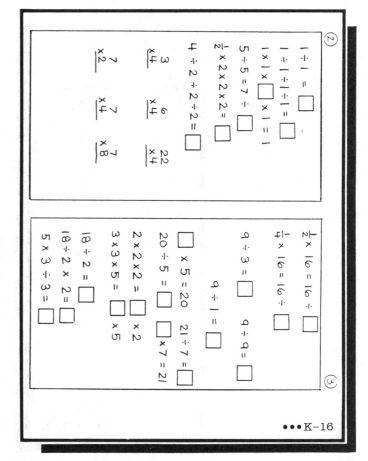

·····K17

Matching word statements with symbolic representation

This lab sheet requires *good* reading ability and is difficult. The child has a choice on how he will approach the work.

a. He may draw lines between the words and the mathematical expression:

seven plus some number ——————— $7 + \square$

b. He may enumerate the word statements and write the numerals next to the matching expression:

   ① three times fifteen   ③ $30 \div 2$

   ② one-half of thirty   ① 3×15

   ③ thirty divided by two   ② $\frac{1}{2} \times 30$

             etc.

c. He may write the mathematical expression under the word statement.

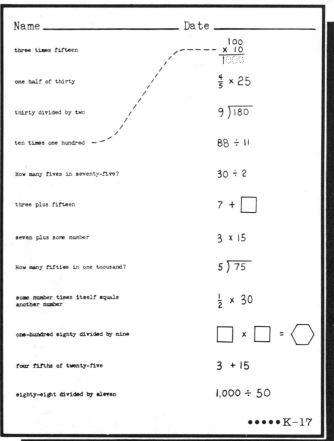

Name_____ Date_____

Use +, −, X, and ( ) to make these sentences true.

2 3 4 = 9	3 2 1 = 6
2 3 4 = 1	3 2 1 = □
2 3 4 = 10	3 2 1 = □
(2 + 3) X 4 = 20	3 2 1 = □
2 3 4 = 14	3 2 1 = □
2 3 4 = 24	3 2 1 = □
	3 2 1 = □
3 3 3 = 9	3 2 1 = □
3 3 3 = 3	3 2 1 = □
3 3 3 = 6	3 2 1 = □
3 3 3 = 12	3 2 1 = □
	3 2 1 = □

•••••K-18

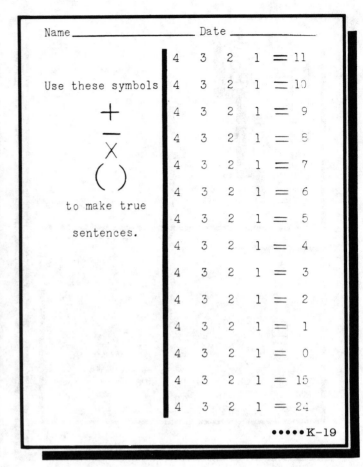

Name_____ Date_____

Use these symbols
+
−
X
( )
to make true sentences.

4 3 2 1 = 11
4 3 2 1 = 10
4 3 2 1 = 9
4 3 2 1 = 8
4 3 2 1 = 7
4 3 2 1 = 6
4 3 2 1 = 5
4 3 2 1 = 4
4 3 2 1 = 3
4 3 2 1 = 2
4 3 2 1 = 1
4 3 2 1 = 0
4 3 2 1 = 15
4 3 2 1 = 24

•••••K-19

••••• K18

Completing the equations

Children are to complete the equations by supplying the correct operational symbols. The teacher should do preliminary work on the chalkboard similar to this before children are given this lab sheet.

Solutions	Some correct solutions
$2 + 3 + 4 = 9$	There are many possible solutions. It is important for children to be aware of the role of parentheses.
$2 + 3 - 4 = 1$	
$2 \times 3 + 4 = 10$	
$(2 + 3) \times 4 = 20$	$3 \times 2 - 1 = 5$
$2 + 3 \times 4 = 14$	*but* $3 \times (2 - 1) = 3$
$2 \times 3 \times 4 = 24$	

Some children will even try negative numbers.

$$3 + 2 + 1 = 6$$
$$3 + 2 - 1 = \boxed{4}$$
$$3 - 2 - 1 = \boxed{0}$$
$$3 \times 2 + 1 = \boxed{7}$$
$$3 \times (2 + 1) = \boxed{9}$$
$$3 \times 2 \times 1 = \boxed{6}$$
$$(3 + 2) \times 1 = \boxed{5}$$
$$(3 - 2) \times 1 = \boxed{1}$$
$$3 - 2 + 1 = \boxed{2}$$
$$-3 - 2 - 1 = \boxed{-6}$$
$$3 \times 2 - 1 = \boxed{5}$$
$$3 \times (2 - 1) = \boxed{3}$$

$3 + 3 + 3 = 9$
$3 + 3 - 3 = 3$
$3 \times 3 - 3 = 6$
$3 \times 3 + 3 = 12$
or $3 + 3 \times 3 = 12$

••••• K19

This is an even more difficult sheet, because the child must follow the predetermined order on the page.

Some correct solutions

$$4 \times 3 - 2 + 1 = 11$$
$$4 \times 3 - 2 \times 1 = 10$$
$$\textit{or } 4 + 3 + 2 + 1 = 10$$
$$4 + 3 + 2 \times 1 = 9$$
$$\textit{or } 4 \times 3 - 2 - 1 = 9$$
$$4 + 3 + 2 - 1 = 8$$
$$(4 + 3) \times (2 - 1) = 7$$
$$4 + 3 - 2 + 1 = 6$$
$$(4 + 3 - 2) \times 1 = 5$$
$$4 - 3 + 2 + 1 = 4$$
$$(4 - 3) \times (2 + 1) = 3$$
$$(4 - 3) \times 2 \times 1 = 2$$
$$(-4 + 3 + 2) \times 1 = 1$$
$$4 \times (3 - 2 - 1) = 0$$
$$4 \times 3 + 2 + 1 = 15$$
$$4 \times 3 \times 2 \times 1 = 24$$

No child is expected to find *all* the answers. Some very analytical children will try very hard and will do very well on this sheet.

Name _____ Date _____

Draw lines from the equation to the rule describing it.

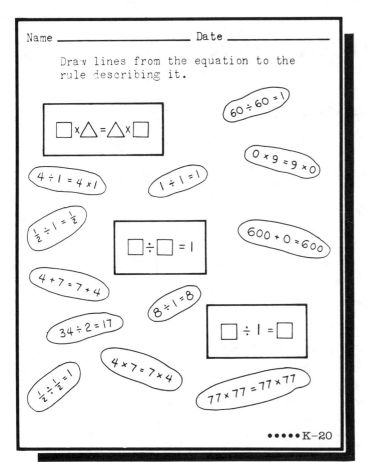

•••••K-20

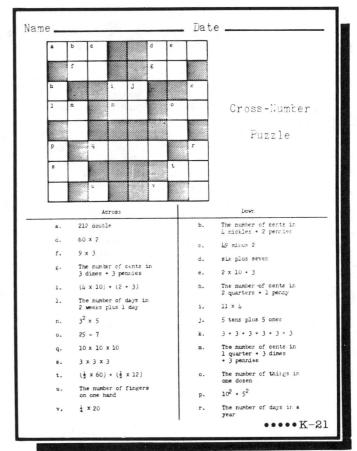

Cross-Number Puzzle

	Across			Down	
a.	212 double		b.	The number of cents in 4 nickles + 2 pennies	
d.	60 x 2		c.	49 minus 2	
f.	9 x 3		d.	six plus seven	
g.	The number of cents in 3 dimes + 3 pennies		e.	2 x 10 + 3	
i.	(4 x 10) + (2 + 3)		h.	The number of cents in 2 quarters + 1 penny	
l.	The number of days in 2 weeks plus 1 day		i.	11 x 4	
n.	3^2 x 5		j.	5 tens plus 5 ones	
o.	25 - 7		k.	3 + 3 + 3 + 3 + 3 + 3	
q.	10 x 10 x 10		m.	The number of cents in 1 quarter + 3 dimes + 3 pennies	
s.	3 x 3 x 3		o.	The number of things in one dozen	
t.	($\frac{1}{2}$ x 60) + ($\frac{1}{2}$ x 12)		p.	10^2 + 5^2	
u.	The number of fingers on one hand		r.	The number of days in a year	
v.	$\frac{1}{4}$ x 20				

•••••K-21

•••••**K20**

The solutions for this sheet are as follows:

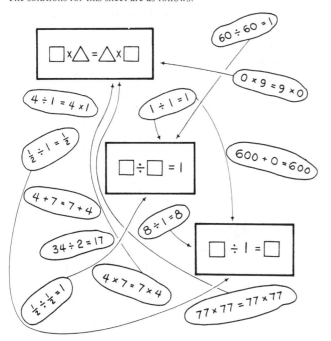

Name _____ Date _____

Dear ___

Please correct my paper. I made some mistakes. Love,

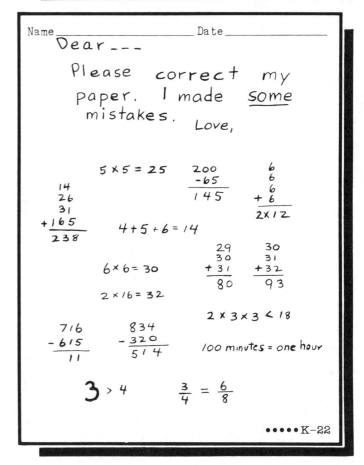

•••••K-22

L   Equalities and inequalities

Kindergarten and first-grade teachers have always considered it their job in "arithmetic readiness" to establish the notions of *less than, more than, same as, not alike*. However, in most instances, no special mathematical symbols are used to express these relationships, and this emphasis is not continued beyond the primary grades. In the Mathematics Laboratory program, inequalities are introduced early.

$3 > 2$ is read as "three is *greater than* two."
$3 < 4$ is read as "three is *less than* four."
$3 \neq 4$ is read as "three *does not equal* four."
$3 \not< 2$ is read as "three is *not less than* two."
$3 \not> 4$ is read as "three is *not greater than* four."
$3 \leq 4$ is read as "three is *less than or equal to* four."
$3 = 2 + 1$ is read as "three *equals* two plus one."

Examples of inequalities

The codification of these relationships can be very useful to the teacher and to the pupil. The examples that follow demonstrate this.

1 Counting

1, 2, 3, $\boxed{4}$, 5, 6, 7 . . .

$4 = \square$ solution set is {4}
$4 > \square$ solution set: {3, 2, 1}
$4 < \square$ solution set: {5, 6, 7 . . .} Any number greater than four is correct.

$1000 > 999$, or any number up to 1000
$0 > -1$
$0 < 1$

2 On the number line

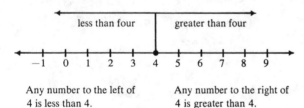

Any number to the left of 4 is less than 4.

Any number to the right of 4 is greater than 4.

3 Addition

$4 + 3 > 4$
$4 + \frac{1}{1000} > 4$

In general, $4 + \square > 4$,   if $\square > 0$

4 Subtraction

$4 - 3 < 4$
$4 - \frac{1}{1000} < 4$

In general, $4 - \square < 4$,   if $\square > 0$

5 Multiplication

$3 \times 4 > 4$
$\frac{1}{2} \times 4 < 4$

In general,
$\square \times 4 > 4$,   if $\square > 1$
$\square \times 4 < 4$,   if $\square > 1$

thus,
$\frac{2}{3} \times \frac{3}{4} < \frac{3}{4}$,   because $\frac{2}{3} < 1$
$\frac{7}{5} \times \frac{3}{4} > \frac{3}{4}$,   because $\frac{7}{5} > 1$
$.3425 \times 4 < 4$,   because $.3425 < 1$

6 Division

$4 \div 2 < 4$
$4 \div \frac{1}{4} > 4$

In general,
$4 \div \square < 4$,   if $\square > 1$
$4 \div \square > 4$,   if $0 < \square < 1$

thus,
$4 \div .95 > 4$,   because $0 < .95 < 1$
$4 \div 8 < 4$,   because $8 > 1$

Use of rods for introductory work on inequalities and equalities

Beginning in kindergarten, children should be given large sheets of paper with equality and inequality symbols drawn on them:

The children are to place piles of rods on either side of a symbol to make a true sentence. By arranging the same amount of wood in identical patterns on either side of the equal sign (as shown under "Proof" below), they will come to understand the idea of equality.

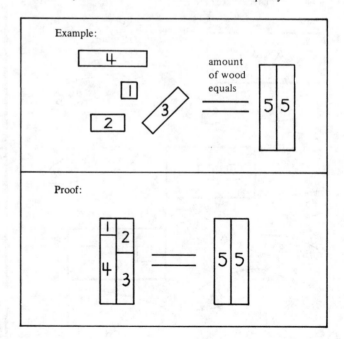

Other techniques to show inequalities and equalities

1 Balance

Two transparent plastic containers, each with four marbles. Children can see that they balance and hence equal one another.

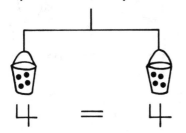

2 Liquids

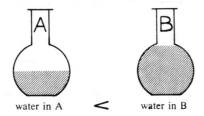

water in A $<$ water in B

3 Money

4 Linear measure

centimeter $\square$ $<$ [meterstick]

Inequalities as tools for estimation

The following problem is presented to a seven-year-old.

$$7 \times 7 \times 7 = \boxed{}$$

He is stumped and does not know the answer. Using rods to help himself, he thinks through the following sequence of steps:

$$7 \times 7 = 49$$
$$49 < 50$$
$$49 = 50 - 1$$
$$7 \times 50 = 350$$
$$350 > 7 \times 7 \times 7$$
$$7 \times 7 \times 7 = 350 - 7$$
$$7 \times 7 \times 7 = 343$$

Or he works on the following problem:

$$\frac{4}{5} + \frac{1}{2} = \square$$
$$\frac{4}{5} < 1$$
$$\frac{1}{2} < 1$$

but $\qquad 1 + 1 = 2$

therefore $\qquad \frac{4}{5} + \frac{1}{2} < 2$

$$\frac{4}{5} > \frac{1}{2}$$

but $\qquad \frac{1}{2} + \frac{1}{2} = 1$

therefore $\qquad \frac{4}{5} + \frac{1}{2} > 1$

Finally he concludes that the answer must be between 1 and 2.

Suggested activity: Guess the Secret Number

This a game second-graders like to play. The teacher announces that the secret number is between 0 and 100, writes a $\square$ on the chalkboard, and writes the answers to the children's questions on the board.

Children's Questions	*Teacher's Answers*
Is it an even number?	$\square$ is an even number.
Is it more than 50?	$\square \not> 50$
Is it more than 25?	$\square \not> 25$
Is it more than 13?	$\square > 13$

Teacher: Now let's review what we know about the number.

Children: The number is: even; can't be 25, because 25 is odd; is either 24, 22, 20, 18, 16, or 14.

More Questions	*Answers*
Is the number in the twenties?	$\square$ is not in the twenties.
Can the number be divided by four, with no remainder?	$\square$ is not divisible by 4.
Is the number 18?	$\square = 18$

Children do not play the game that well at the start, but by playing they soon learn how to use good strategy. (Note: The best questions always cut the number of possible answers in half.)

·L1

It is assumed that before children begin this section, they will play games with piles of blocks or rods heaped on the left and right sides of symbol cards for *equal, greater than,* and *less than.* A blank sheet of paper can serve as a game board on which the children draw a symbol in crayon.

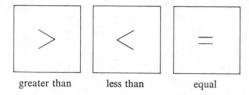

greater than   less than   equal

On L1 children may put rods on the designs and then compare the amounts in the left and right piles by making two trains out of them. They can indicate, in several ways, which pile has more wood:

a. write the word *more;*
b. put >, <, = symbols between pairs;
c. color the side with the most wood.

For an additional activity, the teacher might ask which side of the whole page has the most wood.

·L2

How can we tell on a number line which number is greater than another?

On the conventional number line the farther we move to the right, the larger the numbers. The farther we move to the left, the smaller the numbers.

To find out what to write between '0' and '5', we put one finger on the '0' and the other on '5' and see that '0' is to the left of '5'. Thus $0 < 5$.

A six-year-old told his teacher that the inequality sign < looked like a "wide open mouth." This helped him remember where to write the name for the greater number. It always went on the "wide open side."

Supplementary activity

Children like to play a fast-moving chalkboard game about inequalities. A mathematical sentence such as the following is written on the chalkboard:

$$8 > 1 \quad \text{(true)}$$

Then the teacher asks: 'Who can make it false without crossing anything out or using the eraser?"

Child: $8 > 10$ (false)

Teacher: Who can make it true again?

Child: $28 > 10$ (true)

Teacher: Make it false again.

Child: $28 > 10 + 19$ (false)

Teacher: True again.

Child: $28 > 10 + 19 - 2$ (true)

Teacher: Now make it false.

Child: $28 > (10 + 19 - 2 \times 2)$ (false)

Before long we have the most involved mathematical sentences on the board, and most of the children are alertly watching every change.

·L3, L4

These sheets are for practice on two types of relations:

greater than   >
and
equal to   =

Frames were made large intentionally to encourage children to write interesting ("tricky") statements. Teachers should *not* interfere with a child's "style" in answering these problems.

There are many correct answers to each problem, and children enjoy looking at each other's answers. Notice that all three children in the sample below made the open sentences true.

Which side has more wood?

Use rods.

Name _____

Date _____

·L–1

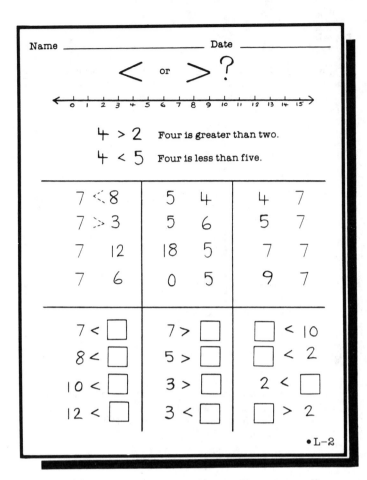

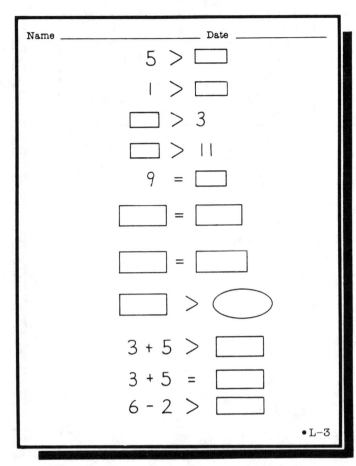

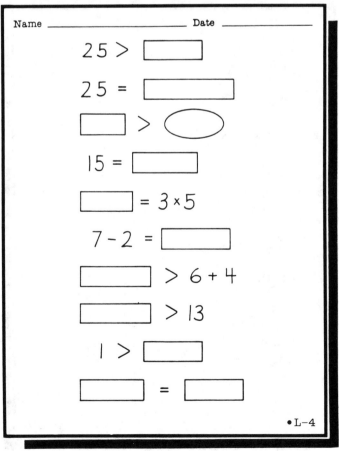

Bill	Nina	Jack
$5 > \boxed{4}$	$5 > \boxed{4\frac{9}{10}}$	$5 > \boxed{-100{,}000}$
$1 > \boxed{0}$	$1 > \boxed{\frac{1}{2}}$	$1 > \boxed{-1}$
$\boxed{4} > 3$	$\boxed{3\frac{1}{4}} > 3$	$\boxed{2436} > 3$
$9 = \boxed{9}$	$9 = \boxed{\frac{9}{1}}$	$9 = \boxed{100 - 91}$
$\boxed{5} = \boxed{5}$	$\boxed{4 \times 8} = \boxed{2 \times 16}$	$\boxed{10\text{-}10} = \boxed{840\text{-}840}$
$\boxed{6} > \bigcirc$	$\boxed{100} > \overline{99}$	$\boxed{1{,}000} > \overline{-1{,}000}$

Bill, a cautious child, made his task simple enough for him to handle it safely.

Nina, an observant child interested in finely drawn differences, tried to make things almost equal.

Jack, a boastful, daring mischief-maker, used his playful, adventurous competence to "go the limit."

Much can be learned about a child by giving him such choices.

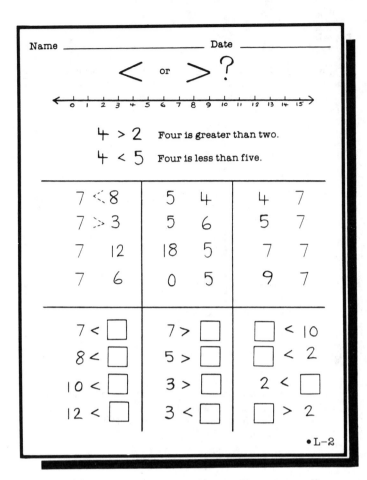

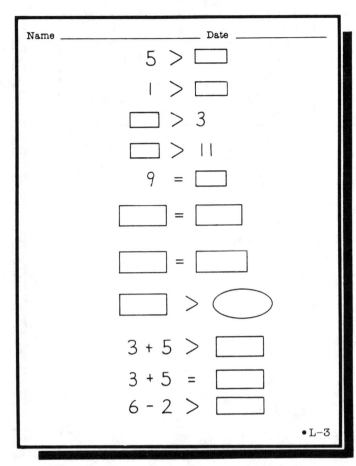

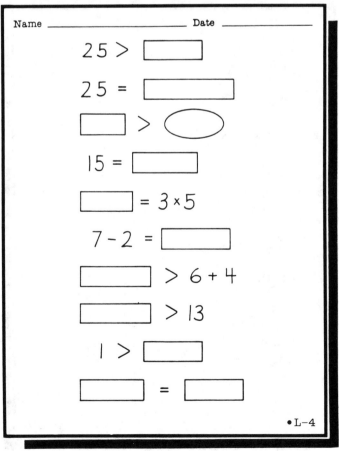

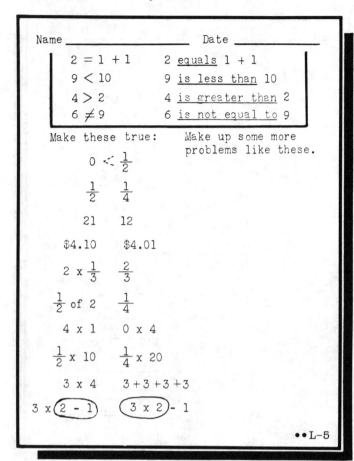

Name _____ Date _____

2 = 1 + 1	2 <u>equals</u> 1 + 1
9 < 10	9 <u>is less than</u> 10
4 > 2	4 <u>is greater than</u> 2
6 ≠ 9	6 <u>is not equal to</u> 9

Make these true: Make up some more
                                    problems like these.

$0 < \frac{1}{2}$

$\frac{1}{2}$ $\frac{1}{4}$

21   12

$4.10 $4.01

$2 \times \frac{1}{3}$ $\frac{2}{3}$

$\frac{1}{2}$ of 2 $\frac{1}{4}$

4 x 1   0 x 4

$\frac{1}{2}$ x 10 $\frac{1}{4}$ x 20

3 x 4   3 + 3 + 3 + 3

3 x ⟨2 - 1⟩   ⟨3 x 2⟩ - 1

••L-5

··L5

This is a good diagnostic page for (1) finding any difficulties children may have on material already taught, or (2) finding discoveries children have made independently on material not yet taught.

$0 < \frac{1}{2}$

$\frac{1}{2} > \frac{1}{4}$

$21 > 12$

$4.10 > $4.01   ⎫ place value in numeral writing

$2 \times \frac{1}{3} = \frac{2}{3}$

$\frac{1}{2} \times 10 = \frac{1}{4} \times 20$ ⎫ different names for same number

$3 \times ⟨2 - 1⟩ < ⟨3 \times 2⟩ - 1$

The loop signals how to read the problem.

··L7

On this sheet we show how expressions can be simplified and then looked at again. Children either may write the simplified form or do this mentally. The sheet is included for those children who may hesitate to write the simplified form.

Name _____ Date _____

$\bigcirc > 8$

$4 > \bigcirc$

$\bigcirc > 10 > \square$

$9 < \bigcirc$

$3 \times 4 > 3 \times \bigcirc$

$29 < 26 + \bigcirc$

$43 - \bigcirc < 43 - 4$

$15 \div 5 < 15 \div \bigcirc$

$3 \times 2 = \frac{1}{2} \times ⟨3 \times \bigcirc⟩$

••L-6

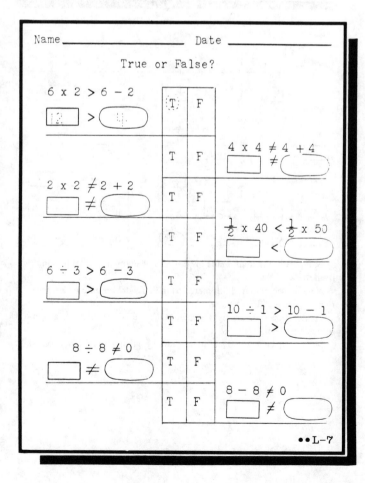

Name _____ Date _____

True or False?

	T	F	
6 x 2 > 6 − 2 [12] > (4)	Ⓣ	F	
		T	F	4 x 4 ≠ 4 + 4 [ ] ≠ ( )
2 x 2 ≠ 2 + 2 [ ] ≠ ( )		T	F
		T	F	$\frac{1}{2}$ x 40 < $\frac{1}{2}$ x 50 [ ] < ( )
6 ÷ 3 > 6 − 3 [ ] > ( )		T	F
		T	F	10 ÷ 1 > 10 − 1 [ ] > ( )
8 ÷ 8 ≠ 0 [ ] ≠ ( )		T	F
		T	F	8 − 8 ≠ 0 [ ] ≠ ( )

••L-7

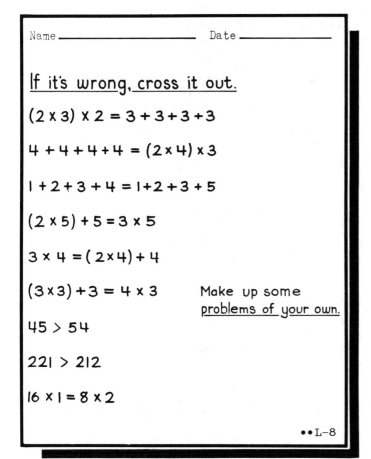

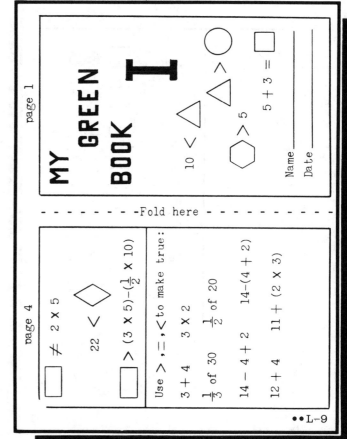

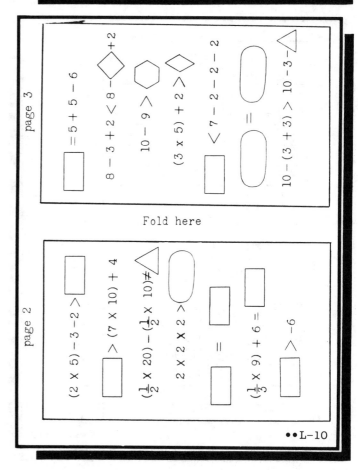

·· L8
True–false

Children can choose several methods of making sentences true.

Instructions: If it's wrong, cross it out.

Problem:	$4 + 4 + 4 + 4 = (2 \times 4) \times 3$
Child:	$4 + 4 + 4 + 4 \neq (2 \times 4) \times 3$

or

$\cancel{4 + 4 + 4 + 4 = (2 \times 4) \times 3}$

The teacher may give some children the additional task of proving their answer: $4 + 4 + 4 + 4 \neq (2 \times 4) \times 3$

because $4 + 4 + 4 + 4 = 16$

and $(2 \times 4) \times 3 = 24$

and $16 \neq 24$

The following pair of problems is included to detect possible confusion in reading numerals.

$$45 > 54 \quad \text{(false)}$$
$$221 > 212 \quad \text{(true)}$$

·· L9, L10
My Green Book

This test booklet contains some of the basic ideas on inequalities and may be used by the teacher to evaluate each child's progress. Children should not be urged to finish every item in the booklet but should be allowed to leave blank what they find too difficult. An especially difficult problem on L10 is the following:

 $> \quad -6$

Name_____ Date_____

Make up some more problems like these.

$$1 < \Box < 3$$

$$9 < \Box < 11$$

$$\tfrac{1}{3} \text{ of } 9 = \Box = \tfrac{1}{2} \times 6$$

$$4 > \Box > 0$$

$$99 < \Box < 109$$

$$1\tfrac{1}{2} > \Box > \tfrac{1}{2}$$

$$\tfrac{1}{3} < \Box < \tfrac{3}{4}$$

$$6 \times 6 > \Box > 4 \times 6$$

$$16 \div 2 > \Box > 16 \div 4$$

•••• L-11

Name_____ Date_____

True or False ?

$6 + 2 = 4 + 4$	T	F
$9 - 3 = 5 + 2$	T	F
$11 - 1 = 10 - 2$	T	F
$11 - 3 = 10 - 2$	T	F
$6 + 8 = 7 + 7$	T	F
$15 - 6 = 10 - 1$	T	F
$3 \times 3 = 3 + 6$	T	F
$5 \times 4 = (4 \times 4) + 4$	T	F
$9 - 3 = 10 - 4$	T	F
$6 + 6 = 5 + 8$	T	F
$9 + 7 = 2 \times 8$	T	F
$3 + 5 = 2 \times 5$	T	F
$100 + 100 = 200$	T	F
$20 + 20 = 10 + 31$	T	F
$60 > (5 \times 10) + 11$	T	F
$34 < 17 + 17$	T	F
	T	F
	T	F

•••• L-12

•••• **L11**
Relations

In the problems on this page, the children must find a number whose relationship is specified in regard to *two* other numbers. This restricts their choices.

Example

$$1 < \Box < 3$$

any number *between* 1 and 3

$$1\tfrac{1}{2} > \Box > \tfrac{1}{2}$$

any number *between* $1\tfrac{1}{2}$ and $\tfrac{1}{2}$

$$4 < \Box > 10$$

any number greater than 4 *and* greater than 10

•••• **L13, L14**
Word problems in inequalities

The child may underline his choice. Usually, he picks the larger quantity, but not always. (Why would one want a large number of wormy apples?)

When the two quantities are equal, the child may either underline the whole sentence or underline the word "or."

•••• **L15**

Lab sheet L15 points out more specifically that each problem has several possible answers, some of which are listed in the right-hand column. If fractions are included, the number of possible replacements is inexhaustible.

Problems	Answers
$8 > \Box > 4$	9, $8\tfrac{1}{2}$, 8, $\left(7\tfrac{1}{2}\right)$, $\left(7\right)$, $\left(6\tfrac{1}{2}\right)$, $\left(6\right)$, $\left(5\right)$, $\left(4\tfrac{1}{2}\right)$
$104 < 109 < \Box$	$\left(190,\right)$ $\left(140,\right)$ $\left(110,\right)$ 107, 100
$1010 > \Box > 1001$	1000, 2006, 999, $\left(1007\right)$
$3 > 6 - 8 > \Box$	1, 0, -1, -2, $\left(-3,\right)$ $\left(-4\right)$
$\Box > 1 > 0$	-5, $\left(2,\right)$ $\left(107,\right)$ $\left(25,\right)$ -2, $\left(1\tfrac{1}{2}\right)$
$\Box < \tfrac{1}{4} < \tfrac{1}{3}$	$\tfrac{1}{2}$, $\left(\tfrac{1}{5}\right)$, 1, 2, $\left(\tfrac{1}{9}\right)$ $\left(\tfrac{1}{100}\right)$

Card L-13

Name_____ Date_____

I WOULD RATHER HAVE:

(a) (4 × 3) balloons or 10 balloons

(b) (7 × 10) pennies or half a dollar

(c) $5\frac{1}{2}$ candy bars or ($\frac{1}{2}$ × 10) candy bars

(d) $\frac{1}{2}$ dozen eggs or 6 eggs

(e) (5 × 5) marbles or 2 dozen marbles

(f) $\frac{1}{3}$ of 30 arrowheads or $\frac{1}{2}$ of 20 arrowheads

(g) (4 × 4)+ 1 gum drops or (2 × 9)-1 gum drops

(h) $\frac{1}{6}$ of a cake or $\frac{1}{3}$ of a cake

(i) ($\frac{1}{4}$ × 100) garnets or 20 garnets

••••L-13

Card L-14

Name_____ Date_____

I would rather have

(3 × 2) wormy apples   or   ($\frac{1}{5}$ × 20) wormy apples

40 pennies   or   (3 × 3) nickles

($\frac{1}{2}$ × 50) marbles   or   (9 × 3) − 2 marbles

(7 × 4) − 2 bees   or   (5 × 4) − 7 bees

$\frac{1}{5}$ of a dollar   or $\frac{1}{4}$ of a dollar

(119 × $\frac{1}{2}$) balloons   or   (3 × 6) − 1 balloons

($\frac{1}{2}$ × 8) cookies   or   ($\frac{1}{4}$ × 100) − 21 cookies

(13 × 2) frogs   or $\frac{1}{2}$ × 50 frogs

P.S. I would rather have one nose than three noses, even though one is less than three

••••L-14

Card L-15

Name_____ Date_____

These are "open sentences" waiting to be made true.	Which of these will make the sentence true? Put loops around the number names that will work.
$8 > \square > 4$	9, $8\frac{1}{2}$, 8, $7\frac{1}{2}$, 7, $6\frac{1}{2}$, 6, 5, $4\frac{1}{2}$
$104 < 109 < \square$	190, 140, 110, 107, 100
$1010 > \square > 1001$	1000, 2006, 999, 1007
$3 > 6 - 8 > \square$	1, 0, -1, -2, -3, -4
$\square > 1 > 0$	-5, 2, 107, 25, -2, $1\frac{1}{2}$
$\square < \frac{1}{4} < \frac{1}{3}$	$\frac{1}{2}$, $\frac{1}{5}$, 1, 2, $\frac{1}{9}$, $\frac{1}{100}$

••••L-15

Card L-16

Name_____ Date_____

$1 > \square$	$34 < 17 + 17$	T	F
$\square > 45$	$60 > (5 \times 10) + 11$	T	F
$9 < \square$	$6 \div 3 > 6 - 3$	T	F
$6 - 2 > \square$	$6 \times 5 \neq (3 \times 5) + (3 \times 5)$	T	F
$3 \times 3 \times 3 > \square$	$221 > 212$	T	F
$6 \div 3 > \square$	$-7 > -5$	T	F
$\square < 11$	$10 \div 10 \neq 0$	T	F
$\square > 5$	$10 - 10 \neq 0$	T	F
$\square > 10 - 3 - 3$	$6 \times 2 > \frac{1}{2} \times 24$	T	F
$9 > \square > \square$	$6 \times \frac{1}{2} \neq \frac{1}{2} \times 6$	T	F
$\square > (6 \times 10) + 3$	$\frac{1}{2} \times 40 < \frac{1}{2} \times 50$	T	F
$10 - 1 > \square$	$(2 \times 4) - 3 - 2 > 1$	T	F
$3 \times 5 \neq \square$			

••••L-16

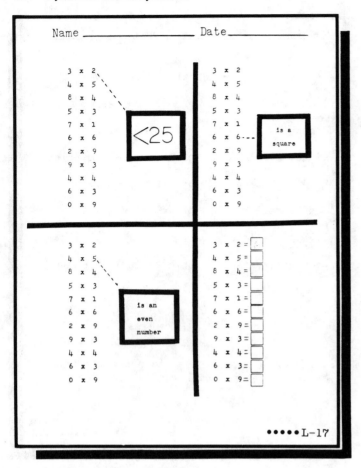

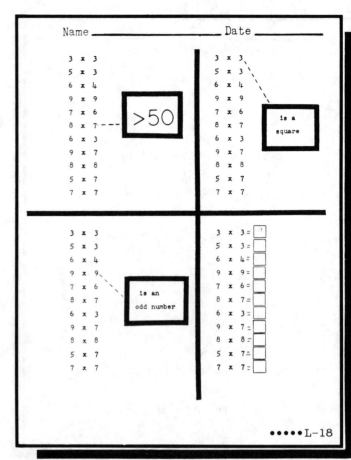

·····L17, L18

Estimation

To do these lab sheets, children must use their knowledge of *greater than* and *less than*, odd-even, and squares, in order to find the answers to the multiplication problems. Such work helps the child to increase his competence in estimation.

Children might not know the answer to the problem 8 × 7. But they have come a long way toward the answer if they can correctly indicate that:

8 × 7 > 50
8 × 7 is *not* a square number.
8 × 7 is *not* an odd number.

The teacher should do chalkboard work to explain this technique. Cuisenaire® rods may be helpful to some children working these sheets. Part of L17, when completed, will resemble the following:

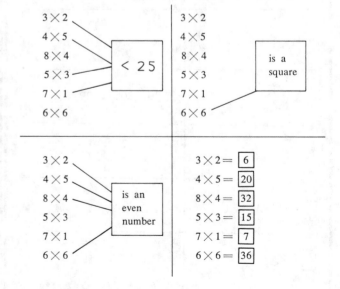

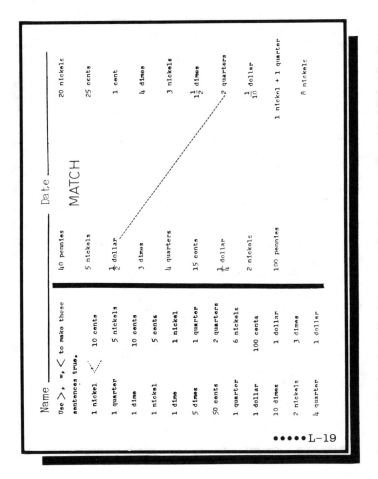

Name _____ Date _____

Make **false sentences** by finishing the following problems.	Make **true sentences** by finishing the following problems.
$9 = 5 + \Box$	$9 = 5 + \Box$
$17 > \Box$	$17 > \Box$
$833 \neq \Box$	$833 \neq \Box$
$5 \times 5 \leqq \Box$	$5 \times 5 \leqq \Box$
$\begin{array}{r}99\\+101\end{array}$ $\begin{array}{r}101\\-\ 99\end{array}$	$\begin{array}{r}99\\+101\end{array}$ $\begin{array}{r}101\\-\ 99\end{array}$
$\begin{array}{r}6000\\-5999\end{array}$	$\begin{array}{r}6000\\-5999\end{array}$

•••••L-20

·····L19

Depending on how familiar children are with money, these lab sheets can be done with or without concrete materials. "Play money" or rods may be used as concrete materials.

Using the white rod for 1¢, then: yellow = 5¢
orange = 10¢
2 orange + yellow = 25¢

·····L20
Make false or true intentionally

To be asked to make false statements is probably an entirely new idea to children. Yet this is an important mathematical device to establish the range of true answers.

False sentences	True sentences
$9 = 5 + \Box$ (any number except 4)	$9 = 5 + \Box$ (only 4)
$17 > \Box$ (17 or any number > 17)	$17 > \Box$ (any number < 17)
$833 \neq \Box$ (only 833 will make this false)	$833 \neq \Box$ (any number except 833 will work)
$5 \times 5 \leqq \Box$ (any number < 25)	$5 \times 5 \leqq \Box$ (25 or any number > 25)

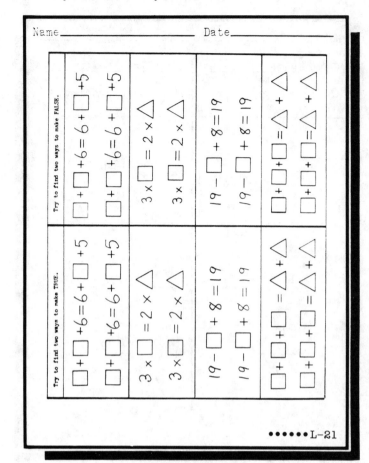

・・・・・・ **L21**

Make true

$$\boxed{5} + \boxed{5} + 6 = 6 + \boxed{5} + 5$$

(no other way)

$$19 - \boxed{8} + 8 = 19$$

(no other way)

Make false

$$\Box + \Box + 6 = 6 + \Box + 5$$

(many ways)

$$19 - \Box + 8 = 19$$

(many ways)

・・・・・・ **L22**

Make true

$$\Box - 80 = 80 - \Box$$

(80 in both $\Box$'s)

Make false

$$\Box + \Box \neq \Box$$

(*only* 0 will make it false)

$$\Box \times \Box \neq \Box$$

(*only* 0 and 1 will make it false)

Make true

$$4 + \Box + 2 = \Box + \Box$$

(6 goes in each box)

$$\Box \times \Box \times \Box = \Box$$

(0 or 1 goes in each box)

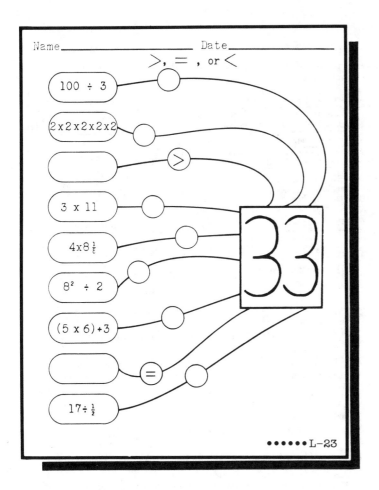

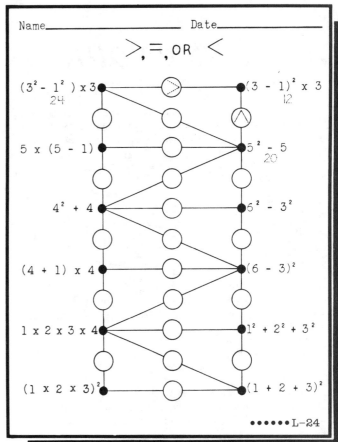

• • • • • • **L23, L24**

These are difficult lab sheets. However, they are very popular with many of the children. Lab sheet L24 presupposes that the children have completed the section on squaring.

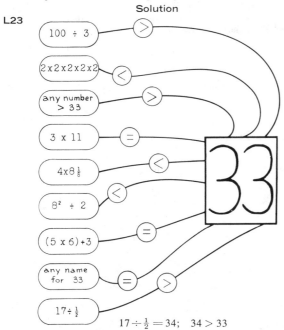

• • • • • **L24**

The children should simplify each expression first. This sheet might be done as a class activity, using the chalkboard. The emphasis is on discovering the importance of parentheses in expressions involving squaring.

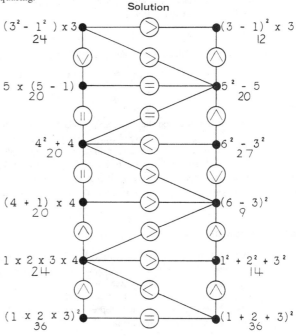

M Place value

What number does a computer mathematician mean when he writes 110101001010? What did a Roman mean when he wrote MMMCDII? What do we mean when we write 3402? *We all mean the same number,* but we use different numerals.

We are thinking of a specific number which we describe, by our notation, in powers* of ten as follows:

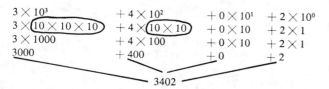

$$3 \times 10^3 \qquad\qquad + 4 \times 10^2 \qquad + 0 \times 10^1 \qquad + 2 \times 10^0$$
$$3 \times (10 \times 10 \times 10) \quad + 4 \times (10 \times 10) \quad + 0 \times 10 \qquad + 2 \times 1$$
$$3 \times 1000 \qquad\qquad + 4 \times 100 \qquad + 0 \times 10 \qquad + 2 \times 1$$
$$3000 \qquad\qquad\qquad + 400 \qquad\qquad + 0 \qquad\qquad + 2$$

3402

In order for children to understand the full impact of this "shorthand" notation, we must build up notions about three basic components of place value:

a. notions about *symbols*
b. notions about *base*
c. notions about *numeral position*

Elementary teachers have long taught the concept of place value. However, new emphasis on this key concept in mathematics requires more comprehensive development of place value than was heretofore done.

Components of place value

Let us develop each of the three basic components of place value independently, and then combine them.

Symbols

We cannot have a written language without a system of notation. This notation is in the form of symbols. In arithmetic, these symbols (numerals) stand for numbers. Our everyday arithmetic uses ten distinct symbols to stand for all sets of numbers:

0, 1, 2, 3, 4, 5, 6, 7, 8, 9.

Other symbols are possible and have been used. The Roman numerals

I, V, X, L, C, D, M   are just one example.

Base

Our system of notation is called the *decimal* system because it is constructed on the base of ten. We have ten separate symbols, nine of which stand for the set of cardinal numbers through the number nine, and one which stands for zero, the empty set. No new symbol exists to represent ten, the number of the base. It is represented by a combination of the two symbols '1' and '0.' It is the smallest two-digit number, written '10.'

Numeral position

This economy of symbols (ten symbols which in combination may represent any number we choose) is made possible by the system of place value. A systematic *value* is assigned to the *place* which each symbol holds in a row of symbols. The numeral that is written in each place tells how often that value is represented in the number. For example, in the number which we express by writing the numerals

'46,' the position (or place) held by the numeral '4' tells us that its value is 4×10^1.

The values of the adjacent digits in a row increase from right to left by successive powers of the base ten.

on and on ← 10^5	← 10^4	← 10^3	← 10^2	← 10^1	← 10^0
on and on ← $\square \times 100{,}000$	← $\square \times 10{,}000$	← $\square \times 1{,}000$	← $\square \times 100$	← $\square \times 10$	← $\square \times 1$

Conversely, they decrease from left to right by powers of ten.

10^5	→ 10^4	→ 10^3	→ 10^2	→ 10^1	→ 10^0	→ 10^{-1}
$\square \times 100{,}000$ →	$\square \times 10{,}000$ →	$\square \times 1{,}000$ →	$\square \times 100$ →	$\square \times 10$ →	$\square \times 1$ →	$\square \times \frac{1}{10}$ →

The '8' in '8' means 8×10^0 or 8×1 or   8 units.
The '8' in '80' means 8×10^1 or 8×10 or   8 tens.
The '8' in '800' means 8×10^2 or $8 \times 10 \times 10$ or   8 hundreds.
The '8' in '8000' means 8×10^3 or $8 \times 10 \times 10 \times 10$ or   8 thousands.

The zeros in each row indicate the absence of some power of ten for which the place is held.

| 800 | = | 8×10^2 | + | 0×10^1 | + | 0×10^0 | | |
| 7604 | = | 7×10^3 | + | 6×10^2 | + | 0×10^1 | + | 4×10^0 |

The numeral symbols

0, 1, 2, 3, 4, 5, 6, 7, 8, 9

are used to indicate how many times the particular power of 10 occurs in a number.

Thus, the '4' in '342' means 4×10^1, while the '4' in '43,200' means 4×10^4.

Mathematicians and scientists simplify the place value notation even further when they write

4.3×10^6 for   4,300,000

and

8×10^9 for   8,000,000,000.

Bases other than ten

In addition to the base-ten system of notation, other positional notation systems are possible and are in use. We may apply the idea of place value to powers of other numbers. *If we choose a base smaller than ten, we need fewer discrete symbols to write with.*

Base two

Let us illustrate this with a base-two system of counting which is used by computers and in the U.S. for buying milk. Dairy products come in half pints (or cups), pints, quarts, half gallons, and gallons. Keeping our positional notation system and the symbols 0 and 1, we can now write a shorthand for 1 quart:

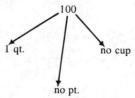

For 1 gallon and 1 pint, we can write:

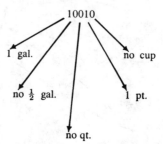

*Read Section P, Squaring, for further comments on "raising to a power."

210

Below is a table of milk measures.

gal.	½ gal.	qt.	pt.	cup	
2^4	2^3	2^2	2^1	2^0	
				1	—— 1 cup
			1	0	—— 2 cups
			1	1	—— 3 cups
		1	0	0	—— 4 cups
		1	0	1	—— 5 cups
		1	1	0	—— 6 cups
		1	1	1	—— 7 cups
	1	0	0	0	—— 8 cups

base ten

Base five

Another illustration is a money system in the make-believe land of Ug, where there are the following coins and bills:

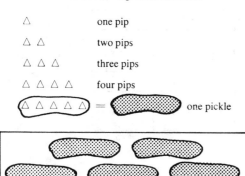

△   one pip

△ △   two pips

△ △ △   three pips

△ △ △ △ four pips

(△ △ △ △ △) = ⬭   one pickle

one pookle

103 means one pookle and three pips:

△ △ △

(Translated into U.S. money this is (1 × 25) cents + (0 × 5) cents + 3 cents.)

In all bases, we need a zero symbol and a unit symbol. In all bases, there are separate symbols for 0 through "one less than the base." Thus, in various bases, the counting begins as follows:

Base two: 0, 1, 10
Base three: 0, 1, 2, 10
Base four: 0, 1, 2, 3, 10
Base five: 0, 1, 2, 3, 4, 10
•
•
•
Base ten: 0, 1, 2, 3, 4 . . . 8, 9, 10

The smallest two-digit number is always the base.

'10' in base five means $1 \times 5^1 + 0 \times 5^0$
'10' in base six means $1 \times 6^1 + 0 \times 6^0$
'10' in base eight means $1 \times 8^1 + 0 \times 8^0$
'10' in base ten means $1 \times 10^1 + 0 \times 10^0$

'101' in base five means $1 \times (5 \times 5) + (0 \times 5) + (1 \times 1)$
'101' in base seven means $1 \times (7 \times 7) + (0 \times 7) + (1 \times 1)$
'101' in base ten means $1 \times (10 \times 10) + (0 \times 10) + (1 \times 1)$

Let us see what the counting series, an addition table, and a multiplication table would look like in some other bases.

Base four

Counting in base four with the symbols 0, 1, 2, 3:

1, 2, 3, 10, ⟶ base four
11, 12, 13, 20,
21, 22, 23, 30,
31, 32, 33, 100 ⟶ base four squared

Addition table for base four:

+	0	1	2	3	10
0	0	1	2	3	10
1	1	2	3	10	11
2	2	3	10	11	12
3	3	10	11	12	13
10	10	11	12	13	20

Multiplication table for base four:

×	0	1	2	3	10
0	0	0	0	0	0
1	0	1	2	3	10
2	0	2	10	12	20
3	0	3	12	21	30
10	0	10	20	30	100

Base two

Counting in base two with the symbols 0, 1:

1, 10, ⟶ base two
11, 100 ⟶ base two squared

Addition table for base two:

+	0	1	10
0	0	1	10
1	1	10	11
10	10	11	100

Multiplication table for base two:

×	0	1	10
0	0	0	0
1	0	1	10
10	0	10	100

Number lines in different bases

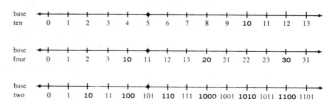

On all of the number lines above the same point has been marked with a dot. That point is '5' in base ten, '11' in base four, and '101' in base two.

When working in other bases, the *number* does not change—only the *name* and *numeral* for the number changes.

The best concrete materials available for developing the ideas discussed in this section are the Dienes Multibase Arithmetic Blocks, although Cuisenaire rods can also be used.

•••• M1–M3

Preliminary activities

It is highly advisable to make or purchase some extensions of the Cuisenaire® rods in order to demonstrate by exact scaling the size relationships between units, tens, hundreds, and thousands.

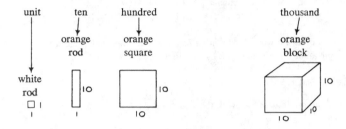

$10 \times 10 \times 1$ cm. orange squares can be cut out of plywood or oaktag paper.

$10 \times 10 \times 10$ cm. orange cubes can be built out of wood or cardboard.

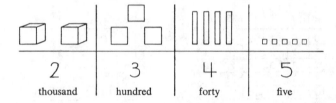

1 Block models are shown to the class; children write down what they see.

2 Teacher or child says a number name; children record what they hear.

3 Children are given a random assortment of rods. They must group them to fit the chart.

Place value games in base ten

After some experiences with scaled models (rods and home-made), children use lab sheet M1 as a code to sort the shapes in the pictures, recording the count in the table.

PICTURE	⬛	☐			•
A		4	4	8
B	3	1	6	6
C	3	4	5	0
D	2	1	4	7
E		2	9	7
F	4	0	0	8
G	6	0	0	0
H		1	0	9

In this exercise the unit is shown as a dot, and the ten as a straight line.

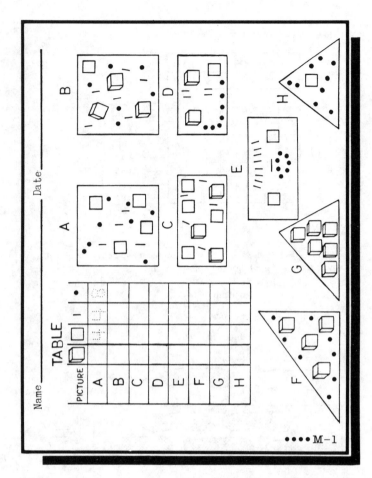

•••• M–1

Code

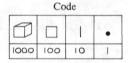

Children enjoy chalkboard sorting games with this code. Here is an example:

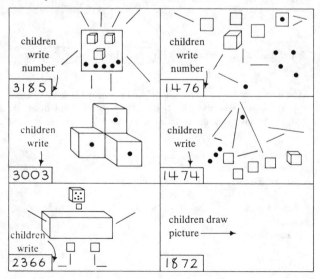

M2 and M3 are similar to M1, except that numerals and abbreviations are grouped according to a base ten place value system.

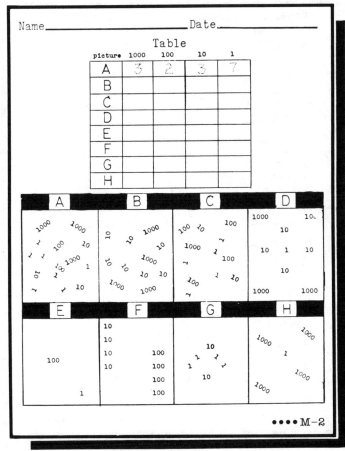

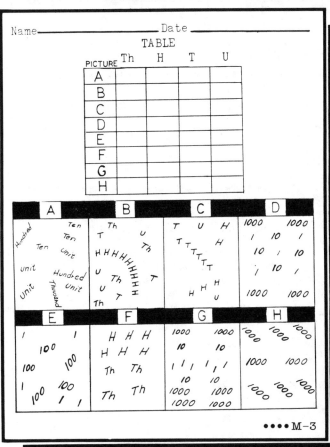

Preliminary activities

It is very important to have some models for "one thousand" cubes. They are easy to make out of posterboard cut in the following pattern and taped together.

Each square *must* be 10 cm. by 10 cm. to correlate with the rods. They can be stored flat.

How many units (white rods) will make one ten (orange rod)? How many tens (orange rods) will make one hundred (an orange square)? How many hundreds (orange squares) will make one thousand (an orange cube)?

Give each child a sheet of paper and two sets of numeral cards 0 through 9. Each child should draw the following diagram on his paper:

thousands	hundreds	tens	units

The teacher (or a child) selects any number (0–9) of the large cubes, squares, orange rods and white rods and arranges them. The children place the corresponding numeral cards on their paper diagram.

Examples

Selected models

thousands	hundreds	tens	units
2	3	1	5

Children's seat work

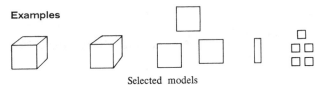

Model (in scrambled order)

thousands	hundreds	tens	units
1	2	0	4

Children's seat work

The children can reverse the procedure by first filling in their individual charts with any numbers they want from 0 to 9. One child is then chosen to build a model of his arrangement. The other children tell from the model what numeral is on the child's card.

Name_____ Date_____

The '5' in [6|3|5] means 5 — thousands / hundreds / tens / **units**

The '7' in [2|7|0|4] means 7 — thousands / hundreds / tens / units

The '7' in [5|7|6] means 7 — thousands / hundreds / tens / units

The '3' in [3|2] means 3 — thousands / hundreds / tens / units

The '3' in 3 4 2 0 means 3 — thousands / hundreds / tens / units

The '8' in 6 0 8 means 8 — thousands / hundreds / tens / units

The '0' in 5 0 8 3 means 0 — thousands / hundreds / tens / units

●●●● M-4

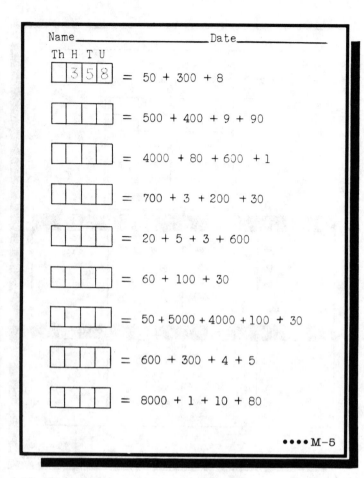

Name_____ Date_____

Th H T U
[|3|5|8] = 50 + 300 + 8

[| | |] = 500 + 400 + 9 + 90

[| | |] = 4000 + 80 + 600 + 1

[| | |] = 700 + 3 + 200 + 30

[| | |] = 20 + 5 + 3 + 600

[| | |] = 60 + 100 + 30

[| | |] = 50 + 5000 + 4000 + 100 + 30

[| | |] = 600 + 300 + 4 + 5

[| | |] = 8000 + 1 + 10 + 80

●●●● M-5

· · · · **M4**

Lab sheet M4 may now be done individually by the children. Those who are still not sure may have the concrete materials to "check" as they work.

· · · · **M5, M6**

Expanded notation and shorthand notation

For some children it will be helpful to label all the diagrams, as

Th H T U
[| | |]

Again the problem is to (1) differentiate between the given powers of ten; (2) add like powers of ten; (3) determine whether the sum includes a higher power of ten; and (4) record in "shorthand" the sum of the powers of ten from the highest given to 10^0.

$$20 + 5 + 3 + 600 =$$
$$600 + 20 + 5 + 3 =$$
$$600 + 20 + 8 = 628$$

Lab sheet M6 is similar to M5, except that words are used, 4 hundreds + 7 tens + 5 units, instead of numerals, 400 + 70 + 5.

Name_____ Date_____

Th	H	T	U

| 4 | 7 | 5 | 4 hundreds + 7 tens + 5 units |

4 hundreds + 7 tens + 5 units

8 hundreds + 2 tens + 3 units

6 hundreds + 0 tens + 6 units

2 hundreds + 5 tens + 0 units

8 hundreds + 9 tens

5 hundreds + 3 units

4 thousands + 7 hundreds + 2 tens + 1 unit

1 thousand + 7 tens + 6 units

0 thousands + 7 units + 0 tens

•••• M-6

Name_____ Date_____

```
  4 0        3          4 3
+ 2 0      + 5        + 2 5


  2 0        7          2 7
+ 5 0      + 2        + 5 2


  1 0 0    3 0    5      1 3 5
+ 4 0 0  + 6 0  + 2    + 4 6 2


  5 0 0    4 0    3      5 4 3
+ 2 0 0  + 4 0  + 2    + 2 4 2
```

•••• M-7

•••• M7, M8

Ruled paper is used in these sheets to guide the children's writing.
The diagram below is not a numeral because it has $\boxed{13}$ units in
the units place.

H	Tens	Units
2	1	13

After we have exchanged 10 of the units for one of the tens, we
have a numeral.

H	Tens	Units
2	1	13
2	2	3

The numeral is 223.

Children learn to put their units, tens, and hundreds into the correct
columns on lab sheets **M7** and **M8**. Regrouping is necessary in only
one problem, and some children may be puzzled by the answer. Subsequent lab sheets will help them solve the dilemma.

Name_____ Date_____

```
  2 4      6 3        5 0        4 4
+ 5 1    + 3 4      + 4 7      + 5 5


  3 4 7    6 5 7      5 4 5
+ 5 3 2  + 2 3 1    + 4 3 2


  7 1 6    4 0 5      3 5 7
+ 1 8 2  + 5 0 3    + 2 4 3


  2 3 2
  3 2 3      0 1 2 3 4 5 6 7 8 9
  1 2 1    + 9 8 7 6 5 4 3 2 1 0
+ 2 1 2
```

•••• M-8

M-9

Name_____ Date_____

1000 = [ ] thousand

1000 = [ ] hundreds

1000 = [ ] tens

1000 = [ ] units

100 = [ ] hundred

100 = [ ] tens

100 = [ ] units

10 = [ ] ten

10 = [ ] units

1 = [ ] unit

•••• M-9

M-10

Name_____ Date_____

13 units = 1 ten + [3] units

17 units = 1 ten + [ ] units

11 units = 1 ten + [ ] units

19 units = [ ] tens + 9 units

10 units = 1 ten + [ ] units

18 tens = 1 hundred + [ ] tens

14 tens = 1 hundred + [ ] tens

25 tens = [ ] hundreds + 5 tens

12 tens = 1 hundred + [ ] tens

16 hundreds = 1 thousand + [ ] hundreds

16 tens = 1 hundred + [ ] tens

16 units = 1 ten + [ ] units

13 hundreds = 1 thousand + [ ] hundreds

•••• M-10

M-11

Name_____ Date_____

3 units + 5 units = [ ] units

0 units + 7 units = [ ] units

4 tens + 2 tens = [ ] tens

6 hundreds + 3 hundreds = [ ] hundreds

5 tens + 7 tens = [ ] tens

5 tens + 7 tens = 1 hundred + [ ] tens

6 units + 9 units = [ ] units

6 units + 9 units = 1 ten + [ ] units

7 units + 7 units = 1 ten + [ ] units

9 tens + 4 tens = [ ] hundreds + 3 tens

6 units + 6 units = 1 ten + [ ] units

5 tens + 8 tens = 1 hundred + [ ] tens

9 tens + 7 tens = 1 hundred + [ ] tens

8 units + 8 units = 1 ten + [ ] units

•••• M-11

M-12

Name_____ Date_____

Th	H	T	U		Th	H	T	U
	8	3	14	=		8	4	4
	2	6	12	=			2	2
	5	13	4	=			3	4
1	6	0	11	=	1	6		1
7	13	4	17	=		8	3	7

7 | 1 | 23 = 7 | | 13 = 7 | | 3

5 | 3 | 9 | 13 = 5 | 3 | | 3 = 5 | | 0 | 3

2 | 9 | 100 = 2 | | 00 = | 000

7 | 9 | 9 | 12 = 79 | | 2 = 7 | | 02 = | 002

•••• M-12

•••• M9–M12

These lab sheets give practice on the place value structure of our base ten arithmetic.

1000 = 1 thousand	100 = 1 hundred	10 = 1 ten
= 10 hundreds	= 10 tens	= 10 units
= 100 tens	= 100 units	
= 1000 units		

Any 10 hundreds make 1 thousand.
Any 10 tens make 1 hundred.
Any 10 units make 1 ten.

M11

5 tens + 7 tens = [12] tens

5 tens + 7 tens = 1 hundred + [2] tens

M12

Th H T U = Th H T U

[1 | 6 | 0 | 11] = [1 | 6 | 1 | 1]

[2 | 9 | 10 | 0] = [2 | 10 | 0 | 0]

9 hundred + 10 tens = 10 hundred

[2 | 10 | 0 | 0] = [3 | 0 | 0 | 0]

2 thousand + 10 hundred = 3 thousand

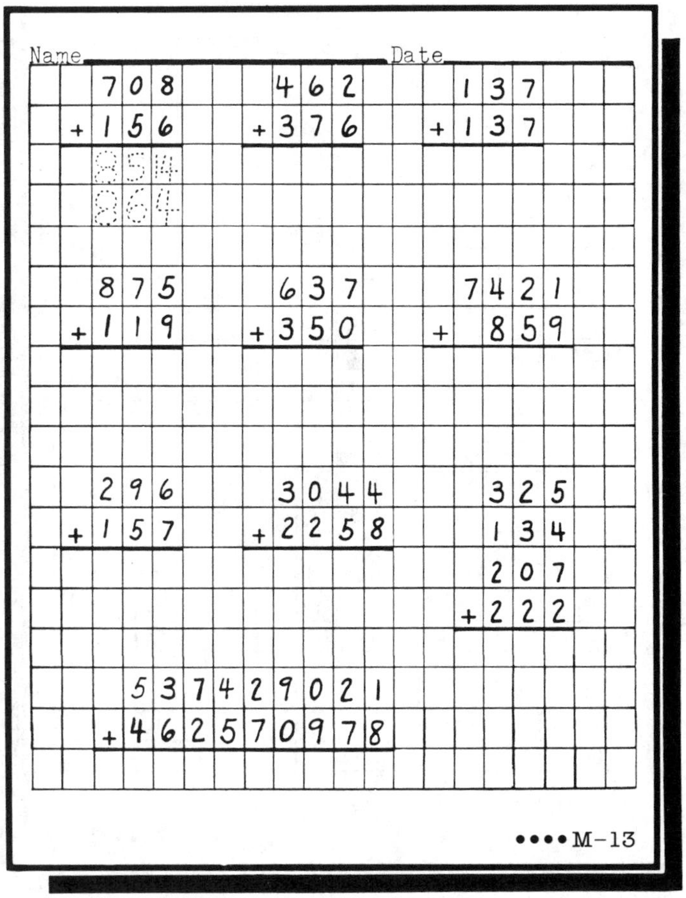

This work shows the series of steps which we must learn to perform mentally when we use the addition algorithm.

$$\begin{array}{r} {\scriptstyle 11} \\ 739 \\ +\,265 \\ \hline 1004 \end{array}$$

These steps are performed gradually, however, so that we understand what we are doing (exchanging units for tens, and so on). The squared blocks (thousands, hundreds, tens, units) can still be used to keep track of the exchanges.

•••• M13–M16

Since in this whole section the emphasis is on place value, the child should be allowed to write down every step.

The steps are:

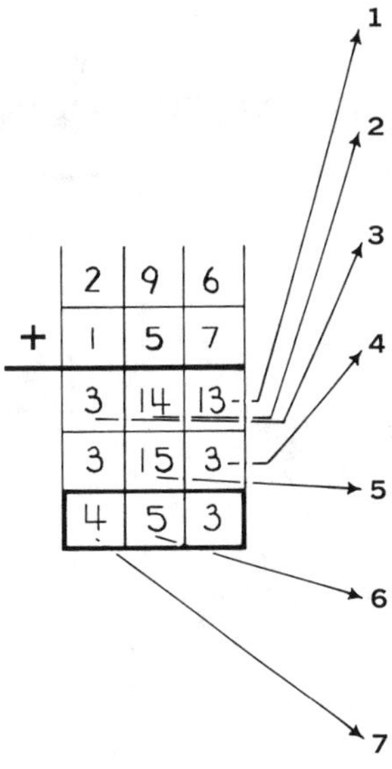

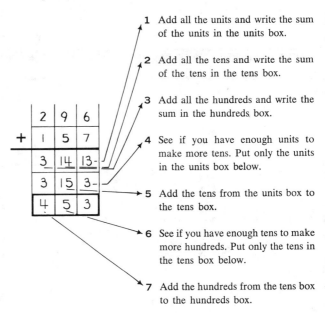

1 Add all the units and write the sum of the units in the units box.

2 Add all the tens and write the sum of the tens in the tens box.

3 Add all the hundreds and write the sum in the hundreds box.

4 See if you have enough units to make more tens. Put only the units in the units box below.

5 Add the tens from the units box to the tens box.

6 See if you have enough tens to make more hundreds. Put only the tens in the tens box below.

7 Add the hundreds from the tens box to the hundreds box.

By the time the children come to the problem

$$\begin{array}{r} 5\,3\,7\,4\,2\,9\,0\,2\,1 \\ +\,4\,6\,2\,5\,7\,0\,9\,7\,8 \\ \hline 9\,9\,9\,9\,9\,9\,9\,9\,9 \end{array}$$

most of them will understand the "system" even if they do not know the oral name "nine hundred ninety-nine million nine hundred ninety-nine thousand nine hundred ninety-nine."

They will know it is *a very large* number. Tell them how to read it if they ask. 999999999 may be written without commas. The commas in 999,999,999 are only for *reading convenience*. They are useful but not essential.

```
   Name                Date

     5 4 7          4 6 3          9 0 5
   + 2 3 4        + 4 6 3        +   6 7


     8 8 8          4 6 7          6 4 2
   +   2 2        + 2 9 8        + 9 8 3


     5 6 2 8 4        1 2 5          9 9
   + 3 4 8 1 6        6 4 2          8 8
                      7 5 3          7 7
                    + 9 4 5        + 6 6
```

••••M-14

•••••M17–M19
Preliminary activity

Following are questions about the number of letters in a word and the number of digits in a numeral. This work can be done at the board.

1 Do the number of letters in a word tell us anything about the size of the thing the word stands for?

world	(5 letters)	The word *world* is smaller than the word *butterfly*, but the thing *world* is bigger than the thing *butterfly*.
butterfly	(9 letters)	
nose	(4 letters)	The word *nose* is smaller than the word *elephant*. A *nose* is smaller than an *elephant*.
elephant	(8 letters)	
tree	(4 letters)	The word *tree* is the same size as the word *leaf*, but the thing *tree* is bigger than the thing *leaf*.
leaf	(4 letters)	
hundred	(7 letters)	*Conclusion:* The size of a word does not tell us the size of the thing the word names.
million	(7 letters)	

2 Do the number of digits in a numeral tell us anything about the size of the number the numeral stands for?

```
    3
  2 1           Conclusion: Yes
4 3 2
etc.
```

3 Ask the same questions about the order of letters as contrasted with the order of digits.

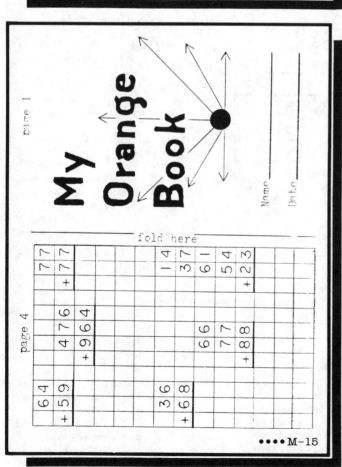

••••M-15

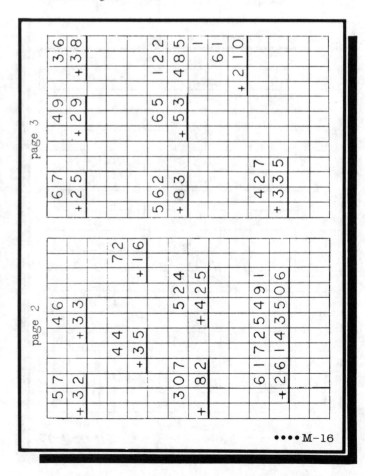

••••M-16

M-17 worksheet

Name_____Date_____	
Seven hundred nineteen	7019
Seven thousand nineteen	7190
Seven thousand one hundred nine	719
Seven thousand one hundred ninety	70019
Seventy thousand nineteen	7109
Seventy thousand one hundred nine	70190
Seventy thousand one hundred ninety	71090
Seventy-one thousand nine	70109
Seventy-one thousand ninety	71900
Seventy-one thousand nine hundred	71009

•••••M-17

M-18 worksheet

What is the smallest number and the largest number you can make with the following digits?

Smallest Number	Digits	Largest Number
	3,7	
	4,2,9	
	7,8,3	
	2,6,2	
	4,2,8,3	
	9,9,2,8	
	0,3,1,7	
	0,3,0,0	
	4,9,2,0	
	3,6,4,0,1,3	

•••••M-18

M17

The importance of 0 as a placeholder for a power of 10 is stressed on this sheet. The numerals '7,' '1,' '9' are used throughout in that order. The numeral '0' is placed between them in many possible ways. Word names and numeral names are to be matched.

Questions

Which is the smallest number listed?
Which is the largest number listed?
Arrange them in size from largest to smallest:

71900	70019
71090	7190
71009	7109
70190	7019
70109	719

M18

A completed chart will resemble the following:

Smallest number	Digits	Largest number
37	3,7	73
249	4,2,9	942
378	7,8,3	873
226	2,6,2	622
2348	4,2,8,3	8432
2899	9,9,2,8	9982
0137*	0,3,1,7	7310
0003	0,3,0,0	3000
0249	4,9,2,0	9420
013346	3,6,4,0,1,3	643310

M-19 worksheet

What is the smallest number and the largest number you can make with the following digits?

Smallest	Digits	Largest
	6,5,8	
	4,0,9	
	3,3,1,3	
	3,2,1,4	
	1,2,3,4,0	

Digits	Write all the possible numbers these digits can make.				
4,2,5	425	452	254		
3,2,3					
6,0,9					
4,7,8					
5,5,5					

•••••M-19

····· **M20**

The change machine

The change machines have been a great favorite with Miquon School children. The machine pictured on this lab sheet is viewed by a child as almost magical and certainly as most useful to a collector of pennies in a piggy bank. (Just think, one could throw all the change one collected into the machine and out would come nothing but pennies! To the child it is incidental that he is at the same time learning something about the value of U. S. coins.)

This sheet is so popular that we had to make a stencil *with machines only*, on which the children themselves could write names of coins and thereby make up their own problems.

Later we "invented" a whole series of machines that worked as follows:

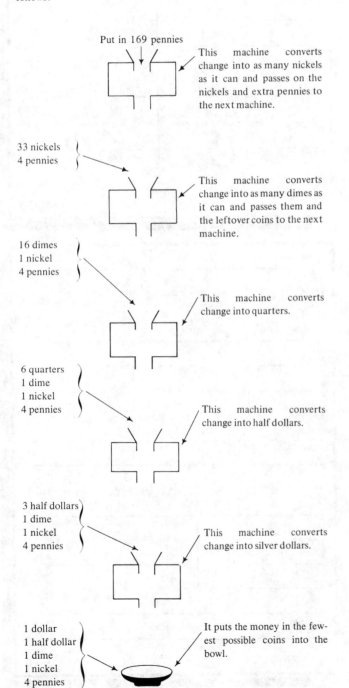

Put in 169 pennies

This machine converts change into as many nickels as it can and passes on the nickels and extra pennies to the next machine.

33 nickels
4 pennies

This machine converts change into as many dimes as it can and passes them and the leftover coins to the next machine.

16 dimes
1 nickel
4 pennies

This machine converts change into quarters.

6 quarters
1 dime
1 nickel
4 pennies

This machine converts change into half dollars.

3 half dollars
1 dime
1 nickel
4 pennies

This machine converts change into silver dollars.

1 dollar
1 half dollar
1 dime
1 nickel
4 pennies

It puts the money in the fewest possible coins into the bowl.

220

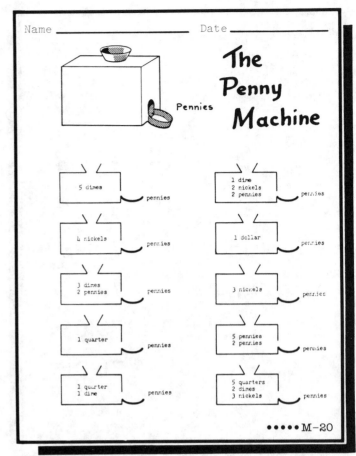

Name _____ Date _____

The Penny Machine

Pennies

5 dimes → pennies

1 dime
2 nickels
2 pennies → pennies

4 nickels → pennies

1 dollar → pennies

3 dimes
2 pennies → pennies

3 nickels → pennies

1 quarter → pennies

5 pennies
2 pennies → pennies

1 quarter
1 dime → pennies

5 quarters
2 dimes
3 nickels → pennies

····· M-20

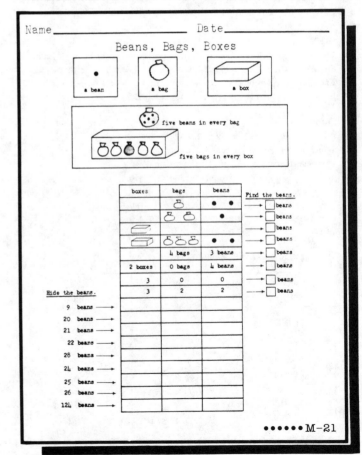

Name _____ Date _____

Beans, Bags, Boxes

a bean   a bag   a box

five beans in every bag

five bags in every box

boxes	bags	beans	Find the beans.
	🛍	• •	→ ☐ beans
	🛍 🛍	•	→ ☐ beans
▭	🛍🛍🛍	• •	→ ☐ beans
	4 bags	3 beans	→ ☐ beans
2 boxes	0 bags	4 beans	→ ☐ beans
3	0	0	→ ☐ beans
3	2	2	→ ☐ beans

Hide the beans.

9 beans →			
20 beans →			
21 beans →			
22 beans →			
28 beans →			
24 beans →			
25 beans →			
26 beans →			
124 beans →			

······ M-21

······ M21
Preliminary activity

Children could be asked to bring in a pound of dried beans, many small paper bags, and empty shoe boxes. Then they could put beans into bags and bags into boxes according to the "five system" (base five) suggested on the lab sheet. This would allow children to play this as a game before doing it on paper.

What do we do with *five boxes* each filled with *five bags* each filled with *five beans*?

It's only logical—to children—that the next larger container must also start with "b" (so as to continue the alliteration). So, the next larger measure is a *bin*. (A bookshelf in the classroom will do.) Now the game is about beans, bags, boxes, bins.

The top of the lab sheet and the upper part of the chart show how the beans have been hidden. The child "finds" them all. The answer is written in the correct base-ten numeral.

means 38 beans

On the lower half of the sheet the child "hides" the beans himself. 69 beans would be hidden thus:

We can see that 2222 in base five = 312 in base ten.

bins	boxes	bags	beans
$5 \times 5 \times 5$'s	5×5's	5's	units
2	2	2	2
↓	↓	↓	↓
$2 \times (5 \times 5 \times 5)$	$2 \times (5 \times 5)$	2×5	2×1

$$250 \quad + \quad 50 \quad + \quad 10 \quad + \quad 2 = 312$$

······ M22
Arithmetic in "milk language"

This is work in what is commonly called base-two or binary arithmetic.

Preliminary activity

1 Ask children to bring empty milk cartons—half pints, pints, quarts, half gallons. (We can tape together two gallon cartons to make a double gallon.)

2 Find out whose birthday is closest and make up a long story about a "pretend" birthday party. A sample story follows.

Teacher: "Elizabeth, your mother says you may invite 13 children to your party. You said that you want Mother to serve chocolate milk. Mother knows that she will need 14 cups of white milk to make chocolate milk for your party.

"Since you also want ice cream and cake and Mother has just done her other shopping, the milk for your party must take up *very* little space in the refrigerator.

"So she sends you to the supermarket to buy *exactly* 14 cups of milk in the *least possible number of containers*. (Here, children can pretend that the empty cartons are on the dairy shelf in the supermarket.) Go and make your purchase, Elizabeth."

If Elizabeth did it correctly, she would bring back

$\frac{1}{2}$ gal.	qt.	pt.	$\frac{1}{2}$ pt.
1	**1**	**1**	**0**

Teacher: "So Elizabeth brings home three cartons of milk: one half gallon (8 cups), one quart (4 cups), one pint (2 cups). That is exactly 14 cups of milk."

3 Make up another party story, inviting all the children in the room, and buy milk for that party. Thirty-five cups of milk could be bought in containers:

1	**0**	**0**	**0**	**1**	**1**
double gal.	gal.	$\frac{1}{2}$ gal.	qt.	pt.	$\frac{1}{2}$ pt.
32		**+**		**2**	**+ 1**

Now let us study the size arrangement of milk containers. They are arranged by powers of two.

2^6 $2\times2\times2\times2\times2\times2$ 4 gal. (64 c.)	2^5 $2\times2\times2\times2\times2$ double gal. (32 c.)	2^4 $2\times2\times2\times2$ gal. (16 c.)	2^3 $2\times2\times2$ $\frac{1}{2}$ gal. (8 c.)	2^2 2×2 qt. (4 c.)	2^1 2 pt. (2 c.)	2^0 1 cup (1 c.)

101 in milk language means **1** quart, no pints, **1** cup (5 cups)

1000 in milk language means **1** half gallon, no quarts, no pints, no cups.

Continued on next page

Name_____ Date_____

Supermarket Dairy Shelf

Buy:	2 gal.	1 gal.	½ gal.	1 qt.	1 pt.	1 c.
17 cups		1	0	0	0	1
11 cups						
4 cups				1	0	0
15 cups						
16 cups						
40 cups						
29 cups						
31 cups						
32 cups						
51 cups						
⬡ cups	1	1	1	1	1	1
⬡ cups		1	0	0	1	1
⬡ cups		1	1	1	0	0
⬡ cups	1	0	1	0	1	0

•••••• M–22

Continued from preceding page.

Lab sheet M22 should now be easy for children to do. Those hesitant may still use the real cartons to do their checking.

Suggestions for activities in binary computation

For the teacher who wants to go beyond this into binary computation (electronic computers use this system), here are further suggestions:

1 Let children make a list of all whole numbers from 0 to 50 in binary notation.

base ten	base two	
0	0	
1	1	
2	10	(pt.)
3	11	
4	100	(qt.)
5	101	
6	110	(qt. + pt.)
7	111	
8	1000	(½ gal.)
9	1001	
10	1010	
11	1011	
12	1100	(½ gal. + qt.)
13	1101	
•	•	
•	•	
•	•	
50	110010	(double gal. + gal. + pt.)

Now we can ask some questions about the patterns we see in the preceding chart:

- How can you tell an odd number in base two?
- What are the special numbers which have a *one followed only by zeros?*
- Which stands for the larger number—100111 or 111000?

2 Give another story problem on the board:

Bob bought this quantity of milk: 10011. Betty bought this quantity of milk: 1011.

Now they have the following six containers of full of milk:

	gal.	½ gal.	qt.	pt.	c.
Bob	1	0	0	1	1
Betty		1	0	1	1

They have a lot of empty containers. Could we put that milk into *four* containers? [Yes]

	gal.	½ gal.	qt.	pt.	c.
Bob	1	0	0	1	1
+ Betty		1	0	1	1
together	1	1	1	1	0

3 pints make a quart and a pint

2 cups make a pint

3 Present another story problem: This milk is in the refrigerator:

$$
\begin{array}{rl}
1101 & (13 \text{ cups}) \\
\text{Sue drinks} \longrightarrow \quad -\ 11 & (\ 3 \text{ cups}) \\
\hline
\text{How much} \longrightarrow \quad 1010 & (10 \text{ cups}) \\
\text{is left?}
\end{array}
$$

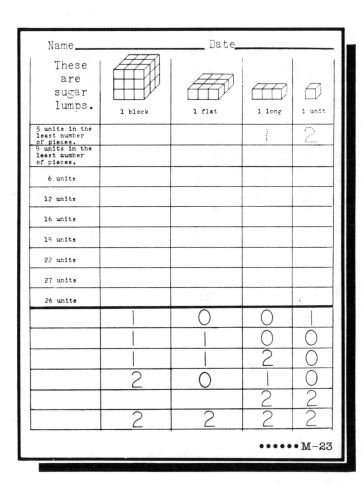

Name _____   **Date** _____

These are sugar lumps.	1 block	1 flat	1 long	1 unit
5 units in the least number of pieces.			1	2
9 units in the least number of pieces.				
6 units				
12 units				
16 units				
19 units				
22 units				
27 units				
26 units				
	1	0	0	1
	1	1	0	0
	1	1	2	0
	2	0	1	0
			2	2
	2	2	2	2

•••••• M-23

Name _____   **Date** _____

9000 – 99	8901
	8999
9000 – 909	8909
9000 – 990	8990
9000 – 109	8919
	8891
one less than 9000	8991
ten less than 9000	8091
eleven less than 9000	8010
	889
eleven less than 900	8989
101 less than 9000	8900
	8890
110 less than 9000	8891
1000 less than 9000 --------------------------- 8000	

•••••• M-24

•••••• **M23**

Base-three sugar-lump problems

We can make a model set with sugar cubes, or we can use rods to make a model set for base three. A base-three "sugar language" goes like this:

base ten	base three	
0	0	
1	1	
2	2	
3	10	(a long)
4	11	(a long and a unit)
5	12	
6	20	(two longs)
7	21	
8	22	
9	100	(a flat)
10	101	(a flat and a unit)
11	102	
12	110	(a flat and a long)
•	•	
•	•	
•	•	
50	1212	(a block, two flats, one long, two units)

Here is an addition problem, expressed in base-three notation on the left and base-ten notation on the right:

$$\text{base three} \quad \begin{array}{r} 1210 \\ +\ 2022 \\ \hline 11002 \end{array} \qquad \text{base ten} \quad \begin{array}{r} 48 \\ +\ 62 \\ \hline 110 \end{array}$$

•••••• **M24**

This lab sheet is similar to M17 except that there are more items in the right-hand column and not all can be matched. One problem is matched as an example.

N Number lines and functions

Fundamental ideas about number lines

1 For any number one can think of, no matter how large, there are always other numbers which are larger (this number plus 1, plus 2, plus 3, etc.). Therefore it is true that there is no "largest" number.

2 To diagram this idea by means of a number-line ray, mark off a point on one end of a line and call it the line's origin (or starting point). Then continue the line as far as the writing surface allows, ending it with an arrow. The arrow indicates that the line goes on and on beyond the edge of the writing surface.

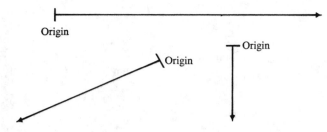

3 If we arbitrarily establish a unit distance and lay that distance off on the line from the point of origin (or 0), then we can find a point corresponding to number 1. This process is continued indefinitely, and the position of any number greater than 0 may be found.

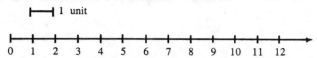

Thus 1 + 1 unit distances away from the origin is the point corresponding to 2; 1 + 1 + 1 + 1 + 1 unit distances away from the origin is the point corresponding to 5, etc. On the number-line ray above, 12 such distances are marked off. The farther we move to the right of the point of origin, the greater will be the number we can expect to find.

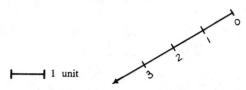

Our diagram could have looked like this, even though the direction of the ray and the unit measure have been changed.

By mathematical convention number lines are usually horizontal, with the numbers increasing as we go to the right. However, there are contrary examples in daily life, such as the vertical number line of the thermometer.

4

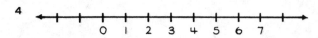

Even in first grade it is advisable to put arrows on both ends of number lines, as shown above, to prepare children for the extension of their number concepts into the realm of negative numbers. Experience has shown that some first-graders will do this on their own and locate, for example, 1 unit to the left of 0 as the point corresponding to 2 – 3.

5 Children should become aware that by estimation they can locate other numbers on the number line beyond the physical representation given. Referring to the number line above, '9' would be slightly off the paper, '25' off the edge of the desk, '1000' probably outside the classroom but still on a straight line with the number line shown. '998' would be found two units to the left of '1000,' etc. Below is part of an imagined extension of the number line above.

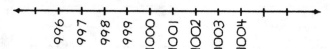

Using the number line

1 Lay off the distance "3 from 0" on the number line.

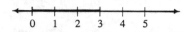

The line segment which results is shaded on the diagram.

2 Lay off the distance "3 beginning at 4" on your number line. You end at ——————?

3 Up to this point, we have not specified that the segment needs to be laid off in the "+ direction". Therefore, two equally acceptable answers could have been given to the preceding problem.

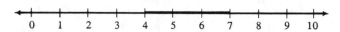

Answer 1: You end at '7.'

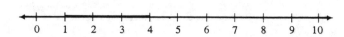

Answer 2: You end at '1.'

Sometimes we may want to be more specific in our instructions. If in the preceding problem we had wished to limit ourselves to only one of the two solutions, our instructions should have been more precise. There are various ways in which this can be done. We can say that we want to lay off on the number line a three-unit segment in the direction of the greater numbers. This can be indicated as follows:

Beginning point	Length and direction of segment	Ending point
0	(+3) →	3
4	(+3) →	7
17	(+3) →	20

If we want to indicate the laying off of a three-unit segment in the direction of the smaller numbers, we may write:

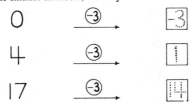

To make our vocabulary less technical when dealing with problems such as those above, we shall frequently refer to the laying off of a segment of a certain length in a certain direction simply as a "move." For example, the segments laid off above might be referred to as "+3 moves" and "−3 moves."

Sample problems

1   Here are a few sample problems to which we can now find the answers by using the number line.

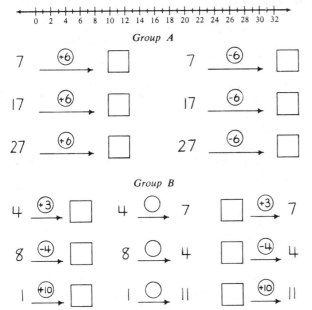

These problems were selected as examples of two observations. Watch the signs over arrows and the last digits of numbers on both sides of the arrows.

Problems in Group B were selected as examples of three types of questions to pose with regard to the same segments on the number line.

a. given: start, size and direction of move
find: . end point

b. given: start, end point
find: size and direction of move

c. given: size and direction of move, end point
find: start

2   Here is a "tricky" problem thrown in for fun. Write in the number that indicates the size of the move.

3   Thus far we have marked off on the number line only those points which correspond to the counting numbers (or natural numbers) and zero. We have indicated that where they are marked off depends *solely* on the original unit of measurement that we have chosen.

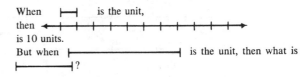

4   a. On the number line below, find the points corresponding to ½, 3½, and 5. Mark these points with dots [Do not hesitate to write in your book.]

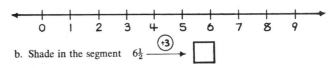

b. Shade in the segment   6½ —(+3)→ □

c. Find the points corresponding to ¼, 5⁄4 and mark them with a cross.

5   For each of the three number lines below, first determine the length of the unit that is being used. Then complete the labeling of the line by writing in a numeral under each cross line.

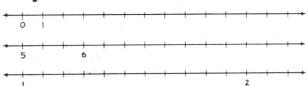

Now make up your own units of measure for the next two number lines and label every cross line.

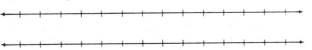

6   Using the unlabeled number lines that follow, show how you would do these problems.

a. How many half units are there in six units?
b. How many half units are there in ten units?
c. How many half units are there in 3½ units?
d. How many ¼ units are there in 1 unit?
e. How many ¼ units are there in ½ unit?
f. Divide a 4-unit segment of the number line into 8 equal segments (pieces). How long is each segment?
g. Divide a 9-unit segment of the number line into 9 equal segments. How long is each segment?
h. Divide a number-line segment into 6 pieces, each ¼ unit long. How long is the segment?

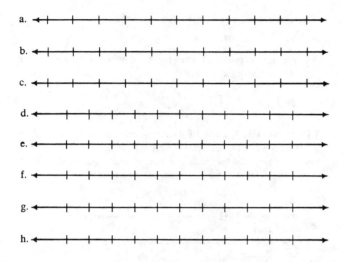

7 Complete these mathematical sentences. Then match them with the word sentences which you have already worked out on the preceding number lines. Place the matching letter beside each mathematical sentence on the line provided.

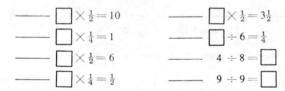

Many more such problems can be made up by the teacher for her pupils. Vary the difficulty according to the age and competence of the group.

Number line and arrow notation

1 We can use the number line for demonstrating addition and subtraction of natural numbers, fractions, and possibly negative numbers.

2 We have devised an arrow notation to express our "moves." (Since this is a "homemade" notation, children and teachers are free to devise their own.)

3 We can use the number line to solve word problems involving multiplication and division of whole numbers and fractions by making a clear diagram of what we are doing.

4 We can also translate a word sentence into a mathematical sentence or equation.

5 From any beginning point, we have been able to make a move of any size in either direction and arrive at an end point.

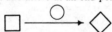

The frames in the expression above may be filled in with numerals for any numbers which make the result correspond to a move on the number line. If any *two* of these frames are filled in with such numerals, there is only *one* possible number that can be named in the remaining frame to make the expression true.

In the examples below, two numbers are given. Determine what number makes the expression true, and write the numeral in the empty frame.

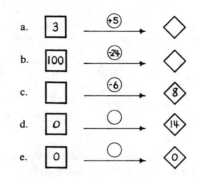

Note that:

In *a, b* and *c,* □, ○, and ◇ stand for different numbers when the problems are solved.

In *d,* ○ and ◇ stand for the same number when solved.

In *e,* □, ○, and ◇ stand for the same number when solved.

Extending arrow notation

How can we extend arrow notation to do the following word problem? We want to make four "+2 moves" on the number line. Where will the end point be? (Always begin at '0' unless otherwise stated.)

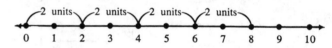

Our end point is at '8.'

We already know how to write *one* "+2 move" with arrow notation:

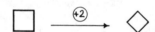

We might write *four* "+2 moves" this way:

Hence our problem would be symbolized thus:

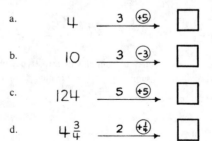

Sample problems

1 Find the end points for the following problems:

a.   4 $\xrightarrow{\;3\;\;(+5)\;}$ □

b.   10 $\xrightarrow{\;3\;\;(-3)\;}$ □

c.   124 $\xrightarrow{\;5\;\;(+5)\;}$ □

d. $4\frac{3}{4}$ $\xrightarrow{\;2\;\;(+\frac{1}{4})\;}$ □

2 Find the following moves:

a.  $12 \xrightarrow{\quad 2 \bigcirc \quad} 20$

b. $0 \xrightarrow{\quad 6 \bigcirc \quad} 2$

c. $50 \xrightarrow{\quad 9 \bigcirc \quad} 5$

d. $10{,}000 \xrightarrow{\quad 100 \bigcirc \quad} 0$

3 Find the starting points:

a. $\triangle \xrightarrow{\quad 6 \; (+1) \quad} 11$

b. $\triangle \xrightarrow{\quad 4 \; (+3) \quad} 36$

c. $\square \xrightarrow{\quad 8 \; (-2) \quad} 20$

d. $\square \xrightarrow{\quad \frac{1}{2} \; (+12) \quad} 13$

4 Find the numbers of the following moves:

a. $6 \xrightarrow{\quad \square \; (+10) \quad} 66$

b. $3 \xrightarrow{\quad \square \; (+3) \quad} 15$

c. $0 \xrightarrow{\quad \square \; (+6\frac{1}{2}) \quad} 26$

d. $44 \xrightarrow{\quad \square \; (-11) \quad} 0$

First-grade notes

The following is taken from an actual class record for October 4–6, 1960. It illustrates arrow notation and number-line games.

Grasshopper game

On the first day the teacher put pictures of grasshoppers and a number line on the board.

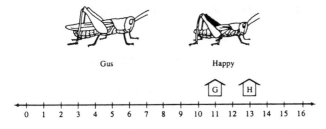

Gus   Happy

Teacher: We shall build Gus's house at point '11' on the number line and Happy's house at point '13' on the number line. Both Gus and Happy are at point '1' on the number line (or racetrack). Gus can make jumps of two units. Happy can make jumps of one unit.

Teacher: Gus jumps from '1' to where?
Children: '3'
Teacher: Happy jumps from '1' to where?
Children: '2'
Teacher: Now Gus jumps from '3' to where?
Children: '5'
Teacher: Happy wants to catch up. How many jumps should she make from '2'?
Children: 3 jumps.

Teacher: Now Gus wants to get to '9.' How far must he jump?
Children: 4 units; 2 jumps of 2 units; $5 + 4 = 9$.
Teacher: Happy wants to land 1 unit ahead of Gus. How far must she jump?
Children: 5 units; 5 jumps of 1 unit; $5 + 5 = 10$.

Teacher: Gus is angry. "I'm going to Happy's house," he says, "and hide inside it." From '9' how many units must he move to get to Happy's house at point '13'?
Jeffrey: 4 units.
Teacher: Gus shuts the door. Nobody can get inside. But Happy does not know what Gus did. So she decides to go to Gus's house. How many units is it to Gus's house? Happy is at '10.'
Children: 1 unit; $10 + 1 = 11$.

Teacher: Now Gus and Happy are at each other's houses waiting for the other to arrive. They wait and wait but nothing happens. They wait a while longer. Now they're tired of waiting. Gus says, "I'm going to move back 3 jumps." Where does he go?
Louis: To '10'; $13 - 3 = 10$.
Teacher: Gus says, "I thought I'd find Happy, but she isn't here. Where is she?" Then he says, "Maybe she's farther back along the track." So Gus goes all the way back to point '3.' How many units does he move?
Anne: 6 units. (The teacher asked Anne to demonstrate on the board the moves that Gus would have to take to get to '3'. Anne did this and found that Gus would have to move 7 units or 3 jumps of 2 units and 1 unit more. $10 - 7 = 3$; $3 + 7 = 10$.)

Teacher: Now Gus decides maybe he'd better go home. How many moves to his house from '3'?
Ruth, Audrey: 8 units or 4 jumps of 2 units; $8 + 3 = 11$.
Teacher: When Gus gets home—much to his surprise—whom does he find waiting for him?
Children: Happy!

After the grasshopper game children came to the board and made up their own number-line problems independently. They were able to do this with little assistance from the teacher.

Start at	Kind of jump	End at	On the number line	The equation
4	$(+3)$	7		$4 + 3 = 7$
7	(-2)	5		$7 - 2 = 5$
5	$(+3 -1 +1)$	8		$5 + 3 - 1 + 1 = 8$
14	$(-4 -2 +3)$	11		$14 - 4 - 2 + 3 = 11$

With the number line on the board, the teacher continued the grass-hopper game on the second day.

Teacher: Gus is at point '30' on the number line. He is going to point '32.' This means he moves how many units?

Children: 2 units.

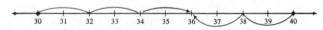

Teacher: Happy is at point '40.' She is going to move *backwards* as many units as Gus moves forward. Where will she land?
Children: At '38.'

Teacher: Gus takes another 2 steps (1 jump). Where is he now?
Children: At '34.'

Teacher: Happy takes another 2 steps (1 jump backwards). Where is she now?
Children: At '36.'

Teacher: Gus wants to meet Happy. How many units must he move?
Children: 2 units.

Teacher: How many units did Happy go?
Children: 4; 40 − 4 = 36.

Teacher: How many units did Gus go?
Children: 6; 30 + 6 = 36.

On October 6, the idea that the number line goes on and on was introduced.

Teacher: The two grasshoppers, Gus and Happy, were jumping on the number line in the second-grade class just before you came in. They jumped and jumped all the way to point '64' on the number line. But there is no point '64' written on the number line on the chalkboard. Where do you think they jumped?

Children's faces showed puzzled looks as they began to look around the room and began pointing outside the door. The teacher then took the group out into the hall and pointed to a spot on the wall.

Teacher: The grasshoppers jumped all the way out here! Suppose they wanted to reach '100'. About where do you think '100' would be?
Children: Right outside the principal's office.

Teacher: What about '500'?
Children: Up the hill!

Teacher: And a million?
Children: In the next town!

The children realized that just because the number line in the classroom extends only to a certain point, this does not mean that the number line stops. Rather, it goes on and on and on—in our minds and in our imagination.

Third-grade notes

In the following class record of October 4, 1960, a slightly different arrow notation is used from that used in the previous section. It is up to the reader to puzzle out this notation.

Grasshopper game

Pictures of two grasshoppers and a number line were drawn on the board.

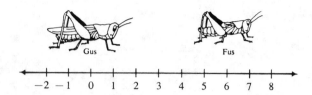

Teacher: Our boy grasshopper, Gus, has learned to make plus and minus hops on the number line. Who can make up a hopping rule for Gus?.

Beth's rule: □ ―Beth→ □ + 4

Teacher: If Gus starts at '6' on the number line, then his next jump would be where?

Children: At '10.'

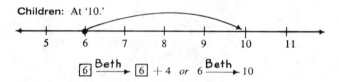

6 ―Beth→ 6 + 4   *or*   6 ―Beth→ 10

Teacher: And his next jump?
Children: '14'.

10 ―Beth→ 10 + 4   *or*   10 ―Beth→ 14

Teacher: And his next?
Children: '18'.

14 ―Beth→ 14 + 4   *or*   14 ―Beth→ 18

Teacher: I lost track of Gus. Now he's at '34.' How many hops has he made since he was at '18'?

Children: 34 − 18 = 16; 16 ÷ 4 = 4; he has made 4 hops since he was at '18'.

Teacher: I've been asleep and lost track again; now Gus is at '69'. If he jumped as he should have done, could he be at '69'?
Children: No!

Billy explained that Gus could not be at point '69' as 69 is odd, and 34 plus 4 times a whole number must be even.

Teacher: Every time Gus jumps to the wrong place, he will have to be penalized. He has to go to jail. Jail will be at point '0' on the number line. What rule must we make to take care of this situation?

Stevie: 69 ―Steve→ 69 − 69

Teacher: Stevie is on the right track. But what if Gus had stopped at point '51'? Would we subtract 69?

Children: No, we would subtract 51:

51 ――→ 51 − 51

Teacher: And for 3:

Children: $\boxed{3} \longrightarrow \boxed{3} - 3$

Teacher: Then our rule must be: box goes to box minus *what?*

Children: Box goes to box minus *box.*

The teacher and children then worked many examples until they saw that this rule would always work. So they formulated *Gus's jail rule:*

$$\boxed{} \xrightarrow{\text{Jail}} \boxed{} - \boxed{}$$

Teacher: If we use Beth's rule and then want to get back to our starting point, what rule should we make up?

Owen:

$$\boxed{} \xrightarrow{\text{Owen}} \boxed{} - 4$$

This will always get Gus back to his starting point.

Teacher: If Gus is at '13', what does he have to do, by using Owen's rule, to get back to point '5'?

Children: Twice Owen's rule.

$$\boxed{13} \xrightarrow{\text{Owen}} \xrightarrow{\text{Owen}} \boxed{5}$$

$$13 - 4 = 9; \quad 9 - 4 = 5$$

Teacher: Billy wants Gus's jumps to be like this:

$$\boxed{} \xrightarrow{\text{Bill}} \boxed{} + 9$$

To reverse this rule what could we do?

Roy:

$$\boxed{} \xrightarrow{\text{Roy}} \boxed{} - 9$$

Next the class worked on rules for Fus.

Teacher: Fus is not allowed to make plus and minus jumps. What can she do then?

Children: She can make "times" and "divide" jumps.

Teacher: If Fus is at point '2' and at each jump doubles her previous jump, where would she be after the 1st jump? [Children: '4'] 2nd jump? ['8'] 3rd jump? ['16'].

Mary's rule: $\boxed{} \xrightarrow{\text{Mary}} \boxed{} \times 2$

Teacher: How would we reverse Mary's rule?

Children: By dividing by 2. By halving it.

The teacher then illustrated, with a piece of chalk, that halving and dividing by 2 are the same—chalk broken in half, or in two equal pieces. The children put this on the board to show the ways to write the inverse of Mary's rule.

$$\boxed{} \longrightarrow \boxed{} \div 2$$
$$\boxed{} \longrightarrow (\boxed{} \times \tfrac{1}{2})$$
$$\boxed{} \longrightarrow (\tfrac{\boxed{}}{2})$$

Then the children decided to hold a race between Gus and Fus.

1 Boys decided to make Gus jump $\left(+1000.\right)$

Gus $\boxed{} \longrightarrow \boxed{} + 1000$

2 Girls decided to make Fus jump $\left(\times 2.\right)$

Fus $\boxed{} \longrightarrow \boxed{} \times 2$

Teacher: Who do you think will win the race if each gets 20 jumps?

Practically all the children thought that the boys' grasshopper, Gus, would win. But Billy said that Fus would win "in the long run."

To find out if Billy was right, the teacher announced that both grasshoppers would start at point '2', and the class worked out the following chart, with the teacher's help.

Jumps	Gus	Fus
1	1,002	4
2	2,002	8
3	3,002	16
•	•	•
•	•	•
•	•	•
10	10,002	2,048
11	11,002	4,096
12	12,002	8,192
13	13,002	16,384

Teacher: Billy was right: Fus would win the race. Fus won on the 13th jump.

As the class ended the boys accused the teacher of being "unfair" to Gus. Some of the children suggested that Gus's jumps next time should be

$$\boxed{} \longrightarrow \boxed{} + 1,000,000$$

and *then* he would win. But Stevie, Billy, and Sarah were sure that he would loose even then "*if* we played a longer game."

Question to class: Make up a "jail rule" for Fus, who cannot go "+" or "−." Next day children reported that they had found the rule

$$\boxed{} \longrightarrow \boxed{} \times 0$$

as a jail rule for Fus. Examples proved that they were correct.

Functions

One of the important topics in mathematics is the study of functions. This is made easy for young children to grasp, through the use of the number line. The work in this unit will introduce the children to the concept of a function, to the concept of the composition of functions, to the concept of the inverse of a function, and to the concept of invariant points.

A function is simply a rule that assigns to each number a second number, called its *image*. For example, the rule might assign to each number the number that is twice the given number. We could write this rule in the form $\boxed{} \longrightarrow 2 \times \boxed{}$,   meaning that any number may be paired with 2 times that number. Any rule can be considered a function so long as it assigns one *and only one* number to each and every given number.

Functions

One of the important topics in mathematics is the study of functions. This is made easy for young children to grasp, through the use of the number line. The work in this unit will introduce the children to the concept of a function, to the concept of the composition of functions, to the concept of the inverse of a function, and to the concept of invariant points.

A function is simply a rule that assigns to each number a second number, called its *image*. For example, the rule might assign to each number the number that is twice the given number. We could write this rule in the form $\square \longrightarrow 2 \times \square$, meaning that any number may be paired with 2 times that number. Any rule can be considered a function so long as it assigns one *and only one* number to each and every given number.

If we have two functional rules, we may make a single rule out of them by applying first one rule, then the other. For example, if rule F assigns to each given number double the given number, that is, $\square \longrightarrow 2 \times \square$, and if rule G assigns to each given number a number which is two more than the given number, that is to say, $\square \longrightarrow \square + 2$, we may combine these two rules to get a rule which first doubles the given number, then adds two, thus:

$$\square \longrightarrow 2 \times \square + 2$$

We call the process of combining rules in this way "composing," and the new rule is called the composition of F and G, written FG, meaning the rule which has the same effect as applying first F, then G.

(Warning: in more advanced mathematics, we would write GF to mean: apply first F, then G. This, however, would be a confusing convention for young children.)

Notice that the rule FG is *not* the same as GF. FG is the rule $\square \longrightarrow 2 \times \square + 2$; GF is the rule $\square \longrightarrow 2 \times (\square + 2)$. Thus FG assigns 6 to the number 2, whereas GF assigns 8 to that number. Composition of functions is *not* commutative; however, it is associative (that is, F [GH] is the same as [FG] H).

Sometimes there are rules which neutralize each other. If a rule Q "undoes" the effect of a rule P, then Q is called the inverse of P. In other words, if PQ is the rule $\square \longrightarrow \square$, then Q is the inverse of P. For example, if P is the rule $\square \longrightarrow 2 \times \square$ and if Q is the rule $\square \longrightarrow \frac{1}{2} \times \square$, then P and Q are inverses. This can be seen because PQ is the rule $\square \longrightarrow \frac{1}{2} \times (2 \times \square)$, which is simply $\square \longrightarrow \square$. (Not all functions have inverses. For example the function $\square \longrightarrow 10$ has no inverse. Any time that one number is the image of two or more numbers, the function has no inverse.)

Some functions leave some of the numbers to which they apply unchanged. Numbers which are the same as their images are called "invariant numbers" for that function. For example, in the function $\square \longrightarrow 4 \div \square$ the number 2 has 2 as its image, and is the only invariant (positive) number. Invariant numbers are also called invariant points, especially when the functions are visualized as mappings or jumps on the number line.

Note: The foregoing is intended only as background information for the teacher. In working with children, the teacher should allow them to use the common terminology given in the lab sheets.

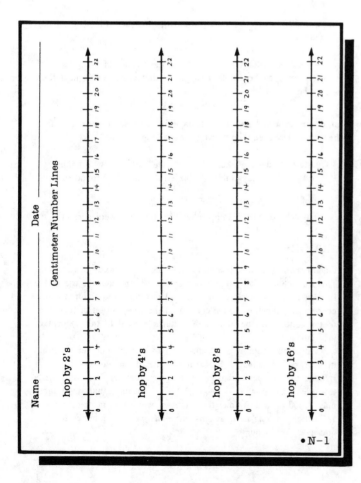

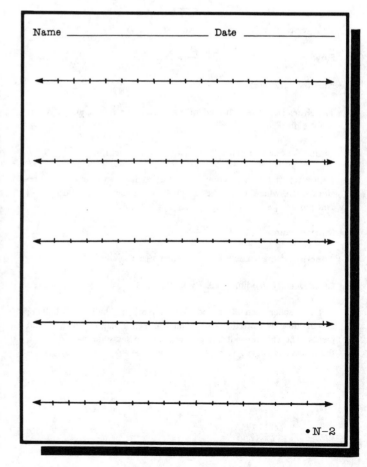

• N1

You may want to tell a story as a preliminary to the "hop by 2's," "hop by 4's," etc.

With some children, it is advisable to have them trace a few hops with their fingers first and put an *x* on each place where they land before they draw the hops.

• N2–N4

Don't always start with 0. Since the arrows indicate that the lines are *slices* from a "very long" number line, we can make the drawing any slice we choose.

We can also use letters of the alphabet for marking the points on a number line. Ask children to make a jump from H to K, then find another jump as long as that jump, etc.

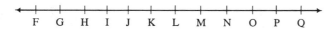

The teacher may use these sheets for the following:

1   Counting sequence

a. counting by 1's, 5's, $\frac{1}{2}$'s, $\frac{2}{3}$'s, etc.

b. counting, beginning, for example, at 97 and going to 111.

c. counting in other bases (work not introduced in the lab-sheet collection until Level 4).

2   Number-line games

$$\square \longrightarrow \square + 4$$

Now "box" goes to "box + 4."

4 jumps to (4 + 4) or 8

3 jumps to 7

3 —→ 7

5 —→ 9

Children label the points on the number line and write the rule they are using. Then they may indicate sample jumps.

Rule: $\square \longrightarrow \square - 5$

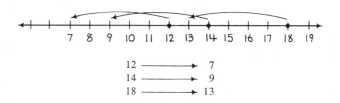

$$12 \longrightarrow 7$$
$$14 \longrightarrow 9$$
$$18 \longrightarrow 13$$

Rule: $\square \longrightarrow 2 \times \square - 1$

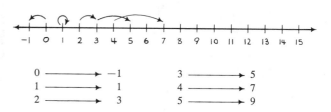

$$0 \longrightarrow -1 \qquad 3 \longrightarrow 5$$
$$1 \longrightarrow 1 \qquad 4 \longrightarrow 7$$
$$2 \longrightarrow 3 \qquad 5 \longrightarrow 9$$

The teacher and her children can make the problems as easy or as difficult as they wish.

Note that the units used on lab sheet N2 are centimeters, so students can use Cuisenaire® rods to measure jumps along these number lines. The units on lab sheet N3 are inches, and lab sheet N4 uses various arbitrary units.

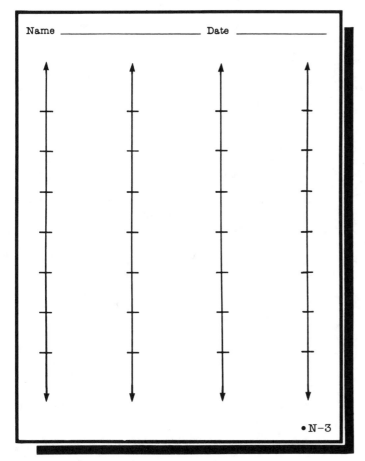

Name _____ Date _____

• N–3

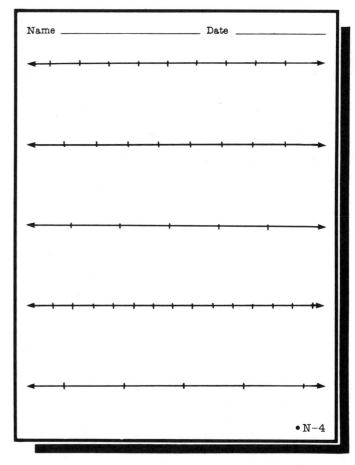

Name _____ Date _____

• N–4

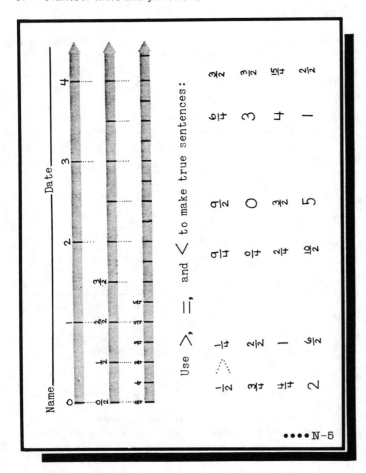

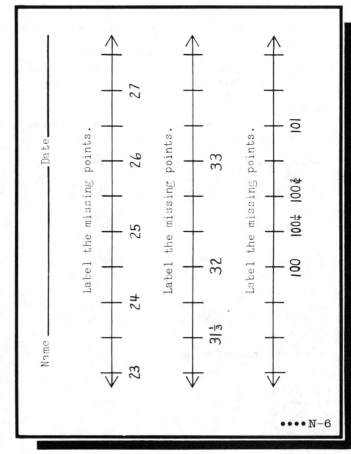

· · · · N5

The children should finish labeling the points marked off on the three number-line segments.

1   How many names for zero are used on our number-line segments? [Three names, $0, \frac{0}{2}, \frac{0}{4}$.]
   How many names for one?   [$1, \frac{2}{2}, \frac{4}{4}$.]

2   Children make the sentences true by writing the correct relationship symbols.

Procedure

$$\frac{1}{2} \overset{\textstyle >}{\underset{\textstyle <}{=}} \frac{1}{4}$$

Child finds $\frac{1}{2}$ on the number line, then traces the distance from $\frac{0}{2}$ to $\frac{1}{2}$ with his finger.

Child finds $\frac{1}{4}$ on the number line, then traces the distance from $\frac{0}{4}$ to $\frac{1}{4}$.

How does the "$\frac{1}{2}$ segment" compare to the "$\frac{1}{4}$ segment"? [The "$\frac{1}{2}$ segment" is greater than the "$\frac{1}{4}$ segment."]

$$\frac{1}{2} > \frac{1}{4}$$

For the problem,

$$\frac{3}{4} \overset{\textstyle >}{\underset{\textstyle <}{=}} \frac{2}{2}$$

the "0 to $\frac{3}{4}$ segment" is less than the "0 to $\frac{2}{2}$ segment," etc.

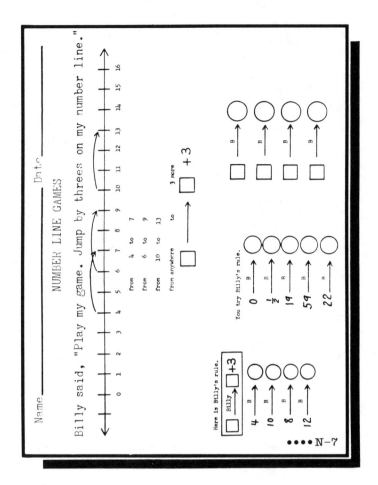

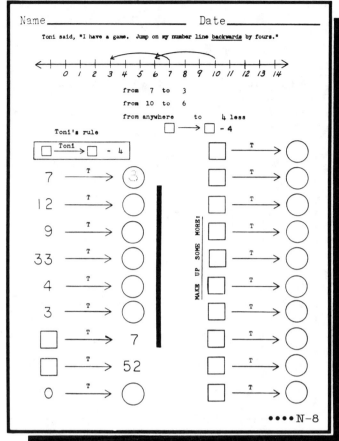

· · · · N7, N8
Preliminary activity

A chalkboard number line can be used to play a game similar to the activity on N7.

If $\square \longrightarrow \square + 4$ is used as the rule, then a strip of cardboard four units long can be cut out to help make the correct jumps.

$$\square \longrightarrow \square + 4$$
$$0 \longrightarrow 4$$
$$5 \longrightarrow 9$$
$$8 \longrightarrow 12$$
$$\text{etc.}$$

The rule is read, "anywhere goes to anywhere plus four," or "box goes to box plus four."

On lab sheet N7 the B over the arrow $\xrightarrow{B}$ refers to Billy's rule.
On the following sheets are other rules, $\xrightarrow{T}$ (Toni's rule), $\xrightarrow{A}$ (Ann's rule), etc.

Many rules can be made in the classroom. All rules take us some place. The children enjoy having rules named after them.

Some other number-line activities not included in the lab sheets are illustrated in the following rules made up by a sample class:

$\square \xrightarrow{Tom} \square + 5$ $\qquad$ $\square \xrightarrow{Sam} 2 \times \square$

$\square \xrightarrow{Mary} \square - 3$ $\qquad$ $\square \xrightarrow{Andy} \square \div 4$

$\square \xrightarrow{Phil} \square + 8 - 3$ $\qquad$ $\square \xrightarrow{Beth} \square - 9$

Sample activities

The children's rules are used in the following game.

1 Start at 12 and do each of the following once:

$$12 \xrightarrow{T} \boxed{17}$$
$$12 \xrightarrow{M} \boxed{9}$$
$$12 \xrightarrow{P} \boxed{17}$$
$$12 \xrightarrow{S} \boxed{24}$$
$$12 \xrightarrow{A} \boxed{3}$$
$$12 \xrightarrow{B} \boxed{3}$$

Question: Did any two rules land us in the same place?

Answer: Yes, rules $\xrightarrow{T}$ and $\xrightarrow{P}$, and rules $\xrightarrow{A}$ and $\xrightarrow{B}$

Question: Will this always happen for these rules?

Answer: Yes for $\xrightarrow{T}$ and $\xrightarrow{P}$. They are the same rule written differently.
No for $\xrightarrow{A}$ and $\xrightarrow{B}$. The rules will land us in the same place only when we start at 12.

Continued on next page

233

Continued from preceding page.

Question: Find a starting place where Tom's rule and Sam's rule land us at the same number.

Answer:

$$\square \xrightarrow{\text{Tom}} \square + 5$$

$$\square \xrightarrow{\text{Sam}} 2 \times \square$$

Begin at 5.

$$5 \xrightarrow{\text{T}} 5 + 5$$

$$5 \xrightarrow{\text{S}} 2 \times 5$$

$$20 \xrightarrow{\text{TM}} \boxed{22} \quad\Big\} \text{ same} \qquad 20 \xrightarrow{\text{MS}} \boxed{34} \quad\Big\} \text{ different}$$
$$20 \xrightarrow{\text{MT}} \boxed{22} \qquad\qquad\qquad 20 \xrightarrow{\text{SM}} \boxed{37}$$

$$20 \xrightarrow{\text{SA}} \boxed{10} \quad\Big\} \text{ same} \qquad 20 \xrightarrow{\text{TA}} \boxed{6\tfrac{4}{4}} \quad\Big\} \text{ different}$$
$$20 \xrightarrow{\text{AS}} \boxed{10} \qquad\qquad\qquad 20 \xrightarrow{\text{AT}} \boxed{10}$$

$$20 \xrightarrow{\text{TS}} \boxed{50} \quad\Big\} \text{ different} \qquad 20 \xrightarrow{\text{MA}} \boxed{4\tfrac{1}{4}} \quad\Big\} \text{ different}$$
$$20 \xrightarrow{\text{ST}} \boxed{45} \qquad\qquad\qquad 20 \xrightarrow{\text{AM}} \boxed{2}$$

2 Find an "undoing" rule for each of the previous rules. (They are called *inverse* rules.)

Doing rule	Undoing rule
$\square \xrightarrow{\text{T}} \square + 5$	$\square \xrightarrow{\text{1}} \square - 5$
$\square \xrightarrow{\text{M}} \square - 3$	$\square \xrightarrow{\text{W}} \square + 3$
$\square \xrightarrow{\text{P}} \square + 8 - 3$	$\square \xrightarrow{\text{d}} \square - 8 + 3$
$\square \xrightarrow{\text{S}} 2 \times \square$	$\square \xrightarrow{\text{S}} \square \div 2$
$\square \xrightarrow{\text{A}} \square \div 4$	$\square \xrightarrow{\text{A}} \square \times 4$
$\square \xrightarrow{\text{B}} \square - 9$	$\square \xrightarrow{\text{q}} \square + 9$

5 Will we find special starting points with any of these rules when, after making a move, we are still at our starting point? (Children often call these "standstill points.")

$\square \xrightarrow{\text{T}} \square + 5$		no "standstill points"
$\square \xrightarrow{\text{M}} \square - 3$		no "standstill points"
$\square \xrightarrow{\text{S}} 2 \times \square$		*zero* is a "standstill point"
$\square \xrightarrow{\text{A}} \square \div 4$		*zero* is a "standstill point"
$\square \longrightarrow 10 - \square$		*five* is a "standstill point"

3 Make up a rule that goes twice as fast as the rules made up before.

Example

Old rule	New rule
$\square \xrightarrow{\text{T}} \square + 5$	$\square \xrightarrow{\text{TT}} \square + 10$
$\square \xrightarrow{\text{S}} 2 \times \square$	$\square \xrightarrow{\text{SS}} 4 \times \square$
$\square \xrightarrow{\text{A}} \square \div 4$	$\square \xrightarrow{\text{AA}} \square \div 16$

On both N7 and N8 a simple addition and subtraction rule is used. It is hoped that children will make up many such rules for themselves.

For part of the lab sheets, the rule and the beginning number are given. The children write down the landing number. Later they write their own starting numbers. When the children are ready, encourage them to use fractions and negative numbers.

Much computation drill is accomplished when we play these number-line games.

4 Will we land at the same place when we use the following rules in any order we want to?

$$\square \xrightarrow{\text{T}} \square + 5$$

$$\square \xrightarrow{\text{M}} \square - 3$$

$$\square \xrightarrow{\text{S}} 2 \times \square$$

$$\square \xrightarrow{\text{A}} \square \div 4$$

Example

$$\square \xrightarrow{\text{F}} \square - 57$$

$$95 \xrightarrow{\text{F}} \boxed{38}$$

$$324 \xrightarrow{\text{F}} \boxed{267}$$

$$1000 \xrightarrow{\text{F F}} \boxed{886} \quad \text{(rule F is used twice)}$$

$$1000\tfrac{1}{2} \xrightarrow{\text{F F}} \boxed{886\tfrac{1}{2}}$$

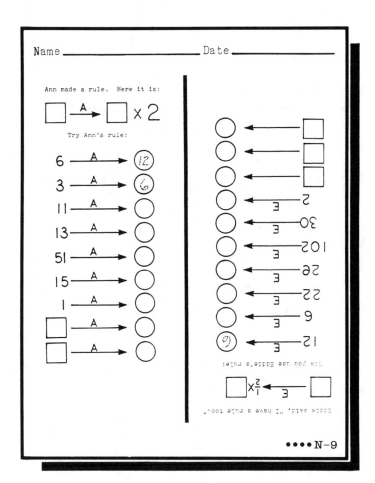

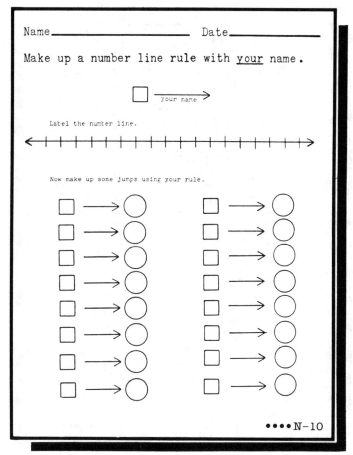

•••• N9

N9 uses two multiplication rules:

$$\square \xrightarrow{\ A\ } \square \times 2$$

$$\square \xrightarrow{\ E\ } \tfrac{1}{2} \times \square$$

Rule E (multiplying by one-half) is the same as dividing by two and is the inverse (undoing) of Rule A.

When children discover this relationship, they may want to make up other pairs of rules like these.

$$\square \longrightarrow \square \times 3$$

$$\square \longrightarrow \tfrac{1}{3} \times \square$$

$$\square \longrightarrow 4 \times \square$$

$$\square \longrightarrow \square \div 4$$

$$\square \longrightarrow \frac{(2 \times \square)}{3}$$

$$\square \longrightarrow \frac{3 \times \square}{2}$$

•••• N10

Lab sheet N10 gives the children an opportunity to make up their own rules.

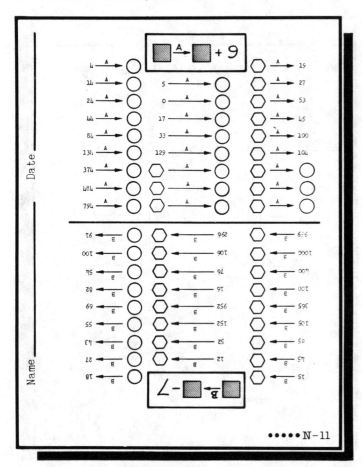

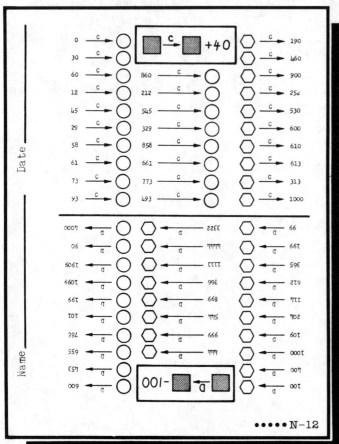

·····N11– N14

Addition and subtraction rules for computation practice

N11

In many of the problems, the *unit* digits of the starting points are the same so that children can build up generalizations about adding and subtracting a specific number.

N12

$$\square \longrightarrow \square + 40$$

When adding tens, the unit digits will be the same for both starting and landing points.

$$\square \longrightarrow \square - 100$$

When subtracting hundreds, the units and the tens digits will be the same for starting and landing points.

N13, N14

More observations similar to the preceding can be made by children.

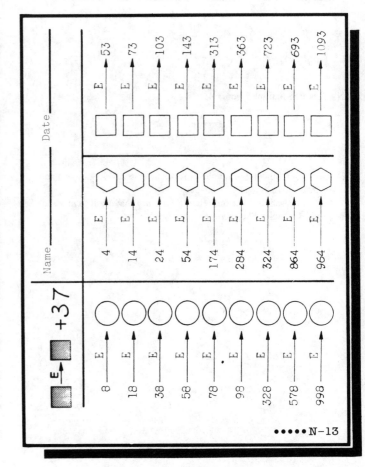

·····N15
Number-line rules

Four number-line rules are given: W, X, Y, and Z.

    W and Y are a rule and its inverse.
    X and Z are a rule and its inverse.

    We will now look at all the moves indicated on the lab sheet and see which of the four rules has been applied.

$$4 \xrightarrow{W} 7 \qquad \blacksquare \xrightarrow{W} \blacksquare + 3$$

$$4 \xrightarrow{X} 8 \qquad \blacksquare \xrightarrow{X} \blacksquare \times 2$$

$$4 \xrightarrow{Y} 1 \qquad \blacksquare \xrightarrow{Y} \blacksquare - 3$$

$$4 \xrightarrow{Z} 2 \qquad \blacksquare \xrightarrow{Z} \tfrac{1}{2} \times \blacksquare$$

$$32 \xrightarrow{Z} 16 \xrightarrow{Z} 8 \xrightarrow{Z} 4 \xrightarrow{Z} 2 \xrightarrow{Z} 1$$

$$5 \xrightarrow{W} 8 \xrightarrow{Z} 4 \xrightarrow{Y} 1 \xrightarrow{X} 2 \xrightarrow{W} 5$$

$$3 \xrightarrow{X} 6 \xrightarrow{Z} 3 \xrightarrow{X} 6 \xrightarrow{Z} 3 \xrightarrow{X} 6$$
or
$$3 \xrightarrow{W} 6 \xrightarrow{Y} 3 \xrightarrow{W} 6 \xrightarrow{Y} 3 \xrightarrow{W} 6$$

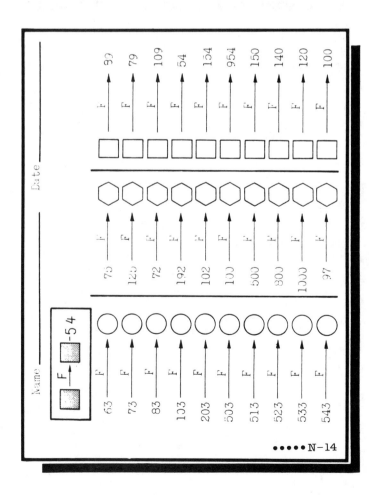

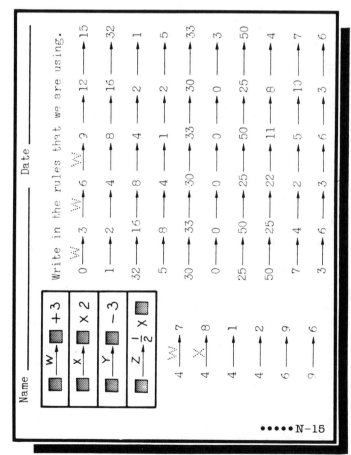

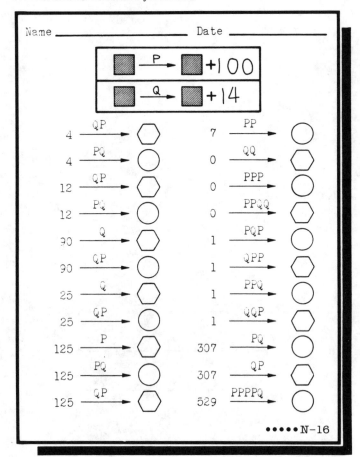

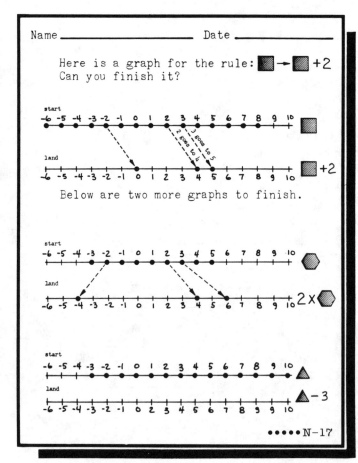

· · · · · **N16**

Combining number-line rules

On N16 we combine two addition rules. We discover (a) that the order in which we add makes no difference, and (b) that we can break up a difficult addition problem into several simpler problems.

$$12 \xrightarrow{Q\ P} \boxed{126} \qquad 12 \xrightarrow{Q} 26 \xrightarrow{P} 126$$

$$12 \xrightarrow{P\ Q} \boxed{126} \qquad 12 \xrightarrow{P} 112 \xrightarrow{Q} 126$$

Remember: If we had a *multiplication* and an *addition* rule, the order of the operation would make a difference:

$$\square \xrightarrow{T} \square + 5$$

$$\square \xrightarrow{U} \square \times 3$$

$$12 \xrightarrow{T\ U} \boxed{51} \qquad 12 \xrightarrow{T} 17 \xrightarrow{U} 51$$

$$12 \xrightarrow{U\ T} \boxed{41} \qquad 12 \xrightarrow{U} 36 \xrightarrow{T} 41$$

· · · · · **N17**

On this lab sheet are pairs of parallel number lines. The top line shows the starting points; the bottom line shows the landing points.

-2 -1 0 1 2 3 4 ... start ■ ... land ■ - 2	□ ⟶ □ - 2	All jumps are parallel to one another and are inclined in the positive direction.
-2 -1 0 1 2 3 4 5 6 7 ... start ⬣ ... land 2 × ⬣	◯ ⟶ 2 × ◯	Jumps are not parallel and fan out. There is a mirror symmetry about the 0 ⟶ 0 axis.
-3 -2 -1 0 1 2 3 4 ... start ▲ ... land ▲ - 3	△ ⟶ △ - 3	All jumps are parallel to one another but are inclined in the negative direction.

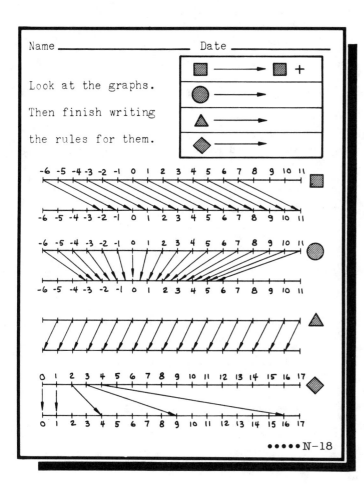

What are the *factors* of 6?

2 is a factor of 6 because three 2's equal 6.
1 is a factor of 6 because six 1's equal 6.
3 is a factor of 6 because two 3's equal 6.
6 is a factor of 6 because one 6 equals 6.

There are not any other factors of 6. For example, 4 is not a factor of 6 since there are not any whole numbers of four that equal 6.

We can say that 3 and 2 make up a *factor pair* for 6 since

$$3 \times 2 = 2 \times 3 = 6$$

1 and 6 are also a factor pair for 6 since

$$1 \times 6 = 6 \times 1 = 6$$

The number 12 has three factor pairs. They are $(1, 12)$, $(2, 6)$, and $(3, 4)$.

The number 5 has only one factor pair: $(1, 5)$.

Any number larger than 1, with *a single factor pair*, is said to be a *prime number*. 2 is a prime number since its only factor pair is $(1, 2)$. 127 is a prime number since its only factor pair is $(1, 127)$. However 10 is *not* prime since it has more than one factor pair: $(1, 10)$ and $(2, 5)$. 16 is not prime since it, too, has more than one factor pair: $(1, 16)$, $(2, 8)$, and $(4, 4)$.

Let us now choose another number which is *not* prime—60, for example. One of the factor pairs for 60 is $(6, 10)$. Therefore

$$60 = 6 \times 10$$

but
$$6 = 2 \times 3$$
and
$$10 = 5 \times 2$$
therefore
$$60 = (2 \times 3) \times (5 \times 2)$$

How about
$$(2 \times 2) \times (5 \times 3)$$
That's equal to 60 too.

How about
$$(2 \times 5 \times 2) \times 3$$
That's also equal to 60.

The numbers 2, 2, 3, and 5 are all prime; when they are multiplied together they equal 60. Therefore, they are called the *prime factors* of 60.

What are the prime factors of 48?

$$48 = 2 \times 24$$
$$= 2 \times 2 \times 12$$
$$= 2 \times 2 \times 2 \times 6$$
$$= 2 \times 2 \times 2 \times 2 \times 3$$

Therefore, the prime factors of 48 are the prime numbers 2, 2, 2, 2, and 3.

What are the prime factors of 99? They are the prime numbers 3, 3, and 11, because $3 \times 3 \times 11 = 99$.

What are the prime factors of 17? 17 is the only prime factor of 17, because 17 is already prime.

What are all the factors of 54? $(1, 54)$.

$54 = 54$	54 is even, so we know we can take out the factor 2.
$54 = 2 \times \boxed{27}$	$27 = 3 \times 9$, so we can take out the prime factor 3.
$54 = 2 \times 3 \times \boxed{9}$	$9 = 3 \times 3$; 3 is prime. Now we are finished.
$54 = 2 \times 3 \times 3 \times 3$	

Name _____ Date _____

Look at the graphs.

Then finish writing

the rules for them.

•••••**N18**

What is the rule?

On N18 graphs of the rules on pairs of number lines are given. The child must discover the rules that made the graphs. The rules are:

■ → ■ + 4
$$\begin{cases} 0 \to 4 \\ 1 \to 5 \\ 2 \to 6 \end{cases}$$

● → ● × ½
$$\begin{cases} 0 \to 0 \\ 1 \to \frac{1}{2} \\ 2 \to 1 \end{cases}$$

▲ → ▲ − 1
$$\begin{cases} 0 \to -1 \\ 1 \to 0 \\ 2 \to 1 \end{cases}$$

◆ → ◆ × ◆
$$\begin{cases} 0 \to 0 \\ 1 \to 1 \\ 2 \to 4 \\ 3 \to 9 \\ 4 \to 16 \end{cases}$$

We see that: (a) only addition and subtraction rules give us parallel lines exclusively; (b) addition and subtraction rules have no "standstill points"; and (c) there can be more than one standstill point.

$$0 \to 0 \times 0$$
$$1 \to 1 \times 1$$
0 and 1 are standstill points for the rule

$$\diamond \to \diamond \times \diamond$$

How many other problems can we make from $2 \times 3 \times 3 \times 3$?

$$(2 \times 3) \times (3 \times 3) = 6 \times 9$$
$$(3 \times 3) \times (2 \times 3) = 9 \times 6$$
$$(2 \times 3 \times 3) \times 3 = 18 \times 3$$
$$3 \times (2 \times 3 \times 3) = 3 \times 18$$
$$2 \times (3 \times 3 \times 3) = 2 \times 27$$
$$(3 \times 3 \times 3) \times 2 = 27 \times 2$$

Thus the factor pairs (6, 9), (3, 18), (2, 27) can be derived by finding the prime factors of 54.

··O1

Introduction to factoring

Factoring is really a subtopic of multiplication. The emphasis in this section is on looking at numbers and finding all of their factors. This activity lets us see that positive whole numbers fall into three distinct groups:

a. Those having only two factors (themselves and one). These are *prime numbers.*
b. Those having more than two factors. These are *composite numbers.*
c. The number *one,* which is neither composite nor prime.

Another aim of the work in this section is to discover that any number can be uniquely represented as the product of its prime factors. No two different numbers will have the same prime factors. For example:

The number 42 is a composite number; it is a product. Its factors are: 1, 2, 3, 6, 7, 14, 21, 42. These factors can be arranged into pairs.

(1, 42)	1×42,	42×1
(2, 21)	2×21,	21×2
(3, 14)	14×3,	3×14
(6, 7)	6×7,	7×6

Thus 42 is the product for four factor pairs. However, 42 has only one unique prime factorization. It is the product of the primes (2, 3, 7). $42 = 2 \times 3 \times 7$.

By using the associative law of multiplication and the commutative law of multiplication, we can reconstruct from the prime factors of 42 all previous pairs of factors.

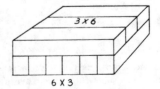

The number 23 is a prime number. It is a product. Its factors are 1, 23. These factors make only one pair.

$$1 \times 23, \quad 23 \times 1$$

Since it is only divisible by itself and 1, it is a prime number.

On lab sheet O1 we single out the brown rod for comparison with the other nine rods. All ten rods fit the diagrams at the top of the sheet. Letters inside the diagrams suggest the color code.

Could the length of the brown rod be built in a color other than brown? [Yes]

8 white rods	$8 \times 1 = 8$
4 red rods	$4 \times 2 = 8$
2 purple rods	$2 \times 4 = 8$
1 brown rod	$1 \times 8 = 8$

8, 4, 2, 1 are the factors of 8.

Brown, purple, red, and white are the one-color patterns of the brown rod.

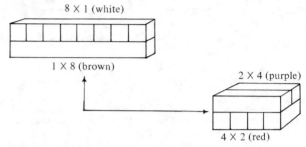

Two pairs of congruent rectangles can be built from these one-color patterns.

From the length "orange-brown" (18 white units) we get the following one-color patterns.

18 white rods	18×1
9 red rods	9×2
6 light green rods	6×3
3 dark green rods	3×6
2 blue rods	2×9
1 orange-brown combination	1×18

The following three pairs of congruent rectangles show these one-color patterns.

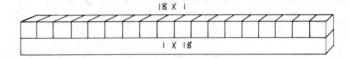

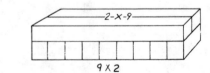

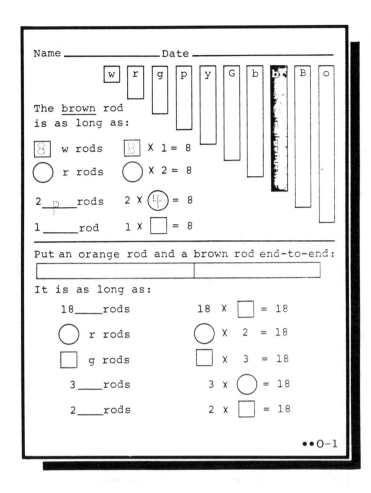

The **brown** rod
is as long as:

8 w rods   8 × 1 = 8

○ r rods   ○ × 2 = 8

2 ___ rods   2 × ④ = 8

1 ___ rod   1 × ☐ = 8

Put an orange rod and a brown rod end-to-end:

It is as long as:

18 ___ rods   18 × ☐ = 18

○ r rods   ○ × 2 = 18

☐ g rods   ☐ × 3 = 18

3 ___ rods   3 × ○ = 18

2 ___ rods   2 × ☐ = 18

••O–1

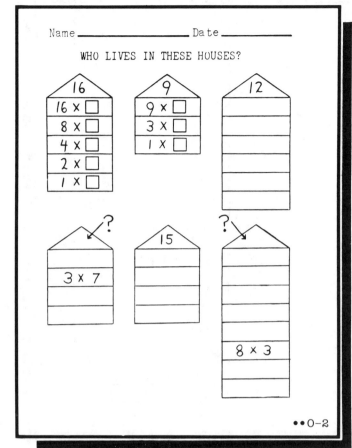

WHO LIVES IN THESE HOUSES?

••O–2

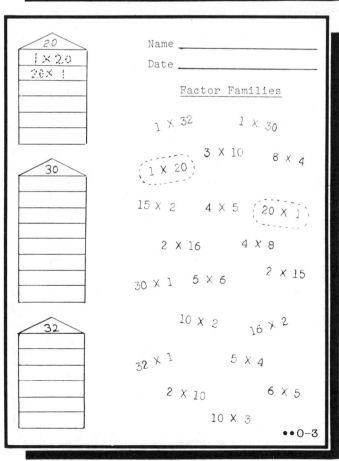

Factor Families

••O–3

••O2
Factor houses

Look at the first house. The house number is written in the gable.
It is 16.

> How many stories does the house have? [5 stories]
> On each floor a factor family lives.
> On the top floor the family 16 × ☐1 lives.
> On the next lower floor the family 8 × ☐2 lives. Etc.

Check your answers with the *one-color* patterns for 16. Do the same
for the other houses whose house numbers you know.

How does the family name "3 × 7" help you find out what house
number that house has? Find the other families who live in that house.

••O3

On this lab sheet all the factor families who live in any one of the
three houses are mixed up. They are on the street.

Make each family go back into its own house. Cross out the
families when they have gone home.

Follow-up activity

Children may draw factor houses of their own, give them house
numbers, and put all the families in.

They may first build one-color patterns with rods and then transfer
the results of their thinking to paper, or they may first do the activity
mentally and then check their answers with the rods.

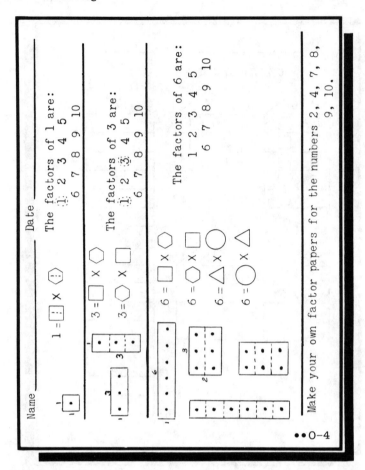

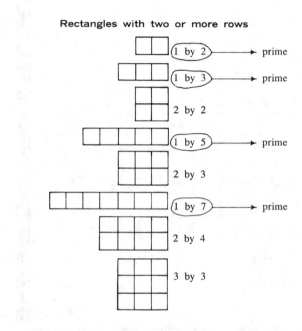

··O4

Rectangles with two or more rows

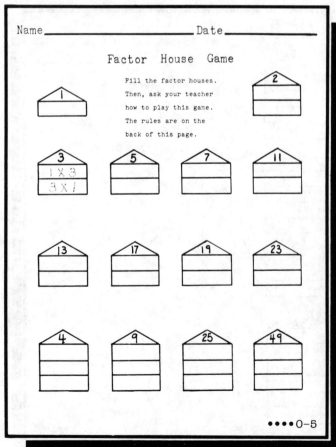

Factor House Game

Fill the factor houses.
Then, ask your teacher
how to play this game.
The rules are on the
back of this page.

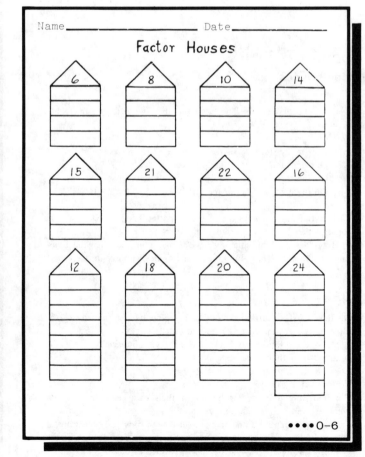

Factor Houses

···· O5, O6

The House Game

This is a factoring game. The objectives are to: (1) help build skills in multiplication; (2) give practice in factoring of integers; (3) give practice in use of prime numbers; and (4) develop a knowledge of squaring.

The children will need Cuisenaire® rods, scissors, and envelopes. Every integer has its own "house." The numeral for a particular number is written in the "attic" of the house.

How many stories tall the house is depends on the number of ordered factor pairs the integer has. Thus, integer 1 lives in a one-story house. Integer 10 lives in a four-story house.

How to play the House Game

1   Children begin by finding all the ordered pairs of factors of a number and writing these on a piece of scratch paper. When they have done this, they must find the correct house for the number and write the number in the attic of its house. Each pair of factors must then be listed on a "floor" of the house. (On lab sheet O6 the house for 16 needs one more floor, and the houses for 12, 18, and 20 have one floor too many.) This is repeated for all the numbers from 1 through 25.

2   The children cut out their houses and write their own names on the back of each house. Each set of houses should be kept in an envelope.

3   The children take partners and one becomes a seller (Child A) and one a buyer (Child B).

Child A places all the houses from one envelope *face down*, before him on a table. Child B tries to buy the houses from Child A by saying, "I want to buy a _____ story house."

Child A asks, "Who lives in it?"

Child B answers, "Number _____."

If B names the right combination of house and number, B has "bought" the house and takes it. He may then ask for another one from A's pile. This procedure continues until B has either bought all the houses or made an error.

If B makes a mistake, Child A must show him his error and read to him all the "factor families" who live in that number's house.

Child A may call "Challenge!" if B is *very* good. Then B must name all the families for that number before he gets the house. No seller may ever ask for more than three challenges during any one game.

The game ends when B has all the houses or makes a mistake. He writes down his score (one point for each house bought) and then takes his place as the seller.

Analysis of house distribution

Note: The material that follows is optional. The teacher may or may not choose to use it with her class.

One-story houses

1 is the only such number; 1 is the unit.

Two-story houses

All prime numbers live in two-story houses.

In the set of numbers 1 through 25, the following are prime:
2, 3, 5, 7, 11, 13, 17, 19, 23.

Three-story houses

The squares of prime numbers live in three-story houses. In the set of numbers 1 through 25, the following numbers are squares of prime numbers:

4   (the square of 2)
9   (the square of 3)
25   (the square of 5)

Four-story houses

The numbers that live in four-story houses have, in addition to themselves and 1, two other factors, of which one is prime and the other is either prime or a square of a prime.

In the set of numbers 1 through 25, the numbers 6, 8, 10, 14, 15, 21, and 22 live in four-story houses. (In this list, 8 has a square of a prime as one of its factors.)

Five-story houses

The square of a square of a prime lives in a five-story house. In the set of numbers 1 through 25, the number 16 is the only number that fits into a five-story house. (16 is the square of 4, which is the square of the prime number 2.)

This analysis can be extended for every group of factors.

Some children may want to make factor houses for numbers from 25 through 50.

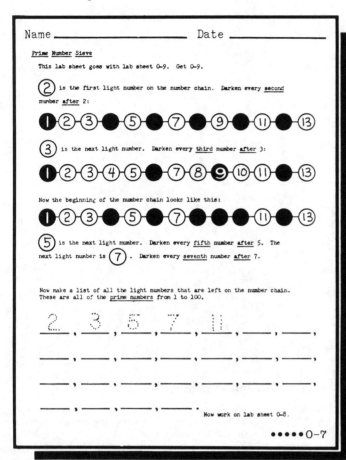

Name _____ Date _____

This lab sheet goes with lab sheet O-9. Get O-9.

2 is the first light number on the number chain. Darken every <u>second</u> number <u>after</u> 2:

①②③●⑤●⑦●⑨●⑪●⑬

3 is the next light number. Darken every <u>third</u> number <u>after</u> 3:

①②③④⑤●⑦⑧⑨⑩⑪●⑬

Now the beginning of the number chain looks like this:

①②③●⑤●⑦●●●⑪●⑬

5 is the next light number. Darken every <u>fifth</u> number <u>after</u> 5. The next light number is **7**. Darken every <u>seventh</u> number <u>after</u> 7.

Now make a list of all the light numbers that are left on the number chain. These are all of the <u>prime numbers</u> from 1 to 100.

2 , 3 , 5 , 7 , 11 ,

____ , ____ , ____ , ____ , ____ ,

____ , ____ , ____ , ____ , ____ ,

____ , ____ , ____ . Now work on lab sheet O-8.

•••••O-7

•••••O7, O9
The Sieve of Eratosthenes

O7 gives the instructions for O9. O9 is the beginning of a number chain (integers 2–100) similar to that which Eratosthenes (Greek mathematician, Third Century B.C.) might have used to sift out the prime numbers from the other integers.

Step 1 leaves the prime number 2, but eliminates all the other multiples of 2 (the even numbers).

Step 2 leaves the prime number 3, but eliminates all the other odd multiples of 3.

Step 3 leaves the prime number 5, but eliminates all the other odd multiples of 5. (Those also divisible by 3 are gone already.)

Step 4 leaves the prime number 7, but eliminates 49, 77, 91. (The other multiples of 7 have already dropped out.)

This leaves only the prime numbers smaller than 100: 2, 3, 5, 7, 11, 13, 17, 19, 23, 29, 31, 37, 41, 43, 47, 53, 59, 61, 67, 71, 73, 79, 83, 89, 97

You may wonder why we can stop after testing for the number 7. We know that $100 = 10 \times 10$. Thus 10 is the largest factor of a number under 101 we need to find. 8, 9, and 10 have already been eliminated because they are multiples of the smaller primes 2, 3, and 5.

Therefore, testing for 7 is the last necessary step for finding the prime numbers under 101.

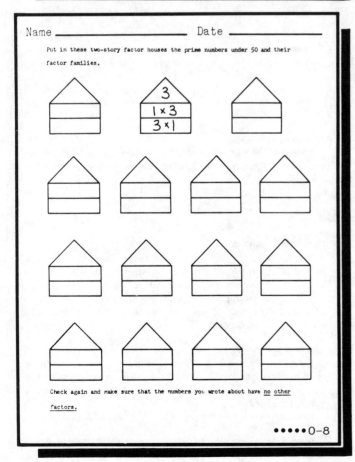

Name _____ Date _____

Put in these two-story factor houses the prime numbers under 50 and their factor families.

3
1 × 3
3 × 1

Check again and make sure that the numbers you wrote about have <u>no other</u> factors.

•••••O-8

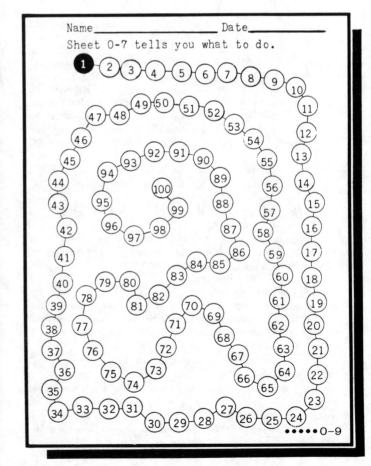

Name _____ Date _____

Sheet O-7 tells you what to do.

•••••O-9

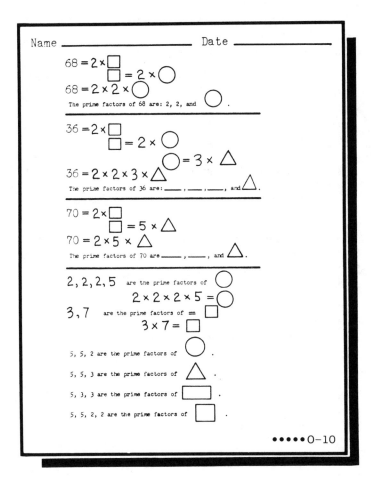

Name _____ Date _____

$68 = 2 \times \square$

$\square = 2 \times \bigcirc$

$68 = 2 \times 2 \times \bigcirc$

The prime factors of 68 are: 2, 2, and $\bigcirc$.

$36 = 2 \times \square$

$\square = 2 \times \bigcirc$

$\bigcirc = 3 \times \triangle$

$36 = 2 \times 2 \times 3 \times \triangle$

The prime factors of 36 are: ____, ____, ____, and $\triangle$.

$70 = 2 \times \square$

$\square = 5 \times \triangle$

$70 = 2 \times 5 \times \triangle$

The prime factors of 70 are ____, ____, and $\triangle$.

2, 2, 2, 5 are the prime factors of $\bigcirc$

$2 \times 2 \times 2 \times 5 = \bigcirc$

3, 7 are the prime factors of $= \square$

$3 \times 7 = \square$

5, 5, 2 are the prime factors of $\bigcirc$.

5, 5, 3 are the prime factors of $\triangle$.

5, 3, 3 are the prime factors of $\square$.

5, 5, 2, 2 are the prime factors of $\square$.

•••••O-10

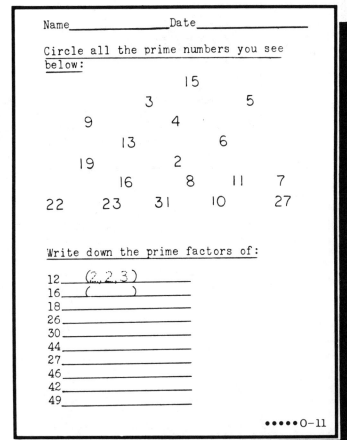

Name _____ Date _____

Circle all the prime numbers you see below:

15

3   5

9   4

13   6

19   2

16   8   11   7

22   23   31   10   27

Write down the prime factors of:

12 ____(2, 2, 3)____

16 ____( )____

18 _____

26 _____

30 _____

44 _____

27 _____

46 _____

42 _____

49 _____

•••••O-11

•••••O10

Take any number—say, 116. Is it prime? [No. It is *even*, and no even number except 2 is prime.] What are the prime factors of 116?

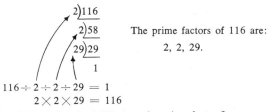

The prime factors of 116 are: 2, 2, 29.

$116 \div 2 \div 2 \div 29 = 1$

$2 \times 2 \times 29 = 116$

Take 243—is it prime? What are its prime factors?

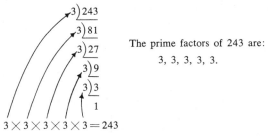

The prime factors of 243 are: 3, 3, 3, 3, 3.

$3 \times 3 \times 3 \times 3 \times 3 = 243$

•••••O11

Answers

At the bottom of the sheet, the prime factors are as follows:

12	2, 2, 3	30	2, 3, 5	42	2, 3, 7
16	2, 2, 2, 2	44	2, 2, 11	49	7, 7
18	2, 3, 3	27	3, 3, 3		
26	2, 13	46	2, 23		

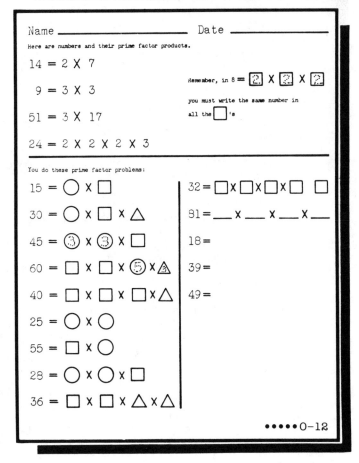

Name _____ Date _____

Here are numbers and their prime factor products.

$14 = 2 \times 7$

$9 = 3 \times 3$

$51 = 3 \times 17$

$24 = 2 \times 2 \times 2 \times 3$

Remember, in $8 = \boxed{2} \times \boxed{2} \times \boxed{2}$ you must write the same number in all the $\square$'s

You do these prime factor problems:

$15 = \bigcirc \times \square$

$30 = \bigcirc \times \square \times \triangle$

$45 = \bigcirc \times \bigcirc \times \square$

$60 = \square \times \square \times \bigcirc \times \triangle$

$40 = \square \times \square \times \square \times \triangle$

$25 = \bigcirc \times \bigcirc$

$55 = \square \times \bigcirc$

$28 = \bigcirc \times \bigcirc \times \square$

$36 = \square \times \square \times \triangle \times \triangle$

$32 = \square \times \square \times \square \times \square \times \square$

$81 = \underline{\ } \times \underline{\ } \times \underline{\ } \times \underline{\ }$

$18 =$

$39 =$

$49 =$

•••••O-12

P Squaring

The sheets in this section are confined to work on "squaring." These general notes, however, provide the teacher with background information on "raising a number to different powers" of which "squaring" or "raising a number to the second power" is only one aspect.

Raising a number to a power as repeated multiplication

Before discussing repeated multiplication, let us first refer to the definition of multiplication that was discussed in Section F. There we defined multiplication in terms of repeated addition, as illustrated by the following examples:

$$2 \times 14 = 14 + 14 \qquad \text{(2 addends)}$$
$$5 \times 7 = 7 + 7 + 7 + 7 + 7 \qquad \text{(5 addends)}$$
$$52 \times 4 = 4 + 4 + \ldots + 4 \qquad \text{(52 addends)}$$

In general,
$$\square \times \triangle = \triangle + \triangle + \ldots + \triangle \qquad (\square \text{ addends})$$

Just as multiplication is a short way of writing repeated addition, "raising a number to a power" is a short way of writing repeated multiplication. It can be considered a fifth operation.

We define 4^2 to mean 4×4 (2 factors), 7^4 to mean $7 \times 7 \times 7 \times 7$ (4 factors), 2^7 to mean $2 \times 2 \times 2 \times 2 \times 2 \times 2 \times 2$ (7 factors), and 4^{36} to mean $4 \times 4 \ldots \times 4$ (36 factors). In general, we define

$$\triangle^{\square}$$

to mean

$$\triangle \times \triangle \times \ldots \times \triangle \qquad (\square \text{ factors})$$

where $\triangle$ is a placeholder for any number in the set $\{0, 1, 2, 3, \ldots\}$ and $\square$ is a placeholder for any number in the set $\{2, 3, 4, 5, \ldots\}$.

$$\triangle^1 \text{ is defined to mean } \triangle$$
$$\triangle^0 \text{ is defined to mean } 1.$$

Terminology

In 5^2 the raised '2' is called the *exponent*. It indicates the power to which 5, the *base*, is raised.

5^1 is read as "five to the first power."
5^2 is read as "five squared" or "five to the second power."
5^3 is read as "five cubed" or "five to the third power."
5^4 is read as "five to the fourth power."
5^5 is read as "five to the fifth power," etc.

Law of exponents

Since, according to the definition above,

$$5^3 = 5 \times 5 \times 5$$
and
$$5^4 = 5 \times 5 \times 5 \times 5$$
we can say that
$$5^3 \times 5^4 = (5 \times 5 \times 5) \times (5 \times 5 \times 5 \times 5)$$
$$= 5^{3+4}$$
$$= 5^7$$

In general, this property may be stated as follows:

$$\triangle^{\square} \times \triangle^{\circ} = \triangle^{\square + \circ}$$

when the exponents, $\square$ and $\circ$, are placeholders for counting numbers, and the base, $\triangle$, is a placeholder for whole numbers.

Properties of the operation "raising to a power"

Briefly, let us look at some of the properties of what is meant by "raising to a power."

1 Raising to a power is not commutative.
For example, we can see that 2^5 does not equal 5^2.

$$2^5 = 2 \times 2 \times 2 \times 2 \times 2 = 32$$
$$5^2 = 5 \times 5 = 25$$
therefore $\qquad 2^5 \neq 5^2$

2 Raising to a power is not associative.

$$2^{(4^3)} = 2^{4 \times 4 \times 4} = 2^{64}$$
$$(2^4)^3 = 2^4 \times 2^4 \times 2^4 = 2^{12}$$
therefore $\qquad 2^{(4^3)} \neq (2^4)^3$

3 Raising to a power has an identity element.

$$5^1 = 5$$
$$17^1 = 17$$
$$1^1 = 1$$
$$1067^1 = 1067$$

4 Another interesting property of raising to a power is illustrated by the following examples:

$$1^3 = 1$$
$$1^7 = 1$$
$$1^1 = 1$$
$$1^{274} = 1$$

Arithmetic and geometric progressions

By repeated *addition* we can make number patterns like the following:

1
$$3 = 1 \times 3 = 3$$
$$3 + 3 = 2 \times 3 = 6$$
$$3 + 3 + 3 = 3 \times 3 = 9$$
$$3 + 3 + 3 + 3 = 4 \times 3 = 12$$
$$3 + 3 + 3 + 3 + 3 = 5 \times 3 = 15$$
$$3 + 3 + 3 + 3 + 3 + 3 = 6 \times 3 = 18$$

2
$$10 = 1 \times 10 = 10$$
$$10 + 10 = 2 \times 10 = 20$$
$$10 + 10 + 10 = 3 \times 10 = 30$$
$$10 + 10 + 10 + 10 = 4 \times 10 = 40$$
$$10 + 10 + 10 + 10 + 10 = 5 \times 10 = 50$$
$$10 + 10 + 10 + 10 + 10 + 10 = 6 \times 10 = 60$$

These patterns provide us with the following sequences of numbers:

$$3, 6, 9, 12, 15, 18, \ldots$$
$$10, 20, 30, 40, 50, 60, \ldots$$

Sequences of numbers like those above are called *arithmetic progressions*. In an arithmetic progression the interval between every two pairs of adjacent numbers is always the same. In the first sequence the interval is 3. The interval in the second sequence is 10.

In like manner, we can also make number patterns by repeatedly *multiplying*.

3
$$3 = 3^1 = 3$$
$$3 \times 3 = 3^2 = 9$$
$$3 \times 3 \times 3 = 3^3 = 27$$
$$3 \times 3 \times 3 \times 3 = 3^4 = 81$$
$$3 \times 3 \times 3 \times 3 \times 3 = 3^5 = 243$$
$$3 \times 3 \times 3 \times 3 \times 3 \times 3 = 3^6 = 729$$

4
$$10 = 10^1 = 10$$
$$10 \times 10 = 10^2 = 100$$
$$10 \times 10 \times 10 = 10^3 = 1000$$
$$10 \times 10 \times 10 \times 10 = 10^4 = 10000$$
$$10 \times 10 \times 10 \times 10 \times 10 = 10^5 = 100000$$
$$10 \times 10 \times 10 \times 10 \times 10 \times 10 = 10^6 = 1000000$$

Upon inspection we can see that the sequences

$$3, 9, 27, 81, 243, 729, \ldots$$
$$10, 100, 1000, 10000, 100000, 1000000, \ldots$$

are not arithmetic progressions, for there is not a constant interval between the adjacent members of the progression. In fact, the interval between adjacent numbers is rapidly increasing. In the first sequence the interval triples each time. In the second, the interval is increased 10-fold each time. Sequences of this type are called *geometric progressions*.

Progressions of squared and cubed numbers

If we look at number pattern 3 above, we can see that the geometric progression

$$3, 9, 27, 81, 243, 729, \ldots$$

can also be written as

$$3^1, 3^2, 3^3, 3^4, 5^5, 3^6, \ldots$$

This sequence is formed by holding 3, the base, constant and, starting at 1, increasing the exponent by one each time.

Let us now observe what happens if we hold the exponent constant at 2 and increase the base by one each time.

$$1^2, 2^2, 3^2, 4^2, 5^2, 6^2, \ldots$$

Since 1^2 means 1×1, 2^2 means 2×2, etc., we can rewrite this sequence in the following manner:

$$1, 4, 9, 16, 25, 36, \ldots$$

Since this sequence was formed by *squaring* each of the counting numbers, it is called the sequence of *squared numbers*.

If we hold the exponent constant at 3, then we get the following sequence of *cubed numbers*.

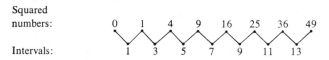

In a similar manner we can form the sequence of numbers to the fourth power, fifth power, sixth power, and so on.

If we study the intervals between the members of the sequence of squared numbers, we notice that the sequence of the intervals is the same as the sequence of odd numbers.

Squared numbers:

$$0 \quad 1 \quad 4 \quad 9 \quad 16 \quad 25 \quad 36 \quad 49$$

Intervals:

$$1 \quad 3 \quad 5 \quad 7 \quad 9 \quad 11 \quad 13$$

Thus, like the arithmetic and geometric progressions, the sequence of squared numbers also increases with regularity. There are also regular patterns according to which the other sequences of numbers raised to a power increase.

An illustration of a progression

The sequences which we have discussed above serve to explain many phenomena that we may observe in the world around us.

Geneology

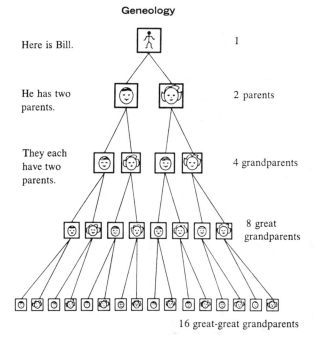

Here is Bill.   1

He has two parents.   2 parents

They each have two parents.   4 grandparents

                                                  8 great grandparents

                                       16 great-great grandparents

How many great-great-great-great-great-great-great-great-great grandparents did Bill have?

•••• P1, P2

Children are to fill in the missing numerals in each grid. The shaded block tells how many unit squares are in each grid. The last numeral in the first row tells us the name of each square. Thus, the first square is a "5 square"; it has 5 rows of 5 unit squares; it contains 25 unit squares.

Lab sheet P2 is similar to P1, but the child must find the total number of units in each square separately, or by rows or columns. The number of units in each grid is to be written in the box below it.

The diamonds contain the same number of dots as the squares above them. It is hoped that some children will notice this without having to count them separately. The children may call the diamonds something like "squooshed squares."

1, 4, 9, 16, 25, 36 are the square numbers produced.

•••• P3, P4

Square centimeters and square inches are introduced. White Cuisenaire® rods have 1 square centimeter faces and can be used to cover squares.

•••• P5, P6

It is assumed that children have built squares with their rods prior to this activity.

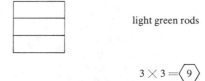

light green rods

$$3 \times 3 = \langle 9 \rangle$$

The same models are used on P5 and P6. The areas of the squares are given on P6. Children should be told that 3^2 is read as "three squared."

Question: How many rods of what length do you need to cover the square?

Answer:

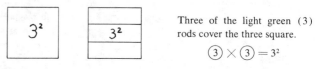

Three of the light green (3) rods cover the three square.

$$(3) \times (3) = 3^2$$

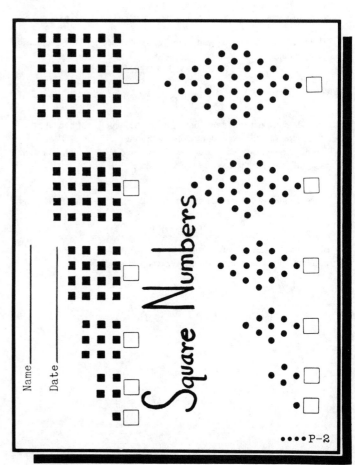

Name _____ Date _____

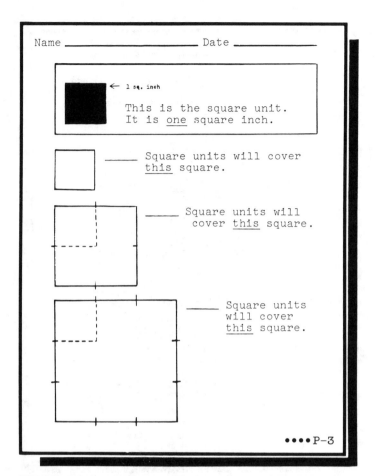

1 sq. inch

This is the square unit.
It is <u>one</u> square inch.

_____ Square units will cover <u>this</u> square.

_____ Square units will cover <u>this</u> square.

_____ Square units will cover <u>this</u> square.

••••P-3

Name _____ Date _____

1 sq. centimeter

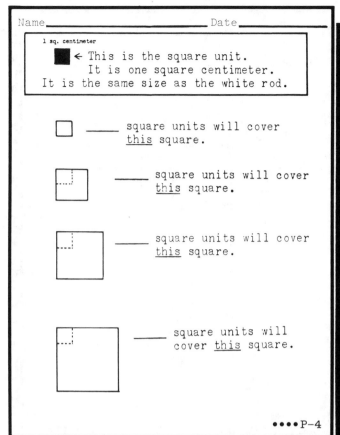

← This is the square unit.
It is one square centimeter.
It is the same size as the white rod.

_____ square units will cover <u>this</u> square.

_____ square units will cover <u>this</u> square.

_____ square units will cover <u>this</u> square.

_____ square units will cover <u>this</u> square.

••••P-4

Name _____ Date _____

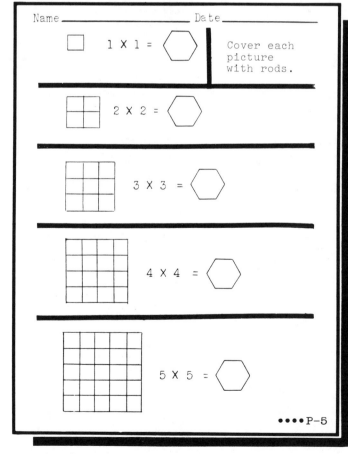

□ $1 \times 1 =$ ⬡

Cover each picture with rods.

$2 \times 2 =$ ⬡

$3 \times 3 =$ ⬡

$4 \times 4 =$ ⬡

$5 \times 5 =$ ⬡

••••P-5

Name _____ Date _____

COVER WITH RODS

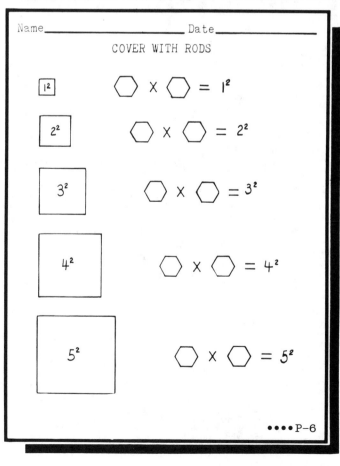

1^2 ⬡ $\times$ ⬡ $= 1^2$

2^2 ⬡ $\times$ ⬡ $= 2^2$

3^2 ⬡ $\times$ ⬡ $= 3^2$

4^2 ⬡ $\times$ ⬡ $= 4^2$

5^2 ⬡ $\times$ ⬡ $= 5^2$

••••P-6

249

Name_____ Date_____

$1^2 = 1 \times 1 =$ ☐

$2^2 = 2 \times 2 =$ ☐

$3^2 = 3 \times 3 =$ ☐

$4^2 = 4 \times 4 =$ ☐

$5^2 = 5 \times 5 =$ ☐

$6^2 = 6 \times 6 =$ ☐

$7^2 = 7 \times 7 =$ ☐

$8^2 = 8 \times 8 =$ ☐

$9^2 = 9 \times 9 =$ ☐

$10^2 = 10 \times 10 =$ ☐

Use
Rods
When
You
Need
Help

•••• P–7

Name_____ Date_____

Find the missing square numbers.
Shade them into the chart.

$1^2 =$ ☐

$2^2 =$ ☐ $5^2 =$ ☐ $8^2 =$ ☐

$3^2 =$ ☐ $6^2 =$ ☐ $9^2 =$ ☐

$4^2 =$ 16 $7^2 =$ 49 $10^2 =$ 100

1	2	3	4	5	6	7	8	9	10
11	12	13	14	15	16	17	18	19	20
21	22	23	24	25	26	27	28	29	30
31	32	33	34	35	36	37	38	39	40
41	42	43	44	45	46	47	48	49	50
51	52	53	54	55	56	57	58	59	60
61	62	63	64	65	66	67	68	69	70
71	72	73	74	75	76	77	78	79	80
81	82	83	84	85	86	87	88	89	90
91	92	93	94	95	96	97	98	99	100

•••• P–8

•••• **P7**

This sheet should not be used until children have built many squares and have experimented with various methods of arriving at the needed product.

Many children get the answers 1^2, 2^2, 3^2, 4^2, 5^2, 10^2 without making models but need models for 6^2, 7^2, 8^2, 9^2.

Here is an example of an ingenious method used by some children.

"9×9? Oh, I can get that from 10×10!" [Child builds 10^2.]
"$10 \times 10 = 100$." [He places a 9^2 on top of 10^2, and then removes extra ten.]
"Now it is 90. Nine 1's are still sticking out. So that is 90, 89, 88, 87, 86, 85, 84, 83, 82, *81*!"

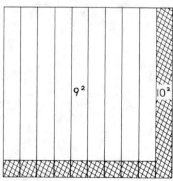

(See annotations for lab sheet P16 for the generalization this child discovered.)

Most children, however, build a certain square and then make a train of the rods to measure the total length, using the orange rods and a smaller rod.

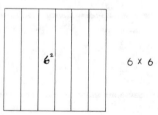

or:

$6 \times 6 = 3 \times 10 + 6 = 36$

Name_____ Date_____

Draw a line connecting names
for the same number.

1^2	4
2^2	25
3^2	36
4^2	81
5^2	9
6^2	100
7^2	64
8^2	49
9^2	1
10^2	16

••••P–9

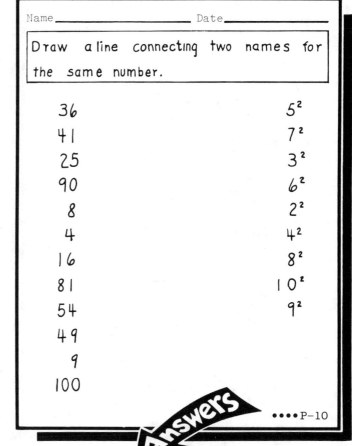

Name_____ Date_____

Draw a line connecting two names for
the same number.

36	5^2
41	7^2
25	3^2
90	6^2
8	2^2
4	4^2
16	8^2
81	10^2
54	9^2
49	
9	
100	

••••P–10

•••• P9, P10
More abstract practice on "square notation"

Children learn to think of $\boxed{}^{2}$ as simply $\boxed{} \times \boxed{}$. They learn to match two different names for the same number.

When children seem confused, they often need no more help than to be asked to say out loud, "four squared" (4^2). They can then find the other name for themselves. Children may check their answers by rod models.

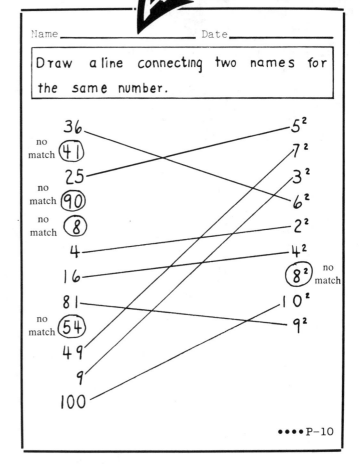

Name_____ Date_____

Draw a line connecting two names for
the same number.

••••P–10

251

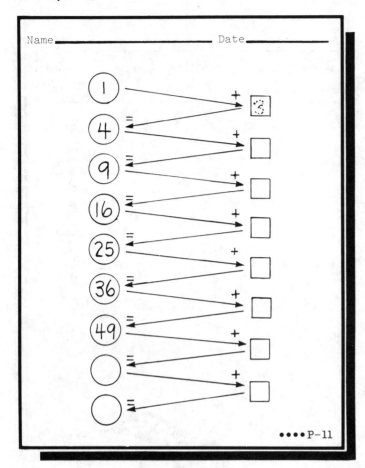

••••P-11

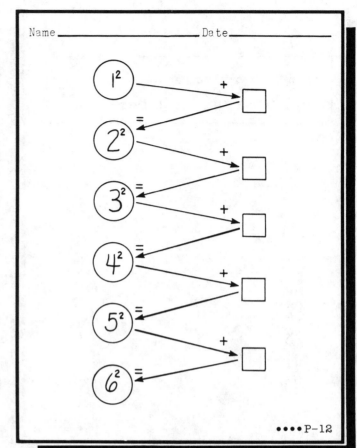

••••P-12

••••P11, P12

Here are arithmetical and geometrical demonstrations of the mathematical fact that the sequence of square numbers is the same as the sequence of the partial sums of the consecutive odd counting numbers.

P11

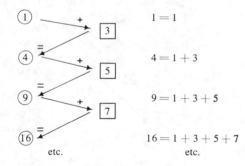

etc.

$1 = 1$

$4 = 1 + 3$

$9 = 1 + 3 + 5$

$16 = 1 + 3 + 5 + 7$

etc.

Name _____ Date _____

$4 = 2 \times \square$

$5 \times \square = 25$

$\square \times 3 = 9$

$1 \times \square = 1$

$10 \times 10 = \square$

$6 \times \square = 36$

$5^2 = \square \times \square$

$9^2 = \bigcirc \times \bigcirc$

$36{,}921^2 = \square \times \square$

$999^2 = \square \times \square$

•••• P–13

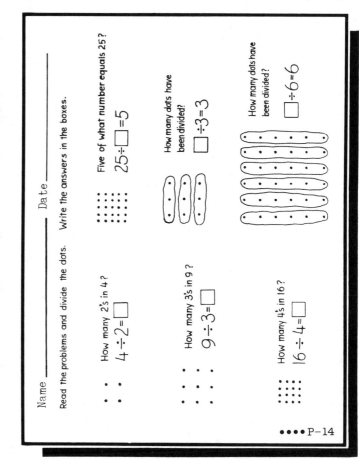

•••• P–14

• • • • P14, P15

Here are problems dealing with the inverse operation of squaring. A square number divided by its square root is equal to the square root.

Name _____ Date _____

$4 \div 2 = \square$ $64 \div 8 = \square$

$9 \div 3 = \square$ $81 \div 9 = \square$

$16 \div 4 = \square$ $100 \div 10 = \square$

$25 \div 5 = \square$

$36 \div 6 = \square$ $\square \div 3 = 3$

$49 \div 7 = \square$ $\square \div 4 = 4$

$\square \div 5 = 5$

•••• P–15

Name _____   Date_____

$$1 \times 1 \quad = \quad 0 \times 0 \; + \; \square$$
$$2 \times 2 \quad = \quad 1 \times 1 \; + \; \square$$
$$3 \times 3 \quad = \quad 2 \times 2 \; + \; \square$$
$$4 \times 4 \quad = \quad 3 \times 3 \; + \; \square$$
$$5 \times 5 \quad = \quad 4 \times 4 \; + \; \square$$
$$6 \times 6 \quad = \quad 5 \times 5 \; + \; \square$$
$$7 \times 7 \quad = \quad 6 \times 6 \; + \; \square$$
$$8 \times 8 \quad = \quad 7 \times 7 \; + \; \square$$
$$9 \times 9 \quad = \quad 8 \times 8 \; + \; \square$$
$$10 \times 10 \quad = \quad 9 \times 9 \; + \; \square$$

$$2^2 - 1^2 = 2 + \square$$
$$3^2 - 2^2 = 3 + \square$$
$$4^2 - 3^2 = 4 + \square$$
$$5^2 - 4^2 = \bigcirc + \square$$
$$6^2 - 5^2 = \bigcirc + \square$$

•••• P–16

•••• **P16**

Children might build pyramids consisting of layers of rod squares beginning with the largest and ending with a 1.

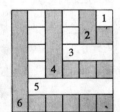

$$2^2 = 1^2 + (2 + 1)$$
$$3^2 = 2^2 + (3 + 2)$$
$$4^2 = 3^2 + (4 + 3)$$
$$\text{etc.}$$

$$6 \times 6 = (5 \times 5) + (5 + 6)$$
$$6 \times 6 = \quad 25 \quad + \quad 11 \quad = 36$$

When children finally discover the generalization that

$$(\square + 1)^2 = \square^2 + 2\square + 1$$

they have a powerful tool for figuring out new square numbers. Thus they can use their earlier knowledge that $5 \times 5 = 25$ to get the product of 6×6.

P16

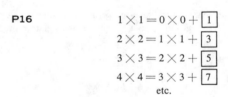

$$1 \times 1 = 0 \times 0 + \boxed{1}$$
$$2 \times 2 = 1 \times 1 + \boxed{3}$$
$$3 \times 3 = 2 \times 2 + \boxed{5}$$
$$4 \times 4 = 3 \times 3 + \boxed{7}$$
$$\text{etc.}$$

The difference between two adjacent squares is the sum of their square roots.

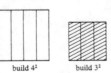

$$2^2 - 1^2 = 2 + \boxed{1}$$
$$3^2 - 2^2 = 3 + \boxed{2}$$
$$4^2 - 3^2 = 4 + \boxed{3}$$

Rod models

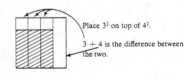

build 4^2 build 3^2 Place 3^2 on top of 4^2.

$3 + 4$ is the difference between the two.

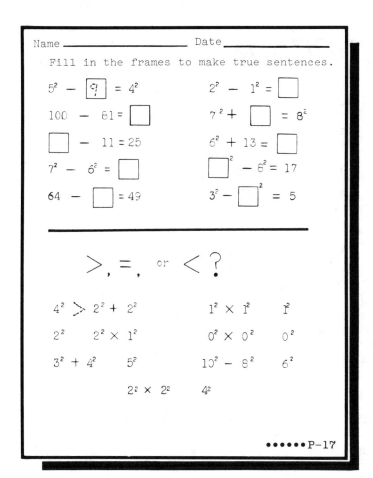

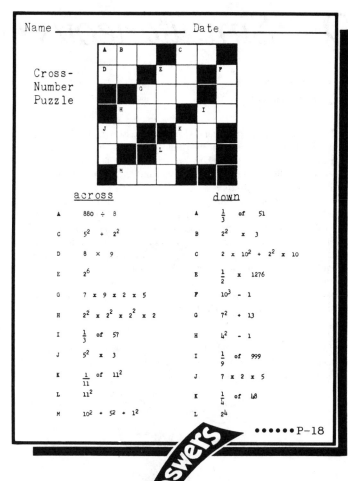

•••••• **P17**

Part of this lab sheet is similar to P16 in Level 4.

$$\square^2 = (\square - 1) \times (\square + 1) + 1$$
or
$$(\square - 1) \times (\square + 1) = \square^2 - 1$$

Knowing square numbers well should help children to figure out other multiplication facts.

From 5×5, we then can get 4×6 by using the following method:

$$(5-1) \times (5+1) = 5^2 - 1$$
$$4 \quad \times \quad 6 \quad = 25 - 1$$
or
$$6 \times 8 = \square$$
$$6 \times 8 = 7^2 - 1 = 48$$

Answers

On the lower half of the sheet, the correct signs are as follows:

$$4^2 > 2^2 + 2^2$$
$$2^2 = 2^2 \times 1^2$$
$$3^2 + 4^2 = 5^2$$
$$1^2 \times 1^2 = 1^2$$
$$0^2 \times 0^2 = 0^2$$
$$10^2 - 8^2 = 6^2$$
$$2^2 \times 2^2 = 4^2$$

•••••• P-18

Q Simultaneous equations

Weight problems

The weight problems that appear on lab sheets Q1 and Q2 provide an excellent opportunity for the child to test his ingenuity. Since these weight problems, with the exception of the first, are actually sets of two linear equations in two unknowns, they may be solved simultaneously by *substitution*.

Thus, in the second problem, since we know that one large cube has the same weight as six marbles, we can replace the large cube on the second balance by six marbles. Now, in order to isolate the small cube on the left side of the balance, we take six marbles from each side of the balance. This can be done without upsetting the equilibrium of the balance, because we are subtracting equal weights from each side. Only the small cube remains on the left side of the balance. On the right side are two remaining marbles. Thus, the small cube is equal in weight to two marbles.

Q1

1   How much does the big cube weigh? To find out, remove the marbles from the pan where the cube is and then take the same number of marbles from the other pan. The big cube weighs $\boxed{3}$ marbles.

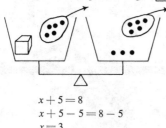

$$x + 5 = 8$$
$$x + 5 - 5 = 8 - 5$$
$$x = 3$$

2   How much does the little cube weigh? The first balance shows that the big cube weighs 6 marbles. Take the big cube out of the one pan in the second balance, and 6 marbles out of the other pan. The little cube weighs $\boxed{2}$ marbles.

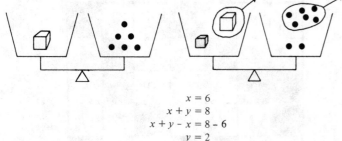

$$x = 6$$
$$x + y = 8$$
$$x + y - x = 8 - 6$$
$$y = 2$$

3   One orange weighs $\boxed{12}$ marbles. ($\frac{1}{2}$ orange weighs 6 marbles.)

Q2

Solutions

4   One ball weighs $\boxed{4}$ marbles.

5   One ball weighs $\boxed{6}$ marbles.

6   The jar *full of water* weighs $\boxed{15}$ marbles.

Solutions

One cube weighs $\boxed{3}$ marbles.

The water in the jar half full weighs $\boxed{3}$ marbles.

A half full jar weighs $\boxed{7}$ marbles.

One black cube weighs $\boxed{8}$ marbles.

The ball weighs $\boxed{4}$ marbles.

Q4

Solutions

1

	1	3	4
	□	□□□	□□□
	A	B	C

$$\begin{cases} A + B + C = ⑧ \\ A \times B \times C = \triangle{12} \end{cases}$$

2

	4	6	2
	D	E	F

$$\begin{cases} D + E + F = ⑫ \\ D \times E \times F = \triangle{48} \end{cases}$$

3

	9	2	2
	G	H	I

$$\begin{cases} G + H + I = ⑬ \\ G \times H \times I = \triangle{36} \end{cases}$$

4

	□	△	○
	K	L	M

$$\begin{cases} K + L + M = 9 \\ K \times L \times M = 24 \end{cases}$$

Any of these six solutions are correct:

K = 2	K = 2	K = 3
L = 4	L = 3	L = 2
M = 3	M = 4	M = 4

K = 3	K = 4	K = 4
L = 4	L = 3	L = 2
M = 2	M = 2	M = 3

5

$$□ + △ + ○ = 6$$
$$□ \times △ \times ○ = 6$$

Solution set for □, △, ○:   {2, 3, 1}   in any order.

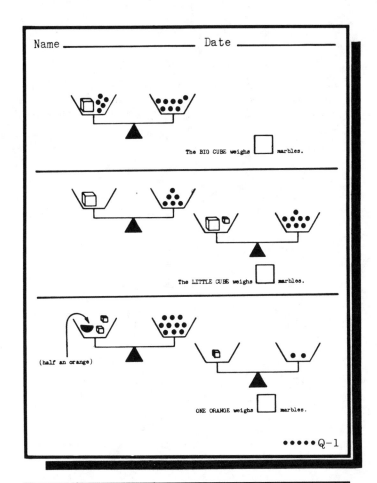

Name _____ Date _____

The BIG CUBE weighs ☐ marbles.

The LITTLE CUBE weighs ☐ marbles.

(half an orange)

ONE ORANGE weighs ☐ marbles.

•••••Q-1

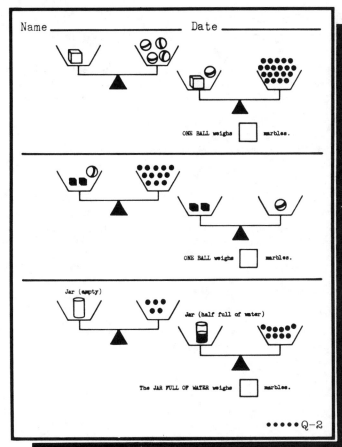

Name _____ Date _____

ONE BALL weighs ☐ marbles.

ONE BALL weighs ☐ marbles.

Jar (empty)   Jar (half full of water)

The JAR FULL OF WATER weighs ☐ marbles.

•••••Q-2

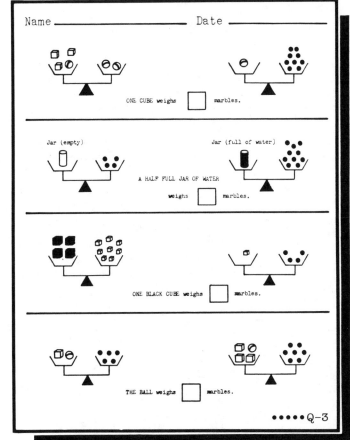

Name _____ Date _____

ONE CUBE weighs ☐ marbles.

Jar (empty)   Jar (full of water)

A HALF FULL JAR OF WATER

weighs ☐ marbles.

ONE BLACK CUBE weighs ☐ marbles.

THE BALL weighs ☐ marbles.

•••••Q-3

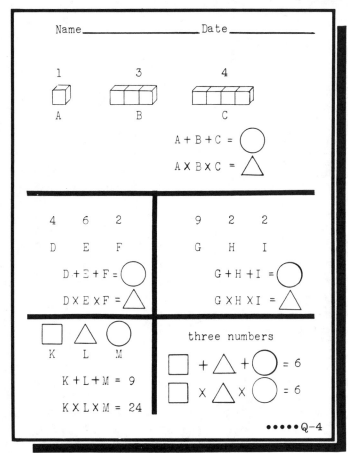

Name _____ Date _____

1	3	4
A	B	C

$$A + B + C = \bigcirc$$

$$A \times B \times C = \triangle$$

4	6	2		9	2	2
D	E	F		G	H	I

$$D + E + F = \bigcirc$$

$$D \times E \times F = \triangle$$

$$G + H + I = \bigcirc$$

$$G \times H \times I = \triangle$$

☐ △ ○

K   L   M

$$K + L + M = 9$$

$$K \times L \times M = 24$$

three numbers

$$\square + \triangle + \bigcirc = 6$$

$$\square \times \triangle \times \bigcirc = 6$$

•••••Q-4

·····Q5, Q6
Preliminary activity

Use a *real* cup (or hat or box) to hide the rods. Let the children guess what rods are under the cup. Build up the game slowly.

Teacher: I have hidden some rods under the cup. When I put the rods end to end they are as long as *ten* white rods. [Or, "Their sum is 10."] What are the rods?

Children will make many guesses:

$$4 + 6$$
$$2 + 2 + 3 + 3$$
$$9 + 1$$
$$3 + 5 + 2$$

The teacher records the list on the chalkboard. The list gets longer and longer—unless, by accident, one of the first combinations is the right one. The teacher volunteers a second clue, letting children pick the question.

Children: How many rods are there?

Teacher: There are three rods.

The children cross from the list all the combinations with more or less than three rods. The following list is left on the chalkboard:

1, 8, 1	3, 6, 1	4, 5, 1
2, 7, 1	2, 6, 2	3, 5, 2
4, 4, 2	3, 4, 3	

Only guessing will determine which combination it is, but the teacher can provide another clue. She tells the children that if the numbers are multiplied, the result is the number 20. The children pick 4, 5, 1 from the list.

$$4 \times 5 \times 1 = 20$$
$$4 + 5 + 1 = 10$$

The teacher lifts the cup. Great joy! Under the cup are a purple (4) rod, a yellow (5) rod, and a white (1) rod.

To make sure that there are no other possible answers (using whole numbers), each of the other number triplets with the sum 10 is multiplied. It can be seen that $\boxed{4 \times 5 \times 1}$ is the only one that fits.

$$1 \times 8 \times 1 = 8$$
$$2 \times 7 \times 1 = 14$$
$$3 \times 6 \times 1 = 18$$
$$2 \times 6 \times 2 = 24$$
$$\boxed{4 \times 5 \times 1 = 20}$$
$$3 \times 5 \times 2 = 30$$
$$4 \times 4 \times 2 = 32$$
$$3 \times 4 \times 3 = 36$$

The game is played a second time. This time, the children insist on more than one clue. *They* ask for the number of rods. *They* ask for the number that results when the numbers, as represented by rods, are multiplied. (The teacher tells them that this number is called the *product*.)

$$\text{sum} = 11$$
$$\text{number of rods} = 2$$
$$\text{product} = 18$$

The teacher writes on the chalkboard:

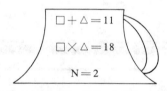

Children may use rods to find the answer.

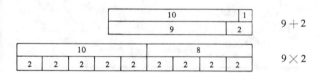

After some more examples, many of which the children furnish, they are ready to do the "cup problems" on lab sheets Q5 and Q6.

WHAT RODS ARE UNDER THE CUP?

Number of rods = 3

$\bigcirc + \square + \triangle = 12$

$\bigcirc \times \square \times \triangle = 54$

Number of rods = 3

$6 + \boxed{3} + \boxed{3} = 12$

$6 \times \boxed{3} \times \boxed{3} = 54$

N = 3

$\square + \bigcirc + \triangle = 11$

$\square \times \bigcirc \times \triangle = 40$

Check your answer with your rods.

N = 3

$\square + \hexagon + \bigcirc = 6$

$\square \times \hexagon \times \bigcirc = 6$

Check your answer with your rods.

••••• Q–5

WHAT RODS ARE UNDER THE CUP?

N = 3

$\square + \bigcirc + \triangle = 6$

$\square \times \bigcirc \times \triangle = 8$

N = 2

$\square + \bigcirc = 2$

$\square \times \bigcirc = 1$

N = 3

$\square + \bigcirc + \hexagon = 3$

$\square \times \bigcirc \times \hexagon = 1$

N = 2

$\hexagon + \bigcirc = 12$

$\hexagon \times \bigcirc = 32$

••••• Q–6

Note: This is only *one* of many hidden-number problems. Here are some other types.

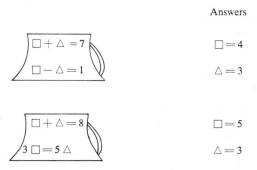

Answers

$\square + \triangle = 7$
$\square - \triangle = 1$

$\square = 4$
$\triangle = 3$

$\square + \triangle = 8$
$3\square = 5\triangle$

$\square = 5$
$\triangle = 3$

$\square - \triangle = 3$
$\square = 2\triangle$

$\square = 6$
$\triangle = 3$

All of these are examples of *simultaneous equations*. Sometimes it is important to sneak in a problem that *does not have a solution*.

$\square + \triangle = 4$
$\square \times \triangle = 50$

no solution

259

Name _____ Date _____

BLOCKS AND CUPS: I have 15 blocks and a large stack of cups. There are many ways in which I can arrange my 15 blocks in the cups. I could put 3 blocks in each of 5 cups like this:

Fill in the ◯'s and ☐'s below to show some of the other ways I can arrange my 15 blocks.

****

3 cups; ☐ blocks in each cup

◯ cups; 15 blocks in each cup

◯ cups; ☐ blocks in each cup

◯ cups; ☐ blocks in each cup

2 cups; 10 blocks in one cup
         ☐ blocks in the other cup

2 cups;   5 blocks in one cup
         (15 − ☐) blocks in the other cup

NOW GO ON TO THE BACK.

•••••Q-7

Name _____ Date _____

ATTENTION! Do the other side of this sheet before you start on this side. THANK YOU!
****
REMEMBER, we have <u>exactly</u> 15 blocks to put into the cups.
****
2 cups; 7 blocks in one cup
         (4 × ☐) blocks in the other cup

3 cups; 3 blocks in one cup
         (3 + ☐) blocks in another cup
         (3 + ☐ + ☐) blocks in another cup

5 cups; ☐ blocks in one cup
         (☐ + 1) blocks in another cup
         (☐ + 2) blocks in another cup
         (☐ + 3) blocks in another cup
         (☐ + 4) blocks in another cup

5 cups; (☐ − 3) blocks in one cup
         (☐ − 2) blocks in another cup
         (☐ − 1) blocks in another cup
         ☐ blocks in another cup
         (☐ + 1) blocks in another cup

•••••Q-8

•••••**Q7, Q8**

Blocks and cups Preliminary activity

Equipment: One egg carton for each child and counters—a pre-determined number of rods for each child.

This is a group game. As an example, each child has 10 rods and an egg carton with 12 compartments.

1 10 things. Use 5 compartments with ☐ blocks in each. What is the ☐ number? [☐ = 2]

2 10 things. Use 3 compartments: 2 compartments with ☐ blocks, 1 compartment with ☐ + 1 blocks. What is the ☐ number?

3 10 things. Use 3 compartments: 2 compartments with ☐ blocks, 1 compartment with ☐ − 2 blocks. What is the ☐ number?

4 10 things. Use 4 compartments: 1 compartment with ☐ blocks, 1 compartment with ☐ + 1 blocks, 1 compartment with ☐ + 2 blocks, 1 compartment with ☐ + 3 blocks. What is the ☐ number?

See lab sheets F43 and F44 for more cup and block problems.

Solutions to Q7

15 things: 3 cups   [5] blocks in each cup

             ① cup   15 blocks

             ⑮ cups   [1] block

             2 cups   10 blocks in one

                      [5] blocks in one

             2 cups   5 blocks in one

                      15 − [5] in the other

Name _____ Date _____

ATTENTION! Do the other side of this sheet before you start on this side. THANK YOU!
****
REMEMBER, we have <u>exactly</u> 15 blocks to put into the cups.
****
2 cups; 7 blocks in one cup
         (4 × [2]) blocks in the other cup

3 cups; 3 blocks in one cup
         (3 + [2]) blocks in another cup
         (3 + [2] + [2]) blocks in another cup

5 cups; [1] blocks in one cup
         ([1] + 1) blocks in another cup
         ([1] + 2) blocks in another cup
         ([1] + 3) blocks in another cup
         ([1] + 4) blocks in another cup

5 cups; ([4] − 3) blocks in one cup
         ([4] − 2) blocks in another cup
         ([4] − 1) blocks in another cup
         [4] blocks in another cup
         ([4] + 1) blocks in another cup

•••••Q-8

R   Graphing equations

Mathematical introduction

We already know that we can take many kinds of trips from $\square = -7$ to $\square = 8$ (and back) on the slice of number line pictured below. Here are some sample trips:

$$3 + 4 = 7$$
$$6 \div 3 = 2$$
$$8 - 10 = -2$$
$$4 \times 2 = 8$$

These trips let us travel to the left ($-$) or to the right ($+$) on this number line.

We can now find answers to certain open sentences.

1   Group A open sentences

$$\square = 4 + 3$$
$$6 - \triangle = 1$$
$$\bigcirc = 27$$

The solution for the first open sentence is the number 7, since $\boxed{7} = 4 + 3$ is a true sentence. The solutions for the second and third open sentences are 5 and 27, since $6 - \triangle\!\!\!\!5 = 1$ and $\bigcirc\!\!\!27 = 27$ are true.

These solutions can be represented graphically as points on *one* number line as shown below.

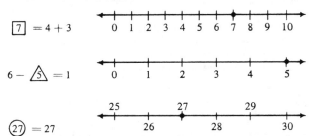

Only *one* number will make each sentence true; only *one* point represents that number.

There are other types of open sentences. Look at the open sentences in Group B. What numbers will make these open sentences true?

2   Group B open sentences

$$\square + \triangle = 4$$
$$\square - 1 = \triangle$$
$$10 - \square = \triangle + 2$$

The first example can be made true by writing '1' in the $\square$ and '3' in the $\triangle$, since $\boxed{1} + \triangle\!\!\!\!3 = 4$ is true. But the first example can also be made true in other ways. Another solution is (0, 4), since $\boxed{0} + \triangle\!\!\!\!4 = 4$ is true. Still other solutions are:

(4, 0)   since $\boxed{4} + \triangle\!\!\!\!0 = 4$

(2, 2)   since $\boxed{2} + \triangle\!\!\!\!2 = 4$

(3, 1)   since $\boxed{3} + \triangle\!\!\!\!1 = 4$

(−1, 5)   since $\boxed{-1} + \triangle\!\!\!\!5 = 4$

($\frac{1}{2}$, $3\frac{1}{2}$)   since $\boxed{\frac{1}{2}} + \triangle\!\!\!\!3\frac{1}{2} = 4$, etc.

Notice that the first number in the pairs is always the one that goes in the $\square$ and the second number is the one that goes in the $\triangle$.

It is impossible to graph the solutions to this example on one number line as we did with the Group A sentences, because here the solutions are two numbers in a certain order (ordered pairs of numbers) rather than single numbers. Also many different ordered pairs solve the same open sentence here, whereas only one number solved the open sentences of Group A.

We must therefore extend the number-line idea to allow us to represent ordered pairs of numbers.

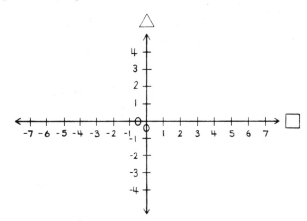

If we have two number lines perpendicular to one another and intersecting, we can move left or right (on the $\square$ number line), up or down (on the $\triangle$ number line) *and* simultaneously right and up, right and down, left and up, left and down in the directions of both number lines.

These combination moves can get us to any location on the plane. No longer need we stay on either $\square$ number line or $\triangle$ number line. Such a pair of perpendicular number lines are called Cartesian coordinates, and their crossing point is the zero point on each line. The $\square$ numbers are measured along the direction of the horizontal number line; the $\triangle$ numbers are measured along the direction of the vertical number line.

The horizontal direction from (0, 0) is given as the first number, and the vertical direction is given as the second number.

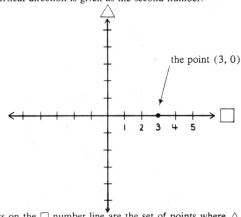

the point (3, 0)

The points on the $\square$ number line are the set of points where $\triangle = 0$ and $\square$ may equal any number.

261

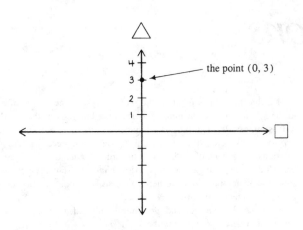

the point (0, 3)

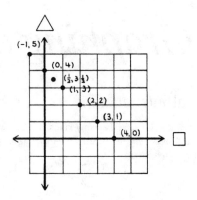

If we continued choosing numbers, we would find that all of these points are in a straight line. Let us draw the line that passes through all of the points.

The points on the △ number line are the set of points where □ = 0 and △ may equal any number.

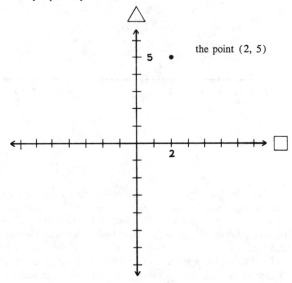

the point (2, 5)

The points which lie on *neither* number line are the set of points where □ = any number except 0 and △ = any number except 0.

Let us now represent the solutions of the Group B open sentences as the points on the plane, by means of the Cartesian coordinates. □ + △ = 4 has the ordered pair (1, 3) as one of its solutions. We represent it as follows:

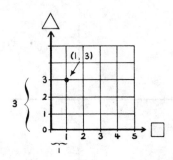

Now let us add to the graph the rest of the solutions of □ + △ = 4 that were previously listed.

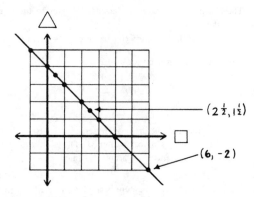

Pick a point anywhere on this line. What ordered pair does the point represent? Put the first number of this ordered pair in the □ and the second number in the △ of the open sentence □ + △ = 4. Does this make the open sentence true? In the diagram above we took the points (2½, 1½) and (6, −2). We can see that these ordered pairs are solutions to the open sentence since

and

$$\boxed{2\tfrac{1}{2}} + \overset{1\tfrac{1}{2}}{\triangle} = 4$$

$$\boxed{6} + \overset{-2}{\triangle} = 4$$

are true. In fact, the ordered pair for *any* point on the line is a solution for □ + △ = 4. Also, the point for *any* ordered pair which solves □ + △ = 4 is on the line.

Following are graphs of the solutions of the other two open sentences in Group B:

□ − 1 = △	
□	△
4	3
3	2
2½	1½
0	−1
etc.	etc.

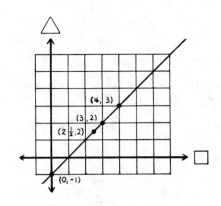

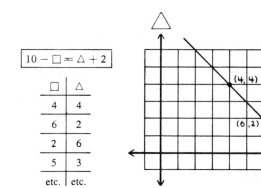

$$\boxed{10 - \square = \triangle + 2}$$

$\square$	$\triangle$
4	4
6	2
2	6
5	3
etc.	etc.

Equations of the type found in Group B are called *linear equations* because, as we just saw when we continued to choose points, these points all lie on a straight line. These sets of solution points divide our plane into various regions. The $\square$ and $\triangle$ number lines are like "fences" which divide the plane into four regions, or *quadrants*.

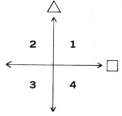

Region 1: $\square =$ any positive number $(\square > 0, \triangle > 0)$
$\triangle =$ any positive number

Region 2: $\square =$ any negative number $(\square < 0, \triangle > 0)$
$\triangle =$ any positive number

Region 3: $\square =$ any negative number $(\square < 0, \triangle < 0)$
$\triangle =$ any negative number

Region 4: $\square =$ any positive number $(\square > 0, \triangle < 0)$
$\triangle =$ any negative number

In the following diagram we have 7 regions, and sets of points on 3 straight lines ("fences") as follows:

Region 1: $\square + \triangle > 4$
$\square =$ a negative number
$\triangle > 4$

Region 2: $\square + \triangle > 4$
$\square =$ a positive number
$\triangle =$ a positive number

Region 3: $\square + \triangle > 4$
$\square =$ a positive number
$\triangle =$ a negative number

Region 4: $\square + \triangle < 4$
$\square =$ a positive number
$\triangle =$ a negative number

Region 5: $\square + \triangle < 4$
$\square =$ a negative number
$\triangle =$ a negative number

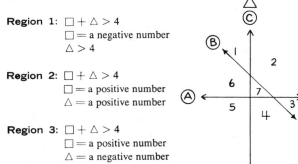

Region 6: $\square + \triangle < 4$
$\square =$ a negative number
$\triangle =$ a positive number

Region 7: $\square + \triangle < 4$
$\square =$ a positive number
$\triangle =$ a positive number

The three straight lines ("fences") are as follows:

A $\begin{cases} \square = \text{any number} \\ \triangle = 0 \end{cases}$

B $\quad \square + \triangle = 4$

C $\begin{cases} \square = 0 \\ \triangle = \text{any number} \end{cases}$

Now we have the tools for identifying
a. a point on a line
b. a point on a plane
c. a line on the plane
d. a region on the plane.

Suggested activities on graphing

There are many games, puzzles, and word problems which a teacher may use orally with her class in order to give children these tools in an interesting way. Most of the following chalkboard activities can be done on geoboards.

The lab sheets in Section R are usable for group or independent written activities *following extensive oral preparation for graphing.* (The sheets do not, however, include any work on identifying regions.)

The dot array

A practical suggestion to a teacher working with graphing: make a semi-permanent dot array with a red felt pen on one part of the chalkboard. (It will not wash off when the board is cleaned, and it can be written over with chalk for other classroom work.) This array, neatly drawn with dots 8 cm. apart, saves a lot of time when the teacher is ready to draw $\square$ and $\triangle$ number lines.

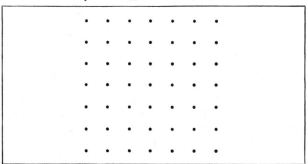

The dot array has the following uses:

1 Graphing

Numerals and axes are drawn with chalk. Points on the plane can now be plotted.

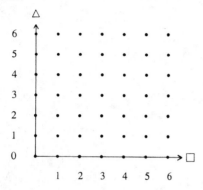

2 Ratios

Shapes are drawn with chalk and labeled. Because the grid is accurate, we can quickly see the ratio between shapes: $B = \frac{1}{8}$ of A, $B = \frac{1}{2}$ of D, $B = \frac{1}{4}$ of C, etc.

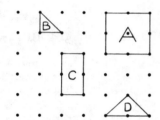

3 Distributive law of multiplication

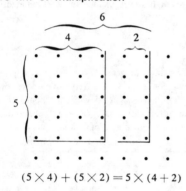

$$(5 \times 4) + (5 \times 2) = 5 \times (4 + 2)$$

Five-in-a-row

Five-in-a-row, a variation on the familiar tic-tac-toe, can be used as an excellent introduction to the Cartesian coordinate system in the primary grades. Five-in-a row is played on a grid of arbitrary size, not less than 6×6. As in tic-tac-toe, there are two players who alternate by marking "circles" and "crosses" on the field; however, in this game marks are made at grid points instead of *in* the squares. Whichever player first manages to place 5 of his marks in a row, vertically, horizontally, or diagonally, wins.

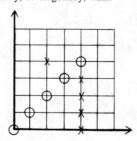

Procedure

Draw a grid on the board. Making the lower-left corner of the grid the origin point (0, 0) of a coordinate system, number the left and bottom edges in the customary way (see below). The children can now be divided into three groups. Group 1 will play against Group 2, and Group 3 will record at the board.

A child in Group 1 names a point in the field by calling out the name of a number pair. A child from Group 3 draws a circle at the named point. Next, a child from Group 2 calls out a point, and a child from Group 3 records a cross on the chalkboard.

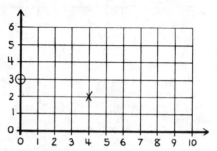

On the grid above, Group 2 has marked a cross at (4, 2) and Group 1 has just marked a circle at (0, 3).

If a team calls for a point already occupied or off the board, it loses its turn.

This arrangement can lead to many variations, of which two follow.

Variation 1

The playing field may be given terrain features, such as a river or a crater. These features are off limits.

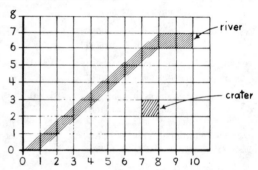

Variation 2

The playing field includes all four quadrands of the plane, not just positive points as in the earlier games.

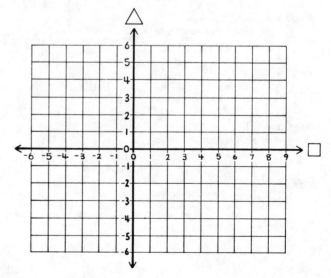

Treasure Hunt

This is a teaching game for locating regions and points on a Cartesian plane. A treasure is hidden at an undisclosed grid point of a given plane. The object of the game is to identify that point in the least number of questions answerable by *yes* or *no*.

Sample play on a sample plane

A Cartesian coordinate system is used to identify all points. The "territory" has 49 points.

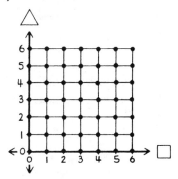

Question 1: Is the treasure any place where □ is less than 3?
Answer 1: No. □ ≮ 3.

The first answer narrows the "territory" to exclude all such points as (0, 0), (0, 5), (2, 3), etc.

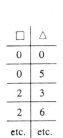
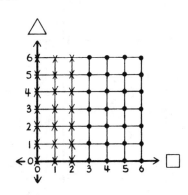

X = points no longer in the game. This leaves 28 points as a spot for the buried treasure.

Question 2: Is the treasure any place where △ is less than 3?
Answer 2: No. △ ≮ 3.

The territory is narrowed further by the second answer. All points such as (3, 2), (3, 0), (4, 1), etc., are ruled out.

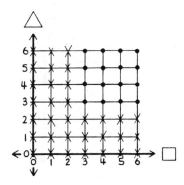

This leaves 16 points where the treasure could be hidden. Treasure is: □ > 2 and △ > 2.

Question 3: Is the treasure any place where either □ or △ equal 3?
Answer 3: No. □ ≠ 3 and △ ≠ 3.

This clue eliminates seven more points, such as (3, 3), (4, 3), (3, 5), etc., and leaves 9 points.

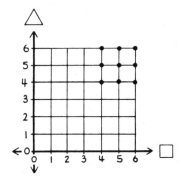

Question 4: Is the treasure where □ is 5 or more than 5 *and* △ is 5 or more than 5?
Answer 4: No. *Either* □ < 5 *or* △ < 5.

This clue eliminates the 4 points (5, 5), (5, 6), (6, 5), (6, 6) where □ and △ both are 5 or more. Five points are left.

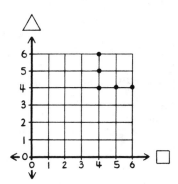

Question 5: Is the treasure where □ equals 4?
Answer 5: Yes. □ = 4.

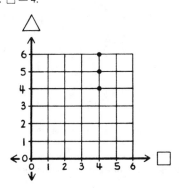

Only 3 points are left: (4, 4), (4, 5), (4, 6).

Question 6: Is the treasure where △ > 4?
Answer 6: Yes. △ > 4.

Territory limits for the game just played

□ and △ numbers are integers.

$$-1 < \square < 7$$
$$-1 < \triangle < 7$$

□ and △ can be any whole numbers between −1 and 7.

After answer 1 the limits are
$$2 < \square < 7$$
$$-1 < \triangle < 7$$

After answer 2 the limits are
$$2 < \square < 7$$
$$2 < \triangle < 7$$

After answer 3 the limits are
$$3 < \square < 7$$
$$3 < \triangle < 7$$

After answer 4 the limits are
When $4 < \square$, then $\triangle = 4$.
When $4 < \triangle$, then $\square = 4$.
When $\square = 4$, then $\triangle = 4$.

After answer 5 the limits are
$$\square = 4$$
$$3 < \triangle < 7$$

After answer 6 the limits are
$$\square = 4$$
$$\triangle > 4$$

Question 7 will determine whether the treasure is at $(4, 5)$ or at $(4, 6)$.

Brief chalkboard puzzles

1   Identifying a line

Here is a secret note. It says: "Follow me and find me. I am waiting for you somewhere on the path $\square = \triangle$." Draw the path.

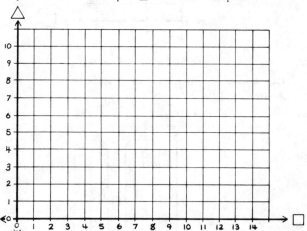

2   Identifying two lines and their intersection

a. Bill walked on the straight-line path from $(-2, 3)$ to $(4, 3)$. He met his friend Ben on the way. Ben was walking on the straight-line path from $(0, 0)$ to $(0, 6)$. Where did Bill and Ben meet? Draw the two paths.

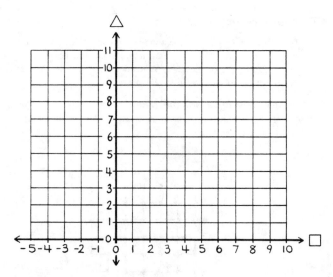

b. Susan biked on the straight-line path $(4, -4)$ to $(-5, 5)$. Sarah biked on the straight-line path $(-4, -3)$ to $(-4, 6)$. The two girls met and had a picnic lunch together. Where did they meet for lunch?

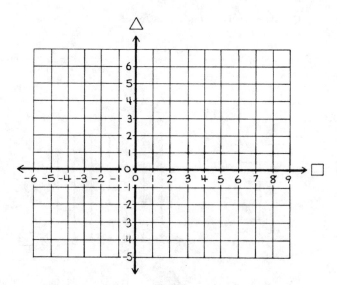

3   Identifying a region on the plane

a. This is a school playground.

A big sign says:

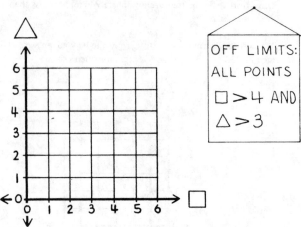

OFF LIMITS: ALL POINTS $\square > 4$ AND $\triangle > 3$

Shade in where the children *can* play.

b. This land is partly swampy and partly dry. The swamp is the part where $\square > 2$ and $\triangle < 3$. Shade in the swamp.

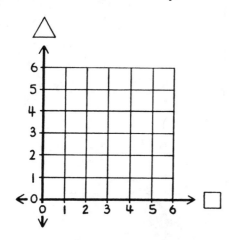

c. A gang fight. Gang A claims all land $\square \geqq 6$. Shade it ▨. Gang B claims all land $\triangle \geqq 6$. Shade it ▨. Will they have an argument? [yes, no]. What territory will they argue about? Territory: [$\square \geqq 6$ *and* $\triangle \geqq 6$] ▨▨▨

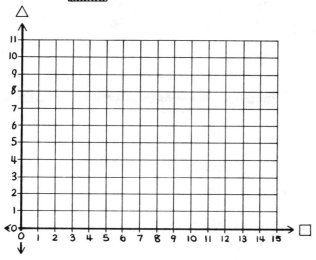

d. Two farmers can't agree on their land. A claims all land ($\square < 6$, $\triangle > 6$). B claims all land ($\square < 6$, $\triangle < 7$). Show with a graph what land they are arguing over.

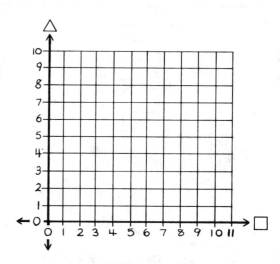

They argue over the double-shaded land: $\square < 6$, $6 < \triangle < 7$. For this land, $\square$ is less than 6 and $\triangle$ is between 6 and 7.

e. A town bought some land for a new school and playground. Draw a map of the land and draw in the part where the new building will be. The land extends from $0 < \square < 10$

$$0 < \triangle < 8$$

The schoolhouse occupies the land from
$$2 < \square < 8$$
$$0 < \triangle < 3$$

f. On this graph color red the shape that has as its borders the following paths:

$\square = \triangle$
$\square = -3$, $\triangle =$ any number
$\square =$ any number, $\triangle = 4$

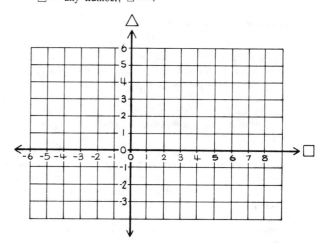

267

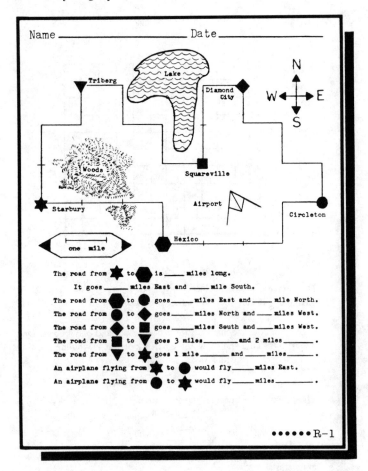

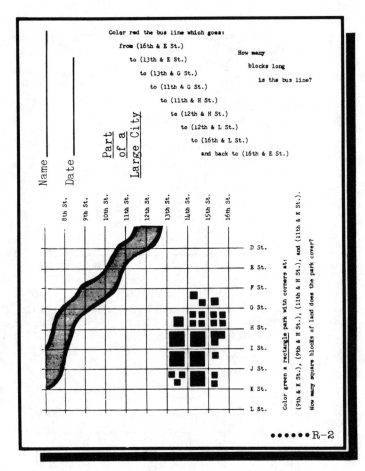

· · · · · · R1

Preliminary activities

1 Let the children study the map on R1 and tell as much about it as they can. It has cities and roads, woods, an airport, and a lake marked off. In the upper right corner it gives the directions for north, east, south and west. The names of the cities and their shapes on the map are related: *Tri*berg (triangle), *Hex*ico (hexagon), etc. The scale *1 in. : 1 mi.* is given and the roads are marked off in miles.

2 If there are children in the class who do not know the north, south, east, west directions, classroom "walking games" should be played before the lab sheet is attempted. Determine the directions in the classroom and label the walls. Where is the sun in the morning? [East.] Where is the sun in the afternoon? [West.]

Give directions such as:

"From your seat walk five steps east, then five steps west."

"Walk two steps south, four steps west."

"To walk from the chalkboard to the door, we can go _____ [number] steps _____ [direction] and _____ [number] steps _____ [direction]."

· · · · · · R2, R3

Play activities

Lab sheets R2 and R3 may be used for play activities before they are used for individual written assignments.

1 Allow the children to look at the diagrams during a "thinking silence" and then ask them to tell what they think they are about.

2 Each child takes a red rod and uses it as a "traveler" on the map on R2. (The rod stands on its square face.)

"Travel on G Street to the river."

"Start on the corner of K Street and 16th Street. Walk on K Street until you get to 13th Street. Now walk on 13th until you get to H Street. Now walk on H Street until you come to the river."

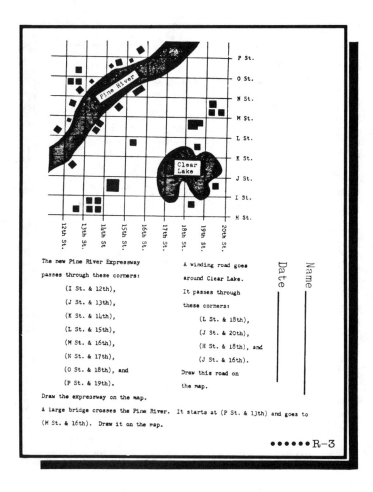

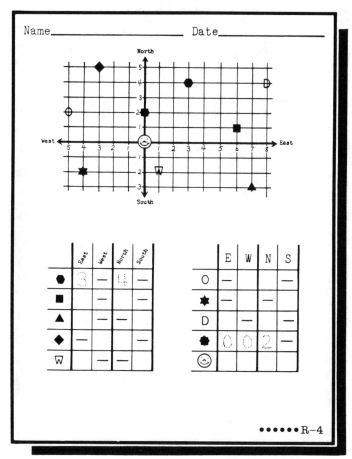

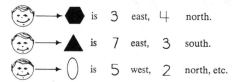

•••••• **R3**

Ask children to tell in words where the largest building is on the map on R3. ["It is between J Street and I Street, and 14th and 15th Streets."] Other directions to give:

Let your "traveler" walk around the biggest building (from J Street and 14th to J Street and 15th to I Street and 15th to I Street and 14th).

Put your traveler on a corner (intersection) where there are no houses in the surrounding blocks. Tell us the name of that intersection.

Put your traveler on a corner (intersection) where there are houses in three surrounding blocks. Tell us the name of that intersection.

•••••• **R4**
East-west north-south

A "rod traveler" can be used to walk from 😊 (the starting place) to each of the intersections marked by designs.

😊 → ⬡ is 3 east, 4 north.

😊 → ▲ is 7 east, 3 south.

😊 → ◯ is 5 west, 2 north, etc.

We fill in the charts beneath the map with the paths traveled (see the two dotted-in samples).

For supplementary work, some children might want to make charts such as:

From ▽ → ▲ is 6 east, 1 south.

◆ → ◯ is 2 west, 3 south, etc.

(We might make the rule that we go east-west first, then north-south.)

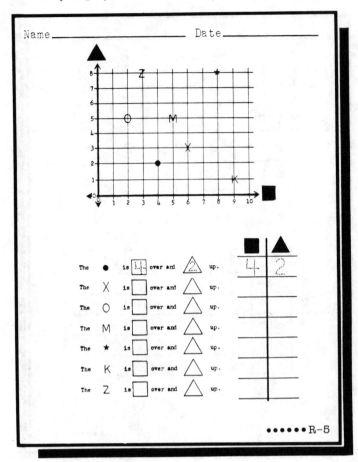

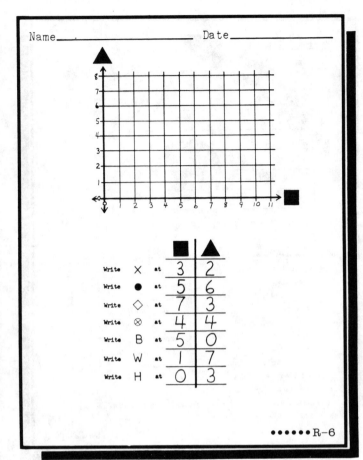

· · · · · · **R5**

□ and △ number lines

Instead of labeling our map with compass points, we now have a map showing two number lines perpendicular to one another and the starting point zero on both lines. One number line (horizontal) is the □ number line; the other (vertical) is the △ number line.

We *always* travel first in the direction of the □ number line, then in the direction of the △ number line. We record our moves on a chart:

	□	△
●	4	2
✗	6	3
○	2	5
M	5	5
★	8	8
K	9	1
Z	3	8

· · · · · · **R6**

This lab sheet is similar to R5. Now the ordered pairs of numbers are given and the child matches them with the corresponding points on the grid. Always start at (0,0).

(3,2) for **X** means 3 right, 2 up.
(5,6) for ● means 5 right, 6 up.
(5,0) for B means 5 right, 0 up.

Thus (5,0) lies *on* the □ number line.

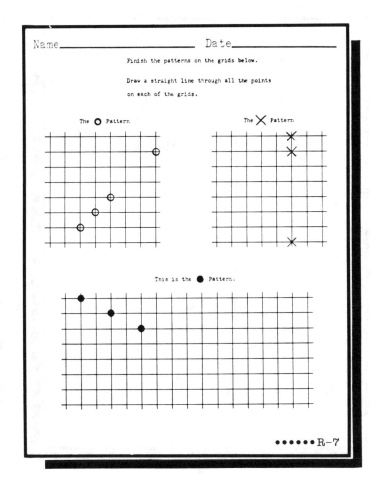

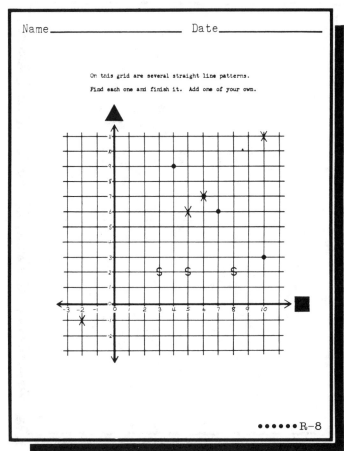

• • • • • • R7

The completed patterns are:

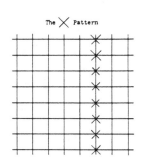

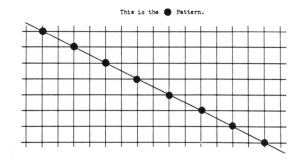

Note: No points are labeled. A variety of slopes for straight line graphs are explored.

• • • • • • R8

The completed patterns for lab sheet R8 are:

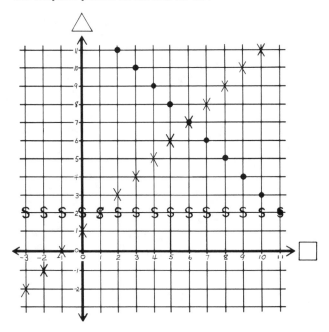

Note: (6,7) is in both the ● and X patterns.
(11,2) is in both the ● and S patterns.
(1,2) is in both the X and S patterns.

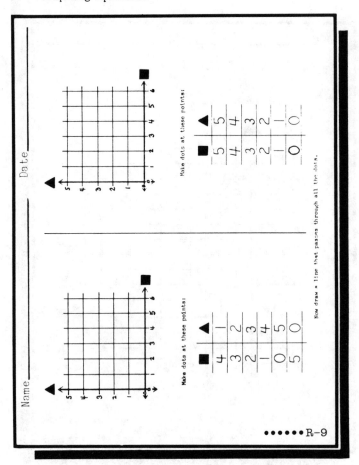

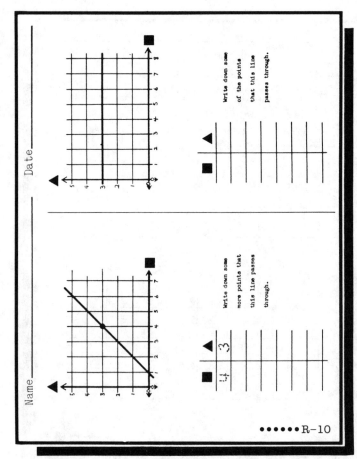

····· **R10**

Most children will fill in the table with whole number pairs.

□	△
4	3
3	2
2	1
1	0
5	4
6	5

□	△
0	3
1	3
2	3
3	3
4	3
5	3
6	3
7	3
8	3

Some ingenious child, however, might include such points as:

□	△
$1\frac{1}{2}$	$\frac{1}{2}$
$3\frac{1}{4}$	$2\frac{1}{4}$

and

□	△
$\frac{3}{4}$	3
$2\frac{1}{3}$	3

Such answers are sound, since the task is to write *any other points* that these lines pass through.

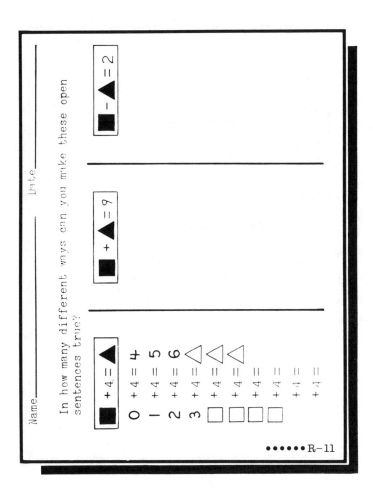

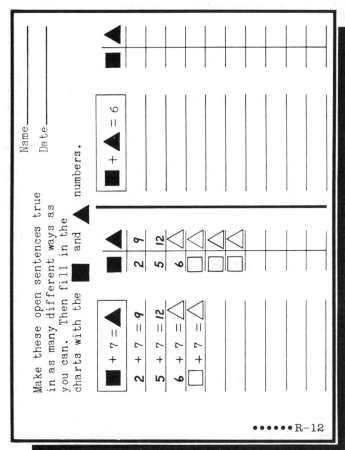

• • • • • • **R11**

For the first problem,

$$\boxed{\Box + 4 = \triangle}$$

$\Box$ may be any number. $\triangle$ is always the $\Box$ number plus four.

For the second problem,

$$\boxed{\Box + \triangle = 9}$$

the answer may be *any* number pair whose sum equals nine; for example:

$0+9$	$5+4$
$1+8$	$6+3$
$2+7$	$7+2$
$3+6$	$8+1$
$4+5$	$9+0$

or, nine as the sum of a negative number and a positive number; for example:

$$10 + {-1} \qquad 11 + {-2} \qquad {-3} + 12$$

or, fraction pairs whose sum is nine; for example:

$$-\tfrac{2}{5} + 9\tfrac{2}{5} \qquad \tfrac{10}{3} + 5\tfrac{2}{3}$$
$$3\tfrac{1}{2} + 5\tfrac{1}{2} \qquad \tfrac{2}{7} + 8\tfrac{5}{7}$$

For the third problem,

$$\boxed{\Box - \triangle = 2}$$

the answer should be any number pair whose *difference* equals two. There are an infinite number of such number pairs.

$$\boxed{12} - \triangle{10} = 2$$
$$\boxed{2} - \triangle{0} = 2$$
$$\boxed{33\tfrac{1}{5}} - \triangle{31\tfrac{1}{5}} = 2$$

etc.

• • • • • • **R12**

Open sentences

This lab sheet is similar to R11. The children are to write their $\Box$ and $\triangle$ number pairs into the charts (see lab sheet).

$\Box + 7 = \triangle$ is called an "open sentence." It is neither true nor false. By replacing $\Box$ and $\triangle$ with certain chosen number pairs, we can make the open sentence into a *true* sentence.

273

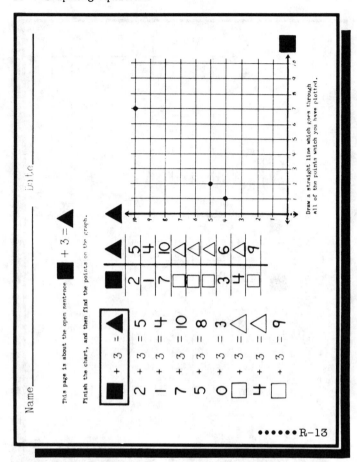

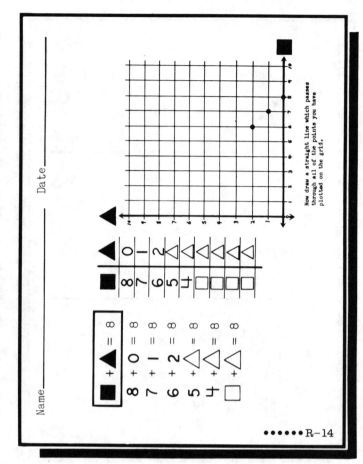

· · · · · · **R13**

1   Make all the open sentences ($\square + 3 = \triangle$) true.

2   Finish the number-pair chart so that it is a list of the pairs ($\square$, $\triangle$) which were used to make the sentences true.

3   Use each pair ($\square$, $\triangle$) in the chart and draw a point for it on the graph. The pairs (1,4), (2,5), (7,10) are given as examples.

· · · · · · **R14**

On R14 we can easily see that the sum of $\square$ and $\triangle$ always equals 8.

$\square$	$\triangle$
8	0
7	1
6	2

274

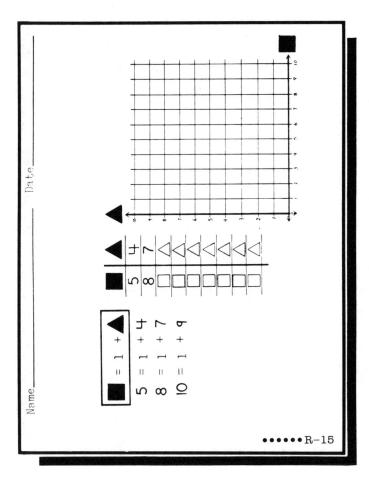

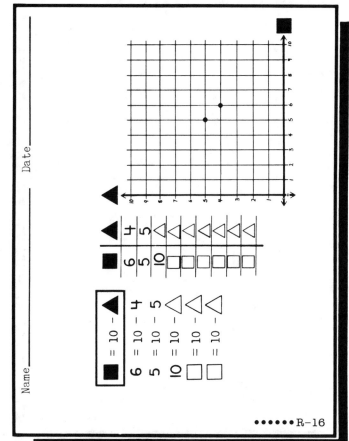

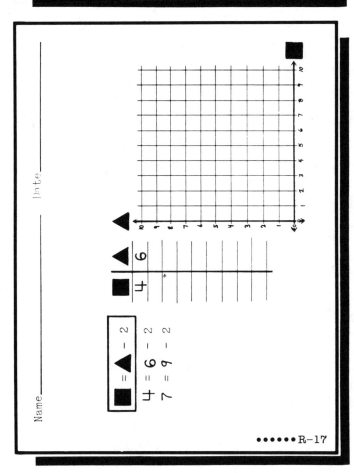

•••••• **R15–R17**

On R15 lab sheet we can see not only that $\square = 1 + \triangle$ but also that
$\triangle = \square - 1$.

$\square$	$\triangle$
5	4
8	7
10	9

On R16 we can see that $\square + \triangle = 10$.

$\square$	$\triangle$
6	4
5	5
10	0

On R17 we can see that $\triangle = \square + 2$ if $\square = \triangle - 2$.

$\square$	$\triangle$
4	6
7	9
3	5

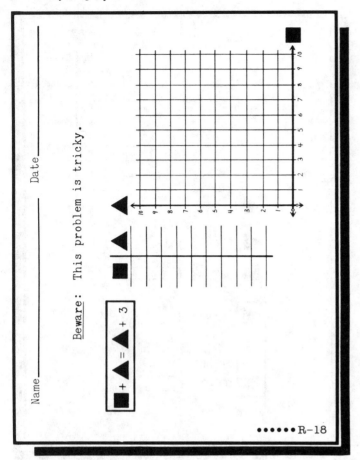

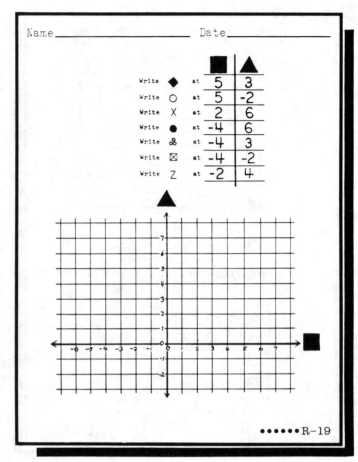

· · · · · · **R18**

Why is this problem tricky?

First hint: Remember our frame rule: *in the same problem like frames are placeholders for the same number.*

Second hint: Is there a simpler way to write the open sentence □ + △ = △ + 3?

· · · · · · **R19, R20**

These two sheets are similar to R5 and R6, except that the grid is extended to include negative values for □ and △.

To the left of 0 are the negative □ values. Down from 0 are the negative △ values.

(4, −2) means 4 units to the right and 2 units down.

(−4, −2) means 4 units to the left and 2 units down.

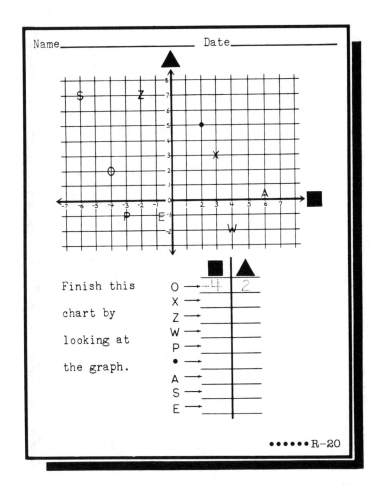

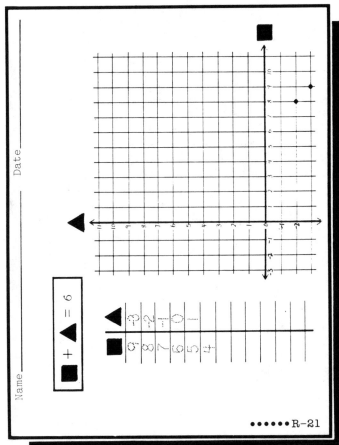

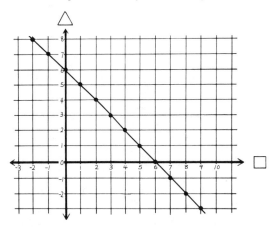

······ R21

Linear equations

What pairs of numbers make this sentence true?

$$\boxed{\square + \triangle = 6}$$

The following are some of the pairs.

$\square$	$\triangle$
9	−3
8	−2
7	−1
6	0
5	1
4	2
3	3
2	4
1	5
0	6
−1	7

etc.

Also:

$4\frac{2}{3}$	$1\frac{1}{3}$
$\frac{3}{5}$	$5\frac{2}{5}$

etc.

Locate some of the points named by the ordered pairs in the list.

All points lie on a straight line. That is why $\square + \triangle = 6$ is called a *linear equation*.

If $\square + \triangle = 6$, then $\square = 6 - \triangle$ and $\triangle = 6 - \square$. Notice the straight line crosses the $\square$ number line at (6,0) and crosses the $\triangle$ number line at (0,6).

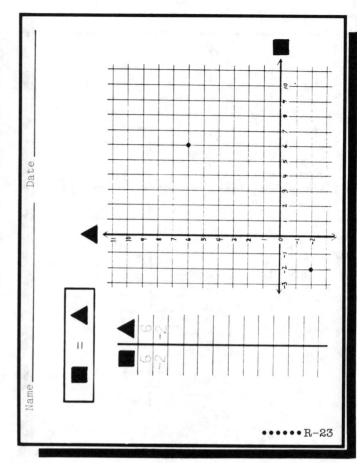

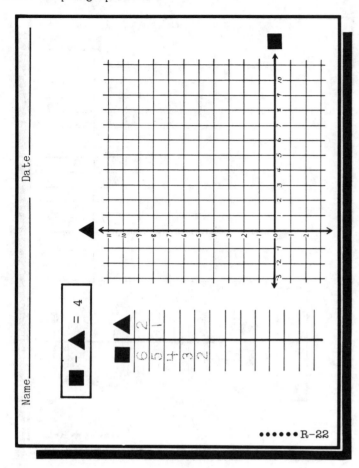

□	△
6	2
5	1
4	0
3	−1
100	96
$4\frac{1}{2}$	$\frac{1}{2}$

•••••• R22

The following is another linear equation:

$$\boxed{□ - △ = 4}$$

A list of pairs that make true sentences follows:

This is a graph of the equation.

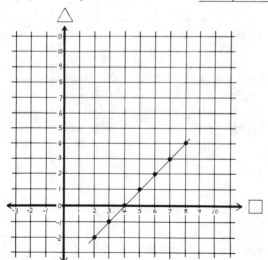

Notice that the line □ - △ = 4 crosses the □ number line at (4,0) and the △ number line at (0,-4).

•••••• R23

The following is a linear equation, with a graph of the equation and a list of numbers that make true sentences.

$$\boxed{□ = △}$$

□	△
6	6
5	5
3	3
0	0
−2	−2
etc.	

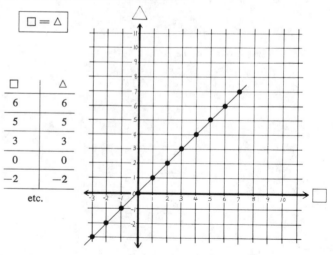

Notice that the line □ = △ crosses both the □ number line *and* the △ number line at the same point (0,0). The line □ = △ makes a 45° angle with each number line.

278

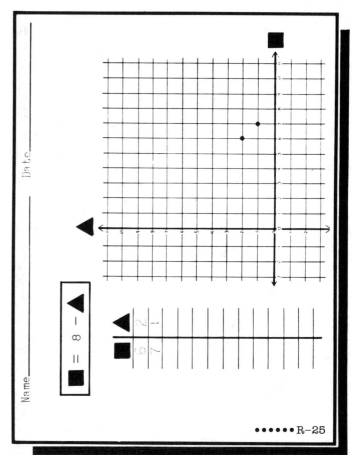

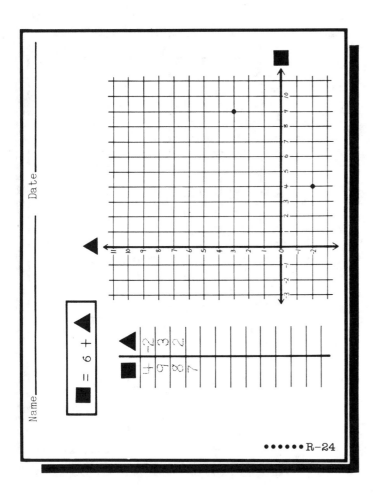

· · · · · · **R24**

The following equation $\boxed{\square = 6 + \triangle}$

is the same equation as $\square - \triangle = 6$.

The graph for this equation is a line parallel to the graphs for the equations on lab sheets R22 and R23.

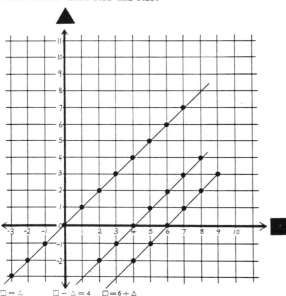

$\square = \triangle$ $\square - \triangle = 4$ $\square = 6 + \triangle$

279

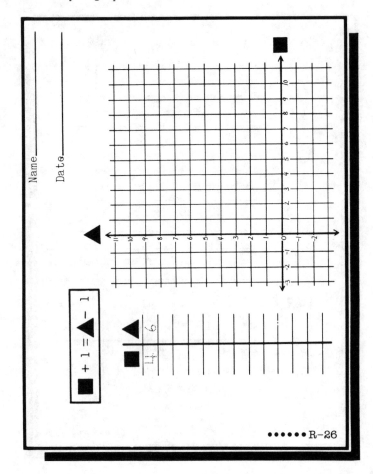

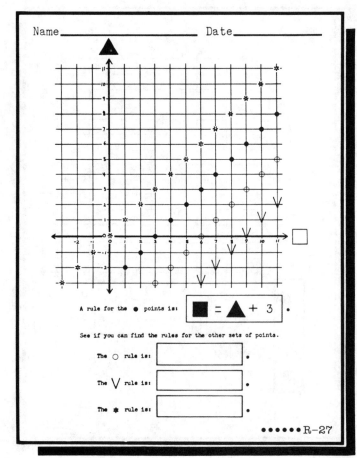

• • • • • • **R26**

Is there a simpler way of writing

$$\boxed{\Box + 1 = \triangle - 1}$$

Yes. It is $\Box = \triangle - 2$ or $\Box + 2 = \triangle$. Graph it.

• • • • • • **R27**

The ● rule is: $\Box = \triangle + 3$
The ○ rule is: $\Box = \triangle + 6$
The V rule is: $\Box = \triangle + 9$
The * rule is: $\Box = \triangle$

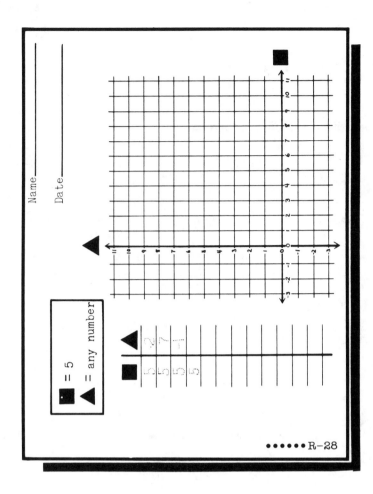

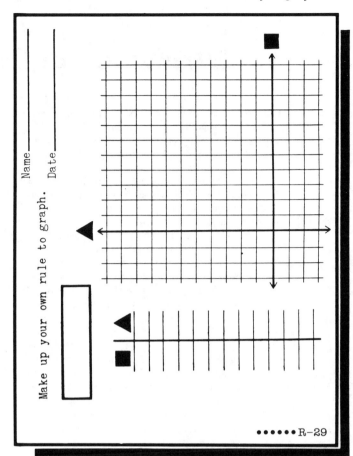

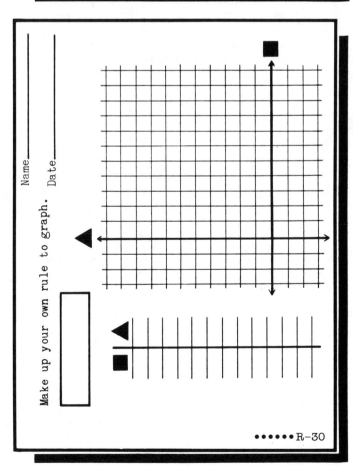

•••••• R28

The graph of these sets of ordered pairs is a straight line parallel to the △ number line (or *y* axis). All points on this graph are equidistant to the △ number line but arbitrary as related to the □ number line. Children might make a graph so that every point is equidistant to the □ number line (*x* axis).

Question: What would the graph look like if every point on the graph were equidistant to a given point?

S Geometric recognition

The work in this section merely attempts to sharpen children's awareness of the variety of regular and semiregular shapes that surround them. The lab sheets provide opportunities for the child to record generalizations that may have been built up from experimentation with the physical realities surrounding him.

Some terminology is introduced because it is convenient to have names for the shapes that we observe. Since it is impossible to represent a three-dimensional figure on two-dimensional paper, all lab sheet examples deal with plane figures only.

First, we must observe that there are different kinds of lines. There are curved lines ⌒ and there are straight lines ——— . There are many lines that may connect two points, but there is only *one* shortest line and that is the straight line.

This can be demonstrated by stretching a piece of string between two objects in the classroom. There are many "string paths" between the objects but the shortest one is the straight path, when the string is stretched and taut.

Now we may examine the things around us that are bounded by straight lines: the walls of the room, the edge of the chalkboard, the panes of glass in the window, the notebook paper on our desk. As we leave the man-made things and look around our natural environment—our own bodies, the contour of the landscape around us, the trees, leaves, clouds, etc.—we find it more difficult to find obvious examples of straight lines. Yet straight lines exist in the path that light travels, in the structure of crystals, etc.

When we draw two straight lines from a common point, we have an angle. We can observe how these two lines are inclined, or bent, toward one another. This inclination varies.

A common example of the inclination of two lines toward one another are the hands of the clock. When the hands are as far apart as this,

we call it a *right* angle. Two right angles together make a *straight* angle.

There are many examples of right angles in our school environment. The edges of books, paper, chalkboards, rulers, and boxes are bounded by right angles. The corner of the wall forms a right angle with the floor.

When we connect four straight lines in such a way that four right angles are formed, the resulting figure is a *rectangle*.

The *square* is a special kind of rectangle which not only has four right angles but also has four straight lines of the *same length*. All rectangles have two pairs of sides of equal length, except for the square, in which *all* sides are of equal length.

Sample classroom activities

1 Straight lines

2 Curved lines

3 Broken straight lines

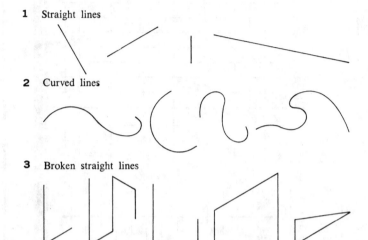

A B C D E

A is made up of 2 straight lines and 1 angle.
B is made up of 5 straight lines and 4 angles.
C is made up of 3 straight lines and 2 angles.
D is made up of 4 straight lines and 4 angles.
E is made up of 3 straight lines and 3 angles.

A, B, and C are *not* polygons. They each have one more line than they have angles. Their end points do *not* join.

D and E are polygons. D and E have as many lines as they have angles. Their end points *do* join. D is a 4-sided polygon (a quadrilateral). E is a 3-sided polygon (a triangle).

Draw a broken line which is made up of 3 lines and 3 angles. Is this a triangle?
Draw a broken line which is made up of 3 lines and 2 angles. Is this also a triangle?
Draw a polygon with 5 sides. How many angles does it have? A 5-sided polygon is a *pentagon*. A 6-sided polygon is a *hexagon*.

· S1–S4
Introduction

These lab sheets deal with the recognition of the properties of simple *polygons*. Polygons are closed plane figures bounded by straight-line segments. They may be precisely defined and classified as follows:

Polygons—many-sided closed curves bounded by straight edges

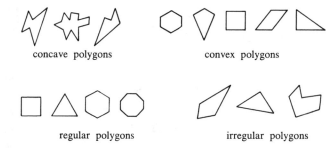

concave polygons   convex polygons

regular polygons   irregular polygons

The following chart singles out the quadrilaterals for a more detailed examination. (The numerals on the left are keyed to the ensuing comments explaining the chart.)

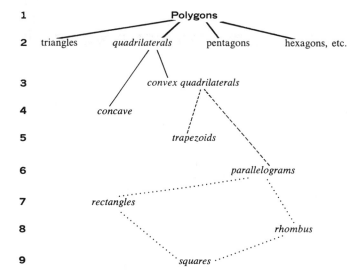

1   **Polygons**

2   triangles   *quadrilaterals*   pentagons   hexagons, etc.

3   *convex quadrilaterals*

4   *concave*

5   *trapezoids*

6   *parallelograms*

7   *rectangles*

8   *rhombus*

9   *squares*

1   A *polygon* is a figure made of closed curves bounded by straight-line segments. Polygons range from triangles to many-sided polygons. They can be broken down into concave and convex polygons. (In a concave polygon one or more of the diagonals lies outside the figure.)

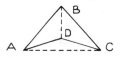

The diagonal $\overline{AC}$ is outside the figure $\overline{ABCD}$.

2   *All* four-sided polygons are *quadrilaterals*.

3   A *convex quadrilateral* is a four-sided figure in which both diagonals lie inside the figure.

4   A *concave quadrilateral* is a four-sided figure in which only one diagonal lies inside the figure.

5   A *trapezoid* is a quadrilateral with one pair of parallel sides.

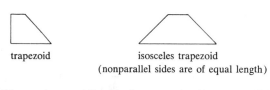

trapezoid   isosceles trapezoid
(nonparallel sides are of equal length)

6   A *parallelogram* is a quadrilateral whose opposite sides are parallel. All three of these are parallelograms:

7   A *rectangle* is a special kind of parallelogram, which is a special kind of quadrilateral. Rectangles are parallelograms with four right angles.

8   A *rhombus* is a special type of parallelogram with all sides of equal length.

9   A *square* is a special kind of rectangle and a special kind of rhombus. It has four right angles *and* sides of equal length.

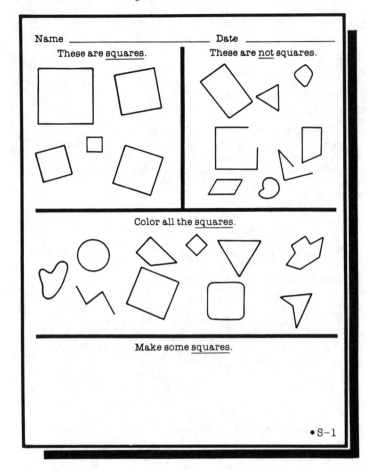

· S1
Squares

These are squares.

We found early in our work with five- and six-year-olds that their concept of "squareness" and "triangleness" was often an unnecessarily restricted concept.

For example, the children did not think that a diamond ⬦ was a square. A square had to rest solidily on its base ▢ . A triangle like this ▽ or this ◹ was not considered a triangle; it had to point up △ to be a triangle. For these reasons, squares and triangles of various sizes and in various positions were included among the squares and triangles in the diagram.

These are not squares.

Other rectangles, triangles, other quadrilaterals, "almost squares," and loops are shown. "Almost squares" (not simple closed curves) are *not* squares.

Color all the squares.

Only 2 of the examples given are squares.

Make some squares.

Some children might worry about how to do this. Let them look around the classroom for small square items to trace. White rods will do, for example.

· S2
Triangles

The remarks about S1 apply to triangles also.

Children might be asked to think of other words beginning with *tri* (tricycle, tripod, triple, trio), and maybe someone will get the idea that *tri* means "three."

There is only one triangle to color.

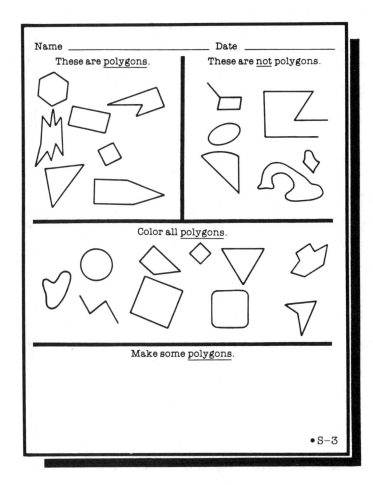

· S3

This sheet is also similar to S1 and S2, but the polygons will require more thoughtful study. What could all these funny shapes called "polygons" have in common which *none* of the "not polygons" have?

Obviously *none* of them have roundness; obviously *all* of them have sharp corners; obviously *all* of them are made of "straight lines hooked together"; obviously none of them have "tails sticking out." (These are child-like observations but *very* germane, nevertheless.)

There are only 6 polygons to be colored. Notice that the coloring section of the three pages is identical, and children now color again the squares and triangle of the previous pages.

Children should know that *poly* means "many."

Note: If you have geoboards and rubberbands, let the children make polygons. Then gradually give more and more restricted and complicated directions. (They, too, can take turns making up the directions.)

1   Few directions
Make many polygons.
Make triangles, little and big ones.

2   More directions
Make a red triangle and a blue square.
Make a blue triangle inside a red square.
Make a square inside a square inside a square.

3   Still more directions
Make a polygon inside a triangle and a square outside a triangle.
Make a green square outside a yellow square which is outside a blue square.

4   All children except Ann are asked to clear their geoboards.

Teacher: Ann, you tell us what is on your geoboard. (No one is allowed to peek.)

Ann: I have a big yellow triangle and a little red square crossing the big yellow triangle.

Teacher: You all be Ann's copy cats. *You* make something that could be Ann's design.

(There are many possibilities that fit the description. One could be a copy of Ann's.) Afterwards another child is chosen as leader.

· S4

S4 is self-explanatory. If the teacher cares to, she can use the opportunity to introduce some of the names, such as *quadrilaterals, rectangles, pentagons,* and *hexagons*. Practice with these new names can be given during the play with the geoboards.

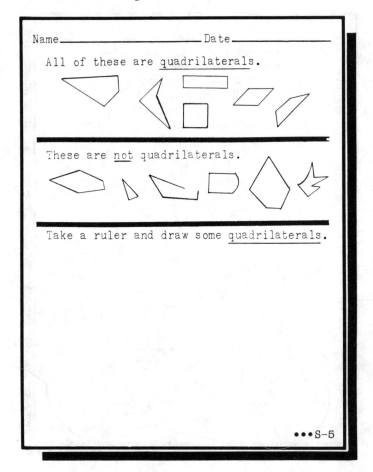

Name_____ Date_____

All of these are quadrilaterals.

These are not quadrilaterals.

Take a ruler and draw some quadrilaterals.

•••S-5

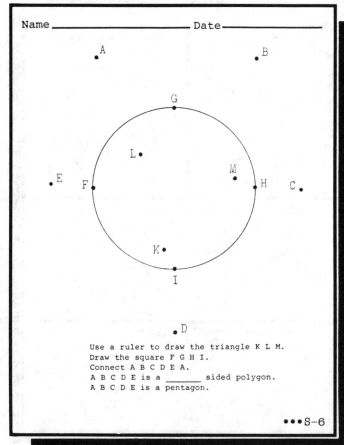

Name_____ Date_____

Use a ruler to draw the triangle K L M.
Draw the square F G H I.
Connect A B C D E A.
A B C D E is a _____ sided polygon.
A B C D E is a pentagon.

•••S-6

••• S5
Supplementary activity

The children enjoy playing games with many fanciful shapes and non-sense names. You can make up as many creatures as you like, but be sure to give all the creatures of the same name some identifying characteristics. Start this game on the board.

Here are some bopeeps:

These are not bopeeps:

Ask the children to color the bopeeps. (Bopeeps have four "antennas" or "sticks" on the outside *and* a dot on the inside.)

Ask the children to draw some bopeeps of their own.

The same procedure should be followed for lab sheet S5. Give the children rulers and ask them to draw some quadrilaterals. This is not a frustrating task for them, for any four straight lines joined to make a closed figure will do. They do not need to worry about right angles, equal lengths, etc.

••• S6

If the directions are difficult for the children to read, the teacher may read them aloud. The children should find the labeled points and trace the figures with their fingers before they draw the figures. You may want to start this lab sheet on the chalkboard. When the page is completed, the following questions may be asked:

Which figure lies *inside* the circle?   [Triangle KLM.]
Which figure lies partly *on* the circle?   [Square FGHI.]
Which figure lies *outside* the circle?   [Pentagon ABCDE.]
Which figures lie inside the pentagon?   [The square, the circle, the triangle.]
Which figure is neither all inside the square nor all outside the square?   [The circle.]

The children may want to make up some pages of their own like this.

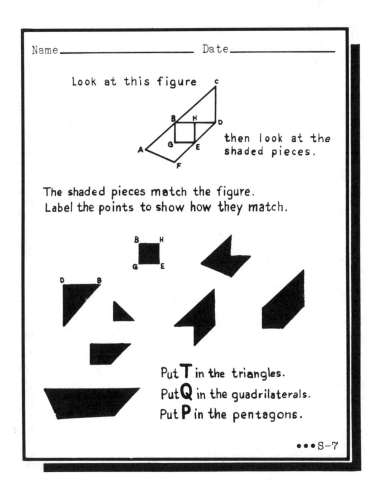

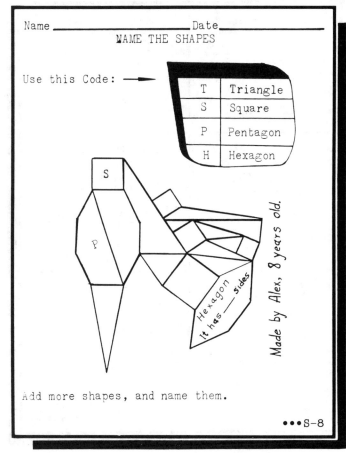

Recognition aids

Oaktag copies of quadrilateral ACDF and the parts cut out of ACDF will be helpful to those children who have difficulty superimposing the cut-outs mentally. One set of these cut-outs should have labeled points.

    With this lab sheet the children should learn:

    (1) to concentrate on specific parts of a geometric figure;

    (2) to recognize congruence even when the figure is rotated;

    (3) to recognize congruence even when a figure is reflected (flipped over);

    (4) to realize that within a quadrilateral there could be other quadrilaterals, triangles, pentagons, etc.

This is one of many examples of papers designed by the children themselves and shared with other children. The teacher should set an upper limit on the number of sides a polygon can have because children have a tendency to make things too difficult for themselves.

287

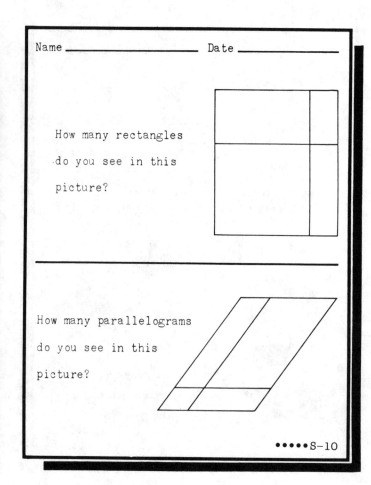

Could you make a
SQUARE with sides
the same lengths
as these lines?

YES   NO

_____
_____
_____

Could you make a
TRIANGLE with
sides the same
length as these
lines?

YES   NO

_____
_____

Could you make a
SQUARE with sides
the same lengths
as these lines?

YES   NO

_____
_____
_____

Could you
make a
RECTANGLE
with sides
the same
lengths as
these lines?

YES   NO

Could you make a
TRIANGLE with
sides the same
lengths as these
lines?

YES   NO

_____
_____

NAME:_____

DATE _____

Now DRAW these
SQUARES,
TRIANGLES, and
RECTANGLES
if you can.

•••••S-9

Name _____   Date _____

How many rectangles
do you see in this
picture?

How many parallelograms
do you see in this
picture?

•••••S-10

····· **S9**

Sample activity

This lab sheet may best be done as a group activity unless some previous work has prepared the children for the thinking involved.

You will need a large supply of thin wooden dowels of various
lengths but with at least four of the same length in each set.

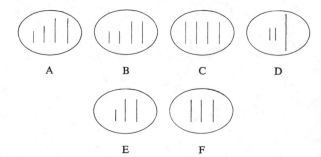

Set A will make a quadrilateral. It will not make a rectangle because
it does not have two pairs of sides of equal length.

Set B will make a rectangle. It will not make a square because not
all sides are of equal length. (It will also make a parallelogram.)

Set C will make a square. (It will also make a rhombus.)

Set D will not make a triangle. The sum of the lengths of the two
short sides is less than the third side.

Set E will make a triangle. (It will make an isosceles triangle, one
with two equal sides.)

Set F will make a triangle. (It will make an equilateral triangle,
one with all sides equal.)

····· **S10**

How many rectangles and parallelograms can you see in this picture?

Notice that there are the same number of rectangles and parallelograms! How many children will draw this generalization *without* re-
counting the number of parallelograms? How does one tackle a counting problem of this type? There are several ways.

How many single rectangles?   [4]

How many ways of combining two rectangles to form a single
rectangle?   [4]

How many ways of combining three rectangles to form a single
rectangle?   [0]

How many ways of combining four (all) rectangles?   [1]   The
total number of rectangles is 9.

288

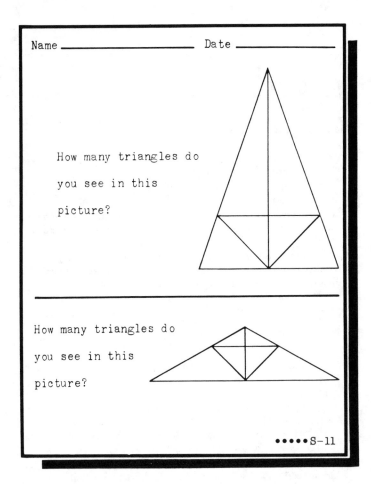

Name _____   Date _____

How many triangles do
you see in this
picture?

_____

How many triangles do
you see in this
picture?

•••••S-11

· · · · · **S11**

The same method used for counting the rectangles can be used for
counting the triangles. Here is another method.

Label each point which lies on more than one line.

Question: In how many ways can we
use points A, B, C, D, E, F, G as vertices of different triangles?

1 Triangles including vertex A:
   A B C   A G C   A G D

2 New triangles including vertex B:
            B C G   B F G

3 New triangles including vertex C:
   C D E   C E F   C D F
         C D G   C G F

4 New triangles including vertex D:
            D E G   D F G

5 New triangles including vertex E:
            E F G

The total number of triangles is 13.

T Length, area, and volume

Basic ideas about measurement

1 In order to measure, we must have a *unit of measure*.

    a. This unit may be arbitrary.

    b. A selected unit of measure may become standardized for convenience of public use.

    c. The most widely used standard unit of measure for small distances is the *centimeter*.

2 After having selected the unit of measure for a given task, we must:

    a. use it consistently throughout the task (hence, we ultimately find ourselves with multiples and fractions of the unit);

    b. label our measurement to indicate what unit we have used.

3 All actual measurements are *approximate*. The degree of accuracy depends upon the following:

    a. the refinement of our measurement tool;

    b. our skill in using the tool we selected.

Basic aims of the lab sheets

1 To present to the child the idea that, by developing appropriate tools (units of measure), he can:

    a. express quantitatively many phenomena in the physical world;

    b. make comparisons among many phenomena in the physical world.

2 To help the child develop judgment as to what units to choose for a given task.

3 To help the child develop ingenuity in the following:

    a. devising units of measure which are reasonable, though not standardized;

    b. using these homemade units to make comparisons among phenomena measured;

    c. discovering that the ratio (relations) of things measured is fixed (constant) and does not depend upon (is not a function of) the chosen unit.

4 To help the child become equally familiar with metric and common measurements:

    a. by frequent use of both;

    b. by surrounding the child with physical equipment which uses one or the other of these units.

Children have been "measuring" long before they enter first grade. But most of their measuring has been either *direct* comparisons between objects, distances, weights, or *indirect* comparisons through the use of their own bodies or strength. The following are examples of direct comparisons:

    a. Given 2, 3, or more sticks of varied length, any six-year-old can put them in order of length.

    b. Given rocks of grossly varied weight, a child can put them in order of heaviness (if he is allowed to lift them). Another child can come along and repeat the same task with the same results.

All that children lack when they are "measuring" in this way is a *unit of measure* by which fine comparisons can be made—a unit of measure which becomes the reference point, the standard by which all subsequent measurements are taken.

Classroom anecdotes

Ann came over to the teacher with her arms outstretched and her hands parallel to say that her desk was "this" long.

"Are you sure, Ann?" her teacher asked.

Ann went back and checked with her hands. She realized that she could not maintain her arms at a constant distance from one another while walking about. She hunted for something that was more reliable.

Ann found a ball of string and measured her desk. She snipped off a piece of string the length of her desk, and announced, "My desk is this long," holding up the length of string.

Then Ann could use her string—which was "a desk long"—to measure other things in the room. The board was more than "6 desks long." The window was "3 desks long."

Ann had devised a crude unit of measure.

Other children made their own units of length. Some measured in "pencils," some in "books," in "sticks," in "paper strips," some in "hands."

Ruth and Louis worked as a team. Ruth measured her desk with a stick. She called her unit a "tock." Her desk was about "8 tocks long." (Louis checked it and agreed.) Then Ruth measured the length of her pencil box; it was "a little more than 2 tocks long."

Louis cut a paper strip for his measure. He called it a "pap." He measured Ruth's desk and pencil box in "paps" while Ruth watched. They found Ruth's desk to be about "4 paps long" and her pencil box to be "about 1 pap long."

Ruth and Louis continued to measure other things in both "tocks" and "paps." They discovered that it always takes more "tocks" than "paps" to measure by, because a "pap" was longer than a "tock"; in fact, a "pap" was about "2 tocks long."

Other teams of children compared homemade units similarly. So many different units of length were used to measure the same objects that *no one* could keep track of them all. A partial list of comparisons on the chalkboard satisfied only a few.

Someone had the bright idea of using the same thing to measure by. What did *everyone* have? Pencils, yes, but some were short and some were long. Sheets of paper, yes, but they were too large to get the "in between" lengths right.

Finally, it occurred to someone to use Cuisenaire® rods to measure by. Everyone had a supply of those.

With new enthusiasm, the children again measured desks, books, pencils, boxes, etc. The unit of measure was sometimes the red rod, sometimes the orange rod, sometimes the white rod. The children could verify one another's measurements. The group had its first standardized unit.

From here on, the transition to rulers was easy. In fact, the teacher had a hard time holding back many of the children who had wanted to measure with rulers or yardsticks before.

Why did the teacher discourage using the ruler? She wanted to make sure that the children had gone through the experience of devising units of their own first. She feared that for some of them, the measuring of length was linked too rigidly to just *one* system of units, namely inches-feet-yards or centimeters-meters.

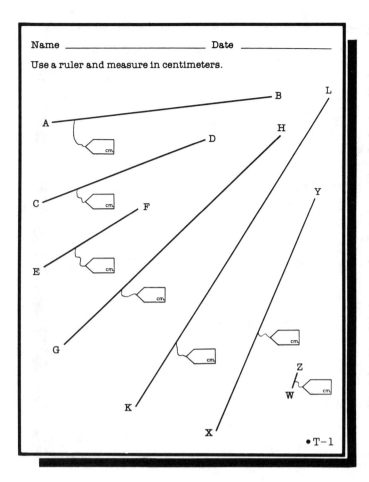

Name _____ Date _____

Use a ruler and measure in centimeters.

• T-1

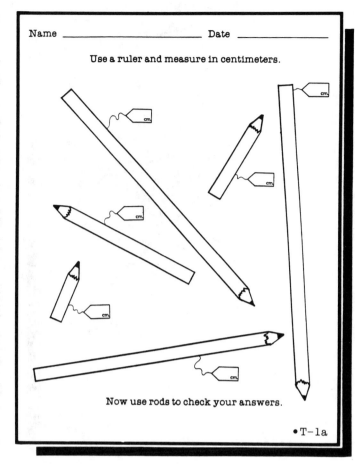

Name _____ Date _____

Use a ruler and measure in centimeters.

Now use rods to check your answers.

• T-1a

·T1–T6

Preliminary activity: play with the ruler

Each child needs a centimeter ruler and an inch ruler. Children should measure the lengths of common schoolroom objects with their rulers. They should have opportunities to measure the lengths of line segments which they themselves draw. Practice should also be provided in laying the ruler parallel to a line segment so that the zero edge of the ruler is lined up with one of the end points of the line segment.

On the chalkboard, children should practice measuring line segments with metersticks, rulers, and yardsticks. There should be some discussion about how difficult it is to measure something *exactly,* and children should be encouraged to say that this line is *"about* so-many centimeters" or *"about* so-many inches long."

The words "centimeters" and "inches" and their abbreviations ("cm." and "in.") should be written on the chalkboard for easy reference. Children should be asked to measure the lengths of their Cuisenaire® rods, using centimeter and inch rulers. To their delight, children discover that all the rods are multiples of one centimeter: white rod = 1 cm., red rod = 2 cm., etc. This establishes a convenient and useful differentiation between the two units of measure—centimeters and inches. The mechanics of measuring the length of a line segment and the concept of length, as measured by implied units of length, have actually been encountered in number-line activities. This will become apparent by the ease with which children read off 3½ cm., 5½ in., etc.

·T1

On lab sheet T1 children measure the given line segments in centimeters. Notice that the line segments to be measured on this lab sheet are labeled.

We can introduce the phrase "line segment" here. Each of the line segments is a part of a line which goes in the same direction as the line segment. The *line* has no beginning and no end point. Thus line segment $\overline{AB}$ lies on a line

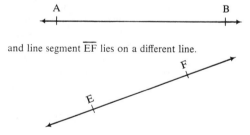

and line segment $\overline{EF}$ lies on a different line.

Sample questions

Which line segment is the shortest?   [$\overline{WZ}$; it is 1 cm. long.]
Which line segment is the longest?   [$\overline{KL}$; it is 23 cm. long.]
$\overline{AB}$ is longer than _____ but shorter than _____.
$\overline{CD}$ is 4 cm. longer than _____.

291

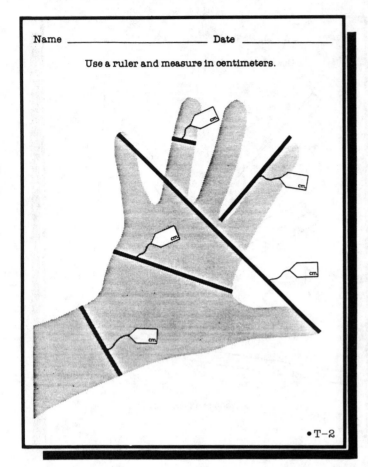

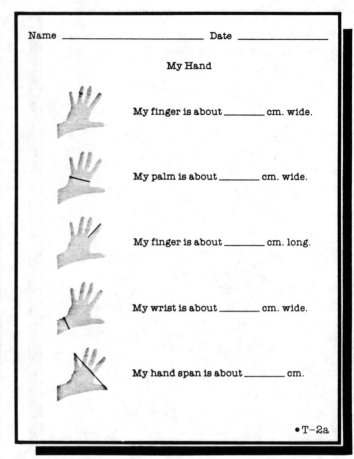

· T2, T2a

Children should use their centimeter rulers or Cuisenaire® rods to measure the indicated parts of this adult hand. Afterwards they can make similar measurements of their own hands and record the results on lab sheet T2a.

The measurements recorded on lab sheet T2a can form the basis for each student's personal measuring system. For example, a child may find that one finger or fingernail is almost exactly 1 cm. wide. Then this finger or fingernail can be used as a measure to estimate the dimensions of larger objects. A book 3 fingers thick will be about 3 cm. thick. If a child's wrist is 4 cm. wide, then a desk top measuring 15 wrists will be about 15 x 4 = 60 cm. across. Emphasize the use of the word "about." This personal measuring system will not be as accurate as a ruler or meterstick, but it is a very effective means of fixing the relative sizes of various measurements in children's minds.

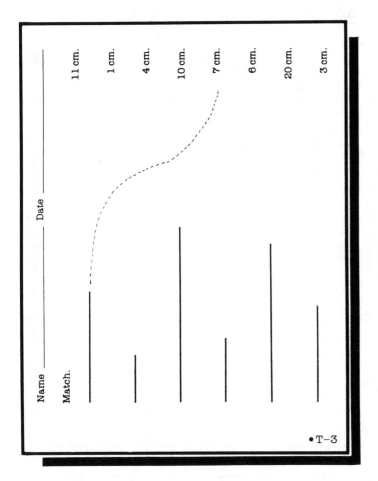

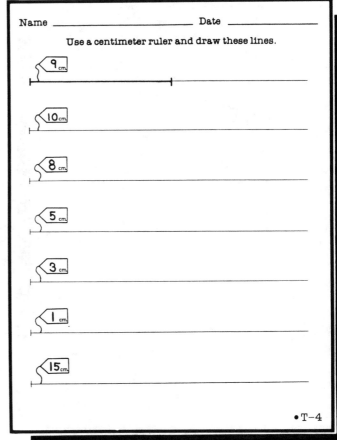

· **T3**

Notice that on this matching exercise two extra measurements have
been given. Some children may realize that 1 cm. is shorter than any
of the given line segments and that 20 cm. is longer than any of the
segments. When these two "extra" measurements are eliminated,
then it is apparent that the shortest segment must be 3 cm., the next
one 4 cm., and so on. In this manner, the matching can all be done
without the use of ruler or rods. If some of the chldren discover this
on their own, fine. Otherwise, they should just go ahead and do the
exercises using ruler or rods.

Name _____ Date _____

Use ruler. Measure in inches.

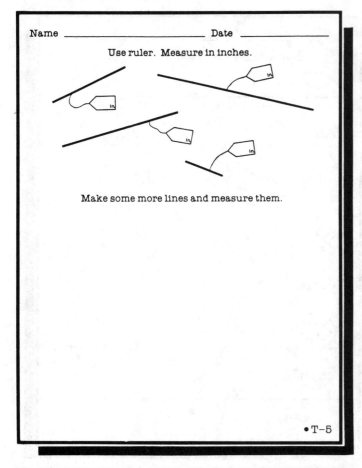

Make some more lines and measure them.

• T–5

Name _____ Date _____

Use an inch ruler and draw these lines.

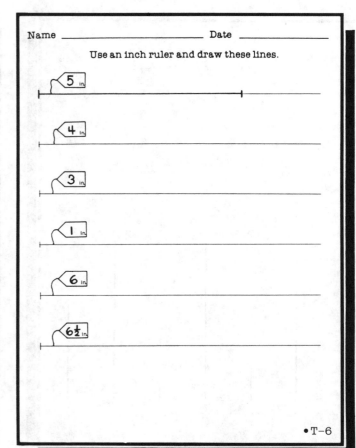

• T–6

Name _____ Date _____

Find the length and width.

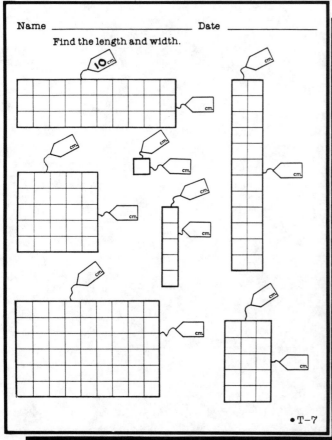

• T–7

Name _____ Date _____

Use the rods to find the length and width.

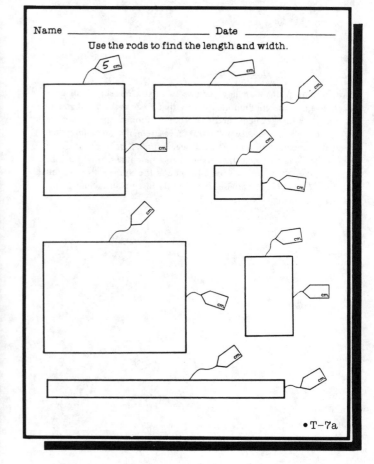

• T–7a

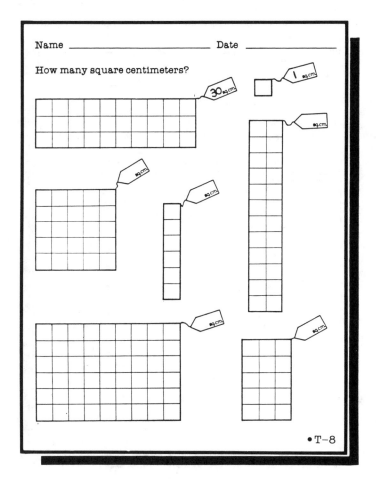

Name _____ Date _____

How many square centimeters?

•T–8

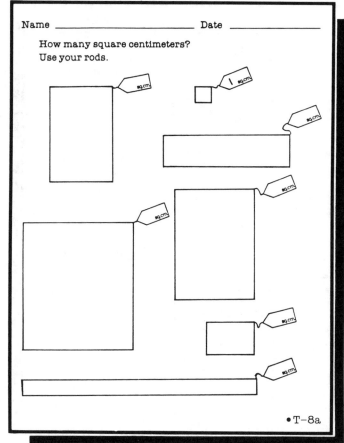

Name _____ Date _____

How many square centimeters?
Use your rods.

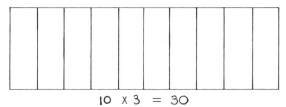

•T–8a

· T5, T6

On these lab sheets children measure and draw line segments in *inches*.

· T7, T7a

On lab sheets T7 and T7a, children determine the length and width of given rectangles. On T7 this can be done by counting. Rods and centimeter rulers should also be used to show that the result comes out the same regardless of the method used. On sheet T7a, no markings are given, so rods or rulers must be used to measure the dimensions.

· T8, T8a

Area measurement is introduced on these two lab sheets. The area of a plane figure is the amount of space inside the figure. Area is measured in *square centimeters (sq. cm.).* One square centimeter is shown at the top of each of these sheets. Each surface of the white rod is one sq. cm., so the area of a rectangle can be determined by counting how many white rods will cover it.

Less counting is necessary if one covers the rectangles with larger rods. For example, the 30 sq. cm. rectangle at the top of lab sheet T8 can be covered using light green (3) rods, as shown below:

$$10 \times 3 = 30$$

Since it took ten 3's to cover this rectangle, the area is 10x3 or 30. The same rectangle can also be covered using orange (10) rods:

$$3 \times 10 = 30$$

It took three 10's to cover the rectangle, so the area is 3x10 or 30. Regardless of what color rods we use to cover the rectangle, the answer is always 30.

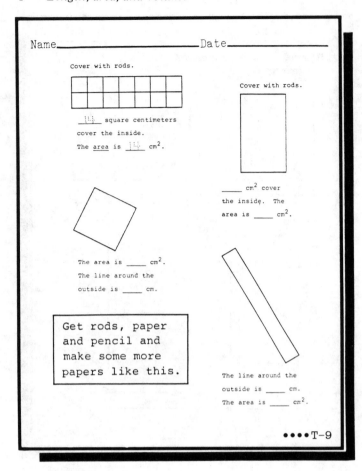

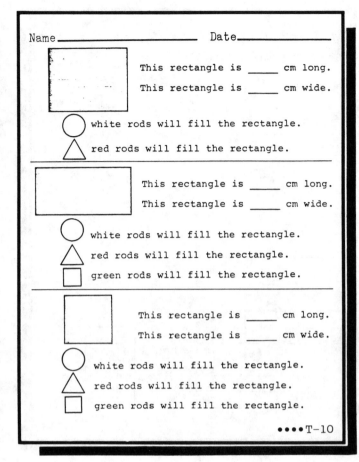

····T9

On this lab sheet the work on area begun on T7 and T8 is continued with more emphasis being put on the word *area*.

In addition to this:

1   The measure of the area is expressed in *square centimeters.* (Both the abbreviations and the whole words are used.)

2   The children are asked to measure *around* the figures. The word *perimeter* is not yet used.

It is important to give the children time to make up some sheets of their own. They can do this easily by tracing around rod rectangles.

····T10

"Long" and "wide" are introduced. Ruler measurement is suggested. Some children will want to use the rods as a substitute for rulers since they know from previous activities that the rods are on the centimeter scale.

When children fill the rectangles with white, red, and green rods respectively, they might discover (*a*) that the rectangles are easiest to cover with white rods, and (*b*) that one-half as many red rods and one-third as many green rods are needed.

Rectangle 1	Rectangle 2	Rectangle 3
20 white rods	18 white rods	9 white rods
10 red rods	9 red rods	$4\frac{1}{2}$ red rods
$6\frac{2}{3}$ green rods	6 green rods	3 green rods

This might be a good time to look a little more closely at the shape of the faces of the white rod. Ask the children to press firmly with the white rod into the fleshy part of their hand. The rod will leave a print on the hand. What shape is that print?   [It is a square.]

Additional questions

This is a square centimeter.
How many square centimeters cover each of the rectangles?
Does the red rod have square centimeter faces?
Make a square centimeter print on your hand with the red rod.
How about the long face of the red rod? How many square centimeters is it?

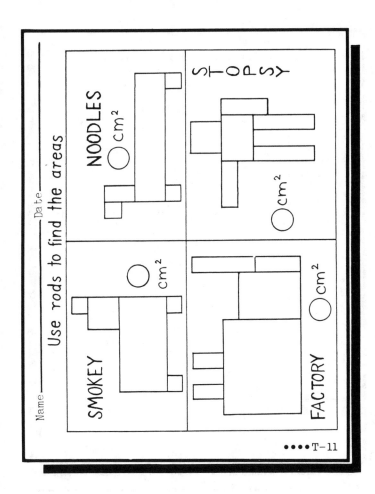

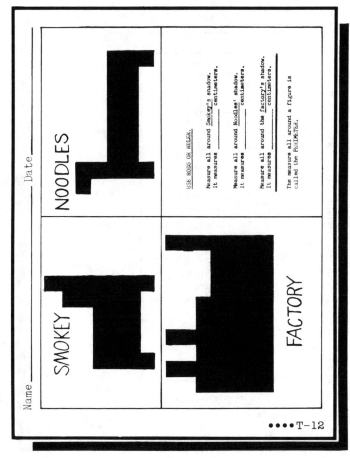

····T11, T12

Area and perimeter

Children cover the pictures with rods and then add up the lengths of all rods used.

Areas

Smokey: 25 square centimeters
Noodles: 21 cm²
Factory: 53 cm²
Stopsy: 24 cm²

It is easier to use rods than to use the ruler to measure around the shadows on T12. Some children need to be reminded to use one rod at a time and to write down the length immediately before measuring the next line.

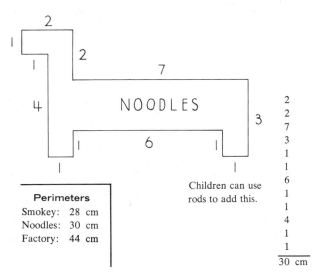

Perimeters
Smokey: 28 cm
Noodles: 30 cm
Factory: 44 cm

Children can use rods to add this.

If interest is aroused, children may be asked to make their own simple shapes by tracing around rods and then figure out the perimeters and areas. They may also want to go back to lab sheets T9 and T10 and figure out the perimeters for these shapes.

A few triangles may be included if you want to make some additional lab sheets or cut-outs for practice with perimeters and areas.

Name _____ Date _____

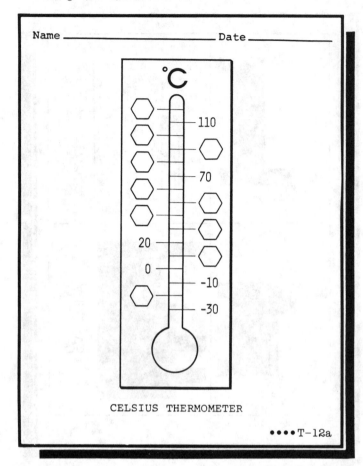

CELSIUS THERMOMETER

•••• T-12a

Name _____ Date _____

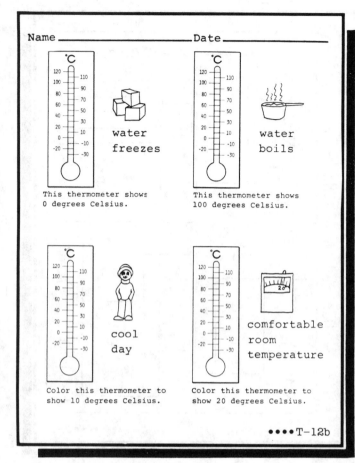

water
freezes

This thermometer shows
0 degrees Celsius.

water
boils

This thermometer shows
100 degrees Celsius.

cool
day

Color this thermometer to
show 10 degrees Celsius.

comfortable
room
temperature

Color this thermometer to
show 20 degrees Celsius.

•••• T-12b

Name _____ Date _____

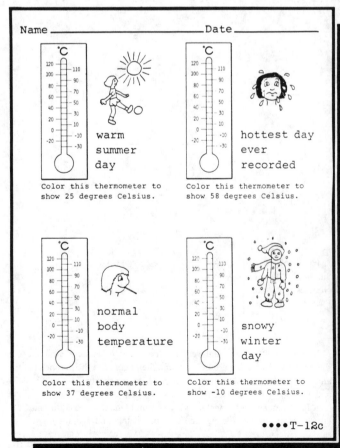

warm
summer
day

Color this thermometer to
show 25 degrees Celsius.

hottest day
ever
recorded

Color this thermometer to
show 58 degrees Celsius.

normal
body
temperature

Color this thermometer to
show 37 degrees Celsius.

snowy
winter
day

Color this thermometer to
show -10 degrees Celsius.

•••• T-12c

Name _____ Date _____

THE TEMPERATURE IS...

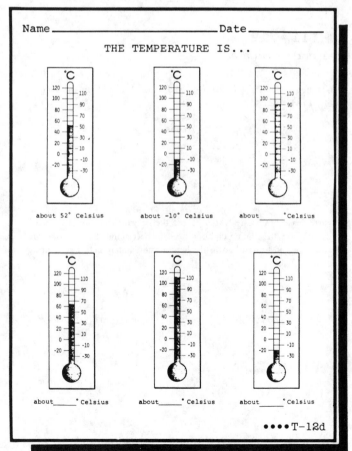

about 52° Celsius

about -10° Celsius

about_____°Celsius

about_____°Celsius

about_____°Celsius

about_____°Celsius

•••• T-12d

Name_____ Date_____

8 pints = 1 gallon

c. ↔ cup
pt. ↔ pint
qt. ↔ quart
gal. ↔ gallon

gal.

16 cups = 1 gallon
8 pints = 1 gallon
4 quarts = 1 gallon

4 quarts = 1 gallon

16 cups = 1 gallon

•••• T–13

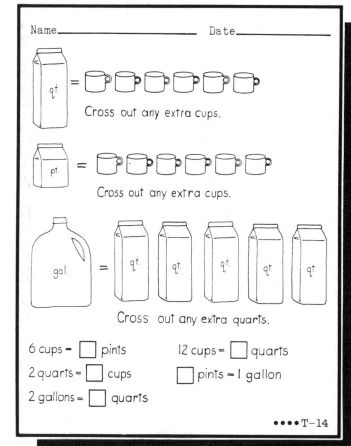

Name_____ Date_____

Cross out any extra cups.

Cross out any extra cups.

Cross out any extra quarts.

6 cups = ☐ pints   12 cups = ☐ quarts

2 quarts = ☐ cups   ☐ pints = 1 gallon

2 gallons = ☐ quarts

•••• T–14

•••• T13–T20
Volume: common liquid measures

You should begin this work using real measuring equipment and water or sand to give the children experience with actual materials.

Demonstrate the relationships illustrated on lab sheet T13 by giving measuring cups to the children and emptying a quart bottle into the cups. Write on the board the number of cups that can be filled from one quart bottle. Ask the children with full cups to pour them back into the quart bottle. (A funnel will help avoid spilling.) Follow the same procedure with pints and gallons. When you have worked through the measures, the children will have made up a measure chart based on their own experience.

•••• T15

Rods can be substituted for the measures to determine the relationships presented on T15.

The children are to draw lines from a word to the appropriate figure. The equivalent measures at the bottom of the page can be checked with rods.

one gallon = __4__ quarts = __8__ pints = __16__ cups

one pint = $\frac{1}{8}$ gallon = $\frac{1}{2}$ quart = __2__ cups

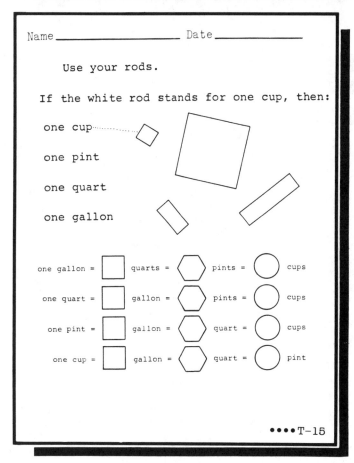

Name_____ Date_____

Use your rods.

If the white rod stands for one cup, then:

one cup ···········

one pint

one quart

one gallon

one gallon = ☐ quarts = ⬡ pints = ◯ cups

one quart = ☐ gallon = ⬡ pints = ◯ cups

one pint = ☐ gallon = ⬡ quart = ◯ cups

one cup = ☐ gallon = ⬡ quart = ◯ pint

•••• T–15

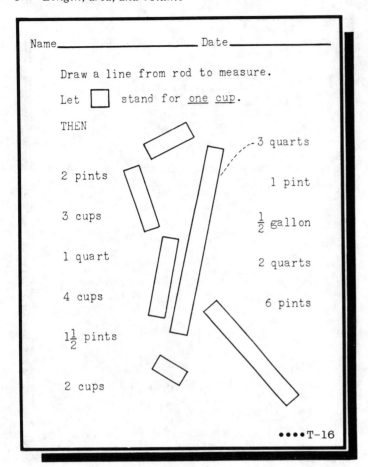

Name_____ Date_____

Draw a line from rod to measure.

Let ☐ stand for <u>one</u> <u>cup</u>.

THEN

2 pints

3 cups

1 quart

4 cups

1½ pints

2 cups

3 quarts

1 pint

½ gallon

2 quarts

6 pints

••••T-16

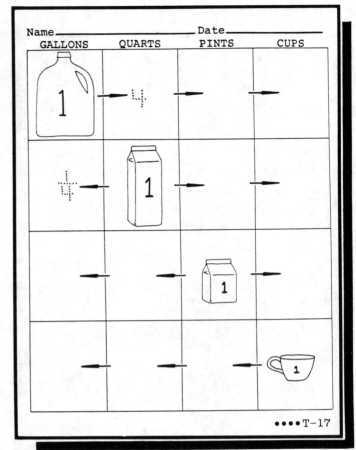

Name_____ Date_____

GALLONS	QUARTS	PINTS	CUPS

••••T-17

••••T17

Follow the arrows and write the numeral for each equivalent measure.

Gallons	Quarts	Pints	Cups
1 →	4 →	8 →	16
¼ ←	1	2 →	4
⅛ ←	½ ←	1	2
1/16 ←	¼ ←	½ ←	⚬

••••T18, T19

Children shade in the amounts requested. The problems on T19 may be answered either by shading in an amount or by writing in a fractional numeral.

Thus, in the second problem the answer could be either

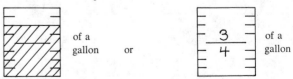

of a gallon   or $\frac{3}{4}$ of a gallon

Name_____ Date_____

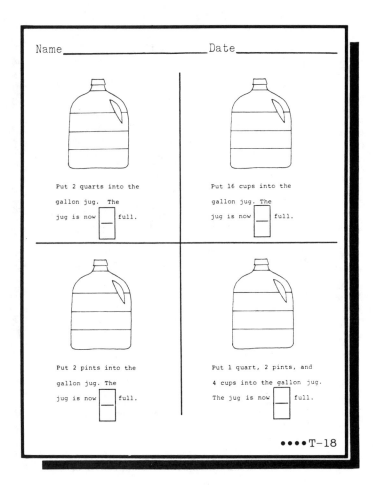

Put 2 quarts into the
gallon jug. The
jug is now ⬚ full.

Put 16 cups into the
gallon jug. The
jug is now ⬚ full.

Put 2 pints into the
gallon jug. The
jug is now ⬚ full.

Put 1 quart, 2 pints, and
4 cups into the gallon jug.
The jug is now ⬚ full.

••••T–18

Name_____ Date_____

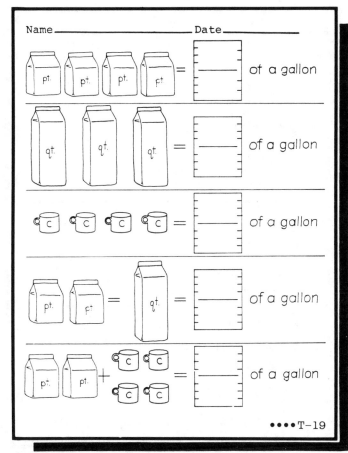

= ⬚ of a gallon

= ⬚ of a gallon

= ⬚ of a gallon

= = ⬚ of a gallon

+ = ⬚ of a gallon

••••T–19

Note: Tables similar to the ones included on gallons, quarts, pints, and cups can be made for other common measures, for example money. Let the white cube represent 1 cent. Then:

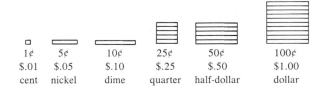

1¢	5¢	10¢	25¢	50¢	100¢
$.01	$.05	$.10	$.25	$.50	$1.00
cent	nickel	dime	quarter	half-dollar	dollar

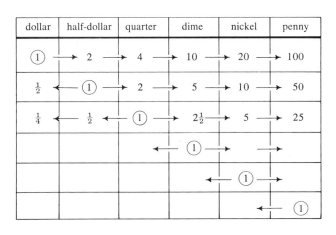

dollar	half-dollar	quarter	dime	nickel	penny
① →	2 →	4 →	10 →	20 →	100
½ ←	① →	2 →	5 →	10 →	50
¼ ←	½ ←	① →	2½ →	5 →	25
			← ① →	→	
				← ① →	
				←	①

Name_____ Date_____

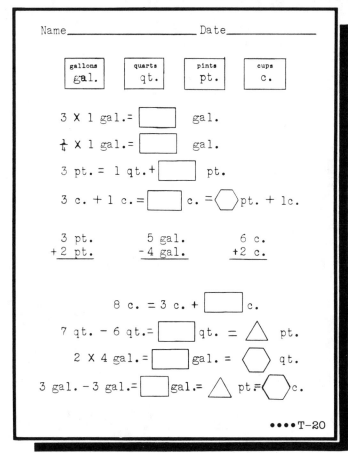

| gallons gal. | quarts qt. | pints pt. | cups c. |

3 X 1 gal. = ⬚ gal.

¼ X 1 gal. = ⬚ gal.

3 pt. = 1 qt. + ⬚ pt.

3 c. + 1 c. = ⬚ c. = ⬡ pt. + 1c.

```
  3 pt.        5 gal.       6 c.
+ 2 pt.      - 4 gal.     + 2 c.
```

8 c. = 3 c. + ⬚ c.

7 qt. – 6 qt. = ⬚ qt. = △ pt.

2 X 4 gal. = ⬚ gal. = ⬡ qt.

3 gal. – 3 gal. = ⬚ gal. = △ pt = ⬡ c.

••••T–20

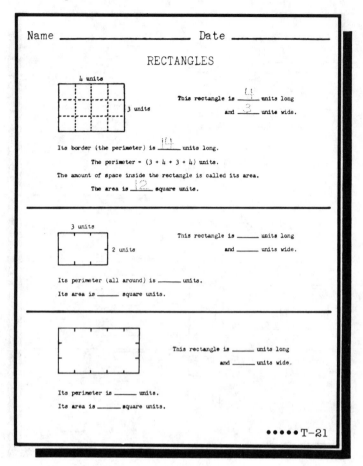

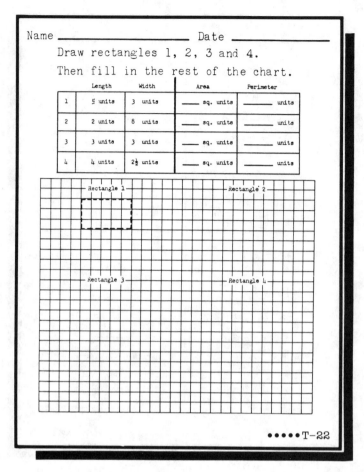

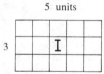

RECTANGLES

4 units

This rectangle is __4__ units long

3 units

and __3__ units wide.

Its border (the perimeter) is __14__ units long.

The perimeter = (3 + 4 + 3 + 4) units.

The amount of space inside the rectangle is called its area.

The area is __12__ square units.

3 units

2 units

This rectangle is _____ units long

and _____ units wide.

Its perimeter (all around) is _____ units.

Its area is _____ square units.

This rectangle is _____ units long

and _____ units wide.

Its perimeter is _____ units.

Its area is _____ square units.

•••••T-21

Draw rectangles 1, 2, 3 and 4.

Then fill in the rest of the chart.

	Length	Width	Area	Perimeter
1	5 units	3 units	_____ sq. units	_____ units
2	2 units	8 units	_____ sq. units	_____ units
3	3 units	3 units	_____ sq. units	_____ units
4	4 units	2½ units	_____ sq. units	_____ units

Rectangle 1   Rectangle 2

Rectangle 3   Rectangle 4

•••••T-22

••••• T22, T23
Area and perimeter

There is enough space on these pages to draw the required rectangles, using one of the given squares as the square unit. On T22 the children should label each diagram by the numeral given.

5 units

3   I

8 units

2   II

Area: 15 square units
Perimeter: 16 units

Area: 16 square units
Perimeter: 20 units

Children should *not* be told formulas for finding areas or perimeters. They will *discover* them even if they cannot or will not verbalize them.

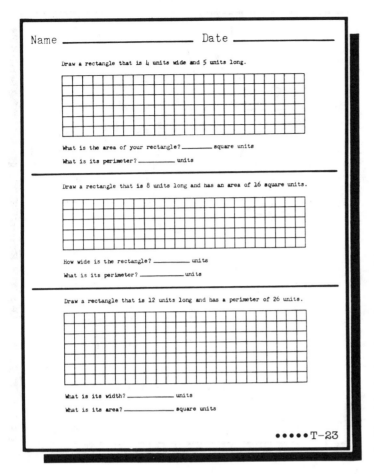

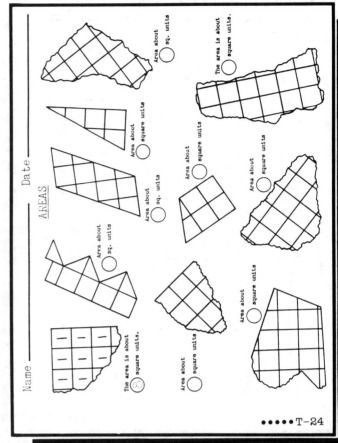

·····T24

All the area measurements preceding T24 have been those of rectangles. We do not intend to do more than suggest that the areas of triangles, circles, and figures with irregular curves can be measured.

The case of the area of a triangle is simple for children to understand. All we need to do is go back to one of the previous sheets (T21, T22, T23) and draw a diagonal through those rectangles for which we know the area and thus cut it into two congruent triangles. Each triangle has half the area of the rectangle. (If that is not convincing, we can take cutout square paper rectangles and fold them on a diagonal and then look at the two congruent triangles which result.)

Exact areas for irregular paper pieces such as some of those shown on T24 are difficult to find. Approximations, however, are not so difficult. Here again squared paper gives us a "hint" about how we might approach a solution to the problem.

Some complete squares are contained within all the figures. We know, therefore, that the area of each figure is greater than the sum of those complete squares but *less* than the sum of the complete *and* partial squares.

Let us look at the shaded example in the upper left corner of the lab sheet. Notice that there are 6 complete squares.

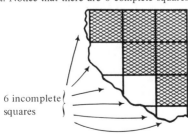

6 incomplete squares

The area of the irregular shape is *more* than 6 squares but *less* than 6 + 6 or 12 squares. It is between 6 and 12 squares. It is *about* 8 squares.

This last statement, "about 8 squares," is based on the judgment that the partial squares add up to approximately 2 complete squares. The symbol for "approximately equal" is ≈ .

Approximations for other shapes on T24:

Top row	A > 4 sq. u. A < 10 sq. u. A ≈ 7 sq. u.	A > 4 sq. u. A < 12 sq. u. A ≈ 8 sq. u.	A > 2 sq. u. A < 6 sq. u. A ≈ 4 sq. u.	A > 3 sq. u. A < 17 sq. u. A ≈ 9 sq. u.
Middle row	A > 3 sq. u. A < 10 sq. u. A ≈ 7 sq. u.	A > 4 sq. u. A < 6 sq. u. A ≈ 5 sq. u.		
Bottom row	A > 8 sq. u. A < 22 sq. u. A ≈ 13 sq. u.	A > 5 sq. u. A < 17 sq. u. A ≈ 10 sq. u.	A > 8 sq. u. A < 20 sq. u. A ≈ 12 sq. u.	

Perhaps it will occur to some child that the smaller the square unit of measure, the more accurate the approximation. The accuracy of the measurement of irregular shapes varies in proportion to the size of the unit of measure chosen.

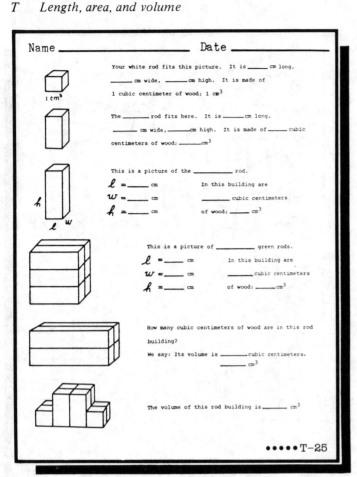

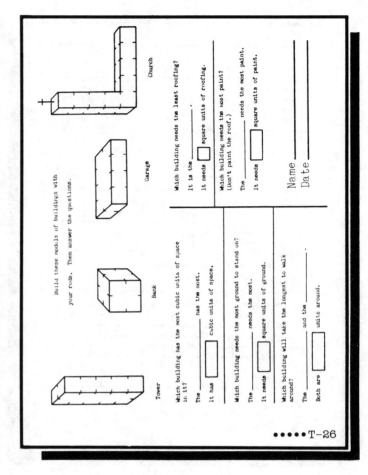

• • • • • T-25

• • • • • T25

Preliminary play with volume

1 Make a rod train out of a white, a red, a green, and a black rod. How many white rods is the train equal to? [13 white rods.]

Each white rod is the size of a cubic centimeter. How many cubic centimeters is the train equal to? [13 cubic centimeters.]

2 Now take the same rods and build any design with them. How many cubic centimeters of wood are in your design? [13 cubic centimeters.]

Build some other designs (using other rods) made out of 13 cubic centimeters of wood.

3 Build a solid box with some rods. How long is your box? How wide is your box? How high is your box? Let's write it down:

$$l = \square \text{ cm.}$$
$$w = \bigcirc \text{ cm.}$$
$$h = \triangle \text{ cm.}$$

How many cubic centimeters of wood is your box made of? (How many white cubes would it take to make your box?)

• • • • • T26

Answers

1 The tower has the most cubic units of space in it. It has 10 cubic units of space.

2 The garage needs the most ground to stand on. It needs 8 square units of ground.

3 The garage and the church take the longest to walk around. The garage and the church are both 12 units around.

4 The tower needs the least roofing. It needs 2 square units of roofing.

5 The tower needs the most paint. It needs 30 square units of paint.

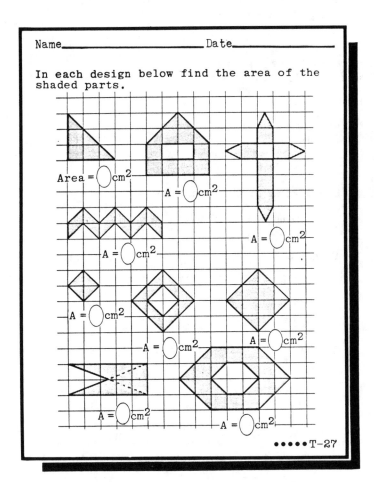

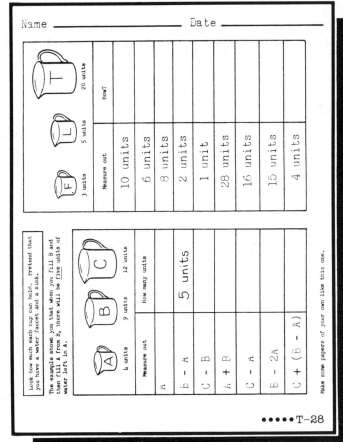

·····T28

The idea presented on this lab sheet may be used as a quick chalk-board game. The number of units each container holds is arbitrary.

There are many ways in which several of these quantities can be measured out. Because the pitchers are unmarked, we cannot say: "We fill a pitcher half full!"

Let's improvise a story to go with the chart on the right.

Teacher: Here is a water faucet, a sink, and three pitchers. Bring me exactly 10 units of water.

F	L	T
3 units	5 units	20 units

Bill: I fill L and pour it into the empty pitcher T. Then I fill L again and pour it into T. $2 \times L = 10$ units.

Karen: I fill T. Then I fill L from T twice and I have 10 units left in T. $T - (2 \times L) = 10$ units.

Answers

Following are solutions to the remaining problems on the right side of the page.

6 units:	2F (in T)
8 units:	F + L (in T)
2 units:	L − F
1 unit:	T − (3F + 2L) *or* 2L − 3F *or* 2F − L
28 units:	T + L + F
16 units:	2L + 2F
15 units:	T − L *or* 3L *or* 5F
4 units:	2L − 2F *or* 3F − L

Don't forget to let the children make up some lab sheets like these.

U Series and progressions

Factorial numbers and permutations

These comments are for the teacher only and are not to be shared in any way with children. The teacher needs to use her judgment as to how much of this she will interpret to the class. (Section P, Squaring, is also pertinent to the topic of series and progressions.

1 The summation of the successive integers equals the *triangle numbers*.

$$1 = 1$$
$$1 + 2 = 3$$
$$1 + 2 + 3 = 6$$
$$1 + 2 + 3 + 4 = 10$$

the triangle numbers

2 The product of the successive integers equals the *factorial numbers*.

$$2! = 1 \times 2 = 2$$
$$3! = 1 \times 2 \times 3 = 6$$
$$4! = 1 \times 2 \times 3 \times 4 = 24$$
$$5! = 1 \times 2 \times 3 \times 4 \times 5 = 120$$

This is a fast way for numbers to grow, as children easily see.

3 The summation of the successive odd numbers equals the *square numbers*.

$$1 = 1^2$$
$$1 + 3 = 4 = 2^2$$
$$1 + 3 + 5 = 9 = 3^2$$

4 Another pattern which produces the square numbers is shown. How is it related to item 3?

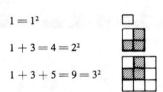

1
2 + 2
3 + 3 + 3
etc.

A table of the preceding						
	1st	2nd	3rd	4th	5th	6th
Triangles	1	3	6	10	15	21
Factorials		2	6	24	120	720
Squares	1	4	9	16	25	36

a. Which number in the table is both a square number and a triangle number? [1]

b. Which number belongs to the factorial numbers and the triangle numbers? [6]

Using rods to show factorial numbers

Let us illustrate how we produce the series of factorial numbers by using rods.

1 In how many ways can we put a white rod and a red rod in a row?

Answer: 2 things, 1×2 ways, $1 \times 2 = 2$.

2 In how many ways can we put a white rod, a red rod, and a light green rod in a row?

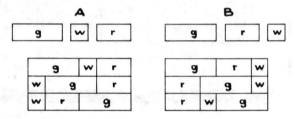

Answer: 3 things, 2×3 ways, $1 \times 2 \times 3 = 6$.

3 We now add a fourth rod (purple) to the previous 3-rod patterns and get the following 4-rod patterns:

a.   wrg   *p*wrg   4 new patterns
              w*p*rg
              wr*p*g
              wrg*p*

b.   wgr   *p*wgr   4 new patterns
              w*p*gr
              wg*p*r
              wgr*p*

c.   rwg   *p*rwg   4 new patterns
              r*p*wg
              rw*p*g
              rwg*p*

d.   rgw   *p*rgw   4 new patterns
              r*p*gw
              rg*p*w
              rgw*p*

e.   gwr   *p*gwr   4 new patterns
                              g*p*wr
                              gw*p*r
                              gwr*p*

f.   grw   *p*grw   4 new patterns
                              g*p*rw
                              gr*p*w
                              grw*p*

Totals: From 6 patterns with three rods we get 24 patterns with four rods.

$$1 \times 2 \times 3 \times 4 = 24, \text{ or } 4! = 24$$

From each of the 24 four-rod patterns we can get 5 new patterns by inserting the yellow rod in all possible ways.

$$5! = (1 \times 2 \times 3 \times 4) \times \mathbf{5} = 120$$

The total number of possibilities of rearrangements for $\square$ number of things will always be $\square$! or

$$1 \times 2 \times 3 \times \ldots \times \square$$

We can do this same thing with 2-digit, 3-digit, 4-digit numerals or letters of the alphabet. Using the numerals '1' and '2' we get the following:

$$\left.\begin{matrix} 12 \\ 21 \end{matrix}\right\}\quad 1 \times 2 \text{ numerals}$$

With the numerals '1,' '2,' '3' we get the following:

$$\left.\begin{matrix} 123 \\ 132 \\ 213 \\ 231 \\ 312 \\ 321 \end{matrix}\right\}\quad 1 \times 2 \times 3 \text{ numerals}$$

With '1', '2', '3', '4' we will get $1 \times 2 \times 3 \times 4$ possibilities or 24 possibilities. These 24 possibilities are also all the possible ways four people can sit in these four chairs: ⋏⋏⋏⋏.

Progressions on the number line

Addition of zero

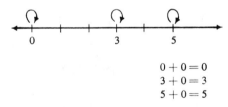

$$\begin{aligned} 0 + 0 &= 0 \\ 3 + 0 &= 3 \\ 5 + 0 &= 5 \end{aligned}$$

Doubling

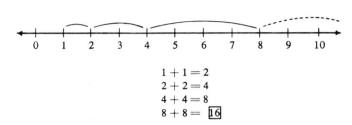

$$\begin{aligned} 1 + 1 &= 2 \\ 2 + 2 &= 4 \\ 4 + 4 &= 8 \\ 8 + 8 &= \boxed{16} \end{aligned}$$

Arithmetic series: adding three

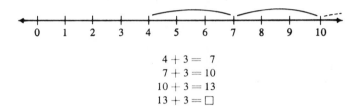

$$\begin{aligned} 4 + 3 &= 7 \\ 7 + 3 &= 10 \\ 10 + 3 &= 13 \\ 13 + 3 &= \square \end{aligned}$$

Triangle series: adding one more number each successive step

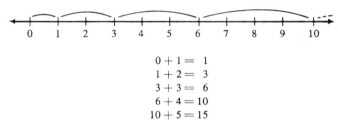

$$\begin{aligned} 0 + 1 &= 1 \\ 1 + 2 &= 3 \\ 3 + 3 &= 6 \\ 6 + 4 &= 10 \\ 10 + 5 &= 15 \end{aligned}$$

Arbitrary selection: no discernible pattern

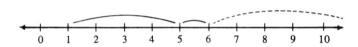

Triangle numbers: preliminary experiences

You may begin work with triangle numbers by building towers of the following types with white rods or any other set of cubes:

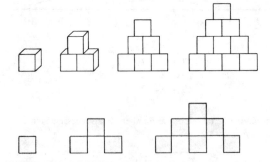

We can also do this with discs (pennies, etc.)

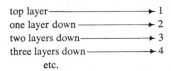

After such model-making, we may ask the following questions:
How many blocks are there in each tower?

1	3	6	10	15	?
block	blocks	blocks	blocks	blocks	blocks

How many blocks are there in each separate layer of a tower?

top layer $\longrightarrow$ 1
one layer down $\longrightarrow$ 2
two layers down $\longrightarrow$ 3
three layers down $\longrightarrow$ 4
etc.

How many blocks are in the whole tower?

T_1 (Triangle Tower One) $= 1$
T_2 (Triangle Tower Two) $= 2 + 1$
T_3 (Triangle Tower Three) $= 3 + 2 + 1$
$T_7 = 7 + 6 + 5 + 4 + 3 + 2 + 1$

We can now build triangle towers with rods of various lengths:

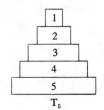

How many white rods? [15.]

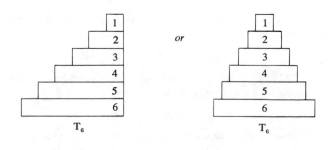

Now build rod tower T_7. How many white rods in T_7?

Now, have the children build a whole family of T towers.

Here is a new series of questions:
What kind of tower can we build out of T_1 and T_2 used together?

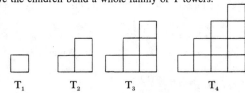

$T_1 \quad + \quad T_2 \quad = \quad S_2$ (Square Tower Two)

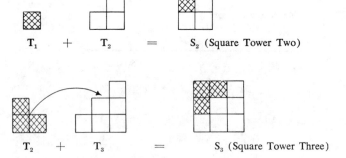

$T_2 \quad + \quad T_3 \quad = \quad S_3$ (Square Tower Three)

Will it work for $T_3 + T_4$ $(T_3 + T_4 = S_4)$
$$T_4 + T_5$$
$$T_6 + T_7$$
$$T_6 + T_5$$

$T_2 + T_3 = (1 + 2) + (1 + 2 + 3) = \square$
$T_3 + T_4 = (1 + 2 + 3) + (1 + 2 + 3 + 4) = \square$

Now the children should be ready to work on lab sheets.

308

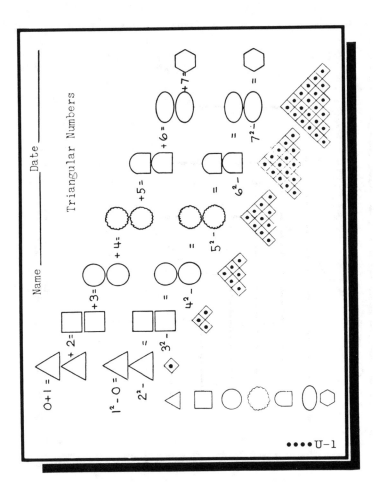

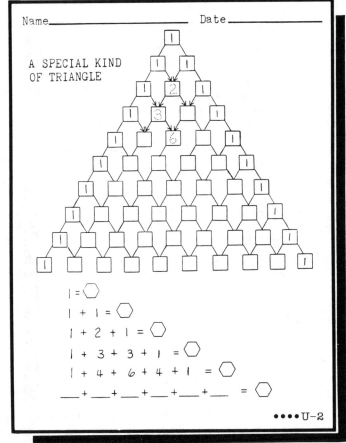

• • • • U1

On this lab sheet, two like frames in a column stand for the same number.

Thus, $0 + 1 = \triangle 1$

$$\triangle 1 + 2 = \boxed{3}$$

$$\boxed{3} + 3 = \bigcirc 6$$

$$\bigcirc 6 + 4 = \bigcirc 10 \quad \text{etc.}$$

$$\bigcirc 10$$

After much trial and error, we have found that children understand this way of presenting a progression without words. The pattern seems to reveal itself easily. The diagrams at the bottom of the sheet reinforce visually the numerical patterns presented above.

Let us look at the relationship between the square numbers 1, 4, 9, 16, 25, . . . and the triangle numbers 1, 3, 6, 10, 15, . . .

Square numbers		Triangular numbers	
1	$\square_1$	1	$\triangle_1$
4	$\square_2$	3	$\triangle_2$
9	$\square_3$	6	$\triangle_3$
16	$\square_4$	10	$\triangle_4$
25	$\square_5$	15	$\triangle_5$
36	$\square_6$	21	$\triangle_6$
49	$\square_7$	28	$\triangle_7$

$$\square_2 - \triangle_1 = \triangle_2 \qquad\qquad \triangle_1 + \triangle_2 = \square_2$$
$$\square_3 - \triangle_2 = \triangle_3 \quad \text{or} \quad \triangle_2 + \triangle_3 = \square_3$$
$$\square_4 - \triangle_3 = \triangle_4 \qquad\qquad \triangle_3 + \triangle_4 = \square_4$$

• • • • U2
Pascal's Triangle

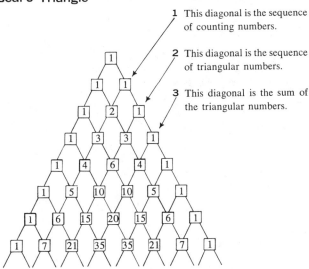

1 This diagonal is the sequence of counting numbers.

2 This diagonal is the sequence of triangular numbers.

3 This diagonal is the sum of the triangular numbers.

What kind of numbers do we get when we add any two adjacent numbers in diagonal 1? [Odd numbers.]

What kind of numbers do we get when we add any two adjacent numbers in diagonal 2? [Square numbers, or perfect squares.]

What are the sums of the numbers in the horizontal rows? [Powers of 2.]   What will be the sum of the numbers in the tenth row?

Note: Find the significance of the sequence of numbers in the horizontal rows by looking up Pascal's Triangle in a mathematics book.

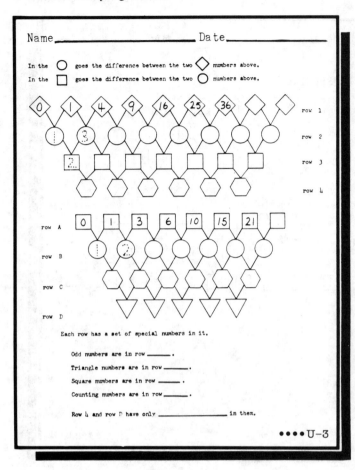

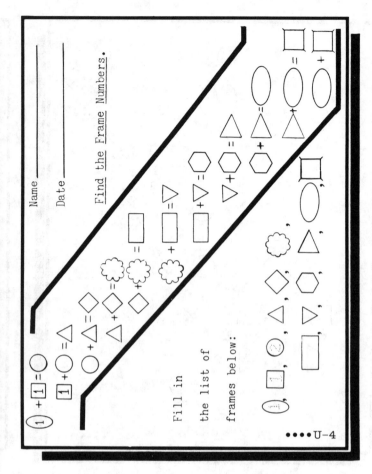

•••• U3

Difference of differences

Top diagram

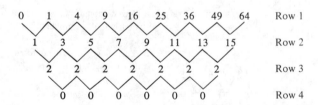

0	1	4	9	16	25	36	49	64	Row 1
1	3	5	7	9	11	13	15		Row 2
2	2	2	2	2	2	2			Row 3
0	0	0	0	0	0				Row 4

Bottom diagram

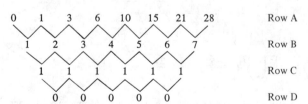

0	1	3	6	10	15	21	28	Row A
1	2	3	4	5	6	7		Row B
1	1	1	1	1	1			Row C
0	0	0	0	0				Row D

Answers

Odd numbers are in row 2.
Triangle numbers are in row A.
Square numbers are in row 1.
Counting numbers are in row B.
Row 4 and row D have only zeros in them.

•••• U4

Fibonacci series

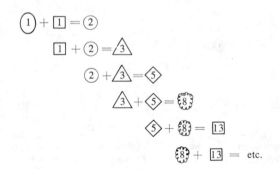

This series of numbers is the Fibonacci series. The next number is always the sum of the previous two numbers.

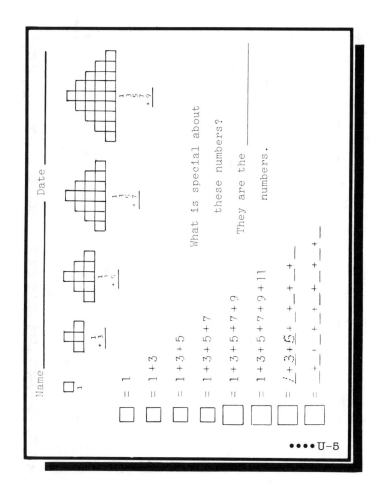

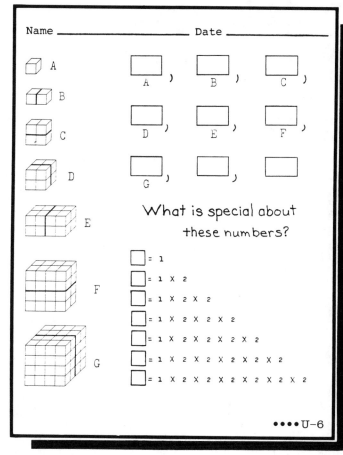

···· **U5**
Square numbers

Square numbers are the summation of the odd integers beginning with 1.

Three squared equals the summation of the first *three* odd numbers.
Four squared equals the summation of the first *four* odd numbers.
Five squared equals the summation of the first *five* odd numbers.

···· **U6**
Doubling or the powers of 2

Children can build this series with rods.

white rod	red rod	two red rods	four red rods	four purple rods	eight purple rods

$$1 = 1$$
$$2 = 1 \times 2$$
$$4 = (1 \times 2) \times 2$$
$$8 = (1 \times 2 \times 2) \times 2$$
$$16 = (1 \times 2 \times 2 \times 2) \times 2$$
etc.

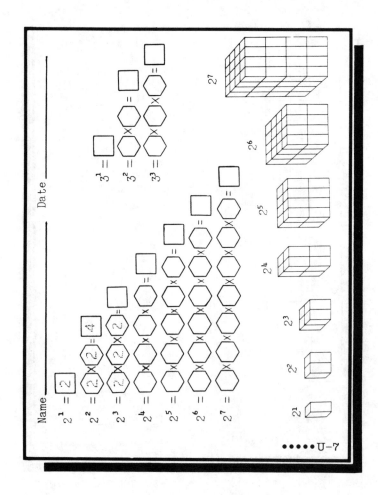

Preliminary activity

Make up a lab sheet for your class similar to the following:

Continue the series:

$(1, 10), (2, 20), (3, \_\_), (\_\_, \_\_), (\_\_, \_\_), (\_\_, \_\_)$
$(1, 1\frac{1}{2}), (2, 3), (3, 4\frac{1}{2}), (4, \_\_), (\_\_, \_\_), (\_\_, \_\_)$
$(1, 1), (2, 4), (3, 9), (4, \_\_), (\_\_, \_\_), (\_\_, \_\_)$

Now you begin some series. Let a friend finish them.

$(\_\_, \_\_), (\_\_, \_\_), (\_\_, \_\_), (\_\_, \_\_), (\_\_, \_\_), (\_\_, \_\_)$

$(\_\_, \_\_), (\_\_, \_\_), (\_\_, \_\_), (\_\_, \_\_), (\_\_, \_\_), (\_\_, \_\_)$

$(\_\_, \_\_), (\_\_, \_\_), (\_\_, \_\_), (\_\_, \_\_), (\_\_, \_\_), (\_\_, \_\_)$

$(1, 10), (2, 20), (3, \square)$ is the beginning of a series of equivalent ratios, or equivalent fractions.

Example: $\frac{1}{10} = \frac{2}{20} = \frac{3}{30} = \frac{4}{40}$

The following ordered pairs of numbers satisfy the equation $\triangle = 10\square$.

$\square$	$\triangle$
1	10
2	20
3	30

$(1, 1\frac{1}{2}), (2, 3), (3, 4\frac{1}{2})$ is part of a series of equivalent fractions, or equivalent ratios where $\triangle = \frac{3\square}{2}$ (The second number is $1\frac{1}{2}$ times the first number.)

$(1, 1), (2, 4), (3, 9), (4, 16)$ is part of a series where $\triangle = \square^2$.

· · · · · U7

On lab sheet U7 the notation 2^1, 2^2, 2^3, 2^4, etc., is introduced.

$$2^1 = 2$$
$$2^2 = 2 \times 2$$
$$2^3 = 2 \times 2 \times 2$$

The exponents [1, 2, 3,] refer to how many times 2 is used as a factor.

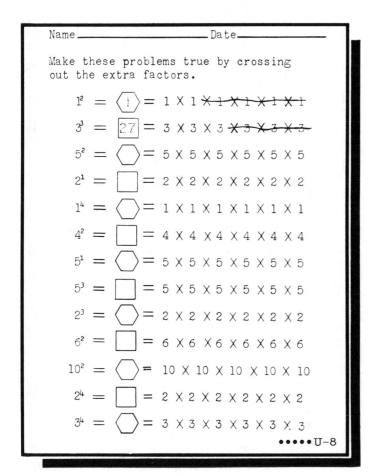

Name_____ Date_____

Make these problems true by crossing out the extra factors.

1^2 = ⟨1⟩ = 1 X 1 X̶ ̶1̶ ̶X̶ ̶1̶ ̶X̶ ̶1̶ ̶X̶ ̶1

3^3 = 27 = 3 X 3 X 3 X̶ ̶3̶ ̶X̶ ̶3̶ ̶X̶ ̶3

5^2 = ⬡ = 5 X 5 X 5 X 5 X 5 X 5

2^1 = ▢ = 2 X 2 X 2 X 2 X 2 X 2

1^4 = ⬡ = 1 X 1 X 1 X 1 X 1 X 1

4^2 = ▢ = 4 X 4 X 4 X 4 X 4 X 4

5^1 = ⬡ = 5 X 5 X 5 X 5 X 5 X 5

5^3 = ▢ = 5 X 5 X 5 X 5 X 5 X 5

2^3 = ⬡ = 2 X 2 X 2 X 2 X 2 X 2

6^2 = ▢ = 6 X 6 X 6 X 6 X 6 X 6

10^2 = ⬡ = 10 X 10 X 10 X 10 X 10

2^4 = ▢ = 2 X 2 X 2 X 2 X 2 X 2

3^4 = ⬡ = 3 X 3 X 3 X 3 X 3 X 3

•••••U-8

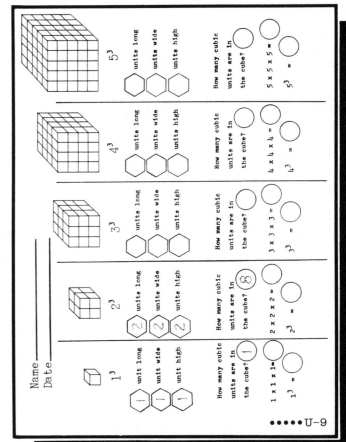

Name
Date

•••••U-9

••••• U8–U10

On U8 the various notations we have used for a number are summarized.

$$3^3 = \boxed{27} = 3 \times 3 \times 3$$
$$5^2 = \langle 25 \rangle = 5 \times 5$$
etc.

3^3 is called "three cubed" or "three to the third power."
5^2 is "five squared" or "five to the second power."
2^4 is "two to the fourth power."

Lab sheet U9 is self-explanatory. You can build a model of this progression with rods.

Lab sheet U10 concentrates on the powers of ten. This is very important in the concept of place value.

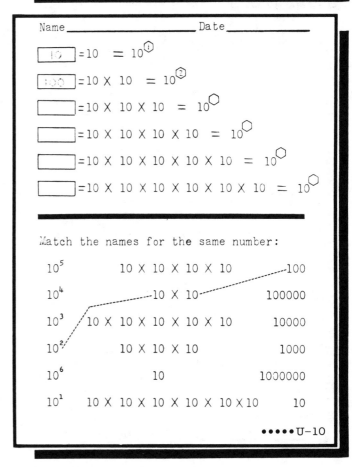

Name_____ Date_____

▭10 =10 = $10^{①}$

▭100 =10 X 10 = $10^{②}$

▭ =10 X 10 X 10 = $10^{⬡}$

▭ =10 X 10 X 10 X 10 = $10^{⬡}$

▭ =10 X 10 X 10 X 10 X 10 = $10^{⬡}$

▭ =10 X 10 X 10 X 10 X 10 X 10 = $10^{⬡}$

Match the names for the same number:

10^5 10 X 10 X 10 X 10   100

10^4 10 X 10   100000

10^3 10 X 10 X 10 X 10 X 10   10000

10^2 10 X 10 X 10   1000

10^6 10   1000000

10^1 10 X 10 X 10 X 10 X 10 X 10   10

•••••U-10

313

· · · · · U11
Points and lines

The work on lab sheet U11 represents a great deal of playful observation if developed slowly. It combines geometric thinking and patterning with the development of progressions, showing the unity of several aspects of mathematics. Let us illustrate this.

2 points, 1 line

1 line from A		all lines together
1 line	=	1 line

3 points, 3 lines

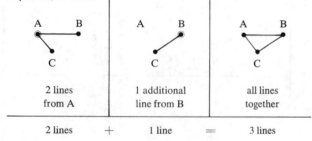

2 lines from A		1 additional line from B		all lines together
2 lines	+	1 line	=	3 lines

4 points, 6 lines

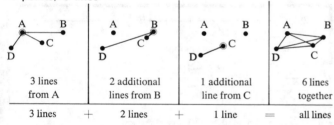

3 lines from A		2 additional lines from B		1 additional line from C		6 lines together
3 lines	+	2 lines	+	1 line	=	all lines

5 points, 10 lines

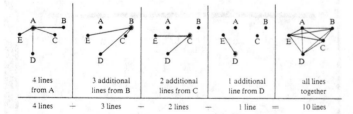

4 lines from A	3 additional lines from B	2 additional lines from C	1 additional line from D	all lines together
4 lines	+ 3 lines	+ 2 lines	+ 1 line	= 10 lines

The number of lines is always a triangular number.

Each point can be connected by one shortest path with every other point, but this will draw each path twice. Therefore, we must count only one-half of the paths.

2 points, 1 line

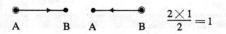

$$\frac{2 \times 1}{2} = 1$$

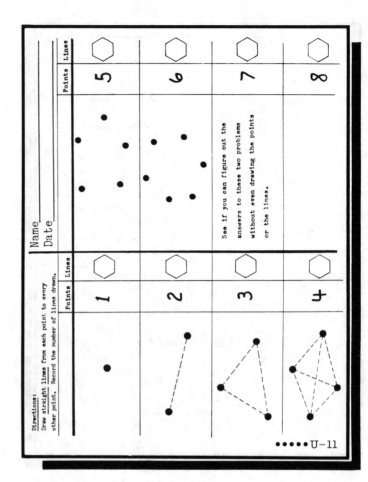

3 points, 3 lines

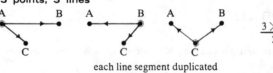

each line segment duplicated

$$\frac{3 \times 2}{2} = 3$$

4 points, 6 lines

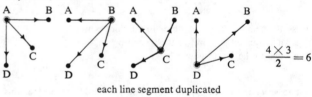

each line segment duplicated

$$\frac{4 \times 3}{2} = 6$$

5 points, 10 lines

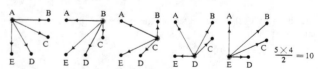

each line segment duplicated

$$\frac{5 \times 4}{2} = 10$$

To get the number of lines, one must:
a. count the number of points;
b. multiply by one less than that number; and
c. divide the product by two.

$$\frac{\square \times (\square - 1)}{2}$$

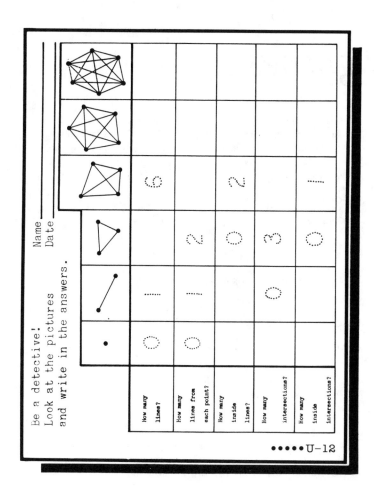

····· U12

Answers

	•	╲•	◁	⊠	⬠	⬡	
1st row:	0	1	3	6	10	15	triangular numbers
2nd row:	0	1	2	3	4	5	counting numbers
3rd row:	0	0	0	2	5	9	diagonals
4th row:	0	0	3	5	10	21	
5th row:	0	0	0	1	5	15	

V Grid and arrow games

The grid and arrow games, a favorite of children, demand concentrated thinking under interesting conditions.

This topic should be developed largely through chalkboard work. The lab sheets are only a small part of the activity on grids with arrows. However, many children can puzzle out possible answers, even when given only one hint such as:

"On this chart [see Array 1 below], 16 $\downarrow$ = 26. Follow this with your finger on the chart." Many children will be able to do the remaining problems without further explanation:

16 → = 17   16 ← = 15   16 ↑ = 6

16 ↗ = 7   16 ↙ = 25   16 ↖ = 5

16 ↘ = 27

The teacher should do very little talking. In fact more can be accomplished in 20 minutes of pantomine than with long verbal explanations.

How to play the game

Procedure: The teacher puts *one* of the following arrays of numerals on the chalkboard. Many other arrays may be used: for example, arrays of even numbers only, odd numbers only, multiples of three, etc.

Array 1

1	2	3	4	5	6	7	8	9	10
11	12	13	14	15	16	17	18	19	20
21	22	23	24	25	26	27	28	29	30

Array 2

30	31	32	33	34	35	36	37	38	39
20	21	22	23	24	25	26	27	28	29
10	11	12	13	14	15	16	17	18	19
1	2	3	4	5	6	7	8	9

Array 3

25	24	23	22	21
20	19	18	17	16
15	14	13	12	11
10	9	8	7	6
5	4	3	2	1

The teacher writes 18 $\downarrow$ on the board and tells the children, "Here is a secret code for a number on the chart. Which number might it be?"

Answer

for Array 1   18 $\downarrow$ = 28

for Array 2   18 $\downarrow$ = 8

for Array 3   18 $\downarrow$ = 13

If children give answers other than those expected, the teacher simply writes the correct arrow notation for the answer the child gave instead of saying that the child is "wrong." Then she asks again. For example, using Array 1,

Teacher: 18 $\downarrow$ = □

Child: 18 $\downarrow$ = 18

Teacher: 18 = 8 $\downarrow$

18 $\downarrow$ = □

Child: 19

Teacher: 19 = 18 →

18 $\downarrow$ = □

Child: 18 $\downarrow$ = 28

Teacher: Right, 18 $\downarrow$ = 28. Now we have an arrow code for 18, 19, and 28.

Writing the following on the board and referring to Array 1, the teacher asks, "What would these mean?"

28 $\downarrow$ = □   16 $\downarrow$ = □   34 $\downarrow$ = □

15 → = □   21 → = □   55 → = □

44 ← = □   16 ← = □   etc.

Combinations of arrows are introduced.

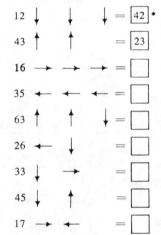

12 $\downarrow$ $\downarrow$ $\downarrow$ = 42 *

43 ↑ ↑ = 23

16 → → → = □

35 ← ← ← = □

63 ↑ ↑ ↓ = □

26 ← ↓ = □

33 ↓ → = □

45 ↓ ↑ = □

17 → ← = □

New kinds of arrows are introduced.

52 ↗ = 43 *

17 ↙ = 26

---

*All answers are based on the use of Array 1.

Computation problems may be tried.

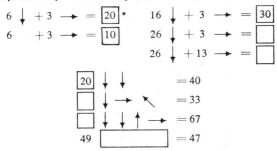

In the last problem, put arrows in the rectangle to complete the equation.

Children's questions and observations

After several arrow games are played with the whole class, the children are ready for some of the lab sheets. Following are samples of the kinds of questions children ask and some of the observations they have made.

1 On Array 1 how do we get from 10 (at the end of a row) to 11? Can we only go the long way backward in this direction (←)? What does 10 → mean?

Answer: The class can make up its own rules about such end points. 10 → , 20 → , etc., can be ruled out as "nonsense." Or, 10 → can be said to mean: "Go back to the beginning of the row" because the chart curves back and is fastened like a cylinder. There are many other possibilities which are acceptable, but they must be simple and logical.

2 If we extend Array 1 upward, we can form a mental image of negative numbers. However, the first row above 1 to 10 does not start with −11. Children are surprised when the "right way" turns out to be:

```
−19 −18 −17 −16 −15 −14 −13 −12 −11 −10
 −9  −8  −7  −6  −5  −4  −3  −2  −1   0
  1   2   3   4   5   6   7   8   9  10
 11  12  13  14  15  16  17  18  19  20
```

3 Some moves are "waste of time" moves because they get you nowhere. For example,

15 → ←   = 15
15 → ↑ ← ↓   = 15
15 ↗ ↙   = 15
15 ↗ ↓ ←   = 15
15 ↖ ↘   = 15

These are really *moves* and their *inverse moves,* as in the operations of arithmetic.

15 + 1 = 16   16 − 1 = 15

4 Some moves are the same as other moves made in a different order. Both moves land at the same place.

7 ↓ → → = 7 → → ↓
68 ↘ → ↓ = 68 ↓ → ↘

These are illustrations of the commutative principle.

$$7 + 10 + 1 + 1 = 7 + 1 + 1 + 10$$

5 We can think of arrows as having numerical values. Thus, on Array 1,

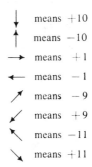

↓ means +10
↑ means −10
→ means +1
← means −1
↗ means −9
↙ means +9
↖ means −11
↘ means +11

6 When we begin on an even number on our array and use ↑ or ↓ moves only, we will land on even numbers.

↓		↓
44	45	46
54	55	56
64	65	66
↑		↑

7 Is there always only *one* shortest way to go from a number to another number? For example:

a. From 5 to 6, the shortest way is 5 →
b. From 18 to 38 there are 3 "two-arrow" paths:

18 ↓↓   18 ↗↘   18 ↘↗

Is one of them *shorter* than the other 2 paths, or are they all the same?

8 When you look at an arrow code with several arrows, mentally cross out all the "waste of time" arrows. Then it is easy to figure out.

31 ↓ → ↗ ← = 31 →
53 ↘ ↓ ↖ ↓ ↑ → = 53 ↘

Name_____ Date_____

Arrow Games

1	2	3	4	5	6	7	8	9	10
11	12	13	14	15	16	17	18	19	20
21	22	23	24	25	26	27	28	29	30
31	32	33	34	35	36	37	38	39	40
41	42	43	44	45	46	47	48	49	50
51	52	53	54	55	56	57	58	59	60
61	62	63	64	65	66	67	68	69	70
71	72	73	74	75	76	77	78	79	80
81	82	83	84	85	86	87	88	89	90
91	92	93	94	95	96	97	98	99	100

Look at the 1-100 number chart when you do these problems.

10 ↓ = ☐   10 ↓↓ = ☐   10 ↓↓↓ = ☐

20 ↓ = ☐   20 ↓↓ = ☐   20 ↓↓↓ = ☐

30 ↓ = ☐   30 ↓↓ = ☐   30 ↓↓↓ = ☐

80 ↓ = ☐   80 ↓↓ = ☐   80 ↓↓↓ = ☐

Make up your own.

•••V-1

Name_____ Date_____

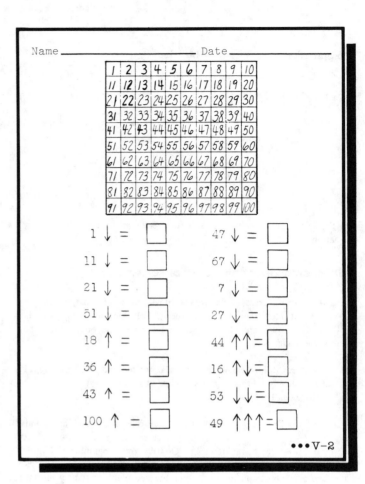

1	2	3	4	5	6	7	8	9	10
11	12	13	14	15	16	17	18	19	20
21	22	23	24	25	26	27	28	29	30
31	32	33	34	35	36	37	38	39	40
41	42	43	44	45	46	47	48	49	50
51	52	53	54	55	56	57	58	59	60
61	62	63	64	65	66	67	68	69	70
71	72	73	74	75	76	77	78	79	80
81	82	83	84	85	86	87	88	89	90
91	92	93	94	95	96	97	98	99	100

1 ↓ = ☐   47 ↓ = ☐

11 ↓ = ☐   67 ↓ = ☐

21 ↓ = ☐   7 ↓ = ☐

51 ↓ = ☐   27 ↓ = ☐

18 ↑ = ☐   44 ↑↑ = ☐

36 ↑ = ☐   16 ↑↓ = ☐

43 ↑ = ☐   53 ↓↓ = ☐

100 ↑ = ☐   49 ↑↑↑ = ☐

•••V-2

••• V1–V4

These grid and arrow activities provide children with practice in adding and subtracting special numbers. The children are to start at the given number and make whatever moves are indicated by the arrows —moving one space for each arrow in the direction that the arrow is pointing. For example, 10↓ = ☐20☐ . On the 10x10 one hundred chart, the arrow moves are equivalent to the following arithmetical operations:

↓	adding 10
↑	subtracting 10
→	adding 1
←	subtracting 1
↘	adding 11
↙	adding 9
↖	subtracting 11
↗	subtracting 9

These problems make good drill exercises in adding and subtracting 9's, 10's and 11's.

Name_____ Date_____

Arrow Games

1	2	3	4	5	6	7	8	9	10
11	12	13	14	15	16	17	18	19	20
21	22	23	24	25	26	27	28	29	30
31	32	33	34	35	36	37	38	39	40
41	42	43	44	45	46	47	48	49	50
51	52	53	54	55	56	57	58	59	60
61	62	63	64	65	66	67	68	69	70
71	72	73	74	75	76	77	78	79	80
81	82	83	84	85	86	87	88	89	90
91	92	93	94	95	96	97	98	99	100

Look at the 1-100 number chart.

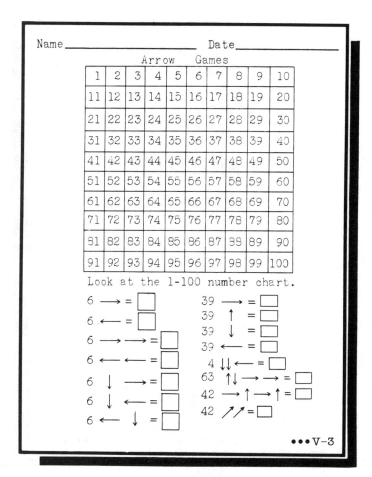

6 → = ☐   39 → = ☐

6 ← = ☐   39 ↑ = ☐

6 → → = ☐   39 ↓ = ☐

6 ← ← = ☐   39 ← = ☐

6 ↓ → = ☐   4 ↓↓ ← = ☐

6 ↓ ← = ☐   63 ↑↓ → → = ☐

6 ← ↓ = ☐   42 → ↑ → ↑ = ☐

               42 ↗↗ = ☐

●●●V-3

Name _____ Date_____

ARROW GAMES

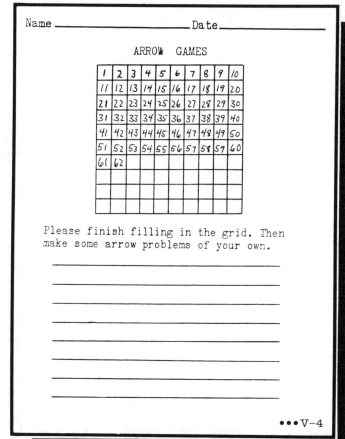

1	2	3	4	5	6	7	8	9	10
11	12	13	14	15	16	17	18	19	20
21	22	23	24	25	26	27	28	29	30
31	32	33	34	35	36	37	38	39	40
41	42	43	44	45	46	47	48	49	50
51	52	53	54	55	56	57	58	59	60
61	62								

Please finish filling in the grid. Then make some arrow problems of your own.

_____

_____

_____

_____

_____

_____

_____

_____

●●●V-4

●●● V5

Solutions

6 [↘ ↘] = 28   has *many* solutions. The simplest solution is indicated.

49 ↓ ↓ = 69

6 → → → = 9

43 ↗ ↑ = 24

100 [↖ ↖ ↘] = 67   has *many* solutions. The simplest solution is indicated.

50 ↓ ↑ ↗ ↗ ↙ ↔ ← = 49

27 ↗ → → ↓ ← ↓ ↙ = 48

4 ↓ ↘ ↘ → → ↓ ↙ = 57

Name_____ Date_____

Arrow Games

1	2	3	4	5	6	7	8	9	10
11	12	13	14	15	16	17	18	19	20
21	22	23	24	25	26	27	28	29	30
31	32	33	34	35	36	37	38	39	40
41	42	43	44	45	46	47	48	49	50
51	52	53	54	55	56	57	58	59	60
61	62	63	64	65	66	67	68	69	70
71	72	73	74	75	76	77	78	79	80
81	82	83	84	85	86	87	88	89	90
91	92	93	94	95	96	97	98	99	100

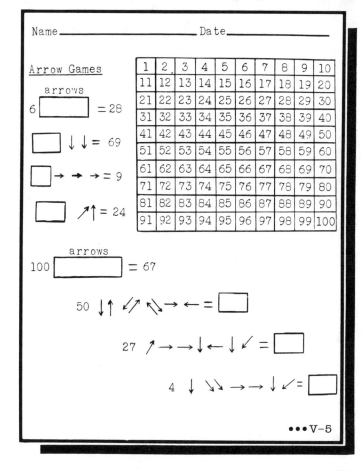

arrows

6 [   ] = 28

[☐] ↓ ↓ = 69

[☐] → → → = 9

[☐] ↗ ↑ = 24

arrows

100 [   ] = 67

50 ↓↑ ↙↗ ↘↖ → ← = ☐

27 ↗ → → ↓ ← ↓ ↙ = ☐

4 ↓ ↘↘ → → ↓ ↙ = ☐

●●●V-5

Name_____ Date_____

Arrow Games

Draw a line from the arrow names for 53
to the big ⑤③ . Make some arrow names
for 53 of your own.

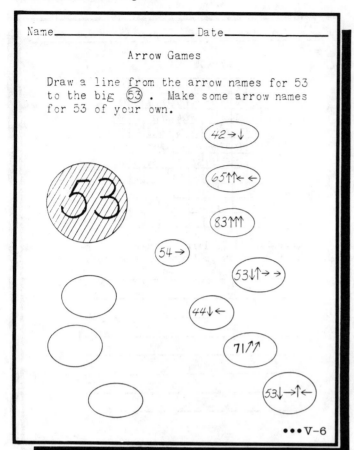

•••V–6

Name _____ Date _____

ARROW GAMES

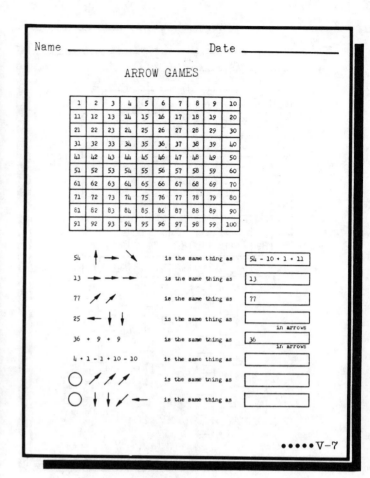

•••••V–7

•••••**V7**

Solutions

13 → → → = 13 + 1 + 1 + 1 = 16

77 ⤢⤢   = 77 − 9 − 9 = 59

25 ← ↓ ↓ = 25 − 1 + 10 + 10 = 44

36 + 9 + 9 = 36 ⤢⤢   = 54

4 + 1 − 1 + 10 − 10 = 4 → ← ↓ ↑   = 4

•••••**V8**

On any rectangular array, regardless of what numerals or pictures are
written in it, these simplifications of moves will be true. This page
then is no longer dependent on the 1–100 chart used on the previous
lab sheets.

••••••**V9**

Comments: Discuss with the children patterns they see on the chart.
Some of the patterns:

The numerals follow the diagonal pattern shown above.

The first row of numbers are the triangle numbers: 1, (1 + 2),
(1 + 2 + 3), (1 + 2 + 3 + 4), etc.

Second row: 2, (2 + 3), (2 + 3 + 4), (2 + 3 + 4 + 5), etc.

Third row: 4, (4 + 4), (4 + 4 + 5), (4 + 4 + 5 + 6), etc.

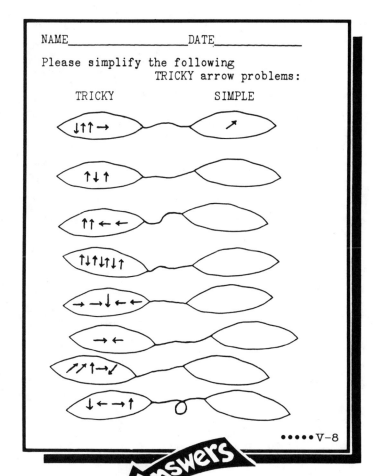

NAME_____DATE_____
Please simplify the following
  TRICKY arrow problems:

TRICKY   SIMPLE

•••••V-8

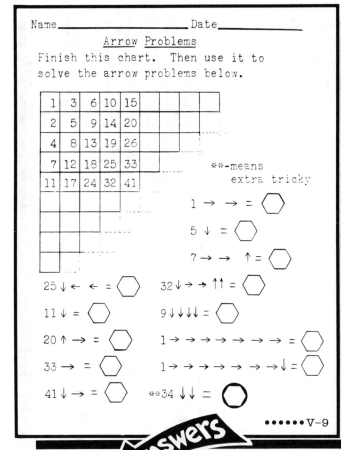

Name_____Date_____
Arrow Problems
Finish this chart. Then use it to
solve the arrow problems below.

1	3	6	10	15				
2	5	9	14	20				
4	8	13	19	26				
7	12	18	25	33				
11	17	24	32	41				

**-means
  extra tricky

1 → → = ⬡

5 ↓ = ⬡

7 → → ↑ = ⬡

25 ↓ ← ← = ⬡   32 ↓ → → ↑↑ = ⬡

11 ↓ = ◯   9 ↓↓↓↓ = ⬡

20 ↑ → = ⬡   1 → → → → → → → = ⬡

33 → = ⬡   1 → → → → → → → ↓ = ⬡

41 ↓ → = ⬡   **34 ↓↓ = ⬠

•••••••V-9

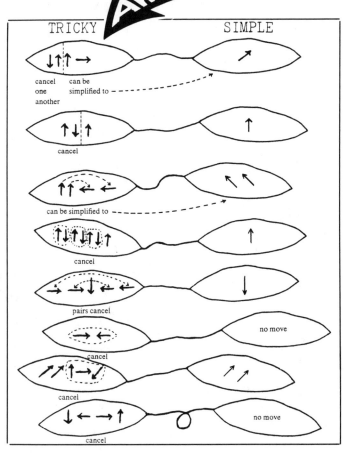

TRICKY   SIMPLE

•••••V-8 (Answers)

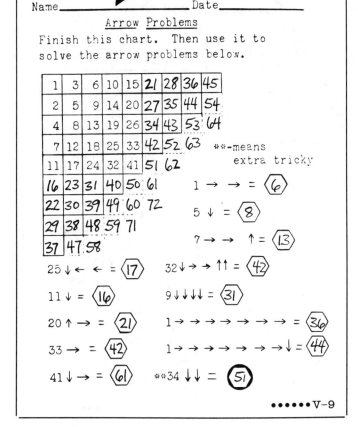

Name_____Date_____
Arrow Problems
Finish this chart. Then use it to
solve the arrow problems below.

1	3	6	10	15	21	28	36	45
2	5	9	14	20	27	35	44	54
4	8	13	19	26	34	43	53	64
7	12	18	25	33	42	52	63	
11	17	24	32	41	51	62		
16	23	31	40	50	61			
22	30	39	49	60	72			
29	38	48	59	71				
37	47	58						

**-means
  extra tricky

1 → → = ⟨6⟩

5 ↓ = ⟨8⟩

7 → → ↑ = ⟨13⟩

25 ↓ ← ← = ⟨17⟩   32 ↓ → → ↑↑ = ⟨42⟩

11 ↓ = ⟨16⟩   9 ↓↓↓↓ = ⟨31⟩

20 ↑ → = ⟨21⟩   1 → → → → → → → = ⟨36⟩

33 → = ⟨42⟩   1 → → → → → → → ↓ = ⟨44⟩

41 ↓ → = ⟨61⟩   **34 ↓↓ = ⟨51⟩

•••••••V-9

Name _____

Date _____

Finish filling
in this grid.

Then solve these
arrow problems.

3	0	1	2	3	
0		2	3	0	1
1	2	3	0		2
2	3			2	3
3	0	1	2	3	0
	1	2		0	1
	3	0			
			1		3

1 → ⬡

2 → ⬡

3 → ⬡

0 → ⬡

2 → → → → ⬡

3 → → → → ⬡

1 ↓↓↓↓ ⬡

⬡ ↓↓↓↓ 3

⬡ ↑↑↑↑ 0

2 → ↓ → ↓ ⬡

1 → ↓↓↓ ⬡

2 → ↑ ⬡

0 → ↑ → ↑ → ↑ ⬡

1 ← ↓ ← ↓ ⬡

3 ← ← ← ↓↓↓ ⬡

0 ↑↑↑↑ → → → → ⬡

2 ↑ ← ⬡

2 ↑↑ ← ← ⬡

2 ↑↑↑ ← ← ← ⬡

•••••• V-10

Answers

Name _____

Date _____

Finish filling
in this grid.

Then solve these
arrow problems.

3	0	1	2	3	0
0	1	2	3	0	1
1	2	3	0	1	2
2	3	0	1	2	3
3	0	1	2	3	0
0	1	2	3	0	1
1	2	3	0	1	2
2	3	0	1	2	3

1 → ⟨2⟩

2 → ⟨3⟩

3 → ⟨0⟩

0 → ⟨1⟩

2 → → → → ⟨2⟩

3 → → → → ⟨3⟩

1 ↓↓↓↓ ⟨1⟩

⟨3⟩ ↓↓↓↓ 3

⟨0⟩ ↑↑↑↑ 0

2 → ↓ → ↓ ⟨2⟩

1 → ↓↓↓ ⟨1⟩

2 → ↑ ⟨2⟩

0 → ↑ → ↑ → ↑ ⟨0⟩

1 ← ↓ ← ↓ ⟨1⟩

3 ← ← ← ↓↓↓ ⟨3⟩

0 ↑↑↑↑ → → → → ⟨0⟩

2 ↑ ← ⟨0⟩

2 ↑↑ ← ← ⟨2⟩

2 ↑↑↑ ← ← ← ⟨0⟩

•••••• V-10

W   Mapping

It seems to us that children need to go through the exercises of enlarging or reducing objects and observing the corresponding changes in their lengths, areas, and volumes. In order to read a map with insight, they need to become aware of families of similarly shaped things. They also need to have experience in building coordinate systems that will help them to locate places on maps.

These experiences are given on the lab sheets of Section W but the suggested preliminary activities are even more important.

Section R, Graphing Equations, and T, Length, Area, and Volume, are directly related to these activities.

In addition to the activities suggested on the following pages, children should also be given opportunities to make their own versions of maps of the schoolgrounds, streets they live on, their classroom, etc.

Building the concept of similarity

Preliminary activities

1   Feeling game
Display a large carton with a hole, containing an assortment of balls, cubes, rectangular prisms, triangular prisms, and solids of other shapes. The child is *shown* a sphere or a cube and asked to find by *feel only* (putting his hand into the carton without looking) the other objects with that shape.

2   Sorting game
Give children a large assortment of solids or paper cutouts and ask them to sort the objects according to like shape.

3   Drawing activity
Give children squared paper and ask them to draw a family of squares, a family of triangles, a family of arrows, or a family of houses.

4   Geoboard activities
Each child works with his own geoboard (geometry board) and colored rubber bands to make designs. (Construction of the geoboard is described in *Part I: Notes to Teachers, Appendix E,* page 45.)

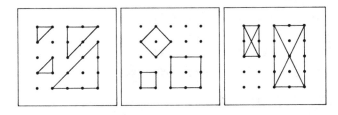

5   Rod activities
Scale can be illustrated with rods as follows:

a. Take a white rod and look at its shape. It is a cube. Make another cube using red rods. What were the fewest red rods you needed to make a red cube? [4 red rods] Could you build that cube out of white rods? How many white rods would it take? [8 white rods]

b. Here is a purple rod. Look at its shape.

Can you build a bigger block that shape?

The new block is twice as long, twice as wide, twice as high as the purple rod. It has the same shape. How many purple rods did it take to build the new block? [8] It has 8 times as much wood in it as the purple rod.

c. Here is a building.

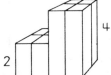

Make a smaller building with the same shape. This is the smallest building with that shape.

It is half as long, half as wide, half as high as the big building. How many small buildings could fit into the big building? [8 small buildings] Children should now make simple buildings of their own.

6   Illustrating similarity of shadows
With a slide projector as a light source and the chalkboard as a screen, we can illustrate the similarity of an object's shadows.

a. Ask a child to move the distance from the projector to the screen. Watch his shadow getting smaller and smaller.
b. Watch the shadow of a ball as we move it back and forth between the projector and the screen.
c. Repeat this for other shapes.
d. Trace the outlines of shadows on the board. Trace small shadows of an object inside large shadows of the same object.
e. Draw a square on the board and then try to fit it inside the shadow of a paper square. Move the paper square farther away from the board and closer to the light source to get a larger square shadow, which is traced *around* the square on the board.
f. Move the paper square closer to the board (therefore farther from the light source) and trace the new square shadow *inside* the square on the board.

7   Puzzles

Which of the snowmen are similar? [A, B, E]

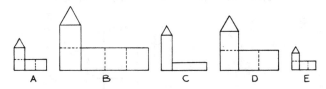

Which of the buildings are similar? [A, D, E]

The notion of a coordinate system

Preliminary activity: a class anecdote

The teacher drew a 1″ square on the chalkboard. [After the first illustration, the squares shown here are greatly reduced.]

Teacher: Write the letter "A" in the square.

Child: That's easy.

Teacher: Write the letter "A" in the square [as she adds a second square].

Child: Which square? The upper or the lower square?

Teacher: The upper one.

Child:

Teacher: Write the letter "A" in the upper square.

Child: Which one, the right or the left one?

Teacher: The upper right square.

Child:

Teacher: Write the letter "A" in the upper right square.

Child: Which upper right square? The inside or the outside one?

Teacher: The inside upper right square.

Child:

At this point there is a protest from the class, "It could be like this."

Teacher: Who is right?

The class decides that this is too confusing and wants to start over again. They demand that we write "good" names for each square.

New system of names:

U—upper
L—lower
M—middle
L—left
R—right

UL	UM	UR
ML	MM	MR
LL	LM	LR

The children are satisfied until the teacher enlarges the grid and asks the children to put a ◯ in the UL square.

⊞ = all squares that can be labeled "upper left," or UL.

There is confusion again. There are too many UL squares. New suggestions are made.

a. Roy suggests that we write numerals in all the squares so we can "talk" about them.

1	2	3	4	5
6	7	8	9	10
11	12	13	14	15
16	17	18	19	20

b. Billy thinks he has a different name for each square.

    20 is in LLRR
    10 is in URR
    9 is in UR
    3 is in UUM

c. Owen says he can simplify Billy's idea.

    20 is in 2L2R
    10 is in 1U2R
    9 is in 1U1R
    3 is in 2UM

Children like the combination of numbers and letters in Owen's system.

d. Karen wants to try *east, west, north* and *south*.

Children don't find Karen's system easier, but the labels E, W, N, S suggest that all the outside rows and columns be labeled instead of the inside rows and columns.

20 is in ID
10 is in IB
9 is in HB
3 is in GA

It works! But Billy says it isn't so good because we have to start relettering every time we make the grid larger.

e. The children finally decide to use numerals for columns and letters for rows. Then they can go on to larger grids.

f. David is worried because there are only 26 letters in the alphabet and asks what the 27th row would be called? The class thinks this system is good enough for now.

20 is in D5
10 is in B5
9 is in B4
3 is in A3

The concept of similarity

All cubes are similar* in shape. Some are also of the same size (volume). All have only *right* angles and only *square* faces. All cubes have the same number of right angles, the same number of square faces, and the same number of vertices.

*Here and below the word *similar* is used as in geometry, meaning "having the same shape, differing only in size and position."

All spheres (balls) are similar in shape. Some are also of the same size (volume). In any sphere, the distance between the center point and any point on its surface is always the same.

All squares are similar figures. Some are also the same size (area). All squares have *four* right angles and *four* equal sides.

All circles are similar figures. Some also are the same size (area). In any circle, the distance between the center point and any point on its circumference always is the same.

Not all triangles are similar triangles.

Not all rectangles are similar rectangles.

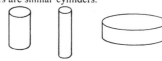

Not all cylinders are similar cylinders.

Here is a family of similar triangles.

Here is a stack of similar triangles. (These are easily made on geoboards.)

Here is a family of similar rectangles.

Here is a stack of similar rectangles.

Here is a family of similar cylinders.

325

· · · · W1, W2

It is assumed that preliminary work has been done with the class as a whole on the major ideas underlying these sheets:

(1) naming and locating the individual squares by two directions (row, column)

(2) idea of similarity of shape (in this case, reducing and enlarging the shape)

(3) combining the two ideas so that (approximately) each square of like name contains the same part of the drawing.

Lab sheet W2 has a large grid on which a child should trace his hand. Hand-tracing gives each child a personal and therefore unique thing to map. It should be stated before children begin that this will, at best, be approximate. Hands wiggle and are not easy to trace. A hand is even harder to copy when reduced in size. (Fingers tightly squeezed together are easier to draw than fingers spread out.) The important thing to watch for is that approximately the same part of the hand reappears in the corresponding smaller square.

1 Child traces his hand.

2 Child darkens area around his hand. (The hand print is then easier to see.)

3 Child shades in the corresponding squares on the smaller grid which will be completely outside his hand print.

4 Child attempts to draw his hand print.

The evaluation of this paper is simply whether or not the child at least understood the problem. This is easily checked by comparing fingertips.

Questions to ask

How much larger is the top grid than the bottom grid?

How much larger is one square in the top grid than one square in the bottom grid?

Which grid has more squares in it, the bottom grid or the top grid? How many more?

How many little squares would make a big square?

How many little grids would make a big grid?

What part of the big grid is the little grid?

What part of one of the big squares is one of the little squares?

How many little hands could fit into the big hand?

The big hand is how many times larger than the little hand?

Supplementary lab sheet

You may want to make a lab sheet like the one below for your children. Again this is a very "personal" type of mapping. The children are to write their names in one grid using separate block letters and then carefully transpose them into grids of different sizes.

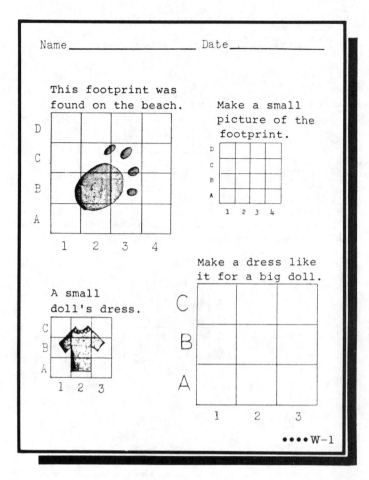

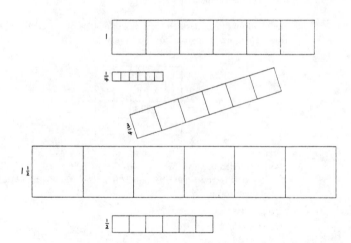

Whatever irregularities occur in the letters in the first grid should be repeated in the other grids.

OwEn
OwEn

Things to watch for

1 What kind of letter was used? That kind of letter must be repeated.

2 Do any letters touch the squares? The same letters must touch the squares in the same spot.

3 Are the letters different sizes? The differences in sizes must be repeated.

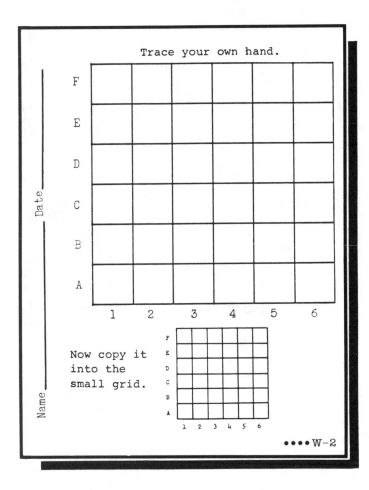

Trace your own hand.

Now copy it into the small grid.

•••• W-2

Name_____ Date_____

A picture of a tree is mapped on Grid I.

We started the picture on Grid II. Finish it.

Map the picture on Grid III and on Grid IV.

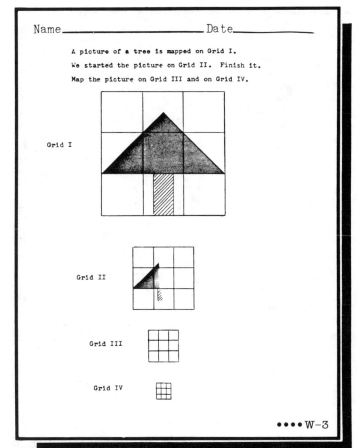

Grid I

Grid II

Grid III

Grid IV

•••• W-3

•••• W3, W4

Lab sheet W3 is simpler than W1 and W2 and is therefore easier for the children to do more accurately. The word *scale* may be introduced here. "We are going to map the tree on a smaller (reduced) scale. Let us call the scale of the tree in the first grid, *1*."

Then the tree in Grid II is $\frac{1}{2}$ as tall as the tree in Grid I. The scale is reduced to $\frac{1}{2}$. (The *area* is reduced to $\frac{1}{4}$.)

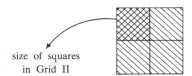

size of squares in Grid II

The length of the tree in Grid III is $\frac{1}{2}$ of the length of the tree in Grid II. It is also $\frac{1}{4}$ of the length of the tree in Grid I.

The length of the tree in Grid IV is $\frac{1}{2}$ the length of the tree in Grid III. It is $\frac{1}{4}$ of the tree in Grid II. It is $\frac{1}{8}$ of the tree in Grid I.

$\frac{1}{4}$ of $1 = \frac{1}{4}$
$\frac{1}{4}$ of $\frac{1}{4} = \frac{1}{16}$
$\frac{1}{4}$ of $\frac{1}{16} = \frac{1}{64}$

By dividing the empty upper left square in each drawing into fourths, the children can see the area relationships.

W4 is the same as W3, except that the children are now *enlarging* the scale instead of *reducing*.

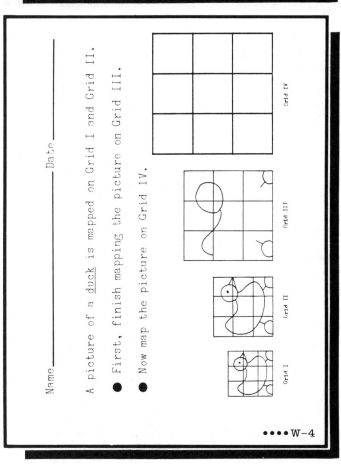

A picture of a <u>duck</u> is mapped on Grid I and Grid II.

● First, finish mapping the picture on Grid III.

● Now map the picture on Grid IV.

Grid I

Grid II

Grid III

Grid IV

•••• W-4

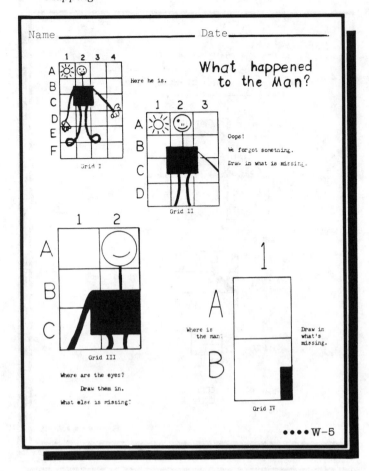

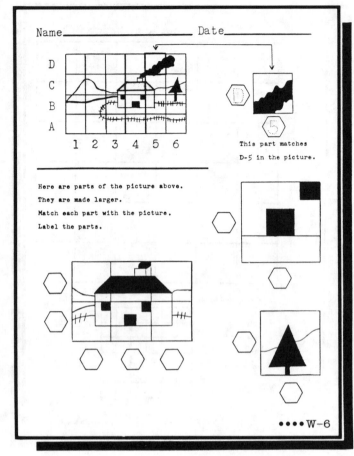

• • • • W5, W6
Enlarging the scale

This time (*a*) the squares are labeled; (*b*) the labeled squares are enlarged (are drawn to different scales); (*c*) the number of labeled squares in each grid decreases. The results are therefore "close-ups" of sections of the original grid.

The children should first study the series of pictures and explain in their own words what is happening.

All of these "mappings" are really readiness activities for map-reading in general. The children might be encouraged to bring in road maps. On such road maps inserts are often found where a detail, such as a city, is shown separately, drawn to a larger scale.

An exercise in "close-ups"

The following is a suggestion for practice on the chalkboard.

Here is a picture of Jack walking up a hill.

All of Jack and most of the hill are in the picture.

Most of the hill is no longer in the picture.

Most of Jack and all of the hill are no longer in the picture.

Solutions to W6

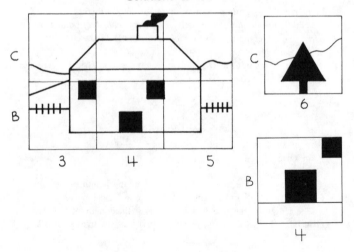

The teacher might play a game with the children by asking them to come to the chalkboard and draw the part of the picture that goes into the following squares. (Children do this from their copy of the lab sheet.)

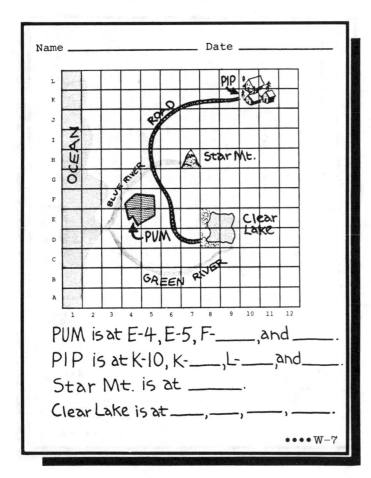

Name _____ Date _____

PUM is at E-4, E-5, F-____, and ____.
PIP is at K-10, K-____, L-____, and ____.
Star Mt. is at ____.
Clear Lake is at ____, ____, ____, ____.

•••• W-7

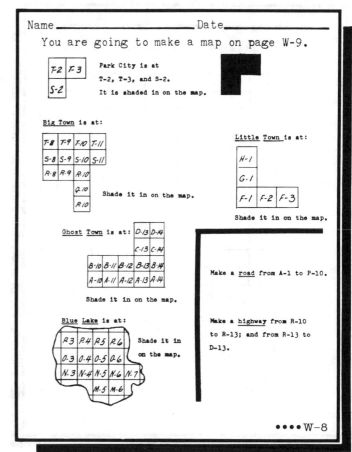

Name _____ Date _____

You are going to make a map on page W-9.

| F-2 | F-3 |
| S-2 | |

Park City is at
T-2, T-3, and S-2.
It is shaded in on the map.

Big Town is at:

T-8	T-9	T-10	T-11
S-8	S-9	S-10	S-11
R-8	R-9	R-10	
	Q-10		
	R-10		

Shade it in on the map.

Little Town is at:

	H-1	
	G-1	
F-1	F-2	F-3

Shade it in on the map.

Ghost Town is at:

		D-13	D-14
		C-13	C-14
B-10	B-11	B-12	B-13	B-14
A-10	A-11	A-12	A-13	A-14

Shade it in on the map.

Blue Lake is at:

R-3	P-4	P-5	P-6
O-3	O-4	O-5	O-6
N-3	N-4	N-5	N-6	N-7
	M-5	M-6	

Shade it in on the map.

Make a road from A-1 to P-10.

Make a highway from R-10 to R-13; and from R-13 to D-13.

•••• W-8

•••• W7–W10

Making maps

On these sheets we ask the children to use the skills for map-reading and map-making built up in the previous sheets. (Most road maps identify regions by a letter-numeral combination.)

Lab sheet W7 contains a very crude geographic map showing an ocean, two rivers, two roads, two cities, a lake, and a mountain. The children are to write in the location of the two cities, the mountain, and the lake.

During class discussion, or as an additional individual activity, they can also locate the ocean and name the squares that the roads and rivers pass through. They may draw in additional things such as bridges, other roads, other cities.

Lab sheets W8 and W9 must be used together. W8 is the instruction page.

Four communities and a lake are blocked out, with their locations given. Children must transfer them to the grid on W9. They can check their work by comparing shapes.

Names of communities should be written on the map. Children are also asked to make a *road* and a *highway*. ("Road" may be interpreted as being a winding, leisurely path. "Highway" means a speedier route.)

Children may make their own map on W10. You probably will need extra sheets of such graph paper because usually an epidemic of map-making breaks out. Don't overlook opportunities for mapping the classroom, the school grounds, the neighborhood, etc.

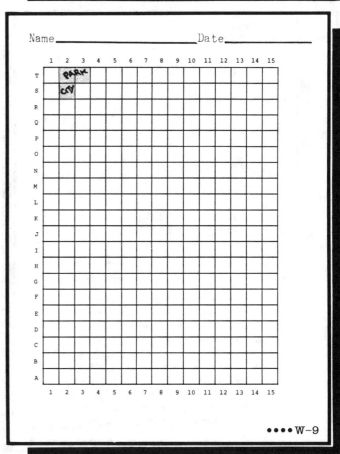

Name _____ Date _____

•••• W-9

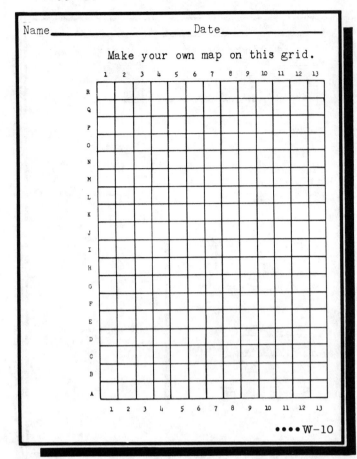

Name_____ Date_____

Make your own map on this grid.

•••• W–10

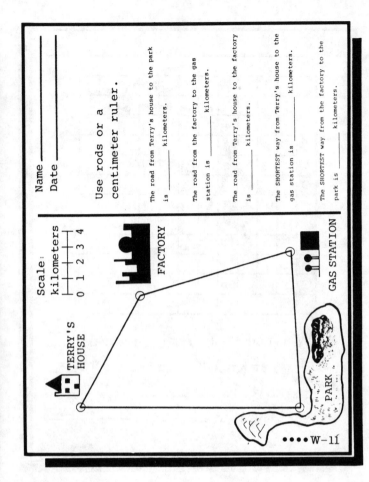

Name_____
Date_____

Use rods or a centimeter ruler.

The road from Terry's house to the park is _____ kilometers.

The road from the factory to the gas station is _____ kilometers.

The road from Terry's house to the factory is _____ kilometers.

The SHORTEST way from Terry's house to the gas station is _____ kilometers.

The SHORTEST way from the factory to the park is _____ kilometers.

Scale: kilometers
0 1 2 3 4

TERRY'S HOUSE

FACTORY

GAS STATION

PARK

•••• W–11

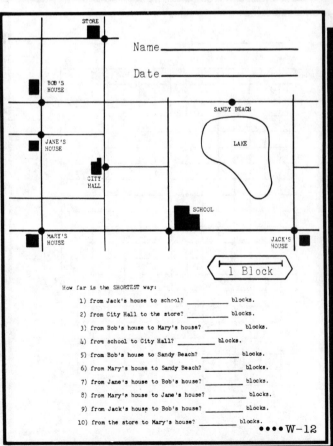

STORE

BOB'S HOUSE

JANE'S HOUSE

CITY HALL

MARY'S HOUSE

SANDY BEACH

LAKE

SCHOOL

JACK'S HOUSE

Name_____

Date_____

1 Block

How far is the SHORTEST way:

1) from Jack's house to school? _____ blocks.

2) from City Hall to the store? _____ blocks.

3) from Bob's house to Mary's house? _____ blocks.

4) from school to City Hall? _____ blocks.

5) from Bob's house to Sandy Beach? _____ blocks.

6) from Mary's house to Sandy Beach? _____ blocks.

7) from Jane's house to Bob's house? _____ blocks.

8) from Mary's house to Jane's house? _____ blocks.

9) from Jack's house to Bob's house? _____ blocks.

10) from the store to Mary's house? _____ blocks.

•••• W–12

• • • • W11, W12

On W11 and W12, roads are to be measured. The scale given on W11 is approximately 1 cm : 1 km. Let the children measure either with rods or with rulers. Measuring with rods is easier.

More road maps appear on W12, but here the roads are measured in length of blocks. *Shortest* roads are asked for.

X Clock arithmetic

Learning to tell time

A unit on the clock is valuable not only for the practical objective of learning to tell time but also as the basis for a fundamental study of the circle, fractional parts of the circle, measurement of angles, and cyclic numbers.

There are many difficulties in the presentation of such material. Some of these basic difficulties are as follows:

1 The inconsistency between our spoken and written language about time:

	"quarter to one"	(spoken)
but	12:45	(written)

	"half past two"	(spoken)
but	2:30	(written)

	"five of four"	(spoken)
but	3:55	(written)

2 Complications in the addition of hours, and hours plus minutes:

$$10:00 + \Box = 2:00$$
$$9:47 + \Box = 10:15$$

3 The fact that:

$\frac{1}{12}$ revolution of the small hand $=$ 1 hour
1 revolution of the large hand $=$ 60 minutes

Objectives

1 To enable children to understand well the synchronized rhythm of the clock so that they will be able to judge time, independently of numerals, simply by noting the size and position of the center angle formed by the hands and the relative positions of the large and small hands.

2 To utilize children's observation of and familiarity with the clock face to help them recognize fractional parts of *any* circle.

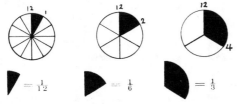

3 To give children a feeling for recording a cyclic movement (and for observing it) in circular patterns as contrasted with the number-line experience.

4 To transpose the cycle observed in a circle to the number line.

5 To have children become aware of numbers and their complements.

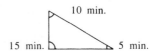

Cycle $= 60$

6 To utilize the children's observation of the movement of the minute hand for measurement of angles. Thus:

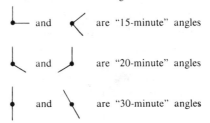

Thus, the triangle below has approximately the angles indicated:

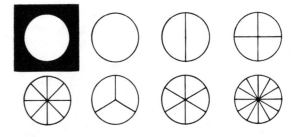

Approach

Equipment

Large fractional puzzle, containing a wooden frame and fractional parts to fit into the frame.

Procedure

1 Children need to learn to identify:

1 whole $= \frac{2}{2} = \frac{4}{4} = \frac{8}{8} = \frac{6}{6} = \frac{12}{12}$

and recognize that $\frac{1}{4} = \frac{2}{8} = \frac{3}{12}$

$$\frac{1}{6} + \frac{1}{12} = \frac{1}{4}, \text{ etc.}$$

2 A paper clock face is fitted inside the wooden frame.

The slice covered is $\boxed{\frac{1}{4}}$.

The slice covering the clock face is $\frac{1}{2}$. It covers ⌈6 hours⌉ ($\frac{1}{2}$ of 12).

3   A minute face is inserted into the frame.

The slice covering the minute face is $\frac{1}{12}$. It covers ⌈five minutes⌉

The slice covering the minute face is $\frac{1}{2}$. It covers ⌈30 minutes⌉

How do we count minutes in an hour (1 to 60)?

10 minutes $= \frac{1}{6}$ hour
15 minutes $= \frac{1}{4}$ hour
30 minutes $= \frac{1}{2}$ hour
60 minutes $= 1$ hour
50 minutes $= \frac{5}{6}$ hour or $\frac{10}{12}$ hour
$\frac{1}{3}$ hour $= 20$ minutes
$\frac{3}{4}$ hour $= 45$ minutes

4   Teach children how to plot hours and minutes on the number line. (Make a large number line that stretches the length of the room.)

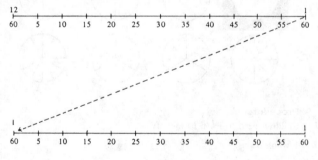

Ask:

a. How far is it from 2:00 to 4:00? [two hours]
b. How many minutes? [2×60 minutes]
c. Where would you look for "quarter after four"?

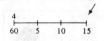

d. Where would you find "half past five"?

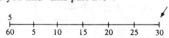

e. Where would you find "quarter to five"?

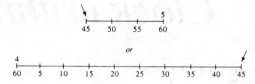

f. How much time has passed between 2:10 and 7:20? [5 hours and 10 minutes]

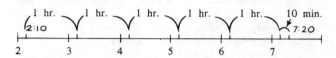

Children are usually very impressed when they discover how many revolutions the minute hand of the clock really has to make and how long this takes, especially since the hands on the clock face do not look so very different!

Making clocks

Use paper plates, cardboard hands, and paper fasteners. Children play chiefly as partners. One child names a specific time, such as "five after four"; the other responds by setting his clock at the requested time.

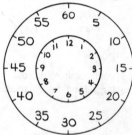

Board work about how to tell time

Teacher: Can you tell the time? [She draws diagrams of clock hands similar to those below.]

Children:

Yes, 12:00   Yes, about 3:20   Yes, quarter to six

Teacher: What do we need to tell time?

Children:

a. A picture of the clock in our heads.
b. Two hands that move a certain way from the points.
c. We don't need numerals.
d. The hands each trace a circle as they move. One circle is inside the other circle.

•X1–X7, X9

On X1 the child is concerned only with hours. Children write in the time shown or draw in the hands for the time given.

On X2 the child is concerned only with half-hours. Children draw in the minute hand and write in the numeral for the time shown.

Sheet X3 takes up "quarter past" the hour and is essentially the same as X2.

X4 and X5 have hours and half hours mixed, and on X6 quarter hours are mixed with the other two.

X7 and X9 are the same as X6 except that all or some numerals are left off in order to focus the child's eyes on the center angles formed by the clock hands. (Some children will write in the numerals. This should neither be encouraged nor discouraged.)

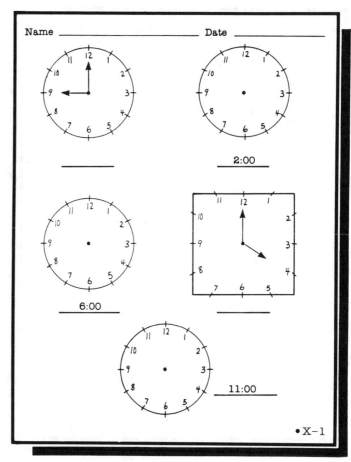

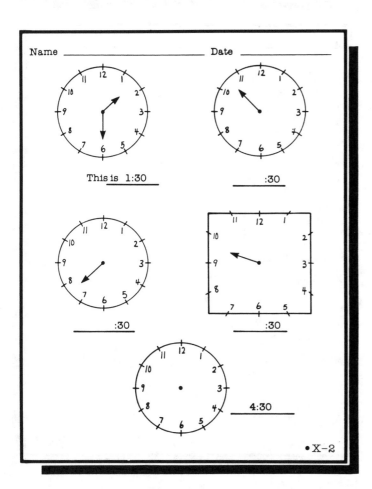

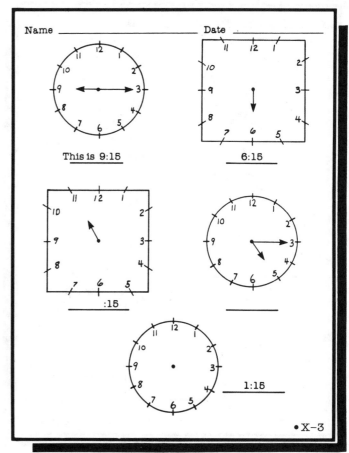

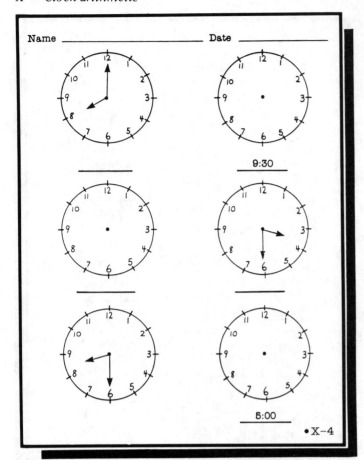

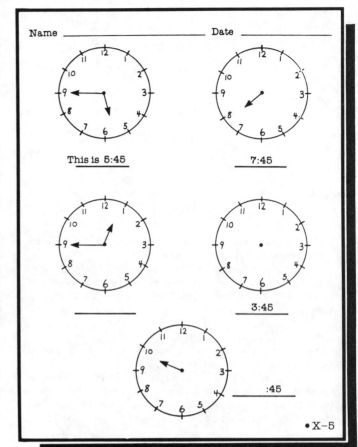

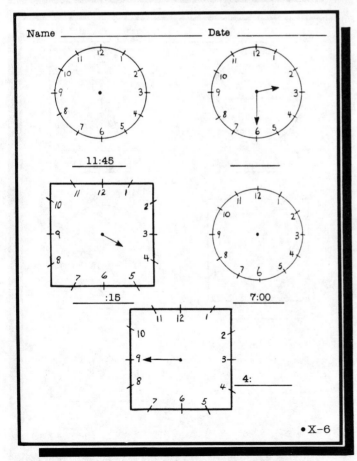

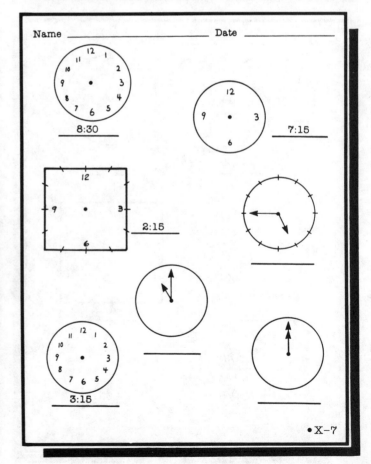

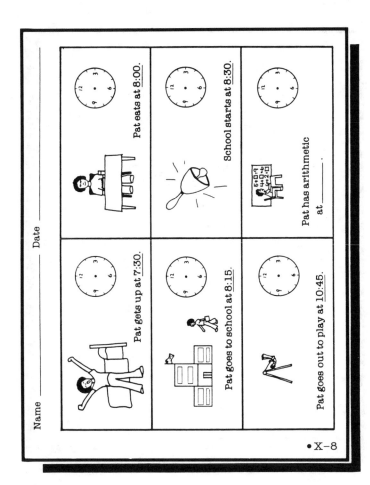

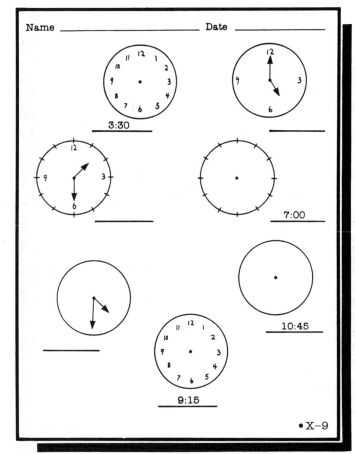

· X8

Additional suggestions

Children put in the hands of the clocks to show the time indicated in the sentences.

In the sixth rectangle the sentence "Bill has arithmetic at _____." must first be completed. Each child may want to make up his own time for the arithmetic period.

The teacher might want to prepare a lab sheet to show the times of her own daily class activities. Children draw in hands to show starting and ending times for each activity.

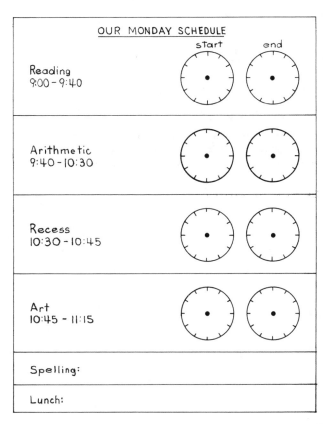

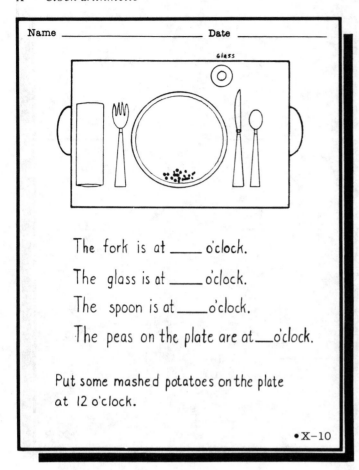

The fork is at ____ o'clock.

The glass is at ____ o'clock.

The spoon is at ____ o'clock.

The peas on the plate are at ____ o'clock.

Put some mashed potatoes on the plate
at 12 o'clock.

•X–10

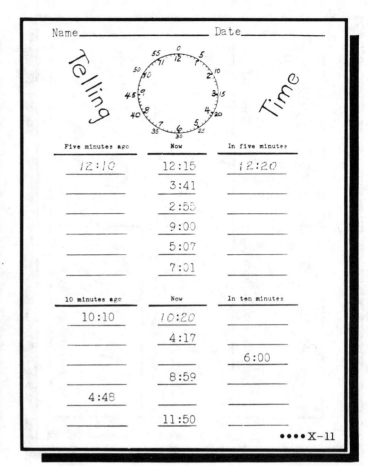

•••• X–11

•X10

The fork is at   [9]   o'clock.

The glass is at   [1]   o'clock.

The spoon is at   [3 or 4]   o'clock.

The peas are at   [6]   o'clock.

Children enjoy the game of arranging objects on their desks using
"clock" instructions. (This system is often used by companions of
blind people to help them unobtrusively in social situations. The system
is also used in navigation.)

•••• X11

The clock face on the top of X11 is a visual clue for those who feel
unsure.

"Five minutes ago" is a type of subtraction with clock numbers
(cyclic numbers). We solve it by moving counterclockwise on the
circle (↶).

"In five minutes" is a clock addition. We solve it by moving clockwise on the circle (↷).

Name _____ Date_____

What time will it be <u>half</u> <u>an</u> <u>hour</u> after:

1:30 ☐

2:15 ☐

5:40 ☐

6:12 ☐

7:55 ☐

9:49 ☐

11:07 ☐

12:38 ☐

$\frac{1}{4}$ of an hour = ☐ minutes; $\frac{1}{4}$ X 60 ☐

$\frac{1}{2}$ of an hour = ☐ minutes; $\frac{1}{2}$ X 60 ☐

$\frac{1}{3}$ of an hour = ☐ minutes; $\frac{1}{3}$ X 60 ☐

$\frac{1}{4}$ of an hour = ☐ minutes; $\frac{3}{4}$ X 60 ☐

$\frac{1}{12}$ of an hour = ☐ minutes; $\frac{1}{12}$ X 60 ☐

•••• X-12

Name _____ Date_____

Days and Weeks

Sun.	Mon.	Tues.	Wed.	Thurs.	Fri.	Sat.

Make a calendar.

The first day is a Tuesday. The month has 31 days.

One week has _____ days.

Two weeks have _____ days.

Four weeks have _____ days.

	Weeks	Days
10 days		
17 days	2	3
21 days		
26 days		
31 days		
35 days		
36 days		

•••• X-13

••••X12

Preliminary activity

The following teaching aid is very convenient for showing that *all* half-hour (30-minute) intervals are *half-circle moves* of the big hand, that *all* quarter-hour (15-minute) intervals are *quarter-circle moves* of the big hand.

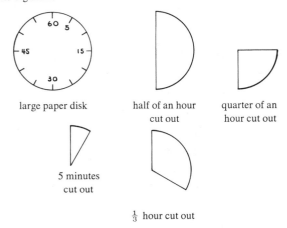

large paper disk

half of an hour cut out

quarter of an hour cut out

5 minutes cut out

$\frac{1}{3}$ hour cut out

Then by placing the cut-outs over the paper disk, we can see that any hour and 40 minutes plus half an hour equals the next hour and 10 minutes, etc.

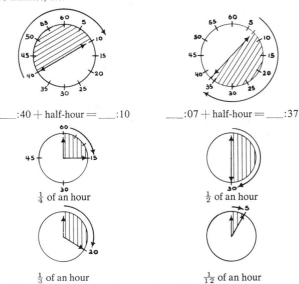

___:40 + half-hour = ___:10

___:07 + half-hour = ___:37

$\frac{1}{4}$ of an hour

$\frac{1}{2}$ of an hour

$\frac{1}{3}$ of an hour

$\frac{1}{12}$ of an hour

Name_____ Date_____

Month		Number of Days		Number of Days and Weeks
January	has	31 days	or	☐ weeks and ⬡ days.
February	has	28 days	or	☐ weeks and ⬡ days.
March	has	31 days	or	☐ weeks and ⬡ days.
April	has	30 days	or	☐ weeks and ⬡ days.
May	has	31 days	or	☐ weeks and ⬡ days.
June	has	30 days	or	☐ weeks and ⬡ days.
July	has	31 days	or	☐ weeks and ⬡ days.
August	has	31 days	or	☐ weeks and ⬡ days.
September	has	30 days	or	☐ weeks and ⬡ days.
October	has	31 days	or	☐ weeks and ⬡ days.
November	has	30 days	or	☐ weeks and ⬡ days.
December	has	31 days	or	☐ weeks and ⬡ days.

Add up the totals: ◯ days or ☐ weeks and ⬡ days.

48 weeks and 29 days = ☐ weeks and 1 day.

There are ☐ months in a year.

There are ☐ weeks in a year.

There are ☐ days in a year.

•••••X-14

Name _____ Date _____

From: Philadelphia   150 kilometers   To: New York

Train speed: 100 kilometers per hour (km/h)
The train will travel ☐ hrs. and ☐ min.

From: Philadelphia
To: Chicago
1200 kilometers

Speed: ☐ km/h

The non-stop plane gets to Chicago in 2 hours.
Its speed is _____ kilometers per hour.

210 km to Washington
Philadelphia
Speed: ☐

The Bing family drove to Washington in $3\frac{3}{4}$ hours. They stopped for gas for 10 min. They stopped 35 minutes for lunch.
What was their speed? _____km/h

•••••X-15

••••X14

Days, weeks, months, year

Here is one eight-year-old's very clever device for adding up all the days of the months:

"I gave February the two extra days from January and March so that each had 30 days.

"Then I added:

> 90 days for those three months,
> 90 days for the next three months,
> 90 days for the next three months,
> 90 days for the next three months.

"That's 360 days.

"Then I collected the one extra day from December, October, August, July, May. That made 5 more days.

"So, there are 365 days in a year!"

Children and teacher should discuss other possibilities for adding this long column of days.

•••••X15, X16

These are "brain-teasers" for the few children in every class who need to be given extra challenges.

km/h (kilometers per hour) will need to be explained.

Solutions to X15

1 The train will travel ☐1☐ hour and ☐30☐ minutes.

2 The non-stop plane gets to Chicago in 2 hours. Its speed is ☐600☐ km/h.

3 The Bing family drove to Washington in $3\frac{3}{4}$ hours. They stopped for gas for 10 minutes. They stopped 35 minutes for lunch. What was their speed? ☐70 km/h☐

Solutions to X16

$1\frac{1}{2}$ hours	=	90	minutes
3 hours	=	180	minutes
$2\frac{1}{4}$ hours	=	135	minutes
6 hours	=	360	minutes
12 hours	=	720	minutes
$1\frac{2}{3}$ hours	=	100	minutes
30 minutes	=	$\frac{1}{2}$	hour
45 minutes	=	$\frac{3}{4}$	hour
75 minutes	=	$1\frac{1}{4}$	hour
1 minute	=	$\frac{1}{60}$	hour
7 minutes	=	$\frac{7}{60}$	hour
10 minutes	=	$\frac{1}{6}$	hour

Teachers may make up similar lab sheets using the community they teach in as a starting point. Make up lab sheets using kilometers and kilometers per hour.

Name _____ Date _____

$1\frac{1}{2}$ hours = ☐ minutes

3 hours = ☐ minutes

$2\frac{1}{4}$ hours = ☐ minutes

6 hours = ☐ minutes

12 hours = ☐ minutes

$1\frac{2}{3}$ hours = ☐ minutes

30 minutes = ◯ hour

45 minutes = ◯ hour

75 minutes = ◯ hour

1 minute = ◯ hour

7 minutes = ◯ hour

10 minutes = ◯ hour

•••••X-16

Name _____ Date _____

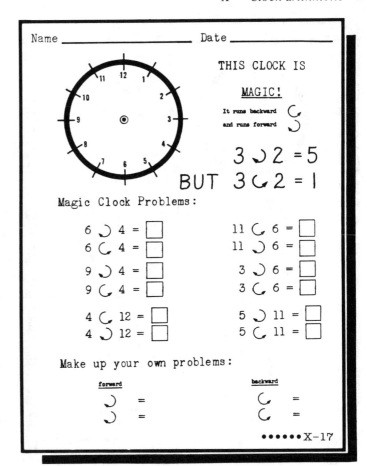

THIS CLOCK IS

<u>MAGIC!</u>

It runs backward ↻
and runs forward ↺

$3 \,↺\, 2 = 5$

BUT $3 \,↻\, 2 = 1$

Magic Clock Problems:

6 ↺ 4 = ☐   11 ↻ 6 = ☐
6 ↻ 4 = ☐   11 ↺ 6 = ☐
9 ↺ 4 = ☐   3 ↺ 6 = ☐
9 ↻ 4 = ☐   3 ↻ 6 = ☐

4 ↻ 12 = ☐   5 ↺ 11 = ☐
4 ↺ 12 = ☐   5 ↻ 11 = ☐

Make up your own problems:

<u>forward</u>   <u>backward</u>

↺ =   ↻ =
↺ =   ↻ =

•••••X-17

•••••**X17, X18**

Here clock arithmetic is presented as a special type of arithmetic with a finite number of numbers.

There is a well-known riddle which asks: "When does $10 + 4 = 2$?" The answer is, "On the clock; when the hour hand records four hours past 10 o'clock, it is pointing to 2 o'clock."

Our 12-hour clocks are examples of a form of finite arithmetic. When twelve hours have passed, we have completed a cycle (a circle) on the clock, and then we start again. The clock does not keep a record of completed cycles; it keeps a record of partial cycles only. It keeps track only of the remainders that are left when we divide by 12 any number of times.

Let's put this to a test.

We give the children several play clocks, each having only one hand but each with an ordinary clock face with 12 divisions. All the clock hands point to the same number.

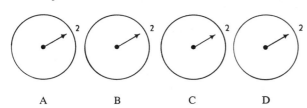

A   B   C   D

We send a child out of the room while the clocks are being reset. Upon his return, the child is to tell how the clock hands were moved.

The clock hands are moved clockwise, one, two, three, and four units respectively.

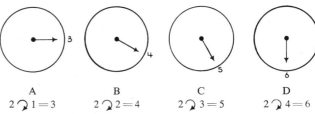

A   B   C   D
$2↷1=3$ $2↷2=4$ $2↷3=5$ $2↷4=6$

The clocks are reset at 2. Another child is sent out of the room. This time the hands are moved in the following ways:

The hand on clock A is not moved.

The hand on clock B is moved 8 spaces clockwise.

The hand on clock C is moved 11 spaces clockwise.

The hand on clock D is moved 12 spaces clockwise.

Here are the results on the clocks:

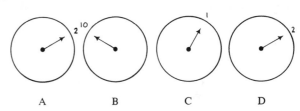

A   B   C   D

Will the child be able to know from the dials what happened? Clocks A and D look alike. Yet the "observers" know that one was turned and one was not.

A   D
$2↷0=2$ $2↷12=2$

Continued on next page

339

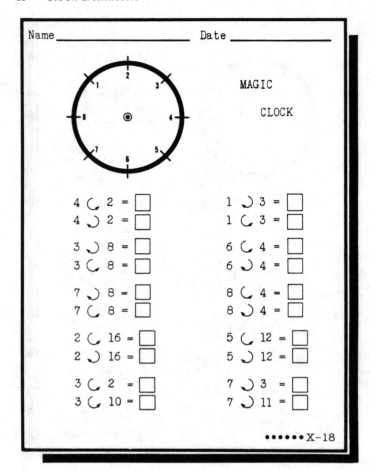

Name_____   Date_____

MAGIC

CLOCK

4 ⌣ 2 = ☐
4 ⌣ 2 = ☐

3 ⌣ 8 = ☐
3 ⌣ 8 = ☐

7 ⌣ 8 = ☐
7 ⌣ 8 = ☐

2 ⌣ 16 = ☐
2 ⌣ 16 = ☐

3 ⌣ 2 = ☐
3 ⌣ 10 = ☐

1 ⌣ 3 = ☐
1 ⌣ 3 = ☐

6 ⌣ 4 = ☐
6 ⌣ 4 = ☐

8 ⌣ 4 = ☐
8 ⌣ 4 = ☐

5 ⌣ 12 = ☐
5 ⌣ 12 = ☐

7 ⌣ 3 = ☐
7 ⌣ 11 = ☐

••••••X–18

Continued from preceding page.

From this we learn that

$0 \times$ a cycle
$1 \times$ a cycle
$2 \times$ a cycle
$3 \times$ a cycle
•
•
•
$\square \times$ a cycle

will not show up on the clock face when $\square$ is a whole number.

Thus:
$12 \curvearrowright (0 \times 12) = 12$
$12 \curvearrowright (2 \times 12) = 12$
$12 \curvearrowright (9 \times 12) = 12$

but:
$12 \curvearrowright (\frac{1}{2} \times 12) = 6$
$12 \curvearrowright (1 + \frac{1}{2} \times 12) = 6$
$12 \curvearrowright (2 + \frac{1}{2} \times 12) = 6$

We can always tell the remainder of cycles and *only* the remainder of cycles.

$$9 \curvearrowright 16 = 9 \curvearrowright (1 \times 12) + 4 = 1$$

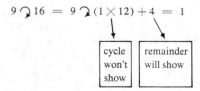

cycle won't show   remainder will show

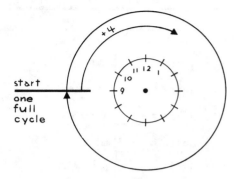

start
one full cycle

Now we might ask ourselves: Do clocks *have to* run clockwise? They do not. We may explore clock moves in the counter-clockwise direction.

$8 \curvearrowright 4 = 12$ but $8 \curvearrowleft 4 = 4$

$12 \curvearrowright 2 = 2$ but $12 \curvearrowleft 2 = 10$

$12 \curvearrowright 6 = 6$ but $12 \curvearrowleft 6 = 6$

Now we might ask ourselves: Do clocks have to have a cycle of 12? They do not. We can have cycles of any length more than 1.

Here is a "six clock."   Here is a "ten clock."

$1 \curvearrowright 4 = 5$ $1 \curvearrowright 4 = 5$
$1 \curvearrowleft 4 = 3$ $1 \curvearrowleft 4 = 7$

The "remainder groups," or answers, will be different on these clocks, but they follow regular patterns.

Background   information   for   the   teacher

Mathematicians call this kind of finite arithmetic *modular arithmetic*.

When they refer to cycles of length 5 (as on a "5 clock"), they call the arithmetic *modular 5*. Thus, 12 modular$_5$ is the same as 2 modular$_5$ or 17 modular$_5$ or 232 modular$_5$. This simply means, in terms of our clock dials, that we will not be able to tell whether we turned our dial 12 spaces or 17 spaces or 232 spaces or 2 spaces. All we can tell is that we completed an unknown number of full cycles and always went 2 spaces beyond our starting place.

2, 12, 17, 232, when divided by 5, all have the common remainder 2.

5, 10, 15, 230, when divided by 5, all have the common remainder 0.

4, 19, 254, 1009, when divided by 5, all have the common remainder 4.

These are written in mathematical sentences as follows:

$$229 \text{ mod}_5 \equiv 4 \text{ mod}_5$$
$$14 \text{ mod}_5 \equiv 4 \text{ mod}_5$$
$$33 \text{ mod}_5 \equiv 4 \text{ mod}_5$$
$$49 \text{ mod}_7 \equiv 0 \text{ mod}_7$$
$$21 \text{ mod}_7 \equiv 0 \text{ mod}_7$$
$$16 \text{ mod}_7 \equiv 2 \text{ mod}_7$$

The symbol $\equiv$ is read as "is congruent to." It means "belongs to the same remainder group when divided by the modular."

Y   *Sets*

Most of the newer elementary-school mathematics programs include some work in set theory and the language of sets.

In this primary math program, vocabulary and symbolism are at a minimum because our experience has shown that formal work in logic and sets is only suitable for older children. We do include the very powerful Venn diagrams, which represent graphically the relationships between things and ideas, to introduce the *concepts* of sets, subsets, union, and intersection. These we can introduce to children in a playful way and without technical vocabulary. Our experimental groups of six-, seven-, and eight-year-olds enjoyed and understood this approach.

Let us illustrate what we mean. Below are three Venn diagrams, each with two loops. Each loop is an imaginary "fence," enclosing the elements of the set.

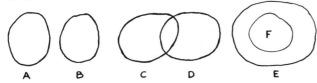

Two categories of things (sets of things) can be related to one another in one of the three ways illustrated by the diagrams.

A and B are completely separate. They have no common elements. No A's are B's; no B's are A's.

C and D are partly separate but also have common elements. Some C's are also D's; some D's are also C's.

E and F have common elements but not all of E is contained in F. All F's are contained in E; some E's are contained in F.

We can arbitrarily pick any two sets of things and discover that their relationships can be portrayed in one of these three ways:

Birds, books

birds   books
                No birds are books.
                No books are birds.

Highways, toll roads

toll roads
                Some highways are toll roads.
                All toll roads are highways.

Girls, people with freckles

freckled girls
                Some girls have freckles.
                Some freckled people are girls.

In the example of birds and books, we have no element of one set which is also an element of the other set. Therefore their *intersection* is the *null* set, $\emptyset$, or empty set { }. Their *union* is all books and all birds.

birds   books
— union —

In the example of highways and toll roads, all the elements of the set of toll roads are also elements of the set of highways. Therefore, their intersection is *not* the empty set. Their *intersection* is the set of toll roads. These are the elements common to both sets. Their *union* is the set of highways. The elements belong either to one of the two sets or to both.

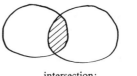

toll roads   highways

In the example of girls and people with freckles, some of the elements in the set of girls are also elements of the set of people with freckles. Therefore, their *intersection* is the set of freckled girls. Their *union* is the set of girls without freckles, freckled girls, and people (except girls) with freckles.

intersection: union: "all girls and all
"freckled girls"   other freckled people"

We can of course use Venn diagrams to portray relationships between three or more things. Here are merely *some* of the possible relationships between three things:

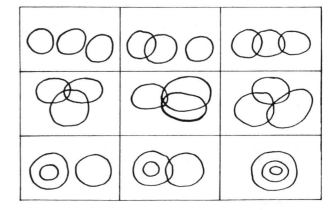

Readiness activities

Episode 1

The following episodes illustrate various readiness activities we have done before the lab sheets were given to the children.

Time: Early afternoon in early November, during a free activity period.

Place: The science corner of a first-grade classroom (could be a second grade).

Participants: Several first-graders, a student teacher.

Props: Assorted sizes of cardboard box lids, many rocks, many leaves (collected by children).

Action: Student teacher encourages children to look at and feel the rocks carefully. She then separates them into two distinct piles, putting each pile into a box-lid tray. She seems to talk to herself: "In this tray are all the speckled rocks and in that tray are all the . . ." Children shout, "Plain rocks."

All the rocks are dumped on the table. She asks children to make up some sorting puzzles of their own. Jessica sorts the rocks into dark and light rocks; Ruthie sorts them into "rocks with holes" and "rocks without holes." Bill sorts them into "dusty rocks" and "clean rocks." Someone else sorts them into "littler-than-a-prune and bigger-than-a-prune rocks." The student teacher makes a list of all the sorting puzzles but stays out of the game.

Without any adult suggestion, another group of children has started on some leaf-sorting games: pointed leaves—round leaves; fuzzy leaves—shiny leaves; red leaves—brown leaves—yellow leaves; zig-zig leaves—straight leaves.

An argument begins about those leaves that are partly red and partly brown and partly yellow. Should they be put into a different pile? Should they be put into the brown pile if they are mostly brown and into the yellow pile if they are mostly yellow? They finally end up in a "mixed pile."

The next day during the free activity period some children resume the sorting game on their own. New variations for sorting are discovered.

Episode 2

Time: Math period, later in the year.

Place: First-grade classroom (could be older children); children sit in a semicircle around a large cleared floor space.

Props: Large colored rope loops.

Action

1 The teacher lays a large red rope loop on the floor and calls some girls by name to step into the loop. She lays a blue rope loop on the floor close by and asks some boys to step into it. The children say correctly that the blue loop holds a set of boys.

   She puts a yellow loop on the floor and she steps into it. The children call the yellow loop the "teacher loop." Everyone is asked to go to his seat.

2 The teacher puts the yellow loop inside the red loop and asks Martha, Mary, and Leslie to stand inside the yellow loop. (The three girls are each wearing red hairbands.) The rest of the children are asked to look carefully for something special about these girls but to keep it a secret if they discover it.

   All the other girls in the class are asked to stand inside the part of the red loop that is *not* inside the yellow loop.

   What is the game now?

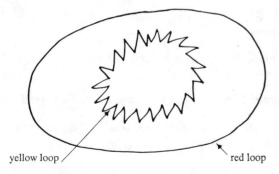

Red loop: all girls in the group
Yellow loop: some girls (those with red hairbands)

The girls without red hairbands are asked if they are inside the red loop [yes]. Inside the yellow loop [no].

Martha, Mary, and Leslie sit down, and a child is asked to draw a picture of this game on the chalkboard.

3 The teacher now puts three loops on the floor in the following way:

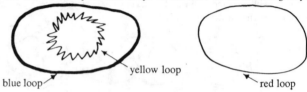

The class is asked to sort the children in order to make a story for this arrangement. These are some of their ideas:

a. Blue loop: boys
    Blue and yellow loops: boys who have blond hair
    Red loop: girls

b. Blue loop: children wearing sneakers
    Blue and yellow loops: children wearing low sneakers
    Red loop: children wearing leather shoes

A picture of this arrangement is drawn on the board.

4 The teacher holds four different-colored loops. She gives the red loop to Bill, Tom, and Sam and asks them to stand inside it.

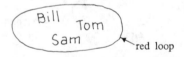

She gives a yellow loop to Mary and Janie, who put it on the floor and stand in it.

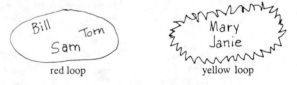

She takes the green loop, and she stands in it.

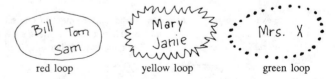

Another child is now given the blue loop and asked to put it around all the people who wear glasses. (These people are not to get out of their other loops.) Mary, Bill, Tom, and Mrs. X wear glasses.

This is the loop formation now:

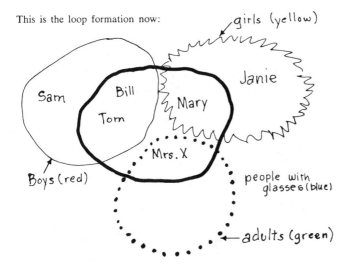

a. Who is a member of the set of girls? [Mary, Janie. They are in the yellow loop.]

b. Who is a member of the set of boys? [Sam, Bill, Tom. They are in the red loop.]

c. Who is the girl who is a member of the set of girls *and* the set of people with glasses? [Mary. She is in the yellow loop *and* in the blue loop.]

d. Who is a member of the set of adults without glasses? [Nobody in the room. The set is empty. Nobody is in the green loop only. Mrs. X, the teacher, is in the green *and* the blue loops.]

e. Is there anybody in both the red *and* the yellow loops? [No. No person is a boy *and* a girl.]

Episode 3

Time: Math period.

Place: Second- or third-grade classroom (seven- or eight-year-olds); children work at tables in groups of four.

Supplies: These may be a variety of leaves; paper shapes in various colors; letters of the alphabet; mixtures of metal, wooden, and paper objects, etc.

Action: Children are asked to use their loops to play sorting games. After completing an arrangement they ask children from another table to guess their sorting principles.

Example A: The supplies are individual pieces of paper with letters of the alphabet (capital and small letters) and various colored loops. Several sortings are made, using different sorting principles.

1

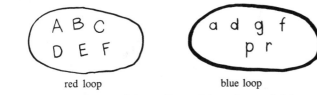

No capital letter is a small letter. No small letter is a capital letter.

2

The sorting principle is as follows:
  Green loop: letters with straight lines
  Yellow loop: letters with curved lines
  Yellow and green loops: letters with both curved and straight lines

3

The sorting principle is the following:
  Green loop: the letters of the alphabet
  Red and green loops: the vowels
  Green loop but *not in* red loop: the consonants

Example B: The supplies are red and black plastic checkers, red and white paper disks, metal washers, paper clips, paper squares, plastic curtain rings, toothpicks, plastic party picks, various colored loops. The following arrangements were made by the children.

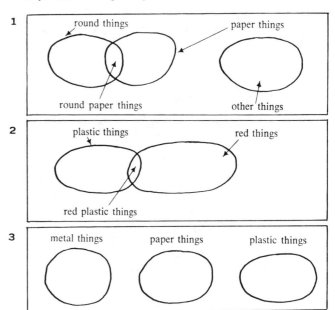

The preceding examples are only a few suggestions. An infinite variety of objects, easily available in the classroom, can be sorted.

Sets extended to mathematics

Just as we can arrange objects (leaves, rocks, people) according to various sorting principles, we can do the same thing with properties of numbers.

Let us choose as a simple master set the counting numbers 1–9. We write:

$$C = \{1, 2, 3, 4, 5, 6, 7, 8, 9\}$$

The capital letter "C" gives the name of the set of the counting numbers 1 through 9. (Sets are usually named by capital letters.) Brackets, { }, enclose the elements of the set.

Sets have subsets. In the example, two of the subsets are the *even* numbers between 0 and 10 and the *odd* numbers between 0 and 10.

Relationships between sets are described by the union of the sets and the intersection of the sets. The symbol for union is $\cup$. The symbol for intersection is $\cap$

Let us now look at set C and some of its subsets:

$$C = \{1, 2, 3, 4, 5, 6, 7, 8, 9\}$$

Subsets:
$E = \{2, 4, 6, 8\}$ even numbers
$O = \{1, 3, 5, 7, 9\}$ odd numbers
$T = \{1, 2, 4, 8\}$ powers of two
$P = \{2, 3, 5, 7\}$ prime numbers
$X = \{3, 6, 9\}$ multiples of three
$F = \{4, 8\}$ multiples of four

1   Subsets E and O

Union of subsets E and O is set C. (The shaded part is the union.)

$$E \cup O = C$$
$$E \cup O = \{1, 2, 3, 4, 5, 6, 7, 8, 9\}$$

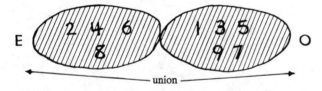

union

Intersection of subsets E and O is the *empty set*. It has no members.

$$E \cap O = \{\ \}$$

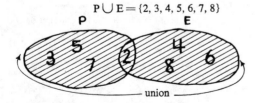

intersection

2   Subsets P and E

Union of subsets P and E.

$$P \cup E = \{2, 3, 4, 5, 6, 7, 8\}$$

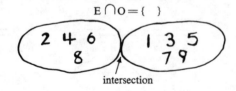

union

The shaded part is the union of P and E.

Intersection of subsets P and E.

$$P \cap E = \{2\}$$

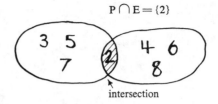

intersection

The shaded part is the intersection.

3   Subsets E and F

Union of subsets E and F.

$$E \cup F = \{2, 4, 6, 8\}$$

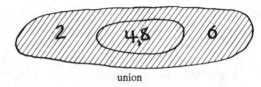

union

The shaded part is the union.

Intersection of subsets E and F.

$$E \cap F = \{4, 8\}$$

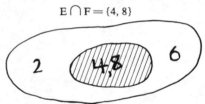

The shaded part is the intersection.

The relationships among the subsets of C can be illustrated by the three following Venn diagrams:

1	2	3
The following sets have no common elements. Their intersection is the empty set.	The following sets have some common elements. (Some elements belong to both sets.) These elements are the intersection of the sets.	In the following sets one is a *proper subset* of the other set. Their union is the larger set; their intersection is the subset.

$E \cup O$	$E \cup T$	$F \cup E$
$P \cup F$	$O \cup T$	
$O \cup F$	$P \cup T$	
	$X \cup O$	
	$X \cup E$	

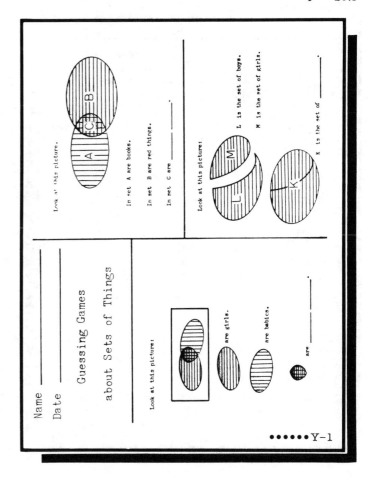

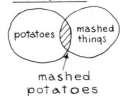

•••••• **Y1**

The following are answers for lab sheet Y1:

1 The intersection of the set of girls and the set of babies is the set of <u>baby girls</u>.

2 Set A are books: little books, blue books, dictionaries, storybooks, etc.
Set B are red things: red dresses, red candy, red beets, red barns, etc.
Set C is the intersection of books and red things. In set C are <u>red books</u>.

3 Set L is the set of boys.
Set M is the set of girls.
Set K is the set of <u>children.</u>
The *union* of set L and set M is the set K.

Make up other examples of such diagrams.

Set of all potatoes in the world.
Set of all mashed things in the world.
Set of <u>mashed potatoes</u>.

Set of stationwagons
Set of new cars.
Set of <u>new stationwagons</u>.

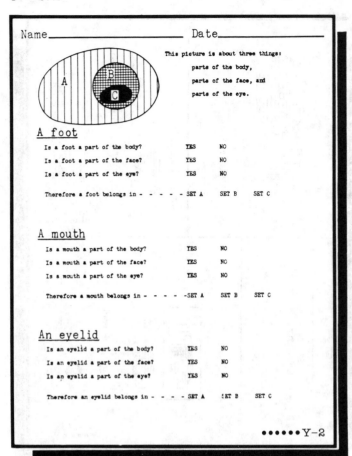

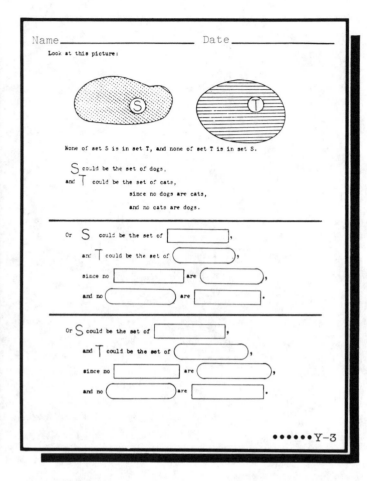

Here the child is taken through a series of questions to establish whether an element belongs to one, two, or all three of three given sets.

Set A

Set B is a proper subset of set A.

(All of B is in A)

(Some of A is also in B)

Set C is a proper subset of set B, which is a proper subset of set A.

(All of C is in B and in A)

(Some of B is in C)

(Some of A is in C)

A foot

(Yes) part of body

(No) part of face

(No) part of eye

A foot belongs to set (A) .

A mouth

(Yes) part of body

(Yes) part of face

(No) part of eye

A mouth belongs to set (A) and set (B) .

An eyelid

(Yes) part of body

(Yes) part of face

(Yes) part of eye

An eyelid belongs to set (A) , set (B) , and set (C) .

346

After the children have completed lab sheet Y2, the teacher may ask the children to locate other elements belonging to sets A, B, C:

an arm (set A)	a shoulder (set A)
a nose (set B)	a cheek (set B)
a shoe (outside set A)	the iris (set C)

The same relationship among sets exists in the following example:

Set A: Cities	Paris, Rangoon, Brasilia
Set B: United States cities	New York, Anchorage
Set C: Illinois cities	Chicago

•••••• Y3

An oral game based on Y3 may be played by the class.

The teacher draws a diagram similar to the one on Y3 on the board. Each child takes a turn and names two disjoint sets. S could be a set of grasshoppers and T could be a set of elephants, since no grasshoppers are elephants and no elephants are grasshoppers.

Should the game become dull before each child has a turn, the teacher can make it a little more challenging by requiring that set T become set S of the next pair:

Set S: {birds}
Set T: {tomatoes}

Set S: {tomatoes}
Set T: {pencils}

Set S: {pencils}
Set T: {stars}

This change in the game demands better listening.

Note: Remember that the two sets on this page are always disjoint sets. The union (∪) of the two sets are all the elements of both sets. The intersection (∩) of the two sets is the empty set or null set.

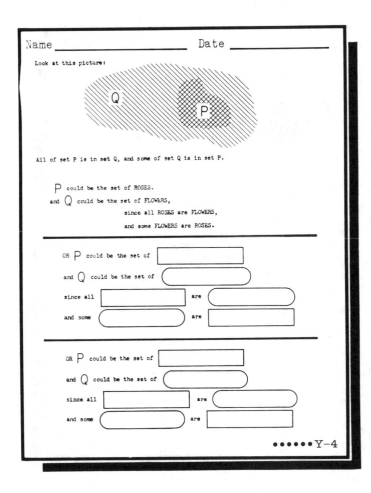

Name _____ Date _____

Look at this picture:

All of set P is in set Q, and some of set Q is in set P.

P could be the set of ROSES.
and Q could be the set of FLOWERS,
            since all ROSES are FLOWERS,
            and some FLOWERS are ROSES.

OR P could be the set of [   ]
and Q could be the set of [   ]
since all [   ] are [   ]
and some [   ] are [   ]

OR P could be the set of [   ]
and Q could be the set of [   ]
since all [   ] are [   ]
and some [   ] are [   ]

••••••Y–4

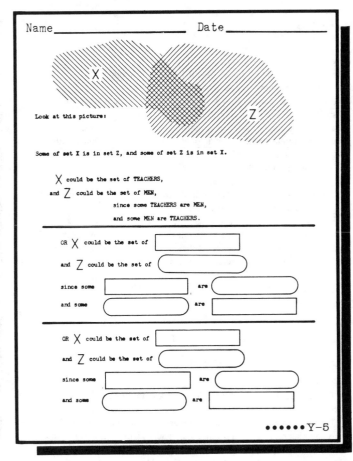

Name _____ Date _____

Look at this picture:

Some of set X is in set Z, and some of set Z is in set X.

X could be the set of TEACHERS,
and Z could be the set of MEN,
            since some TEACHERS are MEN,
            and some MEN are TEACHERS.

OR X could be the set of [   ]
and Z could be the set of [   ]
since some [   ] are [   ]
and some [   ] are [   ]

OR X could be the set of [   ]
and Z could be the set of [   ]
since some [   ] are [   ]
and some [   ] are [   ]

••••••Y–5

•••••• **Y4**

These are the important generalizations on lab sheet Y4:

All P is Q

Some Q is P

Examples

Q		P
set of objects		subset of objects
dogs	→	poodles
soldiers	→	infantry men
doctors	→	surgeons
card games	→	poker
states	→	California
pencils	→	red pencils

Note: The *union* of Q and P is Q. Q ∪ P = Q. The *intersection* of Q and P is P. Q ∩ P = P.

•••••• **Y5**

Again the teacher can draw a diagram similar to that on Y5 on the chalkboard and ask the children for examples of two sets of things which would fit this diagram.

Examples of this relationship are harder to find than for the previous one.

occupation/sex
      mathematicians/women
      doctors/men
shape/color
      triangles/blue things
      cubes/white things
shape/material
      cubes/plastic things
      balls/rubber things
sex/hair or eye color
      boys/brown-haired people
      men/blue-eyed people
function/material
      rain gear/plastic things
      toys/metal things

Some mathematicians are women. *Some* women are mathematicians.

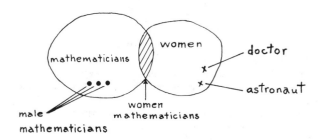

347

The striped circle shows the set of all <u>ducks</u>.
The white circle shows the set of all <u>four-legged animals</u>.
The dark circle shows the set of all <u>dogs</u>.
The <u>cat</u> can be placed anywhere in the white circle except for the
  space occupied by the dogs.
The set of <u>fish</u> should be placed outside all the given circles.
The <u>set of animals with wings and feathers</u> must be provided with a
larger loop around the ducks but outside the territory of the fish and
the four-legged animals.

We often play a board game with diagrams similar to those on Y6.
Every child in the class writes his breakfast menu on a sheet of
paper. The teacher draws a loop on the chalkboard and calls it E. It
represents the set of children in the class who had eggs for breakfast.
She calls on several children to put their initials either inside or outside
the loop, depending on whether they did or did not eat eggs.

The teacher then asks: "What do you know about Mary's breakfast?
What do you know about Bill's breakfast?" etc.

The teacher erases the initials and draws a second loop, for those
who had bacon. She puts a dot in E∩B and asks those children whose
breakfast would fall into that region to raise their hands. Mary and
Tommy do so and then write their initials. The teacher then asks for
children who had E but not B. They put their initials in that loop, and
children who had B but not E follow suit.

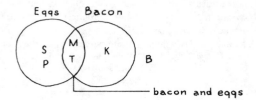

The teacher asks what new things we know about Bill's breakfast,
about Mary's breakfast, etc. (Bill had neither eggs nor bacon; Mary
had both eggs and bacon.)

The teacher erases the initials and draws a third loop. She labels it
C, for those who had cereal. After a "thinking silence," the children
put their initials in the region that describes their breakfast.

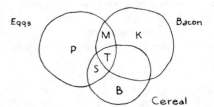

The children who did not put their initials on the board list what
the others had for breakfast. (Note that Paul had eggs; Mary, bacon
and eggs; Kathy, bacon; Tom, bacon, eggs, cereal; Bill, cereal; and
Sue, eggs and cereal.)

Another meaningful personal activity involving sets and subsets is
the personal inventory. Each child is given a questionnaire to check.

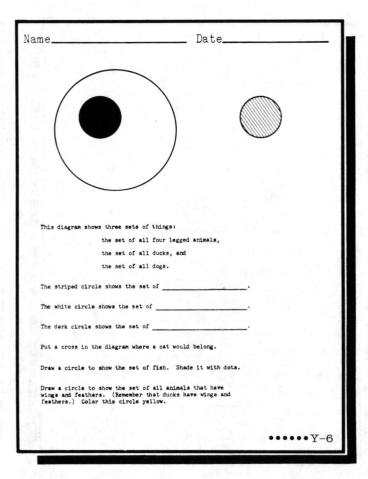

	Yes	No
Are you a boy?		
Are you a girl?		
Are you a swimmer?		
Do you play a musical instrument?		
Do you have a pet?		
Do you live in an apartment?		
Are you more than 8 years old?		

Here are the results of the checklists for four children, Mary, Bill,
Warren, Ellen.

	Mary	Bill	Warren	Ellen
Set B—boys		✔	✔	
Set G—girls	✔			✔
Set S—swimmers		✔	✔	✔
Set I—instruments	✔		✔	✔
Set P—pets	✔	✔		✔
Set A—apartments				
Set Y—older than 8	✔			

Analysis of the chart:
Which set is the empty set [Set A.]
Bill and Warren are the only members of what set? [Set B]
Who is an element of Y ∪ P? [Mary, Bill, Ellen.]
Who is an element of (I ∩ S) ∩ P? [Ellen]

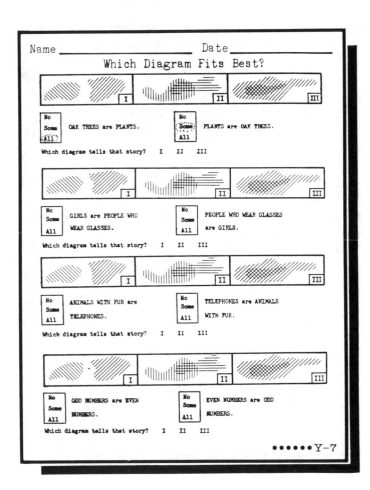

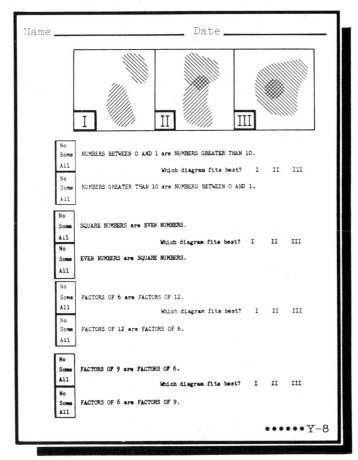

•••••• **Y7, Y8 , Y10**

On these lab sheets it is important to point out that the adjectives *no*, *some*, and *all* are word clues to the relationship between sets. They are correlated with the appropriate Venn diagrams.

The following represent the generalized cases of the three relationships between two sets.

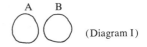

No A is B.	Some A is B.	Some A is B.
No B is A.	Some B is A.	All B is A.

Note: It could be that A and B name the same set. Then, all A is B and all B is A. This would be the case if A represented the set of all feathery animals and B represented the set of all birds.

The children must choose the proper pair of adjectives that make each pair of sentences true. Next they must relate these true sentences to the correct Venn diagram.

On lab sheet Y8 all example sets chosen are subsets of the set of numbers.

Answer

No number between 0 and 1 is greater than 10.
No numbers greater than 10 are numbers between 0 and 1.

 (Diagram I)

Answer

Some square numbers are even numbers.
Some even numbers are square numbers.

 (Diagram II)

A = {1, 4, 9, 16, 25, 36, . . .}
B = {0, 2, 4, 6, 8, 10, 12, 14, 16, . . .}
C = {4, 16, 36, 64, . . .}
A ∩ B = C (the even square numbers.)

Answer

All factors of 6 are factors of 12.
Some factors of 12 are factors of 6.

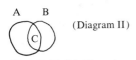 (Diagram III)

A = {1, 2, 3, 6}
B = {1, 2, 3, 4, 6, 12}

A ∪ B = B
A ∩ B = A

Answer

Some factors of 9 are factors of 6.
Some factors of 6 are factors of 9.

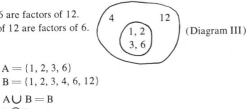 (Diagram II)

A = {1, 3, 9}
B = {1, 2, 3, 6}

•••••• **Y9**

Set of pet dogs.

Set of dogs that bite.

Set of pets that bite.

Set of pet dogs that bite.

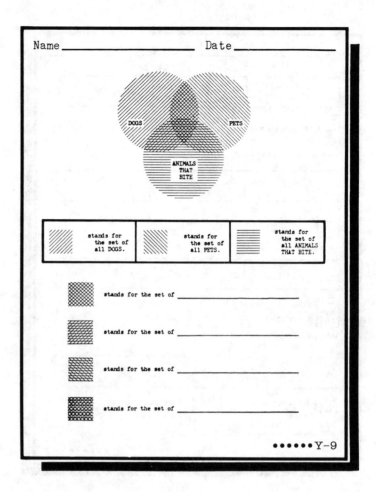

Let us illustrate the use of this Venn diagram to show the relationship between three sets of numbers.

Our universal set is the set of counting numbers less than 37.
Let subset T be the triangle numbers.
Let subset S be the square numbers.
Let subset O be the odd numbers.
Then, $T = \{1, 3, 6, 10, 15, 21, 28, 36\}$
$S = \{1, 4, 9, 16, 25, 36\}$
$O = \{1, 3, 5, 7, 9, 11, 13, 15 \ldots 33, 35\}$

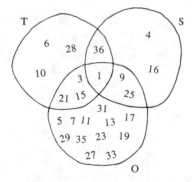

$T \cap S = \{1, 36\}$ numbers < 37 which are both triangle and square.

$S \cap O = \{1, 9, 25\}$ numbers < 37 which are odd and square.

$T \cap O = \{1, 3, 15, 21\}$ numbers < 37 which are odd triangle numbers.

$(T \cap S) \cap O = \{1\}$ numbers < 37 which are odd, square, and triangle.

Additional activity

Illustrate these sentences by a diagram. Write the name of at least one animal for each set.
   Some animals are mammals.
   Some mammals have no legs.
   Some mammals have two legs.
   Some mammals have four legs.

Illustrate these sentences by a diagram.
   Mr. Smith is a father.
   Mr. Smith is a man.
   Mr. Smith is a human being.
   Mr. Smith is a mammal.
   Mr. Smith is a living thing.

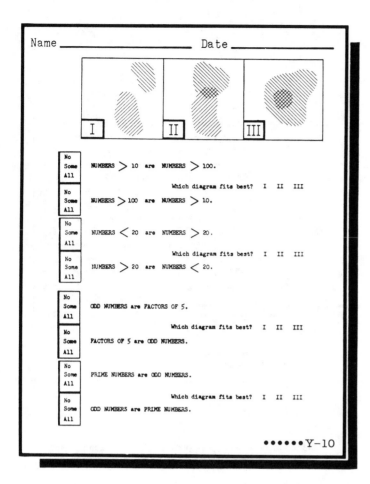

Name _____ Date _____

No Some All	NUMBERS > 10 are NUMBERS > 100.
	Which diagram fits best? I II III
No Some All	NUMBERS > 100 are NUMBERS > 10.
No Some All	NUMBERS < 20 are NUMBERS > 20.
	Which diagram fits best? I II III
No Some All	NUMBERS > 20 are NUMBERS < 20.
No Some All	ODD NUMBERS are FACTORS OF 5.
	Which diagram fits best? I II III
No Some All	FACTORS OF 5 are ODD NUMBERS.
No Some All	PRIME NUMBERS are ODD NUMBERS.
	Which diagram fits best? I II III
No Some All	ODD NUMBERS are PRIME NUMBERS.

•••••• Y–10

•••••• **Y10**

Answers

<u>Some</u> numbers > 10 are numbers > 100.
<u>All</u> numbers > 100 are numbers > 10. (Diagram III)

<u>No</u> numbers < 20 are numbers > 20.
<u>No</u> numbers > 20 are numbers < 20. (Diagram I)

<u>Some</u> odd numbers are factors of 5.
<u>All</u> factors of 5 are odd numbers. (Diagram III)

<u>Some</u> prime numbers are odd numbers.
<u>Some</u> odd numbers are prime numbers. (Diagram II)

Supplementary suggestions

The following are some examples of chalkboard work or lab sheet exercises.

Incomplete word statements

Children choose the right word to complete the following sentences and then illustrate the statements with their own Venn diagrams.

Some boys are bad.

(Choose one)   No / Some / All }   bad people are boys.

Draw a diagram.

All things that are alive grow.

Some / No / All }   things that grow are alive.

Draw a diagram.

This last example is tricky and should lead to some good discussion. A crystal grows. But is it alive? Our answer depends on our definition of "grow."

Z   Word problems

The lab sheets in this section require more advanced reading skills than those of the previous sections; they require careful analytical reading. Few clues are given diagramatically or numerically. The problems often include a subtle twist or an easily overlooked restrictive phrase. These features—and not the mathematics—make the problems difficult.

It is the author's belief that "word problems" must require *analytic thinking* to be mathematically worthwhile in printed materials for children.

This is not to say that word problems about a number of cookies or people (lost, found, left over, etc.,) should never be presented to children. Of course they should. Such "make-believe" story problems are, however, easily improvised by both children and teachers themselves. (And therefore they are pedagogically more interesting too.) In addition, a typical school day presents endless opportunities for numerical problem solving. Any good teacher can see to it that these opportunities are a continuous *oral* part of every lesson.

In this section samples of such improvised oral word problems growing out of school activities or community experiences are provided. When the teacher incorporates such activities into the regular classroom dialog, than *all* six- to ten-year-olds get adequate practice in solving word problems—and not just the good readers.

Every primary teacher knows that the nonreader or poor reader gets stuck on the *words* he is reading, not on the simple mathematics involved. (Would we teachers do better if we had to read these same problems written in the Greek alphabet?) Yet the faces of these same unsuccessful children brighten when a sympathetic adult does nothing more than read the problem, with good phrasing, for them. With an "Oh, that's easy!" the correct answer comes forth in most cases.

When the time comes that most children in a class are ready for written word problems, let the first such problems be ones that *they* helped write or at least those which are based on situations which concern *them*.

The following pages include:

a. sample word problems growing out of such classroom routines as attendance records and temperature readings;
b. sample word problems dealing with personal statistics;
c. sample word problems about "buying food" (consumer problems);
d. word problems about numbers;
e. word problems about money;
f. suggestions about all-school events.

The *First-Grade Diary* includes many illustrations for improvised problems and games. *All such sample problems,* including those on the following pages, *are more effective if they are adapted to the situation in the classroom where they are presented.*

Problems taken from class routines

The class from which the following sample problems were drawn had 30 pupils: 14 girls, 16 boys.

1   Word problems on attendance and calendar marking

October 19___						
SUN	MON	TUE	WED	THU	FRI	SAT
				S ①¹	² C	~~3~~
~~4~~ C	5 S	⑥ S	7 S	8 R	9 C	~~10~~
~~11~~	~~12~~ S	⑬ S	⑭ S	⑮ S	16 S	~~17~~
~~18~~ S	⑲ S	20 C	㉑ C	22 R	㉓ C	~~24~~
~~25~~ S	㉖ S	㉗ S	28 R	29 R	30 C	~~31~~

Legend: X = "not a school day"
O = "all children present"
S = "sunny" when calendar was marked
C = "cloudy"
R = "rainy"

a. How many school days in October?

b. On how many days was the sun shining when we marked the calendar?

c. On how many days were 100 per cent of the children present?

d. On how many days in October was at least one child absent?

e. There were _____ rainy days when all children were present.

f. During October the attendance seemed to be best (all present) on which day of the week? Worst on which day of the week?

g. October has _____ school days.
$\frac{\Box}{21}$ of all school days were sunny days.
$\frac{\Box}{21}$ of all school days were rainy days.
$\frac{\Box}{21}$ of all school days were cloudy days.
$\frac{8}{\Box}$ of all sunny school days had every child present.

h. Today there are three times as many boys absent as girls. Today there are as many boys in school as girls. How many children are at school? (Remember the composition of the sample class.)

2   Word problems on temperature readings

Monday, October 5			
Temperature			
9:00 AM		12:00 Noon	
indoors	outdoors	indoors	outdoors
23°C	19°C	25°C	28°C

The teacher asks the class to make up word problems about the temperature readings for the day.

a. At 9:00 it was 4°C warmer in our room than it was outside; *or* at 9:00 it was 4°C colder outside than in our room; *or* the difference between the outside and inside temperatures at 9:00 was 4°C.

b. The temperature in our room has gone up 2°C between 9:00 and 12:00. The outside temperature has gone up 9°C during the same time.

c. At 9:00 the difference between the inside and outside temperatures was 4°C. At 12:00 the difference between the inside and outside temperatures was −3°C.

Problems based on personal statistics

The sample problems are from a class of 24 children.

1   Chart A: Distribution of birthdays by months of the year

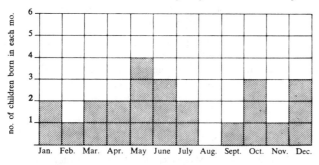

2   Chart B: Number and sex of children in each family

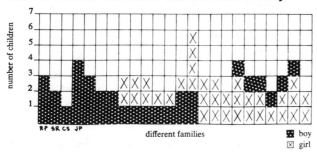

Such a chart is easily made. In this class boys and girls came in turn to the board, wrote their initials under the bottom row, shaded the box above the initials correctly, and each in turn filled out his own family column.

After the chart was completed, the teacher asked for a "thinking silence" in order to study the chart. When the silence was over the children took turns talking about the chart. (It was not necessary for the teacher to ask any questions.)

After the discussion the chart was rearranged by first putting down the families with the least children and ending up with the families with the most.

3   Chart C: Modification of Chart B (rearranged from least to most)

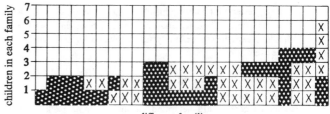

After Chart C was completed the teacher asked children what new things they could discover from Chart C. Some comments made by the children follow.

a. If the families with the most children gave some to the families with the fewest, then almost all would end up with three children.

b. The chart resembles stair steps, only not so regular. Most people in the class have either two or three children. There are:

    1 family with   1 child
    8 families with   2 children
    11 families with   3 children
    3 families with   4 children
    no families with   5 children
    1 family with   6 children

This gave us the idea for Chart D.

4   Chart D

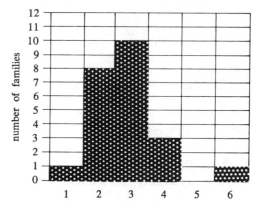

The children saw that this chart was like a multiplication table.

$$(1 \times 1) + (8 \times 2) + (11 \times 3) + (3 \times 4) + (1 \times 6) = 68$$

Our 24 families have 68 children in them.

353

Problems about food buying

It is suggested that such problem solving be done as a class activity, using the board. Teacher and children can bring in newspaper ads, shopping experiences, or empty food packages for study of labels and prices, etc.

1   Comparison shopping in the store

Billy had always insisted that his mother buy him individual packs of breakfast cereal until he found out that a "nine pack" (nine individual boxes) costs 18 cents more than the same amount of cereal packed into one box.

Now he wants his mother to save the extra _____ cents for each individual serving.

2   Comparing prices in newspaper ads

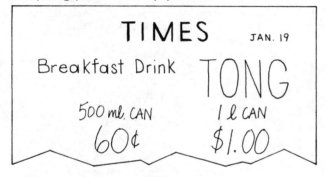

1 *l* of Tong bought in 500 *ml* cans costs _____.
1 *l* of Tong bought in a 1 *l* can costs _____.

3   Buying wisely

Which makes more sense—buying fruit by the pound or by the piece? (You can do both.)

```
Advertisement:
Large Grapefruit (seedless)  5 lb. bag $3.50
Large Grapefruit (seedless)  3 for $1.00
```

Quickies: about numbers

1   Brain teasers for youngest children

At the beginning of the class the teacher makes up the following:

a. Pretend there is a great big father elephant in this room. In comes a mother elephant. Don't lose them. The door opens again and the teeniest, weeniest baby elephant runs up to his mother. How many elephant legs are in the room now? How many elephant ears? How many elephant tails? (Of course it is silly, but children respond happily to this kind of oral nonsense.)

b. Here is a meter of string. (Teacher pretends; she has no real props.) I fold it over carefully so that I have four layers all alike. I snip them where they are folded and give one piece to Mary and one to Bob, one to Bill and one to—yes—Jane. How long is your piece, Jane? And yours, Bob? And yours, Mary? And yours, Bill?

c. Here is another meter of string. Raise your hands if you want a piece. This time I fold it in half and cut it. Brian and David, you may have the pieces. Figure out how long the pieces are *but keep the answer secret!* Now, boys here are the scissors [pretends to hand them scissors]; fold your pieces of string in half and cut them. How long is each piece?

2   Riddles for slightly older children

a. Guess what? My pet cat had kittens yesterday and right on the same day someone gave me the cutest baby chicks! Oh dear, I don't remember how many of each I have! All I remember is that altogether there were 14 eyes and 20 legs among them. Who will tell me how many chicks and cats I have?

b. Let's pretend that Bobby's mother bought him two pairs of new white socks and two pairs of new gloves for his birthday. Okay, Bobby? Now if Bobby is clever he can wear these socks as several different pairs. He can also do this with his gloves. How many different pairs of socks can he make? How many different pairs of gloves?

c. Here is my bag of marbles. [Teacher continues to pretend.] You four children will share them evenly with me. These seven marbles are my share. How many did I pretend were in the bag? [35 marbles] After I divided my marbles evenly among my seven friends, I had none left. How many did I have to start with? [*Any* multiple of seven or zero]

d. Think of a number, double it, subtract three. What number do you now have? Who can tell the starting number. [There are endless variations of this: What number goes into four *and* into seven a whole number of times? What number do four and seven go into a whole number of times?]

e. Here are two cups each with some pennies in them. The pennies in *each cup* can be arranged in rows to make a square pattern. When we put all the pennies together into one pile, they can again be arranged into a square pattern. There are less than 100 pennies. How many pennies are in each of the two cups? [9 in one cup, 16 in the other; 9 + 16 = 25]

f. I am the smallest number that leaves a remainder of one when divided by five and by seven. I am the number _____. [To the teacher: Is the correct answer 36 or is it 1?]

g. After putting the drawing below on the board, ask: What is special about the *neighbors* of the numbers 4, 6, 12, 18? Can you add another number with such neighbors to that list? [Both neighbors are prime numbers. You might have to point out that 7, 8, 9 and 13, 14, 15 are intentionally excluded.]

Problems about money

These sample word problems are probably best done with the entire class or in small groups.

1 Coin problems

a. In how many ways could I carry a quarter's worth of money around in my pocket?

b. I could have change for 34 cents in 18 different ways. Find them. Here is a start.

number of coins	quarter	dime	nickel	penny
6 coins	1		1	4
7 coins		3		4

c. Three children each have four U.S. coins. Each child's four coins are the same, but each child's four coins are different from those the other two children have.

Child A has 100 times as much money as Child B.
Child B has $\frac{1}{25}$ as much money as Child C.
Child A has four _____.
Child B has four _____.
Child C has four _____.

2 Problems about allowances and savings

a. Ben gets 12 cents allowance every Sunday for a whole year. Bruce gets 50 cents allowance the first day of every month for a whole year. Who gets the most money by the end of the year?
Ben gets _____.
Bruce gets _____.

b. Uncle Fred visited Simon and Sue's house for a week. He gave them each a money present, but in a different way.

Sue got a dollar on Sunday. Simon got a penny on Sunday, two pennies on Monday, four pennies on Tuesday—always doubling the previous day's money. Saturday was the last day.

One child complained. Which one? Why? Prove it.

Problems derived from school events

The most important advice about the creation and solving of word problems is that teachers (and children) regularly develop booklets of word problems based on school and community events. At the Miquon School we made such problems based on school fairs and UNICEF collections.

• • • • • • Z1

I had one dollar . . .

model plane kit	$0.25 or $ .25
comic book	$0.20 or $ .20
lost	$0.05 or $ .05
in bank	$0.50 or $ .50
total	$1.00

Mr. Fixit and Mary . . .

Each floor tile is a 10 centimeter square. (That means its area is 100 square centimeters.) Mary's floor was

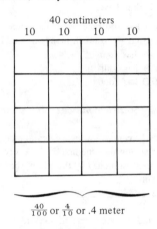

40 centimeters
10   10   10   10

$\frac{40}{100}$ or $\frac{4}{10}$ or .4 meter

The last problem requires careful reading. There is only one correct answer. What do we know?

1. Mother has less than 40 cents.
2. Each of the three boys may have one third of that money. (They share alike in the amount of money.)
3. They will get the same amount of money in different amounts of coins.

Answers

Each boy will get 11 cents in the following coins:

Bill :	two nickels, one penny
Ben :	one dime, one penny
Paul:	eleven pennies

There were 33 cents in the purse. No other combination will work.

• • • • • • Z2, Z3

These lab sheets are about *denominate* numbers—numbers which measure something. The name of the unit of measurement must be indicated. The children should become familiar with the most frequently used abbreviations.

The picture clues allow some of the children to associate the abbreviation with the correct idea without the help of the teacher.

Answers

12 <u>hrs.</u> on a clock
60 <u>min.</u> in an hour
60 <u>sec.</u> in a minute

1 dollar $ 1.00

a 5 ¢ stamp

1 <u>gal.</u>   1 <u>qt.</u>   1 <u>pt.</u>   1 <u>c.</u>

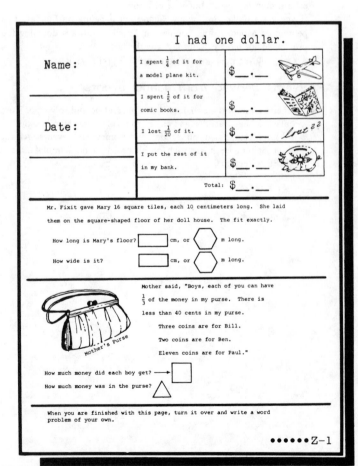

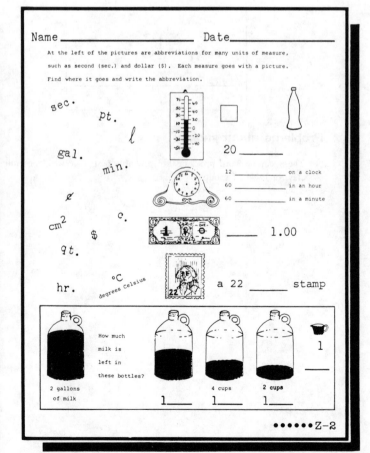

• • • • • • Z3

Answers

1 <u>yd.</u>	1 <u>m</u>
3 <u>ft.</u>	100 <u>cm</u>
36 <u>in.</u>	

11 o'clock <u>A.M.</u>
11 o'clock <u>P.M.</u>   1 <u>kg</u>
1 <u>doz.</u> eggs

New York   15 <u>km</u>

It is reasonable to assume that the children will need more practice with these and other abbreviations. Teachers can make more lab sheets or play chalkboard games using them.

These abbreviations may be written on file cards and given to each child. Each child should find an appropriate object in the classroom to associate it with. Include more metric abbreviations, such as kg (kilogram), km (kilometer), g (gram), l (liter), ml (milliliter), and mm (millimeter).

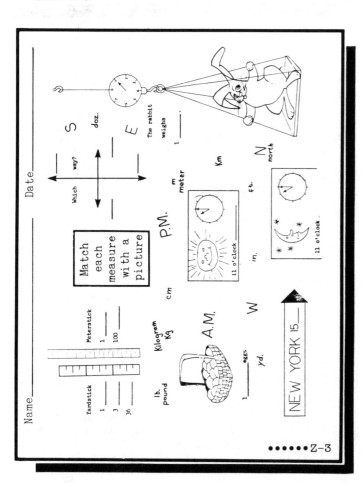

• • • • • • Z4

There are some similarities in the problems about coins and money to the purse problem on lab sheet Z1.

"Most coins" does not mean "most money." 100 of Jim's coins equal in money value (not weight) 10 of Bob's coins and 1 of Carol's coins.

An aside about degrees Fahrenheit

The thermometer shows 70° F (Fahrenheit). Not only should we insist on children saying in the classroom: "It is 70 degrees today," but better yet, "It is 70 degrees Fahrenheit."

70° C means 70° centigrade, which is much hotter than 70° F. The centigrade thermometer is used in our science laboratories (and in most of the rest of the world in everyday life).

  0° C names the freezing point of water at sea level.
100° C names the boiling point of water at sea level.
 36° C is normal body temperature on the centigrade thermometer.

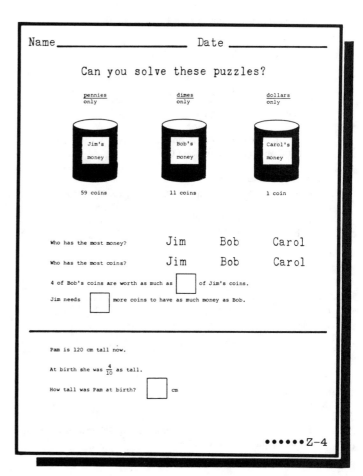

357

• • • • • • Z5

This page is a thought puzzle in the best tradition. Hasty readers will find it hard. Let's not overexplain it and take the detective work (the use of clues) out of the task. But should a whole group find the problem difficult, we can make a demonstration lesson of the lab sheet.

Demonstration procedure

You will need four shoe boxes filled with $7.36 in play money in the denominations shown on the lab sheet. Four children are given the shoe boxes and a fifth child asks for change.

$1.18—I cannot take it out of A or B.

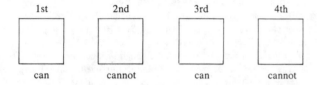

Therefore, the 1st box is not A and the 3rd box is not A; the 1st box is not B and the 3rd is not B.

$5.43—I cannot take it out of A or C.

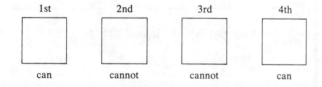

Therefore, the 1st box is not A and the 4th box is not A; the 1st box is not C and the 4th box is not C.

Conclusions thus far

1st box is not A, not B, and not C. Therefore, it must be D.
3rd box is not A, not B, and not D. Therefore, it must be C.
4th box is not A, not C, and not D. Therefore, it must be B.
2nd box must be A.

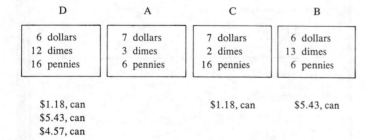

D	A	C	B
6 dollars	7 dollars	7 dollars	6 dollars
12 dimes	3 dimes	2 dimes	13 dimes
16 pennies	6 pennies	16 pennies	6 pennies

$1.18, can		$1.18, can	$5.43, can
$5.43, can			
$4.57, can			

D is the only one which will permit me to subtract any amount of money from the sum of $7.36.

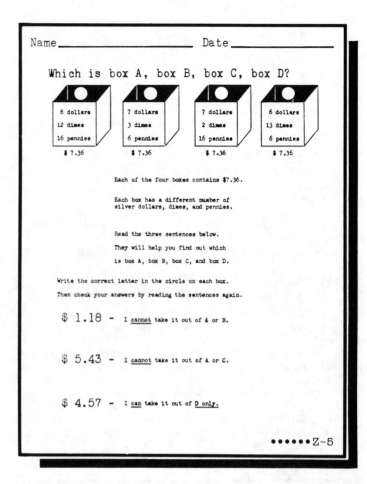

Which is box A, box B, box C, box D?

6 dollars	7 dollars	7 dollars	6 dollars
12 dimes	3 dimes	2 dimes	13 dimes
16 pennies	6 pennies	16 pennies	6 pennies
$ 7.36	$ 7.36	$ 7.36	$ 7.36

Each of the four boxes contains $7.36.

Each box has a different number of silver dollars, dimes, and pennies.

Read the three sentences below. They will help you find out which is box A, box B, box C, and box D.

Write the correct letter in the circle on each box. Then check your answers by reading the sentences again.

$ 1.18 -   I cannot take it out of A or B.

$ 5.43 -   I cannot take it out of A or C.

$ 4.57 -   I can take it out of D only.

• • • • • • Z-5

• • • • • • Z6–Z9
Simon and Sue booklet

This booklet of word problems includes a variety of levels and challenges. It is a sample of school-originated word problems.

Baseball cards
Both have 238 cards together.
They have 226 different cards. (12 cards are duplicates.)

How tall?
Sue is 125 cm.
Simon is 135 cm.

Candy
Each child gets $\frac{3}{4}$ of a candy bar. (Use "rod candy bars" to explain.)

The present
Each child gets $ .08 change.

When was Barbs born?
Barbs was born on Feb. 5.

The guessing game
Sue is a poor player. This should become obvious to the children. She "wastes" questions. A good player always asks a question which cuts the number of possibilities in half.

Sue's worst question is "Does it end with a five?" (She had just found out that the answer is an *even* number.)

Name _____ Date _____

SIMON and SUE

fold here

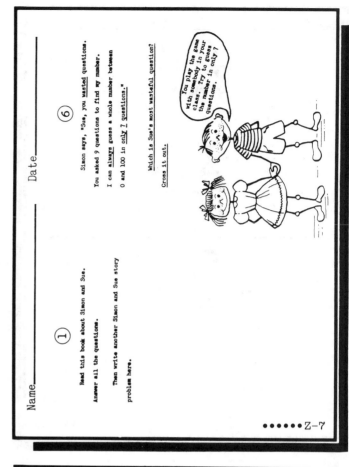

Name _____ Date _____

① Read this book about Simon and Sue.

Answer all the questions.

Then write another Simon and Sue story

problem here.

⑥ Simon says, "Sue, you wasted questions.

You asked 9 questions to find my number.

I can always guess a whole number between

0 and 100 in only 7 questions."

Which is Sue's most wasteful question?

Cross it out.

"You play the game with somebody in your class. Try to guess the number in only 7 questions?"

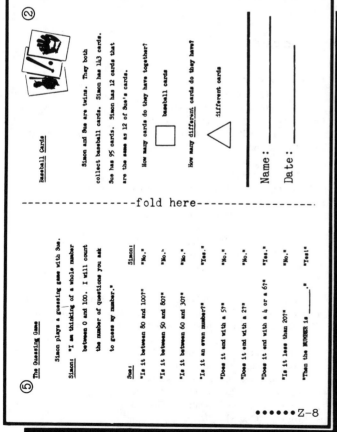

② **Baseball Cards**

Simon and Sue are twins. They both
collect baseball cards. Simon has 143 cards.
Sue has 95 cards. Simon has 12 cards that
are the same as 12 of Sue's cards.

How many cards do they have together?

[ ] baseball cards

How many different cards do they have?

△ different cards

Name: _____
Date: _____

-------fold here-------

⑤ **The Guessing Game**

Simon plays a guessing game with Sue.

Simon: "I am thinking of a whole number
between 0 and 100. I will count
the number of questions you ask
to guess my number."

Sue:	Simon:
"Is it between 80 and 100?"	"No."
"Is it between 50 and 80?"	"No."
"Is it between 60 and 80?"	"No."
"Is it an even number?"	"Yes."
"Does it end with a 5?"	"No."
"Does it end with a 2?"	"No."
"Does it end with a 4 or a 6?"	"Yes."
"Is it less than 20?"	"No."
"Then the NUMBER is ___."	"Yes!"

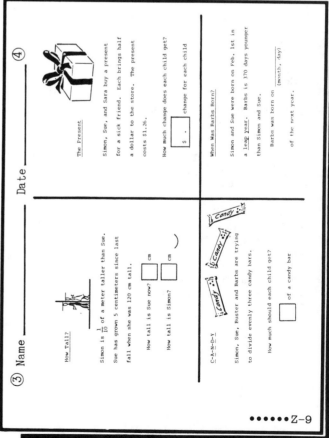

③ Name _____ Date _____

How Tall?

Simon is $\frac{1}{10}$ of a meter taller than Sue.

Sue has grown 5 centimeters since last

fall when she was 120 cm tall.

How tall is Sue now?   [ ] cm

How tall is Simon?   [ ] cm

C-A-N-D-Y

Simon, Sue, Buster and Barbs are trying

to divide evenly three candy bars.

How much should each child get?

[ ] of a candy bar

④ **The Present**

Simon, Sue, and Sara buy a present

for a sick friend. Each brings half

a dollar to the store. The present

costs $1.26.

How much change does each child get?

$ [ ] . [ ] change for each child

When Was Barbs Born?

Simon and Sue were born on Feb. 1st in

a leap year. Barbs is 370 days younger

than Simon and Sue.

Barbs was born on ___ (month, day)

of the next year.

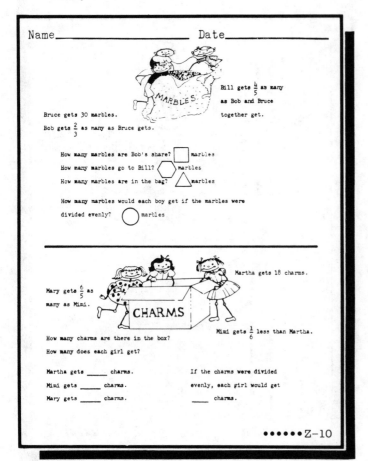

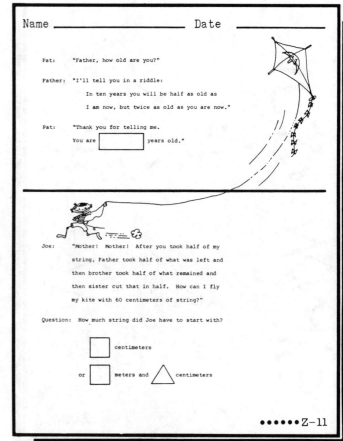

••••••Z10

Marbles

Bob gets 20 marbles. $\frac{2}{3}$ of 30 = 20
Bill gets 40 marbles. $\frac{4}{5}$ of (30 + 20) = 40
There were 90 marbles in the bag.

30	+	20	+	40	=	90
Bruce		Bob		Bill		Total

If the marbles had been divided evenly, each boy would have gotten 30 marbles. 90 ÷ 3 = 30

Charms

Martha gets 18 charms
Mimi gets 15 charms. 18 − ($\frac{1}{6}$ of 18) = 15
Mary gets 18 charms. 15 + ($\frac{1}{5}$ of 15) = 18
There were 51 charms in the box.
If the charms had been divided evenly, each girl would have gotten 17 charms. (Do this with rod models. It works beautifully.)

••••••Z11

How old are you?

Father is 40 years old.
Only if the child is now 10 years old will he or she be "twice as old as you are now" in another 10 years.
So the child will be 20 years old in 10 years, which is half as old as the father is now.

Kite string

Most children start with the 60 centimeters of string and reconstruct the original by doubling.

60 × 2 = 120 before sister cut
120 × 2 = 240 before brother cut
240 × 2 = 480 before father cut
480 × 2 = 960 before mother cut

The original length is 960 centimeters, or 9 meters and 60 centimeters

Here is a "word problem" made up by an upper elementary school child at Miquon School to arouse interest in the Halloween UNICEF collection. It was very popular among the older children:

Mary, Bill, Steve, Joy, and Georgia want you to tell them how much money they collected for UNICEF.

Mary collected 20% as much as Bill
who collected   4% as much as Steve
who collected 25% as much as Joy
who collected 80% as much as Georgia
who collected $12.50.

Name_____ Date_____

Think about these questions and make good guesses. Then check your answers.

If you walk to school . . .

	First Guess	Answer Checked
about how many streets do you cross?		
about how many traffic lights do you pass?		
about how many intersections do you pass?		
about how many houses do you pass?		

If you ride to school . . .

	First Guess	Answer Checked
about how many km away is your home?		
about how many traffic lights do you pass?		
about how many turns do you make?		
about how many minutes does the trip take?		

About your school:

	First Guess	Answer Checked
about how many classrooms are in your school?		
about how many children are in your school?		
about how many children under six years of age are in your school?		
about how many children over nine years of age are in your school?		
about how many books are there in your classroom?		
about how many books are there in your school?		
about how many children in your school are boys?		
about how many children are absent daily in your class? (What is the average number absent daily, counted over a week?)		

•••••• Z-12

Name_____ Date_____

More questions about your school:

	First Guess	Answer Checked
About how many walking steps is it to the principal's office?		
About how many meters is it to the principal's office?		
About how many floor tiles (or boards) are on your classroom floor?		

If your classroom were empty . . .

	First Guess	Answer Checked
about how many people could sit on chairs in it?		
about how many children could lie on the floor in it without touching each other		
about how many children could stand up in it packed like sardines?		

Questions about other things:

	First Guess	Answer Checked
About how many apples are in a kilogram of apples?		
About how many marshmellows are there in a kilogram?		
About how many peanuts in a kilogram?		
About how many apples could fit in a shoe box?		
About how many marshmellows in a shoe box?		
About how many drops of water fill $\frac{1}{4}$ cup of water?		

	First Guess	Answer Checked
About how many times does your heart beat in a minute?		
About how much does a liter of milk weigh?		
About how much does a liter of water weigh?		
About how much does a liter of sand weigh?		
About how many people live in your city?		
About how many people live in your state?		
About how many people live in the United States?		

Are there more dogs than people in the U.S.A.?	Yes	No
Are there more chickens than people in the U.S.A.?	Yes	No

•••••• Z-13

•••••• **Z12, Z13**

Many children are hesitant about guessing, and most teachers discourage it. But good guesses are the best tools for thinking in mathematics and science.

Good guesses are hypotheses. They give the person something to aim at, something to test or try out. They are a kind of rational, but rough, thinking which can be refined with further work. Guesses help a person get started on a problem.

Children should be encouraged to estimate. Here are some examples. Some of the questions have exact answers which can be verified by an observer, whereas others can only be answered within a reasonable range.

Exact answer

About how many classrooms are in your school?

Reasonable range

About how many walking steps to the principal's office?
About how many apples in a kilogram of apples?
About how many drops of water fill $\frac{1}{4}$ cup of water?

There probably are fewer dogs than people in the United States.
There probably are more chickens than people in the United States.

Problems of estimation as on lab sheet Z13 should also be devised using the metric system.

Examples

How many peanuts are in one kilogram?
How much does a liter of milk weigh?
How many grams does a liter of water weigh?
(One liter of water at 2°C at sea level weighs 1000 grams or 1 kilogram.)

Scope and Sequence Chart

Level 1	**Level 2**

Number systems and number operations

Level 1	Level 2
• Natural numbers (0-99): concepts of order, cardinality, "largest," "smallest," "middle," "one more," "one less"	• Natural numbers (0-999)
• Recognition and symbolization of additive and subtractive situations	• Concept of odd and even whole numbers
• Relationship between addition and subtraction	• Concept of order (extended)
• Concept of commutative property of addition	• Additive and subtractive situations (extended)
• Concept of non-commutativity of subtraction	• Relationship between addition and subtraction (extended)
• Concept of identity element for addition	• Concept of commutative property of addition (extended)
• Recognition and symbolization of multiplicative situations of multiplication	• Concept of associative property of addition
• Concept of commutative property of multiplication	• Concept of non-commutativity of subtraction (extended)
• Concept of identity element for multiplication	• Concept of identity element for subtraction
• Recognition and symbolization of unit fractions ($\frac{1}{2}, \frac{1}{3}, \frac{1}{4}, \frac{1}{6}, \frac{1}{8}, \frac{1}{16}$)	• Multiplicative situations (extended)
• Number line (corresponding natural numbers and points on a line)	• Concept of commutative property of multiplication (extended)
	• Concept of distributive property of multiplication with regard to addition
	• Recognition and symbolization of fractions (extended non-unit fractions)
	• Recognition and symbolization of divisive situations.

Numeration

Level 1	Level 2
• Base-ten system (1 through 99)	• Base-ten system (1 through 999)
• Grouping by ones and tens	• Grouping by ones and tens (extended)
• Place value (informal)	• Place value (informal, extended)

Sets

Level 1	Level 2
• One-to-one correspondence	• Odd and even sets
• Cardinality of sets	

Level 1 | # Level 2

Equalities and inequalities

- Concepts of "greater than," "less than," "equal to"
- Recognition and symbolization of "greater than" and "equal to" only

- Recognition and symbolization of "greater than," "equal to," "less than," "not equal to"

Problem solving

- Mathematical sentences

$$10 \div 10 = \square$$
$$3 + 3 - 3 = \square$$
$$\square = 10 - 9$$
$$5 - \square + 7 = 8$$
$$\square = 10 \times 6$$

- Problems such as

$$\begin{array}{r} 4 \\ 5 \\ +6 \\ \hline \end{array}$$

- Subtraction as difference between two numbers (comparison)
- Reasoning games

- More complex mathematical sentences

$$4 + 3 + 2 + 1 + 9 + 8 + 7 = \square$$
$$5 - \square + 7 = 8$$
$$17 - 8 = \square$$
$$\square = 17 - (7 \times 1)$$
$$(2 \times 3) + (\tfrac{1}{2} \times 8) = \square$$
$$\square = (\tfrac{1}{2} \times 14) - (\tfrac{1}{4} \times 16)$$
$$100 \div \square = 10$$

- Problems such as

$$\begin{array}{r} 18 \\ - \ 9 \\ \hline \end{array}$$

- Who lives in this house?

24
1×24
2×12
3×8
4×6
$3 \times 4 \times 2$
$2 \times 2 \times 2 \times 3$

- Reasoning games (extended)

Computation

- Addition: sums up to and including 10 (up to four addends only)
- Subtraction: minuends up to and including 10, subtrahends up to and including 10 (one minuend and one subtrahend only)
- Multiplication: multipliers up to and

- Addition: sums up to and including 50 (up to five addends, two-place addends)
- Subtraction: minuends up to and including 30, subtrahends up to and including 30 (up to five subtrahends, two-place minuends, and two-place subtrahends)

Level 1	**Level 2**
including 10, multiplicands up to and including 10, products up to and including 40	• Multiplication: multipliers up to and including 20, multiplicands up to and including 640, products up to and including 1280
	• Fractions: multiplication of whole numbers only ($\frac{1}{2}$, $\frac{1}{4}$, and $\frac{1}{3}$)
	• Division: dividends up to and including 100, divisors up to and including 10, divisors of mixed numbers ($2\frac{1}{2}$)

Measurement

Level 1	Level 2
• Concept of units of measure	• Concept of square units of measure
• Concept of linear measure	• Concept of standard units: square inches, square centimeters (extended)
• Idea of measurement of area (informal)	• Finding areas: squares (extended)
• Concept of standard units: inch, centimeter, square centimeter, minutes, hours	
• Finding areas: squares and rectangles	

Geometry

Level 1	Level 2
• Recognition of rectangles, triangles, circles, right angles	• Recognition of squares

Number theory

Level 1	Level 2
	• Factors (through 24 only)
	• Prime numbers (through 23 only, optional)
	• Arithmetic and geometric progressions (informal)
	• Even numbers, odd numbers

Applications

Level 1	Level 2
• Use of standardized measurement instruments—clock	

Level 3	Level 4

Number systems and number operations

Level 3

- Natural numbers (0–9,999)
- Additive and multiplicative properties of odd and even whole numbers
- Concept of order (extended)
- Additive and subtractive situations (extended)
- Multiplicative situations (extended)
- Zero property of multiplication
- Distributive property of multiplication with regard to addition (extended)
- Fractions: unit and non-unit fractions (extended) ($\frac{1}{5}$, $\frac{1}{10}$, $\frac{1}{12}$, $\frac{1}{20}$, $\frac{1}{100}$ and $\frac{2}{5}$, $\frac{3}{8}$, $\frac{4}{8}$, $\frac{8}{8}$, $\frac{8}{16}$, $\frac{9}{8}$, $\frac{3}{2}$, $\frac{4}{2}$, $\frac{7}{5}$)
- Mixed numbers ($3\frac{1}{2}$, $4\frac{1}{2}$, $2\frac{1}{3}$)
- Addition of fractions
- Multiplication of a fraction by a whole number (extended)
- Relationship between addition of fractions and multiplication of a fraction by a whole number
- Divisive situations (extended)
- Relationship between multiplication and division (extended)
- Number line (extended to addition, subtraction, multiplication, and division); vertical number line
- Concept of negative numbers

Level 4

- Natural numbers (0–99,999)
- Additive and subtractive situations (continued)
- Comparison of addition and subtraction
- Multiplicative situations (extended)
- Commutativity of multiplication (extended to multiplication of whole numbers and fractions)
- Comparison of multiplication and addition
- Equivalence of multiplication by a fraction and division by its reciprocal
- Relationship between multiplication and division (extended)
- Number line (extended to fractions); use of imaginary number line
- Square root (informal)
- Divisive situations (extended)
- Arithmetic progressions (informal)
- Geometric progressions (informal)

Numeration

Level 3

- Base-ten system (1–9,999)
- Grouping by tens (extended), hundreds
- Place value (extended, informal); additive approach to subtraction (subtraction as difference between two numbers)

Level 4

- Base-ten system (1–99,999)
- Grouping by ones, tens, hundreds, thousands
- Place value (extended)

Sets

- Odd and even sets (extended)

Level 3 | # Level 4

Ratios

- Use of scale on maps (informal)
- Converting units of liquid measure (informal)
- Equivalent ratios
- Constructing maps to scale

Equalities and inequalities

- Concepts of "greater than," "equal to," "less than," "not equal to" (extended to fractions, units of measurement, inches and centimeters only)
- Concepts of "equal to," greater than," "less than," "not equal to" (extended to include dozen, penny, nickel, dollar)
- Connectives, "or" and "not"

Problem solving

- Mathematical sentences (extended) such as:

$$2 + 4 + 1 + 3 = \square + 1 + 3$$

$$\triangle + 2 + \triangle + \triangle = 14$$

$$(\tfrac{1}{2} \times 14) + (\tfrac{1}{2} \times 16) = \square$$

$$10 + 4 = \square + \square =$$

$$(7 \times 10) + 5 = \square$$

$$\square + \square + 3 = 13$$

$$13 + 15 = 2 \times \triangle$$

$$\begin{array}{r} 3{,}642 \\ -\ \ 642 \\ \hline \end{array}$$

$$20 - (3 \times 5) + 20 - (3 \times 5) = \triangle$$

- Mathematical sentences (extended) such as:

$$17 + \square + 10 = 37$$

$$35 \div 5 = \square$$

$$\square \times 5 = 35$$

$$5 \times 6 = \square$$

$$50 \times 6 = \square$$

$$500 \times 6 = \square$$

$$\begin{array}{r} 14 \\ 37 \\ 61 \\ 54 \\ +23 \\ \hline \end{array} \qquad \begin{array}{r} 121 \\ +220 \\ \hline \end{array}$$

- Reasoning games: "What's the rule?"
- If/then reasoning with weights and balances

367

Level 3	Level 4
Computation	**Computation**

Computation (Level 3)

- Addition (maintained, up to seven addends)
- Subtraction (maintained)
- Multiplication: multipliers up to and including 800; multiplicands up to and including 600 (simple three-place multiplicands by simple two-place multipliers; simple two-place multiplicands by simple three-place multipliers)
- Fractions (maintained)
- Division (maintained, two-place dividend by two-place divisor)

Computation (Level 4)

- Addition (maintained, up to seven addends)
- Subtraction (maintained)
- Multiplication: multipliers up to and including 800; multiplicands up to and including 600 (simple three-place multiplicands by simple two-place multipliers; simple two-place multiplicands by simple three-place multipliers)
- Fractions (maintained)
- Division (maintained, two-place dividend by two-place divisor)

Measurement (Level 3)

Measurement (Level 4)

- Concept of standard units (extended) cup, pint, quart, gallon
- Finding volume (informal)
- Finding areas: squares and rectangles (extended)
- Conversion of units of liquid measure

Geometry (Level 3)

- Recognition of semi-circles, quadrilaterals, triangles, squares, pentagons, hexagons
- Vectors (informal)

Number theory (Level 3)

- Grid games

Number theory (Level 4)

- Triangle numbers (informal)
- Factorial numbers (informal)
- Square numbers (informal)
- Introduction to modular arithmetic (informal)
- Exponents (squares only)

Applications (Level 3)

- Concept of coins as fractional parts of a dollar
- Concept of scale on a map
- Use of money (coins through one dollar) in solving problems

Applications (Level 4)

- Use of standardized measurement instruments—clock (extended)
- The calendar
- Liquid measurement

Level 5 | Level 6

Number systems and number operations

- Natural numbers (0–999,999)
- Additive and subtractive situations (extended)
- Addition algorithm introduced
- Subtraction: use of place value to solve subtraction problems instead of "borrowing" algorithm
- Multiplicative situations (extended)
- Divisive situations (extended)
- Fractions (extended): least common multiple; addition of fractions (continued); reduction of fractions; subtraction, multiplication and division of fractions; ratios between geometric shapes; ratios as relationships between semi-concrete representations
- Number line (extended): number-line rules and inverses; making graphs of number-line rules
- Equivalence of multiplication by a fraction and division by its reciprocal
- Relationship between multiplication and division (extended)
- Arithmetic progressions (extended)
- Geometric progressions (extended)

- Natural numbers (0–999,999)
- Additive situations (continued)
- Subtractive situations (extended): use of place value, or regrouping, to solve subtraction problems; working toward the subtraction algorithm
- Multiplicative situations (extended)
- Fractions (extended): ratios between geometric shapes; ratios as relationships between semi-concrete representations; word problems
- Division with remainders

Numeration

- Base-ten system (1–99,999)
- Grouping by ones, tens, hundreds, thousands
- Place value (extended)
- Difference between number and numeral

- Place value (extended)
- Informal work in bases other than base ten: base two ("Dairy Shelf" game); base three ("Sugar Lump" game)
- Difference between number and numeral (extended)

Sets

- Solution sets: graphing number-line rules
- Simultaneous equations

- Intersection of sets (informal)
- Union of sets (informal)
- Logic
- Subsets (extended)
- Guessing games about sets of things
- Solution sets: graphing of linear equations

Level 5

Ratios

- Equivalent ratios
- Ratios between geometric shapes
- Ratios as relationships between semi-concrete representations
- Converting units of dry measure

Equalities and inequalities

- Concepts of "equal to," "greater than," "less than," "less than or equal to," "not equal to," "not greater than," "not less than" (continued)
- Use of "greater than," "less than," "equal to" in estimation of products, in making true and false statements, in work with money

Problem solving

- Completing addition, subtraction, multiplication charts and puzzles
- Problems such as:

$$\begin{array}{r} 52 \\ +29 \end{array}$$

$$362 \xrightarrow{+100} \square \xrightarrow{-100} \triangle$$

$$8\,)\,\overline{80 + 16} \qquad 8\,)\,\overline{96}$$

$\frac{8}{12}$ of $12 = \square$; $\frac{10}{5} \div \frac{2}{5} = \square$

Make False: $9 = 5 + \square$

- Word problems such as: Father bought 6 boards, each 1 yd. long. How many feet of lumber did he buy?
- Rate $\times$ time $=$ distance
- Reasoning games (extended): if-then reasoning with weights and balances; reasoning using simultaneous equations; number-line games

Level 6

- Ratios as relationships between semi-concrete representations (extended)
- Equivalent ratios

- These concepts continued and extended to include "greater than or equal to"
- Use of the preceding concepts in making true and false statements, in estimation

- Problems such as:

$$\begin{array}{r} 2\ 4\ 3 \\ -1\ 2\ 5 \end{array} \qquad \begin{array}{r} 213 \\ \times\quad 6 \end{array}$$

$$7\,)\,\overline{70 + 28 + 3} \qquad 7\,)\,\overline{101}$$

- Make False: $\square + \square + 6 = 6 + \square + 5$

- Word problems such as: There are 7 apples in a bowl. You get half as many apples as mother and twice as many apples as baby. How many apples do you get?
- Story problems
- Reasoning games

Level 5 | # Level 6

Computation

- Addition: sums up to and including 12,435 (five-place and four-place addends)
- Subtraction: minuends up to and including 7,000; subtrahends up to and including 2,540
- Multiplication: multipliers up to and including 1,000
- Fractions (extended)
- Division: dividends up to and including 576 (three-place dividend by two-place divisor)
- Division by fractions

- Addition (maintained)
- Subtraction (extended)
- Multiplication (extended)
- Fractions (extended)
- Division with remainders

Measurement

- Area and perimeter problems
- Finding volume (cubic units)
- Equivalent measures

- Liquid measure
- Time
- Temperature
- Word problems involving measurement

Geometry

- Cubes
- Geometric-recognition games

Number theory

- Prime numbers (extended)
- Factors through 100
- Prime factors
- Square roots
- Exponents
- Grid games (extended)

- Modular arithmetic
- Grid games (extended)

Estimation and probability

- Informal estimation: "guessing" quotients
- Estimation of area

- Estimation of number, distance, averages (word problems)
- Graphing of linear equations

Level 5	Level 6

Applications

- Use of money (bills through $100) in solving problems
- Word problems: addition, subtraction (comparison), mutiplication, and division involving standard measures of length and weight

- Use of money in solving word problems
- Word problems (extended)
- Fractions
- Mapping (extended)
- Map reading

About the author

Born in Germany, Lore May Rasmussen completed her graduate studies in education at the University of Illinois where she met her husband, Donald.

Mrs. Rasmussen has been Assistant Professor of Elementary Education at Talladega College, Research Associate with the University of Illinois Arithmetic Project, and Visting Associate Professor of Education at Temple University. She developed the *Miquon Math Lab Materials* during her eight years as teacher and math specialist at the Miquon School, Miquon, Pennsylvania.

Mrs. Rasmussen has served as math workshop leader and speaker for numerous school districts, universities and professional orgainizations. In 1976 she was presented the John Patterson Award for Excellence in Education by the Philadelphia Citizens' Committee on Public Education for her work as director of the Learning Centers Project of the Philadelphia Public Schools.

Presently Mrs. Rasmussen lives in Berkeley, California. She writes and consults with schools using the *Miquon Materials*. She has three sons, all working in mathematics education.